The High Tide and the Turn

"The high tide," King Alfred cried,
"the high tide, and the turn!"

In G. K. Chesterton's epic poem, *The Ballad of the White Horse*, the Christian King Alfred shouts joyously at the crux of the great Battle of Ethandune that the tide of paganism which has swept his country has reached its crest, and is now turning in the Christians' favor.

The High Tide and the Turn

A crowd emerges from the huge
Yoido Full Gospel Church in Seoul,
South Korea, in 1988. Seating twenty-
eight thousand, the Yoido Church evi-
dences the astonishing success
Christianity was enjoying in Asia,
Africa, and Latin America during the
late twentieth century. It far more
than offsets in numbers the rejection
of Christianity becoming increasingly
evident in western Europe.

A.D. 1914 to 2001

A New Christendom Explodes into Life in the Third World

The.
Christians

THEIR FIRST TWO THOUSAND YEARS

Twelfth Volume

CHRISTIAN HISTORY PROJECT
An Activity of SEARCH
The Society to Explore And Record Christian History

SEARCH CANADA:

The Society to Explore And Record Christian History is incorporated under the Alberta Societies Act. It has been registered as a charity by the Canada Revenue Agency.

Directors:
Ted Byfield, Edmonton, AB, President
Douglas G. Bell, CA, Edmonton, Treasurer
James Fitzgerald, Palmer Lake, CO
Christopher Gerrard, Rockville, MD
Terry Glaspey, Eugene, OR
Jaan Holt, Alexandria, VA
Murray Lytle, Calgary, AB
Allen Schmidt, Chase, BC
Secretary: Keith T. Bennett

SEARCH USA:

The Society to Explore And Record Christian History is incorporated under the Societies Act of the Commonwealth of Virginia. The society has been recognized by the Internal Revenue Service as a 501(c)(3) tax-exempt organization, donations to which are tax deductible.

Directors:
Jaan Holt, Alexandria, VA, Chairman
Ted Byfield, Edmonton, AB, Canada, President
Christopher Gerrard, Rockville, MD, Treasurer
Douglas G. Bell, CA, Edmonton, AB
James Fitzgerald, Palmer Lake, CO
Terry Glaspey, Eugene, OR
George Kurian, Yorktown Heights, NY
Murray Lytle, Calgary, AB
Allen Schmidt, Chase, BC
Joe Slay, Richmond, VA

Administration
General Manager: Keith T. Bennett
Customer Service: Clare Bennett

The High Tide and the Turn A.D. 1914 to 2001, A New Christendom Explodes into Life in the Third World
being Volume 12 of the series: **The Christians: Their First Two Thousand Years**

Writers: Ross Amy, Paul Bunner, Colman Byfield, Link Byfield, Virginia Byfield, Michael Coren, Ric Dolphin, Terry Glaspey, D'Arcy Jenish, Lianne Laurence, Mike Maunder, Thomas McFeely, Mike Wall, Steve Weatherbe
Director of Research: Adam Macpherson
Design and Art Director: Dean Pickup
Indexer: Louise Fairley, Indices

Academic Advisers: Dr. Peter Engle, dean of education at Living Faith Bible College in Caroline, AB; David J. Goa, director of the Chester Ronning Centre for the Study of Religion and Public Life, Augustana campus, University of Alberta, Camrose; Fr. Brian Hubka, priest of the Roman Catholic diocese of Calgary, AB; Dr. Dennis Martin, professor of historical theology, Loyola University, Chicago; Dr. Eugene TeSelle, emeritus professor of church history and theology, Vanderbilt University, TN

Research Readers: Ross Amy, Daniel Amy, Mary Cobb, Annie Colwell, Rachel Friesen, Celia Paz, George Rice, Ann Snyder, Mike Wall
Style Control: Georgia B. Varozza
Proofreaders: Georgia B. Varozza, Annie Colwell, Jennifer Fast

©2013 The Society to Explore And Record Christian History
203, 10441 178 Street, Edmonton, AB, Canada T5S 1R5
Chairman and President, Ted Byfield

Library and Archives Canada Cataloguing in Publication

The high tide and the turn : A.D. 1914 to 2001. A new Christendom explodes into life in the Third World / edited by Ted Byfield.

(The Christians: their first two thousand years ; 12)
Includes bibliographical references and index.
ISBN 978-0-9869396-2-4

1. Church history—20th century. I. Byfield, Ted II. Society to Explore and Record Christian History III. Series: Christians, their first two thousand years ; 12

BR479.H55 2013   270.8'2   C2013-900056-9

PRINTED IN CANADA BY FRIESENS CORPORATION

CONTENTS

FOREWORD

A certain limitation is imposed upon anyone intending to write a history of Christianity—namely that if Christianity is true, the job is technically impossible. For when the story ends, meaning when Christianity ends, everything else will have ended too. Presumably nobody would be left on earth to record any more history, or for that matter to read it. Our more modest effort—an account of Christianity's first two thousand years—at least falls within the realm of the possible, although it necessarily suffers a similar disability in that many of the events described are still going on.

This is one peculiarity of volume 12. Some of its stories have no ending because, of course, the ending has not yet occurred. It has another peculiarity too. Because of the scope and magnitude of recent Christian history, this book is half as big again as any of its predecessors. The twentieth century has seen more Christian trends and events, disasters and triumphs, failures and successes, than any other. Also, some readers may feel that we have paid too much attention to purely secular affairs, but very few events are purely secular. Religious issues often lie behind controversies that seem purely secular. That's why the Christian story cannot make sense unless it is accompanied by the secular, and vice versa.

Finally, most of our readers have a unique perspective on the twentieth century, in that they have lived in it, have taken part in some of the events described here, or have known people who did. Prior centuries they could only read about, but this one they have experienced firsthand. It is *their* century, and for the first time they are viewing it as their successors will—that is, as history—which may have a curious effect, like discovering that a building whose initial construction you recall from your childhood is now being designated an historic site. It makes you feel like an historic site yourself (which you suspect may be the way younger people do in fact regard you). Such are the pangs of old age—or are they actually joys?

We know something about all this, my wife and I, being eighty-three and eighty-four respectively. We began preliminary research for this series in January 1983, thirty years ago, and have been working on it full time for the last twelve. "What a relief it must be," friends say, "to see the job finally finished. What a sense of accomplishment it must bring!" But the job is not finished. In fact, it has barely begun.

The task now is to get the series into the hands of as many Christians as possible, thousands upon thousands of them, and equally important, to get them to actually read it. With more than thirty-six hundred pages this could also be considered a daunting undertaking—at the rate of one chapter read per week, it would require nearly two and a half years to complete. Yet these volumes are not encyclopedic, intended primarily for reference, nor are they "coffee table" ornaments to be casually reviewed, pronounced "beautiful," and set aside. Rather, they offer a vital and coherent story—and for Christians especially, often a gripping one—which starts at the beginning of volume 1 and ends on the last page of this one.

People who have been reading each book as it appeared tell us they make two discoveries. For one, each chapter and each volume creates a certain suspense, so that you want to know what happens next and why, which makes the process both pleasurable and profitable. Beyond this, however, our readers say that as the story unfolds they acquire something they never possessed before, notably a remarkable new comprehension of what is taking place right now, and why. Knowing the past, they find, gives them a better understanding of the present; the current scene, once so baffling, becomes far less fearsome.

As for us, for so much help and faithful support over so many years, we are deeply grateful.

Ted Byfield

General Editor

The Christians

The High Tide
and the Turn

A.D. 1914 to 2001

OUR THANKS GO OUT TO THE PEOPLE WHOSE FINANCIAL
GIFTS TO SEARCH MADE THE PRODUCTION OF
THIS FINAL VOLUME POSSIBLE

PATRONS OF THE PROJECT

Richard Bird, Calgary   L. R. Cable, Edmonton   Dr. Ernest Hodges, Edmonton   John Hokanson, Edmonton
Jack Klemke, Edmonton   Sandy MacTaggart, Edmonton   Gerald J Maier, Calgary   Allen Markin, Calgary
Stanley A. Milner, Edmonton   R. J. Nelson Family Foundation, Lloydminster, AB   Mervin & Faye Schafer, Calgary
Margaret and Ron Southern, Calgary   Tony Vandenbrink, Calgary   Frank Vetsch, Calgary

APOSTLES OF VOLUME 12

Charles Allard, Edmonton   Bill & Linda Britton, Calgary   Leo & Faye Gaumont, Tofield, AB
Wayne Hansen, Sherwood Park, AB   Mark Hicks, Lynden, WA
Saint John's School of Alberta Legacy Foundation, Stony Plain, AB   Masha Krupp, Ottawa
Hugh & Laura MacKinnon, Toronto   Celestine Montgomery, Edmonton
Ed Sardachuk, Calgary   Hank Schoen, Surrey, BC   Al Stober, Kelowna, BC
Herb Styles, Calgary   William & Fern Williams, West Chicago, IL

1119 OTHER NORTH AMERICANS WHOSE GIFTS SAW THE VOLUME FINISHED

A-D

Peter Adema, Acton, ON; Joyce Agnew, Brandon, MB; George Akers, Edmonton, AB; Michael Albrechtson, Crawford Bay, BC; Gloria Alcock, Kenora, ON; Ginny Alexander, 100 Mile House, BC; Scott Allan, Fredericksburg, VA; Charles Allen, Grapeland, TX; Janice Allison, Veteran, AB; Faye Altwasser, Yellow Grass, SK; Bob & Karen Anderson, Orange, MA; Bob Anderson, Colorado Springs, CO; Gordon Anderson, Langley, BC; Peggy Anderson, Calgary, AB; Rachel Anderson, Wellesley, ON; Raymond & Jeanette Anderson, Champion, AB; William Anderson, Anderson, IN; Virginia Andrews, Imperial, MO; Margie Antes, San Ramon, CA; Harry Antonides, North York, ON; Paul & Laurel Armerding, Hood River, OR; Carol Armstrong, Calgary, AB; Kevin Armstrong, Calgary, AB; Peter & Cathy Armstrong, Odessa, FL; Joan Arychuk, Millet, AB; Harold Ashley, Calgary, AB; Art Ashton, Vancouver, WA; Joseph Askin, Calgary, AB; Jim Atkinson, Lutes Mountain, NB; Eckehart Augustini, Gibsons, BC; Virginia Austin, Dunbarton, NH; David Austring, Newmarket, ON; Leslie Avila, Germantown, TN; Linda Ayer, Colchester, VT; John & Linda Bachmann, Mission, BC; Ralph Bagshaw, Vancouver, BC; Helen Bailey, Lillian, AL; Merilyn Baird, Calgary, AB; Owen Baker, Enderby, BC; Irene Bakos, Calgary, AB; Kenneth Bannister, Edmonton, AB; Dorian Barbee, Sevierville, TN; Robert & Isabel Barber, Strasbourg, SK; Barton Barcel, Bellwood, NE; Casey Barendregt, Smithers, BC; Barbara Bargy, Prince George, BC; Marie Barkess, Delta, BC; Doug Barnett, Edmonton, AB; Norman Bartel, Kleefeld, MB; William Barthel, Coalhurst, AB; Brian & Miriam Bartley, Norland, ON; Gary & Elizabeth Bartz, West Caldwell, NJ; Gordon Bauman, Alma, ON; Frans & Cheryl Bax, McLean, VA; Wallace Bays, Richland, WA; Muriel Beatty, Richmond Hill, ON; Kelli Beaucage, North Battleford, SK; Pam Beecher, Concord, NC; Cornelis Beek, Cranbrook, BC; Robert Beekhuizen, Calgary, AB; Hessina Bekkering, Taber, AB; Helena Bell, Saskatoon, SK; Randall Belle, Coronach, SK; Carol Belsheim, Marwayne, AB; Doug Bennett, Nelson, BC; Barbara Benoit, Lloydminster, AB; Elesa Bentsen, Duluth, GA; Michael & Judith Berg, Rosemount, MN; Ronald Berry, Washington, MI; Sidney & Deborah Bertz, Eagle River, AK; Richard Bibby, Camrose, AB; Marguerite Biederman, Calgary, AB; Roberta Biel, Lacombe, AB; Jan Bieler, East Lansing, MI; Alvin Bingaman, Seattle, WA; Leslie & Jeannine Biollo, Lac La Biche, AB; Trevor Birkholz, Fresno, CA; Paul Bistritan, Surrey, BC; David Bjorem, Tempe, AZ; Dorothy Blaak, Abbotsford, BC; Robert & Verna Blackburn, Mississauga, ON; E David Blair, Calgary, AB; Judy Blakeney, Winthrop, WA; Myrna Bloch, Fort Langley, BC; Peter Blote, Edmonton, AB; Marvin Blundell, Hay Springs, NE; Sandra Bogenholm, Los Alamos, NM; Doug Bohn, Greenwood, BC; Lillian Bokenfohr, St Albert, AB; Garry & Gayle Bond, Edmonton, AB; Edna Bonertz, Drayton Valley, AB; Joe Boonstra, Telkwa, BC; Wilma Borger, Jordan Station, ON; Vickie Born, Granby, CO; Richard Borroughs, Kelowna, BC; Clarence Bos, Taber, AB; John Bos, Taber, AB; Helen Bosch, Abbotsford, BC; Royce & Pietie Boskers, Ardrossan, AB; Dale Bowler, Sherwood Park, AB; Chris Boyle, Beausejour, MB; Bill Braak, Abbotsford, BC; Charles Bradshaw, Opelika, AL; Mary Brady, Hemdon, VA; Ray Brandon, Comox, BC; Sheri Braun, Langley, BC; Jonah Braun , Edmonton, AB; Mark Brewster, London, ON; Dorothy E Bright, Coarsegold, CA; Jonathan Brinkman, Chatham, ON; Ralph Brinsmead, Calgary, AB; John Bristow, San Jose, CA; Klaas Brobbel, Oakville, ON; William Bronson, Great Falls, MT; Bill Brough, Cadwell, IL; Jim Brown, Lloydminster, AB; Ray & Beverley Brown, Vista, MB; Lieuwe Bruinsma, Leduc, AB; Kristine Buchholtz, Sherwood Park, AB; Michael Burgard, Bozeman, MT; Patricia Burgess, Edmonton, AB; Andrew Burghardt, Dundas, ON; Harvey Burkholder, Three Hills, AB; Mary Burlingame, Glen Ellyn, IL; John & Margaret Burnham, San Jose, CA; Mary Burnie, Toronto, ON; Stanley N Burris, Waterloo, ON; Carole Burton, Clarkes Beach, NL; Mamie Burton, Fairfax, VA; Graham Butcher, Stouffville, ON; David Butler, Monrovia, CA; Sue Butterfield, Morton, IL; Mary Buzinsky, Edmonton, AB; Carmen Bycok, Kingston, ON; Monte Byrd, Bellville, TX; Roy Calvert, Downers Grove, IL; Don Calvert, Slave Lake, AB; Howard Cameron, Stony Plain, AB; Spiro & Jacklyn Camilleri, Towson, MD; Kenneth W Campbell, Calgary, AB; Tim Campbell, Red Deer, AB; Carol Campbell, Aurora, ON; Eliza Campbell, Queen City, AZ; Elise Campbell, Monroe, CT; Joanne Cannon, Calgary, AB; Rose Carnes, Holland, IN; Pat Carroll, Kamloops, BC; Errol Carruthers, Medicine Hat, AB; Richard & Olivia Carson, Caddo, OK; Robert Case, McMinnville, TN; Pamela Cavey, Janesville, WI; Clarence & Femmie Cazemier, Red Deer, AB; Colin Cazemier, Calgary, AB; James Chabun, Emerald Park, SK; Greg Chalk, Oklahoma City, OK; Garfield Challoner, Norquay, SK; Michael Chambers, Fort Pierce, FL; Larry Chandler, Payette, ID; Stan Chappell, Edmonton, AB; Hazel Chase, Vermilion, AB; Wilma Cheesman, Guelph, ON; Lawrence Cherneski, Taber, AB; Barrett Chevalier, Edmonton, AB; Clem Chiasson, St Albert, AB; Carl Christensen, St. Lina, AB; James Christie, Trochu, AB; Jim Christie, Pickering, ON; Myrna Christopherson, Olds, AB; Dallas Christopherson, Olds, AB; Gayle Church, Drumheller, AB; Don Cinnamon, Edmonton, AB; Judy Clark, Hoonah, AK; Vivian Clark, Alliance, AB; Ross & Sally Cleary, Ottawa, ON; Marie Luise Cleaver, Vancouver, WA; David A Cline, White Rock, BC; David & Sarina Cliplef, Onoway, AB; Patrick Clock, Kalama, WA; Joan Cobb, Nashville, IL; Gerald Cole, Stettler, AB; Donna Coleman, Bellingham, WA; Robert Coleman, Everett, WA; Vonda Coleman, Brewton, AL; Vicki Collard, Bainbridge Island, WA; Stan Collier, Penhold, AB; Stewart & Corinne Collin, Foremost, AB; Mike Cooney, Edmonton, AB; Margaret Cooper, Kitchener, ON; Don Copeland, Calgary, AB;

Dirk & Carol Cornish, Thorsby, AB; Clyde Corser, Yellowhead County, AB; Dan & Joanne Couch, Roseburg, OR; Don Coulter, Calgary, AB; Richard & Lynn Coulter, Grabill, IN; Robert & Edith Coutts, Rolla, BC; Gay Couture, Saskatoon, SK; Adrian Crane, Edmonton, AB; Barbara Crouse, Lebanon, OH; John Crowell, Solvang, CA; Marcia Crumley, Uniontown, OH; Walter Cuell, Peace River, AB; Timothy & Lori Culp, Taylor, MI; Elaine Culp, Battle Lake, MN; Ruth Cummings, Vancouver, BC; Robert Cummins, Birchwood, MN; Bill Curtis, Worcester, PA; James Curtis, Jacksonville, FL; Robert Daino, Kinnelon, NJ; Zoltan & Doris Darvasi, Surrey, BC; James and Marilyn Davey, Portage la Prairie, MB; Maurice de Putter, Richmond, BC; Alphonse de Valk, Toronto, ON; Sandra DeBoeck, Grand Forks, BC; Mary Deboer, Burlington, ON; David Defauw, Casco, MI; Frits Dekker, Bow Island, AB; Amos Delagrange, Woodburn, IN; Fred Demoskott, Langley, BC; Dave Denlinger, Canton, OH; Daniel Dennison, Willowbrook, IL; Jan & Cent DeRegt, Spruce Grove, AB; Marj Derochie, Claresholm, AB; Gerrit & Wilma Dewit, Chilliwack, BC; Andy &

Tara Dewitt, Salem, IL; Brenda Dezeeuw, McBain, MI; Mike Dika, Rycroft, AB; Steve Dion, Sidney, BC; William Disch, Georgetown, TX; Sharon Dittrich, Malibu, CA; James & Janice Dixon, Orchard Park, NY; Laura Dodson, Lagrange, GA; Mark & Adele Dolan, Hudson, WI; Michael L. Doll, Calgary, AB; Alice H Doll, Smithers, BC; Chris Dombroski, Edmonton, AB; Belva Dosdall, Hardisty, AB; Mary Frances Doucedame, Newbury Park, CA; Carol Douglas, Courtenay, BC; Marcia Dow, Rivercourse, AB; Robin Dow, West Vancouver, BC; Don Dowdeswell, Pennant Station, SK; Fred Downing, St. Paul, MN; Peggy Drehmel, Wausau, WI; Steven Driggers, Avon, IN; Robert Drinnan, Dunrobin, ON; Trudy Droogendyk, Lynden, ON; Tera Dueck, Sexsmith, AB; Margo Dunsworth, Edmonton, AB; Milt Duntley, Arkdale, WI; Joe & Marilyn Dupuis, Edmonton, AB; Carol Dyck, Rosemary, AB; John & Gisela Dyck, Brooks, AB; John & Sue Dyck, Calgary, AB; Peter & Agnes Dyck, Linden, AB; Terry Dyck, Clive, AB; Adolph Dykstra, Edmonton, AB; Jacob Dykxhoorn, Calgary, AB; Edward Dzielenski, Longmeadow, MA;

E-I

Don & Anne Eddie, Lisle, ON; Kelly & Caroline Edwards, Calgary, AB; Ann Egert, Cando, SK; Marilyn Elhard, Eastend, SK; Chuck Elliott, Edmonton, AB; Bryan Elliott, Westwold, BC; Lewis & Jane Elzinga, Yellowhead County, AB; Grace Elzinga, Beverly, MA; Brian & Ellen Engbers, Calgary, AB; Peter & Michelle Englefield, Edmonton, AB; Faye Engler, St Albert, AB; William Engvall, Sonora, CA; H David Enns, Vernon, BC; Elizabeth Epp, Surrey, BC; Terry Epp, St Albert, AB; Katie Everett, Windham, NH; Caryl Evjen, Hampton, MN; Gloria Evjen, Stony Plain, AB; Audrey Ewanchuk, Edmonton, AB; Faith Evangelical Free Church, Dallas, OR; Willie Falk, Niverville, MB; Michael Fanning, Calgary, AB; William Faulkner, Cape Coral, FL; Lydia Fedor, Edmonton, AB; Cornelius Fehr, Lowe Farm, MB; Elsie Fehr, Barriere, BC; Ruth Fehr, Kelowna, BC; Peggy Felshaw, Hemet, CA; Fran Fenimore, Blair, NE; Bill Ferguson, North Pole, AK; Norman & Sophie Filtz, Edmonton, AB; Eileen Finlay, Edmonton, AB; Steven & Kristie Firme, Haxtun, CO; Dale Fischer, Didsbury, AB; John Fischer Jr., Inver Grove, MN; Mark Fischer, Mokelumne Hill, CA; Tom & Marianne Flanagan , Calgary, AB; Howard & Veronique Fohr, Ottawa, ON; Virginia Foley, The Woodlands, TX; Marc Fontaine, Vonda, SK; Robert Forbes, Red Deer, AB; Earle Forgues, Calgary, AB; Paul & Sheila Forsyth, Lynnwood, WA; Gord Foster, Fort Vermilion, AB; Larry & Suzanne Foster, Buda, TX; Hipolito Franco, Scarborough, ON; Ron Frank, St. Albert, AB; Edward Peter Franck, Bangor, SK; Wanda Franke, Grande Prairie, AB; Carol Fraser, Calgary, AB; Sandra Frazier, Omaha, NE; Shona Freeman, Amelia, VA; Gloria Freije, Glendale, AZ; Larry Frey, Prince George, BC; Debra Friedli, Ada, MI; Jack Friis, Lawrencetown, NS; Laura Frost, Delta, BC; Gwen Funk, Neville, SK; Brian Galliford, Prince George, BC; Donna Gamble, Fort Saint John, BC; Jonathan & Karen Garner, Stony Plain, AB; Allen Garrett, Okotoks, AB; Herman Gartner, Lloydminster, AB; Deanna Gass, Arrowwood, AB; Margaret Gennaro, Katy, TX; Therese Gervais, Morinville, AB; A Campbell Gibbard, Edmonton, AB; Terry Gibbs, Carnarvon, ON; Ron & Marilyn Gibson, Quesnel, BC; Donald Gibson, Wall Lake, IA; Glenn Gill, Williams Lake, BC; Cliff Ginn, Airdrie, AB; Barry R Giovanetto, Calgary, AB; Roland Girard, Genelle, BC; Dale Glasier, Medicine Hat, AB; Elizabeth Goff, Qualicum Beach, BC; Virginia Golany, High Prairie, AB; Denne Gold, Acme, WA; Chris & Debra Goldring, Calgary, AB; Don Goodale, Edmonton, AB; John Goodbrand, Youngstown, AB; Tim Goode, Lake Country, BC; Jim Goodvin, Edmonton, AB; Peter Gook, Quesnel, BC; Wilhelm Gortemaker, Winnipeg, MB; Mary Gour, Grovedale, AB; Paul Gowdy, Kelowna, BC; W. D. (Bill) Grace, Edmonton, AB; Tom Grainger, Surrey, BC; Gary Graves, Asheville, NC; Ralph Greene, Brampton, ON; Janet Greenlaw, Grande Prairie, AB; Steve Grenat, West Lafayette, IN; David Grier, Saskatoon, SK; Lori Griffin, Owatonna, MN; Norm Grinde, Wetaskiwin, AB; Helen Griscowsky, Medicine Hat, AB;

Anna Groeneveld, Allenford, ON; Arie Grootenboer, Murillo, ON; Valerie Grundke, Dartmouth, NS; George Haack, Ste Anne, MB; Janet Hackett, Murrysville, PA; Arnold Hagen, Camrose, AB; Donald & Jean Hagquist, Johnston, IA; Margaret Hailey, Pennsburg, PA; Doug Hait, Edmonton, AB; Frank Haley, Edmonton, AB; Wilfred Haley, Loretto, ON; Joyce Haley, Anchorage, AK; Lucinda Hall, Barstow, CA; Dennis Haller, Burnaby, BC; Monika Halwass, Calgary, AB; W G Hamilton, Calgary, AB; Elizabeth Hammond, Yellow Springs, OH; Harley Hammond, Tofield, AB; Ken Harcus, Edmonton, AB; John Harder, Calgary, AB; Richard & Gwyneth Harding, Calgary, AB; Myrna Hargrave, Cochrane, AB; James Hargrave, Abbotsford, BC; Arend Harke, St Albert, AB; Norman Harper, Fayetteville, PA; George Harper, Nashville, TN; Leonard Hart, Steinbach, MB; Fred Hauf, Edmonton, AB; Arnot & Lenore Hawkins, Thunder Bay, ON; Margaret Hearn, Victoria, BC; Ken Heavenor, Edmonton, AB; Jakob Heckert, Ann Arbor, MI; Leslie Hedley, Calgary, AB; Ira & Velma Heebner, Cypress County, AB; Art Heinrichs, Calgary, AB; John & Margaret Helder, Edmonton, AB; Susan Helder, Volga, SD; Alan Henderson, King City, ON; George Hennig, Edmonton, AB; Robert Herbst, Carthage, MO; Fred Herfst, Burnaby, BC; John & Jobyna Herman, Colville, WA; Theodore & Lori Herman, Omro, WI; Ernest Herndon, Gloster, MS; Adrian Herren, Pensacola, FL; Lalia Herrera, Calgary, AB; Wayne Hertlein, Langenburg, SK; Harry Hess, Edmonton, AB; Adele Hetherington, Moose Jaw, SK; Brian & Barbara Hewitt, Granisle, BC; Lee & Sharon Hibbard, Nampa, AB; Richard Higgins, Rockville, MD; Ted High, Whitecourt, AB; Lawrie Hignell, Edmonton, AB; Thomas & Catherine Hilton, Gibbons, AB; Doug Hindmarsh, Vancouver, BC; Jeanette W Hines, Martinez, GA; Gary Hinkle, Bremen, IN; Peter Hinterkopf, Waynesboro, PA; Anne Hodgson, Girouxville, AB; Terry Hodson, Golden, CO; Kermit Hoffs, Phoenix, AZ; Fred Hofsink Sr, Smithers, BC; Elaine Hogan, Curtice, OH; Barbara Holan, St Albert, AB; John Holcombe, Phoenix, AZ; Cory & Nora Holden, Finland, MN; Tom Holder, Leduc, AB; Lyn Holloway, Castor, AB; Robert Holmstrom, Vero Beach, FL; Helen & Jaan Holt, Alexandria, VA; Louis Hompoth, Regina, SK; John Hopson, Fairfax, VA; Merwin & Elaine Houger, Creston, WA; Loraine Houston, Red Deer, AB; Rosalie Howerton, Tyler, TX; Harry Hubbard, Lethbridge, AB; Daniel Hudelson, Coopersville, MI; Don Hughes, Edmonton, AB; Bert Huizing, Abbotsford, BC; Caroline Hunt, Dallas, TX; Harold Hunt, Maple Ridge, BC; Peter Hunt, Bragg Creek, AB; Don Hurlbert, Escondido, CA; Jean Husted, Littleton, CO; Kenneth Hutchinson, Calgary, AB; Carson & Vicky Ikert, Sleeman, ON; David Imes, Crawford, TX; Dudley Inggs, St Helena, CA; Kathleen Isely, Redmond, OR; Bonnie Ivey, Chapleau, ON;

J-M

Doug Jackson, Chilliwack, BC; Rick Jahn, Signal Mountain, TN; Vincent James, Fraser Lake, BC; Wallace & Pamela Jans, Medicine Hat, AB; Jan Jansma, Port Alberny, BC; Allen Janzen, Castlegar, BC; Randal & Janice Jewell, Sandusky, MI; Alexei Jernov, Edmonton, AB; Sally Joblonkay, Wetaskiwin, AB; Janet John, Cranbrook, BC; Michael Johnson, Glennallen, AK; Barbara L Johnson, Calgary, AB; Corey & Jennifer Johnson, Hughenden, AB; Bill & Jan Johnson, Fremont, MI; Fred & Nadia Johnson, Calgary, AB; Lucille Johnston, Calgary, AB; Mary Johnson, Gibsonton, FL; Will Johnston, Vancouver, BC; Guy Johnston, Victoria, BC; Allan Johnston,

Big Valley, AB; Robert Johnstone, Vancouver, BC; Glen Jonat, Vernon, BC; F. Pedersen Jones, Stony Plain, AB; Horace Jones, Washington, DC; Keith Jones, Grande Prairie, AB; Oce & Max Jones, Clive, AB; Richy Jones, Bakersville, NC; Susan Jones, Indianapolis, IN; Lee Jorgesen, Ellscott, AB; Ray Joustra, Osgoode, ON; Arthur Jukes, Calgary, AB; Robert O Kalbach, Farmington, NY; Hildred Karlson, Edmonton, AB; John Katrichak, Sparwood, BC; Everett & Marlo Kearley, Saskatoon, SK; Hardy Kehler, Steinbach, MB; Peter Kempe, Taber, AB; Henry Kennedy, Calgary, AB; Ron Kennedy, London, ON; Forrest & Jenny Kennerd, Cochrane, AB;

J-M (Continued)

Verdon & Janice Kerr, Yellowhead County, AB; Steven Keske, Lakeville, MN; Ralph Ketel, Pine River, MB; Alice Kielstra, Calgary, AB; Jim Kienholz, Holyoke, CO; Jim Kiernan, Victoria, BC; Shirley Kiffiak, Picture Butte, AB; Robert Kimball, South Lake Tahoe, CA; Leona King, Tottenham, ON; Steve King, McLean, VA; Jitsche Kingma, Smithville, ON; Donald & Jeanne Kirchner, Franklin, WI; John Kirn, Columbus, OH; Tim Kjorlien, Drayton Valley, AB; Lutz Klaar, Prince George, BC; Henry Klaas, Listowel, ON; Isaac & Trudy Klassen, Prince George, BC; Timothy Klaver, St Thomas, ON; Stacey Kleiboer, Meskanaw, SK; Don Klein, Viking, AB; Barbara Kloster, MacKlin, SK; Dolores Knight, Santa Ana, CA; John & Debra Knowles, Cayley, AB; Dennis Knudtson, Calgary, AB; Yvonne Kobes, Edam, SK; Earl Koch, New Hamburg, ON; Kathryn Koch, Waldorf, MD; Mary Ann Koerschner, Iron Mountain, MI; Alois Kolinsky, Edmonton, AB; Eric Kolkman, Ardrossan, AB; Sandra Konechny, Dalmeny, SK; Dino Konstantos, Woodbridge, ON; Bill Kooman, Red Deer, AB; Phyllis Kopen, Edmonton, AB; William Korvemaker, Dorchester, ON; Cor Korver, Lethbridge, AB; Barry Kossowan, Edmonton, AB; Kim Kostuch, Caledonia, WI; Ed Kowalenko, Calgary, AB; Thomas Krajecki, Aurora, IL; Mary Kreutzer, Plumas, MB; William & Cindy Kruisselbrink, Allenford, ON; Donna Kuhn, Spokane, WA; Virginia Kurtz, Cape Elizabeth, ME; Michael & Cheryl Kuziw, Sherwood Park, AB; Mary Labelle, Cochrane, ON; Marion Labonte, Ottawa, ON; Rozalie Lacoursiere, Delmas, SK; David Lah, O'Fallon, MO; Michael & Rose Marie Lalor, St Albert, AB; Doug Lambe, Nepean, ON; Oakley & Ruby Lambert, Columbus, MS; Kristen Lancaster, San Antonio, TX; Hazel Landgraf, Spruce Grove, AB; Dorothy Lane, Athabasca, AB; Louise Lang, Calgary, AB; Jack Lang, Little River, SC; Elva Langland, Bassano, AB; Wayne & Candy Lannan, Calgary, AB; William Laprise, Elkgrove Village, IL; Marlene Larrabee, Gleason, WI; John & Marjorie Lawrence, Calgary, AB; Anthony Leenheer, Edmonton, AB; Hector Lefebvre, Edmonton, AB; Coral Lehman, Surrey, BC; Ed Lehman, Edmonton, AB; Roger Lenartowski, Lake Mills, WI; Bill Lensmire, Ixonia, WI; Debbie Leslie, Sedgewick, AB; Charles Lester, Tallahassee, FL; Dallas Lester, Yelm, WA; George Lewans, Shaunavon, SK; Cynthia Lewis, Paris, TX; Dawn Lhenen, Calgary, AB; Margie Liberty, Hercules, CA; Harry Lincoln, North Bethesda, MD; Vernal Lind, Battle Lake, MN; Cornelis & Julie Lindhout, Toronto, ON; Victoria Link, San Diego, CA; Wil Link, Vacaville, CA; Walter Lint, Winnipeg, MB; Priscilla Lipp, Rocky View, AB; Gary & Helene Litschke, Calgary, AB; Wendy Livingstone, Langley, BC; Louise Lobdell, Carbon, AB; Betty Lockhart, Dayton, NV; Norm Lorenz, Dunster, BC; Don & Joyce Low, Vancouver, BC; Dorothy Lowrie, St Albert, AB; Paul Lowrie, Anahim Lake, BC; Philip & Sandra Luchka, Lethbridge, AB; John Lukacs, Olds, AB; Wilma Lutke, Maple Ridge, BC; Heather Maahs, Chilliwack, BC; Don & Heidi MacDonald, Priddis, AB; Don & Jean MacDonald, Elrose, SK; John MacDonald, Nevada City, CA; Veronica MacDougall, Green Valley, ON; Brian MacGregor, Ottawa, ON; Roger MacKin, Moose Jaw, SK; John MacLean, Calgary, AB; James MacLean, Thunder Bay, ON; Murdoch & Katherine Macleod, Calgary, AB; Patricia Maczko, Edmonton, AB; Paul Maitland, Peoria, IL; Margaret Malcolm, Calgary, AB; Emmanuel Malterre, Calgary, AB; James Marchant, St. Lambert, QC; Gary & Gladys Marcial, Calgary, AB; Marilyn Margeson, Berwick, NS; Ernie Marshall, Edmonton, AB; James Martens, Wetaskiwin, AB; Joseph Martens, Havelock, ON; Allan Martin, Mount Forest, ON; Phyllis Martin, Royersford, PA; Dean & Anna Martin, Wallenstein, ON; Erma Martin, Cochrane, AB; Denis Mascardelli, Calgary, AB; Rosemary Mason, Lakefield, ON; Clara Matthews, Billings, MT; Lilly Matzigkeit, Kelowna, BC; Vince Mauer, Cincinnati, OH; David Maxwell, Adrian, MI; Phillip Mayfield, Williams Lake, BC; Neil & Nancy McAskill, Burnaby, BC; Dave McCaw, Lloydminster, AB; Brian McClellan, Laurel, MD; Anne Marie McCollum, Arrington, TN; Alex & Ruth McCombie, Chesley, ON; Matthew McCormick, Toronto, ON; Donna McCormick, Toronto, ON; Pat McCoy, Edmonton, AB; Ian McCulloch, Harrisonburg, VA; Don McCurry, Divide, CO; James McDermott, Fayetteville, NC; Joyce McEwan, Tisdale, SK; William & Freda McGill, Edmonton, AB; Joanne McGlinch, Lima, OH; Douglas & Gayle McIntosh, Brooklin, ON; Annie McIntyre, Langley, BC; Evelyn McIver, Grand Forks, BC; Audrey McKay, Blackfalds, AB; John McKean, Edmonton, AB; Marilyn McKenzie, Okotoks, AB; Monty McKenzie, Strasbourg, SK; Candis McLean, Calgary, AB; D M & Margaret McMillan, Huntington Beach, CA; Gary McMillen, Santa Clarita, CA; Leonard Meador, Madison Heights, VA; Adele Meador, Klamath Falls, OR; Evelyn Mealy, Kingwood, TX; Robert Meeks, Saint John, IN; Allan Megli, Linden, AB; Patricia Mehlberg, Lawrenceville, GA; Diana Meinen, Chilliwack, BC; Tom Meland, Clearwater, BC; Norma Melindy, Aspen Cove, NF; Peter Mendes, Edmonton, AB; Karen Mendonca, Edmonton, AB; Thomas Mercer, Murrayville, BC; Jessie Mercer, Calgary, AB; James Merz, Sherwood Park, AB; Marina Mesa, Buena Park, CA; Bill & Claire Middleton, York, ON; John Miedema, Edmonton, AB; Milford Miller, Boise, ID; Virginia Miller, Millville, MN; Dave Mitchell, Vulcan, AB; Jerry & Peggy Mitchell, Radford, VA; Mark Moesker, Wyoming, ON; Candace Molberg, St Albert, AB; Gordon Mollet, Creston, CA; Carol Monk, Delta, BC; Gwendolyn Montrose, Abilene, TX; Michael Moore, Freelandville, IN; Charles & Farrar Moore, Nashville, TN; Gwen Moore, Ottawa, ON; Jane Moore, Selma, AL; Susan Morbey, North Saanich, BC; Fawzy H Morcos, Edmonton, AB; Herb & Eloise Morgan, Nampa, ID; Robert I Morgan, Albuquerque, NM; Casey Moroschan, Edmonton, AB; George & Rhoda Morrison, New Westminster, BC; Tracy Morsi, Waterford, MI; Ron Morton, Calgary, AB; Lyle Mosher, Evansburg, AB; Shirley Moss, Medicine Hat, AB; Sandra Moulton, Melfort, SK; Ivy Moulton, Melfort, SK; Martin & Brigitte Mueller, Ft Saskatchewan, AB; Hugh Mutlow, Fiske, SK; Leslie Myram, Prince George, BC;

N-S

Peter and Lois Nauta, Edmonton, AB; Julie Nellermore, West Fargo, ND; Thomas Nelson, Birmingham, AL; Timothy Nelson, Walnut Cove, NC; Barry Neufeld, La Crete, AB; Chuck & Melva Neufeld, Penticton, BC; David Neuman, Los Alamos, NM; Julie Neuman, Albuquerque, NM; Peter & Anne Neustaeter, La Crete, AB; John Neustaeter, Edmonton, AB; Joanne Neven, Dundas, ON; Philip Ney, Victoria, BC; Ginger Nichols, Columbia, SC; Linda Nickerson, Spencer, NC; Don Nielsen, Red Deer, AB; Jamie Nielsen, Calgary, AB; Doris Nikkel, Lundar, MB; John & Margaret Noorloos, Wyoming, ON; Cathy Nordli, High River, AB; Paul Norris, Westerose, AB; Garth & Cheryl Oberkirsch, Weyburn, SK; Joseph & Jamie O'Halloran, Newberg, OR; Agnes Olfert, Drumheller, AB; Donald Olson, Ohaton, AB; David & Doreen Olson, Camrose, AB; Shawn & Amy Oltz, Niles, MI; Esther S Ondrack, Spruce Grove, AB; Terry O'Neill, Coquitlam, BC; Gloria Opgenorth, Edmonton, AB; John Opmeer, Richmond, BC; Fay Orr, Edmonton, AB; Frank O'Shea, Calgary, AB; Catherine Osterberg, Post Falls, ID; Jeff & Lin Ostrosser, Spruce Grove, AB; Ruth Paceyi, Edmonton, AB; John & Trudy Paetkau, Edmonton, AB; Leanne Pahl, Calgary, AB; Donald & Valerie Palmer, Peace River, AB; Ken Palmer, Calgary, AB; Parish of the Annunciation, Nepean, ON; Karlotta Parry, Saint Anthony, ID; Denise Patrick, Fostoria, MI; Loren Pearson, Edmonton, AB; Yvonne Peirce, Victoria, BC; Philip Pelletier, Calgary, AB; Edna Penner, Linden, AB; Lloyd & Gladys Penner, Stettler, AB; Tim Penner, Clay Center, KS; Ernesto Perez, Lomita, CA; Jean Perkins, Grand Marais, MN; Gloria Peronto, Ishpeming, MI; Elizabeth Perry, Calgary, AB; Gloria Peterman, Hadley, PA; Christine Peters, Tatla Lake, BC; Helmut Peters, Calgary, AB; Keith Peters, Kerrobert, SK; Gene Petersohn, Sheboygan, WI; Donald E Peterson, Rose Prairie, BC; Paul Peterson, Hazelton, BC; Kenneth Petruk, Edmonton, AB; Dallas Petry, Edmonton, AB; Howard Pettengill, Indialantic, FL; Frederick Phelps, Mount Plesant, MI; Eugene Phoa, Sherwood Park, AB; Fred & Marilyn Pilon, Richmond Hill, ON; Rick Plett, Linden, AB; Edward Plume, Calgary, AB; Ellen Poai, Kailua Kona, HI; Mark Poernbacher, Surrey, BC; Paul Pollex, St. Thomas, ON; Kim Poon, Markham, ON; Graeme Postill, Airdrie, AB; Patrick Potter, Wisconsin Dells, WI; Tom Powrie, Edmonton, AB; Priscilla Poynter, Lexington, KY; Gregory & Jacqueline Priatko, Eagle, WI; Roland Priddle, Ottawa, ON; Philip Priddle, Ottawa, ON; Jake Prins, Lacombe, AB; Neil Pronk, Brantford, ON; Dwight Pulsfus, Sauk City, WI; Robert Purdy, Calgary, AB; Mary Pyle, Boise, ID; Kris Raabel, Hinton, AB; Ron and Wendy Radant, Okotoks, AB; Joanne Radstake, Alma, ON; David Rainforth, Lacombe, AB; Cheryl Ranns, Victoria, BC; Eugene Ratsoy, Edmonton, AB; Bill Rawlins, Nanaimo, BC; Terry Raymond, Peace River, AB; Jack Read, Edmonton, AB; Randy Redekop, Vauxhall, AB; Faith Reece, Hazel Park, MI; Holly Reed, Nepean, ON; Brian Reed, Calgary, AB; Anne Reedyk, Three Hills, AB; Nora Reimer, Winnipeg, MB; Elizabeth Rose Reimer, Surrey, BC; Theo Reiner, Calgary, AB; Mildred Reinhart, Lashburn, SK; Fred & Teresa Reitsma, Smithers, BC; Frank Rempel, Swift Current, SK; Lynn Requier, Donnelly, AB; Linda J Reynhout, De Smet, SD; David & Deborah Reynolds, Burnsville, MN; James & Marlene Richards, Cavan, ON; Stephen & Janet Richards, Thorsby, AB; Cathryn Richardson, Arlington Heights, IL; Clayton Richardson, Brownfield, AB; Sam Richter, Calgary, AB; Patti Richter, Heath, TX; Darrell Riemer, Pine Lake, AB; Troy & Laura Rife, Mishawaka, IN; Tom Rigby, Littleton, CO; Jo Ann Rinke, Clinton Township, MI; Dorothy Rivers, High River, AB; David Robbins, Alhambra, CA; Joe Robbe, Portland, MI; William Robertson, Ellijay, GA; Don Robinson, Camrose, AB; Jeff Robinson, Laurel, MD; Dirk Rook, Renfrew, ON; Patricia Rooke, Victoria, BC; John Rosevear, Knowlton, QC; Denise Roth, Saskatoon, SK; Grace Roth, Medicine Hat, AB; David Rousseau, Haverhill, MA; Nathan Rousu, Edmonton, AB; Clay Rowe, Gadsden, AL; Doug & Geri Rozander, Okotoks, AB; Jane Rued, Palmetto, FL; Nancy Ruhlman, Mount Vernon, WA; Roy & Sheila Runzer, Glendon, AB; Carl Rusnell, Edmonton, AB; George Russell, Milk River, AB; Wim Ruysch, Rollyview, AB; Sophie Sadowsky, Edmonton, AB; Suzie Sage, Republic, WA; Jim Sagert, Quesnel, BC; Felipe Sahagun, Bloomfield, NE; Stephen & Laura Salisbury, Ft Washington, PA; Joe Sanche, Beaumont, AB; Diane Sandberg, Lake Elsimore, CA; Evelyn Sandquist, Estevan, SK; Helmut Sass, Winnipeg, MB; Robert Saunders, Winnipeg, MB; Rick Sawatzky, Saskatoon, SK; Bill Saxon, Guyton, GA; Rita Scarpelli, Cranbrook, BC; Matthew & Shawna Schachtner, Green Bay, WI; Ken Schade, Kitchener, ON; Hans Schaffland, Calgary, AB; Peter Schalin, Edmonton, AB; Corry Schalk,

Strathroy, ON; Dorothy Schenstead, St. Walburg, SK; David Schesnuk, St Eustache, MB; Ted & Frieda Schmidt, Kelowna, BC; Allen Schmidt, Blind Bay, BC; Dan Schmidt, Aurora, IL; Garry & Lois Schmidt, Arroyo Grande, CA; Ed Schneider, Grimshaw, AB; Axel Schoeber, Victoria, BC; Jerod Schoof, Ardrossan, AB; Pieter Schoon, Grimsby, ON; Shirley Schuurman, Tillsonburg, ON; Andrew Scotland, Erskine, AB; Ellis Scott, Stratford, ON; Graham Scott, Port Colborne, ON; Alan Scott, Sugar Land, TX; Gordon Setterlund, Sherwood Park, AB; Margaret Sever, Gardnerville, NV; Simon Sevgian, Scarborough, ON; Arnold & Elna Sexe, Worthington, MN; Vivian Shackleton, Calgary, AB; Regina Shanklin, Bloomfield, NJ; Alice Shannon, Innisfail, AB; Stephen Sharpe, Smiths Falls, ON; Grace Shaw, Port Alberni, BC; Peggy Sheafer, Cincinnati, OH; Barbara Shearer, Edmonton, AB; David Shoulders, Monument, CO; Peter Shumelda, Toronto, ON; Doug & Janis Siemens, Morrin, AB; Bryun & Dianne Sigfstead, Edmonton, AB; James Simmons, Murray, KY; Gay Simpkins, Grants, NM; David & Mary Skelton, Edmonton, AB; Don Skolly, Woodstock, ON; Isak Skorohodov, Salem, OR; Joe Slay, Richmond, VA; John Sloan, Devon, AB; Alma Small, Edmonton, AB; Alice W Smith, Hayes, VA; Walter Smith, Shreveport, LA; Elmer Smith, Kelowna, BC; Derrell S Smith, Innisfail, AB; John & Rachel Smith, Cameron Park, CA; Robert Smith, Cedar Park, TX; Oliver Smith, Alix, AB; Adrian Smith, North Vancouver, BC; Cassandra Smith, Alexandria, VA; Irwin Smutz, La Grande, OR, John Snesar, Abbotsford, BC; Sue Snyder, Glendon, AB; Walter Sobole, Las Vegas, NV; Morris & Helen Sobool, Peachland, BC; Russ & Joanne Sochan, Hope, BC; Mabel Sorensen, Berwyn, AB; Muriel Southern, Victoria, BC; Brenda Spark, Lloydminster, SK; Walter Spencer, Rochester Hills, MI; Robert Splane, Boyle, AB; Andrea Spronken, Calgary, AB; Joan St Denis, Ladysmith, BC; Kari Stadem, Blomkest, MN; John & Donna Stadt, Thetis Island, BC; Chris Stafford, Calgary, AB; Paul Staiano Port St. Licie, FL; James Stanich, Rycroft, AB; Carol Stankievech, Calgary, AB; Mark Staples, Calgary, AB; Richard & Karina Staudinger, Alix, AB; Roy & Sarah Steffen, North Collins, NY; Linda Stein, Toronto, ON; Lyle Stein, Etobicoke, ON; Ron Steinbrenner, Edmonton, AB; Joanne Stella, Brandywine, MD; Spencer Stevens, Calgary, AB; Reid Stewart, Lower Burrell, PA; Harold Stiansen, Calgary, AB; Dolly Stinn, Vernon, BC; Chris Stodola, Osoyoos, BC; James Stolee, Edmonton, AB; William Stott, Oak Hill, VA; Don Strang, Sherwood Park, AB; Donna Strange, Sioux Falls, SD; Lil Strangway, Edmonton, AB; Don Strauch, Tucson, AZ; David Strauss, Langley, BC; Martin Stribrny, Edmonton, AB; John Strydhorst, Grande Prairie, AB; Sya Strydhorst, Neerlandia, AB; Sandra Sully, Cary, NC; Richard Sunderlage, Adams, WI; David Sundheimer, Phoenix, AZ; Melissa Suttles, Franklin, IN; Jim Swan, Red Deer, AB; Chip Swanson, Unalakleet, AK; Donald Swinehart, Apollo, PA; Audrey Swinton, Edmonton, AB; Lydia Sych, Millet, AB; Richard Sykes, Aiken, SC; Don Symons, Oshawa, ON;

T-Z

Rosaria Taccone, Oakville, ON; Rick Talbot, Calgary, AB; Lyle Taylor, Medicine Hat, AB; Pauline Taylor, Toronto, ON; Marvin Tegen, Midland, MI; Louis Tekavec, Gold River, BC; Jim Telford, Abbotsford, BC; Dick & Erlyce Tenhove, Blackfalds, AB; Dale Terhaar, Grand Haven, MI; Richard Ternes, Walton, NE; Henry Thalheimer, Kelowna, BC; Larry Theis, Shelbyville, TN; Fran Thevenot, Saskatoon, SK; Horst Thiele, Pitt Meadows, BC; Eldon Thiessen, Crooked Creek, AB; Jim Thiessen, Edmonton, AB; Wayne & Joan Thompson, Cecil Lake, BC; David Thompson, Ooltewah, TN; William Thompson, Winston Salem, NC; Ulrik & Yvonne Thomsen, Silver Valley, AB; Sandy Thomsen, Barrhead, AB; Bonnie Thomson, Pickering, ON; Lynn Thrush, East Vale, CA; Albert & Elizabeth Tiemstra, Barrhead, AB; John & Alida Tigchelaar, Stony Plain, AB; Earl Tilleman, Crossfield, AB; Bruce & Valerie Timm, Sauk Rapids, MN; Will Timmer, Abbotsford, BC; Renita Timmerman, Picture Butte, AB; Bernice Timmerman, Moorhead, MN; Myron & Lynn Toews, New Norway, AB; Peter & Elsie Toews, Olds, AB; Raymond Toews, Glaslyn, SK; Jeffrey Toivonen, Barrhead, AB; Lanora Tolman, Fairbanks, AK; Ivan Tomlinson, Beaverton, ON; John Tors, Toronto, ON; Rose Tratch, Wetaskiwin, AB; Brian Traynor, Edmonton, AB; Carmen Tripp, Tucker, GA; John & Zennia Trollope, Star, AB; John Trueman, Quesnel, BC; Karin Trygg, Burnaby, BC; Jelle & Henrietta Tuininga, Lethbridge, AB; Leslie Tulloch, Sault Ste Marie, ON; Dave Turner, Edmonton, AB; Sharon Turney, Oakland, MD; Alene Tutcher, Lewiston, ID; Judith Tyrrell, Ottawa, ON; Gloria Uldrich, Hot Springs, AR; Martin Ulrich, Cochrane, AB; Christa Unger, Drayton Valley, AB; Gordon Unger, St. Albert, AB; Henry Unrau, Edmonton, AB, Richard Updegraff, Lau Claire, PA, Bob Valek, Columbus, IN; Joe Van Aerden, Okotoks, AB; Evelyn Van Andel, Modesto, CA; Ernie & Helen Van Boom, Sturgeon County, AB; Roy Van Boom, Leduc, AB; Hendrikus & Dianne Van Dalfsen, Leduc, AB; Frans Van de Stroet, Iron Springs, AB; Daniel Van den Berg, Sturgeon County, AB; Ary Van Es, Burdett, AB; Jacob & Mrs Christa Van Gelder, Corner Brook, NL; Harry & Jane Van Gurp, Belmont, ON; Adriaan & Evelyn Van Hoeve, Cochrane, AB; Willy Van Randen, Surrey, BC; Jean Van Wieringen, Picture Butte, AB; Arie Van Wingerden, Sunnyside, WA; Gary Vandenakerboom, Rocky Mountain House, AB; Rick Vandenberg, Telkwa, BC; Helen Vandenhoven, Edmonton, AB; Leonard Vanderhoeven, Woodstock, ON; Hank Vanderlaan, London, ON; Martin Vanderspek, Norwich, ON; Kelvin Vanderveen, Carman, MB; Andy Vanderveen, Carman, MB; William & Tine Vandervelde, Dorchester, ON; Paul Vandervet, Brantford, ON; Brenda Vangaalen, Lethbridge, AB; John Vanhoepen, Chilliwack, BC; John & Teena Vant Land, Lethbridge, AB; Hans & Rita Van'tland, Coalhurst, AB; Chris Varvis, Edmonton, AB; Jon Vaughan, Lindsay, ON; Bram & Joanne Vegter, Spruce Grove, AB; Melvin Veldhuizen, Loveland, CO; Jack Venbrux, Edmonds, WA; Jack Verduyn, Burlington, ON; Peter & Barbara Verhesen, Trochu, AB; Steve & Luella Vetsch, Valleyview, AB; Hans Visser, Taber, AB; Hank Vissers, Qualicum Beach, BC; Tammo Voerman, Exeter, ON; Una Vogel, Leduc, AB; Anthony Vogrincic, Edmonton, AB; Ron & Joan Vorpahl, Randon Lake, WI; Chris Voss, Mission, TX; Henny Vroege, Halifax, NS; Alice Waechter, Grinnell, IA; Don Wakelam, Nanton, AB; Gene Waldo, Crystal Falls, MI; Al Walker, Athabasca, AB; Roger Wall, Durham, NC; Nancy Walton, McLean, VA; Fred Walz, Forest, ON; Antony Ward, Calgary, AB; Barbara Ward, Nelson, BC; Ernest Ward , Wiarton, ON; Daniel Ware, Sherwood Park, AB; Eldora Warkentin, San Luis Obispo, CA; Robert Warneck, Burlington, VT; Mary Waslen, Saskatoon, SK; Reginald Watson, Sundre, AB; Jan Watt, Ilderton, ON; Carson Weaver, Charlotte, NC, Chris Weaver, Boston Heights, OH; Fiorella Weaver, Cleveland, GA; Bill Webb, Innisfail, AB; Tom Webber, Tampa, FL; Esther Weeks, Orion, AB; Alfred Weimann, Sherwood Park, AB; Gordon Weir, Edmonton, AB; John Weissenberger, Calgary, AB; Michael Weller, White Rock, BC; Jean Weltz, Innisfail, AB; Richard West, Carmichael, CA; Thomas Wex, Omro, WI; Gwenne Wheale, Winfield, AB; Bronwen Wheatley, Calgary, AB; Gerald Wheeler, Calgary, AB; Jonny Whisenant, Buford, GA; Christine White, McKinleyville, CA, Robert White, Colborne, ON, Russ White, Holly Springs, NC; Erwin Wiebe, Niverville, MB; Jake Wiebe, Chilliwack, BC; Ida Wielenga, Taber, AB; David Wiens, Duchess, AB; Melvin Wiens, Beechy, SK; Harvey & Coreen Wierenga, Smithville, ON; Henrietta Wieringa, Granum, AB; Bruce Wilkinson, Edmonton, AB; Irvin Willems, Waldheim, SK; Dave Williams, Edmonton, AB; Miriam Williams, Revelstoke, BC; Thomas Williams, Gravenhurst, ON; Faye Willis, Vicksburg, MS; Vic & Dorothy Willms, Montney, BC; Helen Wilson, Calgary, AB; Samuel Wilson, Fox Lake, IL; Robert Wingerter, Zionsville, IN; Glenn & Joyce Winingar, Mabelvale, AR; Olga Winstanley, Langley, BC; Peter Winter, Brantford, ON; John Witmer, Houston, TX; Paul Wittmer, Canton, CT; Peter Wlodarczak, Sherwood Park, AB; Floyd Wollum, St Albert, AB; Peter & Trixie Wonder, Hagersville, ON; Charles Wootten, Matoaca, VA; Wendy Worrall, Abbotsford, BC; Henry Woudstra, Edmonton, AB; Gregg Wren, San Antonio, TX; Elyssa Wright, Roanoke, VA; Iris Wright, 150 Mile House, BC; Jim W Wright, Rouleau, SK; Lyle Wright, Kerrobert, SK; Ronald Wunsch, Lasayette, IN; Sandra Yakimowich, Two Hills, AB; Nancy Yatscoff, Edmonton, AB; Carl & Phyllis Yoder, Goshen, IN; Ralph Yonkman, Enderby, BC; Bob Younger, North Vancouver, BC; Sheila Ypma, Taber, AB; Henry Zekveld, Bowmanville, ON; Jacob Zekveld, Camlachie, ON; Dan Zelinger, Kenosha, WI; Timothy Zerface, Cinnaminson, NJ; Clinton Ziegler, Vegreville, AB; Henry Ziernfeld, Toronto, ON; Donald Zoell, Sherwood Park, AB; Andrew Zuidhof, Lacombe, AB.

Includes donations for this volume received up to December 31, 2012.

*The German painter Otto Dix, who served on the western front in the First World War, returned to Germany to create an
ultra-realist art known as the Neue Sachlichkeit (New Objectivity) in which he depicted his experiences in the trenches in
all their stark misery, as shown here in this detail from his triptych* The War. *A war that most people thought would be
over by Christmas 1914, turned into a fifty-one-month-long war of attrition, which meant digging in and waiting for the
enemy to run out of men and material and struggle, while pounding them incessantly to hasten the process.*

CHAPTER 1

Seventeen million die in a war that becomes the Great Repudiation

All looked to Germany, citadel of culture and progress, to produce the nirvana the era of science had promised, but instead it brought a slaughter hitherto unimaginable

Before the outbreak of the First World War in August 1914, writes the Christian historian Arnold J. Toynbee (who fought in it), "it was expected that life throughout the world would become more rational, more humane, and more democratic and that slowly, but surely, political democracy would produce greater social justice." In fact, he continues in his 1961 *Study of History*, "we thought that mankind's course was set for an earthly paradise." But the Great War, as it was known at the time, became the Great Repudiation. Science and technology, the expected pathway to this nirvana, became instead an instrument of destruction on a scale hitherto unimaginable.

It was somehow poetic, therefore, that this war should be instigated by a nation that in the previous century had come to epitomize progress. Imperial Germany—paramount in science, technology, industry, philosophy, and *kultur*—believed itself destined to lead the world. But Germany needed space, and Kaiser William II, his cadre of Prussian generals, and a docile civilian government had a plan to acquire it. They saw their young, dynamic, and growing German Empire as the Second Reich (Second Empire), the first having been the medieval German kingdom and empire that included much of Italy. By moving eastward into the Slavic lands, they would cement Germany's rightful leadership of Europe. True, this almost certainly would also entail completing the subjugation of archenemy France that had begun with the Franco-Prussian conflict of 1870–1871, so it entailed a two-front war. But Germany was ready for that.[1]

1. Behind the German assumption of a right to seize the Slavic lands lay the widely accepted ideology of eugenics (see chapter 4). A by-product of the nineteenth century Darwinian theory of evolution, it saw some peoples as self-evidently superior to others, conferring on the superior a scientifically authen-ticated duty to supplant the "lesser breeds." Thus General Friedrich von Bernhardi, in his 1912 best-seller *Germany and the Next War*, insisted that the elimination of the Slavs by the Germans was a "bio-logical necessity." Without war, he wrote, "inferior or decaying races would easily choke the growth of healthy budding elements."

2. Franz Ferdinand had upset his uncle, Emperor Franz Joseph, by marrying Sophie, a woman of inferior nobility but whom he loved even more than he loved hunting. (The archduke's numbered and mounted kills reputedly totaled two hundred thousand animals and birds.) He had further annoyed the old emperor with ideas for liberalizing the empire into a "United States of Great Austria." Shortly before his assassination, Franz Ferdinand had decried any war with Serbia: "What would we get, for heaven's sake? A few plum trees, some pastures full of goat droppings, and a bunch of rebellious killers."

In 1905, Count Alfred von Schlieffen, chief of the general staff, had devised a plan of twin attacks. Fulfilling it was entrusted in 1914 to his sixty-six-year-old successor, Helmuth von Moltke, gloomy nephew and namesake of the hero of the Franco-Prussian War. Four-fifths of the German forces—about a million men—would sweep through neutral Belgium, hook around northwestern France, and take Paris and the republic in thirty-nine days. They would then board trains to East Prussia, and with nine hundred thousand troops of Germany's ally Austria-Hungary would defeat the Russians. "Paris for lunch; dinner in St. Petersburg," smirked Kaiser William. But there was one qualification. Germany must not appear as the aggressor, lest it evoke the wrath of the world. Someone else must pull the trigger, and someone else did.

Austria-Hungary also saw an invasion of the Slavic Balkan states as a means of recovering its preeminence among the German-speaking nations, lost to William I's Prussian-led North German Confederation in the nineteenth century. The Ottoman Turks, rulers of the Balkans for four centuries, were crumbling. Austria-Hungary had already annexed Bosnia and Herzegovina and now wanted an excuse to move into Serbia, but they faced a major difficulty. Austria-Hungary was Roman Catholic, the Balkan peoples were mostly Orthodox Christians, and Orthodox Russia saw itself as their protector. If Austria-Hungary invaded Serbia, Russia would declare war on Austria-Hungary. Germany would then come to the defense of Austria and declare war on Russia. France and England, allied with Russia, would come to its defense and declare war on Germany.

Thus on the morning of June 28, 1914, at Sarajevo in Bosnia, when Gavrilo Princip, a scrawny nineteen-year-old Serbian freedom fighter, raised his nine-

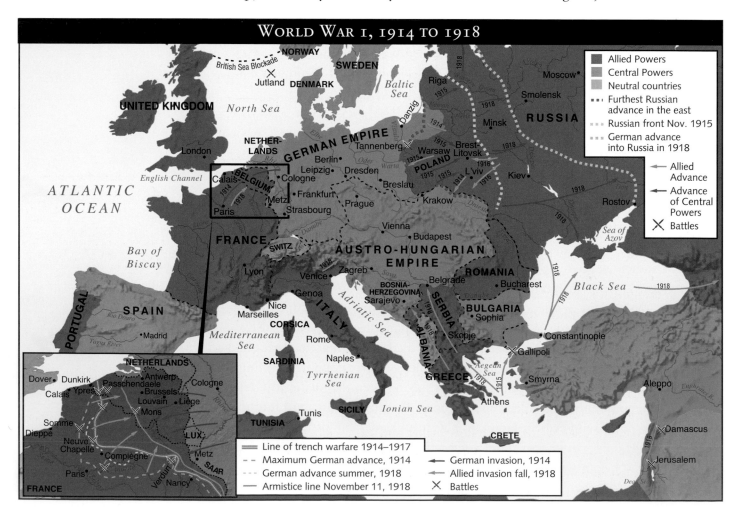

millimeter pistol and killed Archduke Franz Ferdinand, the fifty-year-old heir to the Austro-Hungarian throne, (and his wife, Sophie, Duchess of Hohenberg as well), this produced a crisis. Within a month, Austria-Hungary invaded Serbia, and most of Europe went to war.[2] Much of the world soon followed, the Ottoman Turks joining

Archduke Franz Ferdinand

Gavrilo Princip

Helmuth von Moltke

Kaiser William

Germany and Austria-Hungary, and Italy later allying with England, France, and Russia. (The fact that all but one of these warring nations, Ottoman Turkey, was at least nominally Christian could only further weaken the credibility of that faith in the eyes of the ever more prevalent religious skeptics.) Thus ten million enthusiastic recruits rushed joyously to arms, believing they would be home for Christmas, and Germany could disclaim any responsibility.

Even so, things went wrong with the Schlieffen Plan. The Belgians, expected to collapse immediately, put up an unexpected resistance. The British, mobilizing more

'We believe there's a higher law above that of the state,' wrote the archbishop of Canterbury, while German soldiers were invoking God on their belt buckles.

quickly than foreseen, came to their aid. Though outnumbered three-to-one, they delayed the German avalanche for a vital two days at Mons. The world heard in horror how German artillery virtually leveled the cities of Liège and Louvain (Leuven in Flemish). Stories circulated, many of them later found to be false, that Germany was responding to Belgian resistance by killing ten citizens—men, women, children, priests—for every dead German, torching entire towns, raping women, mutilating children, and sending Belgian men to Germany as slave labor. In the midst of this carnage, the English Red Cross nurse, Edith Cavell, was executed by the German army for aiding the Allied war effort and became a heroine of democracy.[3]

The perception of a villainous Germany made it easier for the Allied clergy to support the war. On the eve of hostilities, Protestants and Catholics from England, Germany, and other European countries had begun to hold international meetings designed to promote brotherhood among the churches and avert war. After hostilities began, these voices were drowned out by colleagues who supported the cause of "spiritual mobilization" against a Germany whose Protestant church, a merger of Lutheran and Calvinist, was wholly subordinate to the state.

"We believe," wrote Archbishop Randall Davidson of Canterbury, "that there does exist exactly what our opponents deny, a higher law than the law of the state, a deeper allegiance than can be claimed by any earthly sovereign, and that in personal and national conduct alike we have to follow higher and more sacred principles." In Germany, however, the soldiers' belt buckles were engraved with the phrase *Gott mit uns* (God with us), and many sincerely believed that powerful conviction indicates the presence of God. Therefore God was directing German armies at war.

3. Edith Cavell, the forty-nine-year-old spinster daughter of an English country vicar and herself a devout Anglican, served during the war in the Brussels hospital she had cofounded in 1910. While tending to the wounded on both sides, she also helped Allied soldiers obtain papers and escape into neutral Holland. She was caught, tried for treason, and executed by firing squad on October 12, 1915. The night before her death, she said to the prison chaplain, "I have no fear or shrinking. I have seen death so often that it is not fearful or strange to me. And this I would say, standing as I do in view of God and eternity: I realize that patriotism is not enough. I must have no hatred or bitterness against anyone."

Theologian Ernst Troeltsch was one of ninety-three prominent German religious leaders who signed the Appeal to the German Nation and the Civilized World, defending militarism as an integral part of Germany's greatness. "We fight not only for what we are, but also for what we will and must become," he declared.

In Rome, the recently elected Pope Benedict XV, fifty-nine, was appalled by the events reported in Catholic Belgium and what they presaged. "The world has committed suicide," he mourned, but stopped short of condemning German atrocities out of deference to the Vatican policy of neutrality. Later on, Pope Benedict would make several attempts to bring the leaders together for peace talks and be rebuffed by both sides. Meanwhile, he threw the resources of the Holy See into international relief work, almost bankrupting the Vatican treasury.

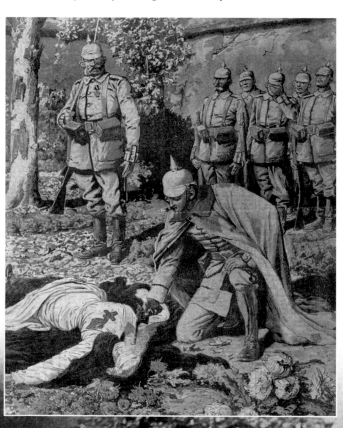

The most galvanizing Christian presence in Belgium was Cardinal Désiré-Joseph Mercier, whose fearless calls to resist what he called "the army of evil" so embarrassed the Germans that they placed him under house arrest (thereby further increasing his popularity).

The German offensive shocked the French, who had expected the attack to come through Alsace-Lorraine, not Belgium. Hence their commander in chief, General Joseph-Jacques-Césaire Joffre, veteran of France's colonial wars, had gathered most of his nine hundred thousand troops in the wrong place. Still clad in the blue coats and bright red trousers introduced a century earlier, Joffre's army met the Germans at the Marne River on September 5. In a three-day battle along a three-hundred-mile front, both armies experienced the lethal might of modern technology, each suffering a quarter of a million wounded or dead. But the French snatched victory at the last, helped by six thousand reserves from Paris, who were rushed to the front in six hundred taxicabs. The French clergy attributed the victory to the

Blessed Virgin, on whose feast day the battle had begun. It was called "the Miracle at the Marne."

Meanwhile, the French church and the once avidly anticlerical Third Republic government (see volume 11, page 62) had put aside their differences, forging what was called the "sacred union." Unlike the British clergy, who volunteered as military chaplains and were told to remain well behind the lines, French clerics were subject to conscription and many served in the front lines, some as armed combatants, but nearly all as medics and stretcher-bearers. These included more than eight hundred Jesuits. A wounded French soldier remembered how the stretcher-bearer Pierre Teilhard de Chardin, the Jesuit philosopher whose writings on evolution would later influence Vatican II, coolly came to him under terrible enemy fire. "I thought I had seen a messenger from God," said the soldier, marveling at de Chardin's calm. "If I'm killed," came the reply, "I shall just change my state, that's all."

In the British lines, Anglican chaplains were not always so readily welcomed, largely because of class differences; most were products of Oxford or Cambridge. But there were also British chaplains like Reverend G. A. Studdert Kennedy, nicknamed "Woodbine Willie" because he was always ready to provide a weary soldier with a cigarette (Woodbines were a popular brand). Kennedy, later a notable poet and rousing Anglican preacher, was awarded the Military Cross for rescuing wounded men under fierce machine-gun fire at Messines Ridge. British Catholic chaplains, who came largely from the Anglo-Irish working classes, also routinely administered the sacraments to wounded and dying men under heavy bombardment.

Senior Anglican clergy lent increasing support to military recruitment, one of the most effective being Bishop Arthur Winnington-Ingram of London, whose earlier missions in the city's tough East End had given him a common touch. Winnington-Ingram considered the war a "great crusade to defend the weak against the strong." Preaching from wagons draped with the Union Jack, he demanded of his audiences, "We would all rather die, would we not, than have England a German province?"

As the war ground on, however, the message of the Anglican clergy subtly changed. Alan Wilkinson writes in *The Church of England and the First World War* (1978), "As it became more difficult to present it as a crusade, clergy turned to expound it as human folly which God could use for his purposes, for example in order to

Senior British clergy participated in the war effort by joining the recruitment campaign of Field Marshal Horatio Herbert Kitchener, the secretary of state for war, whose fearsome visage adorned the famous poster (inset), and whose army of volunteers came to number three million. The lower clergy signed up as chaplains, their main duties being to comfort the dying and bury the dead. In the photo below, a chaplain from the Irish 1st Munster regiment says a burial prayer over the bodies of soldiers killed by a German shell.

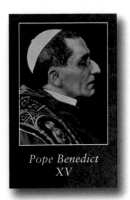

Pope Benedict
XV

Randall
Davidson

Arthur
Winnington-Ingram

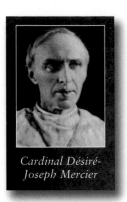

Cardinal Désiré-
Joseph Mercier

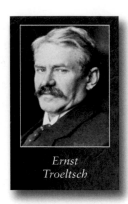

Ernst
Troeltsch

rouse England from selfishness and complacency." Similarly in France, writes Michael Snape in *The Great War* (2008), there was "a tendency in Catholic homiletics to depict the present conflict as a just chastisement of an apostate French nation."

After the Marne, much chastisement lay ahead. The Allies had pushed the Germans back forty miles and then stopped, exhausted. German General von Moltke suffered a nervous breakdown and told the kaiser, "We have lost." In a sense, he was right. There would never be another successful German offensive on the western front, which became a blood-drenched stalemate.

The Germans fared better in the east. Much had been expected from the "Russian Steamroller," which entered the war with 1.3 million men. But superior German organization, superior weaponry, and superior generalship checked the initial Russian advances into Prussian Poland at the Battle of Tannenberg in August 1914, Germany's most spectacular victory of the war. The Russians would struggle on for another two years, but Tannenberg began for them the national tragedy that would end in civil war. (See chapter 2.)

On the western front, however, there unfolded over the next thirty months a gruesome, futile, and ultimately pointless slaughter. Parallel lines of opposing trenches stretched for three hundred and fifty miles from the Belgian coast to the Swiss border, separated by an expanse called "No Man's Land," where most of the killing occurred. One account recalls "the frights, cold, the smell of H. E. [high explosives], the horribly smashed men still moving like half-crushed beetles, the sitting or standing corpses, the landscape of sheer earth without a blade of grass, the boots worn day and night till they seemed to grow on your feet..." This memory of the British lines was recorded by Second Lieutenant C. S. Lewis, aged nineteen, who would later become perhaps the most influential Christian writer of the twentieth century. Lewis's description could have applied with equal accuracy to the German lines.

The stalemate exemplified what would become known as a war of attrition, which meant waiting for the enemy to run out of men and materials and to collapse, while pounding him incessantly to hasten the process. Periodically, one side would launch a major offensive requiring hundreds of thousands of infantrymen, supported by artillery fire, to "go over the top" and into the machine-gun fire and falling shells. These offensives had storied French names—Ypres, Neuve Chapelle, the Somme, Champagne, Verdun, Passchendaele—but ugly results.

One of the ugliest occurred at the fortress city of Verdun. In February 1916, the new German commander, Erich von Falkenhayn, sent a hundred thousand German soldiers over the top, supported by newly devised platoons known as storm troopers, armed with grenades, light machine guns, and flamethrowers.

4. Although nowhere near as great a factor as it would become in the next war, aerial bombing was introduced in 1915 when German Zeppelin airships began to venture over English towns. These raids produced relatively few casualties—some fourteen hundred British dead, against sixty thousand in the Second World War—and provided more British propaganda benefit than German strategic gain. By the end of the war, after airplanes replaced the more easily destroyed hydrogen-filled airships, the British had begun retaliatory bombing of enemy civilian targets.

The infantry was supported by an artillery barrage from behind—a million shells were fired in the first day—with Fokker aircraft strafing and bombing from above.[4] The French were taken by surprise, a key supporting fortress fell, and Germany celebrated "Verdun Day." It was premature. The French held on so grimly that the German attack stalled. For the next ten months the Germans diligently pursued their onslaught and the French just as determinedly opposed them. By December, the Germans gave up. Verdun was still French. Just over seven hundred thousand men were dead: 362,000 French and 336,000 German. Nothing had changed. Falkenhayn, disgraced, was relieved of his command.

What aided the French at Verdun was a British diversionary attack at the Somme River to the west, but it too became an effectual disaster. This stroke was devised by the British commander in chief, Field Marshal Sir Douglas Haig, the fifty-five-year-old Scottish-born scion of the Haig & Haig whisky empire. A strict Presbyterian, he regularly invoked God in his diary. "I feel that every step in my plan has been taken with the Divine help," he wrote to his wife before the battle.

It began in July 1916, with a seven-day artillery bombardment—heard and felt, it was said, one hundred and sixty miles away in London. But it failed. Many shells fell far short of the German bunkers, which were dug thirty feet deep. Others failed to explode. The attacking troops, struggling through barbed wire and mud churned by the artillery barrage, were trudging directly into the machine-gun emplacements of the virtually unscathed defenders. Within twenty-four hours, twenty one thousand British soldiers died and thirty-six thousand were wounded, the worst day's

The deadliest battle of the war for the French was fought around the city of Verdun following a surprise attack by German troops under General Erich von Falkenhayn (below left) in February 1916. The battle raged for ten months, and, as can be seen in the photograph below, devastated the city. The French, under the supreme command of General Joseph-Jacques-Césaire Joffre (right), and with the help of a diversionary attack by the British at the Somme, pushed the Germans back to their lines—but not before almost seven hundred thousand men had perished in total on both sides.

5. Germany hoped to excite a Muslim jihad against the British in the Middle East and thus divert British forces from the western front. In a counter show of strength, General Charles Townsend led a division of Indian and British troops along the Tigris River into Ottoman Iraq, aiming to capture Baghdad. The Turkish Sixth Army, commanded by the seventy-three-year-old German General Colmar von der Goltz, drove them back to Kut, where they were besieged for several months and suffered near starvation. Townsend finally surrendered to the Turks in what historian James Morris calls "the most abject capitulation in Britain's military history." The Allies suffered twenty-three thousand casualties, and of the thirteen thousand taken prisoner, sixty per cent died of disease or were murdered by their Ottoman guards.

casualties in British history. Lieutenant Henry Williamson wrote: "I see men walking forward; and I go forward with them, in a glassy delirium wherein some seem to pause, with bowed heads, and sink carefully to their knees, and roll slowly over, and lie still. Others roll and roll, and scream and grip my legs in uttermost fear, and I have to struggle to break away, while the dust and earth on my tunic changes from grey to red."

The Battle of the Somme dragged on until late autumn, costing 660,000 German and 624,000 Allied casualties. Total ground gained: six miles. Among those casualties were many thousands of Canadians, Australians, New Zealanders, and South Africans, the four largely self-governing "dominions" of the British Empire, the competence and skill of whose troops steadily improved. Haig's diary makes no mention of divine help after the first day. Some historians describe Haig as "the Butcher of the Somme," others as an able general tragically overtaken by the exigencies of a modern war neither he nor his fellow generals, nor the enemy's generals either, had any notion how to fight.

By now the Great War had spread over three continents. The Ottoman Turks enjoyed brief success against Russia. But when winter set in, the Turks, lacking shoes and coats, began to freeze, lost twenty-five thousand men, and were driven back through the Christian Armenian regions of their shaky empire. Blaming the Armenians for colluding with the Russians, the Turks proceeded to instigate the century's first genocide. (See subchapter, page 16.)

The Turks were far more effective against the British. Not only did they stop General Sir Charles Townsend in his advance on Baghdad,[5] they foiled a joint British, Australian, and French landing on the Gallipoli Peninsula, at the mouth of the Dardanelles, the westernmost link in the chain of waterways connecting the Mediterranean to the Black Sea. Winston Churchill, the forty-year-old First Lord of the Admiralty who had conceived the Gallipoli Campaign, had to take blame for its failure and the loss of 250,000 men. Forced from the cabinet, he took command of a battalion in France, and later became minister of munitions. But Churchill's finest hour was still a quarter century hence.

Elsewhere, the Italians were fighting the Austro-Hungarians in the alpine northeast of Italy and losing every battle. In colonial Africa, the Allies were wasting men and resources in a protracted attempt to chase the Germans from that continent. At sea, the British blockade had effectively bottled up the German battleships and was preventing food and natural resources from reaching Germany, while the Germans, using their Belgian ports, retaliated with submarines (U-boats) that became the scourge of Atlantic merchant shipping bound for England. In May 1915, a U-boat sank the ocean liner *Lusitania* off the Irish coast, drowning 1,195 passengers, 128 Americans among them. A year later, in May 1916, the

German High Seas Fleet sallied forth to break the blockade, challenging the British Grand Fleet at the Battle of Jutland in the North Sea. They sank more ships than they lost, but did not break the blockade.

In 1917, two pivotal developments drove the war to a climax the following year. The first was a major change on the eastern front that seemed to portend certain German victory. In February, a mutiny broke out in Russia's army, and the tsarist government fell. Two months later, the second event occurred—the United States joined the war on the Allied side.

In October, Russia's Bolshevik Communists gained control of the government. At Brest-Litovsk they made peace in a treaty that was grossly favorable to the Germans, who retained eastern Poland, the Ukraine, Finland, and the Baltic provinces. So it became a race to see whether Germany could triumph in the west, before American reinforcements could get there.

The aged General Paul von Hindenburg and his chief strategist General Erich von Ludendorff, hailed as heroic victors in the east, had been made supreme commanders and become virtual military dictators of Germany. Ludendorff promptly launched a series of spring offensives in what he saw as a final knock-out blow against the Allies in the west. On March 21, 1918, the Germans struck the Somme region, and in six days British casualties reached three hundred thousand. "Every position must be held to the last man," General Haig ordered. "There must be no retirement. With our backs to the wall and believing in the justice of our cause, each one must fight on to the end." Among the Allied casualties that April was C. S. Lewis. "Just after I was

The Battle of the Somme, which for the British became emblematic of the slaughter and futility of the First World War, was launched in July 1916 by General Sir Douglas Haig (below right). The offensive followed seven days of heavy artillery bombardment that tore up ground and left the Germans virtually unscathed and well prepared when the British went "over the top" (bottom photo) and came under heavy machine gun fire. On the first day, the British dead—some of whom are pictured below left photograph—numbered twenty-one thousand, the highest battle deaths in a single day in British history.

Chief of General Staff Paul von Hindenburg (left), and his chief strategist General Erich von Ludendorff (right) study a map of the western front with Kaiser William II at German command headquarters in the last year of the war. With the war in Russia ended, the Germans had manpower enough to launch a final great offensive in the spring of 1918, hoping to defeat the Allies before American soldiers arrived en masse. They failed.

hit," he would write, "I found (or thought I found) that I was not breathing and concluded that this was death. I felt no fear and certainly no courage. It did not seem to be an occasion for either." The man immediately beside him had been killed.

Continuing their advance through May and June of 1918, the Germans again reached the Marne River, thirty-five miles from Paris. But the morale of their troops, sapped by the privations brought on by the British blockade and crushed by war weariness, was at its lowest ebb. With mutinies in the ranks and widespread drunkenness from wine pillaged in occupied French villages, their advance stalled. Furthermore, American troops had by now appeared in strength in the Allied lines.

Two things had prompted American involvement in the war. The first was a resumption in early 1917 of unrestricted U-boat activity, which was claiming American lives and shipping. The second was the interception by British intelligence of a telegram sent by German foreign minister Arthur Zimmerman to his ambassador in Mexico. It authorized the ambassador to tell the Mexican government that if the Americans joined the war, Germany would support a Mexican attack on the United States—and would reward Mexico with the states of Texas, New Mexico, and Arizona upon America's defeat. The telegram was made public by the British and its impact on American opinion was instant, deep, and decisive.

The United States had declared war on April 6, 1917—Good Friday—with widespread citizen support even from the Lutheran and Catholic Christians despite their large proportion of German- and

The Americans declared war on Germany on Good Friday 1917, launching a splashy recruitment campaign that demonized the "Hun" (illustrated in the poster) and was effective in raising an expeditionary force that eventually reached three million. Some of these "Doughboys," as they were nicknamed (because the buttons on their uniforms resembled lumps of bread dough), are shown in the photograph being welcomed by French soldiers.

Irish-Americans. The flamboyant evangelist Billy Sunday, a former professional baseball player, was among the most impassioned in his exhortations to defeat "the Hun," shouting at his audiences, "If you turn hell upside down, you will find 'Made in Germany' on the bottom." General John Pershing requested an army of three million Americans and by late June 1917, following a splashy recruitment campaign, American troops had begun arriving in Europe.

The Allies had agreed to the single command of French Marshal Ferdinand Foch, the general largely credited with the Miracle at the Marne, and the combined force included more than a million of Pershing's fresh, eager—and tall—Americans. (European recruiters had long since abandoned height requirements.) In July 1918, the "Yanks" and French repulsed the last major German offensive at the Second Battle of the Marne. It was the turning point of the war.

Allied numbers were enlarged by newly conscripted soldiers as old as fifty and by an American force grown to two million. Armaments were enhanced by twenty-five hundred airplanes and hundreds of tanks. The gains of the German spring offensive were soon erased, and by summer's end the Allied armies, often with Canadian and Australian troops leading the assault, were pushing the Germans back. On September 28, General Ludendorff told Kaiser William that he had no chance of winning; his army, he said, was crippled by a sense of "looming defeat." Germany must seek an armistice (a cease-fire). The kaiser, petulant to the last, refused to listen. He replaced Ludendorff. In early November, the U.S. First Division broke through German defenses in the Argonne Forest and reached the hills overlooking Sedan, site of France's decisive defeat in the Franco-Prussian War forty-eight years earlier. Then they moved aside and allowed the French the honor of capturing the city.

Germany had now been driven back to its borders, with its soldiers surrendering in hordes, its navy in mutiny, and Marxist uprisings occurring in major cities. On November 9, the generals informed the kaiser that he no longer had their confidence; he must abdicate or there would be revolution. William retreated to neutral Holland, where Queen Wilhelmina resisted Allied attempts to extradite and prosecute him. He would remain in a country house in Doorn until his death in 1942.

William's abdication terminated the rule of Prussia's Hohenzollerns, and the war would also see the end of three other fabled dynasties: the Romanovs in Russia in 1917, the Habsburgs in Austria-Hungary, and four years later the Ottomans in Turkey. Turkey capitulated when Britain's General Edmund Allenby and his Egyptian Expeditionary Force, aided by an insurgent Arab army guided by the famous T. E. Lawrence ("Lawrence of Arabia"), captured first Jerusalem, then Damascus. The Turks surrendered on October 30, 1918, twelve days before the Germans.[6] In November, 1922, the sultanate was abolished.

General Edmund Allenby enters Jerusalem with a group of Allied officers in January 1918. After some earlier setbacks at the hands of the German-led Turkish army, Allenby and his Egyptian Expeditionary Force, aided by an insurgent Arab army led by T. E. Lawrence ("Lawrence of Arabia"), had pushed back. The Turks surrendered in October 1918, ending the seven-century Ottoman era.

6. The capture of Jerusalem was hailed in the British press as the long-awaited fulfillment of the dream of Richard the Lionheart (see volume 7, chapter 5). In Rome, *Te Deums* were sung in every church. General Allenby, a veteran of the Boer Wars and a master of cavalry, respected the sanctity of the city by dismounting, along with his officers, outside of Jaffa Gate and entering Jerusalem on foot. Allenby placed the city under martial law, but in his proclamation he assured the populace that no brutality would be allowed, nor any damage to buildings and shrines sacred to Jews, Christians, or Muslims. At the end of the war, Jerusalem and surrounding Palestine were placed under British mandate until the creation of Israel in 1948. (See chapter 11.)

By 1918 Habsburg power was also unraveling. There was famine in Vienna and mutiny in the army, and the component states of Hungary, the Balkan possessions, and Czechoslovakia (formerly Bohemia, Moravia, and Slovakia) had all declared their independence. Broken and defeated, Austria sued for a separate peace with the Allies on November 3. A new republican government sent Emperor Karl, just two years on the throne, into exile. Almost seven hundred years of Habsburg rule was also over.

Meanwhile, Germany had proclaimed itself a republic, soon to be called the Weimar Republic for the town where the constitution was later ratified. The Social Democrats controlled the government, allied with the military leadership—a partnership necessary to suppress a revolution that threatened to turn Germany Bolshevik. Hoping for a merciful peace settlement, the government sent a delegation to negotiate an armistice with Marshal Foch in his railway car at Compiègne, where they found no joy at all. As far as Foch was concerned, there would be no negotiation. The Germans must evacuate all occupied territories in Belgium and France, along with the eastern European areas ceded by Russia in the Treaty of

The man who tried to halt the war

For his efforts Karl of Austria was rejected by his enemies and allies, lost his throne and died in exile and poverty, but history vindicates him

How was it that in four long years no significant leader, on either side, seemingly tried to halt the horror and destruction of the First World War? Actually, someone of high authority did try to make peace as early as 1916, and on Christian premises—a fact largely ignored by historians. In any event, the secret overtures of Emperor Karl I of Austria toward France and England were discreetly dismissed after six months as futile by the Allied powers and rejected as treasonous by his German allies, so the slaughter continued.

For Karl Franz Joseph von Habsburg-Lothringen, who was also King Karl IV of Hungary, the outcome could scarcely have been worse. Both his empire and the six-hundred-and-fifty-year reign of the Habsburg dynasty ended with the Armistice in 1918, and he died four years later in poverty-stricken exile at the age of thirty-four. His final words to his wife, Empress Zita, then pregnant with their eighth child, were: "I love you endlessly," and the last name on his lips was "Jesus." His efforts to make peace, and his numerous other Christian endeavors, went almost entirely unrecognized until eight decades later, when Pope John Paul II proclaimed him Blessed Karl of Austria.[1]

Born in 1887 into one of Europe's most powerful houses, Archduke Karl was raised a devout Catholic, and from age sixteen served creditably in Austria's army. His father, the irrepressibly adulterous Archduke Otto "the Handsome," died in 1906, and the assassination in June 1914 of Karl's uncle,

Archduke Franz Ferdinand, made Karl the direct heir of his aged great-uncle, Emperor Franz Joseph. The assassination also plunged Europe into the First World War. Two years later, Franz Joseph died after a sixty-eight-year reign. Karl, aged twenty-nine, inherited an empire straining under the nationalist ambitions of a dozen ethnic groups and rent by two years of warfare.

Introspective in personality, he is said to have faced these formidable odds in serenity, reputedly preceding every decision with prayer. In 1911, he had married the vivacious

The wedding of Archduke Karl of Austria and Princess Zita of Bourbon-Parma in 1911 (above) was one of the last major gatherings of the Habsburg clan prior to the First World War, whose outcome ended the dynasty and the empire. After becoming emperor in 1916, Karl tried to effect a peace and save the empire, but failed on both counts, dying in exile in 1922. Seated next to Karl in the group photograph is his great uncle, the long-serving kaiser Franz Joseph.

Brest-Litovsk. Furthermore, they must hand over their navy and most of their armaments to the Allies, and submit to temporary occupation of the Rhineland.

Agreeing under protest, the Germans signed the armistice at 5:00 a.m. on November 11, to take effect at 11:00 that morning. Fighting continued to the very end. General Arthur Currie, commander of the Canadian Corps, a dogged and tightly organized army that had not lost an action since its arrival in early 1915, was moving on Mons, determined to recapture the Belgian city where the war had begun fifty-two months earlier. Mons was taken, but not before twenty-five-year-old Private George Price of Moose Jaw, Saskatchewan, was killed by a sniper at 10:58 a.m., the last recorded Allied casualty of the Great War. In one sense, however, tens of millions more casualties still lay ahead, for the First World War would not be "the war to end all wars," as the Allied peacemakers hoped, but rather the progenitor of hostilities that would resume twenty-one years later and produce three times the casualties.[7]

Although the Armistice had been signed, the war would not officially end until a peace treaty had been negotiated. The American President Woodrow

7. Some historians link the influenza pandemic to the First World War, adding its casualties to the death toll. Called Spanish Flu because it seemed to first occur in neutral Spain, it raged from January 1918 to December 1919, spread throughout the world, and killed somewhere between fifty million and one hundred and fifty million people, most of them healthy young adults. Although the war did not cause the pandemic, the movement of troops, especially during demobilization in late 1918, probably hastened its spread.

Princess Zita of Bourbon-Parma. Their marriage, unlike many Habsburg unions, proved idyllic, with Empress Zita providing unfailing support and astute counsel. As she cannily observed, for example, one of her husband's attractive characteristics sometimes proved detrimental, namely his Austrian sense of humor: "He saw the funny side of everything. It was one of the many reasons he had such difficulty with the Prussians."[2]

But Emperor Karl's greatest difficulty with his uncongenial ally was Germany's determination to prolong the catastrophic war. In November 1916, he therefore initiated secret peace negotiations with France and England, using one of Zita's brothers, Prince Sixtus, an officer in the Belgian army, as go-between. But Paris broke off the talks six months later, and in April 1918, during a diplomatic row with Austria, published the relevant correspondence (causing what became known as the Sixtus Affair). Emperor Karl's position with his German allies was irreparably damaged.

As a military commander, he consistently did his best to reduce battlefield horrors, writes historian Gordon Brook-Shepherd in *The Last Habsburg* (1968). "I forbid the order to take no prisoners," he commanded his officers, and "I forbid most emphatically stealing and plundering and wanton destruction." To care for the wounded, widows, orphans, and unemployed, he established one of the world's first ministries of social welfare, set up soup kitchens, and had the imperial coaches deliver coal to Vienna's poor. In 1917, persuaded that many political agitators had been unfairly tried, he granted a sweeping amnesty. In 1918, with nationalism threatening the empire, he belatedly tried to transform it into a federation.

Although forced at the Armistice to surrender all authority, Karl stubbornly refused to actually abdicate, contending that his throne was God-given. He fled to Switzerland and, after failing in two attempts to regain the kingdom of Hungary, was exiled in 1921 to the Portuguese island of Madeira.[3] Destitute, he finally resolved to sell the imperial jewelry, sent for safety to a Swiss bank in 1918, and was

informed that the gems—including the 133.5-carat Florentine Diamond—had disappeared, as had the Austrian lawyer entrusted with them.[4] It was a final blow. On April 1, 1922, in a dank, narrow house in Funchal, Madeira, Austria's last emperor died of pneumonia.

His efforts, writes historian Brook-Shepherd, were chiefly defeated by one insoluble riddle: "Karl needed reforms to get his peace, and he needed peace to get his reforms." What history has dismissed as weakness and naiveté, however, has been seen by Christians as heroic fidelity and practical charity. A few others have agreed. "The only honest man to emerge during this war was Karl of Austria," wrote his contemporary, the agnostic French author Anatole France, "but he was a saint and nobody listened to him." ■

1. Blessed Karl's feast day is October 21, the date of his marriage. To proceed from the designation "blessed" to a declaration of sainthood will require confirmation of another miracle attributed to his intercession. The first miracle attributed to him was the curing of paralysis in a Brazilian nun who prayed for his intercession in 2003.

2. Empress Zita proved resilient during her long widowhood. Clad always in black, she raised their eight children, including the daughter born after Karl's death, and lived to see her ninety-sixth birthday in 1989.

3. The imperial family was escorted out of Austria in March 1919 by a British officer sent by the concerned George V of England. Lieutenant-Colonel Edward Lisle Strutt described in his diary how, during their railway journey to Switzerland, he "sat all night at the back end of the Imperial coach on a camp stool with a revolver on my knee." Strutt subsequently helped in Karl's attempt to regain his Hungarian throne (risking consequent punishment at home). He also achieved fame as a mountaineer.

4. Brook-Shepherd speculates that Karl may already have sold some jewels to finance the airplane that flew him and Zita to Hungary for his second attempt to regain its throne. The collection, which included a tiara of Lothringen gems, eight Golden Fleeces, diadems, brooches, and necklaces, was never recovered, although the appearance of the Florentine Diamond was variously reported in South America, the United States, and Vienna.

In this contemporary English illustration, a delegation representing the newly created Republic of Germany is shown acceding to the terms of the Armistice in the railway carriage of French Marshal Foch (standing behind the table) at Compiègne in the early morning hours of November 11, 1918. At 11 a.m. that same morning, the guns were finally silenced.

German prisoners of war taken by British troops at the beginning of the Second Battle of the Somme in August 1918. By now the German offensive had been thwarted and the Allies were well on their way to pushing the Germans back to their own borders.

8. The "Big Three" leaders had originally been the "Big Four" and included Italian Prime Minister Vittorio Orlando. Italy had been promised certain territories formerly belonging to Austria-Hungary in return for fighting with the Allies (and losing seven hundred thousand men). When it became clear that Italy, considered an inept ally, was not to get some of the promised territories in Central Europe and the Middle East, Orlando stormed out in a rage. Italy's meager rewards from the conference, along with her immense war debts, would contribute to the rise and seizure of power by the fascist Benito Mussolini in 1922.

Wilson, who was to broker the terms, arrived in Paris for the peace conference in January 1919, declaring amid immense adulation: "A supreme moment in history is come. The hand of God is laid upon the nations." Sixty-two years old and a devout Presbyterian, with the dry condescending air of the Princeton professor he had once been, Wilson presented his famous "Fourteen Points," a document devised a year earlier that set out terms of the peace, and provided for the creation of "a league of nations." The terms included a general disarmament, the return of occupied territories, and a prohibition of secret alliances between countries. The League of Nations, precursor to the United Nations, was to be a body in which "great and small nations alike" would settle differences peaceably.

Though Germany was not allowed to participate in the Versailles conference, Wilson had hoped for a relatively nonpunitive treaty that would not incite resentment and a resurgence of German aggression, but the two other major players felt otherwise.[8] British Prime Minister Lloyd George had recently won re-election by promising to extract a fantastic $330 billion (U.S.) in reparations from the Germans. French Prime Minister Clemenceau, nicknamed "Le Tigre," spoke for a country whose cities and population had been devastated. He came to the conference insisting that Germany be punished for the war, and that she return to France not only Alsace and Lorraine, but also parts of the adjacent German Rhineland known as the Saar region. None of these three principals liked the others, an animus suggested by Clemenceau when he remarked, "I find myself between Jesus Christ on the one hand and Napoleon Bonaparte on the other." None would leave entirely satisfied, although Clemenceau was probably happiest with the result. "We are carrying the war on into the peace," he commented.[9]

The signing took place on June 28, 1919, five years to the day after Franz Ferdinand was shot; the venue was the same Hall of Mirrors at the Versailles palace where France had surrendered to Prussia in 1871. Under article 231 of the treaty, Germany was made to admit full responsibility for the war. She was forced to give up Alsace-Lorraine, relinquish her overseas colonies to England and France, pay reparations to be determined later by a committee (set at $31 billion in 1921—equal to half a trillion in 2012 dollars), limit her army and navy to the barest minimum, give up her air force and submarines, never unite with Austria, and submit to French occupation of the Saar for fifteen years. Lloyd George, believing the terms too harsh, predicted, "We shall have to fight another war all over again in twenty-five years time." Marshal Foch, believing the terms too soft, predicted, "This is not a peace; it is an armistice for twenty years." Foch's estimate was the closer.

The Versailles Treaty and its companion treaties redrew the map of Europe, divesting Austria of Hungary and its other member states, but leaving Germany largely intact. The Ottoman states in the Middle East became British and French protectorates, as did the former German colonies in Africa. The League of Nations, while it succeeded at first, flopped its crucial challenge by failing to prevent the rearmament of Germany and the rise of a militaristic Japan. Wilson returned to a United States that wanted no further European involvements. He severely compromised his health in a desperate national tour to promote the League, calling it "an unparalleled achievement of thoughtful civilization." Congress rejected American membership in it.

The League's member nations, eventually totaling fifty-eight, had difficulty reaching consensus or abiding by their own rules of disarmament. The horror of a war that had killed seventeen million soldiers and civilians, and permanently maimed as many more, created such a widespread determination not to let this happen again that pacifism proliferated, enabling a pacifist historian like Cecil John Cadoux to rewrite the history of the early church in his *Early Christian Attitude to War* (1919). Cadoux makes the first Christians into pacifists although in fact the faith was in great measure spread by Roman soldiers. Ironically, it was the popular yearning for peace that prevented the Allies from stopping Hitler's rearmament of Germany in the 1930s.

But C. S. Lewis, despite recurring nightmares, would not remain a pacifist. In 1939, he confided to a friend, "My memories of the last war haunted my dreams for years... I think death would be much better than to live through another war." But live through another war he did, and with his broadcasts on Christianity, he helped Britain live through it too, in the process making his voice the second most recognized in the country after Churchill's. No longer an atheist either, Lewis had come to believe that there are worse things than war or death. In a sermon he preached in 1940, he reflected:

"What does war do to death? It certainly does not make it more frequent; one hundred percent of us die, and the percentage cannot be

The signing of the Versailles Treaty in the Hall of Mirrors on June 28, 1919, is depicted below by the Anglo-Irish painter Sir William Orpen. The treaty followed a peace conference in Paris, attended by dozens of countries, but dominated by the American, French, and British leaders. As suggested in this caricature from the French magazine J'ai vu (inset), it was these "Great Shapers of a New World" Lloyd George, Clemenceau, and Wilson who redrew the boundaries of Europe and sowed the seeds of discontent that helped cause the Second World War.

C. S. Lewis, who served as a lieutenant in the British army during the First World War, is shown on the left, beside his best friend Paddy Moore, who was killed by a shell shortly after the snapshot was taken. Like many First War veterans, Lewis would be plagued by nightmares for decades afterwards. But unlike many of his Oxford-trained contemporaries, he would not become a pacifist, and during his Second World War broadcasts would help Britons live through the new nightmare by arguing convincingly that there are worse things than death.

increased. It puts several deaths earlier but I hardly suppose that is what we fear. Certainly when the moment comes, it will make little difference how many years we have behind us. Does it increase our chances of a painful death? I doubt it. As far as I can find out, what we call natural death is usually preceded by suffering, and a battlefield is one of the very few places where one has a reasonable prospect of dying with no pain at all. Does it decrease our chances of dying at peace with God? I cannot believe it. If active service does not persuade a man to prepare for death, what conceivable concatenation of circumstances would?

"Yet war does do something to death. It forces us to remember it. War makes death real to us, and that would have been regarded as one of its blessings by most of the great Christians of the past. They thought it good for us to be always aware of our mortality. I am inclined to think they were right." ■

An attempted genocide, long concealed

The Turkish campaign to exterminate Christian Armenia was kept secret until historians bared the hideous facts on the century's first such horror

W ho, after all, speaks today of the annihilation of the Armenians?" mused Adolf Hitler in 1939 as he contemplated his plan to invade Poland. Since the answer at that time was "Almost no one," the führer confidently instructed his generals "to send to death, mercilessly and without compassion, men, women and children of Polish derivation and language." Germans would gain a great deal of urgently needed living space, was Hitler's rationale, and the slaughtered Poles would soon follow the Armenians into historic oblivion.[1]

Hitler ultimately proved to be right on both points. The slaughter of the Poles is often eclipsed by the contemporary slaughter of the Jews. Similarly, the attempt of a Turkish military junta in the dying days of the Ottoman Empire to exterminate all Christian Armenians was in fact all but disregarded for most of the first half of the twentieth century. But in the last half,

through the diligence of historians, it was revealed as the first genocide of the modern era, and a fit exemplar in mayhem for those that followed.[2]

The name Armenia is said to derive from Aram, the nation's legendary founder and a descendant of Hayk, cherished in Armenian tradition as one of Noah's great-great-grandsons. Since the seventh century BC, the Armenians have inhabited a region southeast of the Black Sea and west of the southern end of the Caspian. Its highlands include Mount Ararat, where Noah's Ark, according to the Old Testament account, came to rest after the Great Flood. Many centuries later, between AD 40 and 60 according to church tradition, two of the twelve apostles, Thaddeus and Bartholomew, brought Christianity to the Armenians, and in AD 301 they became the first nation to proclaim it as their state religion.

By the sixteenth century, like most of the

1. The argument that history had ignored the Turkish massacre of Armenians in 1915, and therefore would similarly soon forget German mass slaughter of Poles in 1939, is attributed to Adolf Hitler by Kevork B. Bardakjian in *Hitler and the Armenian Genocide* (1985). A professor of Armenian Language and Literature at the University of Michigan, he cites evidence introduced at the Nuremberg war crimes trials.

Middle East and North Africa, they had fallen under the rule of the Muslim Ottoman Turks, and in the nineteenth century the Armenian population under Ottoman rule was concentrated in six *vilayets* (provinces) covering some forty-five thousand square miles in the highlands and mountain valleys southeast of the Black Sea. They were a minority people in each of these provinces. Nearly three-quarters of them were poor, illiterate peasants, although increasing numbers were becoming educated, sophisticated, and increasingly western in outlook.

Contemporary reports consistently depict Armenians as suffering even more severely than other Christians in the Turkish Empire. British ethnographer William Ramsay, who visited their country in the late 1890s, wrote: "Turkish rule...meant unutterable contempt... The Armenians were dogs and pigs...to be spat upon if their shadow darkened a Turk, to be the mat on which he wiped the mud from his feet. Conceive the inevitable result of centuries of slavery, of subjection to insult and scorn, centuries in which nothing belonged to the Armenian, neither his property, his house, his life, his person, nor his family. [Nothing] was sacred or safe from violence—capricious, unprovoked violence—to resist which by violence meant death."

Even this was scant preparation, however, for the horrors visited upon Armenia during the First World War. By then, the Ottoman Turks had lost all their European and North African possessions and a group of military officers known as the Young Turks had overthrown the sultan. Just as in Russia there were pogroms from time to time against the Jews, so in Ottoman Turkey massacres of Armenians are recorded in 1890, 1893, 1895–96, and 1909.

Once in power, the Young Turks established themselves as the Committee of Union and Progress (CUP) to rule the remains of the Ottoman Empire. They saw the outbreak of war in 1914 as a chance to reclaim some of its lost domains, and also to create a purely nationalist Turkish state. Its enemies, it was soon decided, included the Armenians. The eastern provinces must be cleansed of them.

Even before the war began, CUP congresses adopted preparatory resolutions and sent out warning orders to provincial governors, while leading party members whipped up their followers with passionate rhetoric. In late 1914, leading Young Turk member Dr. Mehmet Nazim is quoted as briefing a secret party session as follows: "The Armenian people should be destroyed to the roots, in order that not a single Armenian be

left in our country, in order that the very name be forgotten... Now the war is under way. There will be no other favorable occasion like this."

Only a spark was needed, and one was soon provided by the Battle of Sarikamish in the Caucasus (December 22, 1914 to January 17, 1915), in which Russian forces almost obliterated a Turkish army. The Turks claimed that uniformed Russian Armenians had openly fought against them, and that Armenians inside the Ottoman Empire were trying, under cover of war, to make their region autonomous.

So Armenian soldiers in the Turkish army were sequestered in groups of fifty to one hundred, and shot. This eliminated any likelihood of effective armed resistance to the broader campaign, which began Sunday evening, April 24, 1915, later to be commemorated by survivors and descendants as Red Sunday. First to be arrested were two hundred fifty Armenian residents of Constantinople—politicians, writers, intellectuals, teachers, journalists, doctors, and clergymen, among others. They were held in a detention camp near Ankara and later deported, eliminating the educated and articulate Armenian element.

A month later, CUP Interior Minister Mehmed Talat proclaimed a Temporary Law of Deportation that authorized local officials, assisted by army units and citizen volunteers, to begin clearing the eastern provinces of their Armenian inhabitants. Thousands died in this process. In the *vilayet* of Bitlis, for instance, women, children, and the elderly were herded into stables and haylofts and burned alive. Churches, schools, and orphanages were similarly used to kill between seventy and eighty thousand people. There were other methods as well. "The Turkish atrocities in the district of Bitlis are indescribable," wrote British historian Arnold Toynbee (*A Study of History*, 1934–1961). "After having massacred the whole male population...the Turks collected nine thousand women and children

A scene from Turkey's year-long massacre of thousands of its Armenian inhabitants, published in the French newspaper Le Petit Journal, *December 12, 1915. Turkey has never acknowledged that this brutal campaign, begun the previous spring, aimed at total elimination of its Armenian population—although its rulers said so at the time.*

2. The word genocide, defined as the "deliberate destruction of an ethnic, racial, religious or national group," is relatively new. Its invention in 1944 is attributed to Raphael Lemkin, a multitalented Polish lawyer who derived it from Greek *genos* (race) and the Latin suffix *cidium* (killing). Two years later, the concept of genocide would be central when surviving Nazi leaders were held to account at the Nuremberg trials.

having "their eyebrows plucked out, their breasts cut off and their nails torn off... Their torturers hew off their feet or hammer nails into them just as they do in shoeing horses."

Thousands of others were meanwhile forced to trek many miles, in scorching summer heat and with minimal food and water, to detention camps in northern Syria and present-day Iraq. The men were often slaughtered first, in full view of the women and children. When the feeble and the elderly collapsed en route, they were shot or left to die. Rape and robbery were said to be common. Pregnant women gave birth on the road. One convoy, initially numbering some eighteen thousand, was reduced to about one hundred and fifty after marching seventy brutal days to reach its designated camp in the Syrian Desert.

Ottoman Sultan Hamid is portrayed in the French political cartoon (above) as a butcher. The caption translates, "Well then, while they [the Allies] are busy elsewhere, I can bleed some Armenians." To the right, a present-day map of independent Armenia.

from the surrounding villages. Two days later, they marched them out to the bank of the Tigris, shot them all and threw the corpses into the river."

In Trebizond, a coastal province on the Black Sea, thousands of Turkish troops, police officers, and volunteers reportedly rounded up Armenian citizens and loaded them into small sailing vessels. These were towed out to sea and capsized, drowning their hapless, thrashing passengers. Nor was torture lacking. German missionaries reported that they had witnessed or heard accounts of Armenian women

In mid-December 1915, after German officials complained about roads being littered with mutilated and bloating corpses, Interior Minister Talat sent urgent coded orders that bodies be buried forthwith (both to appease German sensibilities and avoid epidemics). Meanwhile, conditions in the twenty-five detention camps were said to be so frightful that death came as a relief. In any case, death was frequent. In late 1916, a final spasmodic wave of killings was recorded. In one camp, great piles of wood were doused in kerosene and ignited, and two thousand orphaned children tossed into the resulting inferno. In another, seventy

The photograph to the right shows Turkish officers standing before hanged Armenian doctors in Aleppo in 1916. At the time, Aleppo was part of the Ottoman Empire, becoming part of Syria after the First World War. A common scene during the summer of 1915 (above): the bodies of Armenians, either deliberately starved or massacred by Turks, often following rape, torture, or both. The photograph was taken by Henry Morgenthau, Sr., American ambassador to the Ottoman Empire, who had the pictures published in 1918.

thousand people allegedly were burned alive in a single week. Sometimes prisoners were herded into caves and fires lit at the entrances, to suffocate them with smoke.[3]

Missionaries, diplomats, refugees, and journalists brought some news of all this to the outside world. In August 1915, the *New York Times* reported that "the roads and the Euphrates are strewn with corpses of exiles, and those who survive are doomed to certain death. It is a plan to exterminate the whole Armenian people." Later that year, a joint statement issued by England, France, and Russia declared that they would hold "personally responsible...all members of the Ottoman government and those agents who are implicated in such massacres."

After the war, the British, French, and Soviet governments did not make good on this threat. Adverse western opinion, however, did force Turkey's new government to set up military tribunals where senior CUP leaders were charged with various war crimes. Most were convicted, and the three men who ruled the party—Interior Minister Enver Talat, War Minister Ismail Enver, and Marine Minister Ahmed Djemal—were sentenced to death. They had already fled the country, but Armenian survivors traced Talat to Berlin and assassinated him in 1921, and gunned down Djemal in Tbilisi, Georgia, in 1922. Ismail Enver escaped the avenging assassins, and was killed fighting the Red Army in Central Asia in the 1920s.

Few noted, let alone emphasized, the shocking fact that the Armenian population of Turkey had been reduced by ninety percent, and that Turks and Kurds now occupied the highlands where Armenians had been dominant since Old Testament times. Those who survived in Russia became just another cowed Soviet minority, hardly daring to practice their ancient Christian faith. Thousands were executed or deported during the Stalinist purges of the 1930s, the deportees joining their brethren of the Armenian diaspora. All of these, scattered in a dozen countries or more around the world, have generally prospered.

They have also worked diligently to document and disseminate the memory of the tragedy that befell their people, conducting scholarly research and producing books and films,[4] and initiating efforts for national and international recognition of the fact of the Armenian genocide by the Turkish government. In this, they have scored some significant victories, such as the introduction of commemorative resolutions in the United States Congress in 1975, and in 1985 the adoption of a report on the massacre by the United Nations Commission on Human Rights. In June 1987, the European Parliament accorded official recognition to the Armenian genocide, and by 2012, more than twenty countries throughout the world had officially recognized it as authentically historical.

But not Turkey. Terrible things happened in their nation's eastern regions, the Turks have acknowledged, and crimes were committed. But they have steadfastly refused to admit that their forefathers deliberately orchestrated a campaign aimed at wiping out an entire people. ∎

3. Steep-sided Kamakh Gorge on the upper Euphrates River reputedly was the site of numerous massacres. In some cases hundreds of people would be stripped naked and tied together at the edge of the cliff. As those nearest the brink were shot and fell over, their weight would pull the rest into the gorge. At one stage, the mass of corpses is said to have forced the river to change course.

4. The movie *Ararat*, a Franco-Canadian coproduction released in 2002, is based on the Turkish siege in early 1915 of the Armenian city of Van, and the heroic resistance mounted by the inhabitants. Produced by Atom Egoyan (a Canadian filmmaker of Armenian descent) at a cost of $15.5 million, it stars Charles Aznavour and Christopher Plummer, but received notably mixed reviews.

These children were among the lucky Armenians to escape and survive the genocide. Having fled into the mountains, they were later rescued by French naval cruisers and taken as refugees to Port Said in Egypt, among the first of an Armenian diaspora that has since scattered itself around the world.

The Soviets destroy an ancient monastic church while the faithful lament in this 1930 painting by the Italian Achille Beltrame. During the Bolsheviks' anti-Christian campaign, many churches and monasteries were converted to use by the state, but many were destroyed, while those clergy who resisted faced death or sentences to the grim gulags in the north.

CHAPTER 2

Clergy slain in droves, church schools close as the Reds take power

Soviet gangs run wild through Russia's countryside, looting, burning, killing; families must watch while priests are tortured, buried alive, strangled, hanged

I t was August of the year 1917, and the occasion was one that would bear witness to one of the greatest misapprehensions of practical reality in the entire history of Christendom. More than five hundred and sixty delegates marched in solemn procession into Moscow's celebrated Church of Christ the Saviour to begin the first "All-Russia *Sobor*" (council) held by the Russian Orthodox Church in 236 years. Laymen, priests, monks, bishops, and archbishops in their traditional habits and headgear debated beneath centuries-old icons, displaying what Metropolitan Hilarion Alfeyev of Volokolamsk would later describe as their church "at its peak of glory and power."[1]

But this appearance was gravely deceiving, for its entire institutional edifice—forty-eight thousand parishes, sixty-seven dioceses, fifty thousand clergy, fifty-eight seminaries, and thirty-five thousand schools—was inextricably linked to the tsarist regime, which had just been supplanted by a provisional government. Russia's Orthodox Church was doubly vulnerable, notes Orthodox historian Dimitry Pospielovsky, because the tsarist bureaucracy had run it as an arm of the state for about two hundred years. Consequently, it now "lacked the organizational mechanism of a self-governing institution." Its leaders did not even know what each other was thinking, let alone what their rank-and-file priests or laity might think.

The delegates did know that they were in the midst of a revolution, and that the "intelligentsia" leading it had long since been lost to the church, the sacraments, and the Christian faith. Typically for subjects of an autocracy, however, these churchmen blamed the autocrat for their own weakness—which is why the

1. Metropolitan Hilarion Alfeyev is the author of forty-seven volumes on theology and history (four of them in English). He also composed oratorios for soloist, choir, and orchestra, including *The Passion According to St. Matthew* (2006), which were well received in Europe and America as well as in Russia. Born in Moscow in 1966, Metropolitan Hilarion studied piano, violin, and composing in Moscow, became a monk in 1987, and subsequently earned theology degrees in Moscow and in England, including a PhD at Oxford University in 1995. He was elected bishop of Volokolamsk in 2002, and seven years later became a permanent member of the Holy Synod of the Moscow Patriarchate and its frequent representative at international conferences.

Lenin holds court at a committee of the Bolshevik party in this 1917 lithograph (above), with Trotsky to the left and Stalin to the right. The January 1920 edition of the English pre-teen periodical, The Children's Newspaper, *weighs in on the leadership of the new party in Russia. A day after taking power in October 1917, the Bolsheviks confiscated all church lands on behalf of "the People."*

2. Grand Duke Michael Alexandrovich Romanov, born in 1878, was the youngest son of the future Tsar Alexander III, and fourth in line for the throne after his father and his elder brothers, Nicholas and George. The assassination in 1881 of his grandfather, Alexander II, put him third in line, and his father's death in 1894 made him second. At the death of his brother George, Michael became heir presumptive until the birth of Tsar Nicholas's son, Alexei. Because Alexei was a hemophiliac and not expected to live, however, Michael was named successor when Nicholas abdicated in 1917. He refused to accept the throne without ratification by a general assembly. Later imprisoned and murdered by the Bolsheviks, Michael Alexandrovich nevertheless is often considered Russia's last tsar.

All-Russia Sobor, after the abdication of Tsar Nicholas II, refused to support his younger brother, Grand Duke Michael Alexandrovich, as successor.[2] It formally welcomed the provisional government instead, proclaiming that "the hour of general freedom for all Russia [has come]; the whole land…rejoiced over the bright new days of its life." It was a major misapprehension indeed.

The center-left government of Alexander Kerensky, which had replaced the tsar and freed the church,[3] would soon be replaced in turn by the dreaded Bolsheviks, whose leaders, Vladimir Lenin and Leon Trotsky, intensely hated religion. Lenin consistently dismissed "every religious idea, every idea of God, every flirting with the idea of God," as "…unutterable vileness…vileness of the most dangerous kind." Under Lenin and successor regimes four-fifths of the bishops attending the 1917 All-Russia Sobor would be executed, die in prison, or be forced into permanent exile. More than twelve thousand clergy would be murdered, and more than one hundred thousand Orthodox Christian lay leaders killed. "The majority were shot; some were beaten; more were hanged; others were drowned," according to the Web page of the Orthodox Church in America in 2012.[4]

The All-Russia Sobor had begun its deliberations by debating whether to replace state control with the church's first patriarchate since 1721. A significant contingent of delegates strongly favored a less hierarchical system, but the growing antireligious violence and street warfare outside the church walls soon brought both trepidation and a measure of unity. By the time Metropolitan Tikhon of Moscow had been enthroned as the new patriarch in early November, both the city and the Kremlin were in Bolshevik hands and the service at the Dormition Cathedral was conducted under the baleful watch of Red soldiers.

The Bolsheviks did not watch quietly for long. Communism's founding ideologue, Karl Marx, had promised that once the workers seized ownership of the factories from the capitalists, the intellectual "superstructure" for capitalism, in which he included liberal democracy and religion, would wither away of its own accord. God was merely the idealization of man's alienation from his own labor, Marx declared, and could be expected to disappear too.

But one thing that distinguished the Bolsheviks from other socialists was their eagerness to speed history's progress with force, and they were more than willing to hasten the withering away of religion. On October 26, 1917, one day after taking power, they proclaimed their Decree on Land, confiscating all church property and buildings for "the People." In November, church weddings were declared legally invalid, along with registration of births and funerals. In January 1918, ecclesiastical control of the nation's public schools was canceled, as were all remaining official links between the Orthodox Church and the state, especially all subsidies.

Lethal violence had begun with the murder of St. Petersburg archpriest John Kochurov by Bolshevik forces on October 31. Kochurov, a former missionary to Russian immigrants in Chicago, was soon followed into martyrdom by Metropolitan Vladimir of Kiev. Red soldiers fighting for control of Russia's ancient capital seized the cathedral in January 1918, and throttled the metropolitan with the chain of his pectoral cross, allegedly while forcing him to surrender church treasures. His body was also found to have two bullet wounds and three stab wounds. Several other bishops and hundreds of priests and laity were killed in 1918, not so much through systematic persecution, since the Bolsheviks were still fighting for military control of the country, as from spontaneous terrorism. (During this period the tsar, tsarina, and their children were executed with little more ceremony. See volume 11, chapter 4.)

Later there would be better-documented executions before firing squads and film crews; what largely characterized this early purge was its ferocity. As Metropolitan Hilarion records: "Clergymen were murdered with particular brutality. They were buried alive, had cold water poured over them in subzero temperatures until they froze, were placed in boiling water, crucified, whipped to death and chopped with axes. Many were tortured before their deaths, or murdered along with their families or in the presence of their wives and children." Moreover, reports Beryl Williams in *The Russian Revolution: 1917–21*, mobilization for the First World War had put firearms into the hands of many Russians, and the war itself may have left veterans indifferent to human suffering. Trigger-happy expropriation squads dispatched by local militias, tribunals, and workers' committees or "soviets," were ready to shoot those who resisted, in the course of "taking possession of shops, banks, and even saunas, while private houses were requisitioned and divided among the poor and homeless."

The revolutionaries shelled cathedrals, even within the Kremlin, covered the walls with graffiti and the floors with feces, and stripped gems from icons and reliquaries. In the early days of the new regime, resistance by the laity was often successful; an unarmed mob of Orthodox faithful would assemble to resist an armed mob of Reds, and the latter would retreat rather than fire on the people. Sometimes they did shoot, as happened at the Alexander Nevsky Monastery in Petrograd in January 1918, and even then the crowd remained steadfast.

3. Alexander Kerensky is the subject of one of history's greatest "What might have been" speculations. Had he remained in office long enough to hold national elections, might the Bolshevik Revolution have been avoided? Although Kerensky was a persuasive orator and a determined reformer, he could not change things fast enough, and his insistence on continued Russian participation in the First World War alienated its leaderless army of mutinous soldiery. He had to ask the Bolsheviks to organize a worker army to oppose them, which they used to seize the government. Kerensky fled Russia and would die in America in 1970. Blaming him for ousting the tsar, no Orthodox church in the United States would bury this grandson and nephew of Orthodox priests; his remains were interred in Wimbledon, England, beneath an Orthodox cross.

4. Statistics from the early days of the Soviet Union vary widely from source to source, especially on the death toll—information the Soviet regime strove to conceal. These numbers came from the Orthodox Church in America Web site. *The New Martyrs of Russia*, a 1972 tribute to Russian Orthodox martyrs, cites a 1930 Russian secret police report putting the number of Orthodox clergy who had died in prison camps at 42,800.

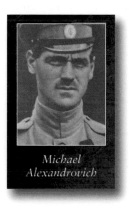

Michael Alexandrovich

In ironic contrast to these acts of random lawlessness, the multifarious new local authorities were busily issuing myriad regulations, including laws banning religious observances. These the Orthodox leadership defied at first, sometimes with fatal consequences. Typical is the account in *The New Martyrs of Russia* (an Orthodox memorial of the persecution) of the death of Bishop Germogen of Tobolsk, who led a defiant procession from his cathedral to the local government building, cross in hand, in protest. At the subsequent Divine Liturgy, he acknowledged to the congregation his fear that "the days of my passion and martyrdom are fast approaching" and asked for their prayers.

Bishop Germogen of Tobolsk (center) is shown in this 1916 photograph with two fellow clerics, the one on the left being Grigorii Rasputin, whose sinister activities were described in the previous volume, and on the right, Sergei Mikhailovich Trufanov (also known as Ilianor), who later became a member of the fascist Black Hundreds anti-Bolshevik group. Germogen was among those who resisted the Bolsheviks and was tortured and drowned for his defiance. Trufanov eventually fled to America and became a Baptist.

Bishop Germogen was indeed soon arrested. A delegation that petitioned for his release was met with a demand for a ransom, but those sent with the required money were imprisoned as well. When rescue by the counterrevolutionary White Army became imminent, the Bolsheviks fled by ferry, taking their prisoners with them. "They took them out on the deck of the steamer and ordered them to take off their upper clothing and shoes…" Then the prisoners, "under a shower of jeers and rude jokes from the guards, were bound and thrown one by one from the deck into the River Tura… Bishop Germogen prayed for his torturers and blessed them… A fist blow to the jaw silenced the old bishop's prayers. Then an eighty-pound rock was tied to his bound hands. The Red guards grabbed the bishop and, after several swings to and fro, roughly threw him into the river."

The New Martyrs notes more briefly the fate of many others. Father Michael Krishanovksy was raised into the air on the tips of several bayonets, for example. Father Koturov of Cherdin was frozen to death with icy water. Archimandrite Benjamin was burned alive. Archimandrite Matthew was slashed to death with swords. Others were shot or killed or simply disappeared. In 1918 and 1919 at least twenty-eight bishops and thousands of clergy and laity were executed.

In January 1918, before most of this occurred, Patriarch Tikhon had issued an anathema against the Bolshevik regime. "Recover your senses, madmen," he exhorted them. "Bring to an end your bloody strife. You are not merely committing cruel deeds, but truly the deeds of Satan, which are condemning you to Gehenna in the next world, and leave a dreadful curse upon your descendants in the present one." Perhaps more serious to the Bolsheviks, for whom the threat of excommunication carried no sting, was the patriarch's call for the Orthodox faithful to "keep away from such monsters…The enemies of the church are trying to gain power over it and seize its property by the force of guns: resist them with the strength of your faith and join your voices in a powerful clamor of protest."

Under a democratic regime, such an exhortation might not be seen as treason, but for the totalitarians now in power in Russia it most definitely was. For several generations, writes historian William C. Fletcher in *The Russian Orthodox Church Underground* (1971), the patriarch's dramatic statement would confirm their ideological belief that the church was their implacable enemy. Yet as Fletcher notes, Tikhon had voiced no antisocialist, procapitalist, or protsarist beliefs; he simply condemned the Bolsheviks for seizing and maintaining power by violence and murder, and for expropriating church property. At the end of that bloody year, on the anniversary of the Communist takeover, the patriarch wrote directly to the government, calling on them to free their political prisoners, reopen the monasteries they had closed, restore the holy images to schools, and end the violence. But he also softened his position somewhat, declaring that it was not the church's role to pronounce on government policy.[5]

The Communists nonetheless put Patriarch Tikhon under house arrest and continued their attack on the Orthodox Church with an assault on its customary veneration of the physical relics of saints. Communist officials opened cherished reliquaries to expose to public view the remains of sixty or more greatly revered saints. The Soviet press gleefully announced that these bodies had invariably deteriorated to bones and dust, thus exploding church claims about their miraculous "incorruptibility." The myth-busting efforts sometimes backfired, and counterclaims circulated that at least some of the hallowed remains in fact *were* incorrupt.

Such reportedly was the case of Saint Sergius of Radonezh, so that the crowd that had been gathered to cheer the unmasking of a supposedly holy fraud fell on their knees in devotion instead—those that weren't busy yanking the Bolshevik commander off his horse and pummeling him. Stories surreptitiously circulated of icons regaining their luster, that the golden domes atop one Kiev church were doing the same, and some ardent Communists were regaining their faith. After 1920, surviving icons were consigned by regulation to such institutions as the Leningrad Museum of Atheism and Religion, located in what had been the Cathedral of Our Lady of Kazan.

These lawless years were especially hard on smaller Christian groups like the Mennonites. They were concentrated in farming

Patriarch Tikhon of Moscow excommunicated the Bolshevik regime in 1918—not for their socialism, but for their violent, anticlerical program. Tikhon was jailed, but later released in the face of international reaction. After a brief period of attempted reconciliation with the Communists, Tikhon was jailed again, died in 1925, and later became an Orthodox saint. Below left, the Alexander Nevsky Monastery in the Kremlin, which was protected from destruction by an unarmed mob of Orthodox faithful.

5. Patriarch Tikhon (Bellavin) (1865–1925) was no stranger to challenge. As archbishop of the Aleutians and North America from 1898 to 1907, he extended the scope of Russian Orthodoxy from Alaska to the eastern United States, to accommodate Orthodox immigrants—Russian and many other nationalities—who were flooding into America. The number of parishes grew to seventy, with two auxiliary bishops, a seminary, and a monastery. Perhaps of greatest significance, he had the Orthodox liturgy and other services very well translated into English. Recalled to Russia in 1907 to become archbishop of Yaroslavl, he served during the early years of the war in Lithuania, and in 1917 became bishop of Moscow.

The anarchist-Communist guerrilla leader Nestor Makhno, terror of Ukraine

6. Nestor Makhno commanded what was known as the Anarchist Black Army, which opposed any attempt by any foreign force—Red Army, White Army, German or Austrian army—to impose a non-Ukrainian government on Ukraine. At one point he allied with the Reds against the Whites, but this did not dissuade the Soviet government from launching a major offensive against him after the Red victory in the civil war. Following numerous narrow escapes, Makhno took refuge in Paris with his wife and daughter. While there, he wrote his memoirs in three volumes, and died at age forty-five in 1934 from a tubercular infection.

7. The Black Hundreds were an ultranationalist and conservative movement that drew on the gentry, aristocracy, middle class, conservative intellectuals, bureaucracy, and clergy. They published newspapers defending the tsar's divine right to rule, and their armed bands, the Yellow Shirts, violently attacked revolutionaries, Jews, and even Ukrainian nationalists.

communes in Ukraine, which made them easy targets for roving anarchistic bands, especially those led by the anarchist-Communist guerrilla leader Nestor Makhno. More pirate than patriot, Makhno became the terror of Ukraine.[6] Some villages broke even their centuries-old pledge of nonviolence and joined with neighboring Catholic and Lutheran settlements to defend themselves, but when Makhno aligned with the Bolshevik government, the Mennonites downed arms rather than resist the government.

In 1919, Makhno's guerrillas herded fourteen men of the village of Molotschna into a basement and threw in hand grenades, then slew the survivors with swords. The women and girls were raped, the village burned down. In Eichenwald village, eighty-one men and four women were murdered in a single night, a story repeated again and again. Next came drought, and with it famine and disease, including venereal disease and typhus spread to the women by soldiery quartered in their homes.

Such suffering became common to most parts of Russia when civil war, which followed the Bolshevik coup in 1917, afflicted the country for the next five years. Russian enemies of the new regime, reinforced by contingents from western Europe, created the loosely led White Army, which was defeated by the Red Army in Ukraine, south Russia, and Caucasus in 1918, in central Asia and northern Russia in 1919, and finally in the Far East and Siberia between 1920 and 1922. Many lives were saved, however, by benefactions from Mennonites in Europe and North America, who by the mid-twenties were also helping their coreligionists to emigrate from the Soviet Union in the tens of thousands. Out of these activities there emerged the Mennonite Central Committee whose worldwide work on behalf of oppressed people was to become renowned through the twentieth century.

These concerns, plus an abortive Soviet invasion of Poland, somewhat distracted the government from pursuing an all-out attack on religion. At one point, Lenin sought assistance from Tikhon to provide relief funds, which the patriarch did provide by chairing a volunteer aid committee and appealing to the pope, other Orthodox patriarchs, and the archbishop of Canterbury to raise funds for Russia within their countries. But the Bolsheviks became so embarrassed by these appeals that they replaced the ecclesiastical committee with one of their own to handle all the money it gathered.

In February 1922, the Soviet government ordered the Orthodox Church to turn over all ecclesiastical art and artifacts; Tikhon agreed to the former but refused to surrender vessels used in the Liturgy (i.e. the Mass, or Holy Communion). Using their total control of the press, the Soviets cited this resistance as proof of the Orthodox leadership's callousness and greed. In a revealing statement made during a politburo meeting, Lenin typically observed that the famine presented a unique opportunity: "Nothing except for a desperate famine can create a frame of mind among the broad peasant masses that might guarantee us their sympathy... We must now wage the most resolute and merciless war against the Black Hundred clergymen and crush their resistance with such brutality that they will not forget about it for several decades."[7]

At first the Orthodox faithful resisted the loss of their church's holy treasures, and many were shot by Soviet police. The Soviets interrogated Tikhon, and arrested, tried, and convicted hundreds of clergy and laity for disobeying the confiscation edict. The biggest show trials, in Moscow and Petrograd,[8] saw more than a hundred people accused. Included among them was Metropolitan Benjamin of Petrograd, executed by firing squad with ten others at a lonely railway station on the city's outskirts in August 1922. Shortly before, Benjamin had declared in a letter to a friend, "My sufferings have reached a peak, but my consolations have increased as well. I am joyful and serene as always. Christ is our life, our light and our peace."

Meanwhile, some two-thirds of Russia's 1,025 monasteries were being closed and their buildings used for barracks, housing, and government offices. As one Soviet chronicler triumphantly recounted, "The black (monastic) clergy were scattered over the face of the Russian land like cockroaches swept out from under the stove by the hand of a tidy housewife." Many monks and nuns would be pioneers of the underground church, which soon formed to maintain the faith across Russia. Firm in their own accustomed communal ways, they allied anew in workers' communes or *artels*—ostensibly good socialists all.

As the dissolution of monasteries struck at the grassroots of the church, the Soviets intrigued cunningly to bring down her leadership. This they did by sponsoring a "reform" group within the church in what at first seemed a surprisingly smooth takeover. Calling themselves the Living Church, or the Renovationists, the reformers persuaded Tikhon, who was still under house arrest, to turn over his administration to them, and to appoint Metropolitan Agafangel of Yaroslavl to act in his place.

But Agafangel, who was not party to their plot, never did reach Moscow; he was imprisoned in the Arctic. The Renovationists took over instead, convening two national assemblies where they pushed through many changes. They deposed Tikhon and abolished his position. They authorized the translation of the Liturgy into modern Russian. They allowed widowed priests to remarry, and permitted married clergy to become bishops. Such reforms greatly pleased many diocesan clergy, who had long felt like an inferior

WOLNOŚĆ BOLSZEWICKA

In this 1920 Polish cartoon, Leon Trotsky is portrayed as a bloodthirsty devil, following a Soviet attempt to annex Poland. The Poles were able to ward off the combined Russian and Soviet Ukrainian force on this occasion, but would not fare so well nineteen years later.

8. Moscow had long been Russia's historic capital, but during the eighteenth century, Peter the Great built the new capital, St. Petersburg, on the Baltic Sea. When the war with Germany broke out in 1914, its name sounded altogether too German, so it was changed to Petrograd. After the Bolsheviks took over in 1917, they moved the capital back to Moscow, and with the death of Lenin in 1924 Petrograd became Leningrad. The name St. Petersburg was restored after the downfall of the Soviet Union. Throughout the whole period, Russians colloquially referred to it as simply "Peter."

Below: Petrograd Metropolitan Benjamin. He was among more than a hundred clerics put on show trial for disobeying the confiscation edict. Shortly before his execution by firing squad, he wrote to a friend, "I am joyful and serene as always."

The cover of a 1929 issue of the Soviet anti-Christian magazine Bezbozhnik *(left) depicting Communist victory over the Gods of Judaism, Christianity and Islam; a Soviet propaganda poster (center) from the 1930s urges the populace to "Ban religious holidays!"; and a 1917 poster (right) depicts Lenin sweeping away emperors, capitalists and clergy. Soviet efforts to marginalize, ridicule and, ultimately, neutralize what Karl Marx had called "the opiate of the masses" faced resistance all the way and would eventually fail.*

caste within Orthodoxy because they were denied leadership by the celibacy requirement for the position of bishop. Historian Hilarion suggests that this partly explains why the Renovationists soon held sway in fifteen thousand parishes, more than half the total. The Soviet regime helped in many ways as well, permitting them to form an administration, to start a theological college, and to publish. It also exiled or executed any clergy who opposed them.

Yet the Renovationists did not prevail. Tikhonites visited churches to persuade their councils to oust Renovationist clergy. Agafangel wrote a letter, which was widely circulated, urging obedience to Tikhon. The faithful responded by spurning the reformers who had captured the cathedrals, and seeking out Tikhonite priests for the sacraments. The Renovationists were just too compatible with the Soviets for many believers to stomach, while they knew that Tikhon still languished in secret police custody. Over the next decade, the Renovationist administration would command fewer and fewer parishes despite state support, and many metropolitans and bishops who initially backed it would recommit to Tikhon.

The Soviet government itself made this rapprochement possible when it released the patriarch in July 1923. For his part, Tikhon publicly admitted his "crimes" against the state and declared himself "by no means an enemy of the Soviet authorities." In an apparent effort at conciliation, he condemned "all threats against the Soviet government" and distanced himself from counterrevolutionaries based abroad. He apparently hoped that by maintaining this neutral position, Orthodoxy could survive. Accordingly, he also secured the public apology and support of Metropolitan Sergius, a devout monk and scholarly bishop who had been jailed by the Bolsheviks and then released to run the Living Church, but who now recanted. Why did the Soviets let Tikhon out at all, when they could have held another show trial? Some scholars suggest it was a nervous reaction to the immense foreign protest against the public trial of seventeen

Catholic clergy in Russia, and the execution of one of them, Monsignor Constantine Budkiewicz.

In any event, Tikhon was back in jail in 1924, where on December 9 he is said to have been saved from assassination by the intervention of his jailer, a man identified as Y. Polozov. Seriously ailing by then, he prudently named three successors, in case the Soviet authorities eliminated one or more by execution or imprisonment. This was indeed what happened to two of them, leaving only Metropolitan Peter of Krutitsa to succeed Patriarch Tikhon when he died in 1925, worn out at the age of sixty, seemingly of an illness.

Before his death the Soviets had been pressuring him to sign another declaration, expressing loyalty to the Soviets and condemning the counterrevolutionary Orthodox clergy outside Russia. He refused, but they published it anyway. The faithful were skeptical of this statement, as they had been of his earlier one. Even if their patriarch had signed it, they believed, he must have been coerced. Throughout his long captivity and afterward as well, Patriarch Tikhon had remained an inspiration and unifying force for the church.

Metropolitan Peter quickly selected three more successors before he himself was imprisoned. One of these was Metropolitan Sergius, who emerged as the new acting patriarch, was promptly imprisoned once more (1926), then released again (1927).[9] Scholars speculate that these shifts in treatment reflected a power struggle within the highest echelons of the government, between those who wanted Christianity destroyed immediately and those who favored a gradualist approach.

No group pursued the gradualist approach more enthusiastically and consistently than the League of the Militant Godless, created in 1925. A party organ, the League soon mobilized eighty-seven thousand volunteer members of its own and could also count on support from labor unions, party members, and

9. Metropolitan Sergius was imprisoned at the Solovki prison camp, a former monastery in the Soviet Arctic that became the prototype of the secret police system of corrective labor camps known as the gulag. Over several decades, at least seventy-five bishops, archbishops, and metropolitans along with thousands of other Christians were worked to death there. The food was inadequate, living conditions primitive, and treatment brutal. Few survived more than a year or two. Sudden disappearance into the gulag, after a brief and secret trial, was an ever-present threat for prominent Christians of any denomination.

In this contemporary illustration Father Constantine Budkiewicz receives a Bolshevik bullet to the back of the head on Easter Sunday 1923. The Polish-born Budkiewicz was at the center of the Roman Catholic resistance to Communist edicts in Petrograd and was put on trial along with Archbishop Jan Cieplak for "anti-Soviet and counterrevolutionary activities." Despite entreaties from Pope Pius XI, Budkiewicz, calm to the last, was executed, although the archbishop received just ten years imprisonment. In the second decade of the twenty-first century, Budkiewicz was still being considered for sainthood.

Metropolitan Sergius of Moscow is depicted in a contemporary painting by Pavel Dmitrievich Korin. Having been jailed and released, Sergius, who emerged as Tikhon's successor, issued a statement in 1927 putting Orthodox support behind the Bolsheviks—a move seen by some as cowardice.

10. Soviet oppression of Muslim subjects was less severe during the 1920s than that accorded Christians and Jews, chiefly for two reasons. Where Muslims were numerous, the Communist Party was weak, with Islam so pervasive in some regions that persecution would alienate the population without destroying the religion. Secondly, persecution would also alienate Muslims in other countries and thus impede the world revolution. Better to win the war on religion at the Soviet center, the Bolshevik strategists reasoned, before moving it to the periphery.

Communist youth clubs, as well as the grudging compliance of many teachers, artists, journalists, and other professions. Its ambitious objective was nothing less than the erasure of "every religious idea, every idea of God," from the mind of every Russian.

Because the League of the Militant Godless believed it was plowing new ground, every tactic must be debated by a relevant committee. Should the state coerce by jailing or fining some believers and keeping the rest out of the best professions, they wondered, or should it merely persuade through propaganda? Should it target Christian believers, whose minds were made up, or concentrate efforts on agnostics, who were more malleable? Should it go after the young in school, or the much-revered *babas*, the grandmothers, who could influence the young regardless of what they were taught in school? Should religious belief be mocked, or scientific and atheist ideas extolled? Should the appeal be to reason, or more crude and sensationalist? Any and all such approaches would be tried in the end, although most confidence probably was placed in the power of the schools to expose religion as unscientific and exploitative. Teachers were urged to identify believers by their lunchroom habits and target them for special attention.

Outside the classroom, adults were reached through posters, newspapers, and films, and by lectures, lectures, and more lectures. One poster, for example, depicted the Soviet Union as a woman combing tiny, lice-like clerics from her hair, and another showed the Virgin Mary considering a film on birth control and thinking, "Oh, why didn't I know this before?" Movies and newspaper articles portrayed Russian Orthodox clergy as capitalist agents, thieves, sexual abusers, and, eventually, Nazis.

Even more than Orthodox believers, Soviet propaganda painted Catholics, Jews, and Protestant sects as traitors and worse, because their leadership lay outside the Soviet Union and their ethnicity was non-Russian. Thus Mennonites, Baptists, and Swedish Lutherans were suspect for their non-Russian origins. Judaism was "impregnated...with greed, love of money and the spirit of egoism," and preached "intolerance and the bloody extermination of peoples of other faiths."

Ironically, Lenin and his successor Joseph Stalin both decried anti-Semitism, which before the Revolution was closely associated with such counterrevolutionary forces as the Black Hundreds, and after that, with the White Armies that fought the Bolshevik forces. According to Lenin, himself part Jewish, anti-Semitism was a tsarist effort to scapegoat Russia's Jews for the failings of the tsarist regime. But Judaism as a faith had to be distinguished from individual Jews, in order to include it in the general campaign against religion, and to allow many individual Jews to maintain positions of leadership within the Communist Party. As for Muslims, they were treated with relative restraint during the 1920s, though their schools and *sharia* law courts were closed.[10]

The relentless persecution of tiny sects such as the Jehovah's Witnesses perhaps reveals more about the paranoia inherent in totalitarianism than it does about the persecuted sects. The Witnesses had only fifty thousand Russian members at the time of the Revolution, but because the Communist ideology regarded

In this 1920 painting by Boris Mikhaylovich Kustodiev, entitled The Bolshevik, *the revolutionary movement is depicted as a giant striding purposefully through Moscow with the support of the multitudinous masses. For Russians of faith, however, the giant had begun to take on the aspect of an ogre.*

all aspects of life as needful of state control and direction, any deviance was suspect. The Witnesses, like the Catholic Church, were special objects of politburo apprehension because they took orders from a leadership beyond the power of Soviet authority to coerce with its customary domestic terrorism. They also posed a particular problem by refusing to serve in the military. Therefore, just as agents were sent to "infiltrate" the Vatican in Rome, other agents penetrated the Witnesses' world headquarters in Brooklyn, New York.

Below: A Petrograd wedding party photographed in 1922. The Bolsheviks attempted to replace Christian and Jewish religious rites with "Red" versions that supplanted the sense of supernatural with one of the Communist collective. Such cultural manipulations proved enduringly unpopular. Soviet weddings ended with the civil registrar declaring, "Congratulations on your lawful marriage. That will be three rubles."

The curious bullet that failed to kill

Pope John Paul II was convinced that the Virgin of Fatima saved his life

Things went so terribly wrong for Mehmet Ali Agca on May 13, 1981, as to later convince the Turk that nothing short of a supernatural power could so completely have thwarted his plan. What could be simpler, the would-be assassin had reasoned, than to work his way close to John Paul II as the pope progressed through jam-packed St. Peter's Square, fire a few pistol shots at close range, and then slip away in the ensuing melee? And Agca was right, too—except for that crucial final clause. Far from "slipping away," the wiry twenty-three-year-old was tackled by a nun, no less, and wrestled down by Vatican security, while the unconscious pope was rushed to the hospital, his blood streaking red on his white cassock.

May 13 is the feast day of Our Lady of Fatima, and Pope John Paul believed that the Blessed Virgin herself had deflected the bullet, which pierced his abdomen but missed vital organs and major arteries. So, it seems, did Agca. The pope recounts in his memoir, *Memory and Identity* (2005), that when he visited Agca in prison in December 1983, he found the Turk fearfully perplexed, and insistent upon knowing "the secret of Fatima."

By this he meant the "third secret of Fatima," the last of the messages reputedly entrusted by the Blessed Virgin Mary to three Portuguese children in 1917. John Paul II revealed this secret in 2000, thus deflating the fascination with it which arguably had obscured the central and enduring Fatima message: the need for prayer (particularly the rosary), penance, conversion, and—most bewildering perhaps to non-Catholics—the benefit of devotion to the "Immaculate Heart of Mary."

The first of the Virgin's celebrated appearances occurred on May 13, 1917, near the village of Fatima, some hundred miles northeast of Lisbon. Ten-year-old Lucia dos Santos and her cousins, Jacinta Marto, seven, and Francisco Marto, nine, were herding sheep in a nearby meadow called the Cova da Iria. As they later recounted, a beautiful woman suddenly appeared, "brighter than the sun, shedding rays of crystal light," who told them that she was from heaven and who promised to return five more times, on the thirteenth day of succeeding months. Word quickly spread, and despite the Great War raging in Europe, increasing numbers of pilgrims braved the obstructionism of Portugal's anticlerical regime to reach Fatima.

Surely, they reasoned, this must be the Blessed Virgin Mary herself. Had she not told the children to pray the rosary daily to end the war? Lucia, who alone spoke on behalf of the vision, said the Lady instructed them to "pray, pray very much, and make sacrifices for sinners, for many souls go to hell, because there are none to sacrifice themselves and pray for them." For her last visit, the wondrous vision promised, there would be a miraculous sign, and so on October 13 some seventy thousand people were waiting, drenched in driving rain. At noon, the crowd saw the sun abruptly emerge. For some ten minutes it seemed to spin and swoop across the sky, exhibiting vivid, changing colors—and when it stopped "dancing," the ground was bone dry. Skeptical newsmen, who had come to scoff, filed wondering eyewitness accounts instead.

Intense conjecture centered on the "secrets" that the children said the Lady had told them, which neither cajoling nor cunning could make them divulge. Although these illiterate little peasants might seem peculiar messengers for the Mother of God, they certainly had been transformed. Abandoning play, they prayed, fasted, and undertook physical discomforts (such as wearing painfully tight ropes around their waists, and drinking no water on the hottest days) as offerings for the conversion of sinners. They also patiently endured repeated interrogations. By August, Fatima's village administrator was so frustrated over the increasing chaos of pilgrims that he seized the three children and tried to make them admit they were lying—threatening to boil them in oil, and jailing them overnight. But their rough cell mates, who at first mocked the pious youngsters, ended by kneeling with them to pray the rosary.

Contemplative little Francisco Marto died in 1919 of bronchial influenza at age ten, and his sensitive sister Jacinta died of pleurisy in 1920. The bishop of Leiria-

Pope John Paul II confers with Turkish gunman Mehmet Ali Agca in a cell at Rome's Rebibbia Prison in December of 1983, a year and a half after Agca's assassination attempt. The pope—and later Agca—came to believe that Our Lady of Fatima had guided the bullet away from any vital organs on the day of the shooting—May 13, 1981.

The three children who reported the vision of the Virgin near Fatima, Portugal, on May 13, 1917 are pictured above left: (left to right) Lucia dos Santos, Francisco Marto, and Jacinta Marto. Lucia survived to become a nun and reveal the three secrets of Fatima. The first was that a world war greater than the First would occur, the second was that Russia would spread communism across the world. At right, a replica of the statue of Our Lady of Fatima.

Fatima arranged for Lucia dos Santos to enter a convent school at fourteen, where she studied, became a nun, and reported receiving further visits from the Virgin Mary. In 1930, the Catholic Church officially recognized the Fatima appearances, and between 1941 and 1943 Sister Lucia wrote out an account of them. She included the three secrets entrusted to the children by the apparition, sealing the third in an envelope marked "1960."[1]

Pope Pius XII released the first and second secrets in 1944. The first is a detailed, vivid, and terrifying vision of hell, which the Virgin showed the children in her July 13 appearance. In the second, she warns that unless people repent, "a worse war than this will follow, Russia will spread her errors across the world, the good will be martyred...various nations will be annihilated..." Further, she explicitly requested that the pope "consecrate Russia to my Immaculate Heart, to save it and the world."

John Paul II authorized publication of the third secret concurrent with the May 13, 2000, beatification of Francisco and Jacinta Marto (the youngest nonmartyrs to be so recognized by the Catholic Church). Among its central features is a vision of an angel with a flaming sword crying, "Penance, penance!" while a "bishop in white" struggles up a steep hill, through a half-destroyed city strewn with the corpses of martyrs, until he is felled at the top by bullets and arrows, beneath a great cross.[2]

Cardinal Tarcisio Bertone, secretary of the Congregation for the Doctrine of the Faith (CDF), affirmed at an accompanying press conference that John Paul II first read the third secret of Fatima while recovering from his bullet wounds in 1981, and believed himself to be "the bishop in white." He sent the near-lethal bullet to the bishop of Leiria-Fatima, who

had it mounted in the golden crown of the Virgin's statue at her Portuguese shrine. Then the pope set about fulfilling her request by consecrating the world, including Russia, to her Immaculate Heart on March 25, 1984. Many, including Sister Lucia, contend that this met the request of the Fatima vision, and that it arguably contributed to the collapse in December 1991 of Russia's atheist Communist regime.

Cardinal Joseph Ratzinger (later Pope Benedict XVI) emphasized at the press conference that Catholic teaching defines apparitions that have been declared authentic, such as those of Our Lady at Fatima, as "private revelation." That is, they add nothing new to the deposit of faith, which is already contained in full in "public revelation." ("Public revelation" ended with the death of the last apostle.) They are "a help which is offered," not an obligation of belief. He said that before Sister Lucia died in February 2005 at age 97, she told him that in her view "the purpose of the apparitions was to help people to grow more and more in faith, hope, and love."

He also explained the significance of "devotion to Mary's Immaculate Heart," and her promise that "my Immaculate Heart will triumph"—surprising ideas, he acknowledged, particularly for the "Anglo-Saxon and German cultural world." But the heart is the center of one's life, and an immaculate heart is one completely open—as was Mary's—to receiving and obeying God's word. Such a heart, Cardinal Ratzinger declared, is "stronger than guns and weapons of every kind." ∎

1. Sister Lucia told Cardinal Tarcisio Bertone (*The Last Secret of Fatima*, 2008) that she thought the third secret would be better understood after 1960.

2. The full story of Pope John Paul II's reign is told in chapter 16.

Moscow schoolchildren ride the escalator in the newly opened and much-publicized Metro in 1935. Science, technology, and atheism were pumped into pupils from an early age—although not altogether effectively. Later on, however, those faithful to their Christian beliefs were excluded from university enrollment and the professions, edicts that discouraged overt religious practice.

Within the Soviet structure, saints' days were abolished or were renamed to honor revolutionary heroes. Church rites of passage gave way to Red Weddings and Red Funerals, distinguished chiefly by bureaucratic paperwork. So banal did these occasions prove to be that the government ultimately built secular wedding palaces to impart some suggestion of transcendence, and secular prayers were added that invoked a future socialist paradise. At one point in the 1920s, writes David Powell in *Anti-Religious Propaganda in the Soviet Union: A Study of Mass Persuasion* (1978), a Soviet wedding would end with the civil registrar declaring: "Congratulations on your lawful marriage. That will be three rubles."[11]

The foot soldiers in the godless cause were the party cadres, the dedicated groups of factory workers and the youth club members, all of whom were instructed to identify, befriend, and persuade believers in God. Their premise was that Christians and other believers were psychologically drawn to religion by loneliness and insecurity. With his new atheist friend, the member was instructed, "the believer will feel that he is not alone, that his fate is not a matter of indifference to his associates. He will understand that he has genuine friends around him." Thus he would be open to scientific exposés of his irrational superstitions. If the premises were wrong, however, and the believer was motivated by neither loneliness nor superstition, but by rational reflection that the world could not have come about by accident, then the approach would fail. To assist the evangelists of godlessness, regional and local "councils of scientific atheism" were therefore established, comprising local intellectuals and paid party officials. Eventually there would be departments of atheism and religion, and even entire colleges, to generate propaganda with earnest statistical studies of belief, and progress toward unbelief.

Such allies in the war against God as filmmakers, intellectuals, and many teachers, proved less than enthusiastic about what they saw as misuse of their time. Further, party workers and the student "godless" often found themselves no match for their believing classmates and workmates in one-on-one discussions. An account from a later era, for example, features a teacher proudly describing the rocket-powered trips of Russian cosmonauts three hundred kilometers into

11. The Soviets tried to replace the sense of the supernatural inherent in Christian and Jewish rites of passage at birth, death, and marriage by enshrining a sense of the Communist collective. The Oktobrist ceremony for newborns, for example, invoked by its very name the Bolshevik insurrection of October 1917, calling on each mother to declare: "This child belongs to me only physically. For his spiritual upbringing I entrust him to society." Red baptisms, funerals, and weddings proved unpopular—even odious. Some later Soviet surveys indicate a majority of even Communist Party members continued to baptize their children in the name of the Father, Son, and Holy Spirit, although other surveys showed that this resort to old rituals was empty of actual belief.

space, emphasizing that they encountered no sign of God. Therefore, the teacher concludes, God assuredly must not exist. Then she asks a second grader, whom she knows to be a Christian, if he doesn't find this argument convincing. Responds the child: "I do not know if three hundred kilometers is very much, but I know very well that only those who are pure of heart will behold God." But for every teacher willing to discourage religious belief among primary school children, there were more who considered it a waste of time—or even counterproductive and likely to produce an "unwholesome interest" in religion.

According to David Powell, museums played a uniquely Russian role in the crusade against faith, perhaps because of the Soviet emphasis on the rationality of

12. Giordano Bruno was celebrated by Soviet museums as a martyr to science, as in fact he was also portrayed by nineteenth-century skeptics in the West. A near-contemporary of Galileo, Bruno was burned at the stake in 1600 after the Roman Inquisition declared him a heretic. His heresy, however, had little to do with science. Rather, it was due to his teaching that Jesus Christ was a skilled magician.

The godless were instructed to befriend believers in God, so that 'the believers would be open to scientific exposé of irrational superstitions.'

scientific Marxism. Especially emphatic were the museums of science, which underlined human mastery of nature by juxtaposing the latest theories on the world's origin posited by natural scientists against biblical treatments of the same subject. They also dramatized such historic events as the Catholic persecution of Galileo Galilei and Giordano Bruno.[12] Art museums presented shows purporting to expose the chronic debauchery of Orthodox clerics, or the allegedly bizarre

In this 1917 cartoon, "Mother Russia" is depicted as being sacrificed on the altar of Bolshevism. Such subversive artistic expression would soon meet with harsh consequences.

indoctrination techniques of Protestant sects. In Muslim areas, historical museums might focus on the harsh punishments inflicted upon those who defied their imams. Powell cites as example the beheading of a driver who refused to deliver imams to their mosque without fee.

Religion, in sum, was depicted as fraudulent, false, dangerous, and—worst of all—unscientific. But museum directors, Powell adds, generally proved as reluctant as teachers to pervert their work for atheism's sake. This necessitated the creation of specialized museums of atheism, usually located in confiscated churches. More effective than anything else in discouraging religious belief, however, or at

Turncoat Anabaptist writers used their inside knowledge of Protestantism to write novels extolling Communist scientific progress.

any rate its overt practice, were such discriminatory practices as exclusion of believers from university enrollment and from the professions.

The stars of the godless campaigns, at least in the early years, were often turncoat clergy, the so-called "Commissars in Red Cassocks," who publicly denounced their former faith and institution, and provided the new antireligious propaganda bureaucracy with valuable insider knowledge and salacious exposés. What motivated these men? Some may simply have needed work. Some had sought reform of the Orthodox Church's rigid hierarchy for decades. But the sincerity of such apostates was always in question, and they were slowly replaced by secular experts.

Similarly, turncoat Anabaptists such as David Schellenberg and Gerhard Sawatsky used their experience of rural Protestantism to write novels and poetry that contrasted the scientific progressivism of communism with the primitive resistance to change found in their own Protestant farm communities. Like the ex-priests, they ultimately became suspect to those with purer radical pedigrees. Schellenberg's novel *The Languishing Land*, for instance, was criticized for making heroes of individual revolutionaries, rather than celebrating the collective struggle of the whole village and community.

In 1926, as these Soviet strategies to destroy Christianity were being mapped out, the new patriarch Sergius was being pushed into drastic action to save it. He issued a proclamation reiterating Patriarch Tikhon's call for the church to remain neutral on political issues, but any hope that this would mollify the Soviets was soon dashed. Sergius was himself arrested; as were the three successors he named, and many other clergy.

For a liturgical and sacramental church, the virtual elimination of the priesthood meant destruction. Sergius made the momentous decision that Orthodoxy could *not* be neutral, but must support the regime to survive. In 1927, he issued a proclamation to this effect, setting the future course for state-church relations. "We wish to be Orthodox and at the same time claim the Soviet Union as our civil homeland, the joys and successes of which are our joys and successes, the misfortunes of which are our misfortunes," he declared, in a statement aimed at both the

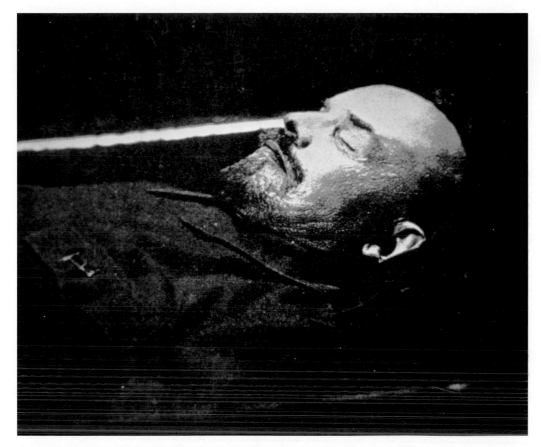

Lenin (shown here lying in state in Red Square) died aged fifty-three in January 1924, having absented himself from politics the previous year following a series of strokes. His death set off a power struggle that would see Trotsky banished and Stalin eventually emerge triumphant in 1927.

faithful and the Soviet leadership, requesting that it officially recognize the church.

The immediate result was negative. On the one hand, Sergius's declaration was seen by many who had suffered under the regime as apostasy and cowardice. Many bishops condemned the declaration, and underground churches formed around them. But most Orthodox believers regarded this decision as a necessary evil, and remained faithful to the patriarchate.

The Soviet leadership simply ignored it altogether, persisting in the position that the Orthodox Church had no formal existence above the parish. Besides, the leaders of the Soviet state were preoccupied with the final throes of the power struggle engendered by Lenin's death in 1925. In 1927, Lenin's malevolent and cunning protégé, Joseph Stalin, emerged triumphant. Cold, heartless, vindictive, brutal by even Bolshevik standards, Stalin soon disposed of all his notable rivals, in particular Leon Trotsky, whom he expelled first from the Communist Party and two years later from the country, finally arranging his assassination in Mexico City in 1940.

Although persecution would not abate under Stalin, Christianity would survive regardless, as would the Russian Orthodox Church. Patriarch Tikhon and his successors had consecrated new bishops and established underground seminaries. Many clergy became itinerant priests. The faithful learned to worship in homes and natural settings far from towns, or traveled long distances to attend an open church, and they prayed for deliverance. But deliverance was not at hand, and the most frightful persecution of all was about to descend on Russia's Christians, as chapter 5 in this volume will describe. ∎

Entitled Christ of Saint John on the Cross, *this 1951 painting by the eccentric Spanish surrealist Salvador Dali, presents the Crucifixion in both a traditionalist and a Modernist light. The angle of view creates a triangle that at once represents the Trinity and also, said Dali, "the nucleus of the atom." These two aspects might also be seen as representative of the battle between Modernism and traditionalism that raged throughout the twentieth century and created turmoil in both Catholic and Protestant churches.*

CHAPTER 3

Rupture, chaos, dismay shatter Christendom as Modernism takes its toll

A new theology, born of 19th-century skepticism, takes root among Catholics, despite a papal ruling, and wreaks havoc among Protestant communions

Two millennia of sometimes bitter experience have taught Christians that it is not the nonbelieving oppressor—the Roman emperor Diocletian or the Soviet General Secretary Joseph Stalin—whom they should most fear. Even more should they beware of the lapsed Christian who remains within their midst, seeking to affirm his own unbelief by undermining the belief of others. As the twentieth century opened, western Christianity, both Catholic and Protestant, encountered an emerging doctrine called Modernism, one that Pope Pius X early on condemned as the "synthesis of all heresies." By mid-century it would disrupt and dominate much of mainline Protestantism and, papal denunciation notwithstanding, create turmoil in Roman Catholicism as well.

Modernism was—and remains—a broadly based attempt by thinkers, popularly described as "advanced," to remake the biblical faith of the less advanced, not to say "backward." That is, to reshape Christian teaching to conform with the latest accepted theories arising out of cosmology, biology, psychology, sociology, and, in particular, history. It arose in the mid-nineteenth century with a new system of historical-critical biblical analysis (sometimes called "higher criticism") at the German University of Tübingen, under the leadership of liberal Protestant theologian Ferdinand Christian Baur (see sidebar, page 42). Bible passages that contradict contemporary science must be regarded as unhistorical myth, said Baur. As symbols, they might express important moral or psychological truths about human nature, but could no longer be seen as recounting actual events. A second assumption was that the books of the Bible merely reflect the unscientific

attitudes and misconceptions of their authors and the communities in which they lived, and therefore must not be regarded as the inspired Word of God. Both premises contradicted all previous Christian theology.

The "school of Baur" would be largely repudiated by subsequent textual discoveries, but by then Modernism had taken deep root, and Tübingen scholarship continued to reject the idea that the Gospels are based on eyewitness accounts of the life of Jesus. They concluded that many key Gospel events, including Christ's miracles and his bodily Resurrection, were merely folktales that arose long years after the events they describe. They doubted, at least implicitly, that Jesus was in any literal sense God. Jesus "transcended death" they said, only in the sense that he remained alive and transformative in his followers' minds.

As the German priest Ludwig Ott explains in his authoritative *Fundamentals of Catholic Dogma* (1952), Modernism is based on agnosticism, the belief that we *cannot* know anything supernatural, because it can't be proven by scientific demonstration. Modernist philosophies treat all spirituality as internal and subjective (the theological term is "immanent"). Man and nature are real, God a mere concept. Modernism therefore easily accepts Charles Darwin's theory of evolution by natural selection and moves comfortably into humanist political philosophies based on selective Christian moral teachings. Christianity, it insists, must change and progress with the growth of human knowledge.

The Resurrection of Christ by the seventeenth-century French painter Noël Coypel. The Modernists, who first appeared at Germany's Tübingen University in the mid-nineteenth century, sought to prove that key Gospel events, including the miracles, and especially Christ's Resurrection, had been composed so long after the events they described that they were merely folktales. Despite later historic evidence that affirmed the dates traditionally assigned to the Gospels, Modernism grew through the twentieth century, superseding traditional beliefs among theologians in many of the mainline seminaries.

In accord with this thinking, Modernism questions all the Christian creeds, the doctrinal statements that worshippers for centuries have regularly recited aloud in church services declaring what they believe to be true. Instead, Modernism seeks common ground with other religions because to Modernists all attempts to describe ultimate reality must be regarded as purely speculative. By any traditional definition, to unreservedly adopt Modernism amounts to apostasy, a total departure from Christianity, so that Modernism effectually becomes another religion. Loss of faith, of course, is hardly new, and had Modernists simply left their churches, they might have been missed, but there would have been no crisis. Indeed, many did leave. Many others, however, chose to stay and tried to change the meaning of Christianity from within.

Fierce conflict was inevitable and it raged through much of the twentieth century between the Christians, those who held to the faith as delivered by the apostles, and the Modernists, the "advanced thinkers" who rejected Christianity. Of the

Christians, some held that the Bible trumps science, others that while God created the laws of science, he also sometimes chose to intervene and suspend them, occasioning thereby the miraculous. The Christians continued to insist on two things: that the Gospels recorded real events, and that the supernatural is just as real as the natural. Taking the Christian position, Scottish Anglican bishop and missionary Stephen Neill explained it thus in *The Interpretation of the New Testament* (1962): "A Christ who is in any way at all less than historical is not the Christ of the Gospels, or of the Church, or of faith, or of glory." Similarly, Reformed theologian Richard Niebuhr commented acidly in *The Kingdom of God in America* (1937), Modernists believe that "a God without wrath brought men without sin into a kingdom without judgment through a Christ without a cross."

By the late 1800s, Modernism was infiltrating both Protestantism and Catholicism, but the Catholics, having a centralized doctrinal authority, were the first to fight it. Pius IX, pope from 1846 to 1878, had vigorously suppressed theological novelties within the Catholic Church. However, his successor, Leo XIII (1878–1903), believed that while the faith must be preserved, Catholicism must better address modernity's challenges. As one of his first acts, Leo published the encyclical *Aeterni Patris* (Of the Eternal Father) in 1879. It formally assigned precedence to the carefully reasoned medieval philosophy of Thomas Aquinas, which begins by offering five ways of reasonably deducing the existence of God. According to Marvin O'Connell, whose book *Critics On Trial* (1994) recounts the Catholic Modernist crisis, Leo's move "was a tacit admission that the church's house of intellect stood in grave need of repair."

Repair was the stated goal of the first Catholic Modernists too, at least initially. Like their Protestant forerunners, these clerics and laymen professed that Christian doctrine must be amended, but not abandoned. But there also began an extreme Catholic Modernism among a small cadre of thinkers. Three were preeminent: the

Pope Leo XIII is pictured waving to a crowd at the Vatican in 1898. Leo had hoped that Catholicism might better address modernity's challenges by pursuing the faith-through-reason approach of Thomas Aquinas. But when Modernist scholars began questioning the provenance and authenticity of the scriptures, he would issue an encyclical affirming categorically that the entire Bible had been written under the direct inspiration of the Holy Spirit.

Anglo-Austrian layman Baron Friedrich von Hügel; the Irish-born Jesuit priest George Tyrrell; and the French scholar and priest Albert Loisy.

The particular contribution of Hügel, born in 1852, was his service for half a century as a sort of clearinghouse for Catholic Modernist ideas. Though personally pious, he became attached to historical-critical thinking during the final years of Pius IX. Fluent in several languages, he used his connections to elite European

How Baur plus Bauer went sour

After the 19th-century Baur failed to prove the New Testament legendary, the 20th-century Bauer fails to prove the Jesus of the Bible a political plot

The Modernist heresy, which afflicted both Protestantism and Catholicism throughout much of the twentieth century, was ostensibly driven by a desire to rediscover and reestablish the beliefs and practices of the first Christians, the "primitive church." However, drawing dramatically new conclusions from patchy documentary evidence eighteen centuries old is by no means a certain science.

The father of Modernist historical-critical analysis (see accompanying chapter) was Ferdinand Christian Baur, a Protestant professor at the University of Tübingen in southern Germany. In the early to mid-1800s, Baur asserted that the New Testament was not written until late in the second century, some three or four complete human lifetimes after the events it describes. His thesis, if true, would have reduced the basis for Christianity to legend or fiction, though Baur saw theological conflict within the New Testament as neither.

But this initial historical-critical attack was debunked comprehensively by subsequent British scholars who were themselves relying on textual analysis, and showed that it was impossible for the New Testament to have been written at so late a date. Though dating debates continue, most specialists in the field now give the New Testament books much the same range of authorship dates as the church has always assigned them, in the last half of the first century.[1]

But doubt springs eternal. Jumping ahead one century, there comes another German professor, this one Walter Bauer (note the "e" in the name) from Göttingen in the north, arguing that the beliefs considered orthodox today—such as the idea that Jesus is God—were rejected by the early church, until the small Christian congregation in second-century Rome imposed them on the larger churches of the Eastern Empire, mainly through bribery and political craft. Bauer said that in many places, what was later considered "heresy" was the first form of Christianity to be adopted. Often these did not deny that Jesus was God; in fact they were sometimes extreme forms of that belief.

These twentieth-century Bauer's ideas were as short-lived as the nineteenth-century Baur's. After translation of his book *Orthodoxy and Heresy in Earliest Christianity* into English in 1971, Bauer was forcefully refuted by other experts, both Catholic and Protestant. For instance, he based his conclusions partly on the apparent silence of the ancient writers about the existence of orthodox communities—communities

Walter Bauer and a first edition English version of his book, which posited that the early church rejected the idea of Christ's divinity. Despite its dubious research, the book became a big hit among the skeptics in the Ivy League universities.

that believed as Roman Christians did—in various other geographic regions. From this Bauer assumed the Christians in these other areas must have believed differently—an "argument from silence" that provoked some scathing responses ("rich use of imagination," etc.) from his academic critics.

Even so, the effect of his speculations was to encourage doubt among academics intent on discrediting the traditional viewpoints. Moreover, as religious skepticism became almost obligatory in the Ivy League universities, quoting Bauer remained fashionable long after his work had been rejected, and few discovered that the most textually authenticated historical literature of any kind during the first five centuries of the Christian era is the New Testament. (See previous volume, *Unto the Ends of the Earth*, page 247.) ■

1. Scholars, however, continue to debate dates within that fifty-year time frame. *The Oxford Companion to the Bible*, for instance, notes that the two epistles to the Corinthians likely consist of several shorter letters or notes written by Paul early in the fifties. *The Oxford Encyclopedia of the Books of the Bible* cites with scholarly authority the probability that 1 Thessalonians dates back to the year 40, though other scholars put it closer to 50.

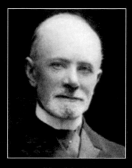

George Tyrrell　　*Alfred Loisy*　　*Maurice Blondel*　　*Friedrich von Hügel*　　*Adolf von Harnack*

Catholic circles to encourage cutting-edge Catholic thinkers to explore new ground.

Tyrrell was born in Dublin in 1861 and raised there in a fatherless and impoverished Anglican household. Drawn to Catholicism by a yearning for the stability and order his family life lacked, he impulsively joined the Jesuit order shortly after moving to London in early 1879. Although Tyrrell was eventually ordained in 1891, from his early Jesuit studies onward he bristled with hostility toward the order's adherence to what he viewed as a sterile and stale theological orthodoxy. In 1897 he came into contact with Hügel, who introduced him to the latest Modernist thought. Especially influential for Tyrrell were the ideas of French Catholic layman Maurice Blondel, whose controversial new immanentist philosophy held that God's existence is affirmed through a sequence of human actions.

Though not himself an original thinker, Tyrrell was a good writer who popularized the ideas of others. Within two years of encountering Hügel, he had published a pair of articles criticizing Catholic theology. Between 1903 and 1907 he published three books articulating his doctrinal radicalism more fully, to the growing dismay of his Jesuit superiors and the Vatican. Now openly dismissive of Catholic authority, Tyrrell defiantly proclaimed "the right of each age to adjust the historico-philosophical expression of Christianity to contemporary certainties, and thus to put an end to this utterly needless conflict between faith and science which is a mere theological bogey."

Catholic Modernism, however, was centered in France, not England, and its undisputed champion was Albert Loisy. When Leo XIII became pope in 1878, Loisy was a twenty-one-year-old seminarian who would be ordained a diocesan priest the following year. Rather than pastoral work, he chose to pursue biblical historical-criticism, and was skeptical of Catholic doctrine from the outset.[1] Installed as an instructor and biblical researcher at the *Institut Catholique* in Paris in the mid-1880s, Loisy set out, he claimed, to "rescue Catholicism from the leaden sheath into which it has been thrust by the philosophy of the Middle Ages and the false science of the Jesuits."

The obscure young priest's commitment to such a church-altering objective might suggest an unseemly arrogance, yet Loisy possessed an intellect and industry to match his ambition. By 1893, as a result of his initial forays into historical-critical territory, he had run seriously afoul of local Catholic authority. The Sulpician priests who directed the education of Parisian seminarians forbade them to attend Loisy's classes, and after yet another provocative lecture, he was forced to resign from the Institut in November.[2]

That very day in Rome, Leo XIII released an encyclical, in direction very different from *Aeterni Patris*. It delineated the principles by which Catholic academics

1. The young Loisy was heavily influenced by Ernest Renan, a Catholic seminarian who later became a renowned atheist scholar. For three years in the early 1880s, Loisy regularly attended Renan's lectures at the College de France in Paris. Renan's 1862 *Vie de Jésus*, according to historian Marvin O'Connell, was "an immensely popular and influential book . . . [which] reduced the person of Jesus to that of an amiable Galilean social reformer with no moral or supernatural significance."

2. Loisy also seemingly did not scruple about lying to his Catholic superiors to advance his theology. In 1890 he publicly swore to interpret sacred scripture "in accord with the unanimous judgment of the Fathers of the Church." From his subsequent work, it appears he had no intention of adhering to this oath, or to other professions of doctrinal loyalty. When he sought a position as a chaplain at an archdiocesan secondary school, Cardinal François Richard of Paris flatly refused him. "If he goes to a place like that, filled with impressionable youth," growled the cardinal, "all he will do is spread his pestilential ideas."

3. Three years earlier, Leo had signaled Rome's rapidly rising displeasure over unauthorized efforts to reconstruct Catholic doctrine to make it more amenable to modern thought. In his 1899 apostolic letter he condemned what he called "Americanism," an attempt to reconcile Catholicism with American concepts such as church-state separation and democratic church government. "The underlying principle of these new opinions," he declared, "is that, in order to more easily attract those who differ from her, the Church should shape her teachings more in accord with the spirit of the age and relax some of her ancient severity and make some concessions to new opinions." Leo was having none of this.

4. Loisy's *L'Evangile et l'Eglise* was too radical for lay philosopher Blondel—a thinker claimed by Modernists and traditionalists alike. The latter may have the stronger case. In correspondence with a priest, Blondel complained about several aspects of the book and took particular issue with Loisy's claim that Jesus was not conscious of his own divine nature. Commented Blondel, "To deny Jesus the consciousness that he was divine is to deny the divinity of Christ." Loisy would later acknowledge that he had already ceased to believe in Jesus's divinity at the time he wrote the book.

should study scripture. It affirmed categorically that the entire Bible had been written under the direct inspiration of the Holy Spirit. While the encyclical acknowledged the right of Catholic scholars "to push inquiry and exposition beyond what the Fathers have done," it insisted that their conclusions must conform with Catholic precedent. Loisy sent a conciliatory letter to the pope, pledging to conform "to all the instructions of the magnanimous pontiff." The pope then advised him to abandon his biblical research completely. Loisy ignored Leo's request, later scoffing, "Since it was merely advice, I was the only judge of my own interest."

Loisy now was indelibly marked as a man of dangerously subversive ideas both by Rome and by France's Catholic hierarchy. Unwelcome as a Catholic teacher, he was forced to accept a chaplaincy to a community of Dominican nuns. From this position, he authored twenty-five new articles between 1896 and 1899, many of them published under a pseudonym. By now he would admit the historical validity of only one creedal statement—that Jesus had "suffered under Pontius Pilate." Unsurprisingly, a number of Loisy's pseudonymous writings later earned formal church censure.

But it was a short book Loisy authored under his real name in 1902—having recently obtained the security of a prestigious secular professorship—that triggered the final showdown. Entitled *L'Evangile et l'Eglise* (*The Gospel and the*

The same year that Pius sought to squelch Modernism in the Catholic world, a similar repudiation of it had proved equally disruptive among Protestants.

Church), it was ostensibly a refutation of claims by the era's leading German Protestant higher critic, Adolf von Harnack. Using his own considerable historical-critical scholarship, Loisy attacked von Harnack's argument that the early Christian church had lacked a Catholic nature. Loisy asserted it had unfolded along Catholic lines from the outset, developing organically from its generation as a "seed" planted by Jesus.

In itself, this might have been applauded by the nonagenarian Pope Leo, still mentally alert though in failing health.[3] However, Leo could hardly praise a historical-critical work that also, as Loisy well knew, transgressed every principle of scriptural analysis the pope had laid down in 1893. Along with its basic premise that every aspect of the Christian church is constantly evolving, *L'Evangile et l'Eglise* asserted that Jesus was completely unaware of his own divinity during his earthly life.[4] Several French bishops quickly condemned Loisy's book, but the Vatican's own response was delayed until after Leo's death the following year.

The new pope was Pius X, who as cardinal archbishop of Venice had established himself as a fierce enemy of Modernism. Soon after his election, five of Loisy's works, including *L'Evangile et l'Eglise*, were placed on the Vatican's Index of Prohibited Books, the list of published works Catholics were not to read (the Index was abolished in 1966). But neither Loisy nor Tyrrell tempered their comments. In fact, in 1903 Tyrrell published *The Church and the Future* in which he declared that Catholic doctrines are a "grotesque...travesty of the whole light of Christ's work as shown us in the Gospels."

Pius was determined to get the Modernist genie back in the bottle, especially in the Catholic heartlands of France and Italy. By early 1907, rumors were rampant that a comprehensive papal denunciation was imminent. It arrived that summer, in two parts. First, a Vatican document condemned sixty-five Modernist propositions; this was followed by the papal encyclical *Pascendi Dominici Gregis* (Feeding the Lord's Flock). Consolidating Modernist thought with a coherence it lacked in practice, *Pascendi* rigorously enumerated its incompatibilities with Catholic orthodoxy, element by element, ideas that in most instances would contradict Protestant biblical tradition as well.[5] Pius concluded his thirteen-thousand-word critique, "And now, can anybody who takes a survey of the whole system be surprised that we should define it as the synthesis of all heresies?"

Though they had been forewarned, the leading Modernists were shocked by *Pascendi*'s scope and force. Most subsequently repudiated their Modernist writings and publicly professed loyalty to Catholic doctrine. Not so the two most prominent of them; Loisy and Tyrrell were excommunicated. (Hügel, having been more publisher than writer, and less personally aggressive, was spared.) Tyrrell, already ousted by the Jesuits, died in 1909, defiant to the end. Loisy continued to be hostile for another twenty-five years. His excommunication came with "infinite relief," he said. He died a pantheist in 1940, his gravestone inscribed: "Albert Loisy/Priest/Retired from Ministry."

Pascendi prescribed several preventive measures to contain the heresy, and these were powerfully reinforced in 1910 when Pius mandated a church-wide "Oath Against Modernism." It required all Catholic clergy and educators to profess that God can be known with certainty through the use of reason; to adhere exactly to all Catholic doctrines; and to renounce completely "the error of the Modernists." While this would be held in great odium by subsequent generations of "advanced" Catholic thinkers, for five decades it seemed to accomplish what Pius intended: Overtly Modernist theologies were excised from formal Catholic education and discourse. However, the movement was far from dead.

This "synthesis of all heresies," meanwhile, had encroached more openly and forcefully into the Protestant churches of western Europe and North America. By the turn of the twentieth century biblical historical-criticism already dominated the Protestant universities of northern Europe, and as early as the 1880s had sunk roots in North American seminaries, causing consternation and dismay.

The same year that Pius X sought to squelch Modernism in the Catholic world (1910), a parallel repudiation of it was voted by the General Assembly of the Presbyterian Church in the United

5. Modernism, declared Pius, is based on agnosticism; it reduces religion to mere human psychology; it gravitates theologically toward pantheism (nature worship); it effectively denies Christ's divinity by separating "the Jesus of faith" from "the Jesus of history;" it reduces Catholic dogma from unchangeable fact to mutable symbolism; and it expects the church to conform its beliefs to those of the civil order and the passing spirit of the age.

Pope Pius X, in his official portrait, and, inset, his 1907 encyclical Pascendi Dominici Gregis *(Feeding the Lord's Flock), which attempted to put the Modernist genie back in the bottle by rigorously enumerating its incompatibilities with Catholic orthodoxy. Pius concluded the encyclical by stating, "And now can anybody who takes a survey of the whole system be surprised that we should define it (Modernism) as the synthesis of all heresies?"*

6. The first prominent American Protestant champion of Modernist biblical historical-criticism was Professor Charles Briggs of Union Theological Seminary in New York. After two earlier acquittals by local Presbyterian authorities, Briggs was convicted of heresy by the General Assembly in 1893 and defrocked as a minister. Union Theological Seminary retaliated by revoking the Presbyterian Church's right of veto over its professorial appointments. Briggs then became Union's president and it was rapidly transformed into America's most theologically "advanced" seminary. Presbyterianism's Princeton Seminary in New Jersey retained Calvinist orthodoxy until the 1930s.

States. It issued a "Doctrinal Deliverance" declaring five "fundamental" doctrines to be "necessary and essential" to Christian faith. Known as the Five Fundamentals, these were scriptural inerrancy, the Virgin Birth of Jesus, his physical Resurrection, that his Crucifixion was atonement for human sin, and the historical and physical reality of his miracles. Although Presbyterians were only America's fourth-largest Protestant denomination at the time, trailing Methodists, Baptists, and Lutherans, the traditional Christian opposition to Modernism became most heated there. In 1892, seeking to remain denominationally aligned with the Calvinism of the 1646 Westminster Confession of Faith, the General Assembly had affirmed biblical inerrancy.[6]

Over the decade of the 1910s, Union Oil cofounder Lyman Stewart, a Presbyterian layman, financed a series of pamphlets entitled "The Fundamentals: A Testimony to the Truth." They were widely read and clearly laid out the lines of the coming battle. It was from these pamphlets that American fundamentalism would subsequently derive its name. However, while the pamphlets rejected Modernism, their doctrinal content was relatively broad and their authors included prominent Presbyterian moderates who later would reject the rigid biblical literalism that came to define U.S. fundamentalism. That is, they came closer to the ancient view of the scriptures—that they were inerrant in that they had been inspired by the Holy Spirit, and that some were history, some poetry, some allegory, and some parabolic.

The most prominent principals in this rhetorical war were two famous

Americans. On the Modernist side was Harry Emerson Fosdick, a Baptist minister and Union Theological Seminary professor who was, by general consensus, his era's finest Protestant preacher and a fervid advocate of the eugenics program (see chapter 13). The fundamentalist champion was William Jennings Bryan, the

Above, inset left, William Jennings Bryan and right, Harry Emerson Fosdick, and below, Fosdick's Union Theological Seminary in New York City. By general consensus the era's finest Protestant preacher, Fosdick earned himself the nickname "Modernism's Moses," but was vigorously challenged by the fundamentalist champion (and three-time failed presidential candidate) Bryan, whose lobbying efforts within the Presbyterian General Assembly helped bring Fosdick to heel, albeit temporarily.

three-time failed Democratic presidential candidate and former U.S. Secretary of State. Now, as a Presbyterian elder, he was campaigning to keep Darwinian evolutionary teaching out of American schools. He viewed evolutionary ideas in the direst terms, protesting that they undermined biblical authority and Christian doctrine. Moreover, writes Bradley J. Longfield in his article "For Church and Country: The fundamentalist-Modernist Conflict in the Presbyterian Church," Bryan declared that Darwinism "cut the nerve of moral reform and destroyed the foundation of Christian civilization."

In early 1922, Bryan and Fosdick skirmished over evolution in the pages of *The New York Times*. Shortly after these exchanges, Fosdick ascended the pulpit of New York's First Presbyterian Church, where he served as a permanent guest preacher, to deliver a famous sermon entitled "Shall the Fundamentalists Win?" Fosdick, who would earn the nickname of "Modernism's Moses," declared belief in the Virgin Birth and the Resurrection to be outmoded and nonessential, and scriptural inerrancy to be flatly incredible. He asserted that his supporters in both

To gain Fosdick's sermon wider audience, New York publicist and Modernist Ivy Lee arranged to have it mailed to America's 130,000 Protestant clergymen.

the Presbyterian and Baptist churches were loyal evangelical Christians who merely sought to reconcile their faith to the findings of contemporary scholarship. Further, Fosdick accused traditionalists of "one of the worst exhibitions of bitter intolerance that the churches of this country have ever seen." To gain Fosdick's sermon a wider audience, New York publicist Ivy Lee, a Modernist whose professional clients included the Rockefellers, arranged to have the sermon printed and mailed to each of America's 130,000 Protestant clergymen.

"Shall the Fundamentalists Win?" provoked speedy rejoinders from traditional Presbyterianism's most prominent defenders. Philadelphia pastor Clarence Macartney fired back with a sermon entitled "Shall Unbelief Win?" It too was converted to a pamphlet and distributed widely, and the Philadelphia presbytery requested the General Assembly to discipline Fosdick's New York church. As well, J. Gresham Machen, an accomplished New Testament professor at the still-traditionalist Princeton Theological Seminary, published a book entitled *Christianity and Liberalism*. It maintained that Modernist theology constituted a completely new religion from which "everything distinctive of Christianity" had been replaced by an empty materialism that led to "a sordid life of utilitarianism." It greatly paralleled the language of Pius X's *Pascendi*, though each would doubtless have found the other an unusual ally.

Bryan joined the fray at the 1923 Presbyterian General Assembly. There he was narrowly defeated in a bid for election as the assembly's moderator, and his initiative to bar evolutionary teaching from Presbyterian schools was also voted down. But at the lobbying of Bryan and other leading traditionalists, the assembly reaffirmed the Five Fundamentals and ordered the New York presbytery to bring the Baptist Fosdick and his Presbyterian flock to heel.

For three years, the Presbyterian Church seesawed institutionally between the two factions. Fosdick's supporters crafted a declaration known as the Auburn Affirmation, objecting that the General Assembly constituted a court rather than a legislative body, and therefore had no right to legislatively impose the Five Fundamentals. The Affirmation also argued that the Five Fundamentals were not settled doctrine, merely theory, and that evangelical Christianity required freedom

The old faith versus the new realities

How to preserve the former while recognizing the latter was the challenge facing the new era's Catholic and Protestant theologians, and some did both

As twentieth-century Christianity collectively wrestled with Modernism, it did not simply divide into opposing camps of rigid reactionaries versus apostate revisionists. Many influential scholars sought to fit intellectual developments into historic Christian belief, but without changing or compromising the basic content of the faith.

One of the first was John Henry Newman, who went from low Anglican evangelical youth to high Anglican priest to Roman Catholic convert. In *An Essay on the Development of Christian Doctrine* (1845), written shortly before his conversion to Rome, Newman acknowledged that from its early centuries the Catholic Church had clarified doctrinal understandings when necessary, but he firmly rejected that this produced new beliefs. To the contrary, he held that all new formulations had been implicit in scripture and Christian tradition from the outset, and were drawn from this unchanging doctrinal deposit to satisfy new circumstances and answer new arguments. He dismissed out of hand the most extreme Modernist contention that Christianity is merely a human invention.

The Catholic hierarchy was initially suspicious of Newman's venturesome ideas, but his approach received official endorsement late in his life when Pope Leo XIII named him a cardinal.[1] This encouraged succeeding generations of traditionalist Catholic thinkers to explore new ground—as long as basic doctrinal integrity was not compromised.

One such thinker was twentieth-century Swiss theologian Hans Urs von Balthasar, who was and remains exceedingly influential. Among his vast body of scholarship, arguably one of the most significant contributions was his articulation of the beauty of the Christian faith in a seven-volume study of "theological aesthetics."[2] Though firmly grounded in premodern Catholic thinking, Balthasar became unusually open to contemporary Protestant scholarship, especially (later in life) that of his friend Karl Barth, a Swiss Reformed theologian with whom he corresponded for decades. Barth rejected the dominant Modernism of early twentieth-century Protestantism; he emphasized the Trinitarian nature of Christianity, and insisted that the Bible contains "divine thoughts about men, not human thoughts about God."

Barth was neither fundamentalist nor Modernist. He rejected strict biblical inerrancy and freely conceded that narrative inconsistencies exist between the New Testament's four Gospels. However, Barth asserted that these must be understood as part of the mysterious method chosen by an incomprehensible God to communicate his divinity to humanity, not as evidence that the Gospels are mere myth. "Do you want to believe in the living Christ?" Barth once commented. "We may believe in him only if we believe in his [bodily] resurrection. This is the content of the New Testament."

Barth's influence extended ecumenically to Protestants and Catholics and beyond. *Time* magazine featured him on its cover during his U.S. tour in 1962, and Pope Pius XII is said once to have described him as the most important theologian since Saint Thomas Aquinas in the thirteenth century. ("This proves," the Protestant Barth is said to have quipped, "the pope's infallibility.") He is sometimes called the founder of Protestant neoorthodoxy, because many Protestant thinkers followed his lead in seeking to combine historical Christianity with elements of recent theology and philosophy.

American theologian Francis Schaeffer, notwithstanding a deep understanding of modern art and thought, remained unconvinced that in the end modernity had much to offer the Christian. An evangelical Presbyterian, he had studied under J. Gresham Machen at Westminster Theological Seminary, and later moved to Switzerland where he founded the L'Abri spiritual community. He concluded that in the end all pseudo-Modernist belief systems, including Barth's, produce disbelief and despair. Schaeffer argued in support of traditional Calvinism. This he saw as logically defensible and founded on solid evidence (including such recent archaeological finds as the Dead Sea Scrolls) that substantiates New Testament components previously dismissed as fictional by skeptical academics. Many drivers of the politically powerful Christian Right in the United States followed Schaeffer.

Roman Catholicism, meanwhile, was experiencing a parallel internal struggle. Though Modernist-inclined scholars often claimed that intelligent Catholic discourse was impossible for five decades after Pope Pius X condemned Modernism in 1907, there was in fact among faithful Catholic intellectuals a vigorous ongoing debate.

By the time of the Second Vatican Council (1962–1965)

of thought to be preached effectively. Encouraged by an outpouring of support for Fosdick across denominational boundaries, the New York presbytery largely exonerated him after investigating his conduct.

Undaunted, the traditionalists rallied at the 1924 General Assembly behind Macartney, who was elected moderator and immediately appointed Bryan as vice-moderator. However, the assembly declined to repudiate the Auburn Affirmation

Theologian Karl Barth makes the cover of Time *magazine in April 1962; and (and left to right) Jacques Maritain, Christopher Dawson, and Francis Schaeffer. All contributed to making the old faith credible to modern doubters. Barth was singled out by Pope Pius XII as the most important theologian since Thomas Aquinas. "This proves," quipped Barth, "the pope's infallibility."*

there were two major schools of thought. There were Thomists, named for the thirteenth-century philosopher saint Thomas Aquinas, who had been trying from the early nineteenth century to refute post-Christian philosophers since Immanuel Kant (1724–1804) by finding counterarguments implicit in the pure rationalism of medieval scholasticism. The second group were Augustinians, named for the sainted North African bishop of the fourth century, who taught that faith leads to reason, not reason to faith.

The interplay between leading exponents of these groups makes a vast field of study. In addition to Thomists there were Transcendental Thomists (Karl Rahner, Joseph Marechal), who in their effort to accommodate Kant were accused of antisupernatural Modernism. Opposing this were neo-Thomists such as Jacques Maritain and Etienne Gilson, who contended that earlier Thomists had misrepresented his philosophy and were trying to salvage it. Opposing both, the Augustinians held that while Thomism was good philosophy, the world could be converted only by hearing and heeding the story of Christ's atoning Crucifixion and saving Resurrection. For most people, the abstractions of philosophy are as inaccessible as a liturgy in Latin. This attitude caused them to be suspected, not of Modernism, but of seeking to sever Catholicism from its roots. Known as the Ressourcement/Communio movement, this school included among its more orthodox adherents Balthasar, Henri de Lubac, Joseph Ratzinger, and Karol Wojtyla.

Because the last two were both numbered among the reformers of the Second Vatican Council and both later

became popes, it led to a sense of shock and betrayal among many more extreme reformers when they later firmly insisted upon retaining and reinforcing Catholic Christianity as objectively true and necessary for salvation. However, unlike the more Modernist of the modernizers, they had never said it was anything else.

American Catholic historian James Hitchcock, himself a young reformist intellectual during the 1950s, makes an interesting point in his 1985 essay, "Postmortem on a Rebirth: The Catholic Intellectual Renaissance." "A little-noticed aspect of Modern intellectual history," writes Hitchcock, "is that although the new theologies, whether Christian or Jewish, were created with the aim of making the old faith credible to modern doubters, this rarely succeeds. What brings over the G. K. Chestertons, Ronald Knoxes, and Edith Steins from the atheistic/agnostic camp is the ancient, unchanging message of the historic faith." ∎

1. Early Catholic Modernists like Albert Loisy and George Tyrell said they were influenced by Newman's arguments regarding the development of doctrine, but then contradicted themselves by insisting he didn't go nearly far enough, and should have accepted drastic "evolutionary" doctrinal developments that contradicted original Christian teachings, such as the Modernist rejection of Christ's physical Resurrection.

2. As might be expected with a groundbreaking theologian, Balthasar's innovative ideas sometimes generated serious resistance and some of his opinions remain controversial. As with Newman, Balthasar's overall approach earned papal endorsement when Pope John Paul II nominated him a cardinal in 1988. Balthasar died two days before his installation ceremony.

A 1922 cartoon by the fundamentalist cartoonist E. J. Pace graphically depicts the descent of the Modernists down an infernal staircase leading to atheism. Pace's views were shared by Clarence Macartney (center), who was elected moderator of the Presbyterian General Assembly in 1924, and by J. Gresham Machen (right), whose attack on liberalism led to his dismissal from the Princeton Theological Seminary.

7. John Foster Dulles, a Presbyterian who in the 1950s would serve as U.S. secretary of State under President Eisenhower, acted as defense counsel for the New York presbytery during the assembly, which also debated the presbytery's recent licensing of two ministers who refused to affirm belief in the Virgin Birth. Ironically, Dulles's son Avery would convert to Catholicism during his college years, become a Jesuit priest, and earn international renown as an orthodox Catholic theologian. In the year 2000, at the age of eighty-two, Father Dulles was elevated to the rank of cardinal by Pope John Paul II.

and renewed its counteroffensive against Fosdick only obliquely.[7] As a Baptist, he would not be reinvestigated, but he would be forced to choose between joining the Presbyterian Church or resigning his preaching post at First Presbyterian. As traditionalists hoped, this stratagem succeeded in removing the nettlesome Baptist Fosdick from his Presbyterian pulpit. Resigning in March 1925, Fosdick was installed shortly afterward as pastor of Park Avenue Baptist Church, largely at the instigation of the world's richest Protestant, John D. Rockefeller Jr. From there Fosdick moved in 1930 to even greater prominence as pastor of the newly built Riverside Church in Manhattan, an extravagant and socially active institution funded by wealthy second-generation business magnates. Rockefeller alone would contribute $32.5 million to church coffers by the time of his death in 1960, part of the more than $500 million dollars he disbursed over his lifetime in philanthropic gifts.[8]

Fosdick's departure did nothing to end the Presbyterians' stalemate. Both sides sniped inconclusively into 1925, with Bryan continuing as a key traditionalist leader. However, his involvement in that year's famous Scopes trial (see sidebar, chapter 4, page 66) proved disastrous for Presbyterian traditionalists and, by extension, for like-minded American Protestants generally. The lampooning Bryan suffered from the news media convinced millions of Americans that biblical fundamentalism amounted to willful ignorance.

The 1926 Presbyterian General Assembly endorsed the Auburn Affirmation's call for acceptance of doctrinal diversity and, over the next decade, led other large Protestant denominations to do the same. In the late 1920s Machen and other traditionalists were purged from their Princeton Seminary stronghold, and the early 1930s saw a shift of emphasis in foreign missions from traditional evangelism to social initiatives and interreligious cooperation. By the mid-1930s Modernist ideas prevailed. This in turn provoked the formation of breakaway denominations such as the Presbyterian Church of America (later known as the Orthodox Presbyterian Church), founded in 1936 by Machen and the traditionalists.

Significantly, however, at no time during the 1920s and 1930s did the theologically "advanced" constitute anything close to a majority of America's Protestants. Generally, Modernism began at the top, and worked downward.

The Modernists won the confrontation partly because Bryan lost in the court of secular opinion, and partly because the Presbyterian General Assembly bungled its imposition of the Five Fundamentals.

But the real reasons the traditionalists lost probably lay deeper. Post-First World War America was rapidly secularizing and harbored a seemingly boundless faith in the power of science. Modernism appealed to many of America's deep-pocketed business elite, and at the same time fit well with the era's populist "social gospel" movement, a powerful reform initiative to legislate against "collective sins" such as poverty and alcoholism. Perhaps most compelling of all was the Modernist argument that a Protestant denomination must embrace all doctrinal differences, based on the interesting but debatable assertion that this was a founding Protestant principle. Debatable or not, many agreed that Modernist-minded ministers like Fosdick should be free to express diverse opinions, even if they denied the Five Fundamentals.

But many did not agree. Thus began a growing exodus of Protestant Christians into new fundamentalist breakaway sects and churches that sprang up largely in reaction to Modernism. During and after the Second World War the mainline churches remained outwardly solid, and provided most members of the nation's governing class. Numerous theologically traditionalist Christians still filled their pews, though they exercised little restraint on the leadership. It seemed undeniable that Modernism reigned supreme. There was, however, one glaring exception, notably what would soon become the biggest American Protestant church of all, the Southern Baptist Convention. They stayed firmly attached to the Five Fundamentals, and became even more traditionalist after the late 1970s.

8. When Fosdick expressed concern to Rockefeller about becoming known as the pastor to one of America's richest men, Rockefeller retorted, "Do you think more people will criticize you on account of my wealth, than will criticize me on account of your theology?"

John D. Rockefeller Jr. is pictured here with his father in a 1915 photograph. The richest man in America at the time, Rockefeller supported both scientific endeavor and Modernism in the Baptist Church, facilitating Harry Emerson Fosdick's move in 1930 to Manhattan's interdenominational Riverside Church, shown below left in a recent photograph.

9. Roman Catholic teaching rejects "atheistic evolution"—the view that no force exists beyond or behind nature, but it allows for "theistic evolution"—that God purposely created the universe and life on earth over long periods of time, and not necessarily in six literal twenty-four-hour "days" as written in the Book of Genesis. The Catholic Church remains similarly uncommitted on whether God developed the human species from other life forms. But it does insist that starting with Adam and Eve, God has specially created each human being in his own image with a unique soul.

10. Teilhard was also a controversial paleontologist. He endorsed the "Piltdown Man"—the name given to bones of an alleged early "humanoid" found in a gravel pit near Piltdown, Sussex, England in 1912. The Piltdown Man was enthusiastically embraced by the scientific community as evidence of evolution, but exposed as a hoax in 1953. The bones were from an orangutan, a chimpanzee and a human. While the forger was never discovered, Teilhard remains on the list of suspects.

The immensity of the crowd at this 1959 Southern Baptist Convention gathering bespeaks the popularity of what by the 1970s had become a phenomenon. In the postwar period, Modernism resulted in a burgeoning membership in a variety of breakaway fundamentalist sects, and helped make America's Southern Baptists the biggest Baptist denomination in the world.

On the surface, it appeared that much of Protestantism had succumbed while Catholicism stood firm. But the Catholic debate was far from finished. In the wake of *Pascendi* and the anti-Modernist oath, "advanced" Catholic thinkers did not disappear. Instead, they learned to communicate their thoughts more obliquely. Up until 1960, borderline heresies were funneled primarily through French Jesuit priest and paleontologist Pierre Teilhard de Chardin and his quasi-scientific theory of cosmic evolution. While Teilhard's ambitious synthesis of faith and science wasn't exactly Modernism, its evolutionary character aligned neatly with Modernist principles.[9] Occasionally Teilhard ran afoul of church authorities, with the Vatican intervening against the publication of some of his books. Indeed, some of his ideas were specifically condemned by Pope Pius XII in a 1950 encyclical. But Teilhard was never ordered to abandon his theological speculations completely. He became adroit at sidestepping Vatican criticism, advancing his controversial ideas only so far as seemed prudent at any given time. "I feel the moment has come for me to disappear for a time from Paris, where things are getting 'too hot' for me personally," he privately explained in 1950 about his decision to undertake anthropological field research in South Africa. "It would be better to give Rome the impression that I am delving back into what people down there call 'pure science.'"[10]

Other problematic Catholic thinkers of the postwar period, such as Germany's Karl Rahner and France's Yves Congar, were similarly deferential to church authority, but continued to push the boundaries without quite crossing them. "Rahner, Congar, [and] Teilhard de Chardin were all suppressed, but they quietly continued working to prepare the future," the Modernist Swiss theologian Hans Küng noted approvingly in 1984. "In a period like this, people must remain rather than be driven out." Two others were Edward Schillebeeckx, a Belgian Dominican theologian, and Raymond Brown, a U.S. Sulpician Bible scholar who frankly doubted (but did not formally deny) the scriptural basis of core Catholic beliefs: the Virgin Birth, Christ's physical Resurrection, and that the apostles founded the order of bishops. Teilhard died in 1955, and the Vatican subsequently issued an official caution about his doctrinal shortcomings in 1962. But Rahner, Congar, Schillebeeckx, Brown, and Küng would all go on to serve as expert advisers during the Catholic Church's worldwide Second Vatican Council, convened between 1962 and 1965. Not all these people were of one mind, not all were ultimately Modernist, and some of their ideas have since been pronounced orthodox; still, they and many more like them contributed to the crisis in faith and morals that shook Catholicism after the Council.

Modernist ideas were also propagated through informal associations such as *La Pensée,* a group of French Jesuits that formed in the 1920s and numbered Teilhard among its members. Jesuit superiors were aware of *La Pensée*'s nonconformist thinking but lacked sufficient grounds—or perhaps will—to disband it; Teilhard boasted that into the late 1940s its members "never ceased advancing in their notions of Christ and Christianity." Vatican policing of doctrinal purity was frequently accused of being overzealous, fostering a lasting sense of grievance among many Catholic intellectuals.[11] And as within Protestantism, theological innovation found additional cover by aligning itself with social and political progressivism, which had church approval. Leo XIII's 1891 encyclical *Rerum Novarum* (On the New Things) had authoritatively condemned unrestricted capitalism and provided official Catholic support for labor unions and government intervention to ameliorate the sometimes desperate conditions of the working classes, a support that continued during the twentieth-century papacies.

So as the 1950s drew to a conclusion, Modernist ideas were present in both major traditions of western Christianity. Mainline Protestantism was guided, in substantial measure, by the intellectual heirs of Harry Emerson Fosdick. Like his famous Riverside Church, the mainliners became identified with progressive social causes; for ecumenical associations that downplayed doctrinal differences; for a psychologized understanding of Christianity that often saw ministers make counseling their primary pastoral activity; and more broadly, for a secularized religion that had discarded "old-fashioned" Christianity with its endless emphasis on the need for salvation from personal sin.

Among Catholics, there was a deceptive peace. The orthodoxy imposed by Pius X remained in place, and outwardly Catholicism seemed healthier than at any time since the Reformation. Opposed to Hitler's Nazism, the Catholic Church had emerged from the Second World War in good standing with western governments. In Europe and North America it was gaining converts, and religious vocations stood at record levels; it dominated Latin America, was making inroads in Asia, and a remarkable Catholic evangelization was under way in Africa. Beneath the surface, however, new undercurrents of all sorts were running strong—some Modernist, some simply antiauthoritarian. No postwar Catholic thinkers of prominence were nearly as radical as Loisy and Tyrrell, but many clergy and laity had quietly concluded that some searching reconsideration of their faith's teachings was overdue.

However, neither the most optimistic Protestant pastor nor the most impatient Catholic intellectual of the 1950s could have predicted how strong a tidal wave of change would hit Christianity in the next decade. ∎

Top: French theologian Yves Congar (right) is pictured in the early 1960s with then Münster University professor Joseph Ratzinger (later Pope Benedict XVI). They, along with Pierre Teilhard de Chardin (below, left) and Karl Rahner (right), sought to move the church into the modern age, but at the same time remain deferential to papal authority.

11. A further complaint of "advanced" Catholic thinkers was that Pius X's *Pascendi* encyclical had demolished a straw man, since no one associated with the small early Catholic Modernist movement had integrated its ideas as systematically as the encyclical did in describing it. True enough, the Dominican theologian Aidan Nichols acknowledged in a centenary reexamination of the encyclical. But he said that Pius was well aware of this, and had deliberately assembled Modernist theology comprehensively in order to critique it coherently.

Lytton Strachey, great debunker of things Victorian and sacred, is pictured at his desk in this postimpressionist pastel by French painter (and Strachey's brother-in-law) Simon Bussy. In his book Eminent Victorians, Strachey attacked his despised forebears, one admirer explained, "by turning his fire on the humbug and hypocrisy that come from organized religion."

CHAPTER 4

God, fidelity, honor, truth —all safe targets for scorn in the era of debunking

After Victorian heroes are smeared by their children, and Bloomsbury's luminaries jeer sexual propriety, Margaret Mead's fantasy dupes a whole generation

The years between the First and Second World Wars, wrote the Christian essayist Dorothy L. Sayers in 1941, "saw the most ruthless campaign of debunking ever undertaken by nominally civilized nations. Great artists were debunked by disclosures of their private weaknesses; great statesmen by attributing to them mercenary and petty motives, or by alleging that all their work was meaningless, or done for them by other people. Religion was debunked and shown to consist of a mixture of craven suspicion and greed. Courage was debunked, patriotism was debunked, learning and art were debunked, love was debunked, and with it family affection and the virtues of obedience, veneration, and solidarity.

"Age was debunked by youth and youth by age. Psychologists stripped bare the pretensions of reason and conscience and self-control, saying that these were only the respectable disguises of unmentionable unconscious impulses. Honor was debunked with peculiar virulence, along with good faith and unselfishness. Everything that could possibly be held to constitute an essential superiority had the garments of honor torn from its back and was cast out into the darkness of derision. Civilization was debunked till it had not a rag left to cover its nakedness." Author Sayers attributed all this to the sin of envy (Latin *invidia*). "Envy," she wrote, "cannot bear to admire or respect; it cannot bear to be grateful."

As the twentieth century dawned, the heirs apparent of Britain's Victorian aristocracy had much to be grateful for, living as they did in the unprecedented luxury of the world's most prosperous country. Their parents and grandparents, aided of course by gifted commoners, had somehow preserved Europe from continent-wide conflict for eighty-five years, had made matchless progress in medicine, transportation, and communication, and had turned a largely agricultural society into a world industrial center. The beneficiaries of this heritage proved singularly ungrateful, however, deriding their Victorian forebears as insufferable hypocrites and lampooning what was now regarded as their sanctimonious and self-serving Christian piety. Nor did they see themselves as motivated by *invidia*, but by righteous indignation.

Preeminent among the debunkers was a frail young Cambridge man named Lytton Strachey, son of a former viceroy of India, who graduated from Cambridge and embarked upon what began as an unremarkable literary career. Exempted from military service as physically unfit, he spent the First World War creating the work that would win him lasting renown among a new literary and

'We were the forerunners of a new dispensation,' exulted John Maynard Keynes. 'We entirely repudiated custom. We were, that is to say, in the strict sense immoralists.'

artistic set. Many of its members also escaped war service, as it happened, generally as conscientious objectors. Strachey attacked the despised forebears, one admirer explained, "by turning his fire on the humbug and hypocrisy that come from organized religion." In his instantly acclaimed *Eminent Victorians*, he singled out for special debunking four "heroes" of the foregoing age. This varied quartet had one thing in common: all were driven by an unreserved belief and trust in God which received Strachey's particular scorn.[1] "To really mean every word when you repeated the Athanasian Creed! How wonderful!" he sneered. "But no doubt the strange notion of taking Christianity as literally true was delightful to the earnest mind."

Strachey gained a further distinction. He was a founding member of a curious circle of geniuses, eccentrics, and sexual perverts (or so they were generally regarded at the time) that took its name from the London district where many of them lived. This Bloomsbury Group originally included the century's most influential economist, its most widely recognized philosopher, and a number of its most acclaimed poets, artists, and novelists. They all despised religion, particularly Christianity, chiefly because it imposed moral restraints on something that they saw as the highest human value. This they called "intimacy," by which they meant sex in all its boundless permutations and variations.

Bloomsbury's philosophical maharaja was George Edward Moore, whose tome, *Principia Ethica*, became the "bible" of the movement, writes Jesse Wolfe in *Bloomsbury, Modernism and the Reinvention of Intimacy* (2011). Among much else, Moore seemed to provide an ethical rationale for whatever "intimate" behavior seemed appealing. "It was exciting, exhilarating, the beginning of a renaissance, the opening of a new heaven on a new earth," exulted another foremost Bloomsbury founder, John Maynard Keynes, a man destined to shape governmental economic policies for years to come. "We were the forerunners of a new dispensation. We entirely repudiated customary morals, conventions and traditional

1. Debunker Lytton Strachey's four major targets were: 1. Cardinal Henry Edward Manning, champion of England's working class, for opposing John Henry Newman's appointment as cardinal; and for foiling Newman's plan to open a Catholic oratory at Oxford, on the grounds that no devout Catholic should attend such an essentially anti-Christian university. 2. Florence Nightingale, for compelling the military bureaucracy to make necessary changes in military medicine and for establishing the nursing profession in the course of this. 3. Thomas Arnold, famed Rugby headmaster, for replacing with Christian-centered education the bullying and vice then characteristic of England's top boys' schools. 4. General Charles "Africa" Gordon, for trying to save Khartoum from Mahdi insurrectionists, against government orders. (Gordon was slain in the process.)

Painter Duncan Grant (left) and economist John Maynard Keynes, both members of the Bloomsbury group, are captured in this photograph from around 1913. This curious circle of geniuses, eccentrics, and homosexuals was the precursor of much that lay ahead in the new century.

wisdom. We were, that is to say, in the strict sense of the word immoralists," Keynes would explain in 1938, having somewhat revised his youthful view of Bloomsbury by then.

Also generally recognized as another Bloomsbury founder was philosopher mathematician Bertrand Russell, whose erudite and much-cited opinions ranged from science, education, marriage, peace, war crimes, and international law, down to the use of lipstick and the practice of wife beating. Russell's radical demonstrations were likewise diverse, from antiwar pamphleteering to public advocacy of lechery, occasionally landing him in jail (the last time at age 88). But his books, interminably denouncing belief in God, heaven, the Bible, and any thing else not "scientifically" sustainable, became required reading in philosophy courses throughout the western world. *Marriage and Morals*, which thoroughly repudiated Victorian morality, won him a Nobel Prize. His personal life ultimately disintegrated into wanton profligacy, however, while his ceaseless stream of comments became so bizarre as to alienate most of his adherents before his death in seeming dementia at age 97.[2]

The Bloomsbury movement grew out of two allied sources. One was the semi-secret study group known as the Apostles, established at Kings College, Cambridge, by evangelical Christians in the early nineteenth century. But by the time Keynes, Strachey, Moore, and Russell were members, the Apostles were not so much distinguished by Christian faith as by religious doubt.[3] Second, notes the American historian of Victorian culture Gertrude Himmelfarb in a 1995 article in *Commentary* magazine, many of the founding "Bloomsberries" (as they called themselves), were direct descendants of the evangelical founders of the nineteenth century Clapham Sect, although they presented quite a contrast to their pious forebears.

For example, novelist E. M. (Edward Morgan) Forster (*Howard's End*, *The Longest Journey*, and *A Passage to India*) was a great-grandson of Clapham founder Henry Thornton. Forster's candid ventures into homosexuality, Himmelfarb writes, "accentuate the enormous difference" between the values of Clapham and those of Bloomsbury. The yawning gulf between the avant-garde poetry of Bloomsbury's R. G. Trevelyan and the zealous evangelism of his great

2. After sixteen years of marriage, Bertrand Russell abandoned his unswervingly loyal wife to take up with the wife of a Liberal member of Parliament. Next came an affair with a teenaged girl from Chicago, then a prolonged relationship with a fellow peace crusader, and then a second marriage that produced two children. This ended when Russell married their governess, who divorced him fifteen years later for his ceaseless liaisons with chambermaids, household servants, guests, casual acquaintances, and other governesses. "Three passions...have governed my life," he once said. "They are the longing for love, the search for knowledge, and unbearable pity for the suffering of mankind." He mentioned no other possible "passions."

3. By the mid-twentieth century, the Cambridge Apostles had acquired a further distinction, namely for espionage and treason. Two members—Donald Duart Maclean and Guy Burgess—both on the staff of MI6, the British counterintelligence agency, were discovered to be spies, but escaped to the Soviet Union. Several other members of the group, including the American magazine publisher Michael Whitney Straight and Sir Anthony Blunt, art curator for Queen Elizabeth II, both confessed. Victor, Third Baron Rothschild, who was also accused, denied any involvement, but was later named as a Soviet spy by six retired KGB colonels.

Bloomsbury group members Virginia Woolf (right) and E. M. Forster (center) as painted by the "Bloomsberry" Vanessa Bell, and Roger Fry (left) in a self-portrait. All despised Christianity for its restraints on "intimacy," by which they meant sex in all its boundless permutations. An early member of the group, economist John Maynard Keynes, renounced the movement in his later years, describing it as "seething with vulgar passions."

4. Lesbianism within the Bloomsbury circle seemed not to preclude a happy marriage. Vita Sackville-West had at least three other partners besides Virginia Woolf, but was deeply devoted to her husband, Harold Nicolson, a diplomat, writer, and politician, and also a homosexual. They had two children. Virginia's marriage to Leonard Woolf likewise appeared undisturbed either by her affairs with women or her fervid anti-Semitism (from which she exempted him). Leonard tenderly cared for her during her mental breakdowns, and her suicide note confirmed her heartfelt love for him: "You have given me the greatest possible happiness. You have been in every way all that anyone could be...I know that I am spoiling your life."

grandfather, Clapham's Zachary Macaulay, offer a further example. For another, the devout Claphamite and slavery-abolitionist James Stephen, who married William Wilberforce's sister, assuredly would have regarded with horror the career of his great-granddaughter, Virginia Stephen Woolf, feminist literary star and Bloomsbury's founding queen.

The Bloomsbury home of Virginia Woolf and her husband, political theorist and publisher Leonard Woolf, is said to have provided the movement with both a geographic center and its name. Virginia's coyly licentious lesbian novels, *Mrs. Dalloway* (1925), *To the Lighthouse* (1927), and *Orlando* (1928), would be resurrected and acclaimed by the feminist movement, enjoying another vogue later in the century. Meanwhile, London society was titillated for decades by her protracted affair with fellow author and poetess Vita Sackville-West. But Virginia Woolf's story ended darkly. After a series of mental breakdowns, she filled her overcoat pockets with stones and drowned herself in England's river, the River Ouse, Yorkshire, at age fifty-nine.[4]

Even from within the cultural community of its day, Bloomsbury did not escape denunciation. Although his own novels also specialized in breaking through moral barriers, D. H. Lawrence regarded the Bloomsbury set with undisguised scorn, saying they were like "black beetles" utterly preoccupied with "their little swarming selves."[5] Keynes later described Bloomsbury as "seething with vulgar passions," its supposed rationalism a disguise for cynicism. Historian Himmelfarb provides another assessment and rationale. Having effectually abandoned its doctrinal Christian origins, she writes, Victorian morality as a whole had "tried to maintain itself without the sanctions and consolations of religion." As a result, it "could not transmit itself to the next generation."

Bloomsbury's corruptive influence, particularly as regards sex, permeated the media through such men as author-publisher David Garnett and literary critic Desmond MacCarthy. (MacCarthy, who wrote for the *New Statesman* and *Sunday Times*, was knighted in 1951.) Bloomsbury values also pervaded the visual arts through painters like postimpressionist Roger Fry and architectural designer Duncan Grant, who was commissioned to design the fabrics for the main ballroom of the luxury superliner *Queen Mary* until the Cunard Line's chairman threw them all out, possibly because of Grant's wide-ranging "intimacies." But the movement's most lasting influence arguably came through Virginia Woolf's sister Alix and her psychoanalyst husband James Strachey, brother of Lytton, who became disciples of (and translators for) another Bloomsbury connection: one Sigmund Freud.

"In America today," writes philosopher Donald DeMarco in *Architects of the Culture of Death* (2004), "Freud's intellectual influence is, in many respects, greater than that of any other thinker."

> He presides in the college classroom, over the mass media, in the chatter at cocktail parties, and in the advice dispensed by sex counselors. His clinical terms—repression, anxiety, guilt feelings, displacement, libido, penis envy, castration complex—are known to a large segment of the population and are traded in common coin.

> All this despite the fact that his philosophy does not hold together, his methodology is inconsistent, and his positive contribution to the world is negligible. Sadly, even though his positive system is not credible, the negative aspects of his philosophy continue to corrode like an uncontrollable acid. Freud's rejection of religion, distrust of fatherhood, suspicion of morality, and reduction of love to sex, have unleashed a plague of problems that has produced widespread and adverse effects.

Like several other Bloomsbury members, James and Alix Strachey had been patients of Freud. Their translation of his works runs to four volumes, and they were centrally responsible for introducing his psychiatric methods to Britain. Freud fit well with the Bloomsberries, his antipathy to all institutional religion being articulate, passionate, and lifelong. Although born into a Jewish family in what is now the Czech Republic, he regarded Orthodox Judaism as scornfully as

5. Lawrence's obscenity-laden novel *Lady Chatterley's Lover*, published in 1928 in Italy, was banned in Britain until Penguin Books released it in England in 1960, thirty years after his death. Penguin was charged under the Obscenity Act, and in the ensuing sensational trial, prominent figures such as novelist E. M. Forster and the bishop of Woolwich, John A. T. Robinson, testified as "experts" for the defense, while writers T. S. Eliot, Aldous Huxley and Iris Murdoch were among the defense reserve witnesses. The company was exonerated, and a year later published the trial transcripts. The bishop went on to publish his own controversial book, *Honest to God* (1963) which questioned orthodox Christian beliefs. Later, however, he developed a much more traditionalist theology based on the historical reliability of the four Gospels.

WHERE CHILDREN DO WHAT THEY LIKE

Earl Russell (formerly Mr. Bertrand Russell) with some of the pupils at his remarkable school at Telegraph House, on the Hampshire Downs. The boys and girls miss lessons when they like, may be rude to their teachers, and are never physically punished. They bathe together, sleep together, and in warm weather run about unclothed. **No** religion is taught.

Philosopher and mathematician Bertrand Russell is pictured among pupils at the Beacon Hill School in this newspaper clip from 1931. During his long life, Russell was an advocate for pacificism, socialism, atheism, and unfettered sex. The experimental school, founded by him and his second wife Dora, did not require its younger students to turn in assignments. The school shunned corporal punishment, and allowed the children to walk the grounds unclothed.

he did Christianity, and married the granddaughter of Hamburg's chief rabbi only on condition that she formally repudiate the synagogue and all it stood for.

Freud's parents managed to provide him with a superb education in law and philosophy at the University of Vienna, followed by medicine, during which his views on religion took their doctrinal shape. Belief in God, he reasoned, resulted from obsessive compulsive disorder rooted in mental illusions, which often issues in neurotic behavior. This could be traced back to the helplessness of the child, he theorized, who longs for the protection of the male parent.

In consequence, sexual "sin," should be treated with therapy, not criminal

The fall and rise of Oscar Wilde

As its wittiest playwright, he was the lion of London society but folly betrayed him, but then, in prison and in despair, he found Jesus Christ, and penned an icon in words

The undoubted forerunner of Britain's debunking Bloomsbury group was the playwright-novelist-poet Oscar Wilde, who died in the year 1900 at the age of forty-six, a decade before Bloomsbury came into being. He possessed in abundance just those qualities the group would cherish, being bountifully literate, sharply perceptive, supremely cynical, contemptuous of convention, bisexual, and wittier by far than any of the Bloomsbury literati. But at the pinnacle of his career, Wilde brought upon himself a disaster that saw him publicly humiliated and abandoned by nearly all his fashionable friends. He died in exile and utter poverty, after composing one of the most moving descriptions of Jesus Christ ever penned in the English language.

Oscar Fingal O'Flahertie Wills Wilde, son of intellectually inclined Dublin parents, excelled at Oxford, then soared soon and high in the arts and in the elegant society of late Victorian England. He married respectably, and fathered two sons whom he dearly loved. By the 1890s, his comedies were the rage of the London theater and the source of epigrams still treasured a century later.

His downfall began when he met the young Lord Alfred Douglas, who (according to Wilde's friends) led him into London's lurid dens of homosexual prostitution. Douglas's father, the marquis of Queensbury, a bluff man famed for codifying the rules for boxing, called Wilde "a posing sodomite." Wilde charged him with criminal libel, and the case backfired. Queensbury was acquitted. Wilde himself was then charged with sodomy and gross indecency, convicted, and sentenced to two years' hard labor. Within a matter of weeks he fell from the top to the bottom of Britain's social hierarchy: imprisoned, deserted by almost all, forbidden to see even his children.

In an astonishing seventeen-thousand-word letter to Douglas, he recorded his desperate struggle to come to terms with what had happened to him, entitling it *De Profundis* from the first line of the psalm: "Out of the deep have I cried unto thee O Lord," a well-known liturgical piece for the neo-

Oscar Wilde (left) is pictured with his young friend, Lord Alfred Douglas, in an 1893 photo. Wilde's ill-advised decision to charge Douglas's father with criminal libel for calling him (Wilde) a "sodomite" backfired. The father was acquitted and Wilde was charged, convicted, and imprisoned for sodomy and gross indecency.

punishment. Guilt feelings, particularly over sex, were induced by religious neuroses. Religion was particularly dangerous to children, he thought, and they should not be exposed to it. Christian Holy Communion was clearly derived from primitive cannibalistic rituals. Despite the air of sanctity derived from its irrational origins, religion was unhelpful to most people. Being not only useless but harmful, it should be replaced by science.

In 1885, at age 29, Freud established a private clinic in Vienna. There he induced one patient to recall through hypnosis some traumatic childhood experiences, which seemed to greatly reduce the severity of her mental disorders. He proceeded to estab-

medieval Romantics of the Victorian period. The letter describes the painful journey of a man from spiritual squalor to the inner grace and triumph that comes through Christ, who "understood the leprosy of the leper, the darkness of the blind, the fierce misery of those who live for pleasure, the strange poverty of the rich…

"There is still something to me almost incredible," the letter continues, "in the idea of a young Galilean peasant imagining that he could bear on his own shoulders the burden of the entire world; all that had already been done and suffered, and all that was yet to be done and suffered: the sins of Nero, of Caesar Borgia, of Alexander VI, and of him who was Emperor of Rome and Priest of the Sun: the sufferings of those whose names are legion and whose dwelling is among the tombs: oppressed nationalities, factory children, thieves, people in prison, outcasts, those who are dumb under oppression and whose silence is heard only of God; and not merely imagining this but actually achieving it, so that at the present moment all who come in contact with his personality, even though they may neither bow to his altar nor kneel before his priest, in some way find that the ugliness of their sin is taken away and the beauty of their sorrow revealed to them."

And then, on the cross: "His own utter loneliness, his submission, his acceptance of everything, and along with it all such scenes as the high priest of orthodoxy rending his raiment in wrath, and the magistrate of civil justice calling for water in the vain hope of atonement from the stain of innocent blood that makes him the scarlet figure of history; the coronation ceremony of sorrow, one of the most wonderful things in the whole of recorded time, the crucifixion of the innocent one before the eyes of his mother…the terrible death by which he gave the world its most eternal symbol."

Oscar Wilde was released from prison in 1897, moved to France, and spent the last three years of his life in penniless exile. On his deathbed he was baptized a Catholic Christian (conditionally, because it was not known whether he had been baptized before). His confidence had been restored by then— or at any rate his sharp comic sense. Near death and realizing that someone else would have to pay for his funeral, he sighed: "Ah, well, then I suppose I shall have to die beyond my means." Later, glancing around his ugly room, he remarked: "Either that wallpaper goes, or I do." ∎

AMONG WILDE'S CLASSIC EPIGRAMS

What is a cynic? A man who knows the price of everything and the value of nothing. (*Lady Windermere's Fan*, 1892)

Democracy means simply the bludgeoning of the people by the people for the people. (*The Soul of Man Under Socialism*, 1891)

I have nothing to declare except my genius. (At U.S. Customs, New York, 1882)

The old believe everything; the middle aged suspect everything; the young know everything.

To disagree with three-fourths of the British public is one of the first requisites of sanity.

Work is the curse of the drinking classes.

Whenever a man does a thoroughly stupid thing, it is always from the noblest motives.

As long as war is regarded as wicked, it will always have its fascination. When it is looked upon as vulgar, it will cease to be popular.

There is only one class in the community that thinks more about money than the rich, and that is the poor. (*The Soul of Man Under Socialism*, 1891)

I couldn't help it. I can resist everything except temptation. (*Lady Windermere's Fan*, 1892)

To lose one parent, Mr. Worthing, may be regarded as a misfortune; to lose both looks like carelessness. (*The Importance of Being Earnest*, 1895)

There is only one thing in the world worse than being talked about, and that is not being talked about.

How else but through a broken heart / May Lord Christ enter in? (*The Ballad of Reading Gaol*, 1898)

Sigmund Freud is pictured below in an 1872 photo at age 16 with his mother Amalia at home in Vienna, and in the portrait photograph taken in 1922 by photographer Max Halberstadt, a friend of Freud's. Freudian psychology came to dominate—some would say poison—the twentieth century.

lish a procedure in which patients were encouraged to retrieve early memories without hypnosis. This effectively healed their minds, he said. By 1920, the technique, known as psychoanalysis, was being professionally practiced throughout the western world. Freud also became famous for his concept of the Oedipus complex, the theory that boys unconsciously harbor in their minds a desire to kill their fathers and sexually possess their mothers.[6] The recommended cure is psychoanalysis. (The possibility that Freudian father hatred might explain the success of *Eminent Victorians* was not noted at the time.)

Freud's professional acceptance was by no means universal; other psychiatrists vehemently disputed his theories. Hans Jürgen Eysenck, a German-born English psychologist renowned for his work on intelligence and personality, accused him of misdiagnosing patients and fraudulently misrepresenting case histories. Hans Israel, a Dutch historian of psychology, claimed that Freud could not document a single unambiguous cure. Philadelphia author, essayist, and English professor Frederick Crews, who actively campaigned against Freudian theories, accused him of inventing success stories to bolster support for a method of treatment that rarely if ever worked.

But such teachings were unreservedly embraced by the liberated generation of the so-called Roaring Twenties, when skirts grew shorter and sexual morals looser still. In America, the long and determined Christian campaign to Ban the Bar culminated in passage of the Eighteenth Amendment and the Volstead Act, which prohibited the legal sale of alcohol while signally failing to prevent its consumption. It was repealed as unenforceable thirteen years later in the Twenty-First Amendment, and the entire experience notably eroded the credibility of Christian moral priorities and noticeably fostered the growth of organized crime in the United States. Meanwhile, errant humanity was being reassured by Freud that a man could no more be blamed for his various weaknesses than for the color of his eyes, causing some to conclude that restraining their various instincts might actually be injurious to mental health.

Freud's life did not end tranquilly. Anti-Semitism, endemic in Vienna, became outright perilous in 1938 when the Nazis took power in Austria. His books were burned and he was publicly denounced. With the help of powerful friends in England and America, his escape was narrowly effected; four sisters would die in

6. In the most common version of the Greek Oedipus myth, the Oracle of Delphi predicts that any son born to King Laius of Thebes will kill him and marry his mother, Laius's queen Jocasta. When a son is born, Laius seeks to thwart the prophecy by tying the infant's ankles together and leaving him to die in the countryside. The child is rescued, grows up, and becomes known from the binding as Swollen Foot (*Oedipus* in Greek). Entirely unaware of the prophecy, he unwittingly kills Laius and marries Jocasta. Terrible natural disasters ensue.

concentration camps. He passed his last days in London, but they were not happy ones, and he died in great pain from cancer of the mouth, in September 1939.

While the influence of Bloomsbury, Freud, and increasing numbers of others was greatly extending the acceptance of sexual profligacy, both in and beyond the arts and intellectual communities, the institution that sexual morality was chiefly intended to protect—namely the family—had not yet come under direct attack. This would soon happen, however, not least through the influence of two women, both American and both named Margaret.

Margaret Mead likely would have been devastated to see herself described as helping to debunk America's Christian cultural mores. Born into a Quaker family, daughter of a professor, she considered herself Christian, opted to become an Anglican, and served on the commission that would rewrite the Anglican Book of Common Prayer in 1979.[7] Earning a master's degree from fashionable Barnard College and a doctorate in anthropology from Columbia University, Mead found a lifetime cause in the mid-1920s when she came into the orbit of Franz Boas, Columbia's sole anthropology professor and a man with a mission.

Boas was convinced that how and where an individual was brought up, not his genetic origins, would determine what he believed and how he acted. It therefore followed, he reasoned, that human society could be engineered as desired by control of education and environment. This idea challenges, among other things, the Christian concept of natural law, which postulates a

Detroit police inspect equipment found in a clandestine brewery in the late 1920s, and a woman in Washington, DC, dressed in the flapper fashion of the era, hides a flask of liquor in her Russian boot, circa 1922. Skirts grew shorter, sexual morals looser, and Prohibition notably eroded the credibility of Christian moral priorities.

striking consistency among the world's moral systems. To back his case, Boas needed what is called "a negative instance," an isolated society whose way of life was radically at odds with the human norm. Such a society might exist among the Pacific islands, it was thought, and he had two assistants, Margaret Mead and Ruth Benedict, both capable of investigating the matter. (The two women enjoyed more than a professional relationship, although the world would not learn of it for many years; they were lovers.) Since Benedict had two children, Boas chose Mead for the South Sea job.

So researcher Mead spent nine months studying some six hundred people on the tiny Samoan island of Ta'u publishing her findings in 1928 as *Coming of Age in Samoa*. This would prove the most highly circulated anthropological book ever

In her nine months in Samoa, Margaret Mead had not lived with a Samoan family, nor learned Samoan, said Freeman. Her account of sexual mores came from two young girls.

written. It became required reading for all first-year anthropology courses, and played a key role in shaping sex education, criminal law, government social policies, and the popular view of acceptable sexual conduct. Furnishing Boas with his indispensable "negative instance," it became a foundational bible for his cultural determinist school of anthropology. Mead herself became the world's most renowned anthropologist, chairwoman of the social sciences division at Fordham University, president of the American Anthropological Association, and head of the executive committee of the American Association for the Advancement of Science.

Coming of Age describes Ta'u as an entirely idyllic South Seas paradise. It was untainted by class struggles. It was unrestrained by the harsh constrictions of Christian sexual morality. Friction between families or individuals was virtually unknown. In particular, it was a veritable Eden of free love. For teenagers, in fact, unrestrained sex with many partners was the recommended pastime. The Samoan girl, Mead wrote, "thrusts virtuosity away from her... All of her interest is expended on clandestine sex adventures. Samoan teenagers know nothing of the pressures and anxiety placed on teenagers in North America." Among boys, the spirit of competition was restrained; a boy "must never excel his fellows more than a little." His elders "are far readier to excuse the laggard than condone precocity."

8. In their famous Canberra encounter, Margaret Mead asked Derek Freeman why he had not delivered to her residence some papers she requested. "Because I was afraid you might ask me to spend the night," Freeman blurted, then instantly apologized. "I don't know why I said that. I was mortified after I said it," he stammered. Later he explained that he was terrified of Mead, not allured by her. "She cast a spell... She mesmerized me." She was known, Freeman said, as "a castrator, who went for men and pulled them down. She had huge power." She often intervened to cost men jobs they had been promised, or to get them fired. "People were really scared of her."

Conclusions drawn from *Coming of Age*, writes economist Todd G. Buchholz in *Commentary* magazine, "were adopted by generations of social thinkers and policy makers who interpreted the Samoan experience as a message to our own society." By the 1930s, it was helping to buttress the novel educational theories pioneered by John Dewey (see subchapter, page 73) and encouraging radically new standards for sexual behavior. In particular, people increasingly questioned whether sexual fidelity in marriage was really so essential anyhow. Divorce rates began to climb.

Then in November 1964, one month short of her sixty-third birthday, dressed frumpily, walking with a cane, Mead

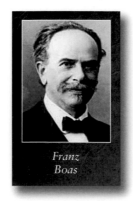

Franz Boas

called on an anthropologist at the Australian National University in Canberra. This was Derek Freeman, who was assembling, she had heard, certain data related to her primal masterpiece. His academic credentials were impressive: he had spent time in Samoa, intended to spend more, and spoke the language fluently. Since it was the only time they met, the Canberra encounter is described exhaustively by University of Colorado anthropologist Paul Shankman in his book *The Trashing of Margaret Mead* (2009). Two impressions are recorded. Mead was said to be visibly shaken by Freeman, while Freeman, who had already suffered two nervous breakdowns, was so frightened of Mead's formidable reputation that he stammered as he spoke, something he had never done before. He would have been aware, of course, that he was threatening to destroy not only the credibility of the world's foremost anthropologist, but also the credibility of anthropology itself, whose luminaries had bestowed so many laurels upon her.[8]

Freeman subsequently returned to Samoa to investigate further, and in 1983 published his detailed conclusions in *Margaret Mead in Samoa: The Making and Unmaking of an Anthropological Myth*. In this book, concludes Buchholz, "in two hundred pages Freeman grabs, tears and shreds Margaret Mead's research to pieces." Female virginity in pagan Samoa, far from being treated as Mead claimed, "was very much the leitmotif of the sexual mores of the pagan Samoans... Virtually every family cherished the virginity of its daughters." Furthermore, far from existing as a paradise of peace and tranquility, the Samoan system was "fraught with intense and long standing rivalries."

In her nine months in Samoa, Freeman emphasized, Mead had not lived with a

The case that put the Bible on trial

Dayton High's football coach had never taught science, but a trumped-up charge that he taught evolution created a media circus in which the Christians lost by winning

It was the seventh day of the trial, viewed then and ever since as the titanic clash of sanity against inanity, or the biblical against the diabolical, depending on who was doing the viewing. Whether from the relentless heat—high nineties Fahrenheit all week—or from the disturbing fact that the second floor of the courthouse in Dayton, Tennessee, was beginning to discernibly buckle under the weight of five hundred sweating occupants, the decision was reached to move the proceedings to the lawn outside.

There, another three thousand rapt spectators could stand and perspire or sit and perspire while Clarence Darrow, preeminent American atheist, trial lawyer, and courtroom acrobat, cross-examined William Jennings Bryan, preeminent Christian antievolutionist, prohibitionist, and three-time presidential candidate, on the scientific veracity of the Bible. Now, on the twenty-first day of July, 1925, the event known as "the Scopes Monkey Trial" was about to reach its zenith.

The background: under the recent Butler Act, Tennessee had forbidden its schools to "teach any theory that denies the biblical account of creation, and that man descended from a lower form of animals." Alarmed at what it saw as an outrageous threat to individual liberty and academic freedom, the American Civil Liberties Union (ACLU) declared from New York that it would defend any teacher so charged. Enterprising Daytonians seized the opportunity. If some teacher could be persuaded to do such a thing, or at least say he did, it would put their eastern Tennessee town of eighteen hundred on the map of America. They found their man in

John Scopes—lanky, twenty-four years old, unattached, religiously indifferent, and new in town. He actually taught football, not biology, but he had once substituted as a science class teacher, and yes, he might well have mentioned something like that. This was good enough for Dayton, Tennessee.

Any hope for an easy ACLU victory disappeared when William Jennings Bryan offered to act *gratis* for the prosecution. Popularly dubbed "the Great Commoner," this famously eloquent and immensely popular Illinois-born progressive and recurrent Democratic presidential candidate was universally recognized at sixty-five as the champion of ordinary Americans against corporate encroachment. Also opposed to militarism, Bryan had resigned as Woodrow Wilson's secretary of state when the U.S. entered the First World War. He later emerged as the charismatic spokesman for a growing Southern antievolution movement, and had advised the Tennessee legislature on the Butler law. But as historian Edward Larson writes in *Summer for the Gods* (1997), Bryan was no biblical literalist. He rejected Darwin's theory of "natural selection," or "survival of the fittest," as a "merciless law by which the strong kill off the weak," which thereby provided philosophical justification for militarism, predatory capitalism, and eugenics.[1] He also held that Christian parents had a right to decide what their children were taught in schools funded by their taxes.

No sooner had Bryan announced his participation than Chicago-based lawyer Clarence Darrow, never a man to miss the main chance, grandly offered to assist the defense (the only occasion he ever worked *pro bono*, Larson notes). Celebrated for saving Nathan Leopold and Richard Loeb, the college boy murderers, from the gallows a year earlier, Darrow at sixty-eight was an untidy, likeable man with an arresting physical presence and an acute intelligence. As eulogized by one New York reporter, "his huge head, leather lined face, square jaw [and] twisted mouth of the skeptic are softened by the quizzical twinkle of his deep-set eyes."

Running for Congress as a Democrat in 1896, Darrow had supported Bryan's presidential bid, and later acted for organized labor before turning to criminal law. A determinist who rejected the idea of free will, he was known for his antireligious writings and lectures and disdain for Christianity. "It is not the bad people I fear so much as the good people," he declared. "When a person is sure that he is good, he is nearly hopeless; he gets cruel—he believes in punishment." Whereas Bryan deplored Darwin's theory because of the "demoralization involved in accepting brute ancestry," Darrow applauded this claim. Man

In this newspaper photo taken at the Scopes Trial, defense lawyer Clarence Darrow (right) questions William Jennings Bryan, director of the prosecution (seated with fan) about the veracity of the miracles in the Bible. "I intended to show the world what an ignoramus he was," exulted Darrow in a letter to H. L. Mencken, "and I succeeded."

Darrow (left) and Bryan share a nonconfrontational moment during a break in the proceedings. At right, accused teacher John Scopes. Scopes was found guilty and fined $100; Bryan died six days later.

got the "idea of his importance" from Genesis, he asserted, whereas "in fact, man never was made. He was evolved from the lowest form of life."

Some ACLU officials were worried by Darrow's bellicose atheism and, fearing that he would sensationalize the trial as a fight between science and religion, tried to eliminate him from the defense, but Scopes wanted him. "It was going to be a down-in-the-mud fight," he commented later, "and I felt the situation demanded an Indian fighter rather than someone who graduated from the proper military academy."

A veritable Pandora's box of publicity was already open on the issue of evolution. In the preceding weeks, prominent Christian fundamentalists like Billy Sunday barnstormed the country, warning of the dangers of evolutionary theory. Darrow embarked on a month-long publicity blitz. Dudley Field Malone, a forty-three-year-old Catholic divorce lawyer (who later would himself be divorced), was the sole Christian on the defense team. Evolution need not contradict belief in a creator, he contended: "There should be no more conflict between science and religion than between the love a man gives to his mother and his wife."

Bryan arrived in Dayton three days early, a pith helmet protecting his bald pate from the sun. He was greeted by enthusiastic crowds and spent much time hobnobbing with reporters. On July 10, while chimpanzees performed in Dayton's streets, steers roasted over pits, preachers declaimed, musicians played, and fluttering banners counseled "Sweethearts, come to Jesus" and "Read your Bible," the trial began. With loudspeakers in place among the cottonwoods, the sleepy town was about to become, as one reporter wrote, "one great sounding board of oratory."

Oratory there was indeed, interspersed with fractious procedural bickering. Darrow, thumbs snapping his unfashionable lavender suspenders, objected to the court's customary daily prayer, arguing that it might "influence the delibera-

tions." Judge John Raulston, an avowed Christian who clearly relished the role, overruled him. Jury selection took just two hours, and with choice restricted largely to fundamentalist-leaning white men, Darrow could only choose some who claimed to be open-minded.

The defense argued that the Butler law was unconstitutional in mandating the teaching of a specific religion. Raulston ruled that Scopes was on trial, not the law. Then, since Butler forbade the teaching of "a theory that denied the biblical account of creation," the defense asked permission to call experts to testify that evolution did no such thing—that Darwin's theories and the Genesis creation account do not conflict. Although seven such witnesses had already arrived, Raulston ruled out expert testimony. Tennessee legislators feared their state was becoming a laughingstock, he knew, and wanted the trial expedited. When Darrow erupted in fury, almost accusing the judge of bias, Raulston cited him for contempt. Darrow apologized, whereupon the judge forgave him in explicitly Christian terms, shaking his hand and advising him to "go back home and learn in his heart the words of the Man who said, 'If you thirst, come unto me and I will give thee life.'"

Meanwhile, whatever the outcome of the trial, one sure winner was Dayton, Tennessee. The volume of news coverage was astonishing. After Darrow's opening oration, a record-breaking two hundred thousand words were telegraphed from Dayton by more than two hundred reporters, and this trial was the first to be broadcast live on radio. Most American newsmen, including the *Baltimore Globe*'s iconoclastic pundit, H. L. Mencken, explicitly favored the defense. So caustically did Mencken mock Bryan, the trial, and Dayton evangelicals that he was advised for his own safety to leave town. He did so after the trial's sixth day, morosely predicting that "the main battle is over, with Genesis completely triumphant."

Mencken therefore missed Darrow's seventh-day master-stroke. Although cautioned by colleagues against testifying, Bryan had declared that he was not afraid to defend the Bible, but in fact he was being set up. "I intended to show the world what an ignoramus he was," Darrow later wrote to Mencken, "and I succeeded." Although Bryan never had been a biblical literalist, when he agreed on the stand that the term "day" in the Genesis creation account could be an indeterminate period of time, the defense claimed that this was a major concession, and creationist supporters were crestfallen. When Bryan not unreasonably asserted that for a Christian "one miracle is just as easy to believe as another," Darrow badgered him to explain how Jonah lived inside a whale for three days, Joshua stopped the earth, or Noah could load the ark with all living animals. "I do not think about the things I don't think about," Bryan snapped.[2]

With Darrow pressing him about the age of the earth, the aftermath of the flood, and the tower of Babel, Bryan became increasingly defensive, reduced to insisting that such things did not matter. While the prosecution made a dozen attempts to end the interrogation, it descended into a shouting match, both men visibly angered and shaking their fists. "The only purpose Mr. Darrow has is to slur the Bible, but I will answer his questions!" Bryan yelled. "I am examining your fool ideas that no intelligent Christian on earth believes," Darrow yelled back. Raulston decided it was time to adjourn.

Exuberant supporters thronged around Darrow, wrote ACLU lawyer Arthur Garfield Hays in a later account, while Bryan "stood apart, almost alone, a strange, tired expression on his face as he looked into the twilight that was closing around him." The next day, Raulston ruled that Bryan would be questioned no further, and his previous testimony struck from the record as irrelevant. The jury deliberated for nine minutes and declared Scopes guilty, and Raulston fined him $100.

Five days later, still in Dayton, Bryan was found dead after his daily nap, probably due to his chronic diabetes.[3] Some people suggested he might have died from humiliation and a broken heart, but Edward Larson notes that Bryan—ever the optimistic and seasoned politician, well accustomed to setbacks—was already planning a vigorous rebuttal campaign. In death, he got a hero's send-off. Many thousands viewed his open casket in Dayton or watched as a special Pullman car carried the body to Arlington National Cemetery, and the pallbearers included senators and congressmen.

Columnist Walter Lippman of the *New York World* wrote that Bryan's death would "weight his words at Dayton with the solemnity of a parting message," and Darrow's "scoffing at the Bible" had persuaded millions that the Scopes Trial truly was just what Bryan claimed it was: a fight "for and against the Christian religion." A New Orleans editorial contended that Darrow's "sneering, 'I object to prayer,'" and his mean-spirited cross-examination had won sympathy for the antievolutionists.

The Tennessee Supreme Court sidestepped the controversy by throwing out John Scopes's conviction, but not ruling on the law itself. It merely advised the prosecution to drop this "bizarre case," for the "peace and dignity" of Tennessee, and the attorney general complied. The Butler law remained on the books until 1967, when the U.S. Supreme Court declared

it unconstitutional. John Scopes left teaching and became a geologist. He refused all opportunities to cash in on the trial, but scientists involved in the case chipped in to pay for his college education.

The Monkey Trial myth meanwhile kept on evolving. Although legally "inconclusive," asserts law professor Phillip Johnson in *Darwin on Trial* (1993), it was "a public relations triumph for Darwinism." The actual trial became largely indistinguishable in the public mind from the 1960s film *Inherit the Wind.* The movie's cast of bigoted Christians features a fanatical pastor and shrill, screaming women, determined to jail a sincere, truth-telling teacher for teaching evolution. Its prosecutor, a gluttonous, sex-hating, ignorant, and manipulative antievolutionist crusader, dies of apoplexy on the courtroom floor while trying to get to the radio microphone.[4] Newsman Joseph Wood Krutch, who had personally covered the Dayton trial, dismissed the movie as a reaction against 1950s McCarthyism that entirely missed the essential "foolishness" of the Monkey trial. "That the trial could be a farce, even a farce with sinister aspects, is a tribute to the twenties, when…we did not play as rough as we play today," Krutch commented in 1967.

Later "rough play" arguably would amply vindicate William Jennings Bryan, the Great Commoner, who discerned evolution's link to eugenics, and who championed parental rights. By 1935, some thirty-five states would adopt laws requiring sterilization of the "eugenically unfit"—largely meaning the mentally and intellectually deficient, habitual criminals, and sometimes even those suffering from certain chronic illnesses. In Germany, the Nazis were a rising power. John Dewey's educational theories were infiltrating American universities and schools (see page 73). Some few of these vital controversies would be resolved within the twentieth century. Among others, as with the Monkey Trial, no clear winner would yet have emerged. ∎

1. Tennessee's high school science textbook, *A Civic Biology*, contained clearly eugenic passages. It noted, for example, that if the mentally ill, the retarded, and habitual criminals "were lower animals, we would kill them off… Humanity will not allow this, but we do have the remedy of…preventing intermarriage and the possibility of perpetuating such a low and degenerate race." As prominent American eugenicist Albert E. Wiggam observed, "Until we can convince the common man of the fact of evolution…I fear we can't convince him of the profound ethical and religious significance of eugenics."

2. Bryan humorously deflected some questions. To Darrow's query, "Do you know where Cain got his wife?" Bryan retorted, "No, sir, I leave the agnostics to hunt for her." Asked if he believed that all life on earth was wiped out by Noah's flood, Bryan mischievously replied, "I think the fishes lived."

3. That William Jennings Bryan was diabetic may account for his famously prodigious appetite. Darrow, asked by a reporter if his cross-examination had caused Bryan to die of a broken heart, replied, "Broken heart nothing—he died of a busted belly." Mencken was even cruder, reputedly crowing, "We killed the son of a bitch."

4. The Hollywood film *Inherit the Wind* (1960) was based on a 1955 Broadway play by Jerome Lawrence and Robert E. Lee, starred Spencer Tracy, Fredric March, and Gene Kelly, and was nominated for four Academy Awards. It presents an almost unrecognizably biased version of the Scopes Monkey Trial.

Samoan family, she had not learned the language, and her description of teen sexual mores was largely based on interviews with two young girls. He found these individuals, by now elderly women, and reminded them of Mead's visit. They began to giggle in embarrassment, he reported, recounting how they had told that white lady such awful lies and stories, not expecting her to believe them. They were sorry now to have so misled her, they said. Had they known that through her they had also misled hundreds of professors, affecting social policy and sexual attitudes throughout the western world, they would probably have been sorry about that too.

Anthropologists, with their entire field of study subject to very upsetting ridicule, renewed their defense of Mead and castigation of Freeman. Some of his data was not properly documented, they asserted. Samoa obviously had changed

Neither Margaret Sanger nor her host of supporters likely foresaw that the ability to 'plan' parenthood might result in quite such an overwhelming reduction in population.

in the decades between her visit and his. In the interim, missionaries had spread Christianity. And what about his propensity to nervous breakdown? Might his book be the product of another breakdown? Freeman soon found himself an outcast among his fellow professionals. But his central contention—that she had been seriously wrong about the Samoans—was hard to deny. For example, Martin Orans, professor emeritus of anthropology at the University of California, Riverside, tried hard to redeem, if not Mead's reputation, at least that of the discipline itself, but was forced to conclude:

> That Mead's seriously flawed work, which is filled with internal contradictions and grandiose claims to knowledge that she could not possibly have had and is so weakly supported by data, could have survived and formed the foundation for an illustrious career raises substantial doubt regarding improved standards of research... That a person of such conspicuous talent could have produced such a flawed work and that it was so widely accepted and praised by so many should serve as an object lesson to us all.

Margaret Mead died in 1978, five years before the publication of Freeman's book, and thus never fully realized the uproar it caused. Something else as well came to light after her death: an active bisexual life. She had been married three times—to Anglican theology student Luther Cressman (1923–1928), to New Zealand anthropologist Reo Fortune (1928–1935), and to English anthropologist Gregory Bateson (1936–1950), by whom she had a daughter, Mary Catherine Bateson. (Her gynecologist, incidentally, was Dr. Benjamin Spock, whose widely influential ideas about child-raising were said to be much influenced by her work.) Her sexual involvement with women, kept secret in her lifetime because it would have cost her both credibility and career, was disclosed in a memoir written by her daughter. It was further elaborated by feminist historian Lois W. Banner in *Intertwined Lives: Margaret Mead, Ruth Benedict and their Circle* (2003), who claimed that her homosexual activity continued into her final years, spent with Rhoda Metraux, who was also an acclaimed anthropologist.

The "other Margaret," presents a very different persona. Born in 1879, twenty-two years before Mead, Margaret Sanger was far more manipulative, cleverer, and less inhibited by scruples. Loudly antagonistic to Christianity and actively destructive of Christian morality, Sanger launched a movement that ultimately would threaten the very existence, not only of anything resembling a Christian society, but of western civilization itself. Although the organization she founded came to be called Planned Parenthood, by the century's end this title would prove to be a misnomer, for the cause she so resoundingly led to triumph was the legalization of birth control. As a human right, it seemed to many people unassailable, but its ultimate consequence was foreseen by few and would probably have appalled even Sanger herself.

For "Planned Parenthood," as one wag put it, quickly came to mean "Planned Barrenhood." Neither Sanger nor her host of supporters foresaw that the ability to "plan" parenthood might result in quite such a wide rejection of motherhood, but the reluctance of women to have children—particularly women with high intelligence and a professional education—would become the chief problem facing the countries of the developed world. In short, the chief consequence of universally available birth control would be the threatened extinction of the ultra-liberal society cherished by Sanger. Her victory, in other words, would arguably turn into a defeat.

Planned Parenthood promoters worked hard and successfully to focus attention on the outstanding virtues and accomplishments of their founder: her undoubted courage in defying officialdom, her adroit handling of the media, her dexterity in managing people, and her tireless devotion to the rescue of oppressed women from what she saw as the slavery of unwanted children. With every published article or biography a hagiography extolling her manifold virtues, Sanger appeared to be a veritable saint.[9] But there were problems. It was not the whole story. In her carefully researched *Margaret Sanger: A Biography of the Champion of Birth Control* (1979), New England writer Madeline Gray would later depict a woman who undeniably did accomplish everything attributed to her. But she was also a ruthless liar, an almost criminally negligent parent, heartlessly contemptuous of a husband who was wholly dedicated to her happiness, and a wanton voluptuary with an unrestrained sexual appetite for males, either young or wealthy or (best of all) possessing celebrity status. This book, with every assertion carefully documented, proved as embarrassing to Sanger admirers as it was difficult to refute.

Sanger was born Margaret "Maggie" Higgins in Corning, New York, in 1879, one of eleven children. Her father, an immigrant Irish stone mason, so fiercely loathed Catholicism—and religion generally—that he refused to let his devout Catholic wife go to church, and when her mother died of tuberculosis during her eighteenth pregnancy, the enraged Maggie bitterly blamed him. Nonetheless, she was very like her father: rebellious, passionate, and driven. She joined the socialist movement, where she met a talented architectural student and would-be artist named William Sanger. They married, and Sanger built a palatial home on the Hudson River for his wife and their three children, at a cost far beyond his means.

But the life of a suburban housewife bored Sanger. She insisted the family move back to the city, where she joined the Greenwich Village crowd, parked her children with whoever would take them, and plunged into such avant-garde causes

Planned Parenthood founder Margaret Sanger on a beach in Nassau in February 1933. Her tireless crusading for birth control would result by the century's end in the threatened extinction of the very type of ultra-liberal society she cherished because its women were increasingly unenthused by the prospect of motherhood.

as eugenics, legal birth control, socialism, and free love. But the idea of extramarital sex appalled William, whose socialism stopped considerably short of wife-sharing. In part to save the marriage, they moved to Paris where he could pursue his artistic interests. Margaret shortly returned home to pursue interests of her own, one of these being other men. William's letters, pleading his love for her—"my Peggy, my own dear Peggy"—are heartrending. His own dear Peggy finally told him to stop bothering her and find himself a mistress, but he wanted his wife. A protracted divorce proceeding ensued.

Meanwhile Margaret was moving into history. Working as a nurse in a New York slum hospital, she became so sickened and aggrieved at the spectacle of poor women dangerously attempting to induce their own abortions that she launched the campaign to revoke the Comstock Law of 1873. An antipornography statute, this law included a clause banning the mailing of information on contraceptives. With a publication called *The Woman Rebel*, Sanger so blatantly defied it that she had to flee the country to escape prosecution. She took refuge in England, where she briefly conducted an affair with sex liberationist Havelock Ellis and another with world-acclaimed novelist H. G. Wells.[10]

But followers back in the United States attracted so much public support that the government had to drop the charges. Sanger returned and founded the American Birth Control League, established the first American birth control clinic,

9. The encomiums applied to Margaret Sanger can scarcely be exaggerated. Writes biographer Ellen Chesler: "Every woman who takes her sexual and reproductive autonomy for granted should venerate Margaret Sanger as a woman of valor." Sex reformer Havelock Ellis: "A great woman, a beautiful spirit, a world's work done." Birth control advocate Dr. John Favill: "Her vision, courage and achievement make her the world's greatest woman." Socialist and civil liberties crusader Helen Keller: "She labored and suffered so that the life of the human race may become sager, finer and more creative." Novelist H. G. Wells: "The greatest biological revolutionary the world has ever known."

'Kissing, petting, and even intercourse are all right as long as they are sincere,' Margaret told her granddaughter, 16. 'I have never given an insincere kiss in all my life.'

and lectured in churches, women's clubs, homes, and theaters. She recruited to her cause thousands of upper-class women, liberal clerics, and scientists, while pouring forth some eight books on birth control, as well as an autobiography. In 1937 the American Medical Association permitted doctors to routinely prescribe contraceptive devices, and the league changed its name to Planned Parenthood, though Sanger objected to this. She considered the new name a limp euphemism.

Her life was not without tragedy. Her only daughter, Peggy, brought up like her two brothers by friends, neighbors, and other relatives, died of polio at age four in a New York hospital. Both sons survived, however, and became doctors. William eventually agreed to a divorce, by which time Margaret had embarked on a fling with J. Noah H. Slee, the Three-in-One Oil Company king, one of her major bankrollers. Slee's wife attempted suicide upon discovering the affair, but J. Noah divorced her anyway. Then he married Margaret, first signing an agreement granting her the freedom to do whatever she liked.

When Slee died in 1943, he left her five million dollars, which she spent traveling the world first class, receiving accolades and awards in almost every country she visited, proclaiming the virtues she perceived in unrestrained sex, and crossing and recrossing the Atlantic to visit the men who provided her with it. "Kissing, petting and intercourse are all right as long as they are sincere," she wrote to her sixteen-year-old granddaughter. "I have never given a kiss in my life that wasn't sincere. As for intercourse, I'd say that three times a day was about right." As she

10. Besides novelist H. G. Wells, sex reformer Havelock Ellis, and Three-in-One Oil tycoon J. Noah H. Slee, whom she later married, Margaret Sanger's lovers included the Spanish anarchist and publisher Lorenzo Portet, lawyer Jonah Goldstein, English author and journalist Hugh de Selincourt, birth control manufacturer Herbert Simonds, *London Times* editorial writer Harold Child, obstetrician Angus MacDonald, and artist Hobson Pitman. Others are identified in her diaries only by initials.

Margaret Sanger (center) and her sister Ethyl Byrne (at her right elbow) on the courtroom steps in Brooklyn, New York, in 1917 during a trial in which they were found guilty of opening a birth control clinic. Right, sexologist Havelock Ellis, partner in one of Sanger's many affairs. Despite the countless hagiographies, Sanger was clearly no saint.

aged, however, she became infirm, developed an addiction to pain-killing drugs and alcohol, and was often found, mud-smeared and bruised, stumbling around the grounds of her Tucson, Arizona, home in the dark.

The Slee inheritance meanwhile was quickly evaporating; when Sanger died of leukemia in 1966, only one hundred thousand was left. In a strongbox, her sons found a letter addressed to their father, written twelve years earlier and never sent, though clearly she meant him to see it. They did not disclose its text, but said it was filled with pleas for William's forgiveness and fond memories of their early years together. But by then William Sanger was long dead.

One of the final distinctions accorded to Sanger was the Gold Medal of Japan, conferred upon her by command of the emperor. Forty years later, largely due to her life's work, Japan would possess one of the world's lowest fertility rates, so low in fact as to threaten the people of this formerly overcrowded island with virtual extinction by the end of the twenty-first century.

The reason was not far to seek. Feminism had promised the woman freedom from the despotism of the man. But the chief oppressor of the woman was not the man, and never had been—it was the child. Now women in their millions were ridding themselves of the tyranny of the child, something Sanger presumably had not foreseen. Neither, of course, had the emperor of Japan. ∎

Dewey and the downfall of the school

Coercion, authority, performance, marks, and structure must all go, said the century's preeminent educator. What matters is self-esteem

None of the early twentieth century's great debunkers looked less dangerous, yet proved far more lastingly destructive of the old Christian order, than the philosopher-revolutionary John Dewey (1859–1952), who can rightly be regarded as the world's first professor of education. A family man and father of six children, he was long and happily married. His views of sexual conduct, at least as practiced in his own life, were entirely conventional. Furthermore, he worked with spectacular success within the established system—but he did so in order to radically, almost unrecognizably, transform it.

Rightly regarded as the foremost educational reformer of the twentieth century, Dewey was not what would later come to be called an "educator." He was a philosopher who reshaped public education—in America almost completely, and to a considerable degree throughout the industrialized world. He did this on the basis of a philosophy known as Pragmatism, which asserts, loosely speaking, that whatever works is right.[1] Predicated on this principle he advanced a whole new educational approach, and in the next half century untold billions would be spent instituting his ideas in primary and secondary schools, with performance standards steadily dropping all the while. Nevertheless, although it would seem ever more evident that "educational pragmatism" was a failure by its own criterion, ridding the schools of Deweyism would not be easy once all the system's practitioners had been trained in nothing else.

A convert himself in this respect, John Dewey exhibited in his thirties the zeal commonly associated with religious awakening. His conversion was not into Christianity, however, but out of it. His father was a Burlington, Vermont storekeeper whose passionate faith led him to stand on street corners asking passersby "Are you right with Jesus?" and at first his son seemed to have inherited the paternal faith. John was a bashful, bookish boy whose acute shyness caused him to fail as an elementary and secondary school teacher in Pennsylvania. But after earning a

doctorate at Johns Hopkins University, he became an outstanding lecturer in philosophy at the University of Michigan, and then head of the department. An active member of the Congregational Church, he conducted weekly Bible classes for the Student Christian Association, warning students in one typical address that "Belief is not a privilege but a duty," and that "Whatsoever is

John Dewey at the height of his influence in 1932, arriving at a conference in Cleveland on social planning and control. Dewey's educational philosophy would almost completely reshape public education in the United States .

1. The Humanist Manifesto of 1933, endorsed by John Dewey and thirty-three other notables, contains a definition of Pragmatism which unwittingly discloses the philosophy's central weakness. That is, what one man might view as a society in admirable working order, another might regard as an utter horror.

2. *John Dewey and the Decline of American Education* (2006) is a comprehensive and understandable critique of Dewey's work written by Henry T. Edmondson, professor of political science and public administration at Georgia State University. He is also director of the Center for Transatlantic Studies.

Dewey in 1902 (left), shortly before leaving the University of Chicago, and, inset, his chief disciple at Columbia Teachers College, William Heard Kilpatrick. Together they spread their gospel of relativism to schools over much of the western world.

not from faith is sin" (Romans 14:23).

But something happened at Ann Arbor, Michigan, that changed young Professor Dewey's life and, some suspect, his religion as well. In 1884 he became fascinated with one of his students, Alice Chipman, who reciprocated his interest. Both twenty-five years old, they were soon married, and she, with his ardent support, launched a vigorous campaign to improve the status of women at the university. Alice described herself as strongly religious, but rejected belief in any dogma, allegiance to a church, and unreserved adherence to the Bible. Before long, John's beliefs began to accord with his wife's, and while teaching at the University of Chicago in the 1890s he seems to have entirely abandoned the beliefs of his Christian upbringing in favor of Pragmatism. Four decades later, his complete conversion would be clearly demonstrated when he championed the first Humanist Manifesto. Its assertions include the following:

- The universe is self-existing and not created. This makes unacceptable any supernatural or cosmic guarantees of human values.

- The distinction between the sacred and the secular can no longer be maintained.

- Worship and prayer must be replaced by a heightened sense of personal life and a cooperative effort to promote social well-being. There will be no uniquely religious emotions and attitudes of the kind hitherto associated with belief in the supernatural.

- Religious institutions and their ritualistic forms and ecclesiastical methods must be reconstituted in order to function effectively in the modern world.

- A socialized and cooperative economic order must be established to ensure equitable distribution of the material means of life.

Dewey began formulating at Chicago an educational agenda to accord with this political philosophy. Like the founders of the United States, he was obsessed with the idea of freedom—but a radically new kind of freedom. He saw people as prisoners of traditionalist thought and morality, and envisioned a new civilization, liberated from outdated taboos, creeds, and codes of conduct, which would use science to reach destinies vastly beyond present human imagination. The road to this nirvana lay not through some Marxist or Fascist revolution but through education, Dewey reasoned. If you changed the way most people thought, after all, the politicians would have to go along with it. He proceeded to publish sixteen books on educational change which would so revolutionize America's public schools as to render them unrecognizable to anyone who had previously attended them.[2]

Following a fierce conflict at Chicago, in 1904 he moved to Columbia University in New York, which became the breeding ground for a veritable educational pandemic.[3] His vision was embraced, indeed devoured, not by teachers but by "educators"—those who teach teachers—a species virtually created by the Dewey revolution. Decade after decade, a torrent of disciples poured forth from Columbia University Teachers College, an establishment skillfully administered by his senior lieutenant in the revolution, W. H. Kilpatrick. They gradually infused his ideas into the new "faculties of education" that began to appear in U.S.

universities, themselves largely a product of Deweyism.

The man himself was meanwhile carrying his ideas worldwide. He referred to his message as "the gospel," and this gospel was embraced not least in the Soviet Union. The schools must be used to eradicate old ideas about human nature, Dewey declared. One Dewey critic, Henry T. Edmondson, in his *John Dewey and the Decline of American Education* (2006), describes what this means: The concept of good and evil must be abolished. Such qualities as honesty, courage, industry, and chastity must no longer be cherished, while such attributes as malice, vindictiveness, and irresponsibility need no longer be deplored, since any individual's conduct is merely his response to surrounding conditions. In fact, all moral authority rooted in the past must go. The student must acquire his own "values" (a Deweyite term) based on his own experience. Similar changes, born of the Enlightenment and the philosophy of relativism, were already changing the schools of Europe, much as Dewey was changing those in America, but the Deweyist movement became much more concerted and bureaucratically driven.

Most important, students must not see themselves as being in any sense "judged." The idea of individual blame must be scrapped, and each individual become in his own eyes a part of the community. If he committed a "crime," he must not be considered responsible; the community had somehow failed him. The concept of "the will" must be expunged, since belief that the individual "chooses" between good and evil leads to the defeat of "selfhood." Gender stereotyping must go. Such distinctions as boys' books and girls' books, or boys' games and girls' games, serve to perpetuate the old, outmoded order. His ideas assuredly would "destroy many things once cherished," Dewey acknowledged, but such was the price of human progress.

Teachers ought not to function as authority figures, he reasoned, but as guides, counselors, and friends. Student desks should be rearranged to banish any suggestion of authoritarian leadership; students must learn to lead themselves. Any attempt by a teacher to impose structure—pass/fail, good/bad, and right/wrong—constituted a form of "pedagogical abuse." All semblance of superiority/inferiority must vanish, along with imposed performance standards. Report cards should no longer carry grade standings, nor any student be singled out for a distinctly good performance—and certainly not for a bad one. The whole notion of good and bad must be removed from the child's mind, with "self-esteem" encouraged in every possible way but never predicated on actual performance. They should esteem themselves because they are selves, he reasoned, not because they have necessarily accomplished anything.

In brief, Deweyism regarded learning as a more or less incidental by-product of education; his central aim was to turn children into "social beings." In the higher grades "critical thinking" should be fostered, which meant questioning the assumptions of the old order, especially parents. A student who challenged parental moral principles was deemed to be "thinking critically." If he continued in dutiful obedience, his education had plainly failed him.

Far removed from Columbia's lofty cerebral latitudes, however, classroom teachers faced the onerous task of applying these elusive theories to such awkward areas as reading, spelling, English grammar, and mathematics. Spelling was particularly distasteful to the Deweyite because it suggested a "right way" to compose a word, and the existence therefore of "wrong ways." Teachers, said the Deweyites, should either overlook errors, or observe them in passing but not "judgmentally." Future citizens didn't need to bother about spelling, even if what they wrote began to resemble gibberish. Grammar posed a further challenge, so teaching it was largely abolished; grammatical rules belonged to the past, and the youthful mind should be freed of the whole concept of "rules."

But grammar had fulfilled another function, serving as a preliminary to logic by requiring students to distinguish whether a group of words was or was not a sentence, and to break sentences into their component parts. It thereby introduced a reasoning process, which to Dewey seemed destructively authoritarian. Formal logic was similarly abolished. This left mathematics, another problematic area where the concept of "mistakes" or

> *The Deweyites said teachers should either overlook errors or observe them in passing, but not 'judgmentally.'*

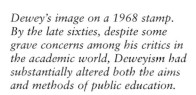

Dewey's image on a 1968 stamp. By the late sixties, despite some grave concerns among his critics in the academic world, Deweyism had substantially altered both the aims and methods of public education.

3. John Dewey's departure from Chicago seemingly centered on his wife. To provide a testing ground for his educational concepts, the University of Chicago had authorized him to establish there the Laboratory School (soon dubbed the "Dewey School"), run by Alice. When the university tried to merge it with another experimental school, Dewey insisted she head the joint endeavor. Fearing Alice's "abrasive style and precipitous dismissal of staff members," writes Thomas C. Dalton in *Becoming John Dewey: Difficulties of a Philosopher and Naturalist* (2002), the university objected. In the ensuing strife, Dewey resigned.

Both presidents Dwight D. Eisenhower (left) and Ronald Reagan launched federal initiatives to combat the destructive effects of Deweyism on the schools. By the 1980s the American school system, once one of the best, had become in some key areas of learning one of the worst.

"wrong answers" was hard to avoid. Five-times-five would insist on equalling twenty-five, however strong one's personal conviction. It was therefore resolved that children should personally "experience" the multiplication table, discovering that things generally turned out more satisfactorily when they made five-times-five equal twenty-five. But other answers should not be harshly dismissed as "wrong," because "right" and "wrong" did not exist.

As for history, clearly it must go, being not only irrelevant but actively dangerous. "It is possible to employ it as a kind of reservoir of anecdotes to be drawn on to inculcate moral lessons on this virtue or that vice," Dewey wrote, "but such a teaching is not so much an ethical use of history as it is an effort to create moral impressions by means of more or less authentic material. At best it produces a temporary emotional glow." Besides, since history was "not useful to contribute to the development of the social intelligence," it was essentially pointless. It was replaced by a new course, "social studies," where fragments from the past could be assembled to reinforce one or another polemical case. Social studies were not meant to present a coherent story, unfolding era by era across time, however, as that would confer upon it a dangerous credibility. Since all existing records were

ultimately somebody's viewpoint—biased, subjective, and essentially fictional—little could actually be learned from the past.[4]

It took about three decades—the 1930s, '40s, and '50s—for Deweyism to engulf the American public school system. From the start, it is true, discordant voices were raised, some of them authoritative. Parents and students, one such voice declared, "must be induced to abandon the educational path that, rather blindly, they have been following as a result of John Dewey's teachings." That voice belonged to President Dwight D. Eisenhower. A more raucous note was sounded by the acerbic Christian novelist Flannery O'Connor. Her advice to parents was unequivocal: "Anything that Wm. Heard Kilpatrick & Jhn. Dewey say to do, don't do."

A notably articulate critic emerged in Canada: Hilda Neatby, professor of history at the University of Saskatchewan, whose book, *So Little for the Mind* (1953), aroused the fury of the new educators. "Deweyism is not liberation," Neatby declared, "it is indoctrination both intellectual and moral, often forced upon the schools by ideological bureaucracies." Such negativity was generally dismissed as the moans of a dying culture.

What became difficult to entirely disregard, however, was the increasing impression of parents and employers that kids weren't actually learning much. The schools were costing more, with teacher salaries, once abysmally low, now appearing quite adequate. But children didn't seem to read so well, many were essentially illiterate, and quite a few could not add, subtract, multiply, or divide. Further, the schools had become laboratories for esoteric experimentation. In the 1960s, for example, "new math" was introduced, which by the 1970s would be quietly dumped as an undeniable failure. "Whole language" reading instruction arrived with the '80s and was mostly out by the end of the '90s. How many lives were ruined by such irresponsible experimentation, no one cared to say.

In 1983, President Ronald Reagan's National Commission on Education produced a report that shook the American educational establishment to the core. Entitled "A Nation at Risk," in clear terms and backed by unassailable data it documented the fact that the American school system, once one of the best in the industrialized world, was now one of the worst. Scores on the Scholastic Aptitude Test (SAT) and the American College Test (ACT) had been dropping for some years. Universities had to provide remedial classes to teach what the elementary and secondary schools no longer did. The performance of American students on international test scores was declining steadily. Knowledge of the great works of literature had largely disappeared. Every test revealed a deepening and dangerous ignorance of historical fact. Finally, the U.S. level of "functional illiteracy" was higher than that of any other industrialized nation.

Many wondered: How had this whole calamity been allowed to happen? Where were the defenders of the literary heritage of the western world when it was being pitched out? Where were the historians, for that matter, when their subject was being reduced to what was at best an eminently dispensable adjunct of sociology? Not least, where were the Christians when the entire premise of their teaching and theology was being eliminated as absurd? (How could Christ have died for our sins, after all, when there was no such thing as sin—or good or evil either, for that matter, or right or wrong?)

It was soon evident that many, if not most, Christian schools had been blind to the fact that "Colleges of Education," where the indispensable government teaching certificate must be earned, were indoctrinating all their students in beliefs and philosophies fundamentally incompatible with the Bible and with Christian doctrine. In Canada,

even most state-supported Catholic schools had so obediently embraced the new ideas that their curriculum was largely indistinguishable from that of the public schools.

Fifteen years later, a follow-up U.S. study—"A Nation Still at Risk"—brought the doleful news that despite supposedly herculean efforts to improve education, nothing much had changed. Some thirty percent of university freshmen still required remedial courses in reading, writing, and mathematics; in California the figure was fifty percent. "Employers report difficulty finding people to hire who have the skills, knowledge, habits, and attitudes they require for technologically sophisticated positions," it noted. On the latest International Math and Science Study, American twelfth graders scored near the bottom. In science they stood nineteenth among twenty-one developed nations, and "our advanced students did even worse, scoring dead last in physics."

Why, asked this second survey, had the many reforms proposed by the first one not been effectively implemented? Then it answered its own question: The authors of the first had "underestimated the resilience of the status quo and the strength of the interests wedded to it." But as one of them, a former Minnesota governor, observed: "At that time I had no idea that the system was so reluctant to change." Reluctant it certainly was, but also incapable. The educators running the school system, although likely unaware of this, were so deeply infected by Deweyist philosophy that they could comprehend no other.

Meanwhile, Alice Dewey had died in 1927. After thirteen years as a widower, John married Roberta Lowitz Grant, whom he had known back in Pennsylvania when he was an unhappy teacher, and they adopted and raised two Belgian orphans. Dewey died at age ninety-two in 1952, thirty-one years before "A Nation at Risk" cast a dark shadow over the educational colossus he had brought into being. Nor did he personally witness the pounding inflicted upon him and all his works by philosopher and classicist Allan Bloom, whose 1987 book, *The Closing of the American Mind*, identified him as one of the chief culprits responsible for closing it.

By then, the catastrophic influence exerted by this educational philosopher-reformer on the allegiance of many Americans to traditional and biblical Christianity was also beyond any doubt. Among the debunkers, his conformist outward appearance notwithstanding, John Dewey unquestionably was a champion. ■

4. The contention that all historical records are somebody's "viewpoint," summoned to discredit history as a source of established fact, is centrally flawed. Consider, for example, four historical statements: 1) "Martin Luther King died." 2) "Martin Luther King was killed." 3) "Martin Luther King was assassinated." 4) "Martin Luther King was martyred." The fourth may be a viewpoint; the other three are facts. It is irrational to contend that if one is a viewpoint, they must all be mere viewpoints. The historical record, and our memories, are clearly subject to error. What we recall happening can differ from what actually happened, but it does not follow that memory is entirely useless, and that in effect we are all no better than amnesiacs.

A barbed wire fence in front of the ruins of a Gulag camp on Vaygach Island in the Russian Arctic pays mute condolence to millions of Soviet citizens who passed through these penal labor facilities between 1929 and their closure in 1960. Instituted under Joseph Stalin's totalitarian regime, the camps' population consisted of as many as two million religious "criminals" at the peak of Soviet persecution.

CHAPTER 5

The Marxist 'paradise' becomes a slave state, avowed to kill off God

Starve the peasants to finance new heavy industry— that's Stalin's master plan to save the economy; the starvation is massive, but the economy fails

The "feared day came at noon on August 6, 1936." So begins Justina Martens's account of how the Cheka—the Stalinist secret police—came to her Mennonite village deep in Ukraine to take her brother Heinrich away.[1] Heinrich had met one evening with other village men to listen as a religious book was read aloud, breaking the laws suppressing religion. An informer must also have been present because the host was swiftly arrested. Her brother "told us to count on the fact he [too] would be arrested."

Two men seized her brother at the collective farm's threshing machine and frog-marched him home to search for weapons. Finding none, they took Justina's books and letters. Heinrich was allowed to hold his children in his arms—for the last time, as it turned out—and was taken by the police to jail, trial, the work camps, and in 1943, death by unknown means. Heinrich's last letter to his sister and his wife came in 1940. "Dear Neta," it read, "if we should not see each other again here, let us earnestly strive to all meet in our heavenly home... And you, dear sister Justina, stay with Neta and the children and strive for those things which are above." Only years after Henrich's death would his family learn of it.

Justina, Neta, and her children, whose family's rich farmlands had been expropriated by the Soviet government in 1930, became waifs in a system that had no place for them. They were derided as "Hitlers" because of their German blood, then conscripted as laborers, and finally, forcibly settled in Siberia with

1. The Soviet secret police would go through numerous organizational shuffles reflected in sesquipedalian names but snappy acronyms. Thus the Cheka was short for Vecheka, which itself was an acronym for the All-Russian Extraordinary Committee to Combat Counterrevolution and Sabotage—the original Soviet secret police. It was soon renamed and re-acronymed as the GPU, a division of the NKVD, then the OGPU, GUGB, NKGB, MVD, and, from 1954 to 1991, the KGB. Many people just kept calling it the Cheka.

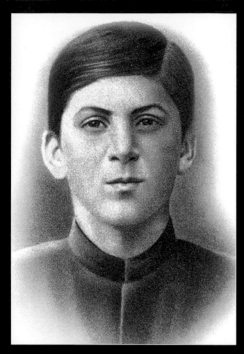  

Three ages of Joseph Stalin: (left) as a sixteen-year-old Orthodox seminarian, still named Besarionis dze Jughashvili, in his home state of Georgia; (center) as a thirty-two-year-old Marxist revolutionary in the Caucasus, having changed his name to "Stalin" (meaning "steel"); and (right) as the sixty-four-year-old secretary general of the USSR in 1942. Stalin's driving aim was to transform the Soviet Union into an industrial power rivaling those in the West and to crush anyone who blocked the way.

2. With the deaths of as many as thirty million Russians in their wake, the Soviets had to search diligently through their scriptures, i.e. the writings of Karl Marx, for some means of justifying this. And they found they need not be too concerned. Marx had assured them that the "essence" of humanity could not be fully realized until all men were completely liberated from the chains of capitalism. Therefore, those thirty million had been slain, worked, or starved to death in the work of achieving the perfect Communist society. However, since they themselves were not yet of the essence, they did not matter.

millions of other undesirables. All were mere digits among the tens of millions of victims of Joseph Stalin's grandiose vision. He was unremittingly transfixed on building what he called "socialism in one country." That country was the Soviet Union. It must become the leading industrial and military power in Europe, he declared. "We are fifty to one hundred years behind the advanced countries," he told party colleagues in 1931. "We must make good the lag in ten years. Either we do it, or they crush us." A decade later, when German armored divisions rolled into the USSR, Stalin's warning would prove prophetic.

Stalin knew that transforming the Soviet Union so wholly and so rapidly would require unimaginable violence against its people—especially against its agricultural peasantry. This, he resolved, must be of no account. What mattered alone was the fulfillment of the Communist vision.[2] To recover from the First World War and the subsequent civil war, the Communists under Lenin had permitted private enterprise and individual farms to flourish during the 1920s, so much so that by 1928 production had recovered to prewar levels overall, while agriculture was twenty percent above. Now firmly in power, however, Stalin decreed that the pace of the Soviet Union's economic growth should be accelerated through nationalization of all enterprises, including farms.[3]

At the same time, Stalin ushered in the first of a series of Five-Year Plans that would squeeze the USSR's production capability to the direst extremes, setting an ill-fated model imitated by left-leaning governments around the world.[4] The first plan emphasized heavy industry and massive public works. The new factories were to be purchased whole from western Europe using trade credits earned by the exports of food products, especially grain, while farm production would be boosted by the "collectivization" of independent peasant holdings into huge, efficient communal and state farms. As for the public works—railways, canals, and power dams—these would be, in Stalin's primitive understanding of economics, built virtually without cost through the use of millions of slave laborers imprisoned in a vast system of work camps run by the secret police and filled by political prisoners, including believers of all faiths.

Superficially and in the accounts of tireless Soviet propagandists, the early Five-Year Plans produced astonishing growth, tripling production in many sectors. Best of all, grain production rose by thirty to forty million tons annually.

But was this true? Big gains in primary industry were indeed achieved, writes the French political and economic philosopher Raymond Aron in his book *In Defense of Decadent Europe* (1977), but only by transferring a disproportionate amount of labor to these sectors. The true result of this misallocated labor, he finds, is that productivity actually declined by 1.9 percent a year from 1928 to

Railways, canals, power dams would be built virtually without cost, in Stalin's primitive economics, through the use of slave labor.

1966 and by 3.9 percent between 1950 and 1962. Moreover, not until 1958 did the real purchasing power of factory and farm workers rise to its 1928 levels. Agricultural production did not reach the 1928 figure for as many years or more; livestock fell in number and kept falling until the 1950s. Furthermore, so much of what was produced was confiscated by the government to finance the Five-Year Plans that famine prevailed over much of the richest grain-producing areas of Russia, a Stalin-made famine that starved millions to death (see subchapter, page 91).

All this notwithstanding, many in the West accepted the Soviet-generated views for decades until the release of Alexander Solzhenitsyn's stinging indictment, his novel *One Day in the Life of Ivan Denisovich*, published in 1962. (He was later awarded the Nobel Prize in Literature, see sidebar, page 337.) The Gulag, he said, was a vast collaboration by its inmates with their jailors to fool the Soviet government into believing production goals had been met.[5] Goods of low quality would be upgraded on paper to a higher quality; goods that were never made would be reported as produced, then written off as spoilage or undeliverable due to transportation shortages. A third type of falsification was the production of goods without value. Some were small; some were very large indeed, such as the Belomor Canal, which Stalin ordered to be built to link Leningrad with the Barents Sea. It was constructed using the most primitive tools between 1931 and 1933 at a cost of five hundred thousand lives. The canal paralleled a railway which rendered it superfluous before it was built, and it turned out anyway to be too shallow to take the ocean vessels for which it was proposed. Yet according to the American economic historian Steven Rosefielde: "Belomor may well explain 11.9 percent of the real growth in Soviet construction between 1928 and 1932."

3. The Soviets were by both ideology and circumstance no friends of the peasantry. By the 1930s, the very existence of a peasant class was an embarrassment to Marxist-Leninist theory, which decreed that the initial revolt of the industrial workers should have made them exceed the peasants both numerically and in political weight. Not only had this not happened, but the independent farmers, favored by Lenin's policies, were establishing new production records and acquiring what to the Bolsheviks was a disconcerting and outrageous wealth. Obviously they had to go.

4. Other governments disastrously copied the Soviet agenda. A five-year plan launched by India in 1956, based on the Soviet model of investment in heavy industry at the expense of agriculture, had the same result, leading India to the brink of famine. Film footage of starving Indian children became common on television and the question arose: Could India ever feed itself? By the twenty-first century the world had the answer. Through technology, better transportation, and management, India had become a net food exporter.

5. GULag or Gulag is an acronym composed of the Russian words meaning "Chief Administration of Corrective Labor Camps," the system of forced labor camps maintained by the Soviet Union until 1960s. (In Russian: *Glavnoye Upravleniye ispravitelno-trudovyh Lagerey*.) Such camps survived as late as 2012 as far afield as Cuba, China and North Korea.

There is another category of falsified economic claims that only someone with Alexander Solzhenitsyn's moral authority could describe. This he called "social bads" in contrast with "economic goods." These were the vast empire of the Gulag camps themselves, built at great expense in material and labor, all dutifully recorded as improvements to the Soviet standard of living and components of its GDP, but which Rosefielde, borrowing a term used by Marxist theorists, calls "immiseration."

Miserable indeed were the lives of workers. Equipped with primitive tools, they would be punished by having their rations halved, ensuring their slow death—and their reduced productivity. Prisoners were regularly strip-searched in subzero weather, both to humiliate them and to provide guards with a chance to rob them. Guards who failed in their duty became prisoners too, and prisoners were punished with solitary confinement and tens of thousands were shot "for continuing anti-Soviet activity during imprisonment." Female prisoners were routinely raped. Hundreds of thousands of the children of Gulag inmates, some as young as three, were consigned to their own special camps where they were raised in the belief that theirs was a normal life.

In the lower photograph, forced laborers toil to build the Barents Sea Canal in 1931. In the (above) idealized Soviet propaganda painting portrays happy workers in a tractor factory around the same time. According to the propagandists, Stalin's five-year economic plans, which relied on slave labor for much of the production, produced astonishing growth; in reality, agricultural and industrial output realized a steady decline for thirty years.

At its peak, the Gulag had eight to twelve million inmates and absorbed one sixth of the Soviet budget. Historian William Fletcher estimates, in *The Russian Orthodox Underground 1917–1970,* that as many as twenty percent were there for specifically religious crimes. Small wonder, for the number of such crimes was burgeoning. The severity of Soviet anti-Christian activity, somewhat mitigated in the early 1920s as the regime sought and largely failed to subvert the faith, abruptly turned more harsh than ever with a 1929 decree forbidding all religious activity outside of worship: no excursions, picnics, sports days, and,

above all, no instruction of children or adults. Then came the wholesale arrest of bishops, which was partially countered by the church's ordination of extra bishops. Clergy of all denominations were executed or "exiled" to work camps; churches were closed on any pretext. Believers were penalized by being denied admission to the secular professions. Even the tolling of church bells was banned.

The Metropolitan Sergius could still count 163 bishops in 1930 and thirty thousand churches. But in 1932, Stalin could with confidence approve a five-year "godless" plan, decreeing: "By May 1, 1937, the name of God must be forgotten across the USSR." And indeed, by 1940, only four bishops remained free and only 4,225 churches were still officially open. In reality, the number of churches was closer to one hundred.

As historian Fletcher summarizes: "The antireligious campaign had achieved almost complete success against the institutional Orthodox Church." When it came to eradicating Christian belief and faith, however, something went shockingly awry with the godless five-year plan, despite the executions and mass arrests, the millions of antireligious pamphlets, tens of thousands of lectures, the creation of more than a dozen universities of atheism, countless school experiments disproving miracles, and the nominal growth of the League of the Militant Godless to 3.2 million. For in 1937, the very year of God's predicted disappearance, the results of an astounding census were revealed. A question, included in the census under Stalin's personal orders, asked the

Moscow's Cathedral of Christ the Savior is demolished in 1931; one of its fallen cherubim is salvaged with a rope, and Soviet workers pile religious symbols they have collected from laborers' dormitories onto a truck bound for the bonfire. Stalin announced his five-year plan to eradicate Christian practice when he declared, "By May 1, 1937, the name of God must be forgotten across the USSR." Yet while his campaign against churches saw some success, the majority of Russians still declared themselves religious in 1937. By the time of the Second World War, Stalin came to see this religious faith as a tool to be used in galvanizing "Mother Russia" against the Nazi invaders.

A selection of wartime Soviet postage stamps with the invocations (clockwise from top left): "Be a Hero", "Death to German Invaders", "The Great Patriotic War for the Complete Rout of the German Invaders", and "Death to German Occupiers." The war cry also went out to Russian clerics. Most answered, but with some exceptions, notably in the Ukraine, where many Christians allied with the Nazis.

6. The *baba* (grandmother) had always been something of an authority figure in Russian culture, and babas were notoriously Christian. Religion, said Lenin in the early 1920s, has now been "largely confined to the babas." No one now remains in the churches, said Stalin in the late 1930s, except the babas. Christian practice, said Nikita Khrushchev in the late 1950s, is now left to the babas. How all these babas kept recurring, no one in authority seemed ready to explain.

respondent whether he or she believed in God. More than half of those polled, fully 55.7 million Russians, regardless of the consequences, answered yes. And before covering up the census, Soviet officials indicated these numbers were probably low by as much as twenty percent due to the ordinary Russian's justifiable fear of retaliation.

The state responded with renewed persecution that coincided with Stalin's paranoid Great Terror. In all, 681,000 Russians were executed, including Communist Party and Red Army leaders, and forty Orthodox bishops. Another twelve died in prison or the Gulag. By 1940, only Sergius and three others were free.

Yet, as was often the case in Russia, appearances were deceiving. However harsh the penalties of faith, the commissars were discovering that it was imperishable. It was soon undeniable that they had grievously underestimated the commitment of ordinary believers, who had found many ways to practice their faith covertly. They had reopened churches unofficially where they could, and stripped the walls of icons and hidden them away where they could not be seized. Rural dwellers in particular remained faithful, often stubbornly petitioning the government for their churches to be reopened. The leader of one local cell of the League of the Militant Godless was found to be keeping icons in his home and to have baptized his children. When the Communist Party began prosecution of a second member who had similarly baptized his children, it was discovered all his fellow local members had done likewise. The matter was dropped. In one collective farm whose leadership was considering antireligious activities, the believers countered with death threats.

Even in the work camps services were held, sometimes in secret, sometimes with the tacit acceptance of the guards. Indeed, historian Fletcher reports that the camps became schools for the underground church. Their priests, pastors, and laity conspired to secretly give and receive the sacraments or hold services. Outside the Gulag, the laity baptized their own children while itinerant priests followed up with mass baptisms and mass confessions. These latter had the advantage of relieving the priests of the pressure from the secret police to betray the secrets of the confessional.

New priests mostly received bare-bones training one-on-one, though an underground seminary operated in Moscow until 1938, having survived two years beyond the execution of its principal, Bishop Bartholomew. Evangelization was performed covertly through public concerts mixing secular, even Communist, songs with hymns. Teaching the catechism became the routine role of grandmothers.[6]

Patriarch Tikhon apparently ordained a Bishop Maxim to lead an organized underground church. It is believed a parallel line of secret bishops existed until each was discovered in turn and shot, ending with Metropolitan Joseph in 1938. Some bishops briefly organized cadres of underground priests to serve the faithful, but the NKVD (the Soviet secret police) had so thoroughly penetrated Russian society with informers that nothing very organized could survive for long. Nonetheless, the steadfastness of so many Christians under oppression inevitably drew the admiration of even the nonbelievers. There was less admiration for Metropolitan Sergius, even from those who admitted his compliance was necessary for Orthodoxy's survival. He denounced the so-called Russian Orthodox Church in Exile and denied its claims of Soviet oppression. He even deposed the leader of the Orthodox Church Outside of Russia for similar remarks.

What finally forced Stalin to reverse his hostility to the church was the rise of Adolf Hitler and the rearmament of Nazi Germany, and the German invasion of Russia in 1941, which Stalin had refused to believe was going to happen until it did. When Germany's armored divisions roared into the Soviet Union, Sergius issued an immediate and sincere call to arms, though he may well have also feared that Stalin would launch another purge out of fear that Russian Christians would ally with the Nazis, as, indeed, they did in parts of Ukraine. As well, one of his bishops defected as soon as the Germans occupied his diocese. Metropolitan Sergius urged all believers to come to the Soviet Union's defense and issued a preemptive excommunication of anyone who disobeyed. Impressed, Stalin allowed more bishops to return from exile, removed restrictions, and, on September 4, 1943, met privately with Sergius and two other prelates. It soon became evident that while people might be reluctant to fight for Bolshevism, they were very ready indeed to fight for Russia, and Russia meant Orthodoxy.

A crowd of parishioners and clergy await Metropolitan Sergius (inset) outside one of the surviving cathedrals in Moscow for his investiture as patriarch in 1943. Sergius had been unpopular with many believers for his collaboration with the Soviets, but the policy was exonerated when the Soviet authorities relaxed their restrictions on the church so as to recruit its support for the war effort.

After this epochal meeting, the whole tenor of church-state relations rapidly improved. Bishops were released from the Gulag; seminaries were opened; a publishing house was granted; and most important, the national church was recognized and permitted to elect a new patriarch: Sergius himself. When he died in 1944, Alexii I was elected patriarch by a council of laity, priests, and bishops. After the Soviet victory in 1945, conditions for the Orthodox Church continued to improve. By 1949, 14,500 churches were operational along with seventy-five monasteries, and ten theology colleges and seminaries.

There were other changes. Several independent national churches were forcibly subsumed into the Russian Orthodox Church, most notably the Ukrainian Catholic Church, which recognized the Roman papacy. Two hundred of its priests were persuaded or terrorized into assembling in 1946 in L'viv to vote in favor of union, though hundreds more suffered imprisonment rather than do so, along with all nine bishops. All the latter died except for the head of the Ukrainian Uniates, Metropolitan Joseph Slipyi who was released after eighteen years in prison and thereafter headed the church from

Moscow Metropolitan Nicolei inspects a Soviet tank which was built in 1944 with funds provided by the Orthodox Church. State-Church relations would continue to improve in the years following the Soviet victory against Germany.

Rome. Meanwhile four million Ukrainian Catholics worshipped either in subjugation to Moscow, or underground. The underground church grew, especially among the young, as a focus for nationalist and anti-Soviet feeling. The Romanian Uniate churches were put under the Romanian Orthodox Church, as was the Autocephalous Ukrainian Orthodox Church which had established itself after the civil war.

In Hungary, the treatment of the church and the torture of its cardinal, Joseph Mindszenty, helped spark a 1956 revolution in that country. As for the Russian Orthodox, Stalin's support soon proved a dubious blessing. The controls he placed on the church proved insidious and corrupting, turning many clerics into puppets of the state. Indeed, according to the 1990 book *The Mitrokhin Archive: The KGB in Europe and the West*, authors Christopher Andrew and Vasili Mitrokhin assert that the KGB's influence was heaviest at the top of Orthodoxy, with several postwar patriarchs and the highly influential Metropolitan Nikodim all identified as KGB agents.

But according to the detailed notes made by Mitrokhin, who was the KGB's chief archivist for many years before defecting, only some of their priest-agents were wholehearted traitors. The book puts the patriarchs Pimen and Alexii II squarely in this category. A second group's members were sincere in their faith, but filed their reports to the KGB out of necessity. The Metropolitan Nikodim, who directed the church's foreign affairs until his death in Rome in 1975, was one of these. Finally, there were the fifteen to twenty percent who refused to serve the state at all. These brave souls were kept in junior posts, and only if they wandered into outright sedition were they charged, convicted, and imprisoned.

The collaborators presented a kind of Potemkin Church, celebrating showy liturgies in Moscow and insisting that the Soviet Union enjoyed perfect freedom of religion. They took the same message overseas, singing the Soviets' praises to foreign church leaders, manipulating the World Council of Churches and the Christian Peace Conference to condemn the western democracies for racism, warmongering, imperialism, sexism, and so on. Thus, in 1969, when the WCC considered a motion condemning the Soviet invasion of Czechoslovakia, Metropolitan Nikodim vowed that the Russian Orthodox Church would never distribute such a declaration to its faithful. The motion was meekly withdrawn.

Outstanding among the third category, but far from alone in his courage, was the priest Gleb Yakunin, who appeared at the 1975 assembly of the WCC in Nairobi and condemned Soviet religious persecution. The Russian delegation returned to Moscow to form a small cadre to collect and publish evidence of religious rights violations. The group survived for four years before the KGB finally had Yakunin tried for antistate activities and sentenced to five years in prison and five in exile. At his sentencing, very much in the spirit of Christian martyrdom, he declared: "I thank God for this test he has sent me. I consider it a great honor and, as a Christian, accept it gladly." Yakunin's sentence would be remitted by Soviet leader Mikhail Gorbachev and he would be elected to the Russian parliament from 1990–1999.

Another famous dissident, Father Dimitri Dudko, did not fare as well. Precisely because he was widely influential and the winner of many converts,

Metropolitan Nikodim of Leningrad, photographed in 1970, and, below, the oppressive entrance to KGB headquarters in Moscow. Several top Orthodox clerics, including Nikodim, were identified as agents for the KGB, the Soviet intelligence service. They refused to support the condemnation of Soviet aggression by outside church organizations.

Above, Hungarian Cardinal Joseph Mindzenty, whose torture helped spark the 1956 Hungarian Revolution and earned him the cover of Time magazine. Top right, Gleb Yakunin, jailed five years for protesting Soviet persecution of Christians, and an Orthodox priest who denounced the Orthodox hierarchy's collaboration with the KGB. After running for office in 1993 despite a church ban against priests doing so, he was defrocked. Bottom right: Father Dmitri Dudko, whose criticisms of the state led to his arrest and imprisonment by the KGB.

7. The deportation of underground Baptist leader Georgi Vins to the U.S. (where he settled with his family in Elkhart, Indiana) was a kind of homecoming. His father, Peter, was the son of Canadian Mennonite leader Jacob Wiens (or Vins). After attending seminary in the U.S., Peter Vins went to Russia to evangelize. He was imprisoned by the Soviets and executed in 1936. Though based in the U.S., Georgi Vins worked hard for the oppressed Baptists behind the Iron Curtain until it fell, and frequently returned thereafter to preach, until his death in 1998.

and his sermons were broadly distributed within the Soviet Union, the KGB imprisoned him in 1980 and interrogated him mercilessly until he broke. His recantation of criticisms against the state was televised and repeated in all Soviet newspapers, destroying his reputation. Dudko died in 2004, tormented by his actions, which he saw as a betrayal of those who had kept the faith. He told a journalist: "I thought if I didn't agree, I wouldn't live... Compared to the hell that I then brought into my soul, anything—even torture or execution—would have been easier to bear."

Stalin continued to show tolerance toward religion until his death in 1953. His successor Nikita Khrushchev, however, though a reformer in other respects, reversed Stalin's permissive religious policies.

Historians such as Christopher Marsh, however, stress the consistency of Khrushchev's actions: since Stalin had repressed freedom of expression in the arts and built the Gulag system, he, Khrushchev, would free the arts and close the camps. And since Stalin had liberated religion, he, Khrushchev, would restrict it.

The regime launched a sophisticated campaign to promote "scientific atheism," ordered as many churches shut as possible, and refused to open new ones. Young people were especially targeted, and so were seminarians: nearly two hundred were induced to renounce their faith in highly public declarations. In 1961, Khrushchev predicted that religion would soon be dead in Russia. Before he was forced from office in 1965, he had closed five thousand Orthodox churches, leaving just eight thousand, while the number of priests had been reduced by half since 1948. In the next twenty years, under Khrushchev's successors, the number of churches fell by another five hundred.

During this period of low-profile oppression, Metropolitan Nikodim played a prominent role in defending Orthodoxy while apparently pleasing his KGB masters. He was especially adroit at using the regime's sensitivity about its international image against it: to prevent the closure of a seminary, he added a department for foreign students; to stop provocateurs from ruining public processions with mocking comments, he invited foreign diplomats and clerics to attend. Playing on the Soviet regime's sensitivities in a very different way was Michael Bordeaux, an Anglican priest who, after witnessing a Moscow church being demolished, returned to England to start Keston College, which served as a clearinghouse for clandestine accounts of Soviet oppression until the Iron Curtain's collapse.

Just as the Soviet Union united Orthodox and Uniate churches to control them, so in 1940 it forced all evangelical Protestants, including Pentecostals and Mennonites, to declare themselves Baptists. But the state could not stifle their evangelical zeal. By such tactics as targeting the unchurched young people, even evangelizing them outside Communist events, these groups grew rapidly to three million by 1960 by their own estimate. (The government admitted to only 545,000.) It responded by forcing the leadership to issue the infamous "Letter of Instructions," ordering member churches to bar youth services, ban youth baptisms, and put a ceiling on baptisms of those aged eighteen to thirty. This prompted radical pastors such as Georgi Vins and Gennady Kryuchkov to form the breakaway Reform Baptists. When the regime refused to recognize them, they assembled from all over Russia, five hundred strong, outside Communist Party headquarters in Moscow, demanding to speak to Soviet leader Leonid Brezhnev. Instead, they were beaten up, and Vins and Kryuchkov were imprisoned for three years.

The state could not stifle the evangelical zeal. By targeting unchurched youth, even at Communist Party events, these groups grew rapidly.

On his return, after being sentenced to another year in prison—this time in the Gulag—Vins went underground, dodging the KGB for three years. When they caught him in 1974, they appeared not to know what to do with him. When his interrogator asked him what concession would bring the Reform Baptists back into the fold, he replied with a list that included the liberation of all religious prisoners, return of children to religious families, and freedom to preach. "That is impossible, that is an ultimatum," replied the shocked KGB agent. Vins was thereupon jailed for a year and then put on trial for defaming the regime and violating the law separating church and state. He refused to defend himself. After four years in the Gulag and much lobbying by Christian groups in the U.S., the regime deported him along with his family to America in exchange for two spies.[7]

Even more troubling for the Soviets than dissenting Baptists were the Pentecostals, who spread into Russia from Soviet territories such as Ukraine and Belarus. While the Baptists had initially pleased the Soviets with their simple, un-Orthodox ways, the Pentecostals' display of "gifts of the Spirit" genuinely alarmed them, as, indeed, it did the Baptists

Soviet Premier Nikita Khruschev is shown here greeting Cuban dictator Fidel Castro upon his arrival in Moscow in 1963, while future leader Leonid Brezhnev grins in the background. Khruschev was viewed as a reformer, compared with Stalin, but his reforms only applied to those areas of society his predecessor had oppressed. Consequently Stalin's liberation of religious practice was reversed, and "reformer" Khruschev restored the persecution of Christians.

The Siberian Seven—the Vashchenko family and two friends—are pictured here in a 1973 photograph, with radical Baptist pastor Georgi Vins (right). Vins and his colleague Gennady Kryuchkov formed a breakaway sect that rejected Soviet restrictions on membership. They were beaten and ordered jailed. The Siberian Seven forced their way into the American embassy and lived there until, with the help of foreign politicians including U.S. President Reagan, they were allowed by Soviet authorities to leave the country.

8. The charge that Russian Christians were sacrificing or, indeed, eating children, echoed the past. Much the same charge had been levied against Roman Christians in the second Christian century, a deduction reached at that time from a conflation of the baptismal rite and the Last Supper. (See volume 2, *A Pinch of Incense*, page 77.)

they were forced to join. The Pentecostals would arrange huge clandestine meetings of twenty thousand people in isolated country locations for mass baptisms.

In terms of audacity, nothing could top the so-called Siberian Seven—Pyotr and Augustina Vashchenko and three of their children plus two friends, all Pentecostals—who in 1978 pushed past guards into the American embassy. The Vashchenkos lived in a jerry-rigged suite in the embassy basement until 1983. They prayed, studied the Bible, and dispatched more than three hundred appeals and visa applications to the Soviet government. President Ronald Reagan made them an issue in his presidential campaign, fifty Congressmen appealed to Brezhnev to let them leave the country, and several visited the family on Moscow junkets. In 1983 the family wrote then-leader Yuri Andropov, telling him "God will force you to resolve our case righteously as he did with the king of Egypt." A hunger strike by Augustina that year helped too. The government finally permitted the Seven and eight other Vashchenko family members to leave the country.

Meanwhile, the authorities continued to vigorously fight the Pentecostals. Against one sect leader, Ivan Fedotov, they concocted wild tales of child sacrifice and produced bogus film footage to prove it.[8] Yet his church continued to attract people. All over the Soviet Union, the government broke up meetings, closed churches, imprisoned leaders in work camps and asylums, and seized children from their parents. But by the waning years of the Soviet Union, a third of the population still openly professed Christianity. As the terrible century's last decade neared, however, their perseverance and their trust in God was about to be rewarded (see chapter 17). ■

Millions die the worst of all deaths

One of every five Ukrainians suffers the lingering horror of starvation,
as planners seize their crops to serve a utopian illusion that didn't work

Famine is arguably the cruelest of all human suffering, for death by starvation comes slowly and painfully over many agonizing weeks or months. A starving man, wrote the twentieth-century Russian journalist and novelist Vasily Grossman, "is tormented and driven as though by fire, and torn both in the guts and the soul." Famished and half-mad, he will wander about like a dazed beast—begging, stealing, and scavenging—until he collapses or crawls home to die and at that point "famine, starvation, has won."

When such agony is inflicted by natural disaster—drought or flood or massive swarms of locusts—it understandably challenges belief in the goodness of God. That it should be inflicted on millions of people through the calculated policy of a governmentally directed ideology boggles the mind.

(Right) A group of starving children during the first Ukrainian famine in 1921–22, and (below) a similarly distressed family. This famine, which occurred under Lenin's leadership, was in part due to bad weather, the factor that allowed for the publication of pictures such as these and also spurred aid from the West, particularly from the United States. The second and considerably more devastating famine in 1932–33 came solely as a result of Soviet collectivization and antikulak policies, and would be concealed by a Soviet regime intent on impressing the world through a facade of Marxist prosperity.

Yet that is the crime of which twentieth-century history unequivocally convicts the atheist Soviet Union in its sixteenth year of experimental communism.

The concept, in fact, came directly from Karl Marx, who saw large industrialized farms as more efficient than small family farms. He also wanted workers' wages kept low to foster rapid industrialization, and food figured prominently in workers' living costs. Economic history provides virtually no support to the first argument. It provides

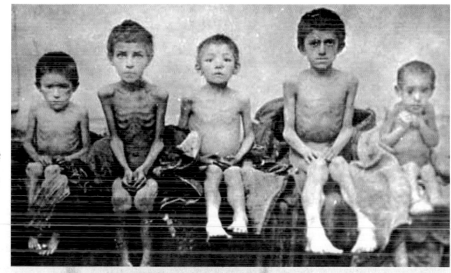

some support to the second, but only if the country has some place to export its industrialized goods at competitive prices, which the Soviet Union did not.

Collectivization was ordered for nearly all Soviet farmers in the early 1930s. Since it was particularly severe and most brutally enforced in Ukraine, the consequences are known historically as the "Ukrainian Famine" or the *Holodomor*. A land of fecund black earth, Ukraine was long the breadbasket of the Russian Empire. Through the winter of 1932–1933 and into the spring, the famine killed an estimated five million Ukrainians out of a rural population of twenty to twenty-five million. In the early stages, peasants ate their farm animals, then the dogs and cats, and then dug acorns buried by snow or collected horse droppings for the undigested grains they contained. By March and April of 1933 they were subsisting on mice, rats, sparrows, ants, earthworms, and snails.

In his definitive history of the famine, *Harvest of Sorrow* (1986), historian Robert Conquest describes it in its full horror. There were food riots by those who still had the strength to riot. Tens of thousands of other gaunt, ragged, wild-eyed humans roamed country roads and urban streets or huddled around train stations begging for scraps. Suicide, usually by hanging, was endemic. Maddened by hunger, people cut up and cooked corpses or killed and devoured their

The price of ruining a media dream

For breaking the story of the Soviet famine Malcolm Muggeridge was blackballed, while the New York Times man who hushed it up was awarded a Pulitzer Prize

In the fall of 1932, Malcolm Muggeridge arrived in Moscow as correspondent for the *Manchester Guardian*, a venerable daily renowned for championing "progressive gradualism." At age twenty-nine he had a solid Socialist pedigree: father an early Labor Party MP, wife the niece of Fabian crusader Beatrice Webb, himself deeply enamored like most young journalists with the perceived dynamism of the Soviet experiment. Less than a year later, he would abandon Marxism and Moscow for good, having uncovered one of the greatest crimes of the twentieth century. His reward for doing so, however, was to be blackballed by most of his profession.

Muggeridge attributed his discovery to sheer boredom, the endless parades of foreign journalists to various "show projects" of the workers' paradise, all paradees obediently regurgitating the Soviet line. Something besides boredom bothered him—how hungry and tired ordinary Muscovites looked. Then there were the rumors of famine in the countryside. Could these be true? One night, a man from the North Caucasus approached him with a startling story. He said his people at home were not just hungry, they were starving, many of them to death.

In March, 1933, he resolved to check the story. But how? Journalists were forbidden to leave Moscow without a governmental escort. Unabashed, he went to the rail station and simply bought a ticket to Kiev, which allowed stopovers. No questions were asked. What he found in Ukraine and North Caucasus turned his disillusionment into raw outrage. He saw peasants

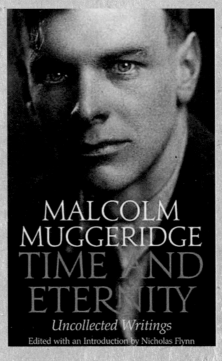

British journalist Malcolm Muggeridge as a young man pictured (left) on the cover of a book of collected essays entitled Time and Eternity, *and (right) the* New York Times' *Walter Duranty. Bribed by the Soviets, Duranty reported that there was no famine in the Ukraine. Muggeridge described the famine in lurid detail, and was for years ostracized by the British press for doing so. He called Duranty "the greatest liar of any journalist I've met in fifty years of journalism." History eventually wholly vindicated Muggeridge.*

dying of starvation while well-fed troops confiscated the grain they had produced. Villages were eerily silent, littered with animal carcasses. People were being loaded onto cattle trucks at gunpoint.

own children. Entire villages eventually were deserted except for the dead. Corpses littered the roads, and municipal authorities had them collected daily (some still faintly breathing) and dumped in mass graves.[1]

But the central and most horrifying aspect lies in the fact that it was man-made—designed and orchestrated by Joseph Stalin and his Communist deputies in Moscow. Historians now generally regard it as nothing less than an undeclared war on the Ukraine's recalcitrant peasantry. It was imposed on peasants in other Soviet regions as well, though with much less determined resolve and calamitous consequences.

The origins of the famine are ideological. After Stalin seized power in the mid 1920s, the Bolshevik leadership was divided, the Right arguing that the peasants must be encouraged to prosper, while the Left held that they should be exploited in favor of the Socialist working class. At first, Stalin favored a prosperous peasantry, but peasant resistance to communism, particularly in Ukraine, soon moved him the other way—with a vengeance. (Conquest writes that Stalin cherished a bitter hatred for Ukrainians, though it has never been made clear why.)

Thus in 1928 under Stalin's First Five-Year Plan all farms in the grain-growing areas of Ukraine, North Caucasus, Siberia, and the Volga were to be expropriated by the government. The farmers were to be

1. A few conscience-stricken Communist officials left haunting personal accounts of the suffering caused by the Ukrainian famine. "The most terrifying sights were the little children with skeleton limbs dangling from balloon-like bellies," wrote one. "Starvation had wiped every trace of youth from their faces, turning them into tortured gargoyles. Everywhere we found men and women lying prone, their faces and bellies bloated, their eyes utterly expressionless." Another wrote: "I shall never forget 1932 as long as I live."

His dispatches were smuggled out of the country via the British embassy and published in the *Guardian*. "To say that there is a famine in some of the most fertile parts of Russia," he wrote, "is to say much less than the truth. There is not only famine but—in the case of the North Caucasus at least—a state of war, a military occupation." The catastrophe was real, he said, and it was man-made by the government.

Such a report, he knew, should have caused a sensation. But the *Guardian*, itself leaning leftward, printed his stories on its middle pages, severely edited. Why, he wondered, was this story being buried? Apparently it discredited too many confident assumptions about Soviet Russia—those of his own editors and certainly those of his fellow Moscow correspondents who regarded his revelations as actively evil. And for the latter, there was a ready explanation.

Holding court most nights of the week at the Hotel Metropol was the *New York Times'* reporter in Moscow, Walter Duranty. This wooden-legged ladies' man had been awarded the 1932 Pulitzer Prize for his coverage of Stalin's Five-Year Plan. He had a flair for grand, sweeping prose, heavily tilted to the government's credit. As to reports of mass starvation, these he airily dismissed. "You can't make an omelet without breaking eggs," he would reply with a wink. Muggeridge found Duranty both fascinating and repulsive. He was "the greatest liar of any journalist I've met in fifty years of journalism," he would later write. The alarming fact, he knew, was that hundreds of thousands would believe Duranty's lies, cherishing a view of Soviet life that was gravely flawed.

Aware that he would soon be deported, Muggeridge left Russia, quit the *Guardian*, settled in Switzerland, and wrote the novel *Winter in Moscow*, describing what he called "one of the most monstrous crimes in history, so terrible that people in the future will scarcely be able to believe it ever happened." Reaction from the press and leftist intelligentsia was hostile. Even his father publicly questioned his son's credibility. No one would hire him as a writer in any capacity. He felt himself an exile or fugitive living abroad or in disgrace.

Meanwhile, Duranty's career soared to its zenith in 1933. Joseph Stalin gratefully acknowledged Duranty's role in establishing U.S.-Soviet diplomatic relations. At a gala in honor of the agreement, he received a standing ovation from New York's elite. Nevertheless, cracks were appearing in his facade. After touring famine-ravaged areas, he denied the famine existed, and extolled the Soviet "accomplishment." By 1940, the *Times* finally realized that their Moscow correspondent had been in the employ of the Soviet secret police, who for years had provided him with money, luxurious living, and women. The *Times* fired him, and Duranty declined into obscurity and impoverishment until his death in Florida in 1957. The *Times* has never apologized for its disservice to the Ukrainian people, though it did concede in 2003 that Duranty was responsible for "some of the worst reporting to appear in this newspaper."

For years, Muggeridge fared little better. In the 1940s he attempted suicide and the accidental death of a son became another blow. "He was haunted," writes his biographer Gregory Wolfe, "by the figure of Christ," but he steadfastly refused to join a church. Yet things were changing in his favor. With the fall of the Soviet Union, his horror stories of the Ukrainian famine were wholly vindicated as historical fact. He became a much respected journalist and television commentator.

Then, while hosting a BBC program entitled *A Life of Christ*, there was a breakthrough. Deeply moved after observing believers at the Church of the Nativity in Bethlehem, he reached a conclusion: "What is not open to question," he said, "is that today, two thousand years later, Christ is alive." From then until his death eight years later, he devoted all his work in both print and television to the Christian cause. Two in particular are noteworthy—*Jesus the Man Who Lives* (1975) and his biography of Mother Teresa of Calcutta, *Something Beautiful for God* (1971). In November, 1982, he and his wife were received into the Catholic Church.

And in one other way, he had long ago helped it immeasurably by teaching a valuable lesson: When something appears to have nearly unanimous consent in the media, this is no guarantee of infallibility. For the media majority, like those described by the media as "experts," can be very, very wrong indeed. ■

ousted from their homes and moved into collectives or communes, with all food production centralized under governmental direction. As the program was put into effect, the peasantry rebelled, most violently in Ukraine.

This was certainly predictable. By the time Bolshevism entered their history, Ukrainians had already endured centuries of domination by neighboring powers—Russia, Austria, Poland, and even at one point Lithuania. Nevertheless, Ukrainians always saw themselves as a distinct people with a unique history dating back some thousand years, when in the year 988 they became the first eastern Slavs to accept the Christian faith. The 1917 Russian Revolution and subsequent civil war initiated four years of chaos that enabled Ukrainians to twice declare their independence. But Russia crushed each revolt with floggings, torture, executions, and mass deportations to Siberia.

Famine first struck in 1921, partly due to bad weather, mostly to early bungled

attempts at collectivization. The then-Leninist government abruptly changed direction, permitting and even encouraging private ownership of land, and allowed farmers to freely sell surplus output, paying taxes on the profits. Agricultural production rose by forty percent in 1922, and the countryside began to recover, though this did little to erase either peasant hostility toward the state or state distrust of the peasantry.

With Stalin, however, there came a new determination to socialize, and in Ukraine this took the form of his *dekulakization* campaign. Peasants known as *kulaks*—meaning any relatively prosperous farmer who might own a few cows or a larger home than his neighbors—were rounded up by the thousands and shot or deported.

Meanwhile, production quotas were set in Moscow for the collectives. In effect, their entire output must be turned over to the state, except for enough to feed the collective and to seed the fields next spring. Scores of small-scale rebellions erupted, and Soviet food production precipitately declined. Moscow responded by increasing the quotas. By 1932 these proved impossible to meet, and the order went out to confiscate the entire output. It would be shipped to other parts of the Soviet Union, Moscow decreed, or sold abroad to finance Stalin's industrialization projects.

Things went wrong from the start. The bureaucratic estimates of possible production levels proved ludicrously optimistic. Transportation problems saw tens of thousands of tons of grain stored in granaries in Ukraine, and when these were full the residue was heaped in rotting piles by railway sidings, protected from the desperate populace by guards under shoot-to-kill orders. Russian novelist Boris Pasternak visited some newly collectivized regions to gather material for a book. "There was such inhuman, unimaginable misery," Pasternak

A starving girl is photographed in the Ukrainian city of Kharkov in 1934. By now families were exhuming dead children to supplement their diets while excess grain lay in storage, kept from them by armed guards.

recalls, "such a terrible disaster, that it began to seem almost abstract... I fell ill. For an entire year I could not write."

The collectivization process, writes historian Andrea Graziosi (*Hunger by Design: The Great Ukrainian Famine and Its Soviet Context*, 2009) was so ruthless and vicious that it actually amounted to "generalized plunder and ravage." To rid Russia's peasantry of the despised kulaks, vandal brigades were formed that might range from starry-eyed young Communist believers to criminal thugs. According to historian Graziosi, these brigades "drove the *dekulakized* naked into the streets, beat them, organized drinking parties in their homes, shot over their heads, forced them to dig their own graves, undressed women and searched them, stole valuables."[2] Further, in 1930 and 1931 alone, more than 1.8 million people were forcibly deported from Ukraine.

Meanwhile the first great wave of collectivization had begun in February 1930, stripping some eight million families of their lands and putting them to work on communal farms. Precisely 13,754 peasant protests are recorded across the Soviet Union, ten times more than the previous year, nearly a third of them in Ukraine. Recurrent crackdowns failed to suppress the unrest through 1931.

Opting for total war, in 1932 Moscow issued decrees that local officials were ordered to carry out, using whatever force was necessary. Grain produced on collective farms was declared state property. None was to be given the workers until production quotas were met, and these were set at impossible levels. The theft of two sheaves of corn, for instance, carried a death sentence. Internal passports were introduced to control the movement of the peasants, and prevent them seeking relief elsewhere.[3]

Towers were erected for surveillance over workers in the fields, while zealous activists searched their huts for hidden grain, taking every scrap of food they could find and any "surplus" clothing. They also dug up graves, on the pretext that grain might be interred with the dead, and left the corpses lying unburied. The dead and the dying were carted together to mass graves, for the sake of efficiency. In Ukraine, local Communists who argued with Moscow's demands were accused of sabotage or other crimes, purged, and replaced with Russians.

On the other hand, cooperative party officials at the local level received ample rations and townsfolk also had food, albeit basic and limited. As for the dining halls of

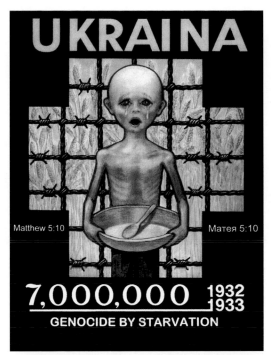

UKRAINA

Matthew 5:10 Матея 5:10

7,000,000 1932–1933

GENOCIDE BY STARVATION

district officials, these are said to have been veritable cornucopias of abundance and even luxury, carefully guarded by armed militias. According to an eyewitness report, the privileged elite at one such facility had their choice of "white bread, meat, poultry, canned fruit and delicacies, wines and sweets" and all at very low prices.

By the end of May 1933, having won the war with the peasants, Moscow began to release foodstuffs that might restore survivors to some semblance of health. After all, there was another crop to be sown and future quotas to be met, even if the workers could barely stand and eighty percent of the livestock had perished. The war on the countryside left behind a defeated and demoralized peasantry. It created a generation of scarred and traumatized children who would know better than to question the wisdom or dictates of the party. Not least, it created a cadre of loyal Communist officials who had so thoroughly stifled their consciences that they were henceforth prepared to employ brutality and terror as routine administrative tools. It was small wonder, therefore, that when the Nazi invasion began in 1941, the Germans were initially welcomed by many Ukrainians as deliverers.

Stalinist Muscovites could count yet another credit in regard to the 1932–1933 Ukrainian famine, namely their claim that it never happened. Any such reports were entirely fictitious, they insisted—the work of biased journalists and western propagandists. And for nearly half a century, much of the world believed them. ∎

2. Historian Robert Conquest observes that the local division of the secret police was given a quota of kulaks to be removed. It then decided which kulaks were to be shot and which imprisoned. Soon, however, the task became too large for the police to handle. Local party activists were mobilized to assist in the deportations. However, many of those charged with carrying out the confiscation of grain and meat from the peasants found themselves unable to do so, quietly smuggling food into the villages. "Buskyr brigades," little more than thugs, were then assigned to collect the grain, usually by beating people up. Some, in addition to taking food, commandeered clothing, icons, painted carpets, samovars, and metal kitchen utensils.

3. Nadezha Alliluyeva, Stalin's second wife, is said to have heard reports of famine and terror in the countryside, of bands of starving orphans begging for bread, and people arrested for selling corpses. She informed Stalin, but he dismissed the stories as "Trotskyite rumors." According to some historians, she and Stalin had a public quarrel over this at a dinner party on November 5, 1932. Alliluyeva was later found dead in her apartment with a revolver at her side, an apparent suicide, though some believe Stalin himself pulled the trigger.

Half a million troops belonging to the SA (Sturmabteilung or Stormtroopers), the SS (Schutzstaffel or protection service), and the SD (Sicherheitsdienst or intelligence service) gather at the great park in Nuremberg for the annual Nazi rally in November 1935. Choreographed by master propagandist Dr. Joseph Goebbels, these shows of military strength and German rebirth were part of the mass mobilization effort that helped transform Adolf Hitler's National Socialist Party from a motley group of eccentrics and thugs in the mid-1920s, to the most powerful dictatorship Germany had ever seen.

CHAPTER 6

Exhausted by the war, wrecked by the peace, the Germans go Nazi

With inflation running wild and their savings lost,
they reject the Weimar democracy, blame the Jews,
and let a thug-enforced ideology take absolute power

In the hours following the armistice that ended the First World War on November 11, 1918, a twenty-nine-year-old Austrian-born corporal with a toothbrush mustache and a feverish belief in his own destiny was recovering from a British mustard gas attack in a German field hospital. Adolf Hitler had been a dispatch runner in a Bavarian regiment of the German army on the western front, had been wounded twice, and had received two Iron Crosses for valor. Now he was hearing that his kaiser had abdicated and Germany's new leaders had agreed to humiliating terms of surrender in French Marshal Ferdinand Foch's railway carriage in Compiègne. "And so," said Corporal Hitler, "it has all been in vain."

The remaining twenty-seven years of Hitler's remarkable career would be spent proving that Germany's 1914–1918 war of aggression had not been in vain. In doing so he would return his adopted country to the height of its power as an economic and military force and make himself the most powerful leader in the history of the German-speaking peoples. But in achieving this, Hitler and his National Socialist (Nazi) Party would stamp out democracy, subjugate Christianity, and instigate a brutal, racially prideful brand of German exceptionalism that was to exterminate millions of Jews and others whom the Nazis and a sizable portion of Germany's sixty-six million citizens considered contaminants to the purity of the superior Germanic race. In the end, he would bring down upon Germany massive destruction inflicted on all its major cities by Allied powers whom he had forced into a second and disastrous European war.

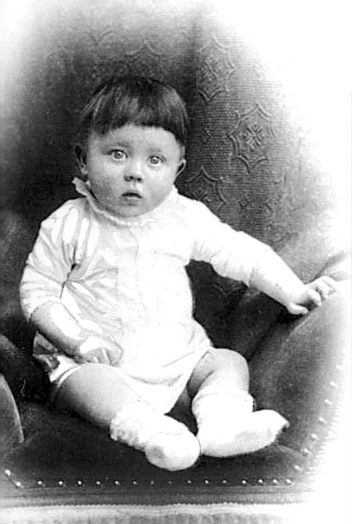

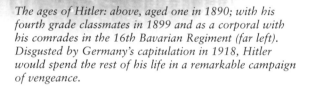

The ages of Hitler: above, aged one in 1890; with his fourth grade classmates in 1899 and as a corporal with his comrades in the 16th Bavarian Regiment (far left). Disgusted by Germany's capitulation in 1918, Hitler would spend the rest of his life in a remarkable campaign of vengeance.

1. In 1919 Kaiser William, exiled in Holland, described his enforced abdication as the "deepest, most disgusting shame ever perpetrated by a person in history, the Germans have done to themselves...egged on and misled by the tribe of Judah... Let no German ever forget this, nor rest until these parasites have been destroyed and exterminated from German soil!"

He expressed these views in a letter to a German general. The Jews were a "nuisance that humanity must get rid of some way or other," he wrote. "I believe the best would be gas!"

This was the first mention of the extermination method to be used in the Nazi death camps. Hitler himself only once mentions actually killing Jews. In *Mein Kampf*, he blames the Jews for stirring up the rebellion in 1919 and regrets they had not been forced to submit to poison gas.

In effect, Hitler resumed Germany's war for European domination that had ended so humiliatingly in Marshal Foch's railway carriage. And if the two million German lives lost in the First World War had been in vain, the more than six million lost in the Second World War died for worse; for they had died defending Nazi totalitarianism, one of the two great and godless evils to tear bloody scars through the twentieth century.

The decidedly anti-Christian roots of Nazism can be found in the nationalist and nihilistic writings of nineteenth-century German intellectuals like Friedrich Nietzsche, who believed the mercies of Christianity to be weakness; they can be found in the eugenicist social Darwinism of racial evangelists like the Anglo-German Houston Stewart Chamberlain and the Frenchman Arthur de Gobineau, who believed that Jews and other "inferior" races were tainting the purity of the Aryan race (see volume 11, page 244); and they can be found in Norse mythology dredged up in the mid-eighteen hundreds from Germany's pre-Christian past and celebrated in the operas of Richard Wagner (Hitler's favorite composer).

Such notions had been burbling in the streams of German consciousness for a half century, and rivulets of it had run through the higher levels of Kaiser William's Second Reich.[1] But it took a convergence of fateful events, and a master exploiter of these events, to turn it all into the fiery torrent that was National Socialism.

Born and raised a Catholic in Austria near Linz, Adolf Hitler had grown up a restless romantic, with few friends, an addiction to the Wild West novels of the German pulp writer Karl May, and an aptitude for drawing. Resisting the intent of his father, a customs official, that he become a civil servant, Hitler left home at seventeen for Vienna. There he had hoped to become a painter, and later an architect, but was twice refused entry into the Academy of Fine Arts for lack of talent. So he lived in flophouses, took odd jobs, sold hand-painted postcards, and read those aforementioned authors whose call for a strong, Jew-free (*Judenfrei*), pan-Germanic nation would become the Nazis' main platform.

Hatred of Jews, though far from unknown elsewhere, proliferated in Germany and Austria, where the Jewish minority (about one percent of the population in Germany, three and a half percent in Austria) had achieved disproportionate representation in the arts, professions, and financial sphere, and tended to be blamed for every setback or threat to the nation. In his autobiography *Mein Kampf* (*My Struggle*), the bible of the Nazi movement published in 1925, Hitler explained the genesis of his anti-Semitism during his time in Vienna, a cosmopolitan city with a substantial Jewish population:

> Wherever I went, I began to see Jews, and the more I saw, the more sharply they became distinguished in my eyes from the rest of humanity... Was there any form of filth or profligacy, particularly in cultural life, without at least one Jew involved in it?... I didn't know what I was more amazed at: the agility of their tongues or their virtuosity at lying. Gradually I began to hate them.

As a boy, Hitler, by one account, had wanted to become a monk, but he abandoned his faith during his days of disappointment in Vienna. Henceforth, he denigrated Christianity in private, referring to it as the "satanic superstition," whose clergy were solely interested in "raking in the money" and "befuddling the minds of the gullible." In one of his dinnertime monologues (recorded by his personal secretary Martin Bormann), Hitler said, "The heaviest blow that ever struck humanity was the coming of Christianity. Bolshevism is Christianity's illegitimate child. Both are inventions of the Jew."

Freikorps troops assemble in the northern German town of Wismar in 1920 during the time of the Kapp Putsch, an attempt to topple the Weimar government, unsuccessful because this paramilitary corps withdrew its support. Soon afterward, however, members of the Freikorps, many of them First World War veterans unhappy with its outcome, would join Hitler and become the core of National Socialism.

Various factors facilitated the rise of Hitler and National Socialism, including a shambled economy with runaway inflation and degeneracy among the urban population. In this 1920s Berlin club, one of one hundred sixty homosexual and transsexual cabarets in the city, the only woman in the picture is seated at the extreme left. Inset, a fifty-million mark note in 1923. At the time it would have taken more than three hundred such notes to buy one American dollar.

2. Martin Luther was originally sympathetic to Jews, believing their rejection of Christianity to be a result of Catholic theological error. He grew vehemently anti-Semitic in the last nine years of his life, however, following his failure to bring Jews to the Protestant faith. In his sixty-five-thousand-word treatise, *On Jews and Their Lies*, he portrayed Jews as "full of the devil's feces...which they wallow in like swine," and called on Christians to burn down synagogues and Jewish homes, confiscate Jewish writings, and put the Jewish population to work as slave labor. The treatise was prominently displayed at Nazi rallies in the 1930s, was regularly cited in the party newspaper *Der Stürmer* (*The Attacker*), and its recommendations became one basis for the Nazi persecution.

Politically, however, Hitler admired the Catholic Church for its longevity, its reach, and its tight control over its followers. During the rise of Nazism, he recognized the usefulness of the conservative and nationalistic elements in both the Catholic minority and the Protestants, whose church was the state church of Germany. He never did publicly renounce his Catholicism, and in speeches he often invoked God and "Providence" and paid dutiful homage to Martin Luther, whose anti-Semitic passages proved a propagandist windfall to the party.[2]

Hitler's rise to power occurred during the fourteen-year span of the Weimar Republic, which provided him and his followers with both a foil and a political path to power. Germany's capitulation in signing the armistice in November 1918, and the Versailles Treaty the following year, had occurred partly because of the threat of a Communist coup. The leaders of the Weimar government had made an alliance with the army to suppress the Communists, and the army created the *Freikorps*, a citizens' militia comprised mostly of Great War soldiers who excelled at their task. They murdered the two principal Communists, Rosa Luxemburg and Karl Liebknecht, and they crushed the brief rule of a Communist council in Munich in 1919, lynching many of the would-be commissars.

It was such restless ex-soldiers, bitter over the German defeat and contemptuous of the flaccid liberal democracies that tried to shape the peace, who formed the core of the oncoming totalitarian movement. In particular, they were enraged at the Treaty of Versailles, which effectually held Germany fully responsible for the war, took away her overseas colonies, reduced her European territory by more than thirteen percent, separated from Germany the industrial region of the Saar, ceded to France resource rich Alsace and Lorraine, confined her army to one hundred thousand men, forbade her to have any U-boats, restricted her new naval construction to ten-thousand-ton coastal defense ships, and denied her any air force at all. Finally, it required Germany to make reparation payments to France and England totaling thirty-three billion dollars (close to half a trillion in 2012 dollars).

The Weimar Republic soon proved incapable of governing this emasculated land. Unable to achieve a majority in the Reichstag, the Social Democrats ruled through the twenties as a "grand coalition" with the slightly rightist Catholic Center Party (the *Zentrum*), the liberal German Democratic Party, and an assortment of smaller groups of the right and left. By 1923, the economy was in a shambles. When the government defaulted on its reparation payments, France occupied the industrial Ruhr region unopposed, a further humiliation. Hyperinflation ran rampant. Where in 1921 it had taken four German marks to buy one U.S. dollar, by late 1923 it took seventeen billion. Workers' salaries were next to useless and savings were rendered worthless.

A mood of ennui and abandon set in. Nihilistic and absurdist art, pseudo-religious cultism, pornography and sexual abnormality blossomed in the cities, especially in Berlin. The capital alone accommodated one hundred and sixty homosex-

A mood of ennui and abandon set in; nihilistic and absurdist art, pseudo-cultism, sexual abnormality blossomed; the 'new woman' made her debut.

ual and transsexual cabarets during the mid-1920s, nudism became a popular pastime, and the "new woman"—short-haired, short-skirted, and sexually liberated—made her debut on the streets of the big cities. However, by the mid decade, a conservative backlash began to develop, and churches and nationalistic groups began speaking out against the moral degeneration of youth, calling for an end to the *Schmutz und Schund* (filth and trash). The result was the election of the rapidly ossifying Paul von Hindenburg, the Great War general, to the presidency in 1925. However, for all his monarchist sympathies and bellicose speechifying about the fatherland, Hindenburg agreed to abide by the Weimar constitution.

By 1923 Hitler was living in Munich and was head of the National Socialist German Workers Party, Nazi for short, founded in 1919 out of the extreme right racist *völkisch* German nationalist movement and the Freikorps. In three years its membership rose from a few hundred to fifty-five thousand, thanks largely to Hitler's oratory, which he had honed in front of the mirror and was soon delivering to crowds as large as six thousand in auditoriums and beer halls around Bavaria. Beginning in low, hesitant tones, and slowly building into an operatic crescendo, blue eyes bulging, hands carving and chopping the air, Hitler could mesmerize an audience. His speeches excoriated Jews and Marxists, whom he blamed for the "shame" of the Versailles Treaty, the degeneracy of the nation under the Weimar government, and the emasculation of Germany as a world power. His message of German rebirth appealed especially to the young, whose prospects under the Weimar Republic appeared dim.

By 1923, the Nazis were well established in Bavaria. They had adopted the swastika emblem and were publishing their own newspaper, the *Völkischer Beobachter*, (*People's Observer*).[3] Hitler had the support of the respected former Great War general Erich Ludendorff, and gathered around him the core of lieutenants who would accompany him through his rise and fall. These included the spectacled agronomist Heinrich Himmler, later to mastermind the extermination campaign against the Jews;

3. The swastika is an ancient and ubiquitous symbol occurring in artifacts and archaeological sites including those of the Persians, Greeks, Hindus, Vikings, North American Indians, and Medieval Christians. Its popularity in Germany surged in the 1870s following the excavation of ancient Troy by the German millionaire and amateur archaeologist Heinrich Schliemann, who discovered the symbol and associated it with the migrations of the Proto-Indo-Europeans who, according to dubious Nazi Aryan racial theory, were the ancestors of the superior Nordic races. Hitler used a black swastika on a white circle in a red field when he drew the Nazi flag in 1920. "A symbol it really is!" he enthused in *Mein Kampf*. "In red we see the social idea of the movement, in white the nationalist idea, in the swastika the mission of the struggle for the victory of the Aryan man."

Former General Erich von Ludendorff speaks to a crowd of would-be Nazi revolutionaries in Munich on the morning of November 9, 1923. The so-called Beer Hall Putsch, organized by Hitler the night before in the Bürgerbräukeller *(a beer hall), failed when police fired on the Nazi marchers, dispersing them, and forcing Hitler to change tactics.*

4. Hitler was not one of those quaffing beer. During his years in Vienna he had sworn off alcohol, having got drunk once and not liked it. He also became a vegetarian, and forbade smoking in his presence. Hitler showed little interest in women for the first four decades of his life. Although some of his detractors, pointing to effeminacy in his mannerisms, suggested he might be homosexual, there is no evidence of this. When he was thirty-eight he became infatuated with his pretty blonde twenty-year-old niece (through a half sister) Geli Raubal, who lived with him in Munich for two years until her suicide in 1931. Two years later Eva Braun, a flighty twenty-one-year-old photographer, became his mistress and, for forty hours before their mutual suicides in 1945, his wife. But Hitler confided to a friend that Geli was the only woman he had ever loved.

5. Hitler drew much of his "evidence" of a Jewish conspiracy from *The Protocols of the Elders of Zion*, published in 1903 in Russia and widely translated and distributed around the world in the first decades of the century. The *Protocols* are the supposed account of a late nineteenth-century meeting of Jewish leaders at which they discussed how to achieve world hegemony by subverting the morals of Gentiles, and gaining control of the world's press and international finance. Once in power, the Nazis forced schools to use it as a textbook, even though the book had been conclusively proven a forgery by the *Times* of London in 1921.

and Hermann Göring, the jolly and corpulent First World War flying ace, who would head the *Luftwaffe* (air force) and become Hitler's second-in-command. Ernst Röhm, the scar-faced former captain in the German army, was the homosexual commander of the *Sturmabteilung* (SA or Stormtroopers), a paramilitary group of fifteen thousand thugs, uniformed in brown army-surplus shirts from the Great War; he would be of immense assistance in Hitler's rise.

On November 8, 1923, Hitler attempted a coup. Backed by the SA and supported by Ludendorff, Hitler interrupted a speech being given by a Bavarian leader at the Bürgerbräukeller, one of Munich's capacious taverns, filled with three thousand stein-thumping Bavarians.[4] Forcing at pistol point the acquiescence of the Bavarian leader for the takeover of government, he led a march on the Bavarian War Ministry the next day. But the Bavarian police met the Nazi rabble in the street and a brief fire fight ensued. Sixteen Nazi "martyrs" were created before the marchers dispersed. Hitler was given a five-year sentence, and pardoned after serving twelve months. His trial, however, had provided his movement with international publicity, and while in jail he dictated *Mein Kampf.*

The wordy tome, which became a best seller in Germany, described Hitler's hatred for Jews and went into great and dubious detail about the rise of "International Jewry" and its insidious conspiracy to gain world domination.[5] Hitler was also quite forthright about his plans for furthering Germany's "historic destiny" once he gained power: how he would dispense with the corrupt parliamentary system, defy the terms of Versailles, rearm the country, ally with Britain and Italy, annex Austria and the Germanic regions of Czechoslovakia and Poland, and then move on the Soviet Union, creating a vast *Lebensraum* (living space) for an Aryan German *Volk*, free of the "verminous" Jewish (and Slavic) races. (Whether Hitler then, or indeed ever, intended the actual extermination of Jews is something historians have argued about since.)

Ostensibly the putsch had made the Nazis ridiculous to respectable German society. The party was banned in Bavaria and all but disappeared during Hitler's incarceration. But driven by a single-minded belief in his "destiny," Hitler regrouped after his release, and changed his strategy to one of achieving power through constitutional means. As a result, the party's legal status was reinstated.

Hitler's followers now included Joseph Goebbels, a thin, dark, pockmarked and clubfooted intellectual from the Rhineland, with a doctorate in history and literature and a genius for promotion. He became the Nazis' master of propaganda. Rabidly anti-Semitic, he had emerged from the "socialist" side of the National Socialist Party, whereby capitalism—seen as rife with Jews—would be abolished and the wealth of the aristocracy redistributed in a peoples' revolution. This position, also held by SA commander Röhm, appealed to the working classes and, along with the organizational efforts of left-wing Nazi Gregor Strasser, helped the spread of Nazism outside of Bavaria.

But Hitler, who was to obtain much financial support from capitalists like the Krupp steel and armaments manufacturer, suppressed what he called the "National Bolsheviks," and wrested complete control of the party for himself. He had a talk with Goebbels that cemented the latter's undying fidelity. "I love him..." Goebbels wrote in his diary after the meeting. "He has thought through everything. Such a sparkling mind can be my leader. I bow to the greater one, the political genius." Strasser, whose divergent views were to result in his elimination, called Goebbels "Satan in human form."

As the decade unfolded, the Nazi Party was transformed into a national organization. But it failed to win more than six percent of the vote or more than six seats in the 608-seat Reichstag. The economy improved, wrote journalist William Shirer in the *Chicago Tribune*, and the Weimar Republic "seemed to have found its feet."[6] However, it soon lost them as the U.S. stock market crashed in October 1929. Heavily dependent on American loans, Germany's economy crashed

6. The recovery of the Weimar Republic is widely laid to the success of Gustav Streseman, its foreign minister between 1924 and 1929, who renegotiated treaties with France, England, and the United States that enabled Germany to regain the occupied Ruhr region, join the League of Nations, prolong the terms of the reparation payments, and secure American loans with which to make the payments and repair the economy. He won the Nobel Peace Prize in 1926.

Below left, Hitler with some of his original lieutenants in 1927, including Heinrich Himmler (to the right of the banner), Herman Hess (to the right of Himmler) and Gregor Strasser (behind and to the right of Hitler). Strasser, part of the left-wing Nazi faction that sought a people's revolution and a redistribution of wealth, later fell victim to Hitler's 1934 purge, called the Night of the Long Knives. Right, a first edition copy of Hitler's memoir and manifesto, Mein Kampf, *and, above, the swastika flag and symbol devised by Hitler in 1920.*

with it. With the unemployed soon numbering more than six million, extreme solutions became more attractive. In the 1930 elections the Nazis polled eighteen percent of the vote, gained 107 seats in the Reichstag, and became a major party.

That same year, the Grand Coalition split, and Chancellor Heinrich Brüning, a conservative Center Party deputy, found it impossible to form a working majority. He had to rely on emergency decrees imposed by President von Hindenburg to roll back wages, tighten credit, and levy other unpopular austerity measures. Hitler soon saw in Hindenburg his ticket to power. In 1932 the old general replaced Chancellor Brüning with Franz von Papen, a colorful and aristocratic Center Party

Göring transformed a small department of the police force into the Geheime Staatspolizei, or Gestapo. It would become a primary agent of Nazi terror.

Field Marshal Paul von Hindenburg, the Great War commander elected president of the Reich in 1926. Although no fan of the man he disdainfully called "the Austrian corporal," it was Hindenburg who eventually acquiesced and made Hitler chancellor in 1933.

deputy who also failed to form a workable government. The elections in July brought the Nazis 230 seats, making them the largest party, but one without a majority in an increasingly chaotic parliament. The Reichstag was dissolved and another election held in November, with the Nazis actually losing thirty-four seats. But von Papen was forced to resign by a cabinet revolt engineered by General Kurt von Schleicher, who took his place. Schleicher attempted to neutralize the Nazis by dividing their ranks, and then offered to form a coalition with them.

He failed on both counts. Behind the scenes, von Papen, now a sworn enemy of Schleicher, joined Hitler in an intrigue with those close to Hindenburg to engineer a coalition of the Nazis and the leading right-wing German National People's Party, with Hitler as chancellor and von Papen as vice-chancellor. Although he'd never liked the "Austrian corporal," Hindenburg, eighty-five years old and verging on senility, was convinced by his friend von Papen that the Nazis could be managed. Hindenburg appointed Hitler chancellor on January 30, 1933. There were to be certain safeguards, including a limit of three Nazis in the cabinet, with the other eight being old-school conservatives, including von Papen, who believed they could control Hitler. "Within two months," von Papen confided haughtily to a friend, "we will have pushed Hitler so far into a corner that he will squeak." Von Papen was neither the first nor the last to underestimate the Austrian corporal.

As part of the deal, Hermann Göring was made interior minister of Prussia. As such he was head of the police in this largest and most important of federal states. Göring used his power to purge the Prussian government of non-Nazis and to transform a small department of the police force, which served as a political intelligence gathering service for all of Germany, into a secret state police called the *Geheime Staatspolizei* (Gestapo). It would soon become a primary agent of Nazi terror.

Heinrich Brüning

Reinhard Heydrich

Heinrich Himmler

Elsewhere, the Nazis were establishing control of the various provincial governments through their own Reich commissioners, who were appointed on the pretext of quelling "revolutions." These fake uprisings were staged by members of the SA and its increasingly powerful spin-off, the black-uniformed, racially pure *Schutzstaffel* (SS or Protection Squad) under the command of Heinrich Himmler, and his tall, blond, stone-hearted second-in-command Reinhard Heydrich.

But the Reichstag was still not under Nazi control, and thus Hitler convinced the cabinet to dissolve it, with an election called for March. During the campaign, a fire destroyed the Reichstag building, which might well have been set by the Nazis themselves.[7] But Hitler blamed the Communists, who during the Weimar years had been stronger in Germany than anywhere else outside of the Soviet Union, and held a hundred seats in the Reichstag. Goebbels mounted a skillful propaganda campaign portraying the act as a diabolical attempt to reduce Germany to anarchy, with Hitler posing as the "reasonable man" appealing for national unity at the polls. Hindenburg was persuaded to issue the Reichstag Fire Decree, under the emergency powers of the constitution, suspending various freedoms, including security of the citizen from house searches, phone taps, or summary arrest. This enabled the Nazis to eliminate the German Communist Party and, with the help of the SA, now numbering half a million men, arrest four thousand of its members.

The Nazis won 288 seats in the election, but still lacked a parliamentary majority and were forced to rule in a coalition with the rightist National Peoples group. To gain full control, Hitler's government brought forward the Enabling Act, which would give it full legislative powers for four years on the pretext of stabilizing the country. As a constitutional amendment, however, the act required a two-thirds majority to pass. Although the Communists were gone, the Social Democrats were expected to oppose the amendment.

7. Göring was able to blame the fire on a Communist plot because the Dutch Communist bricklayer Marinus van der Lubbe had been found in the burning building. However, a number of eminent historians claim van der Lubbe was a Nazi dupe. William L. Shirer in his definitive *The Rise and Fall of the Third Reich* (1959), writes of van der Lubbe as a "Dutch half-wit ...only had his shirt for tinder. The main fires, according to the testimony of experts at the trial, had been set with considerable quantities of chemicals and gasoline. It was obvious that one man could not have carried them into the building, nor would it have been possible for him to start so many fires in so many scattered places in so short a time." Nonetheless the supreme court at Leipzig, subservient to the Nazis, sent van der Lubbe to the guillotine.

The Reichstag building in flames on the night of February 27, 1933. Although the Nazis blamed the arson on the Communists and used it as a pretext to suspend civil liberties, it is suspected by some that they deliberately set the fire.

The Mussolini flop

By beatings, arson, vandalism, and assassination, Fascism takes power in Italy, but its armies are repeatedly defeated, and its leaders wind up hanged at a gas station

In a daring daytime raid in September 1943, twelve gliders carrying Nazi commandos crash-landed on a rocky slope near a remote mountain hotel north of Rome. The object of their mission could be seen at a second-story window: five feet five inches tall, barrel chested, massively lantern jawed, dark eyed, and pale of face. Storming the hotel, Otto Skorzeny's commandos found the deposed Italian dictator suitably grateful. "I always knew," declared Benito Mussolini, "that my friend Adolf Hitler would not let me down." With such a friend, however, the once undisputed leader of Italy now became an indisputably Nazi pawn.

He was not the man to relish a subordinate role. Born in 1883 in Predappio, Romagna, Italy, son of a socialist blacksmith and a Catholic school teacher, Mussolini became a scrappy free-thinker. He refused to attend Mass, and was expelled from his Catholic boarding school for knifing another student. After a brief teaching career, at nineteen he became an eloquent Socialist agitator and reporter in Switzerland, undeterred by arrest.

Returning to Italy two years later, he fell in love with Rachele Guidi, sixteen, daughter of his widowed father's mistress. A strong-willed blonde peasant girl whose mettle matched that of her arrogant and volatile lover, Rachele moved in with him in 1910, the year their daughter Edda was born—first of their five children. They married in 1915, and biographer Jasper Ridley (*Mussolini*, 1997) writes that although Rachele furiously resented Benito's many infidelities, the marriage was remarkably stable.[1]

With the First World War, Mussolini radically shifted his ideological stance. He resigned as editor of the Socialist paper *Avanti!* and was expelled from the party. Though many Socialists condemned the war as imperialist, he backed the Allies and enlisted in the army. Nearly six hundred thousand Italians would be killed, almost a million wounded, and Mussolini himself severely injured.

Postwar Italy, humiliated by its treatment at Versailles and wracked by political and economic chaos, proved amenable to Mussolini's thrusting rhetoric. In short, dramatic sentences, his right arm cleaving the air, he preached militaristic nationalism, authoritarian leadership, and contempt for socialism, liberalism, and unions. His newspaper, *Popolo d'Italia* (*The People of Italy*), in whose office he stockpiled guns and bombs, appealed to ex-servicemen, students, the politically malcontent, and the generally disenchanted. In 1919, some two hundred such supporters met in Milan to form his first *Fasci di combattimento* (fighting bands).

The Fascists, lacking authority, relied on brute force. Action squads known as Blackshirts, often backed by landowners and industrialists, attacked Socialists, Communists, Catholic unionists, and left-leaning local councils, with beatings, arson, vandalism, and assassination. The Socialist Party, fractured by the war debate, and the Liberals, immobilized by anti-Socialist animosity and ties to business, offered scant opposition.

Meanwhile the Vatican policy *"non expedit"* (it is not expedient), adopted in 1868 to protest Italy's seizure of the Papal States, had effectively banned Catholics from voting. In 1919, however, a gaunt Sicilian priest, Father Luigi Sturzo, founded the anti-Fascist Italian Popular Party (PPI) with Vatican permission. The PPI won 101 seats that November, the Socialists 156, and the Fascists none.

But the setback was temporary; by 1922, the Blackshirts had crushed all opposition. That fall, Mussolini organized the March on Rome, exhorting some twenty-five thousand Blackshirts to take the government by force, while he left for Milan to distance himself from the consequent violence. On October 29, with Rome surrounded by belligerent Fascists, King Victor Emmanuel III summoned him to form a government. At thirty-nine, Benito Mussolini became Italy's youngest prime minister.

When the Fascists swept the April 1924 elections, the fiery lawyer and Socialist leader Giacomo Matteotti accused them of fraud and intimidation. His body was found some weeks later. Leading Fascists were implicated in the murder and Mussolini himself brazenly claimed responsibility. He further proceeded to ignore the constitution, censor the press, form a secret police, and outlaw Freemasonry, unions, and political

The dead Benito Mussolini and his mistress Clara Petacci are displayed outside an Esso gas station in Milan following their capture near Lake Como and summary execution by Communist partisans in April 1945. Their bodies were shot at by townsfolk, hung upside down on meat hooks, then stoned.

parties. More positively, he built infrastructure and subsidized grain production. By November 1926, Italy was a Fascist dictatorship, and Mussolini was *Il Duce*—The Leader.

He sought conciliation with the Catholic Church after the Vatican vetoed a proposed coalition between the PPI and the Socialists, the only possible political alliance that might challenge the Fascists. Father Sturzo of the PPI had resigned and was exiled in 1924, the same year the church endorsed the pro-Fascist party, the Union Nationale. With the 1929 Lateran Treaty, Mussolini recognized Vatican City as an autonomous state, and compensated the Vatican for its lost papal lands. Pope Pius XI, naturally grateful, called him "a man sent by providence."

However, Pius was to drastically revise his opinion, as would other western leaders who had lauded Mussolini for leading, as Winston Churchill put it, a "triumphal struggle against the bestial appetites and passions of Leninism." But his 1935 invasion of Ethiopia became an eight-month terror, featuring massacres and poison gas, and making Italy a pariah among most western nations. Victory in Ethiopia brought Mussolini domestic popularity, however, and support from Germany's bellicose Third Reich. His Ethiopian venture had still wider implications. The failure of the League of Nations to respond effectively to the invasion saw the emperor Haile Selassie challenge the conscience of the world, and led to the effective end of the League.

Although Mussolini and many Fascists mistrusted the Nazis, Germany and Italy drew inexorably together in a "Rome-Berlin axis" that supported Francisco Franco in the 1936 Spanish Civil War (see page 112). When Germany annexed Austria in 1938, Mussolini, who had hoped to dominate Austria himself—and not forewarned—nonetheless publicly endorsed the occupation. Not previously notable for anti-Semitism, he now banned Jews from the army, government, teaching or attending school, entering Italy, or marrying "Aryans." This brought sharp rebuke from the pope, as did Il Duce's efforts to supplant the lay association, Catholic Action, with Fascist youth groups.

Italy and Germany formed a military alliance in 1939 known as the Pact of Steel, but when Germany invaded Poland that September without Mussolini's foreknowledge, he reluctantly held back. However, in June 1940, with France falling, he declared war on the Allies, despite the vehement objections of his son-in-law Galeazzo Ciano, the foreign minister.

Italy's wartime role would prove what Churchill would call "a flop." In 1940 Mussolini's attempted invasion of Greece proved so disastrous that German troops had to be sent to rescue the invaders. So ill-equipped were Italy's soldiers, so low their morale, and so incompetent their generals, that within three years the Italians had lost in every theater they entered, with German troops repeatedly called in to replace them.

Hitler and Mussolini walk before saluting troops during the German leader's visit to Venice in 1934. Mussolini had thought Hitler an upstart and a buffoon in the early days of Nazi rule, an attitude that would soon change with Germany's rapid rise to European domination. By the time of the German-Italian Pact of Steel during the Second World War, Mussolini and his poorly performing army had become the buffoons.

When the Allies landed on Sicily in July 1943, the Fascist Grand Council, including Ciano, had Il Duce imprisoned in the remote mountain hotel. After Skorzeny rescued him, the Germans installed Mussolini as puppet leader of the Italian Social Republic, headquartered near Lake Garda, where he proceeded to execute those who had ousted him. Ciano was tied to a chair and shot, despite the urgent pleas of his wife, Mussolini's daughter Edda—who refused to see her father again.

The new Italian government of Marshal Pietro Badoglio surrendered to the Allies in September 1944. The Germans took over northern and central Italy, occupied Rome, and deported nearly nine thousand Italian Jews to extermination camps. The entire country became a grimly chaotic war zone with Italian partisans battling Germans and Fascists as the Allies fought their way north. Mussolini, rarely seen, ordered all captured partisans shot.

In April 1945, with defeat clearly imminent, he and what was left of his government headed for Switzerland, with Il Duce in a German uniform, and were captured by Italian partisans. His mistress of nine years, Clara Petacci, 28, refused to desert him; next day, the partisans shot them both.[2] As a final indignity, their bullet-riddled bodies, along with those of twelve other executed Fascists, were hung upside down at a gas station in a public square in Milan. ∎

1. An energetic womanizer, Mussolini fathered a son in 1914, Benito Albino, with one of his mistresses, Ida Dalser. After Ida sued Il Duce for alimony in the 1920s, she reportedly was confined in various mental hospitals and died in 1937 at age fifty-seven. According to historian Jasper Ridley, allegations that Fascists murdered her and her grown son remain unproven. Friends of Benito Albino claim he joined the navy and was lost at sea.

2. Rachele Mussolini, her son Romano, and her daughter Anna Maria, were arrested in Como by partisans and interned for several months. Rachele died in 1979; Romano, who became a jazz pianist, died in 2006, and Anna Maria died in 1968.

Formerly a Calvinist, Gerlich converted to Catholicism after reporting on a village stigmatic called Therese Neumann, about whom he wrote a book refuting her medical detractors. Fired as the editor of the *Münchner Neuesten Nachrichten* (*Munich's Latest News*) for over-imbibing wine in the office, Gerlich was made editor of a new Catholic newspaper *Der gerade Weg*, where his assaults on the Nazis mounted: homosexual infiltration of top Nazi ranks, and headlines such as "Lock up the Führer" and "Has Hitler got Mongol blood?" In March 1933, Gerlich was arrested by the SA, beaten, imprisoned in Dachau, and soon murdered.

Hitler with Herman Göring (left) and Ernst Röhm (center) in 1931. Three years later Göring was Hitler's most powerful and trusted henchman; Röhm, whose Stormtroopers were eclipsing the German army in number and power, was shot.

Thus the approval of the Center Party, the third largest in the house, was seen as crucial by Hitler. Monsignor Ludwig Kaas, Center leader, must be persuaded to have his party vote with the Nazis.

Kaas, a priest and a professor, as well as a deputy, was a friend and adviser to Cardinal Eugenio Pacelli, the former papal nuncio to Germany and future Pope Pius XII (see sidebar, page 142). Kaas had helped conclude the successful Vatican concordat with Prussia in 1929, and had been working with Pacelli, who had since returned to Rome as the cardinal secretary of state for Pope Pius XI, on the formulation of a concordat with the German Reich as a whole—a concordat whose passage now depended on the Nazis. Thus Kaas was in a difficult position. On the one hand, he and most of his Center colleagues were wholly aware of what opposition to the Nazis might bring, having seen the random brutalities meted out to opponents by the SA. The Center Party—and the Vatican—were also anxious to preserve a common front against communism. Moreover, since the Nazis were likely to achieve an authoritarian state, there would seem little future for an opposition party.

On the other hand, a growing number of Catholic bishops and writers opposed Nazi policy on race and religion. Fritz Gerlich, the acerbic editor of the Catholic newspaper *Der gerade Weg* (*The Straight Path*), had written "National Socialism means: Enmity with neighboring nations, tyranny internally, civil war, world war, lies, hatred, fratricide and boundless want," and spoken of Hitler's "unconditional propensity to evil."[8] Bishops in several provinces had prohibited Catholics from joining the Nazi Party, and denied Nazis the sacraments. Ludwig Maria Hugo, bishop of the venerable diocese of Mainz, declared that Nazism and Catholicism were simply irreconcilable. "The Christian moral law is founded on love of our neighbor," he said. "National Socialist writers do not accept this commandment in the sense taught by Christ; they preach too much respect for the Germanic race and too little respect for foreign races."

Chief among the writers Hugo referred to was Alfred Rosenberg, the party's major racial theorist and editor of the *Völkischer Beobachter*. Three years earlier he had produced *The Myth of the Twentieth Century*, a book second only to *Mein Kampf* in its influence on Nazi ideology. In it, Rosenberg expounded on the superiority of the Nordic races, arguing that God had chosen them to rule. Like Houston Stewart Chamberlain and other *völkisch* writers before him, he declared that Jesus was not a Jew but a member of an isolated Nordic tribe, and that Christianity had been an "Aryan" religion until corrupted by the followers of Paul of Tarsus. He dismissed Catholicism and Protestantism as "negative" Christianity, and proposed a new, race-based version of the faith devoid of any

Nazi ideologue, author, and publisher Alfred Rosenberg is shown seated in the bar at the Berlin Sportspalast in 1932 with propagandist Joseph Goebbels whispering in his ear. The official Nazi newspaper Völkischer Beobachter (People's Observer, below), edited by Rosenberg, on the "historic day"—January 31, 1933—that Hitler became chancellor. The journal Der gerade Weg (The Straight Path, below right), edited by the Catholic subversive Fritz Gerlich (top right), publishes one of its anti-Nazi spoofs, the main headline reading "Does Hitler have Mongol blood?" Gerlich was later disposed of at Dachau.

Judaic "contamination" or such "enfeebling" concepts as original sin or the brotherhood of man.

Such histrionics would in time help inspire the "German Christian Church," the short-lived Nazi institution designed to replace the old German Evangelical Church to which two-thirds of the population at least nominally belonged. A union of Lutherans and Calvinists, it had been the state church of Germany since the early 1800s. In the new Nazi church, pictures of Hitler replaced crucifixes and Mein Kampf replaced the Bible. But for the time being, Hitler was portraying himself as a good, old-fashioned German Christian, having long believed that the support of the churches was a crucial component of his plans for total domination. Indeed many practicing Christians, including Catholics, had already been drawn to Nazism by its promises of political stability, national renewal, and the suppression of communism.

Among the prominent Protestant clergy favorable to Hitler's ascension was the Reverend Martin Niemöller, a much-decorated First World War submarine commander, best-selling author of From U-Boat to Pulpit, and pastor of the Jesus Christus Kirche in the affluent Berlin suburb of Dahlen. Niemöller enthusiastically spoke out for the Nazi Party, believing Hitler to be a savior from the "years of darkness" of the Weimar Republic. Nazism, he wrote, offered "a renewal movement based on a Christian moral foundation." He would very soon see things differently, however.[9]

Meanwhile, Kaas and his colleagues in the Center Party were coming around. Hitler, after all, had distanced himself from the more extreme elements of his party, and had stated that Rosenberg's religious ideas would not be put into practice. In the lead-up to the Enabling Act vote, he had promised, through Vice

9. Within a year after his declared support for Nazis, Niemöller began opposing them, joining with theologians Karl Barth and Dietrich Bonhoeffer to establish the Confessing Church, distanced from the state church that generally supported the government. He also vigorously protested Nazi treatment of the Jews. He was arrested in 1937 and spent eight years in Sachsenhausen and Dachau concentration camps. After the war he served a term as president of the World Council of Churches. Niemöller became famous for penning the self-condemnatory maxim: "First they came for the Communists, and I didn't speak out because I wasn't a Communist. Then they came for the trade unionists, and I didn't speak out because I wasn't a trade unionist. Then they came for the Jews, and I didn't speak out because I wasn't a Jew. Then they came for me, and there was no one left to speak out for me."

In this detail from the official cabinet photograph of June 1932, Franz von Papen is seated to the left, with rival General Kurt von Schleicher standing behind him. Seated to the right is Foreign Minister Konstantin Neurath, who would play a major part in advancing Nazi policy to undermine the Versailles Treaty before he was replaced by the more compliant Joachim von Ribbentrop in 1938.

Chancellor von Papen, to respect the church's liberty; its involvement in the fields of culture, schools, and education; the concordats already signed by German states; and the continued existence of the Center Party itself. Hitler further vowed that a letter reiterating these promises was being drafted. On the assurance of this letter all thirty-one Center members voted for the Enabling Act on March 24, 1933. Only the Social Democrats voted against the bill—despite the intimidating presence of SA thugs inside the opera house that housed the Reichstag after the fire. The act passed easily by a vote of 441 to 94, thus extinguishing democracy in Germany for the next twelve years. At forty-three, Hitler was the de facto dictator.

The Center Party's support of the Enabling Act would fuel criticism of German Catholicism for years to come. The Catholics, it would be charged, enabled Hitler to take power, implying that they agreed with him and supported him. Hitler, however, reneged on every promise he had made. Had he kept those promises and had a vibrant Christian presence survived in Germany, perhaps the whole course of world history might have been different. But he did not. He simply lied to the Center Party legislators and cheated them. This undoubtedly proves them foolish, but it does not prove them closet Nazis. The Protestant state church of Germany, meanwhile, appears to have offered no resistance whatever to the Nazis—unlike the Confessing Church, nearly eight hundred of whose pastors and laymen were arrested in a massive Nazi crackdown in 1936.[10]

Instead of delivering on his promises, Hitler launched a charm offensive. "The national government," he said in a speech two days after the vote, "seeing in Christianity the unshakable foundation of the moral and ethical life of our people, attaches utmost importance to the cultivation and maintenance of the friendliest relations with the Holy See... The rights of the churches will not be curtailed; their position in relation to the state will not be changed." This seeming respect for their religion, along with Hitler's promise to negotiate a concordat with Rome, persuaded the bishops to give the National Socialist leader a chance. They released a joint statement supporting the Nazi government (with some reservations) and lifted all proscriptions against Nazis joining the Catholic Church or partaking of the sacraments.

With the Catholics pacified for the time being, and the Protestants (except for the Confessing Church) largely complacent, Hitler could continue implementing the blanket policy of *Gleichschaltung*, roughly translatable as "forcible

10. There was limited resistance to the Nazis among Germany's twenty-two million Catholics and forty-four million Protestants. True, there were undeniable martyrs like Bonhoeffer and Niemöller and numerous individual Catholics (see subchapter, page 150), but the overwhelming majority of the German clergy, Protestant and Catholic, and their congregants acquiesced. Such resistance as there was tended to be regional—from the Bonhoeffer-Niemöller group in Berlin, from certain conservative Lutheran bishops in Bavaria, and from Calvinists in the Rhineland. The Calvinist theologian A. C. Cochrane, in *The Church's Confession Under Hitler* (1962), describes the Christian response as "a sad tale of betrayal, timidity, and unbelief."

coordination." It was the process of bringing every sphere of German society into line with Nazi ideology and putting every public body under the control of the Nazi government. In essence, the aim was to have the whole population marching in lockstep in preparation for the war ahead.

Part of the process was mass mobilization. This involved the huge, theatrical rallies at Nuremberg (Goebbels' masterwork); the creation of the Hitler Youth to indoctrinate the young and prepare them to fight for the Reich; the quasi-religious deification of Hitler with oaths of allegiance, *Heil Hitler* salutes, and photos of the führer in every public office and classroom; and the suppression of all "degenerate" art, music, and letters.[11]

The synchronization of government institutions—carried out with the help of the SS and the Gestapo—put all eighteen state governments under the control of Nazi Reich governors, abolished state elections, replaced government officials and judges with Nazis, and outlawed labor unions and replaced them with the Nazi-controlled National Labor Front.

Policies relating to Jews and other "undesirables" began to be implemented soon after Hitler's seizure of power. The Law for the Prevention of Progeny with Hereditary Diseases not only called for the sterilization of the mentally ill—a policy volubly condemned by the Vatican and by the defiantly outspoken Catholic Bishop von Galen of Münster—but it also paved the way for a euthanasia program that involved the execution of about two hundred thousand "useless eaters" toward the end of the decade. The accompanying Law for the Restoration of the Civil Service, passed the same day, included the Aryan Clause, which excluded Jews from the bureaucracy as well as from universities, schools, courts, and the legal profession. Successive laws banned Jews from serving in any profession, from working in the cultural and entertainment industries, and from owning or working for newspapers (which soon came under government control).

These Nuremberg Laws of 1935, aimed at preventing "racial pollution," forbade marriage or sexual relations between Aryans and Jews. They also accorded Jews second-class citizenship status, prohibited them from displaying the national flag, and forbade them to employ female citizens of German blood younger than forty-five years of age. Penalties for breaking these laws ranged from fines to imprisonment in one of the new concentration camps. Similar proscriptions were also applied to Gypsies, mulattos, and homosexuals. But much worse was to come, as described in the subchapter on page 118.

Meanwhile Hitler had his eyes on the not-too-distant horizon of war. For this he needed a second segment of the establishment on his side: the military. In order to earn their allegiance, however, he must first deal with the SA, which the veteran Prussian officers loathed. This private army of bullies had proven indispensable in Hitler's rise to power, but was now an encumbrance. Its leader, Ernst Röhm, was looking to effect a "second revolution" to oust the capitalist classes, as well as the army's generals whom he considered to be dotards and whose army he wished to replace with his four million Brownshirts. It was also strongly rumored that Röhm was planning a coup against Hitler, who, as he had confided to a member of his homosexual

11. Goebbels organized a famous book burning by the German Student Union in May 1933 in which the works of such pacifist, socialist, and/or Jewish authors as Karl Marx, Albert Einstein, Émile Zola, Jack London, Ernest Hemingway, and H.G. Wells were consigned to the flames by enthusiastic students in bonfires held in thirty-four university towns. In 1937, Goebbels staged an exhibit of "degenerate" art in a Berlin warehouse, featuring works that supposedly embodied the "perverse Jewish spirit" by such non-Jewish artists as Van Gogh, Picasso, and Gauguin. It was intended to unfavorably—and instructively—contrast with the approved Roman and Greek inspired works in the newly opened, palatial House of German Art. After four months, the degenerate art had attracted over two million visitors, almost three and a half times the number of visitors to the approved gallery

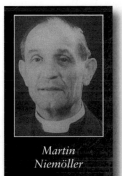

Martin Niemöller

Ludwig Kaas

Ludwig Maria Hugo

Spain's bad man/good man

Hitler and Il Duce see strongman Franco as a certain ally and help him gain power, but he rebuffs them in the war, spares Gibraltar, and lays the ground for democracy

While the world cringed in pain, horror, and fear in the late 1930s and 1940s, Spain settled into what many onlookers considered an obscure, comfortable neutrality. But it had already gone though its own internal paroxysms, and the Spanish Civil War is seen by some people, both Left and Right, as a preparation for the world war that was to come. Effectually, they say, it was a rehearsal for the greater conflict. It was an opening scene that set the stage and the players—Fascist and Democrat—for the war that would turn Europe and much of North Africa into a furnace of struggle and battle.

However, in many ways this is a falsely romantic and politicized interpretation of what was, in effect, a purely local conflict that hardly resembled the Second World War at all. While Fascists, Communists, and Democrats all participated in the Spanish Civil War, it had little to do with the new Europe, and far more to do with the old Spain and its divided history. The country had declined from imperial superpower in the seventeenth century to a nation conquered by Napoleon in the nineteenth, to an economically inferior state in the twentieth.

On the one side of Spanish society were the intrinsically conservative and deeply Roman Catholic peasants, led by similarly traditional landowners, and a military class that mourned its former glories. Aligned with them were various regional interests ambitious for increased autonomy but often committed to ancient Spanish values as well. On the other were the urban working class, the labor unions, the Socialist, Communist, and Anarchist parties, and Catalan nationalists. It was an unwieldy and polarized state of affairs and one that simply could not be long sustained.

There were a number of elections and subsequent governments in the early 1930s. After Bourbon King Alfonso XIII abdicated in 1931, anticlerical violence broke out with rioters targeting churches and convents. This continued sporadically for the next five years. Then in February 1936, a strong, united front of left-wing parties won a majority, and promised to transform the country in its own image. This "Republican" government quickly proceeded to limit the role of the army and socialize the economy, which it had promised to do. But it also went further; it tried to bar various religious orders from teaching, and banned many Catholic processions and holidays. This seemed to many Spaniards to be the shape of

These maps of Spain in 1936 and 1938 show the advances made by the Fascist-assisted Rebel (Nationalist) forces led by General Francisco Franco (top left, foreground) against the Communist-assisted Republicans (Reds). The Spanish Civil War (1936–1939) began as a military coup against the coalition of Socialist and antireligious parties elected in February 1939. The conflict is often portrayed as a prototype for the Second World War, but in many ways this is a false interpretation of a war that had far more to do with the old Spain and its divided history.

SPANISH CIVIL WAR
AUG. TO SEPT. 1936

- Initial Nationalist zone
- Nationalist gains
- Republican zone

SPANISH CIVIL WAR
NOVEMBER 1938

- Nationalist zone
- Republican zone

Below, the remains of the Basque town of Guernica, bombed by the German Luftwaffe's Condor squadron of bombers in 1937 on behalf of the Nationalists, killing as many as four hundred civilians, was the greatest civilian mortality from bombing to date, but a mere trifle against the civilian slaughter in the world war that lay ahead. At top, Spanish Cubist artist Pablo Picasso's representation of the event, painted at the behest of the Republicans, is portrayed in the United Nations' tapestry on a visit to a London gallery in 2009. During the Spanish Civil War, both the Soviet Communists and the German and Italian Fascists, supporting the Republicans and the Nationalists respectively, tested their military capability.

things to come. While the policies may have been popular with the government's most loyal supporters, they struck the rest of Spain as intolerable.

A military coup failed in July 1936, and the bloody war that followed would be fought until April 1939. Neither side was particularly surprised that it came to arms, and both had been preparing for such an outcome. The actual fighting began when a group of generals led by Jose Sanjurjo declared its opposition to the government, and refused to obey its legislation or recognize its authority. It was supported by organized conservative Catholic groups, the small but well-armed Fascist Falange Party, monarchist activists and, importantly, the Carlists, a large group with a militia loyal to the memory and tradition of the Bourbon monarchy. The generals formed and led a Nationalist bloc, used Muslim African troops from Spain's colonies, and were supported to varying degrees by Nazi Germany and Fascist Italy. The Republican Left also formed a coalition of supporters, and were backed by the governments of Mexico and the Soviet Union, and thousands of volunteers, usually Socialist or Communist, from Europe and North America, known as International Brigades.

There were brutalities and massacres on both sides, civilians were sometimes targeted, and the country was used by both Soviets and Fascists as a testing ground for their weaponry and propaganda. From the Nationalists, the war saw one of the first examples of mass bombing on nonmilitary targets. From the Republicans, there were numerous examples of groups of priests, nuns, and monks being indiscriminately murdered.

General Francisco Franco became the dominant military and political figure on the Nationalist side, and by 1939 he had largely exhausted his enemies. This was also, of course, the year that the world had other matters on its mind and Spain was forgotten, thrown into the corner room of selective historical and political memory; it simply didn't matter very much anymore. Both German Nazis and Italian Fascists tried to persuade Franco to form an alliance with them in the

Second World War, but in spite of their support for his cause during the civil war, he insisted on neutrality.

In truth, Spain had neither the economic strength nor the armed forces capable of participating in a global conflict, but Franco's refusal to allow German troops and ships access to Spanish harbors was vital—Gibraltar may well have fallen otherwise, and the Mediterranean and perhaps the whole war lost by the Allies. He also allowed Jewish refugees of Sephardic or Spanish origin to escape into Spain, and showed more compassion to fleeing Jews than some in other countries. A Canadian government official allegedly said of Jewish refugees that "none is too many."[1] While no particular friend of the democratic powers, Franco was singularly detested by Hitler.

He became the self-styled *Caudillo* or leader of Spain, and established a government of various conservative and right-wing interests. Much to the annoyance of the Fascist leaders, he gained personal control of their party, though he was not a Fascist himself. In effect, he made Spain more a reactionary country looking to the past, than some communal, eugenicist state looking to some darkly utopian future. He ruled as a pragmatic authoritarian, and made anticommunism and

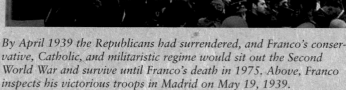

Franco's Nationalist soldiers, bearing food, march into Barcelona in February 1939, and are greeted by a war-weary and hungry populace. Franco's forces had little trouble capturing this Republican government stronghold, and two months later would achieve total victory.

By April 1939 the Republicans had surrendered, and Franco's conservative, Catholic, and militaristic regime would sit out the Second World War and survive until Franco's death in 1975. Above, Franco inspects his victorious troops in Madrid on May 19, 1939.

nationalism the cornerstones of his period in power.

While numerous opponents of the regime were exiled or left the country—and there was certainly persecution and prosecution of those who remained—this was not a society of concentration camps and mass slaughter. In other words, Franco was no Hitler and Spain no Nazi Germany. There was a commitment to what were considered Catholic values and social conservatism, but even many Catholics, Spanish and otherwise, questioned the authenticity of all this.

The country was, however, isolated after 1945, resembling some geopolitical anachronism, an international museum piece. The civil war had seen the departure of many of the country's intelligentsia and business class, and the economy was effectively stagnant. Largely because of this, and much to the chagrin of Spain's Fascists, Madrid entered into an alliance with the United States in 1953. U.S. investment began to improve Spain's economy, and tourism and foreign trade at last brought the country's finances into the postwar world. But when Franco died in 1975, Spain was still the poor man of western Europe, and would not come close to reaching the level of the rest of most other countries outside the Soviet sphere.

Later in Franco's regime, he abandoned most of the final vestiges of a tightly controlled society and economy and looked to technocrats to propel the economy forward. Some of these men were members of Opus Dei, an orthodox Roman Catholic lay organization, and because of this a mythology developed that serious Catholics were universally supportive of General Franco. This was untrue. Opus Dei members were also exiled during the Franco years, and those who were recruited into his government were advocates of a new and not old form of government.

Within Spain, nongovernment trade unions as well as Liberal, Socialist, and anarchist parties, and Basque and Catalan separatists were banned or tightly supervised. Homosexuality, prostitution, and public lewdness were illegal, and the notion of Catholic Spain, imbued with the Christian qualities of faith, family, country, and service dominated cultural and public discourse. In some ways it was remarkable,

but in many others a sham. When Franco's grip loosened and finally disappeared, the country was exposed as a nation not fundamentally different from the rest of the western world, and embraced abortion, same-sex marriage, and much else that would have shocked Francisco Franco.

However, the Generalissimo was far from unblemished. Without doubt he allowed atrocities to be committed during the civil war, had enemies murdered after the war (though nowhere even remotely close to the scale of slaughter in the Soviet Union), and suppressed basic freedoms for decades. He also resisted the demands of the European Fascist powers, and stood firm against the Soviet Union.

The novelist George Orwell, who went to Spain to fight for the Republicans, was swiftly disabused of sympathy with it. He described how the Communist Party tried to commandeer the Republican movement, how it lied about its supposed allies among the Socialists and anarchists, and would certainly have formed the government if Franco had lost the war. Would such a pro-Moscow administration have allowed the German army marching rights during the Nazi-Soviet nonaggression pact? Moscow had certainly been openhanded to the Germans in Poland and elsewhere. If so, this would have been a disaster for the free world.

Franco entrapped Spain in the past, but he also kept it from becoming a puppet of either of the social engineering dictatorships, whether Communist or Fascist. On retirement he handed power to King Juan Carlos, grandson of Alfonso XIII, who instituted a constitutional monarchy and a constitutional democracy, with hardly a fist or gun raised in anger. The transition was smooth and effective, and by the twenty-first century the years of dictatorship were a faded memory—a remarkable achievement that stands tall in the Generalissimo's record. ∎

1. The remark, "None is too many," is attributed to an unnamed Canadian immigration official in a book with that title, published in 1983 by Canadian writers Irving Abella and Harold Troper. They contend that Canada did less than other countries to help Jewish refugees between 1933 and 1948.

coterie, was becoming too cozy with the conservative elites and letting the whole heart and soul of the movement disintegrate. Hitler, however, moved first. With the assistance of Göring, Himmler, and Herman Hess, he prepared a hit list. In the early hours of Sunday, July 1, 1934, Hitler, Goebbels, and a contingent of SS officers traveled in three black Mercedes-Benz automobiles to the resort town of Bad Wiessee and descended on the hotel where Röhm and his closest lieutenants were vacationing. Röhm's deputy Edmund Heines and an eighteen-year-old youth with whom he was sleeping were taken outside the hotel and shot. Röhm was driven to Dachau and offered a revolver. When he

In April 1933, the Nazis instigated the first of their pogroms against Jews by organizing a boycott of Jewish businesses. During that boycott, Stormtroopers, seen here in uniform, forced Jews to march in the streets. They bore anti-Semitic signs emblazoned with such statements as "Don't buy from Jews" and "A good German doesn't buy from Jews." The anti-Semitic measures grew progressively more severe, culminating with the Nuremberg Laws of 1935 that forbade marriage or sexual relations between Aryans and those considered too Jewish.

refused to take his life, an SS guard shot him. Assorted other SA leaders met similar ends that same weekend, along with other perceived "enemies of the Reich" who were not in the SA, including the Catholic editor Gerlich. About eighty-five people died in the slaughter that became known as the Night of the Long Knives.

In one brutal weekend, Hitler had curtailed a possible rival, won over the generals, and forged a reputation for himself as a man who was not to be disobeyed. Himmler's SS, as a reward for its help, was split off from the SA and would soon become more powerful than its predecessor had ever been. Speaking on July 13 in the Reichstag (now meeting in its opera house near the derelict building), Hitler described his actions as an emergency measure against treasonous forces, and received thunderous applause when he declared, "in the state there is only one bearer of arms and that is the army."

Most Germans felt relief, believing the end of SA terror meant a return to law and order (the message was broadcast on Nazi-controlled radio and crafted by Goebbels, who accentuated the SA's homosexual culture). Even Hindenburg, two weeks away from death, sent Hitler a telegram congratulating him for having "nipped treason in the bud and having saved the nation from serious danger."

Hitler had thus eliminated the final threat to his power, secured the loyalty of the army, sent a deadly warning to potential opponents, and convinced an increasingly pliant populace that he not only stood for law and order but was, as he told the Reichstag, "the highest judge of the German people." With Hindenburg's death and the merging of the offices of chancellor and president on August 2, 1934, Hitler became commander in chief of the armed forces. Thereafter all soldiers—and all civil servants—were required to swear a sacred oath promising "unconditional obedience to Adolf Hitler." Alan Bullock, who

Although Germany won most medals at the 1936 Summer Olympics in Berlin, the black American athlete Jesse Owens put the lie to "Aryan" supremacy by winning four gold medals in the 100-meter and 200-meter sprints, the 4x100-meter relay, and the long jump. Shown here receiving his gold for long jump, Owens gives the American salute while silver medal-winning German Luz Long delivers the Nazi version. Above, the Canadian Olympic team receives autographs from Hitler and Goebbels. The postcard below shows Hitler turning the earth for the construction of an autobahn, part of the world's first freeway system which by 1940 would stretch to 2,300 miles. Such events and projects, high employment, burgeoning production, and an openness to outside scrutiny (unlike Soviet Russia), convinced many in the world that Germany and Hitler were to be applauded, not feared.

23.9.1933 Erſter Spatenſtich
23.9.1936 1000 km Autobahn fertig

wrote *Hitler: A Study in Tyranny* (1952), saw all this in another light: "The street gangs had seized control of a great modern state. The gutter had come to power."

Hitler and his generals, at first surreptitiously, embarked upon the road to war, creating an army in the guise of a domestic security force and building warplanes and warships ostensibly within the limitations of the treaty. Arms manufacture and the construction of major public works like the autobahns, together with the elimination of trade unions and the ingenious monetary manipulations of finance minister Hjalmar Schacht, had a near miraculous effect on the German economy. Between 1932 and 1936 unemployment dropped from six million to less than one million, national production rose 102 percent, and the national income doubled.

The Germany that the world viewed during the glittering 1936 Olympic Games was, as the journalist Shirer noted, a seemingly sublime land. "The visitors, especially those from England and America, were greatly impressed by what they saw: apparently a happy, healthy, friendly people united under Hitler..."[12]

In his speeches, Hitler professed himself a man of peace, who merely wished for defensive equilibrium with the other European members of the League of Nations. Germany had been admitted to the League in 1926. When it became known, however, that France had no intention of acquiescing in European disarmament and was maintaining a huge army, Hitler withdrew Germany from the League in November 1933, afterward submitting his decision to the people in a plebiscite to provide the patina of democracy. The vote was ninety-five percent in favor. And in case the world might perceive this as a belligerent act, he proceeded to sign a nonaggression pact with Poland, which had acquired Posen and Silesia from Germany under the Versailles Treaty—areas that Hitler and the generals longed to repatriate. "All of our agreements with Poland have a purely temporary significance," Hitler told a confidant, with a wink.

Such subterfuge largely lulled the leaders of Britain and France into believing that Germany posed no threat to world peace. Indeed Britain was actively pursuing a policy of disarmament. One man, however, remained firmly undeceived. This was Winston Churchill, by now a backbench MP widely viewed as a worn-out warmonger by the pacifistic Stanley Baldwin cabinet. Churchill repeatedly warned against the idiocy of British disarmament in the face of a resurgent Germany. Few paid him any heed until Hitler's war machine roared into Poland in 1939. ■

12. Among the more illustrious visitors was David Lloyd George, who had campaigned as Britain's prime minister in 1918 under the slogan "Hang the Kaiser." He visited Hitler at his mountain retreat in Berchtesgaden in 1936, and came away charmed, calling Hitler "the George Washington of Germany" and declaring: "The Germans have definitely made up their minds never to quarrel with us again." Canadian Prime Minister William Lyon Mackenzie King, after meeting Hitler in 1937, wrote in his diary, "My sizing up of the man as I sat and talked with him was that he is really one who truly loves his fellow-men, and his country, and would make any sacrifice for their good."

A mass of exultant Berliners, below, greet Hitler as he arrives for the Olympics. (Inset) Hitler and Goebbels watch a Nazi parade in Stuttgart in an early color photograph. Having successfully suppressed all opposition and resurrected the economy, Hitler could now move on to the next phases of his plan: a war of expansion and the complete elimination of the Jews.

The ancient question: Why the Jews?

Persecutions and hatred of this gifted people predate the Christian era, but never was it more sweepingly efficient than in the Nazi Holocaust

1. The word "Semitic" is derived from Shem, one of the three sons of Noah, rendered in Greek as *Sem*. It refers to all the peoples, including Arabs and some Ethiopians, that use one of the languages in the Semitic language family. That is, in addition to Hebrew, Arabic and five Ethiopian languages are also Semitic tongues. "Anti-Semitism," however, refers only to hostility toward the Jews. The term was coined in the nineteenth century in Germany as a more scientific-sounding term for *Judenhass* (Jew-hatred.)

It seemed literally beyond imagination that in twentieth-century Europe there could occur a genocide so immense and so grotesque that the world would have serious trouble believing it really happened. But happen it did, when Germany became the scene of the Holocaust (in Hebrew, the *Shoah*), in which some six million European Jews were rounded up to be tortured, abused, and finally murdered. Moreover, as was clearly acknowledged at the time, this was nothing less than an overt attempt to expunge the Jewish people from human history—to be remembered, if remembered at all, as exhibits in museums.

That Germany, the nation of Beethoven and Goethe, should be the scene of this extraordinary manifestation of obsessive Jew-hatred was a major part of the shock. For centuries, Jews in Russia and much of Eastern Europe had generally lived on suf-

ferance, a barely tolerated foreign element subject to intermittent persecution, seldom fully accepted. Elsewhere, in Britain and Scandinavia, for example, by heroic striving to become model citizens they would often achieve limited acceptance, although challenges and social difficulties usually would persist. But in Germany, by contrast, life for most Jews was not significantly different than for anyone else. They typically regarded themselves as Germans first and Jews second, volunteered for military service in the First World War, won Iron Crosses, represented Germany in diplomacy and in sports, and became politicians and notable public figures.

But perhaps this acceptance was not all that it seemed. Hitler's Nazis, deliberately pumping the toxins of anti-Semitism into the national bloodstream, were able to pursue with remarkable ease the task of denigrating,

Left, two members of the Nazi SA (Sturmabteilung, *or Stormtroopers) stand in front of a Jewish store in Berlin in 1933 with signs reading "Germans, defend yourselves against Jewish atrocity propaganda, buy only at German shops!" Below, a chart from 1935, an adjunct to the racial Nuremberg Laws, was an aid in determining who was an Aryan and who was a Jew. For example, only people with four German grandparents (four white circles in top row left) were of "German blood." Such measures marked the halfway point between the Nazis' campaign of marginalization, and their "Final Solution" to the "Jewish question" in the 1940s—that is, extermination.*

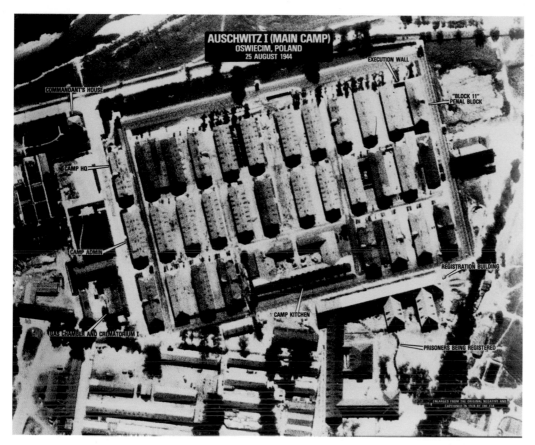

An aerial view of the Nazi's Auschwitz death camp in Poland with the various departments labeled; and, above, a cart with bodies removed from the Gusen Concentration Camp after the war. The effort and organization that went into this machine of mass death indicated how important the German government believed the killing of Jews to be. It saw an eternal struggle between two superpowers: Aryans and Jews. For the former to survive, the latter needed to disappear.

arresting, and finally almost annihilating Europe's Jews.[1] First came a public campaign of abuse and marginalization, when they were blamed for unemployment, defeat, and even disease. Then came incidents of casual violence, escalating to organized brutality. Finally there were the legal attacks: removal of citizenship, firing from government posts, and forced segregation.

All this culminated in what the Nazis termed their Final Solution, which aimed to systematically identify and eliminate anyone who had even a single Jewish grandparent. When shootings proved inadequate for such a mammoth task, they began to force Jews into ghettos, and later into concentration camps, there to be used as slave labor and in dubious medical experiments, and then ultimately gassed and incinerated. As the Second World War progressed, German-occupied countries also became part of a gigantic system for eliminating the Jewish race.

Arguably more amazing yet is the fact that this enormous project was carried out while Germany was fighting a war on two fronts, and was desperately short of food, fuel, and materiel of every sort. Yet time, effort, and scarce resources were devoted to loading millions of Jews on railroad cars and transporting them many miles to specifically built concentration camps where they

were housed, fed, clothed (even if minimally), and systematically tattooed and inventoried—all to kill them.

One explanation attributes this to Nazi ideology. The Hitler government clearly believed that killing Jews was as important as winning the war, maybe more important. This was an eternal struggle, they contended, between two superpowers: the Aryans and the Jews. For the former to survive and prosper, the latter must disappear. Nor was this presented as mere gutter racism or street thug prejudice. There were intellectuals, doctors, scientists, and scholars involved in the Holocaust, every aspect of which was planned and organized. The children, who numbered more than a million, were usually killed first, followed by the elderly and the sick. Able-bodied men and women survived longest, to be used in various ways, but their fate was inevitable. Some few people tried to help the Jews (see subchapter, page 150), and the response of one nation was exemplary.[2]

The Holocaust, of course, is unique in scope but not in kind. Other twentieth-century examples were provided by the Soviets in Ukraine, the Turks in Armenia, the Communists in Cambodia, and the Hutu in Rwanda. That it could happen in twentieth-century Germany, however, made many conclude that similar persecution of Jews can

2. In October 1943, Hitler ordered the arrest of all the Jews in Denmark, which was under Nazi occupation. The Danish resistance movement, aided by the citizenry, successfully evacuated eight thousand Danish Jews to neutral Sweden. Danish intercession also secured the release of other Danish Jews already in transit to Nazi extermination camps. Because of these two initiatives, ninety-nine percent of Danish Jews survived the Holocaust.

German civilians from nearby towns are forced to witness the corpses at one of the concentration camps liberated by the Allies in 1945. Few German Jews in the 1930s could have predicted such horrors. They assumed Hitler to be a vulgar little Austrian corporal who was being used by the German ruling class to destroy communism, and that he would be done away with as soon as possible. Unfortunately for many of them, Hitler's demise would come only after their own.

occur anywhere. The pattern might be interrupted, the eras of coexistence might lengthen, but in the end a scapegoat would be needed again, and no people have fulfilled that role better than the Jews—from Rome to Moscow, from Cairo to Berlin, from ancient to modern. This argument is difficult to refute.

It is sometimes assumed that the hatred of Jews originated with Christianity, but this is not a tenable theory. Persecutions of the Jews recur in pre-Roman history. In the first century of the Christian era, long before Christianity was strong enough to persecute anybody, Sejanus—who was effectively the ruler of Rome under Tiberius Caesar—developed a visceral hatred of the Jews. After they had twice rebelled against Roman rule in Jerusalem, they were forced out of Palestine. Later there were Christian people and Christian states that treated Jews badly, sometimes very badly, but they just as often lived unpersecuted for centuries in Christian countries, generally to the mutual profit of themselves and the Christians. Anti-Semites often argue that persecution was due to Jewish behavior. But no "typical Jewish behavior" has been in fact traceable, and Jews demonstrably have often been stellar citizens in their countries of birth.

Or could it perhaps have something to do with their biblical role as a chosen people? The Jewish precept is that God chose one initially insignificant people in the Middle East to hear his divine message, to carry it through the world, and to remain steadfast and faithful even—in fact, especially—when all around were sinful and disobedient. Therefore, the Jews religiously separate themselves as special, and in that way arouse antipathy.

To the Christians, however, the Jews were chosen to produce the Messiah, in Greek *Christos*, the "designated one." They were not chosen to serve themselves, but for all the nations, for the whole world. They were the carriers of the Word of God. But when the Messiah appeared among them in the first Christian century, he was slain—just as the Jewish prophets had foreseen, say the Christians, and the death of the Messiah and his subsequent Resurrection redeemed the fallen human race, Jews as well as non-Jews. However, the Jews, his own people, rejected him and still await the Messiah. Even so, the great Christian teacher Saint Paul warned Christians to respect and love the Jews who, he said, have been rendered "blind" until "the fullness of the Gentiles shall come in" (Romans 11:25).

Moreover, the chosen people concept was never meant to indicate that Jews were better than everyone else. It only meant that they were different from everybody, not in respect of goodness or excellence of character, but in being given a burden to carry for all time. This burden—preservation of God's Word—necessitated that they not marry non-Jews, not break the dietary laws given them in scripture, and not behave in many other ways like the people around them. They were to be a living reminder that God has given his people a code and vocation that must never die. They must reflect absolute truth and act as a mirror held up to the rest of society. Thus their differentness, their insularity, and their separation from the society around them were inescapable, and frequently resented.

When disease strikes, crops fail, and armies invade, these people who live differently from the rest of society, who pray and wash and eat and sing and speak and believe in a different way, can become the first targeted for persecution and blame. If, as is frequently the case, they have also become prosperous because their religion commands education and hard work, it is all the easier to hate them as opportunistic profiteers. Contrary to anti-Semitic lore, Jews have never dominated any one field, but because they are known as Jews, it is easy and tempting to generalize. As one Hungarian aphorism puts it, "Anti-Semitism is hating Jews just a little more than is absolutely necessary."

The American author Mary McCarthy, who was raised a Catholic but later became an atheist, wrote that "anti-Semitism is a horrible disease from which nobody is immune, and it has a kind of evil fascination that makes an enlightened person draw near the source of infection, supposedly in a scientific spirit, but really to sniff the vapors and dally with the possibility." This is an instructive comment in that it shows how a non-Jew sees the potential for anti-Semitism in everybody, including the informed and intelligent.

German Jews in the 1930s had certainly assumed that culture cured racism. Many of them despised the idea of Zionism, of establishing a Jewish state, because they deeply resented the idea that they were anything other than German, and that they had any need for a home outside of the fatherland. People marvel at how late the Jews of Germany waited before fleeing the country, and many seem never to have considered it. This was because they, and many of their Gentile friends as well, assumed Hitler to be a vulgar little tin pot dictator who was being used by the German ruling class to destroy communism, and that they would get rid of him as soon as possible.

There was even resentment among some German Jews at coreligionists arriving as refugees from Poland, who were regarded as foreign, odd, and alien. German Jews were acutely aware that twelve thousand of their number had died in the First World War, fighting for Germany and the kaiser. Many of them were angry at Britain and France for the way Germany had been treated after 1918, and many sided with the Nationalists when the country seemed on the brink of civil war between Right and Left. By the time the Nazi extermination policy engulfed them, and could not be stopped, they were in shock as much as terror.

One consequence of the Holocaust was to rouse surviving Jews, indeed sympathetic people all over the western world, to advance the cause of Zionism and the establishment of the state of Israel in 1948 (see chapter 18). The early twenty-first century found Israel prosperous, yet still under siege from enemies intent on its destruction. So the Jew is not secure in Israel, nor anywhere else in the world. The burden of "the chosen" remains. ■

> Contrary to anti-Semitic lore, Jews have never dominated any one field or profession, though this is easily generalized.

Lords of all they survey, Adolph Hitler and associates stroll along Paris's Champs-Élysées in June of 1940 following the six-week Nazi conquest of France that had cost the German Army a mere five hundred lives. For a decade, Hitler's audacity had brought him one victory after another to the point where his dream of a Thousand-Year Reich stretching from the Atlantic to the Pacific seemed within grasp. But the Russians, Americans, and British would not be so easily dispensed with as the French, so his plan to remodel Paris in the architectural style favored by Nazis had to be put on hold. He is accompanied here by his master planners, architect Albert Speer (on his right), and sculptor Arnold Breker (on his left).

CHAPTER 7

How the insistent cry for disarmament led to the worst war ever

Posing as a man of peace, Hitler lulls the Allies, mobilizes, and comes close to world conquest, but his blunders lead to his defeat and suicide

By late autumn of 1941, things were going rather well for Adolf Hitler and his ferociously vaunted Thousand-Year Reich. The German dictator's main strategic aim, made abundantly clear in his book, *Mein Kampf*, was to charge eastward into the Soviet Union, overwhelm its pitiful army, topple its "Jewish-Bolshevik" regime, replace its "subhuman" Slavs with purebred Aryan Germans, exterminate or enslave its conquered populations, and extend German *Lebensraum* (living space) from the Atlantic to the Pacific. And this, it appeared, was exactly what he was doing.

Here it was November, and the main force of Germany's powerful *Wehrmacht*—one hundred and fifty-two divisions and three and a half million men strong—had advanced along an eighteen-hundred-mile front, had flung the Soviet Red Army out of Poland and the Ukraine, and was now extending its mechanized pincers around Moscow. From the wall above the führer's desk in the *Wolfsschanze* (Wolf's Lair), his East Prussian headquarters, a portrait of Frederick the Great peered down upon him. Did Frederick's lugubrious gaze betray just a hint of approval? Hitler thought so.

"*L'audace, l'audace, toujours l'audace!*" had been Frederick's war cry as he invoked the audacity that launched the rise of Prussia into modern Germany. Now here was Frederick's effectual successor, a lowborn Austrian corporal, about to force mighty Russia to its knees and transform Frederick's acorn kingdom into a great oak whose limbs would span two continents. He, Adolf Hitler, could teach Frederick lessons in audacity. Only twenty years earlier, he alone had

Frederick II

1. On November 12, 1933, a plebiscite was held in which the German people were asked two questions: whether they approved Germany's withdrawal from the Geneva-based League of Nations, and whether they agreed that only Nazi candidates should be eligible for election to the Reichstag. Ninety-six percent of registered voters cast their ballots. Ninety-five percent approved withdrawal from Geneva, and ninety-two percent sanctioned a Hitler-controlled Nazi government. Historian William Shirer calls this "a staggering victory for Adolf Hitler." In defying the outside world, it was beyond doubt that he had the "overwhelming support of the German people."

2. "Whoever lights the torch of war in Europe can wish for nothing but chaos," Hitler told the Reichstag in May 1935. He renounced any German claim to the long-disputed Alsace-Lorraine region of France; he promised not to annex Austria; he assured Poland, "the home of a great and nationally conscious people," of strict adherence to their nonaggression pact. No impartial mind could doubt, opined the *Times* of London, that the führer's proposals would form the basis of a complete settlement with Germany.

foreseen this triumph. Then he had been audacious with words. He was "a man of peace," he said, and fooled them all—the French, the British, the Bolsheviks, even the German elite. Now he was audacious with Panzer divisions and *Luftwaffe* (air force) squadrons, and there was no fooling about it.

With what telling skill had the "man of peace" deluded them back in 1933? He assured the League of Nations that he would eliminate what little arms Germany had left if other countries abided by the League's charter and did the same. But France was unwilling, so Hitler withdrew Germany from the League, contravened the Versailles Treaty, and rearmed. How else, he argued, could a peace-loving Germany defend itself against a dangerous belligerent like France?[1]

Hitler was gambling that the Allied nations were "too divided, too torpid, too blind to grasp the nature or the direction of what was building up beyond the Rhine," writes journalist and historian William Shirer in his *Rise and Fall of the Third Reich* (1959). He therefore instituted military conscription, authorized the construction of pocket battleships, and secretly remobilized the Versailles-prohibited Luftwaffe under the direction of the fat, jovial, and increasingly morphine-addicted Hermann Göring. Hitler's speeches—studies in honeyed mendacity—were designed to persuade the world that he sought only peace and prosperity.[2] Secretly, however, he and his generals made quite different plans.

In March 1936, they audaciously marched their still minuscule army into the industrial western Rhineland, which had been designated a neutral demilitarized buffer zone under the Versailles Treaty. This was necessary, Hitler explained, because France had signed a pact with the Soviet Union, threatening Germany from both east and west. Though the French had one hundred divisions to call up against him, he was confident that they would not fight; the people wanted peace, he believed, not war. He proved right, and he reclaimed the Rhineland unopposed. Britain objected, but mildly. The move "deals a heavy blow to the principle of the sanctity of treaties," observed Britain's foreign secretary Anthony Eden. "But fortunately," he added "we have no reason to suppose that Germany's present action threatens hostilities."

The British government headed by Stanley Baldwin was pursuing a policy of partial rearmament, largely in reaction to backbencher Winston Churchill's rev-

British Prime Minister Neville Chamberlain (left of center, in the black coat, holding his hat) is received at the Oberwiesenfeld airport in Munich by various dignitaries including German foreign minister Joachim von Ribbentrop (in the overcoat to the left of Chamberlain) on September 28, 1938. They would discuss Hitler's plans to acquire the Sudetenland, if necessary by invading Czechoslovakia of which it was then a part. The resulting Munich Agreement, infamously touted by Chamberlain as "peace in our time," merely confirmed Hitler's belief that the western Allies were "little worms" and posed no consequential threat to his plans for German expansion.

Members of the Reichstag salute Hitler (front row, to the left of the aisle) during its April 28, 1939, session abrogating Germany's nonaggression pact with Poland. Having engineered a fake insurgency by Poles (actually SA operatives) against Germans in the border regions to sway public opinion, Hitler was now ready for the first major push eastward. Among those visible in this photograph are propaganda minister Joseph Goebbels (front row, second from left) and Reichsmarschall Hermann Göring (on the podium directly below the eagle's swastika). By now Hitler had also made himself de facto commander in chief of the army, replacing his top generals with the always amenable Wilhelm Keitel (inset left) and Alfred Jodl (inset right).

elations about Nazi airplane production.[3] But Britons, still reeling from the appalling losses of the First World War, wanted peace above all and Baldwin knew it. So did Hitler. Archbishop Cosmo Lang of Canterbury likewise favored appeasement, although he had condemned Italy's invasion of Ethiopia by the Fascist autocrat Benito Mussolini. "An appeaser is one who feeds a crocodile," Churchill commented, "hoping it will eat him last." In his opening history of the Second World War, *The Gathering Storm* (1948), Churchill describes in persuasive detail how the zeal to preserve peace led democratic Europe directly into the worst war yet.

France and England stood aside when Hitler signed an agreement with Austria's Chancellor Kurt von Schuschnigg, ostensibly to guarantee Austrian sovereignty. But it also acknowledged Austria as a "German state," thereby preempting Mussolini's plan to make it an Italian dependency, and opening the door to Nazi infiltration of the Austrian government. Nor did they object when Hitler partnered

3. Churchill, now in his early sixties, had been out of the cabinet since 1929. He had rejected the government's policy for self-rule in India. He had supported King Edward VIII's right to marry a divorceé, Wallace Simpson, while most of the cabinet wanted (and got) the king's abdication. On these two issues, Churchill was banished to the political wilderness. However, his acid wit in the House and in print, along with revelations he received from sources in British Intelligence showing Germany's military buildup, prepared the way for his return to wartime leadership.

Berlin citizens, two of them apparently delighted, pass the smashed windows of Jewish stores on Friedrichstrasse following the Kristallnacht *pogrom of November 11, 1938. In this precursor to the Holocaust, Jewish businesses and synagogues were destroyed in a Nazi-staged pantomime of public outrage over the assassination of a German diplomat. The Nazis' anti-Semitic programs followed them into each conquered territory, initially consigning Jews to concentration camps and slave labor, later to the extermination camps built mostly in Poland beginning in mid-1941.*

4. Hitler's Spain-bound Condor Legion, composed of some twelve thousand volunteers, brought with it tanks, U-boats, and planes to fight the Soviet-backed Spanish Republicans. It was here that the German Luftwaffe pioneered the technique of carpet bombing, obliterating the town of Guernica and killing several hundred of its civilian inhabitants. This technique would be further developed by the Germans in the bombing of English cities in 1941, and reach its apogee in British and American bombings of German cities later in the war.

5. Czechoslovakia (population ten million) was assembled in 1919 from territories removed from the broken-up Habsburg Empire, including the former kingdom of Bohemia. In the interwar years it became a democratic and prosperous central European state, but was riven by domestic unrest from minorities with loyalties to other nations, including a million Hungarians (loyal to Hungary), half a million Ruthenians (loyal to Ukraine), and three and a half million Sudeten Germans (Austria/Germany). Two and a half million Slovaks were also pushing for more autonomy within the Czechoslovak union.

with Mussolini in providing military aid to the Franco revolt in Spain,[4] nor later when Germany joined Italy and Japan in the anti-Comintern Pact. Initially an anti-Communist alliance, this agreement also foreshadowed the triune Axis that would oppose the democratic Allies and Soviet Russia in the upcoming Second World War. Within Germany, Hitler tightened his hold by making himself supreme commander of the armed forces, to whom every German soldier must take a personal oath. High officers who were not malleable were dismissed in favor of toadies like General Wilhelm Keitel and Colonel Alfred Jodl, who were.

Hitler's next two objectives were exceedingly hazardous. He must somehow absorb Austria, which was German, and Czechoslovakia, which was in part German, without triggering a war with France, whose armed forces vastly exceeded his own, or with England.[5] The first move was on Austria. By March 1938, he had coerced Austrian Chancellor Schuschnigg into allowing Austrian Nazis to virtually control the government. Therefore when German troops marched in they were unopposed, and an *Anschluss* (political union) with Germany was declared. "The only shots fired in anger," writes historian Andrew Roberts in *The Storm of War* (2011), "were by the many Jews who committed suicide."

Germany's anti-Semitic policies followed its armies. In Austria, the three percent of the population who were Jewish (against one percent in Germany) lost their citizenship, were forbidden to marry non-Jews, and could not retain or achieve professional status. That November, throughout all German territories, came *Kristallnacht* (night of [broken] glass), organized by Propaganda Minister Joseph Goebbels as a "popular" uprising to protest the assassination of a Nazi

In the closing years of the century's fourth decade, the Nazi juggernaut rolled unresisted into Austria and Czechoslovakia. Top, Hitler and his Nazi motorcade, flanked by an enthusiastic crowd, process through the streets of Vienna in March 1938. Center left, watched by a rather more sullen throng, German armored cars patrol the streets of Prague following their annexation of Czechoslovakia. Poland by contrast put up a valiant but futile fight, unaided by its new allies France and England, holding off for five weeks before falling to the opposing jaws of the German and Soviet forces. The city of Warsaw, center right, is bombarded by the Luftwaffe on September 9, 1939; and a ten year-old Polish girl grieves over her older sister, one of the civilians killed in the bombardment.

Chamberlain, like Baldwin before him, did not believe that Germany posed much threat to Britain. It was well known by the late thirties that Hitler's ambitions lay to the east, and that he wished to avoid a two-front war. Hitler himself believed until mid-1939 that he might reach an accommodation whereby Germany would leave Britain and her empire alone in return for a free hand in Europe. Due to Britain's pledge to Poland, however, avoidance of war became impossible, although Germany continued to make overtures.

diplomat in Paris. Synagogues were smashed and burned (ninety-four in Vienna alone), thousands of stores were wrecked, about one hundred Jews were beaten to death, and some thirty thousand were sent to concentration camps.

Thus began the Holocaust, which over the next eight years would see six million Jews perish, most of them in the death camps that Reichsführer-SS Heinrich Himmler began operating in occupied Poland in 1941. "Racial hatred and hysteria seemed to have taken complete hold of otherwise decent people," wrote the London *Daily Telegraph*'s Berlin correspondent. "I saw fashionably dressed women clapping their hands and screaming with glee, respectable middle-class mothers held up their babies to see the 'fun.'"

For Hitler to challenge Czechoslovakia was much more perilous. The Czechoslovak government was defiantly hostile, and although by September 1938 he could line up one and a half million troops on the Czech frontier, the Czech forces opposing him were impressive, well armed, and would put up a fight. His principal risk, however, was France. If it chose to attack, there was scarcely a single German soldier between the French frontier and Berlin. A French attack would bring the

Throngs of cheering supporters met Chamberlain's plane and wept with joy as he declared, 'Peace in our time.' Churchill did not congratulate him and he was right.

immediate fall of the Nazi government, and a cadre of German generals stood ready to depose the Nazis when the French arrived—which they fully expected.

But England and France desperately wanted peace, and were sure they could reach a diplomatic understanding with Hitler. Prime Minister Neville Chamberlain flew to Munich, and along with the premiers of France and Italy

Winston Churchill, who became prime minister in 1940 following Chamberlain's resignation, had correctly read each of Hitler's moves as the Nazis rearmed Germany and had accurately warned of what they were planning. Thus he spoke with profound credibility as he took direction of a Britain that was perilously besieged. This classic photograph was taken by the Armenian-Canadian Yousuf Karsh in 1941 following Churchill's speech to the Canadian House of Commons. The bulldog glower was achieved after Karsh impertinently snatched the cigar from Churchill's mouth just before releasing the shutter. It is claimed to be the most reproduced photographic portrait in history.

conferred with the führer. When he came home with a signed treaty, throngs of cheering supporters met his plane and wept with joy as he proclaimed that he had achieved "peace in our time." The Germans would assume control only of the Sudetenland, the German part of Czechoslovakia. The agreement, Chamberlain told Parliament, "has saved Czechoslovakia from destruction and Europe from Armageddon." Peace had been preserved. Archbishop Lang congratulated him, as did the new king, George VI. Churchill emphatically did not congratulate him. "England has been offered a choice between war and shame," he charged. "She has chosen shame, and will get war." He was right. German troops occupied the

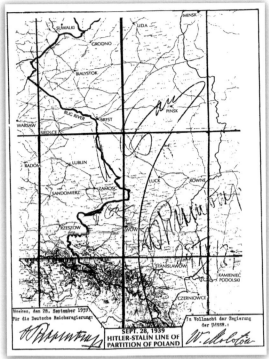

Soviet foreign minister Vyacheslav Molotov, aided by a translator, signs the German-Soviet nonaggression pact on August 23, 1939, watched by Joseph Stalin (second from right), and German foreign minister Ribbentrop (center). Bottom, German troops examine Soviet armored cars, when the still-friendly armies met in early October 1939 following the invasion of Poland. The German-Russian division of Poland is drawn on the map (top right) signed by Ribbentrop and Stalin on the same day as the pact.

Sudetenland, and six months later took over the rest of Czechoslovakia unopposed. Hitler now undertook his next objective, Poland.

Here he confronted a new problem. Soviet Russia, as he well knew, was not likely to stand quietly by and see Poland absorbed into the Nazi orbit. But the Soviets had territorial ambitions of their own. Mutual gain was therefore possible, and Germany's foreign minister Joachim von Ribbentrop traveled to Moscow and negotiated a nonaggression pact with Soviet foreign minister Vyacheslav Molotov. Poland would be divided between Germany and Russia, they decided, and the latter would be given "a free hand" in the Baltic—that is, freedom to seize Lithuania, Estonia, Latvia, and Finland. Meanwhile, Britain and France, finally conscious that appeasement was in fact bringing on a war, guaranteed to defend Poland. This time they meant it.[6]

In August 1939, Hitler was ready to invade Poland; by now the risks were substantially reduced. German rearmament was reaching gargantuan dimensions, and he headed what would soon become the world's most powerful military machine.[7] In an address to his generals he portrayed what their *modus operandi*

7. In a document appended to *The Gathering Storm*, Churchill explains the process of rearmament. In first year, he wrote, a nation produces almost nothing, a little in the second, substantial armament in the third, and an avalanche of arms in the fourth. Since Germany began surreptitiously to arm soon after Hitler took power, it reached the "avalanche" stage by 1940, well ahead of Britain and the United States.

The British retreat from the beaches of Dunkirk is shown here in a realistic contemporary painting. Cornered by the Germans in late May 1940, the British expeditionary force was spared annihilation, first by a mysterious halt order from Hitler's office, second by unusually calm seas that made possible the evacuation of 338,000 troops over nine days, an event the dean of St. Paul's dubbed "the Miracle of Dunkirk."

must be: "Close your hearts to pity. Act brutally... The wholesale destruction of Poland is the military objective. Speed is the main thing. Pursuit until complete annihilation!" As for the Allied leaders, he said, he had met them in Munich and they were "*kleine würmchen*" (little worms). On September 1, the Wehrmacht invaded Poland. Two days later Chamberlain and French Prime Minister Edouard Daladier declared what would become the bloodiest war in history. The Germans employed their new *blitzkreig* (lightning war) tactic: mass tank attacks, and heavily focused air assault, always with great speed in order to achieve total surprise. Poland soon went down, while Russia easily occupied eastern Poland, Lithuania, Estonia, Latvia, and far less easily, part of Finland.[8]

The six months that followed became known as the "phony war." The French, whose military strength still exceeded Hitler's, crouched defensively behind their Maginot Line of fortifications, while Britain sent three hundred and fifty thousand troops to guard France's northwestern borders. On April 9, 1940, Hitler's next blow fell. He took Denmark unopposed, then crossed the straits and seized Norway, handily defeating a British naval attempt to stop him, and sinking some twelve British ships in the process. Chamberlain resigned, and the sixty-five-year-old warhorse Churchill became prime minister on May 10. On that same day the Hitler blitzkrieg screamed west into Holland, Belgium, and France.

The German onslaught easily subdued the Netherlands and Belgium, both of them neutral and unprepared. But the largest concentration of men, tanks, and Stuka dive-bombers came from the northeast, through Luxemburg and the Ardennes forest. They bypassed the Maginot Line and Sedan, site of the great French defeat in the Franco-Prussian war seventy years earlier, and easily overwhelmed the thinly scattered French troops. Soon the German forces were curving around the French from the south, sweeping them northwestward toward the English Channel. On May 16, Churchill flew to Paris and found the government burning archives and preparing to evacuate. Peering at the map depicting the invasion, he inquired concerning the location of the French reserves, a standard contingency in such circumstances. "*Aucune,*" the French general laconically replied—meaning, there are none. Churchill was aghast.[9]

8. The Baltic countries provided Stalin with a buffer against Germany, but Finland posed a different threat. Its boundary came within artillery range of Leningrad. To remove this threat, Stalin attacked Finland on November 30, 1939, and was held back by a Finnish army a tenth the size of the Soviet force, equipped with antiquated artillery and homemade gasoline bombs. (They were named "Molotov cocktails" for the Soviet foreign minister.) Soviet casualties were eight times the Finnish toll, leading Hitler to mistakenly conclude that the Russians could be easily defeated.

The British were now being beaten back to the Channel beaches near the town of Dunkirk. German commander in chief Walther von Brauschitsch ordered General Ewald von Kleist, whose panzer division was just eighteen miles away, to take the town, but before Kleist could act, Hitler ordered Brauschitsch to halt—just why has never been conclusively explained. This saved the British force, and has been called Hitler's first major error. During nine days when the seas remained still as a mill pond, some thousand ships and small boats evacuated 338,000 troops, who therefore lived to fight another day. Walter Matthews, the dean of St. Paul's in London, christened the evacuation "the Miracle of Dunkirk." The miracle did not include his own son, killed on the bridge of the first Royal Navy destroyer to reach the French shore at Dunkirk.

As the French were driven back, Mussolini attacked France from the south. It mattered little. France gave up on June 22, defeated in six weeks. Fewer than five hundred Germans had been killed. Hitler, remembering his misery twenty-two years before, personally accepted the French surrender, using the same railway carriage in which the kaiser's generals had signed the 1918 German capitulation. The Germans were occupying three-fifths of France, including Paris. The remainder was named Vichy France for the town in which its government, under the aging First War general, Marshal Henri Pétain, was established. Created as a Nazi puppet state, it included French colonial

9. "I was dumbfounded," wrote Churchill in his history of the Second War. "What were we to think of the great French Army and its highest chiefs? It had never occurred to me that any commanders having to defend five hundred miles of engaged front would have left themselves unprovided with a mass of maneuver. No one can defend with certainty so wide a front; but when the enemy has committed himself to a major thrust which breaks the line, one can always have, one *must* always have, a mass of divisions which marches up in vehement counterattack at the moment when the first fury of the offensive has spent its force."

Above, a London bus lies in a huge crater created by German bombers during the Battle of Britain in September 1940, and (below) the dome of St. Paul's still stands amid the smoke and flames of the heavy air raid of December 29. The German bombing of civilian areas of cities, known as the Blitz, began as a prelude to Operation Sea Lion, the planned invasion of Britain, but continued for nine months after the Nazis had called off the invasion, killing more than forty thousand Britons.

10. Fearing that Vichy French vessels would be commandeered by the Germans, the British asked the captains of the Free French ships off the coast of Algeria to turn them over for decommissioning. When they refused, Churchill ordered the Royal Navy to attack, sinking one battleship, damaging five others, and killing 1,297 French servicemen. Although the act exacerbated tensions between Churchill and de Gaulle, it showed the Germans that the British were serious about continuing the fight, and helped convince the Americans that Britain was an ally worth supporting.

11. The carnage of the First World War made Britons unwilling to rebuild their armed forces during the interwar years. Further, an inordinate number of fine young officers had been killed in the First War, robbing the Second War of a pool of competent generals. After Dunkirk, General Alan Brooke, who later became chief of the general staff, opined that half the commanders were unfit. Meanwhile, the growing fear of attack by bombers in the late 1930s, along with Britain's historic concern about invasion by sea, spurred the growth of the Royal Air Force and antiaircraft defenses, and the bolstering of the Royal Navy.

North Africa. Another and very different French government in exile was established in England under General (and future president) Charles de Gaulle.[10]

It was now Britain's turn. Realizing that peace could not be negotiated with Churchill, Hitler embarked on an invasion known as Operation Sea Lion. The Luftwaffe was to smash British air and naval bases, communications centers, and war industries. Twenty divisions of troops would then be ferried across the Channel, make short work of the plainly inferior British army, and occupy England. German bombers duly appeared in British skies in early August 1940 and the Battle of Britain began. With Germany now controlling much of the continent, and allied with Italy and Russia, Britain's prospects were dim. Yet she had certain key advantages. Her two fighter aircraft, the Hurricane and the Spitfire, were nimbler than the Luftwaffe's Messerschmitt 109Es. She had superb pilots, including many Poles and Czechs.[11] She had a new device—radar—that could trace the movement of attacking aircraft. And she had broken the top secret German code, called Enigma, which for the rest of the war enabled her to anticipate almost every major move Hitler planned.

In late August, Göring changed his strategy to bombing airfields farther

Pilot Officer Eugene "Red" Tobin, an American serving in the RAF, sits at the cockpit of his Hurricane fighter in March 1941, and a Spitfire from the Polish Kosciuszko Squadron soars above the fields of southeastern England. The combination of highly motivated pilots and nimble airplanes gave the British the edge they needed to ward off the Luftwaffe menace. "Never in the field of human conflict," said Churchill, "was so much owed by so many to so few."

inland. This might have proved decisive if continued, but a Heinkel bomber, possibly off course, attacked London, and Churchill retaliated by sending eighty-one bombers over Berlin. Although this raid did little damage, it caused the infuriated führer to send Luftwaffe bombers against British cities instead of inland airports, enormously increasing civilian casualties. The main target of what became known as the Blitz was London, and the first raid created an inferno more damaging than the Great Fire of London in 1666. In the next eight months more than eighteen thousand tons of high explosives would rain down on London,[12] and more than a thousand tons each on Liverpool, Birmingham, Plymouth, and Glasgow. In total, the Blitz killed more than forty thousand, and damaged or destroyed more than a million houses in the capital alone. But British resolve held, the production of planes and antiaircraft batteries soared, and Churchill's tribute to British airmen entered the canon of English rhetoric: "Never in the field of human conflict was so much owed by so many to so few." Operation Sea Lion was abandoned in the fall of 1940, and the Battle of Britain was won.

But by now, Hitler's armies had conquered the western Balkans and Greece, crossed the Mediterranean, and landed in North Africa. There the skillful general Erwin Rommel and his Afrika Korps were threatening Egypt and the Suez Canal, intent upon opening a German path into Asia. German U-boats meanwhile, operating like wolf packs, were all but cutting off supplies reaching Britain from overseas.[13]

By the spring of 1941, Hitler's gaze had turned east to his major quarry: Soviet

In total the Blitz killed more than 40,000 and destroyed or damaged a million houses in London alone. But the British resolve held, and Sea Lion was abandoned.

Russia. Operation Barbarossa, the largest invasion in history, started more than a month late, a delay that would have unpleasant consequences for Germany. However, when 152 German divisions crossed the Bug and Neman rivers on June 22, 1941, few believed they would fail. Had they not conquered France in less than forty-five days? Expecting Barbarossa's success by September, British Intelligence warned Churchill to anticipate an invasion of Britain in the fall.

Early results appeared to vindicate the pessimism: four thousand Russian planes destroyed on the ground; three German armies advancing along an eighteen-hundred-mile front; one entire Soviet army destroyed, though it almost matched the Germans in planes, tanks, and heavy guns. General Franz Halder, commander in chief of Germany's eastern armies, pronounced the war all but won in four weeks. Stalin himself—short, stocky, and vicious at age sixty-three—was so alarmed that his berating of the Red Army reduced Chief of Staff Georgi Zhukov to tears. At that, Stalin himself crumpled. "Everything's lost," he wailed. "I give up." After a two-day drunk in his dacha, he was cajoled back to Moscow by his deputies.

Persuaded that he alone could stop Hitler, he now issued his infamous Order 270. Surrounded soldiers must fight to the death. The family of any man who surrendered would be arrested. Those fleeing battle must be shot by their comrades; any soldier failing to do so would face execution himself. Whether inspired by Stalin's brutality or by fury at the invaders, the Russians did slow the enemy

VICTORIA

LA CROISADE CONTRE LE BOLCHEVISME

Above right, a Vichy French poster shows on a map the massive German attack on the Soviet Union launched in July 1941, known as Operation Barbarossa, declaring it "A Crusade Against Bolshevism." Left, German soldiers attack a Russian bunker with the latest model flamethrower, capable of shooting fire one hundred feet. The German blitzkrieg advanced six hundred miles and was at the gates of Moscow when Stalin finally recovered his resolve and galvanized his people to fight back.

advance. Nevertheless, by September the Germans had pushed eight hundred miles into Soviet territory, taken two million prisoners, and besieged Leningrad. This city (formerly and latterly known as St. Petersburg) would remain cut off for two-and-a-half years, and would suffer more than two million military and civilian deaths.

By October 5, with German tanks eighty miles west of Moscow, Hitler prepared to finish off the "Slavic rabbit family" and defeat Bolshevism forever. But Stalin had been reading General Mikhail Kutuzov's account of the Russian withdrawal from Moscow during Napoleon's 1812 invasion. He too was arranging a strategic evacuation; already fifteen hundred factories, along with their workers, had been moved in a million railway cars to the other side of the Urals. However, as he was pacing the station platform in a tattered great coat in preparation for departure, Stalin made the decision to go Kutuzov one better. He would save Moscow, as well as saving Russia.

Setting Communist ideology aside, he pronounced the Russian campaign "the Great Patriotic War." He invoked the religious past to rally the defense of Mother Russia, cited the example of Ivan the Terrible versus the Tatars, aired on Soviet radio a dramatization of Leo Tolstoy's *War and Peace*, opened many of the churches closed by the Communists in their campaign to destroy Christianity, and promoted a popular poem on the war invoking heavenly help. One verse of this ran: "It was as if at the graves in each Russian village, guarding the living with the sign of the cross, our ancestors were gathering to pray for their grandsons who no longer believe in a God."

On December 2, 1941, with German advance units just a dozen miles from the Kremlin, Russia's old ally, winter, lent a hand. Temperatures dropped to thirty below zero, and tank and plane engines had to be heated for hours before they could be started. Many German soldiers, victims of the delay in beginning the campaign, lacked winter clothing. Thousands lost ears, noses, fingers, and even limbs to the frost. General Zhukov, seizing the opportunity, launched a counterattack that

A National Socialist propaganda poster shows German soldiers on the eastern front gamely learning how to ski; meanwhile the reality outside of Moscow during the winter of 1941–42 more resembled the Soviet cartoon below. Russia's old ally, winter, had come to the rescue; the tide slowly but surely was turning.

plowed into the frozen Nazi pincers around Moscow. The Germans were driven back a hundred miles and the Russians, after six months of defeat and a million casualties, had finally realized a victory.

Their offensive would falter in 1942 when the Nazis launched successful counterstrikes, swarming south into the Caucasus oilfields and besieging Stalingrad to the north. Nevertheless, Hitler's audacity, having paid off handsomely for a decade and a half, had at that point turned against him. He had proved fallible, and as the year 1941 began drawing to its close he made one of the worst errors of his career. He gravely underestimated the Americans.

On December 7, 1941, two days after Stalin began driving back the Germans, the Japanese attacked the American Pacific fleet at Pearl Harbor in Hawaii. This was a day, President Franklin Roosevelt immortally predicted in his speech to Congress, that would "live in infamy." It also brought the hitherto divided Americans with a single resolve into the war, and turned the conflict into a truly global event.

In half a century, Japan had grown into Asia's major industrial power, had more than doubled its population to eighty million, and expanded its empire to include Korea, Formosa (later Taiwan), Manchuria, and an assortment of South Pacific islands. But its supply of raw materials and food had been severely curtailed during the Depression when western nations erected tariff barriers to protect their economies. Japan's militaristic government, acting in the name of Emperor Hirohito, consequently launched a campaign of domination in Asia, beginning with attacks on China in 1931.

By 1940, led by its bellicose prime minister, General Hideki Tojo, Japan was threatening colonies in the region, including those controlled by the British (Burma, Hong Kong, Singapore, India), the Dutch (Indonesia), the French

Black smoke pours from the USS California following the Japanese air attack on the American naval base at Pearl Harbor, Hawaii, on December 7, 1941. President Roosevelt's "day that will live in infamy" brought the Americans, with their awesome wealth of resources, into the war, first against Japan, and then against Germany and Italy. Winston Churchill could not have been better pleased. "So we had won after all!" he exulted.

After Pearl Harbor the Americans threw themselves into the war effort with zeal, submitting willingly to rationing and other belt-tightening measures. This selection of posters exhorts Americans to buy war bonds, car pool, donate scrap metal, and join the Women's Army Corps. Even Batman, Superman, and Donald Duck joined the fight.

(Vietnam and Cambodia), and the Americans (the Philippines). When the Japanese refused to cease their incursions into Vietnam and Cambodia, the United States placed an embargo on oil. (Japan was then buying seventy-five percent of her oil from America.)

Tensions increased, but peace negotiations were still in progress in Washington, when at six a.m. (Hawaii time) on Sunday, December 7, 1941, three waves of Japanese aircraft carrier-borne planes swooped down on the base at Pearl Harbor, with its eight docked battleships and five hundred parked airplanes.[14] Catching the Americans totally unprepared, they killed 2,403 servicemen and civilians, sank three ships and capsized another (the USS *Oklahoma*), and destroyed half the planes. Winston Churchill heard the news with unabashed jubilation. He knew then, he would later write, that "the United States was in the war up to the neck, and in to the death. So we had won after all! Hitler's fate was sealed. Mussolini's fate was sealed. As for the Japanese, they would be ground to powder." He was to prove right on all three scores.

Since the invasion of Poland, Churchill had continually encouraged Roosevelt's efforts at gaining congressional support for war. The president had succeeded in supplying Britain with arms under the Lend-Lease program, and American warships had attacked several German U-boats that were menacing merchant shipping in the Atlantic.[15] "When you see a rattlesnake poised to strike," he contended, "you do not wait until he has struck before you crush him." But resistance to direct involvement seemed insurmountable.

The day after the attack on Pearl Harbor, however, Congress voted to declare war on Japan, 470 to 1. (The pacifist Montana Republican congresswoman Jeannette Rankin was the sole dissenter.) Three days later, Hitler declared war on the U.S., which was a major blunder. Roosevelt might still have encountered overwhelming resistance to a "two-front" war against both Japan and Germany; Hitler solved his problem. Perhaps the führer overestimated Japanese military strength. Perhaps he underestimated both America's resources and her will to

14. Mitsuo Fuchida, the lead Japanese pilot at Pearl Harbor, became a national hero and was accorded the rare honor of an audience with the emperor. After the war, believing that the Americans had treated the Japanese with brutality, he questioned returning prisoners, who told him they had on the contrary been treated with respect and even kindness. This was inexplicable to Fuchida, whose own *Bushido* code called for revenge. These and other stories of Christian forgiveness led him to the Bible. He became a Christian, moved to the United States, co-wrote several Christian books, and toured America as a member of the Worldwide Christian Missionary Army of Sky Pilots.

15. The Lend-Lease program was the legislative means by which the United States aided first Britain, and later other allies, by providing materials for the war effort. Initially it allowed for the "lending" of "surplus" American ships, weapons, and ammunition in return for the "leasing" of British colonial naval bases to the U.S. Navy. "What should I do when my neighbor's house is burning down?" Roosevelt demanded, in response to the program's critics. "I don't say... 'Neighbor, my garden hose cost me fifteen dollars, you have to pay me fifteen dollars for it.' I don't want the fifteen dollars. But I do want my garden hose back after the fire is over."

The May 1942 bombing of Cologne, Britain's first "thousand-bomber raid," is shown in all its haunting reality in a painting by wartime artist W. Krogman. below. The Cologne raid killed just 411 civilians, a toll that would be much escalated as carpet bombing techniques developed. By late 1943, waves of bombers dropped high explosives, and second waves dropped incendiaries through the blown-off roofs. This resulted in firestorms of great intensity that could kill tens of thousands in a single night's raid. At right, survivors sort through the bodies of those killed in the February 1945 firebombing of Dresden by both American and British bombers, which killed more than twenty thousand civilians.

Rommel's advance upon the Suez Canal was finally stopped at the Egyptian town of El Alamein in the first significant British military victory of the war. It took longer than expected to drive him out of North Africa, but by summer 1943 this was accomplished. Sicily was the next step. General Bernard Montgomery's Eighth British Army, and General George S. Patton's Seventh American took the island from its Italian and German defenders in six weeks, although casualties were high, and rancor between the competing generals was extreme.[19]

When the Mediterranean campaign was conceived, Mussolini's armies still occupied the Italian peninsula and, given the sorry record of the Italian army, Churchill thought victory would be easily won. But by the time the British and American armies landed in Taranto and Salerno on September 8, 1943, Mussolini had been captured, his troops had laid down their arms, and they had been replaced by a German army under the estimable General Albert Kesselring. What was envisioned as a "walk in the sun" turned into a murderous slog up the mountainous spine of Italy over the course of a long, cold, wet winter, with Kesselring's troops exacting an appalling toll for every surrendered mile. Battles like those at Anzio, Ortona, and Cassino would live long afterward in the nightmares of American, Canadian, and British troops. Viewing the wasteland that remained after the four-month battle to take Cassino in early 1944, an English officer who had fought in the First War grimly commented, "It looks just like the Somme."[20]

By the time General Clark marched his American soldiers into Rome on June 5—disobeying orders from General Command to give the more battle-scarred Canadians the honor of liberating the Eternal City—the Allies had lost thirty thousand men. In the remainder of the campaign, they would lose a further thirty thousand while forcing Kesselring northward, ultimately suffering the highest death rate of American or British soldiers in any campaign of the war.

But very soon neither the Italian campaign nor Clark's triumphal entry into Rome would top the headlines, for on June 6, 1944, General Dwight D. Eisenhower, supreme commander of Allied forces in Europe, had given the go-ahead for the D-Day landings in Normandy. Although the Germans had long expected this invasion, due to a diligent Allied campaign of deception they did not know where or when. Hitler, insistent as always on his own infallibility, believed it was coming at the Pas de Calais where the Channel is narrowest. Instead, five Allied assault divisions in seven thousand vessels—history's largest naval invasion—landed on the beaches of Normandy.

Always insistent on his infallibility, Hitler expected the attack at Calais. Instead, history's largest naval invasion materialized on the beaches of Normandy.

Resistance was especially sharp on the American landing sites code named Utah and Omaha. Because the German forces had been concentrated around the Pas de Calais, however, the Allied divisions, massively supported by bombers and paratroops, established beachheads in Normandy and began their protracted push toward Berlin. Within three months they had landed two million men and half a million vehicles. Paris was liberated by the end of August. The Germans pushed back with all they had, which by now included teenagers and middle-aged men conscripted to augment the ranks. Hoping to buy time to fully utilize German "super weapons" such as jet-engine fighters and V-2 rocket missiles, Hitler mounted a desperate last-minute offensive through the Ardennes, creating a major dent in the Allied line. This was the Battle of the Bulge, fought in the bitterly cold and snowy months of December and January 1944–45. The American divisions were stopped, suffering severe casualties, but with a spectacular flanking movement by General Patton's Third Army from the south, they succeeded in breaking through. In March 1945, they crossed the Rhine River into Germany.

By now, the Soviets were advancing on Berlin from the east, the Red Army having finally turned the tide on Hitler in the winter of 1942–1943. After his armies captured the Crimean peninsula in August, his generals wanted to concentrate on the Caucasus and its oil fields, but Hitler wanted the industrial city of Stalingrad taken first to restore German morale after the Allied victories at El Alamein and Midway in the Pacific. Between November 1942 and February 1943, the German troops were stopped, then encircled and forced to surrender.

19. General Bernard Montgomery, known as "Monty," became a celebrity in England after his defeat of Rommel at El Alamein. With his clipped, slightly lisping Sandhurst accent, his propensity for military shorts, and his birdlike prancing before cameras, Monty seemed destined to clash with his American rival. General George S. Patton, "Old Blood and Guts," was a former Olympic equestrian, a member of the southern American military aristocracy. He wore high boots, carried a riding crop, holstered an ivory-handled revolver on his hip, swore freely and expressively, and believed he had been reincarnated several times, always as a warrior.

20. The Germans defended the town of Cassino from Monte Cassino, site of the monastery built by Saint Benedict fifteen centuries earlier. Unable to take the hill in four months, British Major General Francis Tuker called in 229 American bombers which reduced the abbey to rubble. Allied soldiers and war correspondents cheered. Pope Pius XII, who had removed all moveable treasures from the monastery, said nothing. But his secretary of state, Cardinal Luigi Maglione, called the bombing "a colossal blunder...a piece of a gross stupidity." Since the rubble made the mountain even harder to take, it took another four months to apprehend the town.

The hot-seat throne of Pope Pius XII

He was labeled 'Hitler's Pope' in a Soviet-funded film—was the charge true? To save the church, he let Hitler take power, but the Jews themselves defend him

When Eugenio Pacelli, better known as Pope Pius XII, died in 1958, the official cause was heart attack. His doctor denied it. The pope died of utter exhaustion, he said, "overworked beyond limit." Since Pius had presided over the most trying era in the twentieth-century papacy and lived thirteen more years beyond it, the doctor was widely believed, and Pius died beloved of God and man. Or so it seemed. Had he lived longer, however, he would have discovered his wartime papal record condemned and himself denounced as "Hitler's Pope," a weak enabler of fascism, perhaps an accomplice in the attempted extermination of the Jews.

Just how Pius would have responded to this avalanche of invective is hard to say. He was a riot of contradictions, a man of immense courage yet physically and emotionally frail, by turns indecisive and impulsive, compassionate and harsh, charismatic and yet cold, principled but given to expedience. And although he was deeply traditionalist, his inner circle included a woman, a Bavarian nun, Sister Pascalina, nicknamed La Popessa.

Descended from a long line of church bureaucrats, Pacelli seemed born to the papal administration. He was ordained as a priest in 1899 and assigned immediately to the church's foreign affairs branch. There he became an expert on church-state concordats, and helped develop a code of canon law, further centralizing church authority in the papacy. After the First World War began, the welfare programs he established on both sides soon saw him made papal nuncio in Munich.

Two encounters he made in those years had lasting implications. The first was his meeting with a farm girl, Josefine Lehnert, by all accounts whip smart, opinionated, adventurous, hard-working, and beautiful. As a willful teenager, she had surprised everyone—especially the local boys—by dedicating her life to Christ. As the nun Pascalina, she set up a

retreat in Switzerland for ailing clergy. One patient was Pacelli, now a bishop and suffering from acute exhaustion. Thus began an extraordinary lifelong platonic relationship. Pascalina would serve as Pacelli's nurse, secretary, policy adviser, political protector, and even the voice of his conscience.

In the other, he conferred a substantial church donation on a young man starting a movement to oppose communism, which Pius regarded as the gravest threat to Christian civilization. The young man was Adolf Hitler. The report of their meeting appears in *La Popessa*, Paul I. Murphy's 1962

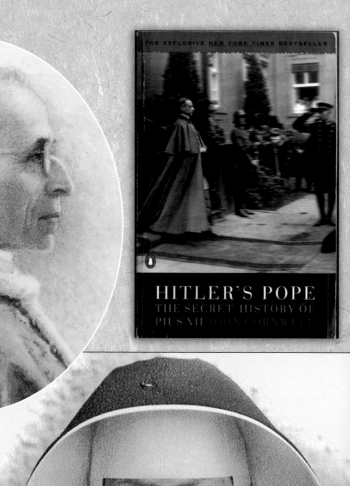

(Counterclockwise from top left) A portrait of Pope Pius XII in 1939; the cover of John Cornwell's 1999 book Hitler's Pope, *which with artful blurring and cropping misrepresents Pius as leaving a post-1933 meeting with Hitler—in reality, the original photo is not blurred and clearly depicts a civilian chauffeur and two Weimar soldiers guarding President Hindenburg's palace door after then-diplomat Pacelli met with him in 1927, five years before Hitler's rise to power; Pius's Bavarian friend and adviser, the 'Popessa' Sister Pascalina.*

Cardinal Pacelli, then papal nuncio to Berlin, is shown with government dignitaries in 1929 prior to his departure for Rome, having effected concordats with Bavaria and Prussia that would serve as models for the 1933 concordat with the Third Reich as a whole. In exchange for Hitler's promise to leave Catholic schools and property unmolested, Pacelli and the Vatican supported the Enabling Act, which allowed Hitler to become dictator of Germany. At right, Pacelli as a youth.

biography of Sister Pascalina, and is drawn from her diaries.

Pius's assessment of the Communist peril became altogether palpable in 1919, when a Russian-backed government was established in Bavaria. Heavily armed Communists descended upon the Munich nunciature and demanded possession of its limousine. In Sister Pascalina's account of what followed, Pacelli simply told them to go away, which they did. What did not go away were the brief nervous breakdowns and nightmares which plagued him for years, a closely guarded Vatican secret. The Bavarian Soviet, however, proved short-lived.

Meanwhile, Pacelli developed the policy that would see him denounced sixty years later. Catholics, representing a third of the German population, supported the moderate Center Party, which was strong enough in the Reichstag to outvote both Hitler's rising National Socialists and the Communists. Pacelli worked hard to negotiate concordats with Bavaria, Prussia, and finally the entire German Reich, retaining papal control over the selection of most bishops, Catholic schools, and church property. But the church agreed to stay out of politics, thus opening a path for the Nazis. The same thinking produced the Lateran Treaty with Mussolini in 1929, which made Catholicism the official religion of Italy, provided financial compensation to the then cash-strapped church, established the sovereignty of Vatican City, and required the Italian clergy to swear allegiance to the Fascist government, abandoning the old centrist Catholic party.

Pacelli, now recalled to Rome as secretary of state, continued pursuing this policy. In exchange for Hitler's promise to respect Catholic schools and church property, he threw church support behind the Enabling Act which allowed Hitler to take power. The Nazis then launched the persecution of the Jews and loosed the thuggish Brownshirts on the many Catholics who spoke out against him (see subchapter, page 118 and subchapter, page 150).

The concordat with the church represented a colossal propaganda coup for the Nazis, and the political power of Germany's twenty-three million Catholics was neutralized. Thousands of Catholic anti-Nazi dissidents were arrested. The louder the church protested, the greater the Nazi reprisals. When an exasperated Pius XI (Pacelli's predecessor) issued an encyclical categorically condemning National Socialism in 1937, Hitler forbade its distribution in Germany. When it was smuggled in, the Nazis confiscated every copy they could and imprisoned the printers, while Hitler pilloried the church as an enemy of the German nation. In a 1938 statement, to which Pacelli contributed, Pius XI declared anti-Semitism inadmissible. "Spiritually," it said, "we are all Semites." On the eve of war the following year, Pacelli was elected his successor.

Six months after Pacelli's coronation, the Nazis invaded Poland and the Second World War began. The new pope vainly pleaded for peace, and finally declared the church's official neutrality. Privately, he took part in a German plot to overthrow Hitler, but it failed and some blamed him. Some assume he became reluctant to implicate the vicar of Christ in an assassination. But in 1940 he tried clandestinely to warn the Allies of Hitler's plan to invade the Low Countries and was discovered. Hitler termed this an act of espionage.

One of Pius's worst trials came in the Balkans. When Hitler and Mussolini overcame the stubborn resistance of the Yugoslav government and forced it into alliance with them, Orthodox Serbian rebels overthrew it. They were soon

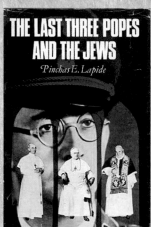

Pinchas Lapide's 1967 book, below, refuted charges that Pius had done nothing to save the Jews from the death camps. According to Lapide, as many as 860,000 Jews escaped the Holocaust through the pan-European rescue efforts of Catholic churchmen directed by the Vatican and Pius XII. After the war Pius was feted by Jewish organizations for his efforts, and Israeli Foreign Minister (later prime minister) Golda Meir, seen above on a 1957 visit to Rome, sent praiseful condolences when he died in 1958.

people, to the best of our ability. But everything we do must be done with much caution. Otherwise the church and the Jews themselves will suffer great retaliation."

However, when Mussolini's government fell and the Nazis occupied Italy, loosing their fury against Italian Jews, the church's response was very different. Pascalina launched a program to rescue Rome's Jews by issuing forged identity cards gaining them entry to Vatican City. Tens of thousands were harbored in the catacombs of the Vatican and the papal retreat of Castel Gandalfo, then smuggled to safety in trucks. Many found sanctuary in Spain or Switzerland. Hitler ordered the pope kidnapped, but local Nazi authorities resisted, fearing a huge political backlash, and the kidnap scheme was abandoned.

The liberation of Rome in mid-1944, followed by the assassination of Mussolini, Hitler's suicide, and the end of the war, brought only uneasy peace for Pius XII. Communism controlled much of Europe, and still threatened to gain sway in Italy. The Vatican worked tirelessly to prevent a Communist coup.

But the world's judgment began to turn against Pacelli with the mid-century rise of secularism and agnosticism. His wartime record came under increasing scrutiny, and five years after his death a much-publicized play called *The Deputy* portrayed the pope as an active accomplice in the Holocaust. It was written by former Nazi youth member Rolf Hochhuth, to worldwide acclaim. (Soviet archives have since disclosed the play was planned and orchestrated by Moscow.) Many other biographers would plow the same ground, culminating with a scathing attack on Pacelli by British author John Cornwell in his 1999 book *Hitler's Pope*,[1] a work much repudiated by Ronald Rychlak's *Hitler, the War, and the Pope* (2000). Behind all this, however, lay the implicit assumption that Pius knew then what we know now, notably that Hitler would lose. But he did not know any of this and had to act on what he did know.

Was his vilification justified? One answer had already come from the Jews themselves. The World Jewish Congress expressed its gratitude with a two million lire donation to the church. Upon Pius's death, then-Israeli Foreign Minister Golda Meir sent praiseful condolences. Perhaps the most effective response came from the Jewish historian Pinchas Lapide, whose 1967 book *The Last Three Popes and the Jews* found Pius's fears of Nazi reprisals altogether valid. From Holland, where local Catholic clergy were most outspoken against the Nazis, more Jews were dispatched to death camps than from any other occupied country. In sum, said Lapide, as many as 860,000 Jews escaped the Holocaust through the pan-European rescue efforts of Catholic churchmen directed by the Vatican and Pius XII. ■

crushed by the Axis powers and Yugoslavia was partitioned. Most of it went to Catholic Croatia, which promptly launched such a ferocious slaughter of the Jews and Orthodox Serbs that even the Nazis were horrified. The Vatican refused to recognize the Croat regime, but did nothing to restrain the bloodbath it was conducting. "From its experience of the 1930s," writes Canadian historian Peter C. Kent in *The Lonely Cold War of Pope Pius XII* (2002), "the Vatican was aware that, where Croatian nationalism was concerned, it could exercise little control over the Croatian clergy." An estimated half million Serbs—Jews, Communists, and Gypsies—were killed.

Hitler's invasion of Communist Russia created for Pius a further problem. With the church's worst enemy, Soviet Russia, now under attack from its second worst enemy, Nazi Germany, whose side would the Vatican take? Pius's effectual answer was neither. While he authorized Catholic chaplains to accompany the German invasion, he refused in any sense to bless it. Similarly, as tens of thousands of Jews all over occupied Europe were being shipped into slavery or extermination, the church remained silent. When individual Christians protested or sheltered Jews, they met the same fate. Yet what could the church do? As Pius told Pascalina: "The Holy See must aid the Jewish

1. Cornwell himself has a curious religious history. Brought up an English Catholic, he enrolled in a seminary, dropped out to attend Cambridge, became an agnostic, married a Catholic, and later rejoined the church as what some call a "revert." Several years after publishing *Hitler's Pope*, he withdrew his denunciation of Pius's wartime inaction, but blamed him for not publicly confessing his errors in the postwar period.

The entire German Sixth Army of three hundred thousand men was lost, with a total of one million military and civilian deaths for both sides. The Soviets took a hundred thousand prisoners, among them twenty-two generals, including Sixth Army commander Friedrich Paulus, who surrendered despite Hitler's stand-and-die order. Hitler was furious, remarking to an aide that Paulus "could have freed himself from all sorrow and ascended into eternity and national immortality, but he prefers to go to Moscow."

After the German loss in Stalingrad, those Nazi generals who had not been captured urged Hitler to create an "East Wall," based on river barriers, as a strategic defense against Soviet advance. Hitler, still firm in his audacity, gambled instead on an offensive. Using their newly developed heavy Tiger tanks, the Germans engaged the Soviets' T-34s near Kursk, west of Stalingrad. German General Erich von Manstein, regarded as Hitler's best strategist, had hoped to encircle the Red Army in a pincer blitzkrieg movement. But the pincers were held back by a series of eight heavily fortified and extensively mined

British General Bernard Montgomery, top left, atop a tank in Egypt, and U.S. General George S. Patton, speaking to an officer from his tank on his way to Messina, combined forces in North Africa in early 1942, moving onto Sicily in 1943, squabbling all the way. It was Churchill's idea for the Anglo-American force to attack the Axis from the Mediterranean, which he called Europe's "soft underbelly." American General Mark Clark called it "one tough gut." By the time it ended, the Italian campaign cost sixty thousand Allied lives, the highest fatalities of any Allied campaign in the war. The lower photograph shows the monastery at Monte Cassino being reduced to rubble fourteen hundred years after St. Benedict built it.

The Third Canadian Infantry Division lands on Juno Beach on D-Day, June 6, 1944, among the 160,000 Allied soldiers deposited on five Normandy beaches by seven thousand vessels in the largest seaborne invasion ever. Top left, two French children watch an American Army jeep driving through the ruins of Saint-Lô, almost totally destroyed by Allied bombers ridding the town of German troops. Above, some of the more than two hundred thousand German soldiers captured during Operation Overlord. Their expressions suggest some relief at having been spared from fighting to the death in Hitler's now hopeless war.

defense zones prepared by Zhukov. Aided by British intelligence, he had learned two months earlier of the attack.

Once stalled, the Germans were pounded by Zhukov's armored divisions, which possessed more and better tanks, more planes, and more antitank guns, and whose troops had orders to shoot any comrades who tried to fall back. Blitzkrieg, in other words, had met its match, and the German offensive line not only was stopped but was broken, allowing the Soviets to move through the gap and push into Ukraine. Kursk was the largest tank battle in history, with Russian deaths exceeding the German four to one. Sixty-seven hundred tanks and twenty-three hundred planes were destroyed.

So began the relentless advance of the Red Army, which occupied Ukraine by the end of 1943, the Baltic States in early 1944, and Warsaw in January 1945. In April 1945, the Russians were on the outskirts of Berlin, notwithstanding a surprisingly fierce resistance from the geriatric and adolescent remnants of the once mighty Wehrmacht. Russian soldiers had become notorious in Germany for raping any woman unlucky enough to find herself in their path. An estimated twenty million women met this fate, sometimes several times over. Stalin approved, remarking that the Red Army had lost eight million soldiers to the Nazis, and "deserved a little fun."

The fifty-six-year-old führer, his once mesmeric eyes clouded, his left hand shaking from the aftereffects of the conspirators' bomb that nearly killed him the previous July, had moved underground in January. In a two-story concrete air-raid bunker fifty-five feet below the rubble of bombed-out Berlin, he continued to move his armies about on old battle maps, imagining last-minute breakthroughs and ordering counteroffensives by generals who were no longer there—or who, if they were, ignored their delusional commander in chief.

Of his early Nazi comrades, only Goebbels remained loyal to the last, reading to his führer from a history of Frederick the Great even as the Red Army blasted its way through the city. Before a small staff of functionaries and Gestapo, Hitler married his mistress, Eva Braun, on April 29. Next afternoon, the newlyweds retired to their quarters and killed themselves: she with a cyanide capsule; he with a revolver to the mouth. Aides carried their bodies up to the garden and, during a lull in the Russian bombardment, placed them in shell holes where they were drenched with gasoline and burned. Goebbels and his wife went out the same way on May 1, after poisoning their six children.

Six days later, General Eisenhower accepted Germany's unconditional surrender, Hitler's Thousand-Year Reich having lasted for a little over twelve. Four months after that, America's atomic bombs, their development significantly aided by Jewish scientists who had fled the Nazi regime, were dropped on Hiroshima and Nagasaki. Japan's surrender immediately followed. The Second World War was officially over.[21]

In Berlin, General Zhukov, presiding over the Soviet-occupied capital, phoned Stalin to tell him of Hitler's suicide. "So the bastard's dead?" Stalin responded. "Too bad we didn't capture him alive." But the Soviet leader was now absorbed in postwar problems and possibilities. Just as his soldiers deserved a little rapine, Stalin reasoned, clearly the Soviet Union, which he felt had broken the back of the Nazis while its Allies dithered in Italy, was entitled to the lion's share of the territorial spoils. In other words, the Cold War was about to begin. ■

21. Total fatality statistics for the Second World War have been estimated at anywhere between fifty and seventy million soldiers and civilians. Likely second to the Soviet Union (twenty-three million) was China, with between ten and twenty million. Next was Germany at about seven million; Poland at more than five million (many of them Polish Jews exterminated in death camps); the Dutch East Indies (Indonesia) at between three and four million; Japan at about three million; India between 1.5 and 2.5 million; and the Philippines, French Indochina (Vietnam), and Yugoslavia at about one million apiece. France (550,000 dead), Italy (454,000), and Britain (451,000) all suffered fewer fatalities than they had in the First World War. In fact, the Soviets lost twice as many people in the siege of Leningrad alone as the British lost in the entire war. The American dead, 418,000, was more than triple the 117,000 American dead in the First World War.

A million Russians died defending Stalingrad during its siege in 1942–43 (depicted at top in a 1964 Soviet painting). As many Germans died trying to take the city, but were finally defeated, losing an entire army. Thus began the final Russian offensive, as is neatly illustrated in the 1944 Soviet cartoon (bottom right). On April 30, 1945, with the Red Army blasting its way into Berlin, Hitler put a gun in his mouth and pulled the trigger. Two days later, as shown in the iconic photograph bottom left, the Soviets were raising their red flag over the ruins of Berlin. And while the Second World War in Europe had been won, the Cold War was about to begin.

Some Christians spoke out and died

Most failed to oppose the Hitler regime, but some few did. Five were Allied spies in German intelligence, who were caught as the Nazis fell. One was Dietrich Bonhoeffer.

Organized opposition to the Nazi regime, much of it Christian, existed through the whole Hitler era, and many of its participants may accurately be described as having gone to a Christian martyrdom. All but one of these endeavors, however, failed to even retard the Nazi horror, and that one came to an unsuccessful end with the bodies of five naked men swinging from makeshift gallows at the Flossenbürg concentration camp, two weeks before the Second World War in Europe ended.

It was remarkable they survived so long. Throughout most of the war all five had been involved with the *Abwehr*, the German counterintelligence agency specifically charged with discovering plots against Hitler. They were, that is, both the hunters and the hunted, and they were in active communication with British intelligence nearly the whole six years of the war. One of the five hanged provided their key link with the British, though he is far better known to Christian history, not as a spy, but as the great German twentieth-century theologian Dietrich Bonhoeffer.

Central to this astonishing endeavor was the inscrutable figure of Wilhelm Franz Canaris, a skillful naval intelligence officer and later U-boat commander in the First World War, who had remained in the navy between the wars. He had backed Hitler as the only man who could salvage Germany economically, then became utterly revolted by the Hitler-ordered slaughter of the Jews and Catholic clergy in Poland. His extraordinary record is recounted in a 2008 biography by the German journalist Michael Mueller (*The Life and Death of Hitler's Spymaster*). Soon after the war's outbreak, Canaris was made an admiral and chief of the Abwehr, which he subversively turned against Hitler, setting up communication with the British through the Vatican, warning the Allies of Nazi plans to attack France through the Netherlands, helping persuade Spain's Franco, whom he knew well, to foil Hitler's plans to take Gibraltar, thwarting a Hitler plot to kidnap Pope Pius XII, helping numerous Jews escape from Germany, and saving from arrest many German army officers who thrice plotted Hitler's overthrow.

In February of 1944, the Schutzstaffel (known as the SS) were finally able to cast sufficient suspicion on Canaris to secure his dismissal from the Abwehr, and in June he was placed under house arrest. He was not charged for months, however, probably because the SS commander Heinrich Himmler hoped to use him as a channel to the Allies when Himmler carried out a plan to seize power from Hitler as the Nazi defeat became inevitable. When the Himmler coup failed to happen, the fate of the five was sealed, and at six in the morning of April 9, 1945, with American artillery fire booming in the distance, the five bodies were thrown on a woodpile and cremated.[1]

Canaris and his three fellow Abwehr officers cannot be described as Christian martyrs, except in the sense that they gave their lives for a Germany that had once been Christian but was now run, in their view, by atheist barbarians. They longed and plotted for the return of the Germany that once had been Christian. As for Bonhoeffer, however, his was clearly a

Sophie Scholl, played by Julia Jentsch, takes the stand before the notorious Nazi judge Roland Freisler in the award-winning 2005 German film about the youthful member of the student resistance movement White Rose. Sophie and her brother Hans Scholl, both Lutherans, were arrested by the Gestapo while distributing anti-Nazi leaflets at the University of Munich. Both were guillotined for treason. Opposition to the Nazi regime existed through the whole Hitler epoch, much of it Christian, and with many of its participants being martyred.

Christian martyrdom. In the name of Christ, he had opposed Hitlerism defiantly and publicly, always knowing the inevitable outcome. A medical doctor who survived Flossenbürg describes Bonhoeffer in his dying hour:

> Through the half-open door of his cell, I saw the pastor kneeling in prayer. I have never been so moved as I was then. His devotion was absolute; he appeared almost cheerful. Later, in front of the gallows, he repeated a short prayer, then climbed up to the rope with complete composure. He was dead in a few seconds. During my fifty years' experience in medicine, I have never seen anyone die so calmly and so trustingly.

Other Christian martyrdoms were plentiful, some of particular note. There was medical student Hans Scholl, age twenty-five, for instance, and his student sister, Sophie, arrested by the Gestapo at the University of Munich while distributing anti-Nazi leaflets. Printed by the clandestine student organization White Rose, the pamphlets protested the killing of three hundred thousand German Jews and denounced Hitler as a diabolical liar. Even more galling to the Nazis was the graffiti stenciled by White Rose members on Munich city walls after Germany's crushing defeat in the Battle of Stalingrad—such sentiments as "Freedom!" and "Down with Hitler!" On February 22, 1943, after a brief visit from their staunchly Lutheran parents, brother and sister were guillotined for treason, along with Christopher Probst, another student, baptized just before his execution. Two more White Rose members—philosophy professor Kurt Huber and Russian-born student Alexander Schmorell—were executed that July. Schmorell would be declared a saint by the Orthodox Church.

Willi Graf (twenty-three), also of the White Rose, was executed that October after six months of solitary confinement and torture. White Rose members who were subsequently condemned included Hans Liepert (twenty-five), beheaded January 1945, and Curt Ledien (fifty-two) and Gretl Mroske (thirty), both hanged within a month of the

'Through the half-open cell door, I saw the pastor kneeling in prayer. I was never so moved in my life.'

war's end. Many White Rose members died in concentration camps. One escaped. Heinz Kucharski was sentenced to death and fled a train during an Allied bombing attack.

The Nazi regime posed a particular problem for the Protestant churches, however, with their strong historic affiliations to German nationalism. In fact, the state church of Prussia had combined both Calvinists and Lutherans since the 1930s. From 1930 onward, a Nazi movement called the German Christians waged an effective campaign for control of the country's German Evangelical Church. Many clergy and parishioners alike had viewed Hitler as offering the first rays of economic hope for their country. But they found themselves increasingly conflicted over various crucial matters, including the treatment of Jews, and particularly for the persecution of Jewish converts to Christianity.

Prominent among Lutheran clerics who spoke up and eventually acted as well, was Pastor Martin Niemöller, who helped found a breakaway organization in 1934 known as the Confessing Church. Declared illegal three years later, it went underground, and Niemöller spent the next eight years in Sachsenhausen and Dachau concentration camps. By one estimate, ten percent of the inmates of the latter were clergy, Catholic and Protestant. Even so, until his death in

Some of those martyred while involved in anti-Nazi activities have been canonized, beatified, and commemorated on stamps. Clockwise from bottom left, Lutheran pastor Martin Niemöller, Münster Bishop Clement August von Galen, Polish priest Maximilien Kolbe, the attempted Hitler assassin Claus Schenk Graf von Stauffenberg, the Scholls, Sophie and Hans, and Catholic convert Edith Stein. Below, the statue of Dietrich Bonhoeffer at the west door of London's Westminster Abbey (furthest right) in the company of Mother Elizabeth of Russia, Rev. Martin Luther King, Jr., and Archbishop Oscar Romero.

1. The three other men hanged with Canaris and Bonhoeffer were Major General Hans Oster, deputy head of the Abwehr; Captain Ludwig Gehre, an Abwehr staff officer; and Dr. Karl Sack, judge advocate-general of the German army and closely associated with the Abwehr.

From left, Wilhelm Canaris, Dietrich Bonhoeffer, and Father Hugh O'Flaherty. Canaris and Bonhoeffer both lived remarkable double lives during the war, working for and against the Nazis, but eventually both were caught and hanged. O'Flaherty, on the other hand, was able to assist Jews in occupied Rome and lived to return to his native Ireland.

2. Urging the faithful to stand fast, outspoken Bishop von Galen accused the Nazis of "a deep-running hatred of Christianity, which is scheduled to be rooted out." Rather than arrest this high-profile ecclesiastic, because they feared it would make him an acclaimed martyr in the eyes of many young Germans, the Gestapo instead seized thirty-seven priests, ten of whom, to von Galen's bitter sorrow, died in the concentration camps His sermons are also said to have inspired the Lübeck Christians—priests Hermann Lange, Eduard Müller, and Johannes Prassek, and Lutheran pastor Karl Friedrich Stelbrink, who were executed together in 1943 for preaching against the Nazis. When their blood ran together on the floor, it was seen by the faithful as the coming together of all Christians to oppose the Nazi regime.

1984 at age ninety-two, Niemöller regretted his own attitudes and policies toward the Jews. At the war's end, he was one of the originators of the Stuttgart Declaration of Guilt, whereby the German Evangelical Church expressed remorse for not more courageously resisting the Nazis.

Dietrich Bonhoeffer, on the other hand, was never duped by Nazi rhetoric. He spoke out for the Jews, and was so determined to stop the Nazis that he took on a double life—becoming an Abwehr agent and ostensibly working for the Reich, but in reality subverting it along with Canaris's resisters.

As his biographer Eric Metaxas recounts in *Bonhoeffer* (2008), young Dietrich dodged his military call-up in May 1939 by accepting a teaching position in New York. But within a month, convinced that God wanted him home, he was back in Germany. There he ran an underground seminary, used his international connections to aid refugees, and accused inactive fellow Christians of relying on "cheap grace." "Only those who cry out for the Jews," Bonhoeffer declared, "can sing Gregorian chants." Under cover of the Abwehr, he served as a courier connecting the German resistance movement to Allied intelligence.

For Catholic prelates, the church's disposition toward the Nazis left little in doubt. Cardinal Michael von Faulhaber of Munich, for example, helped to draft the anti-Nazi encyclical issued by Pope Pius XI in 1937 and read in all Catholic churches. In *Hitler, the War and the Pope* (2000), author Ronald Rychlak describes this as one of the strongest condemnations the Holy See ever published of any national regime. The Nazis seized all copies and arrested distributors. (The charge that Pius's successor, Pius XII, was effectually "Hitler's Pope" was made by

Soviet propagandists in 1945, and made the subject of a play by a Marxist eighteen years later. See sidebar, page 142.)

Bishop Clement August von Galen (known as the Lion of Münster) preached a series of sermons excoriating in particular the Nazi euthanasia program begun in 1939, under which an estimated two hundred thousand mentally or physically handicapped persons would be gassed. It is believed that these sermons, broadcast by the BBC, circulated secretly throughout the Reich, and airdropped by the RAF over its major cities, reached some forty million people. They are thought to have inspired Hans Scholl and his friends to organize the White Rose.[2]

The bishop's words are said to have also encouraged resistance in German-occupied Holland, where Catholics who joined the Nazi Party were excommunicated and church newspapers were forbidden to print party propaganda. Carmelite scholar Titus Brandsma, spiritual adviser to Netherlands Catholic journalists, was arrested in January 1942, ended up in Dachau's dreaded hospital, was subjected to medical experimentation, and was killed by lethal injection on July 26. That same day an episcopal letter publicly protested the deportation of Dutch Jews, which caused the German occupying forces to arrest all Dutch Catholics of Jewish ancestry. Among these was Edith Stein. A German Jew and atheist philosopher who had converted to Catholicism at age thirty-three, she had become a Carmelite nun nine years later. Edith Stein and her sister Rosa (also a convert) died at Auschwitz on August 9, 1942. Edith would be canonized in 1998 under her religious name, Sister Teresa Benedicta of the Cross.

Auschwitz had produced another recognized saint a year earlier, when its commandant selected ten men for death by starvation, as punishment for the escape of three prisoners. One of them burst out sobbing, "My wife... my children..." and a Polish priest named Maximilian Kolbe volunteered to take his place. After weeks in a cramped cell, singing hymns and comforting his comrades, Father Kolbe was killed by injection of carbolic acid. He was canonized in 1982.[3]

Meanwhile, Provost Bernard Lichtenberg of St. Hedwig Cathedral in Berlin (aged sixty-eight) had been arrested for offering public

> 'The Jew is my neighbor with an immortal soul shaped in God's image,' prayed the pastor. He died en route to Dachau.

prayers for Jews. He was called upon to love his neighbor as himself, Lichtenberg protested, "and I recognize the Jew, too, as my neighbor, who possesses an immortal soul, shaped after the likeness of God." Offered his freedom two years later if he would cease preaching, Lichtenberg asked to be deported to Poland instead, to give spiritual aid to Jews and Jewish Christians, but died en route to Dachau in November 1943. Beatified in 1996, he later was named Righteous Among the Nations by *Yad Vashem*, Israel's Holocaust Memorial Center.

Also recognized by Yad Vashem is Hungarian Sara Salkahazi, a former journalist who became a nun in 1930 (giving up a chain-smoking habit to do so). On December 27, 1944, the morning meditation she offered to her fellow Sisters of Social Services was on martyrdom. She was arrested that noon, the authorities having discovered some residents with suspicious identifications at her home for working women. Lined up that evening on the banks of the Danube with eighteen others, Sister Sara was shot as she made the sign of the cross.

Not least effective among rescuers was Monsignor Hugh O'Flaherty, a six-foot-two Irishman who was serving as a Vatican notary when the Germans occupied Italy in September 1943. In *The Vatican Pimpernel* (2008) Brian Fleming recounts how O'Flaherty used his diplomatic immunity, consular connections, and extensive knowledge of Rome, to save nearly eighty-seven hundred of that city's Jewish residents. He was good at disguises, too—street cleaner, nun, whatever—and once gave the slip to brutal Gestapo chief Herbert Kappler by escaping through a coal cellar.[4]

Among those who planned the complete overthrow of the Nazis, one came closest to success. He was Lieutenant Colonel Claus Schenk Graf von Stauffenberg, scion of a Catholic family in Swabia who planted a bomb beneath a big table at a general staff meeting in Hitler's eastern front headquarters. The bomb wounded Hitler, but did not kill him. Stauffenberg was executed that night by firing squad along with four coconspirators. The ensuing purge, writes William Shirer in *The Rise and Fall of the Third Reich* (1959), would result in another 4,980 executions.

Caught up in this sweep was Helmuth James Graf von Moltke, a Lutheran and an Abwehr lawyer, who had assembled a secret organization of intellectuals, politicians, and clerics to plan a Christian-based society in

Germany after the fall of the Third Reich. Von Moltke was hanged. Part of his last letter to his wife survives. "God endows me with faith, hope and charity," he wrote, "in such measure as is really overwhelming."

That many of these suffered as Christian martyrs seemed undeniable, and yet it was Bonhoeffer who questioned the use of the term. He blamed himself and all German Christians for permitting the Nazi revolution to occur. In 1932, the year before Hitler took power, he foresaw what would happen: "The blood of martyrs might once again be demanded," he said, "but this blood, if we really have the courage and loyalty to shed it, will not be innocent, shining like that of the first witnesses for the faith. On our blood lies heavy guilt, the guilt of the unprofitable servant who is cast into outer darkness."

The whole Nazi experience raised a further question for church historians, which was undertaken by the American political scientist Guenter Lewy, in *The Catholic Church in Nazi Germany* (1964). While the response of some individual Christians to the Nazi outrage shines brightly, he writes, institutionally the church "vacillated and compromised." How much is the sheer survival of the institution to count against the preservation of moral integrity? "There comes a time when all temporizing has to be abandoned. In the eyes of many observers, the church in Germany still pays the price for not having listened to the voice of conscience." ■

Reichsmarschall Herman Göring (the fat man in the light-colored uniform) shows fellow Nazis the damage caused by the July 20, 1944, blast caused by the bomb that Claus von Stauffenberg (inset) had planted in the conference room at the Wolf's Lair to kill Hitler. The bomb, contained in a briefcase placed between a table support and the führer, only slightly injured him. Stauffenberg and his co-conspirators, along with 4,980 others implicated in the plot, were summarily executed.

3. Franciszek Gajowniczek, the man whom Father Kolbe saved, survived the war and returned home to find his two sons had been killed but his wife had survived. He was present at both Maximilien Kolbe's beatification and canonization, and died in 1995 at age ninety-four.

4. Monsignor Hugh O'Flaherty reportedly often slept on the floor so that an exhausted Jewish refugee could have his bed. His chief opponent was Rome's Gestapo chief, Herbert Kappler, notorious for the March 1944 Ardeatine Cave massacre in which three hundred Italians were shot in retaliation for a guerrilla bomb attack. In 1947, after Kappler was sentenced to life imprisonment, O'Flaherty visited him monthly, and twelve years later baptized him. The story was dramatized in a 1983 TV movie, *The Scarlet and the Black*.

An aircraft descends out of the fog into Gatow airport in December 1948 during the Berlin Airlift. In the early years of the Cold War, the Soviets blocked passage to the western-allied sectors of the divided capital, which now lay as an island under siege within Communist East Germany. Accordingly, food and fuel were flown into the besieged city in hundreds of American and British aircraft, ensuring the survival of West Berlin.

CHAPTER 8

Three Christian politicians bring unity to Europe grounded in their faith

Adenauer, De Gasperi, and Schuman foil the Soviets, and Christian Democrats unite the democracies after the Airlift thwarts the Red plan to grab Berlin

Among the thousands rounded up in Nazi Germany following the attempt to assassinate Hitler in 1944 was a sixty-eight-year-old former lord mayor of Cologne. To the Nazis he had been a long-time nuisance, going back to 1933 when he ordered police to take down swastikas from a Cologne bridge. He had been imprisoned and freed several times in the war. In his latest endeavor, he had been fatefully slated for transportation to the ominous Buchenwald concentration camp, but had escaped. Now, emaciated, ashen-faced, and caught again, he was entering the Brauweiler prison. The Gestapo forced him to hand over his tie and suspenders. "You're an old man," sneered the guard, "and you have nothing more to live for." But the prisoner had a great deal more to live for, and because of that so did Germany. For the old man's name was Konrad Adenauer.

Adenauer was to become the leader of a new Germany. He was one of several politicians, all Christians and all consciously and forthrightly acting in accord with their Christian convictions, who would shape the Europe that was rising out of the ashes and rubble of the war. They called themselves Christian Democrats, a political-religious movement that went back to the late nineteenth century. They appeared at a momentously critical point in their continent's history. There were two directions Europe could turn after the war—toward the rising power of communism and totalitarianism in the East, or toward the principles of freedom and democracy represented by the West.

Adenauer stood for the West. So did two other leaders, both key, Robert Schuman of France and Alcide De Gasperi of Italy. For all three, democracy was firmly rooted in the Christian faith. As Schuman put it: "Democracy will either be Christian or it will not exist. An anti-Christian democracy will be a caricature which will founder into tyranny and anarchy."

The fight for Europe was the first major battle in the Cold War—a confrontation not only of armies and weapons, but more centrally of ideas and culture. Its main battleground in the five years that followed the Allied victory in 1945 would center on France, Italy, and Germany. The prior lives of the trio had prepared each to play the pivotal role that befell them.

De Gasperi would be the first to move into a position of power, becoming premier of Italy in 1945 at age sixty-four. He came from the Trentino, an Italian-speaking region in Austria prior to the First World War where he won a seat in the Austrian parliament. After the Trentino region became part of Italy, he won a seat in the Italian parliament. Imprisoned during the Mussolini era and then freed, he first worked as a Vatican librarian, and then in the Saint John Lateran Seminary, a center of subversive church resistance to German anti-Jewish activity in Italy.[1] As the Fascist state crumbled, De Gasperi began reviving his old party, *Democrazia Cristiana* (the Christian Democrats).

The death struggle with communism had not yet begun in those days. Christian Democrat De Gasperi often shared the platform with Communist leader Palmero Togliatti, whose party had a strong Italian following. Moreover, Soviet Russia was then a powerful ally of the democracies in the war against Nazi Germany. De Gasperi later recalled a speech he made to a largely Communist crowd. They must travel together a hard road up the mountain, he said. "But up there on the incline walks another Proletarian, also Jewish, like Marx. Two thousand years ago, he established the International based on equality, universal fraternity, the Fatherhood of God. He aroused ardent love, untold heroism, and sacrifices to the point of immolation." His speech then became a sermon: "It is necessary to take to the road once again, to follow that Divine Figure. Has not each one of you already encountered that Proletarian Christ, with his kind look, during the days of pain and tragedy in the shelters, in the prisons, or in the darkness of the catacombs?"

After the war De Gasperi and others tried to sustain the spirit of the wartime Resistance, building coalitions with individuals, not parties. In the atmosphere of chaos, conflict, strikes, and demonstrations after the war, however, it proved impossible. Adherents of one party would break up meetings of other parties; parliamentary coalitions were created and collapsed. De Gasperi himself survived an assassination attempt. In this turmoil in December 1945, he was installed as premier, presiding over an interim coalition of five parties. That the coalition could survive even until the first popular elections six months later was in grave doubt.

Meanwhile in France, things were even more chaotic. Like De Gasperi, Robert Schuman was a man of the borderlands. He was born in 1886 in Luxembourg, then moved to his family's homeland

Alcide De Gasperi, shown here in a 1944 photo, was the first of the postwar Christian Democrat leaders to gain power, becoming premier of Italy in 1945. In those days the death struggle with communism had yet to begin, and De Gasperi could share a platform with Communist leader Palmero Togliatti and speak of Christ and Marx as fellow travelers on the road to universal fraternity.

POSTWAR EUROPE DIVIDED, 1955

European members of the North Atlantic Treaty Association (NATO)
Members of the Warsaw Pact
Non-aligned states
Other Communist states

of Lorraine, over which the French and Germans had been fighting for at least three centuries. Though German speaking, he regarded himself as of the French culture. He traveled in 1909 to Rome for the beatification of France's heroine, Joan of Arc, who, like Schuman, came from Lorraine. He gave thanks at Lourdes in 1914 for being exempted from serving in the German army.

In 1918 Lorraine was returned to France, and Schuman was elected to the Paris Assembly. When Germany invaded in 1939 he was appointed undersecretary for refugees and worked tirelessly to find food, lodging, and medical care for those fleeing the Nazis. He was arrested by the Gestapo when France fell, but escaped and spent the war in hiding. With Liberation, he returned to Paris, but in the atmosphere of purges and waves of terror, he was accused of being a collaborator. He followed the liberating troops to his home town of Metz, where he was acclaimed as a member of parliament and a member of the Liberation Committee, which administered the city.

Those same troops battled on, crossed the Rhine, and soon after took Cologne. One of the first men they looked for was Konrad Adenauer, who showed in the records as having been lord mayor before the Nazis took over. They wanted to reinstate him. He was an old-timer, had been elected deputy mayor back in 1912, and at one point had even rivaled Hitler for the chancellorship of Germany.

1. The Lateran Seminary was a refuge for many in the dying days of the war: Jews hiding from the German patrols that were packing railway cars to Auschwitz, military men who had expressed their disapproval of Mussolini, members of almost every party to be represented in the postwar parliament. Elisa A. Carrillo, in his biography, *Alcide De Gasperi, The Long Apprenticeship* (1965), recalls conversations between De Gasperi and Pietro Nenni, the leader of the Socialist party: "Later, when De Gasperi and Nenni became political enemies, there remained the memories of the friendly debates in the Lateran Seminary, held in what seemed an oasis of security amid the military terror which then gripped Rome."

The Americans knew that though Adenauer had three sons in the German army, the Nazis plainly had marked him as an enemy. In 1934, they put him on trial for accepting bribes, but their case fell apart after Adenauer assailed their star witness, pointing to a crucifix in the courtroom, and commanding: "In the name of all that is sacred to you, tell the truth." The witness broke down, burst into tears, and admitted he was lying. In this way Adenauer could somehow move the most improbable people—like the Communist and the Luftwaffe officer who helped him escape Buchenwald.

Back in the lord mayor's office, he began work parties to clean up the war-ravaged city, sent buses to pick up Cologne citizens in concentration camps, and drew up plans for rebuilding. But his future did not lie in municipal politics. With the war's end, Germany was divided into four zones of occupation—Russian, British, American, and French—and because Cologne was in the British zone of occupation, the Americans left. The British wanted things done differently and were not happy with Adenauer's approach, so they fired him. This left him free to begin working at his real political dream—rebuilding a Christian Democratic party. He decided it must take the lead in creating a new Germany and a new Europe out of the smoking ruins of bombed-out cities, ruined industries, starving populations, unheated houses, and municipal services largely destroyed. Such would be the battleground for the Cold War.

The first victories all went to communism. The Russian zone of East Germany quickly vanished into the cold, joyless structures of a Communist state, and soon all Eastern Europe lay in the darkness of the Soviet sphere: Poland, Czechoslovakia, Hungary, all but Greece in the Balkans, and all three Baltic states. Winston Churchill added a new term to the western world's vocabularies in an historic speech at Fulton, Missouri on March 5, 1946: "From Stettin in the Baltic to Trieste in the Adriatic, an iron curtain has descended across the continent."

Postwar French statesman Robert Schuman, shown here in a limousine in 1950, had grown up in German-speaking Lorraine, but was a Francophile who resisted the Nazis during the war. For him, as with his fellow postwar western European leaders, Christianity was the key to holding back the Russians. "Democracy will either be Christian or it will not exist," Shuman said. "An anti-Christian democracy will be a caricature which will founder into tyranny and anarchy."

Communist parties were on the ascendant in many countries, both east and west. In Milan and other cities, Communist banners flew over factories and public buildings. In the Paris to which Robert Schuman returned in 1945, left and right jockeyed for political ascendancy. Wartime Free French leader Charles de Gaulle—excluded from the Big Three conference at Yalta (and refusing to meet Roosevelt in Algiers)—instead flew to Moscow to sign a treaty with Stalin. Russia, after all, had been France's continental ally against a strong Germany throughout the twentieth century. The French leader of the Communist party, Maurice Thorez, had spent the war in Moscow and now returned with Russian backing and finances. Even the Christian Democratic *Mouvement*

Républicain Populaire (MRP), in its 1944 campaign literature, spoke of "breaking with the capitalist system, putting a stop to the omnipotence of 'King Money,' overthrowing financial oligarchies and trusts, and retaking economic liberty."

By 1945 MRP leader Georges Bidault changed this rhetoric as he attempted to move the party more toward the center: "We must face things head on," he told a party convention. "If we have a bipartite (Communist-Socialist) government, the United States will find good reasons to hold up imports and to refuse credits. We can't get on alone. If a huge effort is not made, we'll be out of bread in six weeks… What we need now, more than political programs, are imports and American aid."

The plight of France mirrored the basic reality that was shaping up across Europe. American aid was needed to rebuild. Nevertheless, there was an inherent resentment of American dominance, particularly in France. For instance, an American aid package in 1946 of $650 million included the condition that French cinemas must show more Hollywood films. Despite the ruins around them, feelings of French *grandeur* still stirred.[2] It therefore came as no surprise when the first French postwar election gave the largest share of seats to the Communists. The implications were ominous. "If France is lost, Europe is lost," read a CIA report to U.S. President Harry Truman.

A series of coalition governments came and went. In January, 1946 Charles de Gaulle resigned as president, and was subsequently bypassed for the next twelve years

2. French sentiment against American domination reached a head in 1948–1949 in a battle over allowing Coca-Cola into the country. In 1950 winegrowers sponsored a bill which would investigate the content of all drinks in the country. *Le Monde* wrote: "We have accepted chewing gum and Cecil B. De Mille, Reader's Digest and be-bop. It's over soft drinks that the conflict has erupted." A court decision ultimately allowed in the soft drink giant. The incident showed that the Cold War was just as much about culture and ideas as it was about military and economic alliances. Mao Zedong once called American culture "sugar-coated bullets."

Below, the bomb-devastated German city of Cologne in 1945 and, inset, its reinstated lord mayor, Konrad Adenauer. Cologne was in the British zone of postwar occupation, but the British fired Adenauer as mayor, allowing him to follow his preferred path: rebuilding the Christian Democrat party.

Foreign ministers from the main victors in the Second World War are shown in Moscow in 1947 during one of the meetings that took place to decide the fate of Europe. From left: Britain's Ernest Bevin, U.S. Secretary of State George C. Marshall, Russia's Vyacheslav Molotov, and France's Georges Bidault. American aid to a devastated Europe under the European Recovery Program (soon to be known as the Marshall Plan) was largely welcomed by the Christian countries, but not by the Soviet Union, which feared that American money would result in American control. When the western powers signed the North Atlantic Treaty (NATO) in 1949, the Soviets saw it as proof of their fealty to a rich and heavily armed benefactor—as illustrated in the Russian cartoon below.

(although his party remained a strong presence). Instead, a "Third Force" emerged, centrist governments claiming to offer an alternative between right-wing nationalists (de Gaulle) and left-wing Communists. The Christian MRP was the glue that held this very tentative alliance together. Then in May 1947, the United States announced the Marshall Plan, the most comprehensive United States aid package ever offered.[3]

Buying into it, the centrist parties dismissed all Communist members from cabinet posts. A subsequent wave of strikes and demonstrations were coordinated by the Communist-run labor unions. Schuman, appointed premier in November, broke the back of the strike with a variety of tools. One was the appointment of Socialist Jules Moch as interior minister. The left was pitted against the left as Moch led the battle against the strikers. Also playing a major role was an American Federation of Labor organizer who helped in the creation of a non-Communist union, thereby splitting the ranks of the strikers. U.S. Ambassador Jefferson Caffery said breaking the power of the Communist strike "was the most important event that has occurred in France since the Liberation." He meant that the Third Force, and its Christian Democratic component, were establishing control of France.

In Italy as in France, it was clear that American aid would not flow quickly to governments with Communist affiliations. A 1945 memo from U.S. Acting Secretary of State Joseph Grew to President Truman states the Italian case: "Our objective is to strengthen Italy economically and politically so that truly democratic elements of the country can withstand the forces that threaten to sweep them into a new totalitarianism... The time is now ripe when we should initiate action to raise Italian morale, make a stable representative government possible and permit Italy to become a responsible participant in international affairs." Prescient words, considering Italy had been an enemy two years before.

The 1946 election returned De Gasperi, but just barely. His party received thirty-five percent of the vote; Communists and Socialists together forty percent. But one wing of the Socialists refused to join a Communist/Socialist coalition, and instead joined De Gasperi to form an anti-Communist coalition. De Gasperi would successfully meld the Christian Democrats and other allies to form the government for the next eight years, a record in Italian politics. This was in no small measure due to De Gasperi's curious ability to make friends. In 1946, faced with an imminent grain crisis, he made an emergency phone call to Fiorello LaGuardia, ex-mayor of New York, who arranged to convert troop ships into grain ships and send them to Italian ports. De Gasperi's one-on-one discussions with Truman laid the groundwork for the Marshall Plan. By 1948, however, all De Gasperi's powers of persuasion were wholly called upon when mounting tension between East and West focused the world's attention on the Italian general election, which took on the hallmarks of a crusade.

"The 1948 elections were fought exclusively in terms of Christ versus communism," asserts historian S. J. Woolf in his 1972 study *The Rebirth of Italy, 1943–50*. The Catholic Church provided all-out support for Christian Democrats (the pope excommunicated Communist supporters the next year). The U.S. intervened covertly and in public: fund raising among Italians in the U.S. brought in $2 million, while Italian Americans also wrote tens of thousands of letters to their relatives in Italy encouraging them to vote for the Christian Democrats.

3. General George C. Marshall, U.S. secretary of state, disclosed the historic European Recovery Program that bears his name. To help administer the Marshall Plan, the Organization for European Economic Cooperation (OEEC) was created which became the Organization for Economic Cooperation and Development in 1961. The OEEC also made it possible for other countries, notably Canada, to contribute funds for European reconstruction. By the twenty-first century this institution would become the economic club of rich nations that also includes South Korea and Mexico, among others.

Catholic girls parade in support of the Christian Democrat party in Milan in 1948 (left). The election was, according to one historian, "fought exclusively in terms of Christ versus communism." The United States intervened both covertly and openly to help elect the Christian Democrats, with assistance from Time-Life publisher Henry Luce, his wife Clare Boothe Luce, and the Italian-American teen heart-throb of the day, Frank Sinatra.

De Gasperi was on the cover of *Time*; Frank Sinatra made a Voice of America broadcast urging Italians to vote for the Christian Democrats. The Christian Democrats won forty-eight percent of the vote, the highest result ever won by an Italian party in free elections. In 1949 Italy entered NATO as a founding member.[4] The place of Italy in the Cold War was now assured.

Postwar Germany differed from Italy and France. The country had ceased to exist. Instead there were zones: the Russian zone, now wholly communized, and three western zones. In the West, occupation by Allied troops initially was total. No travel was permitted between zones of occupation, no national political parties, no national assembly, no national bodies. Instead, the Allied Control Commission became the government, administering a denazification program that wiped out the entire existing civil service.

Such an arrangement could scarcely be regarded as permanent. So where was Germany to go from there? The U.S. was anxious to restore the economy, to reestablish industries, to fuse the three western zones into one, and to allow more central administration. France deliberately slowed this process. Still fearing a historic enemy, France sought to strip German power, particularly the economic

Since the last thing the Soviets wanted was a prosperous western Europe, they had to strike at the Marshall Plan, and they knew the West was most vulnerable at Berlin.

4. The creation of NATO (the North Atlantic Treaty Organization) in 1949 was a significant step in the Cold War. It united the five signatories of the 1948 Brussels Treaty (Britain, France, Belgium, the Netherlands, and Luxembourg) with the United States, Canada, Italy, Portugal, Norway, Denmark, and Iceland. In 1952, Greece and Turkey joined. The addition of West Germany in 1955 led to the creation, on the Communist side, of the Warsaw Pact, uniting countries behind the Iron Curtain.

lifeblood of coal and steel. Neither did they want to see the rebirth of national institutions in Germany for at least twenty years. They carefully guarded the autonomy of the French zone. To every initiative aimed at German recovery, they had the same response: "No."

In this hostile atmosphere, Adenauer strove to revive the Christian Democratic Union (CDU). As usual, he moved brazenly. When party delegates met regionally in January, 1946, he blandly declared himself senior member present, assumed chairmanship of the meeting and, ultimately, of the entire party. Osnabrück industrialist Paul Otto described it as a coup d'état accomplished on the principle of "president by seniority."

Despite the restraints, Adenauer worked to establish the CDU throughout the free western zones. His party had endured the "Hunger Winter" of 1946–47 and now in the following June the announcement of the Marshall Plan came as sunlight through storm clouds. Billions of U.S. dollars would be devoted to the recovery of the free nations of Europe. Adenauer knew that Germany must be central to such an endeavor. He also knew that the Soviet Union was determined to prevent Germany's economic recovery. Worse still, the French were still dominated by their nationalist fears. When their foreign minister Georges Bidault had signed a defence treaty with Britain in 1946, he insisted it be directed against Germany, not the Soviet Union.

Since the last thing the Soviets wanted was an economically prosperous western Europe, they had to strike back against the Marshall Plan. They also knew where the West was most vulnerable, notably at the city of Berlin. It had been captured by the Red Army in the dying days of the Nazi regime in May 1945 at a

FOR EUROPEAN RECOVERY
SUPPLIED BY THE
UNITED STATES OF AMERICA

A worker using a jackhammer helps build a dam for the European Recovery Program-sponsored Hydro Electric Project in Ligne, France, in the 1950s. Top right, the insignia used on the goods shipped by the Americans under the ERP to rebuild Europe; and a 1960 West German postage stamp recognizing the author of what had become known as the Marshall Plan, U.S. Secretary of State George C. Marshall. More than $26 billion worth of aid was directed at Germany, France, England, and the other war-ravaged areas of non-Soviet Europe for reasons both political and humanitarian. The Soviet Union and its Communist friends in the West, however, saw the program as a new form of imperialism based on money instead of arms.

cost of eighty thousand lives on the Soviet side. Even so, the Russians had agreed to give up two-thirds of the city to the French, British, and Americans. Berlin was accordingly divided into four sectors, just as all Germany had been split into four zones. However, the city lay within the Soviet zone, and its livelihood depended on supplies moving from or through Soviet-controlled territory. West Berlin was therefore an unwanted "island" of capitalism in the midst of a Communist state. Ousting from it their three former allies became a top priority on Stalin's agenda. The Marshall Plan afforded him the pretext for doing it, and simply blockading the three western sectors was the way to force the issue.

What the Soviets did not know, however, was the likely western response. Would they fight, or would they meekly acquiesce? Neither for that matter did the three powers themselves—except for France, which had made clear from the beginning it was not prepared to enter into a war with the Soviet Union to maintain a French presence in Berlin. The American decision came right to the desk of the president. "There is no discussion on this point," said Harry S. Truman. "We stay in Berlin—period!" British Prime Minister Clement Atlee backed him up.

But how would they stay there? More specifically, how would the two million Berliners in the American, French, and British sectors survive with food, fuel, and everything else cut off? Six months after the Marshall Plan was announced the Soviets began their countermeasures with a series of increasingly hostile moves. On New Year's Day, 1948, they announced tight new controls on all goods traveling

Children eagerly await one of the first planes to arrive in West Berlin in 1948 during the airlift, orchestrated in large part by USAF General Curtis LeMay (inset), a man normally associated with American bombing campaigns, including the one that ended in the dropping of atom bombs on Hiroshima and Nagasaki three years earlier. During the eleven months of the Soviet blockade of Berlin, the allies sent 277,569 flights into the city, eventually causing Stalin to lift the siege.

from the West into Berlin. Two weeks later they cancelled all travel between the Soviet Zone and West Berlin, and ten days after that they began obstructing military trains moving into Berlin's British sector. On March 20, the Soviet delegate walked out on the Allied Control Council. Early in April, as the U.S. Congress approved the Marshall Plan, the Soviets blocked all water and ground transportation into the three western sectors. On June 1, all train and road traffic into Berlin from the West was halted.

If these moves were intended to frighten the British and Americans from seeking to establish economic stability in West Germany they were not succeeding. In June, the U.S. and Britain issued the D-mark (deutsch mark) for use in all western zones, followed by the B-mark (Berlin mark), for use in Berlin. This provided a stable currency for the first time since the war.[5] Then on June 24, the Soviets abandoned assorted harassment tactics and instead implemented a full blockade on West Berlin. All land and water routes from the West into Berlin were closed. Coal deliveries that supplied electric power plants were cut off. West Berlin was under siege.

In *The Blockade Breakers* (2008), American historian Helena P. Schrader provides a captivating play-by-play account of what followed. The American commander in Berlin, Lucius D. Clay, favored sending supplies into the city by heavily armed truck convoys because he was sure the Russians no more wanted a war over Berlin than the West did. The problem was, however, that immediately available Russian troops in Europe outnumbered the American

and British by astronomical numbers, and the rest of Europe could fall to the Soviets before a sufficient defense could be mounted. So if Berlin was to be supplied it must be done by air.

The requirements for such an undertaking were staggering. All Berlin's coal, milk, fruit, and vegetables came from the Soviet zone. More than two thousand tons of food must be flown in daily, plus twelve hundred tons of coal in sacks, enough to keep the citizenry alive and warm and supplied with coal-fueled electricity, but just barely. The airlift itself would consume nearly three hundred thousand barrels of aviation fuel a month before it was over, requiring twenty-five ocean tankers to deliver it to West Germany. The standard light freight aircraft of the day, the two engine DC3, could carry three tons, the four engine DC4 could carry nine tons, the big new C 47s could carry twenty-five tons. Two new runways would have to be added immediately to both Tempelhof and Gatow airports in Berlin. All told, more than seventy thousand people, military and civilian, would be involved.

On June 25, one U.S. aircraft, improvised as a freighter, made its way into Berlin, the first of 277,569 such flights into the city over the next eleven months of the blockade. The following day Truman approved the airlift; British approval soon followed, and a joint coordinating body was set up to run it. The notably missing partner was France. Air crews, military and civil, were directed to Berlin from every quarter of the free world as the massive program came into being.[6] By August it was up and running, but the big test would come in the winter when the demand for coal would soar. So often the winter had won for Russia. Stalin was confident it would do so again.

By December 1948, in the sixth month of the airlift, it looked certain he was right. Though the supplies arriving daily constantly increased, shortfalls were alarmingly asserting themselves. Fuel supplies were falling short by seventy tons a day; winter flying conditions would cut food shipments by thirty-three percent. The American operation required 224 big freighters and it had only 169. The situation called for technological and organizational genius. Both were found. Flight patterns and timetables were adjusted, turnaround times cut, a new bad-weather navigation system was installed in the aircraft, more planes were added. January of 1949 was the win-or-lose month. When it was over, the result was undeniable. The airlift had worked.

Knowing this, Stalin put out diplomatic feelers for change. His Berlin policy, he decided, did not seem to be working, and he called off the blockade in May. Distrusting him, the U.S. and Britain kept the airlift going for two more months. He had lost the first great test in the Cold War. He had also lost the Berliners, who for months had taken to crowding around Gatow airport to cheer in the planes as they landed, one every four minutes. The last British plane landed on August 26. Painted on its fuselage was a verse from the twenty-first Psalm: "For they intended evil against thee; they imagined a mischievous device, which they were not able to perform."

Yet there remained one major uncertainty and that was the role of France. Even before the success of the airlift, however, French thinking had begun to change. Whether it was the influence of American financing through the Marshall Plan, or the appointment of forward-thinking Robert Schuman as French foreign minister, France began to develop a policy of cooperation with western allies,

5. To counter the popular confidence in the West's D-mark and B-mark, the Soviets issued what was called the East-mark, currency they created by pasting a sticker on their original occupation money. However, the stickers kept falling off, and the Berliners called it the *tapetenmark* (wallpaper mark) indicating what they saw it best used for. The Soviets then passed a regulation outlawing use of the B-mark anywhere in Berlin. The regulation was ineffective, since the Soviet authorities had no jurisdiction outside their own sector.

6. At the time the airlift was triggered, General Clay called General Curtis LeMay, U.S. Air Force commander in Europe. In her book on the blockade, historian Schrader recounts their conversation:

Clay: Have you any planes that can carry coal?

LeMay: Carry what?

Clay: Coal.

LeMay: We must have a bad connection. It sounds as if you were asking if we have planes for carrying coal.

Clay: Yes, that's what I said—coal.

LeMay: General, the Air Force can deliver anything. How much coal do you want us to haul?

Clay: All you can.

rather than confrontation. When France and Britain signed the Brussels Treaty, expanding their defensive alliance to include Belgium, the Netherlands, and Luxembourg, the new treaty was directed against all aggressor states, not just Germany. Then the London conference of western allies in June, 1948 resulted in France agreeing to an international control body to allow coal and steel developments in the Ruhr and appointing Germans to begin a constitutional process to gain sovereignty for a West German state.

With the success of the airlift, events now moved swiftly. The three western zones were united into the Federal Republic of Germany; the eastern zone became the German Democratic Republic. In the Federal Republic's first election on August 15, 1949, the Christian Democrats were the strongest party, forging a coalition with the Bavarian Christian Social Union and the Free Democratic Party to form the government. On September 16, Adenauer at seventy-three became chancellor, a position he would hold for fourteen years, earning the nickname *Der Alte*, the Old One.

'This merging of our interest in coal and steel production will make it plain that war between France and Germany will be not only unthinkable, but materially impossible.'

Under Adenauer, 1949 was the turnaround year for Germany.

In March, he delivered the first major speech of a West German politician on an international stage since the war. Speaking in Switzerland he gave a detailed account of the economic situation in Germany, including criticisms of the allies for dismantling German industries to eliminate competition for their home industries. He said the time for the allies planning Germany's economy "down to the trouser buttons" was past. He praised the Marshall Plan but said it must be accompanied by growing German industrialization and employment. He called for a strong Germany taking its place in a unified Europe. His speech struck a chord with fellow Germans, who felt that someone was finally speaking up for them.

In April, Robert Schuman, as French foreign minister, was in Washington to sign France into NATO. Thanks to the new French spirit of cooperation, a meeting of foreign ministers established a framework to move ahead quickly in Germany. Among the directives, France merged its zone with the other allies. In November the Allied High Commission met with Adenauer at their headquarters at Petersberg Hill, near Bonn. Among other terms, the resulting Petersberg Accord invited West Germany to join the Council of Europe as an associate member and allowed the state to establish consular and commercial relations abroad. For the first time since the war's end, West Germany was gaining equality with other nations. The Federal Republic received "virtual sovereignty in 1952" and full sovereignty three years later.

Schuman was staking his political reputation on these concessions to the old enemy. The French newspaper *Le Monde* reported his speech to the deputies: "I do not mean to minimize the concessions we have granted but I am convinced we have done the right thing. We cannot remain stuck in a negative attitude... True, Frenchmen do not have the right to forget the past, with its suffering and cruelties;

7. The key architect of the Schuman Plan was France's most entrepreneurial civil servant, Jean Monnet. The son of a brandy producer, Monnet had played a key role in the war, acting as liaison with the U.S. in supplying the French and British armies. Following the war, his relations with the allies made him realize that, if France was to receive American aid, the country needed to develop a more comprehensive system of national planning. He'd created the supra-ministerial *Commissariat Général du Plan* in 1946 and been appointed its director. The Schuman Plan was the fruit of Monnet's planning philosophy.

but we who are responsible for the future of France, of Europe, and even humanity, we must avoid the repetition of previous mistakes."

Schuman's greatest contribution to Europe and humanity came the next year. The major threat to France had always been Germany's industrial capacity—its ability to manufacture munitions in wartime and its superior industrial capabilities in peacetime. Coal and steel were the lifeblood of both countries—and that blood had run red three times in wars since the Franco-Prussian war in 1870. In May, 1950 Schuman announced a revolutionary plan (which Adenauer had approved) to place all production of coal and steel in France and Germany under the control of one common European authority.[7]

"The pooling of coal and steel production will immediately assure the establishment of common bases for economic development as a first step for the European Federation," said Schuman. "It will change the destiny of regions that have long been devoted to manufacturing munitions of war, of which they have been most constantly the victims. This merging of our interest in coal and steel production and our joint action will make it plain that any war between France and Germany becomes not only unthinkable, but materially impossible."[8]

The Schuman Plan was the seed from which a united Europe would grow. The major countries of western Europe were, for the first time, united in an economic alliance. They were united too in their vision of the future—a democracy based on western principles of freedom, principles which had grown from Christian roots and were carried by three avowedly Christian leaders. Moreover, the Cold War in western Europe had effectually been won. But forty-seven days after Schuman announced his plan, Communist North Korea invaded South Korea. The focus of the Cold War moved to Asia where it was not destined to result in an unequivocal western victory. And where it would no longer be a cold war but a very hot one. ■

Chancellor Konrad Adenauer leaves the Hotel Petersberg in Berlin on September 21, 1949, flanked by an honor guard of ten soldiers from Britain, France, and the United States, after being presented with the new statute which laid out the terms of occupation in West Germany. When he had been imprisoned five years earlier by the Nazis, a Gestapo officer had told him, "You're an old man; you have nothing more to live for." But Adenauer would resurrect the Christian Democrats and shape the Germany that arose out of the ashes of war.

8. A process for the canonization of Robert Schuman was initiated by the bishop of Metz in 1991. By the year 2004, the diocesan role was closed and the documents sent to the Vatican. But the initiative was halted while evidence was sought of the miraculous in Schuman's life and work.

The resentful peasant boy who grew up to become modern China's creator and a noted mass murderer

History seems to bestow its favors capriciously. In the early 1900s, none of the pigtailed peasants in the south-central Chinese farm town of Shaoshan could have predicted that Mao Shun-sheng's oldest boy, an ungainly, unremarkable, somewhat resentful youth named Mao Zedong, would emerge as the Great Helmsman who would steer China into the modern age, and also become, arguably, humanity's worst-ever mass murderer.

Mao Zedong came to hate his father, a self-made Hunan "rich peasant," grain dealer, and mortgage lender. Zedong likewise came to hate China's ancient Confucian moral order, which he considered regressive. He hated and refused to acknowledge the marriage his father arranged for him when he was thirteen. He loved only his mother, Wen Ch'i-mei, even in his midteens briefly adopting her Buddhist faith. But he left home as soon as he could, at age eighteen.

Mao was an undermotivated, unsuccessful student. His real interest was political ideology. In his late teens and early twenties he gravitated from republican nationalist supporting Sun Yat-sen (a baptized Christian), to become a founding member of the tiny, Moscow-sponsored Chinese Communist party in 1921. During these years Mao practiced a stern personal asceticism and began to distinguish himself as a military leader amidst the besetting civil unrest of the period. Unlike most Marxists, Mao remained a strong Chinese nationalist and put more revolutionary faith in China's peasantry than in its nascent proletarian and bourgeois classes.

In 1925 centrist leader Sun died and was succeeded by the right-wing Chiang Kai-shek, leading to twenty years of bitter, bloody strife between the Communists and the Nationalists. It was alleviated only by two temporary truces when the two sworn enemies allied against the invading Japanese. However, the twelve-year period from 1937 to 1949 was a prolonged three-way war, resulting first in Japan's defeat in 1945, followed by Chiang Kai-shek's defeat in 1949. Chiang's remaining forces retreated to and occupied the island of Taiwan.

It was during these crucial years that through ruthless military and political skill, and with the backing of Soviet leader Joseph Stalin, Mao rose to become military and political leader of China. After the Communist victory he proved far less adept at governing, but maintained power by keeping the loyalty of his army. The first thing he did was move into the imperial palace at Beijing and build a private swimming pool. There he stayed, governing in a bathrobe beside his pool, neither taking a bath nor brushing his teeth, until his

Mao Zedong, center, as a young revolutionary in 1920. A mediocre student who hated his bourgeois father, Mao was first attracted to the republican nationalist Chinese led by Sun Yat-sen (top left). He later gravitated to Marxism and his forces were soon in bloody conflict with the Nationalist forces of Sun's right-wing successor Chiang Kai-shek (top right). The civil war between Mao's Communists and Chiang's Nationalists was interspersed with truces during which they combined to take on—and eventually defeat—the invading Japanese. After the war, however, the Communists prevailed, driving Chiang's forces onto the southern offshore island of Formosa (now Taiwan), where by the first decade of the twenty-first century efforts were being made to reconcile the differences between capitalist Taiwan and the People's Republic of China—a thawing of relations evidenced from the sale of the three smiling paperweights featuring (left to right) Sun, Mao, and Chiang at a Taipei 7-Eleven store in 2008.

death in 1976. Like Stalin, he ruled autocratically, using mass starvation as a means of political control, and on a larger scale. Like Stalin, he relied for personal security on systematic propaganda, terror, and a "cult of personality." Though his policies were as harsh and cold-blooded as Stalin's, it was said that he was personally less sadistic, though it is hard to know. His personal physician from the mid 1950s until his death twenty years later, Li Zhisui, later moved to the U.S. and in *The Private Life of Chairman Mao* (1994) describes him as aloof, manipulative, shallow, addicted to pills, cigarettes, and promiscuous sex, and increasingly self-obsessed as he aged.

University of Hawaii emeritus political scientist Rudolph Rummel estimated in a study on "democide" (a term he coined for mass killings by governments) that Communist China from 1949 to 1987 (years of peace) killed somewhere between 35 million and 103 million Chinese and Tibetans, mainly under Mao. Rummel estimated the Soviet total to be higher—56 million to 115 million—but that was over a longer period (1917 to 1987), including the Second World War, and under more leaders. Whether Mao was a more accomplished mass murderer than Stalin therefore remains unsettled. ■

In the early days of the civil war, Chiang Kai-shek's National forces drove back Mao's Communists into northern China in the 1935 Long March (an eight-thousand-mile retreat much mythologized in Red Chinese lore). With their ranks increased by peasants, and their arms and communications enhanced by the Soviet Union, Mao's forces pushed southward and eventually drove the Nationalists across the Taiwan Strait to the island of Taiwan. In June 1949, the People's Liberation Army takes Beijing (below), which Mao made the Chinese capital again. (It had been Nanking.) Mao declared the inauguration of the People's Republic of China on October 1, 1949. Left, Mao (extreme right in picture) is shown with his comrades, including future prime minister Zhou Enlai (second from left), in northern Shaanxi province following the Long March.

Korean attack challenges western resolve in the Pacific; the war becomes a stalemate, but South Korea is saved

Jutting south from the Chinese mainland lies the peninsula of Korea, 625 miles long and a mere 125 miles from the coast of Japan. The resolve of both Communist China and American-occupied Japan to secure this strategically placed mountainous nation after the Second World War led to one of the twentieth century's more vicious lesser wars, one which produced some two million dead and maimed, mostly Korean civilians. It was the first open, armed clash wherein the Cold War became a hot one.

When Japan surrendered in 1945, its conquered vassal Korea was divided at the 38th parallel of latitude between the Communist Russians in the north and the Americans in the south. By 1950, however, both superpowers had withdrawn their troops and turmoil reigned, the South Korean government distinguished by crippling corruption. In the midst of this on June 25, 1950, Communist North Korea invaded South. They were led by dictator Kim Il-sung, and had Stalin's blessing, Soviet weapons, and Communist China's active support and they included battle-hardened Korean veterans of the Chinese civil war. They swiftly captured the southern capital of Seoul and by August had the South Korean army and an initial contingent of U.S. troops bottled up in the southern tip of the peninsula.

The day after the invasion, U.S. President Harry Truman—with no permission from Congress—ordered men and arms deployed to South Korea. Naval forces supported them. With the Soviets absent from the Security Council for the crucial vote, a mistake it would never make again, the United Nations condemned North Korea, and an international force representing twenty-two nations reinforced the south.

They included Canada, Britain, and Australia, but almost ninety percent of the UN force was American.

The UN commander in chief was celebrity, corncob-pipe-smoking General Douglas MacArthur. He performed brilliantly at first, shoring up the beachhead in the south, and then recapturing Seoul by means of a daring assault on the nearby port city of Inch'on. The North Korean army was soon in full retreat, and by mid-October UN troops were nearing the Yalu River, Korea's border with China.

Then they met disaster. Red China warned that if American troops neared the Yalu, it would consider China invaded. When MacArthur pressed on regardless, a Chinese force crossed the Yalu, confronted MacArthur's troops, and withdrew into China. MacArthur defied his orders and continued advancing, which, by one account, is exactly what Mao was hoping he would do. Three hundred thousand Chinese crossed the Yalu, driving MacArthur's army back into South Korea with terrible losses.

But the Chinese assault into the south was no more successful than MacArthur's assault into the north, and the war soon stalemated. When a truce was finally reached in July, 1953, the border had hardly moved from 1949. Atrocities, frightful and widespread, were attributed to both sides, perpetrated

President Harry Truman (above) meets General Douglas MacArthur on American-held Wake Island during the deployment of American troops into Korea in 1950. They comprised ninety percent of the United Nations force. MacArthur performed brilliantly at first, shoring up the beachhead in the south, and then recapturing Seoul from the North Koreans by means of a daring assault on the port city of Inch'on (left). His exuberance, however, would later prove his undoing.

especially by the Koreans. Famous battles became part of North American vernacular: Heartbreak Ridge, T-Bone Hill, Pork Chop Hill. MacArthur continued to press for an invasion of China until Truman sacked him in April, 1951. The objective of the "Truman Doctrine," as it became known, was to contain communism, not to attempt its defeat. It lasted until the Reagan Doctrine ("we win, they lose") succeeded it in the 1980s.

The price of the war had been steep: 33,600 American dead, 16,000 from other UN nations, and perhaps 400,000 Chinese, 415,000 South Korean, and 520,000 North Korean (estimates of Asian casualties vary considerably). The whole country was pretty much leveled, and it took a decade before South Korea began recovering, eventually to become a global manufacturing giant. The Communist north became a Stalin-style Communist catastrophe with widespread poverty, contrived famines that claimed hundreds of thousands of lives, and slave labor camps for those opposed to the regime. ■

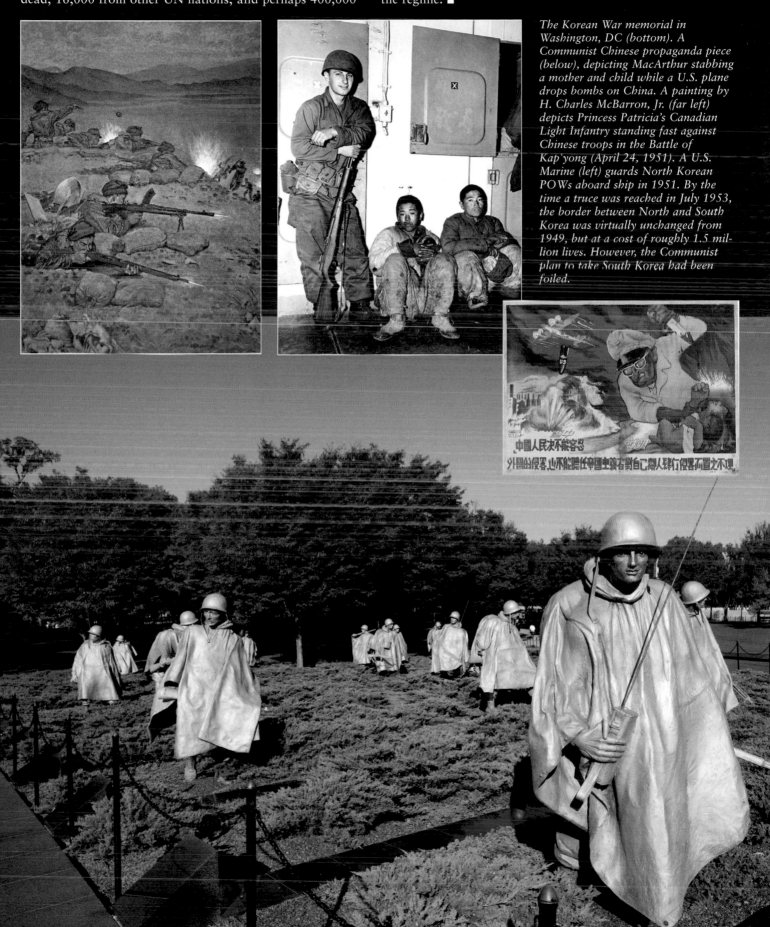

The Korean War memorial in Washington, DC (bottom). A Communist Chinese propaganda piece (below), depicting MacArthur stabbing a mother and child while a U.S. plane drops bombs on China. A painting by H. Charles McBarron, Jr. (far left) depicts Princess Patricia's Canadian Light Infantry standing fast against Chinese troops in the Battle of Kap'yong (April 24, 1951). A U.S. Marine (left) guards North Korean POWs aboard ship in 1951. By the time a truce was reached in July 1953, the border between North and South Korea was virtually unchanged from 1949, but at a cost of roughly 1.5 million lives. However, the Communist plan to take South Korea had been foiled.

Members of the Red Guard shout Maoist slogans as they occupy the Orthodox Saint Nicholas church in the northern Chinese city of Harbin in August 1966 at the beginning of the ten-year-long Cultural Revolution. Both traditional Buddhism and imported Christianity came under attack as Chairman Mao Zedong attempted to rid his socialist state of all "impurities" and "superstitions." Shortly afterwards the Red Guards attached a fire truck to the church and pulled it down. This rare photograph, snapped during the Cultural Revolution, is among those taken by a then member of the Red Guard, Li Zhensheng, who secreted his photographs and later sent them to the United States for publication.

CHAPTER 9

In pain and persecution history's curtain rises on Chinese Christianity

Despite death, prison, and humiliation under Marxism, Christians grow twelve-fold to more than fifty million, and Beijing finds Christianity is the West's strength

When Mao Zedong looked out over Tiananmen Square in October 1949 as the new ruler of the world's most populous country and declared, "China has stood up!" there were only four million Christians in his enormous domain. Half a century later—despite executions, imprisonment, torture, and ten years of "cultural revolution"—the number of Christians had grown at a minimum twelve-fold, to fifty million. Western researchers put it at sixty million, the Chinese churches themselves at over eighty. All of these sources reported continuing and extraordinary Christian growth.

The story of how Chinese Christianity has thrived and grown through years of persecution by Mao and the Communists echoes the story of how the church prospered and grew through its first centuries of persecution under the Roman imperium. True, there were differences. Instead of ravenous lions loosed upon them, the faithful in China were subjected to "struggle sessions" in the town square with prison, torture, or execution to follow. Instead of secret meetings in the catacombs, there were secret meetings in the "house churches." But the similarities were nevertheless undeniable—miraculous healings, heroic evangelism, proliferating sects, and the omnipresence of the cross, witnessing once again to a hostile world which it was commissioned to save through love.

The Christianity that has evolved in China is largely homegrown. History professor Lian Xi of Hanover College, Hanover, IL, attributes Christianity's phenomenal growth to its transformation "from an alien faith preached and presided over by western missionaries into an indigenous religion of the masses." In *Redeemed by Fire: The Rise of Popular Christianity in Modern China* (2010*)*, he paints a vivid picture of the Chinese church that grew so explosively: "With a predominantly rural and lower-class membership, the homegrown Christianity has been characterized by a potent mix of evangelistic fervor, biblical literalism, charismatic ecstasies and a fiery eschatology [end-times teaching], not infrequently tinged with nationalistic exuberance."

A tradition of homegrown churches in China predates the rise of Mao, Lian notes. The cross-fertilizing of doctrines from different foreign missions often resulted in dynamic new beliefs and prophets. These were not always fortunate, the most famous centering on Hong Xiuquan, whose belief that he was the younger brother of Jesus led his rural followers into the disastrous Taiping Rebellion of 1850. Ultimate toll: twenty million deaths (see volume 11, page 202). But dozens of small and large churches sprouted and grew prolifically in the "good earth" of the Chinese soil from the 1920s and the early years of the Communist takeover.

Probably the country's best-known evangelist at the time of Mao's triumph was "Man of Iron" Wang Mingdao. Born in 1900 in Beijing at the height of its Boxer Rebellion, he became a Christian as a fourteen-year-old in a Christian missionary school. He was fired from teaching at a Presbyterian school when he found fault with Presbyterian baptismal practices. Speaking out against perceived wrongs in the church, he conducted Bible studies that grew until in 1937 he built his own church, the Christian Tabernacle. That year, the Japanese marched into Beijing, but the Man of Iron refused to bend to them. He traveled as an itinerant minister throughout China preaching a simple, Bible-based faith. He had no choir in his church, was known to refuse baptism to converts who were just "rice Christians" (people who feign to Christianity in exchange for food), and resisted all attempts to control him—whether by the Japanese, foreign churches or soon, the Communists. But he was to pay a heavy price for his resistance to the latter.

The largest indigenous church in 1949 was the True Jesus Church, with one hundred thousand followers. It stressed speaking in tongues, lengthy public confessions, miraculous healings (particularly among opium users), and a focus on the coming end of the world. To peasants enduring drought, famine, civil war, and the Japanese occupation, it was a potent message.

Another sect, the Little Flock, had about seven hundred churches throughout China in 1949. They were aggressive evangelists, following China's

Chairman Mao proclaims the founding of the People's Republic of China from a podium overlooking Tiananmen Square in Peking (later Beijing) on October 1, 1949. "China has stood up," he declared. At the time there were just four million Christians; fifty years later, despite much hardship and persecution, that number had grown more than twelve-fold.

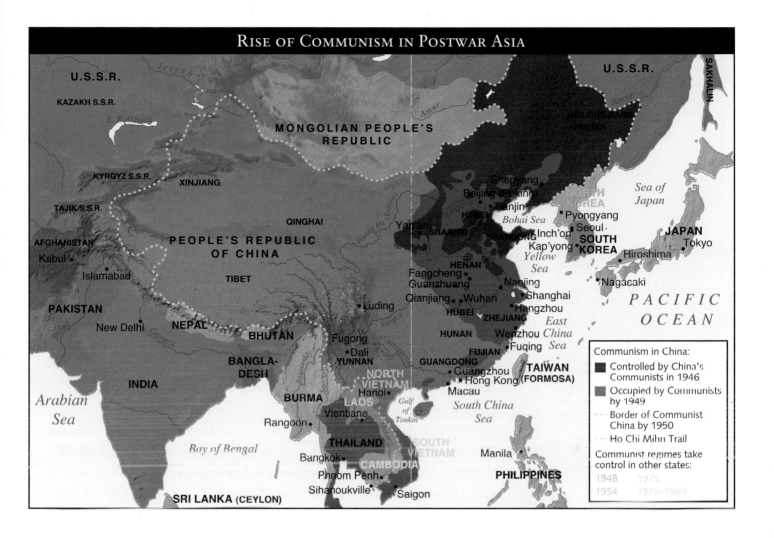

Communism in China:

■ Controlled by China's Communists in 1946

■ Occupied by Communists by 1949

- - - Border of Communist China by 1950

- - - Ho Chi Minh Trail

Communist regimes take control in other states:

1948   1975
1954   1975–1989

railways into the interior to evangelize where missions had not reached. The theology of their founder, Watchman Nee (1903–1972), stressed a personal, mystical, and highly energetic link with God. There were wealthy Chinese patrons. Watchman Nee himself owned a pharmaceutical company. One "giveaway service" in Shanghai netted five hundred thousand dollars with churchgoers giving stocks and bonds and one, an auto dealership. Their generosity might have been spurred by the approaching Communists. The prayer that day was for the invaders to be swept away in the Yangtze River. But the Communists did advance, and Watchman Nee would be among the first Christians arrested.

Still another homegrown church was the Jesus Family, a Christian commune in Shandong province in northern China with branches all over the country. Its leader, Jing Dianyang (1890–1957) was raised in Confucian and Taoist traditions. He converted to Christianity when a boy at a Methodist mission school and later embraced rapturous trances, talking in tongues, and other Pentecostal practices. Many of the Pentecostal usages of Jing's church were similar to the spirit-possessing experiences of China's traditional folk religions. The commune provided a neutral middle ground as Shandong province changed hands between Nationalists and Communist troops during the civil war: "Cannons and guns are but firecrackers, and warplanes are our paper kites," says one of the Family songs, pointing to Chinese visions of heaven: "Isn't this the land of the immortals?... Isn't this the world beyond the spring of the peach blossoms (*shiwai taoyuan*)?"[1]

1. "The world beyond the spring of the peach blossoms" (*shiwai taoyuan*) is a well-known story attributed to Tao Yuanming (Eastern Jin Dynasty, 317–420). A fisherman squeezes through a cave and finds an unexpected gateway into a mystical village, a paradise hidden from the outside world. It is a place of joy and happiness, without hardship or oppression, where everybody lives and works in peace and contentment. The fisherman leaves the villagers and goes home. Although he searches, he can never find the village again. The story is echoed in the mystical story of Shangri-la.

By far the largest Christian group in 1949 was the Roman Catholics. Three of every four Christians were Catholic—three million faithful. Many of them were in rural communities whose conversion went back to the Jesuit missions of the 1600s (see volume 11, page 200). For many years Catholic missions had eschewed individual conversions and focused instead on communal conversions. Thus entire villages in the countryside were Catholic, villagers living their lives, doing their farm labors, and called to prayers by the bell in their local church. There were Catholic churches, schools, and hospitals. In 1926, the first Chinese-born bishops had been consecrated in Rome; by 1940, there were twenty-three Chinese-born bishops. However, in 1949 four out of five dioceses were still under European prelates. The Chinese Catholic Church was part of the worldwide Roman communion, under the pope, and although the church itself was increasingly Chinese in character, in Communist eyes it was imperialistic and counterrevolutionary.

There was a third distinct group of Christians in China in 1949: established Protestant denominations like the Chinese Episcopal Church, the Methodist Church, the Church of Christ, and others.[2] The attention of the Communist government was drawn to one group in particular among these Protestants—those with left-wing views. Many Chinese Protestants were in sympathy with the Communist party. In the chaotic years of civil war after the collapse of the national government in the 1920s, they had made alliances with Communists rather than with Chiang Kai-shek's Nationalist party. From their social gospel perspective, they saw the Communists as representing a true peasants' revolt, the best chance for security and order after so many years of conflict.

The Communists, for their part, viewed these Christians of the political left as the best way to establish stability and order over Christianity. The Chinese for centuries had been nourished on Confucian values of order and stability and accepting the authority of elders and superiors. These values definitely included religion. Since the Song Dynasty (960–1279) there had been a government-appointed Board of Rites that supervised temples and licensed clergy. Such controls had lapsed during the years of civil war but now the Communists revived them, establishing

(Left to right): "Man of Iron" Wang Mingdao, in a photograph taken at the Christian Tabernacle in Peking in 1950; Little Flock founder Watchman Nee, circa early 1950s; future Anglican Bishop K. H. Ting as a young priest. Ting acquiesced with the Communists, accepting their decree that the Protestant churches be self-governing and free of western influences. Wang and Nee were not so compliant and were to suffer the consequences.

a Bureau of Religious Affairs that would have much the same powers. They declared five official religions—Buddhism, Taoism, Islam, Catholicism, and Protestantism—and established controls over religious observances and practices. The religious were then given a choice: accept and abide by the controls or face persecution, torture, and death.

Chinese Protestant leaders like Anglican Bishop K. H. Ting (1915–2012) decided to take what was offered. Like many, he believed the best choice was to work out an agreement with Mao. Over several years of negotiating, they accepted the government demand that Protestants be part of communism's "United Front," partners in advancing the causes of socialism and the people's revolution. To fulfill this mandate, they created a mass-culture agency—the Three-Self Patriotic Movement (TSPM)—a phrase meaning that Protestant churches should be self-governing, self-supporting, and self-propagating—in short, free of western influences.[3]

Ting's critics have accused him of watering down Christianity to include Communist concepts. He certainly played major roles in the 1950s in trying without success to reconcile churchmen like the Man of Iron, Wang Mingdao, with the new order of things. Others acquiesced, however, and he preached sermons and worked with clerics and

Father Bernard Druetto, a French Franciscan priest whose former diocese was in Hunan province, is shown here in the late 1950s after years of imprisonment and torture on suspicion of being a spy and an anti-Communist agitator. Most Catholic churches refused to cut their ties to Rome and their foreign clergy were the first to be rounded up, with many being tortured or undergoing brainwashing. Druetto was exiled to the then British colony of Hong Kong following his release, later moving to Taiwan to resume his mission.

doctrinaire Communists to try to find a possible middle ground. One speech to students in 1957 used the argument of intelligent design to defend theism against Marxist materialism: "We cannot deny that behind the manifestations of nature, there must be a mind, an intelligence, a purpose."

By 1957, all Protestant churches were required to join the TSPM. Traditional liturgies were sustained by the same clergy who had used them before, provided they met with the approval of the TSPM. New clergy and church workers would be trained in the one remaining theological school (Nanjing Union Theological Seminary) and would include lessons on communism. Bishop Ting was appointed chairman of the Three-Self Patriotic Movement and head of the seminary.

The new order for Catholic churches went much less smoothly. A similar body, the Chinese Catholic Patriotic Association (CCPA) was established, but almost all Catholics resisted it. The authorities moved decisively. Foreign priests

2. One prominent Chinese Christian family was the Soong family. Charlie Soong had traveled to America when he was fifteen, been baptized there, and returned as a Methodist missionary. But he soon abandoned that for a successful business career. He married in 1890. His wife's family had been Christian for three hundred years dating back to the early Jesuit missions. Their children included three daughters, each of whom became famous in her own way. Ailing married China's richest man, H. H. Kung (a direct descendant of Confucius). Shingling married Sun Yat-sen, the founding president of the Republic of China (1912). Mao appointed her joint president of the People's Republic of China (1968–1972), undoubtedly recognizing the legitimacy that would be added to his government with the appointment of Sun Yat-sen's widow. The youngest Soong sister, Mayling, married Nationalist leader Chiang Kai-shek (who had to convert to Christianity in order to marry her). She thus became known to the world as Madame Chiang Kai-shek. She did not receive any honorary appointments from Mao.

3. The "three-self" policy was originally developed by missionaries themselves to enable their missions to be transformed into indigenous churches. Henry Venn, who was the secretary of Britain's Church Missionary Society from 1841 to 1873, coined the "three-self" term. Venn often talked of the need for the "euthanasia of missions" to allow indigenous churches to develop.

Bishop Kung Pinmei of Shanghai, shown here in 1949, was among the fifteen hundred Catholics arrested in Shanghai in 1955. Kung suffered five years of "reeducation" and was sentenced to life imprisonment for treason. He was secretly named a cardinal in 1979. It has been estimated that five hundred thousand Christians died from Communist persecution between 1950 and 1978.

4. The Legion of Mary, founded in Ireland in 1921, was the largest Catholic lay organization in the world by the dawn of the twenty-first century, with three million members in 170 countries. Its activities include door-to-door proselytizing, visiting the sick, helping the destitute, and enabling women to escape from prostitution. Its China mission, begun in 1931, survived the Japanese invasion and the Great Leap Forward. In the Cultural Revolution, the government cracked down hard, however, after its members refused to accept governmental control, and it was vigorously suppressed.

were the first to be rounded up, and many were tortured and forced to undergo brainwashing. The two-year ordeal of one Italian priest identified only as Father Luca was described in Robert Jay Lifton's book, *Thought Reform and the Psychology of Totalism* (1961). It recounts endless days in handcuffs and chains; being slapped night and day by fellow prisoners so he couldn't sleep; long "study sessions" alternated with interrogations; physical beatings that left him with broken bones so that for months other prisoners carried him to the toilet and much of the time he lay in his own waste; confusion and disorientation so great that finally he signed documents confessing he was a "running dog of imperialism" whose work with Legion of Mary children had recruited them into "counterrevolutionary" cadres committing sabotage and treason.[4]

Soon it was Watchman Nee's turn. The leader of The Little Flock was arrested in 1952 as part of a purge of industrialists and business people in the "Five Antis" campaign, targeting five economic crimes: bribery, tax evasion, fraud, stealing of state property, and theft of economic secrets. Following three years of "thought reform," he was imprisoned until his death in 1972. Jing Dianyang, who had melded Pentecostal and traditional Chinese rites and created the Jesus Family commune in Shandong was also arrested in 1952 and his commune disbanded. He too endured thought reform, until he died in prison in 1957. Through the unexpected gateway of a prison cell, he entered, at last, his hidden land of *shiwai taoyuan*, "the world beyond the spring of the peach blossoms."

Wang Mingdao stood defiantly among the Christians who had steadfastly refused to join the TSPM. He did not shrink from saying why. "These people have no faith," he spoke of the TSPM clerics. "Masquerading as Christians, they mix with church people and spread some kind of ambiguous, false doctrine to lead astray true believers and corrupt their faith." But in 1955 the Man of Iron was finally reined in, as the government launched an all-out purge on "superstitions and counterrevolutionaries." Although his totally Chinese church had always been self-governing, self-supporting, and self-propagating, Wang and other members of the Christian Tabernacle were arrested.

In prison, he learned firsthand the new Chinese practices of thought reform and reeducation. Fellow prisoners filled his mind with stories of torture and terror and the Man of Iron broke. He confessed his counterrevolutionary tendencies and promised to join the Three-Self Patriotic Movement. But immediately after his release, he became a tormented man. He attended Christian meetings where his confession was read aloud but he felt only shame. He couldn't bring himself to join the movement and so he and his wife were once again arrested. He recanted his previous confessions, denied all that he had been forced to say, and strongly reaffirmed his beliefs. He would spend the next twenty-two years in prison. Although he would not play a direct role in the Christian resurgence to come, Christians in China knew that he had stood firm for the faith.[5]

Moses Xie (1918–2011) was the director of the Chinese Christian Mission in Shanghai and resolutely refused to join the Three-Self Patriotic Movement. He was arrested in 1956. During his interrogation he was handcuffed continuously for the first 133 days. The cuffs cut into the bone of his wrists, guards pulled his hair, kicked him with boots, and relentlessly tried to convince him to abandon his faith. In an interview with former *Time* magazine correspondent David Aikman, Xie described how the pain and torment drove him to attempt suicide by jamming his hand into an open light socket. "Late that night, anguish and contrition flooded his soul," wrote Aikman in *Jesus in Beijing* (2003). As he sobbed in prayer, a voice spoke to him in Chinese, "My grace is sufficient for you." Xie insists to this day that "it was God's audible voice. After that incident, God's grace was really strong. When I was beaten after this, I didn't feel the pain."

Allen Yuan (1914–2005), born as Yuan Xiangchen, was a preacher who had his own baptismal ministry in Beijing. He too refused to join the TSPM, mainly, he said, because he believed that Jesus Christ, not some political group, was the head of the church. He also objected to the theological modernism that characterized Bishop Ting and other TSPM leaders. He was arrested in 1958, ten days before Wang Mingdao was rearrested, and was sentenced to twenty-one years in labor and reeducation camps.

In the fall of 1955, the government moved violently against the Catholics. By the end of that year, fifteen hundred priests, nuns, and lay workers had been arrested in Shanghai alone, including the bishop of Shanghai, Kung Pinmei (1901–2000), and the Jesuit seminarian Jin Luxian. Kung Pinmei suffered five

Moses Xie was handcuffed continuously for 133 days. The cuffs cut into his wrists, guards pulled his hair, and relentlessly tried to convince him to abandon his faith.

years of "reeducation" and was sentenced to life imprisonment for treason. Jin Luxian was kept mainly in solitary confinement for five years and then sentenced to eighteen years for counterrevolutionary activities.

In their *History of Christianity in Socialist China* (1997) Jonathan Chao and Rosanna Chong record one estimate that between 1950 and 1978, five hundred thousand Christians died from Communist persecution. But they were a mere fraction of the total toll among all Chinese from Mao's economic experimentations, which came in two periods of horror. The first, known as the Great Leap Forward (1958–1961), sought to swiftly change the economy from agricultural to industrial by collectivizing farms, prohibiting private gardens, and the imposing slave labor. Tens of millions died—the estimates range from eighteen to thirty-two million. The Dutch historian Frank Dikötter (*Mao's Great Famine*, 2010) says the "Great Leap" triggered "one of the most deadly mass killings of human history."

The second horror was known as the Cultural Revolution (1966–1976). During this time, Mao sought to recover his credibility through a massive campaign against incipient capitalism and anti-Marxist ideology which he said was infiltrating the Communist state. Youths were recruited into the Red Guards and commissioned to ferret out revisionists, seize the properties of the wealthy, and force the owners to work the land. Historical relics and artifacts from the past were destroyed and Christians were especially targeted.

Bibles and hymn books were burned, churches converted to granaries, and leaders subjected to mock trials and humiliations. There were constant campaigns—"Oppose America, Defend Korea"; the "Anti-Rightist" movement; the "Five Antis"; the "Four Olds"—and all of them provided occasions for police and townspeople to make accusations, and round up teachers and ministers and

5. Wang Mingdao refused to leave prison until the government admitted they had wrongfully jailed him. In 1979, he was tricked into believing the government had apologized and accepted release from prison. He lived his final days in a Shanghai apartment, nearly blind and deaf, a critic of the TSPM until his death in 1991. "No Christian Chinese leader in the twentieth century has more clearly articulated the power of the Gospel of Jesus Christ, or more poignantly experienced what the Apostle Paul described as 'the fellowship of sharing' in his sufferings." Thus wrote James Hudson Taylor III, grandson of India's great missionary Hudson Taylor (see volume 11, pages 202–203).

A designated female member of the Red Guards reads a local newspaper to bystanders in front of the railway station in Shenyang in August 1966, conveying the ideas of Chairman Mao to a largely illiterate public. A component of the Cultural Revolution was the constant bombardment of the populace with Communist shibboleths. Another component was the "Struggle Sessions" wherein those considered insufficiently onside with Mao's teachings—and these included Christians—were publicly shamed. Below, two Chinese men, with signs around their necks proclaiming them to be antirevolutionary elements, are driven through the streets of Beijing in January 1967.

landlords and managers. Then, the "brainwashing" in the prison cell, the "struggle session" in the town square as comrades yelled denunciations for hours, with prisoners handcuffed and humiliated, and confessions drawn out of them. Finally came the triumphant parade through the village with the "running dogs" walking on all fours, wearing dunce hats and jeered by their former friends and neighbors.

One Lutheran minister remembered his friend, a teacher. His former pupils and the Red Guards put him naked inside a bamboo cage, dragging him through the village with a "cow" label around his neck, leaving him uncovered in the cage for weeks. They forced him to eat pages from his own schoolbooks covered with excrement. He was skeletal after they finished with him and had nowhere to live because his home was confiscated. The minister took him home and nursed him, but he refused to talk, for fear of implicating his rescuer. After a few days he vanished. "I knew instantly what had happened," recalled the minister. "He had chosen to kill himself. Some time later, his body was found hanging from a tree."

This memoir appears in *Households of God on China's Soil* (1982), a collection of stories by the World Council of Churches recounting the suffering of ordinary Christians in the 1950s and early 1960s, as well as the attempt to abolish all religion during the Cultural Revolution in the 1960s and 1970s. There are fourteen other accounts in this book, with the names of many of the people involved withheld because the days of persecution were not yet over. Here in summary are three:

A GRANDMOTHER'S STORY: "Towards the end of the Fifties," writes one, a grandmother, "Pastor Pi lost his church and asked my husband if he and others could use our home for prayers. That was how this home meeting began." About fourteen people "all housewives like me" attended. After Pastor Pi's death in 1963, the house group continued, praying, reading scripture, and singing hymns. Attendance dropped. People had to take street patrol duties, work in canteens, queue in line for food, and attend twice-weekly political studies classes. But gradually adult children and grandchildren joined and the group sometimes reached twenty people again.

Then the Cultural Revolution began. "One day, my neighbor's fourteen- or fifteen-year-old son with two friends wearing the Red Guard armbands, came to my door and quietly tipped me off about a 'house confiscation' visit by Red Guards anytime." They told her to get rid of her "Jesus things." Three days later a squad of about forty youths came with banners and placards. They announced they were there to eliminate the "Four Olds"—old culture, old ideas, old customs, old habits. They destroyed her Bible, hymn books, and an ivory cross and took away all of her furniture leaving only two chairs and a table.

Wooden statues from a Buddhist temple in Beijing lean against a wall after being knocked off their pedestals by Red Guards in the summer of 1966, a part of their bid to destroy what Mao called "the old superstitions of old China." The Red Guards also burned Christian hymn books and Bibles and converted churches into granaries.

"You have too much, others have none," they said. Several days later, two other families moved into the house. In 1980, four years after Mao's death, the official church nearby was reopened. She attended one service. "It was heavenly. My heart was full of blessings and my eyes full of happy tears. I shamelessly clutched the arm of an old man sitting next to me, wetting his jacket with my tears."

HOW ONE VILLAGE BECAME CHRISTIAN: A young woman, part of a Korean minority brought to northern China to work in the steel mills, tells how a generous gesture by one Christian man started a movement that brought a whole village into the Christian faith. The Koreans at first were not welcomed by their Han neighbors and lived separately.[6] But gradually the Han settlement expanded to include the Korean village, and Korean men began marrying Han women. Around 1973, there were about forty Christian families who met for Sunday prayer in a building with a big courtyard. They also met for prayers in different homes. Her father's home was a meeting place for about twenty families.

That winter a conflict arose in the village. Homes were heated with coke from the steel mill, and many families felt that families with Han wives were getting a

6. The Han people make up ninety-two percent of China's population, and take their name from the Han Dynasty, which ruled a vast area from 206 B.C. to 220 A.D. The Han Dynasty created one strong administrative unit for most of what is now China, centered on the valleys of the Huang He (Yellow) and Yangtze Rivers. With periodic disruptions, this region has maintained a loose unity and cohesion for over two thousand years. Alien peoples like the Mongol and Manchu Dynasties may have ruled it but they were ultimately absorbed by the culture of China. For millennia, the Han have defined that culture.

larger quantity of coke. When a baby died because of the cold, the village held an angry meeting. At this meeting, one of the Christian husbands, Brother Lee, offered to share his family's coke. His wife was Han and nobody took him seriously. But the next day, after work, he brought coke to several Korean families. The following day, he visited other families.

That Sunday at church, the elder praised Brother Lee for following Christ and showing the way. After church, all of the Christian families started to share their coke. Within a year, all the families in the Korean village became Christian.

A PREACHER'S DAUGHTER REMEMBERS HER FATHER: One young woman tells how her father, who had been part owner of a spinning and weaving mill, gave up his position to pastor a Christian congregation in the 1950s. He also joined a group of clergy studying Marxism. There were five Protestant churches in their town and soon all but one were taken over for municipal purposes. Her family's home was spacious so they began holding church services there. Baptists and Presbyterians joined them. At one time, there were over a hundred in the home for a Sunday service. With so many different believers, there was conflict about who could receive communion. Her father prayed for guidance, and then welcomed all with a stirring sermon, "The Blood of Christ washes away all our sins."

His sermon led to a great revival. "People at the house meeting broke down, embraced each other and openly confessed their sins. They went home and did the same to their relatives and families. Next morning, a lot of people gathered at our door, waiting to confess to my father." Then the Red Guards came. A few days later, he and other leaders were paraded through town in a mock parade with

This selection of Red Chinese propaganda posters illustrates the regime's efforts to inculcate the population with the belief that all was well and would remain so, provided everyone fulfilled his duty to the Chairman. (Top) Mao is portrayed in 1971 as a man in his prime (he was actually seventy-seven and ailing) touring a power station, with the inscription "Caring deeply, encouraging diligently." (Below from left) An idealized Chinese worker marches forward clutching the "red book" of Mao's thoughts in his right hand above the heading, "Make the great leader proud, make the great socialist motherland proud." A schoolgirl with a ping-pong paddle and a book about Mao at hand, ponders her role in the Communist future, with the caption, "Continue the revolutionary tradition, become revolutionary successors." Third, in a 1967 poster the man himself waves like a benevolent giant to the masses gathered below with red books in every hand. "Long live Chairman Mao," it reads, "the reddest sun in our hearts; long, long live Chairman Mao!"

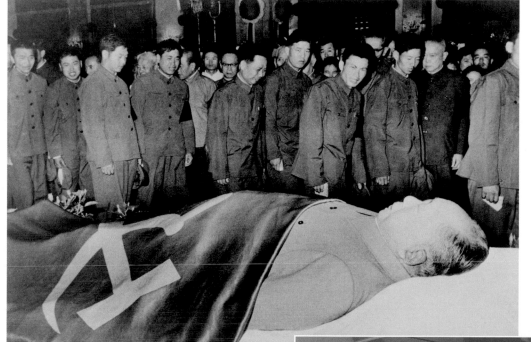

Mao, shown here lying in state in Beijing's Great Hall of the People, died in 1976, setting the stage for a new era of reform under Deng Xiaoping. It seemed remarkable that any churches had survived in China, but in fact an astonishing explosion of Christian belief was starting to take place, not in churches, but in tens of thousands of private homes. Below, one such home is pictured in Dali, Yunnan province, in 2007.

dunce's caps on their heads. He died soon after. "Our prayer meetings could not go on. We could not even be seen greeting each other in the streets." After 1976, certain reforms were made. Pastor Chung of "what used to be the Presbyterian church" began working to have one of the churches reopened. Her family began house meetings again with about fifty people attending, half over sixty, the rest young people. "We have many needs," she said, "But the main thing is we have survived and have not dishonored the name of Jesus."

By 1976 when Mao died, it seemed remarkable that any churches at all had survived in China. But in fact an astonishing explosion of Christian belief was starting to take place, not in churches but in tens of thousands of private homes, where fathers, mothers, and children had somehow kept the flame of faith flickering. By then, life was gravely diminished in the official churches of the TSPM, and the churches of the Chinese Catholic Patriotic Association had been closed down or destroyed during the worst days of the Cultural Revolution.

Deng Xiaoping, who assumed the leadership of China two years after Mao's death, ushered in a new spirit of "reform and opening." By then, certain realities had become inescapable. Mao had promised the proud Chinese a Communist utopia—but thirty years of indoctrination and isolation from the outside had not produced it. The great hopes of the parades and the slogans, of the Great Leap Forward and the Cultural Revolution, had produced instead a great disappointment. Communism did not fulfill the dream it had promised and everybody knew it. Economically, the country was ever more widely embracing capitalism. Politically, it would not be many years before students would carry a statue of

The New Revised Standard version of the English-Chinese Bible; famed house church leader Zhang Rongliang (top) and American missionary and Bible distributor Dennis Balcombe. Both were instrumental in establishing Pentecostalism in China. For his efforts, Zhang was sentenced in 2006 to seven years in prison.

liberty through Tiananmen Square.[7] The ideology fervently embraced by so many was now gone, leaving a huge spiritual hunger. The government still ruled, the "mandate from heaven" was intact and the dynasty stable, but no one believed the ideology anymore. There were still years of persecution ahead, but now, in this great spiritual void, the Holy Spirit stirred.

How else can what happened be explained? There was no central authority, no evidence of an organized campaign or mission, no circulation of printed tracts or appeals or calls for a massive movement. Yet one certainly occurred and on a scale of unaccountable dimension. Suddenly, first hundreds and then thousands of little Christian meetings started taking place in homes all over the country. Almost overnight the "house church" sprang into existence as an omnipresent phenomenon. In addition, supposedly long-dead churches came back to life. In 1978, a former sailor and True Jesus Church follower, Wang Yuansong, evangelized through seventeen provinces, reconnecting True Jesus followers and leaders. By 1980 more than ninety percent of the True Jesus Church congregations that had been disbanded in Fuqing county of Fujian province were reported as reactivated. In the same county, twenty thousand Little Flock followers were active. These numbers grew to the hundreds of thousands when a strongly Pentecostal strain of the Little Flock called the "Shouters" began spreading their message. In Shandong province a small Jesus Family emerged that had managed to survive as a commune all through the years since Jing Dianyang had died in prison in 1957.

Converts were not limited to the old homegrown churches. In southern China, hand in hand with economic liberalization, new five-story churches were built in cities like Wenzhou. But nowhere in the entire country did the Spirit stir as strongly as in the central province of Henan. The name means "south of the river" (the Yellow River) and it has traditionally been the center of the Han civilization and the center of China. In the years ahead, it would be known by the authorities as "the Jesus nest," and the name was not intended as a compliment.

Typical was the explosive growth in Fangcheng County. Gao Yongjiu had been a young soldier with the Nationalists but after he converted to Christianity he began evangelizing in Fangcheng. He was jailed in the 1950s. During the Cultural Revolution he was beaten so hard in the winter that all the stuffing had come out of his coat. He was released in 1970, and wrote a letter to his older brother-in-law asking if he would come back to his home province to help organize Christians. His brother-in-law, Li Tianen, had grown up in Fangcheng and had been a member of the Jesus Family. He had led a house church in Shanghai and was sent to labor camps in the early 1960s. Li arrived at the village of Guan Zhan and met the young Christians. At the time he arrived, there were ten Christians in a village of about two hundred. Their numbers would grow to include all but three villagers.

7. Tiananmen is the center of China's life and identity. Tiananmen Gate is the major entrance to the Forbidden City and fronts the world's largest public square. Its name captures China's understanding of itself. Commonly translated as "The Gate of Heavenly Peace" Tiananmen actually comes from a longer phrase—"receiving the mandate from heaven and stabilizing the dynasty." These concepts encompass the historical Chinese view of China's central place in the cosmos, and the Confucian values of stability and order.

Many of these congregations had begun in secret. One woman, Chen Yurong, remembers how her younger brother, a Communist official, would persecute them. One day, his two young boys were playing near the village well, and one fell in. Chen rushed to the well. "Lord, save this boy, let me die instead," she cried. The boy was saved, and when he surfaced, he told everyone a man in white holding him up had saved him. After this, persecution stopped. Christians in the village prayed for the sick and there were many healings. Gradually their numbers grew.

Meanwhile, Li traveled throughout Fangcheng, training up to twenty young evangelists at a time. They would then travel in pairs to distant parts of China. The young evangelists were often arrested, beaten, and tortured, but this did not inhibit their zeal. The Fangcheng Fellowship, as it came to be called, spread through China until by the 1990s its numbers were running into the millions. Li passed on much of the work of leading the growing fellowship to a younger leader he had trained, Zhang Rongliang.

Nowhere did the Spirit stir as strongly as in the province of Henan. The authorities would know it as 'the Jesus nest.' The name was not intended as a compliment.

Born in 1950, Zhang had barely survived the famine during the Great Leap Forward and became a Christian in 1969. He had been sentenced to a labor camp in Henan province where he became friends with another Christian, Feng Jianguo. Both men's labor involved work in the countryside and they used their time to establish churches in villages around the prison camp. After their release Zhang worked in the Fangcheng fellowship and Feng developed the Tanghe Fellowship. Zhang would be imprisoned many times. He called prison "God's seminary."

In 1974, Zhang was arrested again, and this time the "struggle sessions" in which he faced accusers and denouncers were televised, and particularly shown to school audiences, as lessons against the evils of "counterrevolution" and "superstition." One young girl who watched the television persecution of Zhang was Ding Hei, then thirteen, who had been baptized of her own volition the year before. She felt the denunciations of Zhang were denunciations of her. She joined and rose quickly in the Fangcheng Fellowship until she became a leader. She was on the same podium with Zhang in 1981 when the Fangcheng Fellowship organized a public meeting of five hundred young evangelists. It was the first time house churches—by definition ten or twenty people—had held such a huge public meeting in the face of the authorities.

Both the Tanghe and Fangcheng fellowships were becoming strongly Pentecostal in the 1980s after encounters with an American missionary named Dennis Balcombe. Running an agency called "Donkeys for Christ" (much as in English one might say "workhorse") and under the guise of teaching English, Balcombe met many leaders of the unofficial church when he delivered Bibles to China. His films of Pentecostal trances and speaking in tongues led to similar manifestations in the growing fellowships. At one meeting, seventy young couples (some still in their teens) were given two hundred dollars each and sent to twenty-two provinces. They were to evangelize for six months and then report back.

The efforts of one young pair of women sent to China's far north province, Heilongjiang, produced a church that had grown to five thousand members by 2002.

Allen Yuan resumed his baptismal ministry in Beijing after his release from prison. In August 1998, David Aikman described visiting him in his tiny apartment on a night when twenty-six people were jammed in for a nightly Bible study. Aikman recounts in his book *Jesus In Beijing* (2003) something Yuan told him: "We have a saying in Beijing. If you dare to preach, people will believe. In Hong Kong and Taiwan they have everything, but here they have nothing. It is just like the Apostles' time… We have so many limits on what we can do, but this work now is just like that of the first Christians. We have miracles now… There is a saying that persecution is the growing pain of the church. It is good for the church."

A few months after Allen Yuan's conversation in 1998, the representatives of four of the major house churches in China issued a Confession of Faith about the central principles which bound them together. They declared that their house churches represented eighty million Christians in China, in addition to the ten million then attending official Protestant services in TSPM churches. There is little reason to doubt these figures, which would make the "unofficial" house churches in China the home for the vast majority of the country's Protestants.

What in the meantime had happened to the Catholic Church? The Communist persecution of 1955 had all but terminated the Catholic clergy in China, but in the absence of priests, Catholic villages and neighborhoods quietly began organizing themselves to carry out their own devotions. Catholics did not have the same long-established methods of house meetings and lay leaders that indigenous churches like Little Flock, True Jesus,

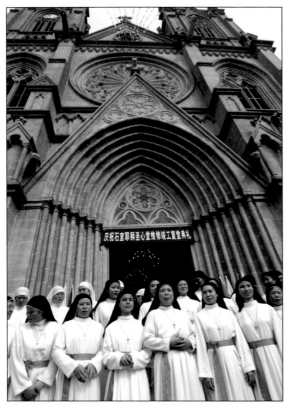

and the Jesus People did, but they quickly adapted to the house church structure. They shared strong community spirit in their rural and neighborhood concentrations. Lay people quickly learned new skills, not the least of which was democratically choosing their leaders. One villager had kept the rafters of his desecrated church in a shed. Years later, he organized villagers, raised funds, and rebuilt the church.

What they missed most, of course, were priests and the celebrations of Mass in the church or cathedral. Whether because some priests recognized this need, or whether they were at heart in sympathy with the People's Revolution, enough priests joined the CCPA that a semblance of public worship was continued in the official churches. Meanwhile, the surviving Chinese bishops also worked with the

The Cultural Revolution burst with particular fury on the Catholics. The devout endured the 'struggle sessions' with dunce caps. Some churches became pig barns.

CCPA to consecrate fifty-one new Chinese bishops, without Vatican approval. The Vatican recognized these bishops as "valid," meaning they could perform sacraments, but "illicit," meaning they were not accepted by the pope and should not be accepted by Catholics except *in extremis* (near death or in extreme danger). Even so, it was now possible for churchgoers to attend weekly Mass, even if ambivalent about the clergy serving.

The Cultural Revolution burst with particular fury on the Catholics, with consequent scenes of horror: parishioners made to kneel on the broken glass of their church, the usual "struggle sessions" with dunce caps and humiliations in the village square, churches desecrated and converted to pig barns and granaries. But in 1979, there came a period of economic and political reform. Priests and bishops began to be freed from prisons. Many operated in the unofficial Catholic house churches. They were able to secretly ordain new priests and bishops whom the pope, in a secret agreement, recognized as both "valid" and "licit." Many priests began serving in the official church.

These authorized churches began operating at capacity, with thousands attending Mass. Richard Madsen, in *God and Caesar in China* (2004), recounts a visit to a Catholic cathedral in Tianjin in the 1980s that illustrates the kinds of distinctions that Catholics made. He attended an early morning Mass celebrated by a priest who had never accepted the CCPA and had suffered for his resistance, but was now being allowed by the government to resume his priestly functions. The Mass was crowded. After the first priest finished, another priest came out to begin a second Mass. All at once, with almost military precision, the whole congregation stood up, turned their backs to the altar, and with a loud stamping sound walked out of the church. The second priest was called "Father Unbeliever" by the Tianjin Catholics and was widely despised because of his collaboration with the government.

One priest who was released from prison but who also decided to work within the official CCPA structure was Jesuit Jin Luxian, jailed since 1955. Rome told him to wait for the Communist collapse, but, as he said, "they underestimated the Chinese Communist Party." Adam Minter quotes him in *The Atlantic* (July, 2007): "After much prayer... I didn't obey the directive of Rome. I said, 'Let the Catholic Church survive.'" In the politics of the underground church he was regarded as a Judas; but *The Atlantic* story quotes Jerome Heyndrickx, a Belgian priest who has served as a Vatican emissary to China since the early 1980s, in conversation with Pope John Paul II about Father Jin: "If he is not faithful, then neither am I."

Since 1982 Jin has worked tirelessly with the CCPA, reopening churches and seminaries, training more than four hundred priests, many recognized by Rome, and changing services to a Chinese language liturgy, which includes prayers for the

Saint Ignatius Catholic Cathedral stands in front of Shanghai's growing skyline in 2005. Below is its bishop, Jin Luxian, in 2011. In the new, increasingly materialistic China, Jin sees a threat greater than persecution.

pope. In 1985, he was ordained bishop-in-waiting of Shanghai by the CCPA, a position he accepted reluctantly because the true bishop, Kung Pinmei, was still in prison. Kung was released the next year, made a cardinal by the pope, and traveled to the U.S. where significant supporters established the Cardinal Kung Foundation to provide assistance for the underground Catholic Church in China. Early results, however, were not encouraging. For instance, in 2012, when Thaddeus Ma Daqin renounced governmental controls on the church while he was being consecrated as auxiliary bishop of Shanghai, he was stripped of his title by the government.

The official churches of the Protestants are also swelling beyond capacity. Megachurches are being constructed in southern China, many of them with TSPM sanction.[8] Bishop Ting, who had so much to do with creating the TSPM in the 1950s, is credited with bringing the TSPM back after the Cultural Revolution. He established the Amity Foundation through which westerners provide Bibles, teachers, seminars, and much rapprochement with the Chinese church. At his death in 2012, obituaries around the world hailed him as a patriot to his country and a visionary to his church.

Whether this rise of Christianity in China will prove permanent was still open to doubt in the opinion of Jin Luxian. Now accepted as Catholic bishop of Shanghai, he was quoted in Richard Madsen's *China's Catholics* (1998): "I had no fear for our Catholics facing the challenge of persecution. But now, facing the challenge of modernization, of pure materialism, of the idolatry of money, of individualism, I have fears… Now, all Chinese grow up in the atmosphere of atheism… Parish activity is reduced only to the religious service, to brief homilies, and short catechism on Saturday evening and Sunday morning. Children's homework is so heavy that they have very little free time… adults talk mostly about money, business, stock market, speculations. Every family has a TV set. They watch TV through the satellite; they watch videocassettes imported from Hong Kong, Taiwan and America. They play cards and mah-jongg. They find little time to pray. They go to church but they begin to find the Mass too long."

Such concerns notwithstanding, it remained true that by the dawn of the twenty-first century there were signs of a growing interest in Christianity at all levels of Chinese society. For government authorities, writes the historian Philip Jenkins in *The New Christendom* (2002), "one of the most alarming signs of this religious upsurge is the number of defections to Christianity by party cadres and even officials. In the 1980s alone, the number of Catholics in central Henan province grew from four hundred thousand to one million." Again, in the mid-90s a Chinese translation of the ponderous five hundred-page *Principles of Christian Theology* was printed in China and sold out its 190,000 press run in eighteen months. More pertinently still, in 2002 a scholar from the Chinese Academy of Social Sciences told a visiting group of American Christians something of which the western world itself might take note:

"We were asked," he said, "to discover what accounted for the success, in fact, the pre-eminence of the West all over the world. We studied everything we could from the historical, political, economic, and cultural perspective. At first, we thought it was because you had more powerful guns than we had. Then we thought it was because you had the best political system. Next we focused on your economic system. But in the past twenty years, we have realized that the heart of your culture is your religion: Christianity. That is why the West has been so powerful. The Christian moral foundation of social and cultural life was what made possible the emergence of capitalism and then the successful transition to democratic politics. We don't have any doubt about this."

But the intelligentsia of Europe and much of America often appear to have a great deal of doubt about it—an omen perhaps that the center of Christianity, and with it the center of civilization, may once again be moving to a more receptive part of the wide world. ■

8. In 2002, a Christmas Eve story in the *Washington Post* described a service for youth from Wenzhou: "On a recent Saturday, in the city's Ouhai district, hundreds of youth gathered for an afternoon of Christian rock music at a massive government-sanctioned church. 'Lord I worship you' read a banner above the altar. Between rousing tunes with a heavy backbeat, the assembled—young families, clean-cut boys straight from Wenzhou's shoe factories, and pink-cheeked girls fresh from the countryside—were treated to a series of stories about how faith-healing could cure cancer."

The bustle of a 1963 session of the Second Vatican Council in Rome is captured in a photo-graph by the young Lothar Wolleh, who began his celebrated career photographing this momentous meeting of bishops called by Pope John XXIII in response to the social and politi-cal issues specific to the postwar era. Cardinal Montini, who would succeed John as Pope Paul VI, feared the pontiff was stirring a "hornet's nest"—a prescient observation, as it turned out.

CHAPTER 10

Cries for change assail the changeless church in the Vatican II tumult

'Good Pope John 23' didn't know the hornets' nest he was stirring, says his successor, who must tame the wild results after radical clergy work mayhem

After Pope John XXIII died in 1963, Catholics, especially those in the liberal-progressive wing of their church, remembered him as "Good Pope John." This admiration was not solely, or even mainly, for the pope's manifest virtue and genial, grandfatherly demeanor. Rather, it was for his unexpected decision to convoke the Second Vatican Council in 1962. By this one act Good Pope John plunged Catholicism into a maelstrom of division and dissent. Perhaps it was necessary and inevitable, given the changing state of the world and the corresponding pressures building within the Catholic Church. Either way, within one decade it would transform much of Christendom's largest church, hitherto a bastion of traditional faith and pious obedience, into an incubator of political, social, and religious ferment.

Pope John probably would have been shocked to learn that he would soon become an icon for religious radicalism, for he was certainly not radical himself. Baptized Angelo Giuseppe Roncalli, eldest son of a devout family of sharecropping farmers in the foothills of the Italian Alps, he was ordained a priest in 1904. After the First World War, at the young age of thirty-three, Roncalli was tapped for Vatican service and appointed a titular bishop by Pope Pius XI in 1925. This credentialed him for senior diplomatic posts over the next three decades. He was papal representative to Turkey and Greece from 1935 to 1944, where he helped thousands of Jews escape from Greece's Nazi occupiers. He served in France from

1944 to 1953, and then rose to cardinal and became patriarch of Venice. This put him in line as a possible successor to Pope Pius XII.

Vatican watchers in the 1950s expected Archbishop Giovanni Montini of Milan to be the next pope, but when Pius died in 1958 he had not made Montini a cardinal, a rank essential for any serious papal candidate. So when the cardinals assembled at the Vatican to elect a new pope, they looked for a steady, reliable, elderly hand to guide their church for a few years while the less-seasoned Montini could be put in line. The 1958 conclave went to an eleventh ballot to settle on Roncalli, who named himself John XXIII.

In January 1959, a mere ninety days into his reign, Pope John announced without forewarning that he was summoning an ecumenical council—a very rare worldwide council of bishops. This astonished the entire Catholic Church.[1] There were no unresolved questions of doctrine, so why do this? The last such get-together was the First Vatican Council of 1870, and it was thought to have obviated future councils by declaring the doctrine of papal infallibility and of papal primacy over the church. So even if Pope John had evinced an interest in further doctrinal refinement—which he had not—he did not need a general council of bishops to do it.

More alarming to many, the western world was in a period of massive social flux, involving moral issues on which the church traditionally took firm and previously unarguable positions. Therefore in calling the council Pope John was exposing his church to the same grave danger of division that was already sundering western society. Divisive doctrinal issues might also arise. Ever since Pope Pius X had condemned in 1907 the initial outbreak of Catholic Modernism (see chapter 3, page 39), doctrinal authorities had rigorously repressed all efforts by revisionists to remove the mystical and supernatural aspects of Catholic faith. Yet it

1. According to Father Ralph Wiltgen, whose book *The Rhine Flows into the Tiber* is widely regarded as the authoritative record of the Second Vatican Council's day-to-day proceedings, the universal surprise over John XXIII's decision extended even to his closest collaborators in the Roman curia, the Catholic Church's central administration.

was well known—though hard to gauge—Modernist sympathies survived among some Catholic intellectuals. A church council could become the instrument for their wider propagation, triggering a ruinous doctrinal debate similar to those that had been roiling within Protestant denominations throughout the century.

So why did Pope John call a Second Vatican Council—or, as it was dubbed, "Vatican II"? Some traditionalists attribute it to impulsiveness and naiveté. For example, Montini (whom John immediately elevated to cardinal) commented privately, "This holy old boy doesn't realize what a hornet's nest he's stirring up." But such an assessment is questionable. John had never been inclined to impulsiveness in his long diplomatic career. He feared that Catholicism, which still spoke of metaphysical certitudes in a dead language, was losing its ability to engage contemporary people, whose certainties were increasingly found in science and whose moral values were increasingly flexible and subjective. And with irreligion and atheism spreading relentlessly in consequence of these changes, ways must surely be found to present Christian truth more convincingly. To do this, said his defenders, John must have concluded that the church needed to reassess how it professed its beliefs, taking into account the findings of modern science and of contemporary historical and biblical scholarship.

On October 11, 1962, twenty-four hundred bishops from around the world, seen here amassed in Saint Peter's Basilica, listened as the octogenarian Pope John XXIII delivered his formal conciliar charge. The council would be "predominantly pastoral in character," he instructed, and its greatest concern should be "that the sacred deposit of Christian doctrine should be guarded and taught more efficaciously." While most bishops expected to ratify some uncontroversial documents and then go home, the northern European progressives, led by Cardinal Joseph Frings of Cologne (shown, inset, in a commemorative plaque in his hometown), had different ideas.

Current events served as a terrifying reminder of the new realities of modern existence. The council began in the same month as the Cuban Missile Crisis in which nuclear war became an imminent possibility. John XXIII warned the council that in today's world, "experience has taught men that violence inflicted on others, the might of arms and political domination, are of no help at all in finding a happy solution to the grave problems which afflict them."

Hearing the liberalizing liturgical proposals put forward by the Germans, Holy Office chief Cardinal Alfredo Ottaviani, seen here, rose in protest and began warning of the dire potentialities, exceeding his ten-minute time allotment. The two cardinals in charge of the debate cut his microphone, and Ottaviani stumbled back to his seat in humiliation. Writes historian Ralph Wilgen: "The most powerful cardinal in the Roman Curia had been silenced, and the Council Fathers clapped in glee."

Then too, Pope John was known to believe that Catholicism must offer a Christian response to the social and political issues specific to the new era. Christianity is not solely about eternal personal salvation. It must also at all times convey a positive message about the dignity of human beings and about how they can live to good purpose, individually and collectively, in this world.[2] Since the First World War Catholic scholars and thinkers had been developing effective answers to the dark, atheistic philosophies of Nietzsche and Marx that had inflicted such pain and misery across the globe in the twentieth century—answers they were extracting from the patristic writings of the early church. But for the world to hear and receive those answers, the church must first reengage the world in a new wave of Christian evangelism.

Finally, there was the continuing scandal of Christian division to consider. The Roman Catholic Church had been separated from the Eastern Orthodox churches for almost one thousand years, and for the last four hundred from the Protestant churches of the West. Perpetuation of these divisions violated Jesus' command that his followers be "one flock," and it grievously undermined their collective witness. If Christians couldn't even agree among themselves about basic doctrinal and disciplinary matters, why should nonbelievers listen to them? In sum, Pope John judged that his church faced very pressing pastoral concerns. The watchword for his council became *aggiornamento*, an Italian term implying an "updating" of the church's message—or more accurately, the way the message is expressed.

So on October 11, 1962, some twenty-four hundred bishops from around the world gathered in a body ahead of their octogenarian pope, and trooped in religious dress through Saint Peter's central square into Catholicism's greatest basilica. Inside, Pope John gave them his formal conciliar charge. The council would be "predominantly pastoral in character," he instructed, and its "greatest concern" would be "that the sacred deposit of Christian doctrine should be guarded and taught more efficaciously." It must "look to the present," he declared, "to the new conditions and forms of life introduced into the modern world, which have opened new avenues to the Catholic apostolate." In effect, he was telling the Catholic Church that its continuing relevance was predicated on its capacity to become an instrument of what would later be broadly described as a "new evangelization" of the modern world to the old faith.

Most council bishops expected to ratify the uncontroversial draft documents prepared by the council's Vatican organizers and go home. Not so, however, the predominantly progressive bishops of northern Europe, led by the Germans. With characteristic

organization and industry, they had mobilized beforehand, identifying key points they wanted included in conciliar documents, and installing reformers in key council positions to accomplish this.[3]

Their traditionalist counterparts conspicuously failed to do the same. This was partly because many assumed the powerful cardinals in the central curia would block excessive innovation, and partly because they believed no liberalizing threat existed since Pope John had ruled so categorically against doctrinal revision. But the reformist European bishops, under the de facto leadership of Cardinal Joseph Frings of Cologne, knew better. With the council undertaking a comprehensive restatement of Catholic belief and its contemporary application, opportunities would abound to insert novel ideas into conciliar documents, especially since

The predominantly progressive bishops of northern Europe had installed reformers in key positions. Their traditionalist counterparts had conspicuously failed to do the same.

modernizers largely controlled the council staff. The most noted of these was council consultant Father Hans Küng, a thirty-four-year-old progressive theologian from Tübingen University.

From the outset, this northern "European Alliance" recruited like-minded bishops from other regions and moved fast. Within days, discussion of the draft document on liturgy—the forms of Catholic worship—went to the top of the council agenda, because the modernizers believed they had control of its content, unlike several other draft documents bordering more directly on doctrine. Those they wanted shelved until next year, allowing time and opportunity for revision. Cardinal Frings spoke first as the council commenced formal deliberations, to consider the draft proposal on liturgical reform. Resorting immediately to a trademark European Alliance tactic, he pressed for reintroduction of reform components that had been deleted during its preparatory phase. The most significant was a provision to allow national bishops' conferences to authorize use of the vernacular (the language spoken locally) in place of Latin in the Catholic Mass.

This, along with other liberalizing liturgical proposals, mightily alarmed the traditionalists. Cardinal Alfredo Ottaviani, head of the Vatican's Holy Office (renamed in 1965 the Congregation for the Doctrine of the Faith), rose in protest. Speaking without notes and caught up in the moment's passion, the powerful curial cardinal continued several minutes past his allotted ten minutes as he enumerated the dire consequences that would ensue from ill-considered liturgical reform. Suddenly, at the instruction of the two European cardinals in charge of that day's debate, his microphone went dead. "After confirming the fact by tapping the instrument, Cardinal Ottaviani stumbled back to his seat in humiliation," writes conciliar historian Ralph Wiltgen in *The Rhine Flows into the Tiber* (1978). "The most powerful cardinal in the Roman Curia had been silenced, and the Council Fathers clapped in glee."

Their delight may have reflected more their resentment of overbearing Roman centralism than any aversion to Catholic tradition. Still, Cardinal Ottaviani's humiliation was symbolically significant. At the First Vatican Council ninety years earlier, the curial cardinals had led a strong majority that imposed its will on a

3. The terms commonly used for the factions which dominated the council are "reformers," "progressives," or "modernizers" on one side, and "traditionalists" on the other. However, most traditionalists could accept moderate change, and a "modernizer" was not necessarily a "Modernist," meaning one who denied the possibility of supernatural intervention in the physical world. Some modernizers probably were Modernists, just as some traditionalists were undeniably reactionaries opposed to any change at all. But most bishops fell somewhere in the middle. The term "conservative" can confuse the issue, because when the council ended, most traditionalists, whatever their personal misgivings, accepted its decisions, following a precept of obedience attributed to Saint Augustine in the fifth century: "Rome has spoken, the matter is ended."

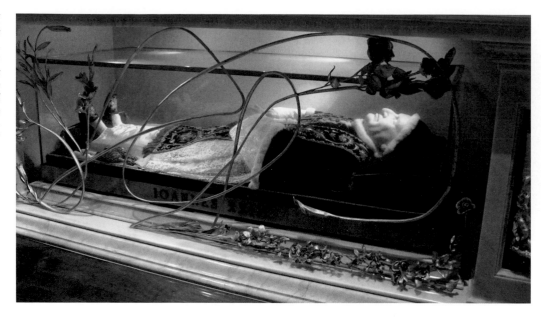

The preserved body of John XXIII lies in its glass coffin at Saint Peter's. By the spring of 1963, while still closely engaged with preparations for the second sitting of the ecumenical council, the pope's health was deteriorating, and on June 3 he died. Thereafter, he would be revered by the liberal progressives as "Good Pope John."

4. Küng, appointed by John XXIII as an expert adviser to the council, was exuberant over the unexpected scope of the modernizers' success during a press panel as the first session ended. What had previously been only the dream of an avantgarde minority, he said, had "spread and permeated the entire atmosphere of the church due to the council." Even after Rome revoked his licence to teach as a Catholic in 1979, Küng remained a widely quoted dissident hero to Catholic and secular progressives. To traditionalists he was an inflated, heretical gadfly. By 2012 he was calling for priests to organize and depose the pope.

5. These prominent *periti* would fare variously after the council ended. Father Joseph Ratzinger, then a priest serving as Cardinal Frings's personal theologian, was elevated to cardinal and served as the Vatican's senior doctrinal official for more than twenty years before being elected Pope Benedict XVI in 2005. In striking contrast, Canada's Gregory Baum, a *peritus* on ecumenical issues, dissented completely from Catholic teachings on sexuality after the council and, while technically still a priest, later wed a previously married former nun whom he subsequently divorced.

reformist minority concentrated in France and Germany. This time, as Ottaviani's silencing made plain, the northern Europeans held the upper hand. The European Alliance then went from symbolic to substantive victory, when the council acceded to Cardinal Frings's request for the reinstatement of all the liberal elements excised earlier from the liturgy draft. The modernizing bishops secured a string of similar organizational victories with respect to other key documents during the council's first session, preventing ratification of any initial drafts before it concluded in early December. This proved decisive to the outcome of the four-year-long council. The reformers had secured procedural control, and could now effect deep and permanent change.[4]

By the end of the first session it was learned that Pope John was suffering from advanced stomach cancer. Still, he remained closely engaged into 1963 with preparations for the council's second session. But by mid-May his health was collapsing, and on June 3 he died. Although John XXIII had never precisely endorsed the aims of the more radical European progressives, he had been undismayed by the ferment they had generated and consequently would be revered ever after by Catholic reformers.

The conciliar reform faction now needed to discern the attitude of his successor, who, if he chose, could shut down the whole enterprise. As expected, Cardinal Montini was elected, taking the name of Pope Paul VI. Though seen to be inclined toward modernization, his warning in 1959 about "stirring up a hornet's nest" generated alarm among progressives. This was allayed, however, when he opened the council's next session in September. He declared that he was speaking "from the window of the council, opened wide to the world." The council should benefit the Catholic Church in three ways: bring the church to a deeper understanding of its own nature; renew the church; and open greater dialogue with contemporary humanity.

Flushed with their 1962 victories, and now even better organized, the European Alliance continued to dominate proceedings in 1963 and 1964. Their preferred liturgical changes were ratified quickly, and other innovations continued to be added at every opportunity into the various drafts that eventually formed the council's sixteen final documents. All the same, it is clear from the lengthy

discussion that most bishops had no wish to dissent from foundational Catholic beliefs. In fact many had scant interest in doctrinal debates, being more concerned with the practical challenges of managing their dioceses. And collectively, the bishops present were much like popes John and Paul: they were modernizers, not Modernists; *aggiornamento* Catholics wishing to restate the traditions of their church more effectively, not revise its faith and morals.

But the council's *periti*—its expert theological advisers—were a very different matter.[5] Many—like Küng—were seeking to engineer a break from the past and to create a new Catholicism. And in the confusion it might even have happened had Pope Paul not intervened decisively near the end of the council's third session in late 1964. He had watched with rising concern as potentially radical ideas were insinuated in key documents. Traditionalists had been calling alarm for months, but Pope Paul had accepted reformers' reassurances that the problematic passages bore no radical meanings. His acquiescence ended when an overconfident reformer circulated a paper to confidants, affirming a collective intent that after the council was over, they could reinterpret conciliar statements about the "collegiality of bishops," thereby weakening papal authority.[6] When Pope Paul happened to see a copy of this he reportedly wept, realizing the radical faction had colluded to dupe him.

A few days later, he sent the council a note, ordering that collegiality not be

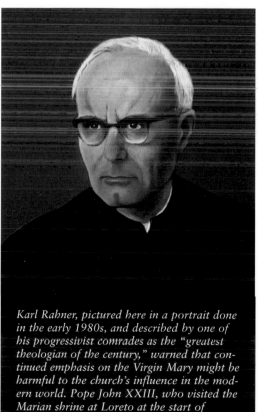

Karl Rahner, pictured here in a portrait done in the early 1980s, and described by one of his progressivist comrades as the "greatest theologian of the century," warned that continued emphasis on the Virgin Mary might be harmful to the church's influence in the modern world. Pope John XXIII, who visited the Marian shrine at Loreto at the start of Vatican II for guidance, viewed such suggestions negatively.

6. In its extreme form, "collegiality" holds that because Christ's disciples were in some sense equals, therefore all bishops have equal authority, making the pope a merely symbolic head of the church. It brought a scathing retort from the still-formidable traditionalist Ottaviani. Scripture offers only one example of the apostles acting as one, he said: when Christ was arrested, "they all fled."

interpreted in a manner adverse to papal authority. Three more papal directives followed, involving the council's teaching on religious liberty, ecumenism, and Mary. The more radical progressives would forever remember this as "Black Week."

Paul VI's subsequent caution, combined with better organization among traditionalists, resulted by council's end in a collection of conciliar documents that would afterward be judged as doctrinally sound, even by most conservatives.[7] Sound, perhaps, but unsettling. Hastily implemented liturgical reform

Ratzinger: the man who finished the job

John Paul's top aide and successor ends the chaos that followed Vatican II, but he doesn't blame the council, only those who 'interpreted' its decisions

By the early twenty-first century, after so many of its participants had died or left the Catholic Church, at least one remained who could say with authority what the Second Vatican Council really meant. This was Joseph Ratzinger, the young conciliar theologian who forty years later became Pope Benedict XVI. A native of Catholic Bavaria, the German priest was only thirty-five when he became an official *peritus* (theological expert) during the council's first session. No one then doubted his reformist credentials. Indeed, in 1964 he was a cofounder of the theological society that began publishing *Concilium*, which became progressive Catholicism's leading international journal.

Even as it began, however, Ratzinger was parting ways from other *Concilium* theologians. During the council, German bishops asked him to collaborate with the most renowned of their more radical modernizers, Jesuit theologian Karl Rahner. Among other things the two were asked to write a replacement text for the draft document *Dei Verbum* (the Word of God), the council's Dogmatic Constitution on Divine Revelation, explaining the authority of the Bible. Ratzinger was willing to work with Rahner, but did not accept his implicit starting assumption that the Bible is an authority within itself. The Catholic faith has always held that God's self-revelation consists of the Bible and Catholic tradition. Some tradition predates scripture, and ultimately, according to Catholic understanding, neither one makes sense

without the other.

The idea that the Bible constitutes a supreme authority in and of itself goes back four centuries to Martin Luther and the founding Protestant Reformation doctrine of *sola scriptura* (scripture alone). However, where to Luther and Calvin the Bible was the supernatural and authoritative Word of God, to the Modernists, neo-Modernists, and quasi-Modernists of 1960s Catholicism, it was merely a human compilation whose contents can be interpreted properly only through the latest academic research into its origins and development. The consequence of this approach to revelation and its interpretation, Ratzinger comments in his book *Milestones: Memoirs 1927–1977*, is that it reduces Christian faith to mere "opinions…in need of continual revision."

Ratzinger, who possessed an encyclopedic knowledge of contemporary theologies, was certainly not an ecclesiastical reactionary. He was prepared to consider the findings of historical-critical scholarship, but regulated always by the settled understanding of Christian truth communicated through the early Church Fathers and later papal and conciliar authorities. That was the view that, in the end, informed *Dei Verbum*, approved by the council and promulgated by Pope Paul VI in 1965. Ratzinger's wholehearted endorsement of this approach placed him in permanent opposition to modernistic biblical exegetes and theologians.

Joseph Ratzinger, shown here as a professor of theology at Tübingen University in 1977, was a Bavarian priest who at thirty-five became a peritus *(expert) at Vatican II. The gap between Ratzinger and the progressivists, small at the time, would grow in the forty years between Vatican II and his election as Pope Benedict XVI in 2005. His transformation was accelerated by such incidents as the occupation of the university by Marxist radicals in 1968.*

was already transforming the solemn, four-century-old Catholic Mass in some locales into something almost unrecognizable. There were other dramatic early shifts. Catholics had already renounced their centuries-long focus on highlighting the perceived errors of other Christians in favor of emphasizing common ground and pursuing as much unity as theologically and practically possible, alongside a new friendliness and respect toward major non-Christian religions, and a clear statement that Jews were no more responsible for Jesus' Crucifixion than anyone else, including Christians.

The second defining crucible of conciliar reform, recounts Ratzinger in *Milestones*, concerned the liturgy. The French and German bishops who pressed the case for liturgical reform had no desire for a radical break from the past. Instead, recalls Ratzinger, the objective was "the purest possible restoration of the ancient Roman liturgy, to which belonged the active involvement of the people in the liturgical event"—something that over time had been lost. Following a relatively short debate in 1963, the Council Fathers ratified this approach in the council's Constitution on the Sacred Liturgy. Ratzinger comments: "It would not have occurred to any of the [bishops at Vatican II] to see in this text a 'revolution'."[1]

As the council ended, Ratzinger publicly signaled his independence from the theological radicals behind *Concilium*. During the council he had followed Rahner's lead as directed by the German bishops, but now that he had faithfully discharged this trust he would state his own, often quite different ideas.[2] By this time, Catholic theologians were radicalizing collectively in another key manner, politicizing themselves in what Ratzinger describes as a new "ideological paradigm" that overtook many theology faculties.

He was exposed personally to the full force of it in 1968, when radicals seized control of the University of Tübingen campus where he taught dogmatic theology. "A few years before, one could still have expected the theological faculties to represent a bulwark against the Marxist temptation," Ratzinger remarks. "Now the opposite was the case: they became its real ideological center."[3]

After completing his book *Introduction to Christianity*, widely regarded as one of the twentieth century's best theological treatises, Ratzinger retreated from Tübingen's radicalized environment to the more settled atmosphere of the University of Regensburg in his native Bavaria. Shortly afterward, Pope Paul VI appointed him to the International Papal Theological Committee. In 1972, he joined with several other prominent theologians in launching the journal *Communio* as an orthodox Catholic counterweight to *Concilium's* increasing extremism. Between 1977 and 1981, he became the archbishop of Munich, next a cardinal, and then was named by Pope John Paul II as head of the Vatican's Congregation for the Doctrine of the Faith.

This made him Catholicism's doctrinal supervisor, and from this lofty perch Ratzinger analyzed postconciliar developments in *The Ratzinger Report*, his 1985 book-length interview with Italian journalist Vittorio Messori. In it, Ratzinger asserted that the Second Vatican Council's authentic vision of faithful renewal, as stipulated in its official texts, had been hijacked. "I am convinced that the damage that we have incurred in the [past] twenty years is due, not to the true council," he commented, "but to the unleashing *within* the church of latent polemical and centrifugal forces; and *outside* the church it is due to the confrontation with a cultural revolution in the West… [one with a] liberal-radical ideology of individualistic, rationalistic and hedonistic stamp."

Such pointed "Rat-zingers" (as they became known) provoked angry accusations by *Concilium* theologians that the cardinal had betrayed his earlier reformist principles. Hardly, he retorted to Messori. When he agreed to join *Concilium*, he recalled, he insisted that the magazine observe "two prerequisites." The first was to eschew "any kind of sectarianism or arrogance, as if we were the new, the true church, an alternative magisterium with a monopoly on the truth of Christianity." The second was to refrain from "any individualistic flights forward" that substituted "an imaginary Vatican III" in place of the actual substance of Vatican II.

The *Concilium* crowd chose to abandon these agreed-upon ground rules, Ratzinger observed, so "it is not I who have changed, but others." ∎

1. "It follows that we must be far more resolute than heretofore in opposing rationalistic relativism, confusing claptrap and pastoral infantilism," Ratzinger commented acidly in 1975, at a time when postconciliar liturgical abuses had become widespread. "These things degrade the liturgy to the level of a parish tea party, and to the intelligibility of the popular newspaper."

2. His collaboration with the radicals convinced Ratzinger that they and he "lived on two different theological planets," an impression that grew with time. Though Rahner remained in good standing with the church, and did not exactly join the progressive onslaught against *Humanae Vitae*, his philosophy of Transcendental Thomism did lead him to increasingly radical political conclusions prior to his death in 1984. Perhaps more significantly, his whole rationalistic approach was sidelined by the more evangelistic theology of John Paul and Benedict, drawn from the early church.

3. In the *Ratzinger Report*, the then-cardinal draws a direct connection between the intellectual and moral decadence of the secular West and the rising politicized theological dissent among Catholics. He also saw the Marxist forms of "liberation theology" introduced from Europe to Latin America as a "kind of cultural imperialism."

Even before the council ended, some of its periti *were publicly attacking the council's refusal to embrace more of their Modernist-tinged theological ideas. Swiss theologian Hans Küng, pictured right, published a book in 1965 chiding the council for failing to include the participation of his favorite progressive German biblical scholars.*

8. The Second Vatican Council's debate on religious freedom was the most fractious of all, as reformers sought repeatedly through procedural maneuvers to extensively reshape it. Pope Paul intervened during "Black Week" after a substantively altered draft had been introduced without prior debate of its new elements. He delayed that vote until the following session. Many council bishops and *periti* were openly incensed, with press reports predicting a "massive revolt" of American bishops which didn't happen. But Father John Courtney Murray, the leading American *peritus* on religious freedom, later acknowledged during a talk at Georgetown University that Pope Paul's action was justified, as the draft was effectively a completely new document.

9. Though overt Modernism was suppressed after 1910, Benedictine theologian Aidan Nichols would later write that its underlying principles remained very much alive in several widespread forms of "neo-Modernism," which for practical purposes amounted to the same thing.

10. Pope Paul VI had foreshadowed that he might hold the line on contraception during the Second Vatican Council debates in the fall of 1965. At his personal instruction, four significant amendments were made to the council's texts on marriage, highlighting the Catholic Church's opposition to artificial contraception and abortion.

A new, largely American understanding of religious freedom had been developed, recognizing a right of religious liberty that applied equally to believers of all faiths.[8] And infused throughout all the conciliar documents was a fresh Christian "personalism," a philosophy that proclaimed the profound worth (or "dignity") of each and all humans, their individual and collective rights and responsibilities as creatures created in the image and likeness of God, and the obligation of every faithful Catholic—layperson as well as cleric—to participate in a "new evangelization" of the modern world. If all this were not enough, one day before the council ended in December 1965, Pope Paul initiated one of the most comprehensive reorganizations of Vatican institutions in Catholic history.

Though the conciliar documents seemed balanced enough after four long years of conciliar infighting, the Catholic bishops would find the global church they were heading home to shepherd much altered. The struggle between progressives and traditionalists had created—or formalized—an enduring factionalism, with the most extreme partisans on both sides believing that they—and the Catholic Church as a whole—had been betrayed by the council's process and outcome. The protracted impasse led to unprecedented theological revolt on a scale not seen since the Protestant Reformation. Even before the council had ended, some of its most prominent *periti* were publicly attacking its refusal to embrace more of their Modernist-tinged theological ideas. Swiss theologian Küng went so far as to compile and publish a book in 1965 that he titled *The Changing Church*, listing grievances such as the council's failure to invite the participation of all of his favorite progressive German biblical scholars.

In 1967, rebellious theologians were handed what they took as permission to express dissent when Pope Paul revoked the Oath Against Modernism, demanded since 1910 of all Catholic clergy and teachers in Catholic universities and seminaries.[9] Removal of this much-criticized oath, they announced, proved that their ideas had been legitimized—and indeed authoritatively institutionalized, falling as they did within what these dissidents called the "spirit of Vatican II." By further extension, this "spirit of Vatican II" had created a "second magisterium" (church teaching authority)—this being themselves; and in their view, their views trumped any other conciliar interpretation, specifically including the pope's.

It was an unfortunate time for such rifts to develop. By now the sixties revolution was in full swing, with its comprehensive rejection of settled beliefs about truth and authority—including Christian morals, and especially teachings about sexuality. Any pope would have found it difficult to keep his footing amid such turbulence, and in the summer of 1968 Paul VI—through no choice of his own—was forced into a minefield of doctrinal controversy whose detonations would continue into the next century. The issue was artificial contraception.

This had been a live issue in all churches since at least the 1930s, when the Catholic Church held firm against it, but one by one, Protestant churches had begun to relax and then abandon the ancient Christian prohibition against contraception for married couples. The legal approval of the world's first contraceptive pill in 1960 again forced the issue to the fore for Catholics. Shortly after the start of the Second Vatican Council, Pope John XXIII had formed a theological commission of clergy, theologians, doctors, and laity to reconsider whether it is ever morally licit for married couples to use birth control. That report had been in Pope Paul's hands for three years, and word had leaked out far and wide that the overwhelming majority supported contraceptive use. The Pill having been enthusiastically received virtually everywhere else (see sidebar, p. 227), it was assumed the pope would now, however reluctantly, allow it too.[10]

But Pope Paul VI did not allow it. Instead he shocked the world. On July 25, 1968, he published his encyclical *Humanae Vitae* (Of Human Life), categorically rejecting as immoral all forms of artificial contraception. And while *Humanae Vitae* was directed primarily at contraceptives, it reaffirmed that both abortion and sterilization were "absolutely excluded" as licit methods of controlling fertility, even within marriage.

This undoubtedly took courage. The pope knew full well the contraceptive ban would be widely unpopular among Catholics, and said so in *Humanae Vitae*: "There is no doubt that to many it will appear not merely difficult but even impossible to observe." However, objective moral truth allowed the church no other conclusion.[11]

Still, Pope Paul was not prepared for the instant backlash which came from Catholic theologians, especially in the United States. There, Father Charles Curran, armed with an advance copy of the encyclical leaked to him by a sympathizer in the Vatican, had assembled a list of dissenting theologians, whose names were provided to reporters along with a joint

11. According to *Humanae Vitae*, "natural law" (the moral law known to all people) indicates only two "noble and worthy" purposes for human sexuality, these being the procreation of children and the strengthening of the conjugal bond between husband and wife. These two purposes, it says, are inseparable. Rupturing the procreative dimension from marital intercourse through contraception, *Humanae Vitae* warned, must "open wide the way for marital infidelity and a general lowering of moral standards," and would encourage men to reduce women to "mere instruments" of sexual pleasure. Though this teaching is binding on Catholics, progressives generally ignore it and hope that because it has not been infallibly declared, a more liberal pope will someday change it.

The bishops are shown emerging from Saint Peter's following one of the later Vatican II sessions, and, inset, the November 22, 1968, cover of Time *magazine, reporting on the furor created by Pope Paul's publication of the encyclical* Humanae Vitae, *which sustained the prohibition on artificial contraception. In the United States a group of theologians was quickly assembled to give the impression of mass dissension in the ranks over these and other forbidden practices including homosexuality and female clergy.*

12. Bobby Kennedy took his Catholic faith more seriously than his older brother, U.S. president John F. Kennedy. In his 1960 run for president, older brother Jack had to assuage Protestant fears he would be directed by the pope by insisting his religion had nothing to do with his politics. "I think it's so unfair of people to be against Jack because he's a Catholic," his wife Jackie remarked at the time. "He's such a poor Catholic. Now if it were Bobby, I can understand."

statement rejecting *Humanae Vitae*. This convinced the news media that the encyclical was completely contrary to informed Catholic opinion. It did not bother them that Curran had been fired one year earlier from the theology faculty of the Catholic University of America in Washington D.C. because of his dissenting beliefs (only to be rehired and promoted shortly afterward due to progressivists' protests). The press coverage of *Humanae Vitae* elated Curran. "Our quick, forceful response…accomplished its purpose," he wrote. "The day after the encyclical was promulgated American Catholics could read in the morning papers about the right to dissent and the fact that Catholics could in theory and practice disagree with the papal teaching, and still be loyal Roman Catholics."

The pope and his loyalist bishops didn't agree, of course, but they were both slow and disorganized in countering the rebel theologians. Using a secular media campaign to change Catholic doctrine was a tactic they had never encountered, though it would be regularly repeated in controversies to come. In this case, the media-initiated uproar accelerated, with the encyclical being denounced seemingly from every quarter in western countries. The pope, the critics declared, "should stay out of our bedrooms." Despite this avalanche of protest, the American bishops supported the pope, publicly at least. Not so in Canada where Canadian bishops released their "Winnipeg Statement" in the fall of 1968. It said—or was taken to mean—that faithful Catholics were free to disobey *Humanae Vitae* if they honestly believed the pope was wrong.

The timing of all this could hardly have been worse: 1968 was the year of a pitched battle between police and antiwar protesters outside the Democratic Party convention in Chicago. It was the year that two heroes of many Catholics—civil rights leader Martin Luther King and Catholic presidential candidate Robert F. Kennedy—were both assassinated.[12] Across western Europe, student and labor unions were staging strikes and seizing control of universities. With political and civil authority under comprehensive attack, Pope Paul's

Right, members of the Parents Aid Society demonstrating in Hempstead, New York, are captured by a fish-eye lens as they demonstrate against the encyclical Humanae Vitae *in 1968, while, below, about three thousand similarly minded Italians fill the Piazza Navona in Rome, calling for Catholic reforms including divorce, and marriage for priests.*

effort to ban something as popular as the Pill on the basis of religious authority seemed downright ridiculous. But to Catholicism's dissident theologians, it was outrageous. Father James Burtchaell, chairman of the University of Notre Dame's theology department, in addressing an audience of four thousand, spoke for many: The papal call for obedience to the "grossly inadequate and largely fallacious" encyclical amounted to "blackmail," he snapped, and it required "a reevaluation of authority in the church."

The revolt over *Humanae Vitae* was the first phase of a church-wide war over what the Second Vatican Council was all about. Behind the "spirit of Vatican II" banner were men and women determined to rewrite Catholic faith and morals. In addition to contraception and abortion, they promoted acceptance of nonmarital sex and homosexuality. They demanded married priests and women priests. They advocated top-to-bottom liturgical revolution, substituting for the old God-centered liturgy a novel "horizontal" worship seeking to energize the now much-invoked "people of God" with contemporary music and activist sermons, rather than endlessly confessing sins and praying rosaries. Churches were remodeled, altar rails torn out, and statuary in many churches not just removed but deliberately smashed. Militant progressives plunged into a gamut of left-wing social causes, some going so far as to formulate a "theology of liberation" conflating the Christian Gospel with Marxist ideology. And like their liberal Protestant forerunners, they subscribed in varying degrees to the Modernist disbelief in Jesus Christ as God.

Against these "spirit of Vatican II" iconoclasts stood Pope Paul and a large contingent of loyal modernizers who accepted the documents as written, but went no further. The Second Vatican Council had endorsed none of these radical things, more moderate Catholics insisted. Indeed the Catholic deposit of faith had been transmitted through the council with no significant alteration, as anyone interested could discern by simply reading the conciliar texts. And while the moderate modernizers did agree that the Second Vatican Council was a church-altering event, it was no revolution. Its evangelical ambition was to strike out boldly with a vital new proclamation of the Gospel of Jesus, doing so in continuity and conformity with nineteen centuries of church history and doctrine.[13]

Theoretically the orthodox Catholics held the upper hand, since their position was supported both by the conciliar texts and the pope's spiritual authority over the church. During the chaotic years of the late 1960s and early 1970s, however, these weren't especially effective tools. With stunning speed Modernist-leaning Catholics had acquired key positions within the newly powerful national bishops'

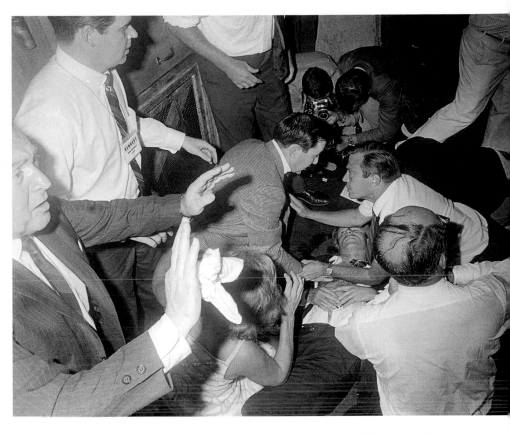

Presidential candidate Robert F. Kennedy is attended to on the floor of the Ambassador Hotel on June 5, 1968, after being shot by Sirhan Sirhan, a Palestinian upset with Kennedy's support of Israel. Kennedy, whose Catholicism ran deeper than that of his brother John, was a hero to many in the faith, as was civil rights leader Martin Luther King, gunned down two months earlier.

13. A relatively small but resolute number of traditionalist priests categorically rejected the council's legitimacy, on the grounds that in some instances (in their view) the texts heretically contradict previous church doctrine. They formed the Society of Saint Pius X (SSPX) in 1970 under the leadership of French Archbishop Marcel Lefebvre. The society later broke from the Catholic Church, though the break was not complete. In 1988 Pope John Paul II restored limited use of the older form of the Mass, easing but not ending the disagreement, and discussions of reunion were ongoing in 2012. In 2009 SSPX reported having eight hundred priests and religious, and two hundred seminarians, in thirty-one countries, all still using the pre-Vatican II traditional Latin liturgy and sacramental orders.

conferences, as well as charitable institutions, universities, and seminaries.[14] From these redoubts they could disregard, and even mock, Vatican disciplinary directives with impunity.

The radicalization of Catholic priestly and monastic orders was equally encompassing. It was conspicuously displayed in the largest of all Catholic orders, the Society of Jesus (the Jesuits), during a late-1960s ordination. This was performed by American Catholicism's most prominent bishop, Cardinal Francis Spellman of New York, who happened also to be the archbishop for the U.S. military. Two of the Jesuit candidates for ordination distributed flyers immediately beforehand, satirizing Spellman as a military "Sky Pilot" and accusing him of war crimes. Yet the cardinal duly ordained both as priests. One of the protesters doubled down on his earlier insults by refusing to exchange the traditional Catholic "kiss of peace" with the cardinal immediately afterward, instead seizing a microphone to urge him to "resign as vicar to the military forces of war."[15]

The Jesuits were among the most radicalized orders, but hardly alone in their fusion of sacred doctrine with secular left-wing activism. It was suddenly all through the church. By the end of the 1960s radical clergy supported by national conference staffs were a permanent and much-valued contributor to leftist social and political causes on everything from disarmament to abortion. Most bishops, having already been burned on the touchy topic of contraception, grew ever more timid about declaring the orthodox faith, even to their own flocks.

For the laity, the most obvious changes could be seen each Sunday, and for many—though by no means all—they were a source of pain. The form of the Catholic Latin Mass had not changed since the councils of Trent four hundred years earlier. Sixteen generations of Catholics had lived from baptism to burial with it, not knowing exactly what it said, but knowing what it meant. Now it was gone—first the Latin and the Gregorian chant, and then, after 1969, the form of the Mass itself. The sense of discontinuity arose in part from the new official Latin form of the Mass, but even more (in English-speaking countries at least) from a deliberate mistranslation to make it more about people and less about God.

The shortened vernacular liturgy was welcomed by many as long needed, and by many others as grievously banal. Caught by surprise in 1963 by the council's sudden decision, the Vatican could offer little guidance, leaving bishops completely at sea about what should be allowed and what should not. The result was liturgical chaos, amounting in some notorious examples to the bizarre, such as masses themed as "Clown," "Jazz," "Eskimo," and "Peace Festival."[16] Most new liturgies were less avant-garde, but generally they emphasized communal togetherness around the "Lord's meal." Though limited use of Latin was restored in later years at Rome's insistence, gone from most parishes was the solemnity and quiet, prayerful piety of the old Latin Mass, or the capacity of many priests to speak the language. This change was reinforced by new hymnals featuring guitar melodies and lyrics in the style of that era's folk-music genre. In effect it inserted the symbols and values of a secular belief system unique to the 1950s and '60s into Catholic worship, particularly in the English-speaking world.

Of more immediate concern to bishops, however, was the continued increase in Catholic faithful and Catholic parishes, with no corresponding rise in the number of priests. As fast as new seminarians arrived, older priests died, retired, or quit prematurely, either to get married or to have a more normal job, or both.

14. Although national bishops' conferences have no canon-law authority over individual bishops, or anyone else, they exert within their own national borders a pervasive and compelling influence.

15. Diocesan bishops and religious orders have almost total oversight of Catholic seminaries, where the effects of progressivism after Vatican II rapidly became acute. In the U.S., for example, total seminary enrollment declined from forty-nine thousand in 1965 to only eleven thousand in 1984. Only after the 1990s did it slowly begin to recover. At the same time the student populations of many seminaries came to contain a significant proportion of actively homosexual men, a fact that would become scandalously contentious twenty years later (see sidebar, p. 326).

According to statistics from the Center for Applied Research in the Apostolate, the total number of active U.S. priests held at fifty-nine thousand from 1965 to 1975, while the number of seminary graduates plunged by thirty-six percent, and kept dropping for twenty more years. As a result, after 1975 the number of priests decreased steadily as well, with only thirty-nine thousand remaining in 2012.

There was after the mid-1960s a sense of things coming apart. Mass attendance probably declined, though it would be impossible to prove, regular confession of sins declined, and children's catechism in many parishes ceased to be taught well or at all. Catholic students felt less obliged to attend Catholic universities, and the major Catholic universities soon began to look and sound as heterodox as secular ones. And through all of this, progressives and conservatives kept blaming each other, and the fault line deepened.

By the early 1970s, Pope Paul was exasperated. "The smoke of Satan has entered the Temple of God," he declared in 1972. "It is doubt, uncertainty, questioning, dissatisfaction, confrontation... We thought that after the Council a day of sunshine would have dawned for the history of the Church. What dawned, instead, was a day of clouds and storms, of darkness, of searching and uncertainties."

Whether or how he could have done things differently will long remain a matter of dispute for Catholic historians. Traditionalists have blamed him for being so trusting he failed to foresee obvious pitfalls, too slow to recognize an unfolding disaster, and too irresolute to do much about it afterward. Others are kinder. Papal historian George Weigel, for one, has described Paul VI as a "process pope" *par excellence*, whose stewardship bequeathed to Catholicism a comprehensive reform that, at least in theory, has constructively regenerated every aspect of its institutional, intellectual, and liturgical life.

After more than a decade of postconciliar turmoil, Pope Paul died in August, 1978 from a heart attack. After his funeral, Catholicism's hundred-plus voting cardinals knew it was critical to select the right successor. Remedying the demoralizing discontinuity wrought by men like Küng and Curran would not be easy. Clearly, it did not call for another process pope. It would require instead a uniquely persuasive and charismatic leader—a spiritual superman of heroic strength of heart. But where could such an inspirational man be found? Did he even exist? The answer, in fact, was at hand. (See chapter 16, page 205.) ■

The aging face of Vatican II liberalism: an unidentified woman, one of twenty thousand celebrants, is captured in full rapture at the fiftieth anniversary of the Second Ecumenical Council in Lyon, France, in October 2012. Twenty thousand gathered to celebrate the council that in the sixties and seventies put guitars in churches, brought Marxism into theology, and offered versions of the Mass that shocked traditionalists.

16. Local bishops were frequently afraid to enforce Vatican directives. "I'll tell them to stop and they say they will, but they won't," one U.S. bishop complained in the wake of a Vatican attempt to curb widespread liturgical abuses. "What do the Pope and Knox (Cardinal James Knox, the Vatican's top liturgical official from 1974 to 1983) expect me to do? Fire half the priests in my diocese?"

Hostile media and rising public opposition cause America to lose its first war ever, as Marxism triumphs in Vietnam

In 1950, the year that North Korean Communists launched the Korean War, Communists under Ho Chi Minh took over French-controlled northern Vietnam. Both revolutions were backed by the Soviet Union and by newly established Communist China, which adjoined the borders of the two. The western democracies—especially the United States—saw both moves as the next steps in the Communist master plan for world conquest. The Korean War ended in July, 1953 with the Communist invasion stopped at the 38th parallel. The following year, the next blow fell in Vietnam when Ho decisively defeated the last French forces there.

This presented U.S. President Dwight Eisenhower with a crisis. Communist insurgencies were also growing in neighboring Laos and Cambodia. Even more problematic, the South Vietnamese government was yet more corrupt, unstable, brutal, and incompetent than South Korea's had been. Having just extricated the U.S. from the conflict in Korea, why start again? The Eisenhower answer was a compromise, and for the next eight years Washington provided arms and training to South Vietnam to quell Communist infiltration and insurrection supported by the north. But the situation was nevertheless deteriorating, and President John F. Kennedy increased support in 1961. By 1963, there were sixteen thousand American military personnel in South Vietnam.

That year the Americans' unsatisfactory Vietnamese puppet, Ngo Dinh Diem, was murdered by his generals, an act encouraged by the American CIA. However, this led to a series of factional coups, allowing the southern Communist Viet Cong a much freer hand than before. In August, 1964, two alleged torpedo boat sneak attacks by North Vietnamese on U.S. warships in the Gulf of Tonkin (one possibly real, the other definitely fictional) led Congress to permit the president—now Lyndon Johnson—to make war in Southeast Asia without declaring it (see map, page 175).

And make war he did. With one hundred thousand black-clad Viet Cong in the south, armed and equipped from the north via the Ho Chi Minh Trail through Laos, the U.S. began a massive campaign to "bomb [the north] back to the stone age" if necessary, according to Air Force General Curtis LeMay. By December, 1965, America's now two hundred

Ho Chi Minh (top right) took over North Vietnam in 1950, then four years later defeated the colonial French forces in the south (featured on the cover of the May 22, 1954, edition of Paris Match, *top left), presenting the Eisenhower administration with a dilemma: Should they involve America in another Asian entanglement like Korea, or risk the further spread of communism? The United States chose to provide token support until the mid-1960s when President Lyndon Johnson committed U.S. troops to a full-out ground and air attack. Above, in the White House family sitting room in 1967, Johnson (far right) confers with (left to right) General Earl Wheeler, General William Westmoreland, and Secretary of State Robert McNamara.*

thousand troops were increasingly confronting North Vietnamese regulars. In 1966, U.S. Commander William Westmoreland launched a ground attack on the Viet Cong, predicting victory by 1967.

What came in November, 1967, was not victory but the Tet Offensive, when the Communists sprang a concerted, bloody assault on one hundred South Vietnamese towns and cities. The Americans and South Vietnamese managed to drive them off, but it shook American public confidence that the war could be won, and it finished the careers of both Westmoreland and President Johnson. In-country American troop numbers peaked at 543,000 in 1969. Ironically, however, a North Vietnamese commander later disclosed that the defeat of the Tet Offensive had destroyed North Vietnam's military capability, meaning that the Americans had won and didn't know it.

The next president, Richard Nixon, de-escalated the American ground war, leaving it to the hapless southern republic, and focused on massive bombing, including Communist base operations in ostensibly neutral Cambodia. Flattening North Vietnam was not aimed at winning the war, only on pressuring the Communists to allow "peace with honor," Nixon's euphemism for a dignified way for America to lose its first war ever without losing face. By now antiwar sentiment in the United States was at fever pitch. A Vietnamese truce was signed in Paris in 1973, the Americans left, and South Vietnam fell to the Communists in 1975. Although American soldiers were routinely depicted as demoralized cannon fodder drafted from the ghettos and deeply into drugs, the facts belie this. Blacks were (slightly) underrepresented, ninety percent of the soldiers who saw action were proud of their service and thought their own country let them down, desertion and drug problems in the ranks were rare, and two-thirds were volunteers, compared to only one-third in the Second World War. Fifty-eight thousand Americans were killed, and one hundred and fifty thousand were wounded. The price paid by the Vietnamese was far higher—an estimated two million civilians dead and almost as many soldiers from both sides. Thirty years later the debate continued as to whether the war had done anything to contain communism in Southeast Asia. ■

U.S. Marines board a helicopter (above) to be carried into action in Vietnam in 1965. In a classic photo from June 1972 (above, right), South Vietnamese children flee an accidental napalm attack of their village. A U.S. Air Force B-52 (left) discharges its bomb load over North Vietnam in the attempt to "bomb them back into the stone age," as Air Force General Curtis LeMay immortally put it. North Vietnamese troops enter Saigon on a tank in April, 1975 (right), following President Richard Nixon's decision to end the conflict "with honor."

This picture, taken during the Woodstock music festival in 1969, shows the new ideal: a hippy family living in a psychedelic bus. In ten short years the younger generation, aided by drugs, free love, social utopianism, and an unprecedented amount of disposable income, had instituted a chaos that would transform the world.

CHAPTER 11

The tale of the sixties: from Alabama valor to Woodstock squalor

Somehow the same generation that won at Montgomery became the drug-zapped zombies of Haight-Ashbury, and the counterculture suddenly became the culture

The United States emerged from the Second World War in 1945 as the most powerful, technologically advanced, and arguably the most benign world empire in history. Yet two short decades later it was being lured into chaos by a younger generation addled by hallucinogenic drugs, unrestrained sex, and social visions which its parents tended to regard as mindless fantasy. Young people across the globe were emulating this peculiar "counterculture," even (with great difficulty) in the Soviet Union, and with lasting consequences. It is hard to dispute that the 1960s, often dubbed the Youth Decade, changed the world.

Many of the origins of that great shift can be found in the immediately preceding years. Beneath the placid surface of 1950s America, a profound transformation had been taking place. Though most people still went regularly to church, and God was undeniably important, the assumption was gradually asserting itself that the essence of "the American way of life"—indeed, the whole purpose of American liberty—was material prosperity.

At the same time, the deluge of postwar babies began creating a distinct demographic class, known as "youth."[1] In their parents' day, such a status scarcely existed. People were either children or adults: the former did what they were told by the latter. Those parents had been a remarkably accomplished generation. They had grown up in the worst global depression in modern history, gone on to win the largest-scale war humanity had ever fought, and finally had built the biggest, most productive, most affluent consumer economy the world had ever

1. Though the birth rate of the postwar era was greater than that of the preceding Great Depression and far greater than that of the years that followed the sixties, it was not unprecedented. Young Americans were proportionately no more numerous in the 1960s than they were in the early twentieth century. The postwar birth bonanza increased the percentage of Americans aged fifteen to twenty-five from 14.5 percent of the U.S. population in 1950 to 17.6 percent in 1970. It remains an open question whether the sixties revolution was caused by a two percent increase in the proportion of young adults, or by moral irresolution among their parents' generation.

making himself an issue by startling innovations that older people found disgusting or dangerous or just silly. "You can't be sexy if you smile, and you can't be a rebel if you grin," he explained to a photographer from the national weekend newspaper supplement *Parade* in 1955. His first big hit, "Heartbreak Hotel," topped the teen charts across America in 1956 and reached second place in Britain. By 1957, aged twenty-two, when he did his trademark pelvic thrusts on the Milton Berle Show while singing "You Ain't Nothin' but a Hound Dog," he was an international icon.[3]

To the great satisfaction of many parents, Elvis was drafted into the army in 1958, and though he could probably have bought his way out, he did the patriotic thing and accepted. Worse for him, before he shipped out to Germany his mother died of hepatitis, brought on by too much weight, drinking, and maternal worry. It was an emotional blow from which Presley never fully recovered. After his military discharge in 1960 he made a series of light-comedy movies celebrating himself, performed to more sedate, more adult audiences in Las Vegas, and produced many more hit songs (such as his 1960 "Are You Lonesome Tonight?" and "It's Now or Never"). Though rarely topping the charts by the latter sixties, he remained immensely popular through the early seventies, and not only with the fifties kids who launched him. After 1973, however, his career dissolved into a fog of Demerol, alcohol, gluttony, and sex. He died in 1977 of an undiagnosed cause stemming from his enlarged heart and his prodigious overconsumption of prescription drugs.[4]

Elvis's meteoric ascent in the fifties demonstrated the new speed and force with which the news and entertainment media could lead and change the culture. And though early Elvis music was not in any sense political, he also, perhaps unintentionally, led young, mainstream America more readily to accept racial desegregation. Older folk—and not just in the South—objected as much to the fact that young Presley sang

Elvis Presley gyrates his hips in a promotion for the film Jailhouse Rock. *Presley had the sort of narcissistic ambition stardom seems to demand.*

3. In 1957 Presley bought his mama, Gladys, a pink Cadillac and brought her from the projects to live in his beautiful new suburban home on Audubon Drive, Memphis. His neighbors were not happy. Elvis thought they were simply jealous—but perhaps it had more to do with the large quantities of laundry Gladys was hanging out in plain view now that at last she had a washing machine, or the chickens she kept in the backyard, or the endless comings and goings of Elvis's growing retinue of redneck drinking buddies and helpers, or the female fans perennially camped on his front lawn. Regardless, a year later the entire household moved to the more secluded Memphis mansion named Graceland he would make world famous.

4. Presley was fascinated by both television and guns. He was said to watch several TV sets at once, and would occasionally put a bullet through one when irritated.

5. The Jim Crow laws were believed to be named for an 1830 comedy act in which a white man in black face sang a comic song with the name in it. The segregation laws varied by state, and were not restricted to the South. Almost every state in the late nineteenth century had laws against mixed-race marriages and conjugal cohabitation; the last few would not be overturned until the 1960s. States of the former Confederacy also had a wide variety of laws requiring literacy and the paying of a tax in order to vote, thorough separation of public facilities of all kinds, enrollment restrictions in schools and colleges, bans against blacks serving on juries and holding public office outside their own community. In South Carolina, for example, a black who aspired to any work apart from field hand or domestic servant required a special permit from a judge.

Left, a segregated drinking fountain in Halifax, North Carolina, in 1938. below, youthful Ku Klux Klansmen make their feelings about integration known during a Klan motorcade in Gwinnett County, Georgia, in 1956. Challenges launched by the National Association for the Advancement of Colored People (NAACP) to the Jim Crow laws triggered a resurgence of the Ku Klux Klan through mid-century. The Klan's membership reached four million.

like a Negro as to his pelvic gyrations. Rock 'n' roll itself was an African-American derivation, and the spectacle of the youth of both races playing it, singing it, and dancing to it, often together, sent shudders up many white spines.

A century after the Civil War, America was still racially divided. Southerners had lost that war in 1865, but many—or most—had never accepted that a black man could ever be equal to a white man in any meaningful sense. In addition, whites lived in fear of black uprisings or "negro rule." Thus, after the last Union troop garrisons left the South in 1877, whites immediately set about neutralizing the three post-Civil War constitutional amendments liberating and enfranchising the once-enslaved race. Ironically, the movement to neutralize them through new racial segregation laws was led by the Democratic Party, later the champion of interracial tolerance.

These Black Codes, known as "Jim Crow laws," were state laws that effectively barred blacks from political office, voting and jury duty, from testifying against whites, and from carrying weapons in public. Some states were harsher than others, but by 1880 throughout the South, blacks found themselves little better off than in slave times.[5] The Jim Crow laws were in the main approved by the Supreme Court in 1896 (*Plessy v. Ferguson*), provoking a "Great Migration" of blacks to industrial jobs in the North.[6] There, however, they found themselves almost as thoroughly segregated and impoverished as in the South. White trades unions, industries, and school and civic administrations ensured that blacks remained in the lowest-paid occupations and the poorest neighborhoods, and also remained subservient.

The National Association for the Advancement of Colored People (NAACP) was formed in 1909 to challenge Jim Crow in court, and little by little it succeeded. But they found that every courtroom victory could be circumvented or simply ignored.

6. The court reasoned that constitutional equality allowed for racially segregated public services provided they were of equal quality—which, of course, they never were. Negro schools and colleges, travel facilities, and commercial services were consistently and shockingly below the white standard. However, *Plessy v. Ferguson* was overturned by the Supreme Court in its *Brown v. Board of Education of Topeka* decision of 1954, which outlawed all forms of racial segregation.

7. Jim Crow laws did not physically isolate the two races, which had always lived in close proximity and often in affectionate relationships. Blacks served whites as housemaids, nannies, cooks, drivers, gardeners, valets, and sharecroppers. The point of the Jim Crow laws was to enforce white supremacy and black subservience in public.

By the 1940s, things like bus boycotts and workplace protests were common, but these did little to change the reality that for black Americans in both North and South, being a Pullman porter was a high-end job. In the 1920s the Ku Klux Klan—effectively suppressed after the Civil War—revived and spread north and west across the country, reaching a membership of four million. They marched in city parades, and terrorized anyone, white or black, intent on weakening the color bar.[7]

After the Second World War, in which black soldiers served in large numbers, social prejudice began, slowly, to melt. Ridding America of the ingrained attitudes and practices of white supremacy might never have happened, however, had it not been for one truly remarkable black Baptist pastor. In 1955 Martin Luther King Jr. took his first pastoral charge in Montgomery, Alabama (population then 125,000), and was promptly drafted to head an African-American boycott of the city bus service. It was instigated by a firm-minded activist named Rosa Parks, one of whose earliest memories was of her grandfather guarding their door with a shotgun while the Klan paraded down the street. One day in 1956 she refused to surrender to a white man her seat at the front of the bus where the law required that only white people sit. Such protests were not uncommon in the South, but were short-lived and did little to change the system. Under the magnetism of King's oratory and political leadership, however, the Montgomery boycott dragged on for thirteen months, and blacks walked to work or used church-organized car pools (which were promptly outlawed but continued regardless). The longer it continued, the more black demands escalated beyond merely improving the details of segregated bus seating. It ended with the complete desegregation of the Montgomery transit service.

The 1963 march on Washington and, inset, Rosa Parks. Parks touched off the civil rights movement when, in 1956, she refused to surrender her seat on a Montgomery, Alabama, bus to a white man.

The Montgomery boycott launched the great black civil rights crusade of the early sixties. Anyone watching the news footage of that movement is struck by the elemental dignity of its participants. They wore suits, ties, and dresses, and spoke in calm but compelling language. Their deportment stood in sharp contrast to the open malevolence of their segregationist opponents. Most striking of all, however, was that the endeavor was almost entirely Christian. It was led by Christian pastors and seminarians—both black and white; its organization was based in churches—both black and white. Its songs were hymns, its

Left, one of four buses occupied by civil rights "freedom riders," burns after being firebombed by angry southern segregationists in Anniston, Alabama, in May 1961. Below, Benny Oliver, a former Jackson, Mississippi, policeman, kicks a black student who had attempted to be served at a whites-only lunch counter, while onlookers cheer. Such actions against peaceful protesters, featured in the national media, helped the cause of desegregation.

texts those of the prophets and Gospel writers, and its thinking and rhetoric were biblical. The church, after all, had been the predominant institution in black communities since the Civil War, its clergy were among its most educated and independent members, and black church leadership in the 1950s was unusually strong.[8]

"They were caught up," Bernard Lafayette would later write in *The Role of Religion in the Civil Rights Movements* (2004), "not only in a social, but also a religious movement born of the church and directed by church leaders." As they marched and rode and sweated in prison work gangs, when they were clubbed and their homes and churches were firebombed, they didn't fight back. They sang hymns: "I'm on my Way to the Promised Land," and "Paul and Silas Bound in Jail." They took their strategy from the Indian leader Gandhi, but their inspiration and conviction came straight from the Bible. "Let justice roll down like waters," declared King, quoting the Jewish prophet Amos (5:24) in his opening address to the Montgomery boycott organizers, "and righteousness as a mighty stream."

After Montgomery, the movement broadened to other states and to different issues, and not all its actions were organized by King. In 1957 President Dwight D. Eisenhower had to federalize the Arkansas National Guard and command it to protect the court-ordered integration of a Little Rock high school, where nine

8. Behind King stood a throng of other blacks: James Lawson, a Methodist pastor from Pennsylvania; Ralph Abernathy, a war veteran and Baptist pastor from Alabama; James Bevel, a Baptist seminarian from Mississippi who became King's youth organizer; James L. Farmer, a divinity student from Texas; Bernard Lafayette, a Florida seminarian who after eight years in the movement became a Baptist pastor; hotheaded Birmingham, Alabama Baptist pastor Fred Shuttlesworth; famous Alabama housewife and activist Rosa Parks, a lifelong Methodist; and Baptist seminarian John Lewis of Alabama, who led the first Freedom Ride, was beaten nearly to death, and as of 2012 had been elected eighteen times straight as Democratic representative for Georgia's Fifth Congressional District. Forty-eight years after the event, in 2009, Elwin Wilson, the man who pummelled Lewis so savagely, became a Christian, and sought and received the congressman's forgiveness.

Civil rights demonstrators, left, listen to Martin Luther King Jr., inset, during the fifty-mile protest march from Selma to Montgomery in 1965, inspired by an Alabama police attack on a voter registration drive in Marion, Alabama. Such endeavors were almost entirely Christian, led by pastors both black and white, but also, as can be seen here, including Jewish rabbis.

WE MARCH TOGETHER
CATHOLIC
JEWS
PROTESTANT
FOR DIGNITY
AND BROTHERHOOD
OF ALL MEN UNDER GOD
NOW!

black students were being barred from entry by a large, angry white mob and an intransigent state governor, the Democrat Orval Faubus. It was the first time since Reconstruction that federal troops had been deployed to enforce federal law on rebellious southern states.

The following year, black students began "sit-ins" at segregated lunch counters in Oklahoma City. They had to keep at it until 1963, but eventually they succeeded. Sit-ins spread in 1960 to Nashville, Tennessee; Richmond, Virginia; Greensboro, North Carolina; and other southern cities. Dozens of students were jailed or beaten, but they kept coming back, and bringing more with them.

In 1961, four Greyhound and Trailways buses set out on scheduled passenger runs from Washington, D.C. and Nashville for New Orleans. Aboard each were "freedom riders" in mixed-race, mixed-gender teams of six university students. Upon entering the South they refused to comply with Jim Crow seating restrictions, rules that had already twice been held to be unconstitutional by federal courts. In Alabama and Mississippi they were met by howling mobs shouting "burn the niggers" who firebombed the buses and clubbed the passengers with steel pipes while police and state troopers stood by. In Mississippi, riders were denied bail and sentenced immediately to hard labor at the notorious Parchman Farm state prison. News pictures of these frightful events shocked the country. More freedom riders arrived, and then more, from all the states in the union— 430 were arrested, and over 300 did time at Parchman. Freedom riders became known as the shock troops of the desegregation army, and Parchman the "University of Nonviolence."

As the turmoil mounted, King and other leaders discussed the paradox of using nonviolence to provoke white violence, even against black women and children. For on this point they were under no illusions. When national news cameras showed white men—and even white women holding white babies—screaming "kill the niggers," the desegregation cause moved ahead. Whenever the world watched state troopers using clubs and vicious dogs to stop black men, women, and children from walking peacefully in public, the white folks up in Washington had to send in federal troops. The Kennedy brothers, John and Robert, were reluctant allies, because desegregation was shattering the Democratic Party, bitterly split between its loyal prosegregationist "Solid South" wing and most of the rest of the party. FBI director J. Edgar Hoover, meanwhile, was running an open campaign to expose the movement as a Communist front. So to move ahead, the civil rights movement had constantly to force the issue through nonviolent civil disobedience, more moderate actions having proved ineffective. By the mid-1960s southern segregation was legally and politically defeated, though the murders, bombings, and intimidation associated with maintaining it continued several years longer. In 1963 King was awarded the Nobel Peace Prize, which he accepted on behalf of all desegregation campaigners. In 1964 two-thirds of the states ratified the Twenty-Fourth Amendment, ending the poll tax in federal elections.[9] The Civil Rights Act followed, outlawing major forms of discrimination against racial, national, and religious minorities and women. President Johnson famously predicted that this would cost the Democratic Party its formerly solid support in the South, but he signed the bill anyway because he considered it just. His

James Earl Ray

The 'freedom riders' were met by howling mobs shouting 'burn the niggers' who firebombed the buses and clubbed the passengers with steel pipes while police stood by.

prophecy proved correct and the Republicans developed their "Southern Strategy." A major political realignment began.

The movement's last big march came in 1965, after Alabama police attacked a voter registration drive in Marion, killing two and seriously injuring scores of others. The shock and outrage of that atrocity inspired a famous fifty mile march from Selma to Montgomery, headed by King and the entire leadership of the movement—white and black, Protestant, Catholic, and even southern Jewish rabbis. They had defeated legalized segregation, but it was plain to King and many others that race prejudice remained almost as deeply rooted as before, and as much in the North as the South. When King led a desegregation housing drive in Chicago in 1966, his marchers were pelted in all-white neighborhoods with rocks, bottles, and firecrackers. King said he had encountered no more vicious opposition in the South.

Uncertainty of purpose blurred King's last years. Racial prejudice, unlike racial segregation, could not be legislated out of existence, and with no police clubbing or fire-hosing them, nonviolent confrontation didn't work. King tried shifting his focus to poverty in general and to the war in Vietnam. As America's troop deployment expanded under President Lyndon Johnson, King took a political risk and became a vocal critic of the war—a full year ahead of U.S. public opinion.

On April 3, 1968, he addressed a rally in Memphis, Tennessee, saying, "I just want to do God's will. And he's allowed me to go up to the mountaintop. And I've looked over, and I've seen the Promised Land. I may not get there with you. But I want you to know tonight that we as a people will get to the Promised Land. So I'm happy tonight... I'm not fearing any man. Mine eyes have seen the glory of the coming of the Lord!" The following evening he was shot dead on his motel room

9. After 1877, states of the former Confederacy imposed a flat tax (or poll tax) of $1 to $1.75 per adult, and voting required proof of payment. This was to reduce the electoral influence of black voters, Mexicans, and also poor white populists. Texas, for example, enacted a poll tax in 1902, reducing the turnout in the presidential election from 60 percent in 1900 to 29 percent in 1904.

The Beatles (left to right): John Lennon, Paul McCartney, Ringo Starr, and George Harrison arrive at New York's Kennedy Airport in February 1964 for their first U.S. tour. Below, hysterical teenaged girls react to the sighting of the "Fab Four" at Los Angeles International Airport. Beatlemania put the Elvis phenomenon in the shade, and there was more than a little truth to Lennon's controversial statement that the group was "more popular than Jesus Christ."

balcony. His assassin, a career criminal and thorough-going racist named James Earl Ray, was arrested in Britain two months later, pleaded guilty in Tennessee, and died in 1998 serving a 99-year sentence.

King's death marked the end not only of the civil rights era, but also of the last successful Christian moral crusade in America. For according to authors such as David L. Chappell and Timothy Keller (*The Reason for God*, 2009) that is exactly what it had been: a Christian revival among blacks that gained crucial support from white secular liberals. But where liberals saw segregation as a result of poor education, black leaders saw it as a direct result of human evil, correctable ultimately by conversion alone. Blacks did not appeal to white America to be more liberal, but to be more Christian.

But by the mid-sixties, America was not becoming more Christian; it was becoming an increasingly wild and frightening place. The mild youth revolt of the 1950s was escalating to outright revolution. This was especially apparent in music. A change began in 1962 with the trans-Atlantic success of the Beatles. Throughout Canada and the United States, the four Liverpool "mop-tops" were besieged by shrieking, crying, fainting girls. Beatlemania put the Elvis phenomenon of the fifties in the shade. The Beatles remained very respectful of Elvis, even though they were more popular. In fact, said Beatle John Lennon, they were "more popular than Jesus Christ"—which infuriated Christians but was, among the sixties set at least, self-evidently true.

If Beatlemania was annoying and alarming to parents, what came next was even worse. The modish, longish hair was lengthening, beards were sprouting, and pop singers were starting to look like Jesus. They traveled in packs and chose strange names—the Kinks, the Animals, the Troggs, the Byrds, the Cream, the Rolling Stones. It almost seemed at first that some of the more bizarre performers might be on some kind of mind-altering drug. Then it came out. The Beatles and Rolling Stones were arrested for marijuana. They were *all* on drugs, as in ever more alarming numbers were their swarms of youthful, lemming-like fans and followers.

One of the most idolized was Bob Dylan, who began life as Bob Zimmerman, a skinny young man from Hibbing, Minnesota near Duluth, and by any traditional standard not much of a singer. Already renowned for folk music—"The Answer Is Blowing in the Wind," and "The Times They Are a 'Changing"—Dylan was the first big star to merge the seriousness of acoustic folk music with the wild electric sound and rhythm of a new rock. When he hit the first loud chord of "Maggie's Farm" at the 1965 Newport Folk Festival in Rhode Island, he was booed by the folksy audience and panned by media; but young record buyers loved it. Another instant musical giant was Jimi Hendrix, a black, drugged-out virtuoso from the rougher parts of Seattle, who was considered by many the best ever electric blues guitarist. Another counterculture meteor was methamphetamine "speed-freak" Jim Morrison and his musically tight group The Doors. Morrison grew up a "navy brat," and got so carried away in performance he was charged with exposing himself on stage in 1969. Equally significant were Grace Slick and the Jefferson Airplane, singing about the wonderland of the hallucinogenic drug LSD, transcending "logic and proportion."

Mid-decade found much of the generation going from the juvenile "bubblegum" teen-love pop of the early sixties into the drug music of the Age of Aquarius. In 1965, Beatles John Lennon and Paul McCartney wrote "Day Tripper," and in 1967 "Lucy in the Sky with Diamonds," both about LSD, the latter so obviously that the BBC refused to play it; however, it went on to become the best-selling studio album in music history. The Rolling Stones followed with "2,000 Light Years from Home," a haunting psychedelic masterpiece Stones' leader Mick Jagger was said to have written in Brixton prison in 1967, following his conviction for drug possession.

By now the news media were starting to write much about "hippies," a term first used in 1963 to indicate young, beatnik-type nonconformists and drug users in New York's Greenwich Village and the San Francisco Bay Area. (Newly-elected California governor Ronald Reagan quipped that a hippie "dresses like Tarzan, has hair like Jane, and smells like Cheetah,"—their pet chimp.) In 1964 beatnik-hippie Ken Kesey and a crew of friends calling themselves the Merry Pranksters drove a psychedelically painted school bus across America to the World's Fair in New York, handing out free LSD to anyone willing to try it. Legal until 1966, the hallucinogen had been discovered in rye fungus and had been synthesized by a

Popular music changed during the 1960s from juvenile love songs to the edgier, more sexualized, and drug-influenced psychedelic, progressive, and hard rock of the later decade. Some of the classic album covers from the decade are shown here. At the center, Cheap Thrills, *the 1968 album by Janis Joplin's band Big Brother and the Holding Company, with artwork by classic counterculture cartoonist Robert Crumb; and clockwise from top left: the Beatles'* Sergeant Pepper's Lonely Hearts Club Band *(1967); The Doors' self-titled debut album (1967); Bob Dylan's* Highway 61 Revisited *(1965); Jimi Hendrix's* Are You Experienced *(1967); the soundtrack album from the rock musical* Hair *(1968); and the Rolling Stones'* Their Satanic Majesties Request *(1967).*

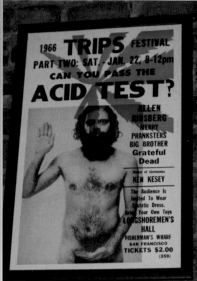

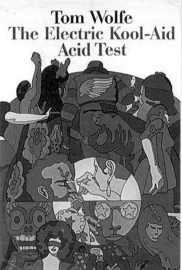

"Merry Prankster" Ken Kesey, with his back to the camera, is shown conducting one of his "Acid Tests" with a group of LSD users at his ranch near San Francisco in 1966. The poster advertising the event (top right) features poet Allen Ginsberg, one of the counterculture group that included Kesey and Timothy Leary. Their travels in a psychedelically painted bus (below right) were immortalized in the classic "New Journalism" book of the era (below left) by Tom Wolfe.

Swiss chemist in 1938. By the 1950s LSD was being used for truth serum experiments by the CIA, and recreationally by a Who's Who of the emerging counterculture—novelist Aldous Huxley, Harvard psychologist Timothy Leary (later fired from the faculty for absenteeism), British expatriate philosopher and Episcopal priest Alan Watts, poet Allen Ginsberg, and a roster of new Bay Area rock acts such as the Grateful Dead, Jefferson Airplane, and electric blues diva Janis Joplin, cruising in her psychedelic Porsche convertible.[10]

The Mecca of hippiedom was San Francisco's Haight-Ashbury district, a pleasant neighborhood of Victorian gingerbread houses west of downtown. Spurred by a sudden media fixation on hippies, mobs of young Americans from all parts of the country descended on the district in 1967 for a spontaneous "Summer of Love." It began in January with a "Human Be-In," which drew an estimated twenty-five thousand to nearby Golden Gate Park. There Timothy Leary, pioneer acid-head, proclaimed the new counterculture catechism for the first time: "Turn on, tune in, drop out." With spring break, the influx began in earnest, swelling to an estimated one hundred thousand by July. Despite overcrowding and filth, excitement was in the air. "Diggers," adopting the name of a seventeenth-century British

A hippie girl smokes a pipe of marijuana on the tour plane of the band, The Monkees, in 1967; and drug use advocate and counterculture guru Timothy Leary is shown at a New Year's LSD party the same year. During the "Summer of Love" in San Francisco, Leary led a "Human Be-In," which drew twenty-five thousand hippies and popularized the catch-phrase "Turn on, tune in, drop out."

radical movement, gave away free food and clothing, strangers banded together and headed off to start "back to the land" communes, rock stars could be met on the street, enthused Berkeley professors spoke to thousands of youths in open parks about the new consciousness, and everywhere were cheap drugs, free sex, stoned hippies, friendly police, bizarre costumes and hairstyles, and nonstop music.

The same media-driven subculture was forming almost overnight in cities across North America and the rest of the free world. However, the "summer of love" theme soon vanished. Within a year the new watchword was "power"— black power, student power, women's power, and, after the 1969 riots by homosexuals at New York's Stonewall Inn, gay power. In fact the last years of the decade presented a whirlwind of riots, sit-ins, bombings, beatings, murder, and endless confrontations with police, troopers, guardsmen, and soldiers.

Among these empowerment groups, the more threatening were students and blacks, who often worked together in pursuit of somewhat differing objectives. (Feminists and gays came to the fore in the 1970s.) The galvanizing issue for students was the Vietnam War. After the 1968 Communist Tet Offensive, U.S. military strength rose to 540,000 servicemen in-country. Of these, twenty-five percent were draftees, mostly infantry who stood a one percent chance of getting killed, and a three percent chance of being seriously injured. But for antiwar students, the biggest issue was not the odds of survival; it was why the U.S. was there at all.

The student movement had grown up as Students for a Democratic Society (SDS), founded as a small anti-ballistic-missile campus network in 1960. It also emerged through the Free Speech Movement that radicalized the Berkeley campus in 1963-1964 near San Francisco, the first instance in which students took control of a university's administration, curriculum, and policy. The antiwar movement—which as the decade progressed also became generally antimilitary, anti-drug laws, antipolice, anti-university rules, and antibusiness—pretty much took over campuses across the country in the late sixties.[11] Takeovers were initiated locally, but were inspired and often assisted by the SDS, and after 1967 by the

10. The intimate connection between sixties music and psychoactive drugs was emphasized by the deaths-by-overdose of Morrison, Hendrix, and Joplin in 1970 and 1971. Morrison killed himself by accidentally sniffing heroin he thought was cocaine and bled to death internally while his passed-out female companion was too stupefied to call for help. Hendrix killed himself, apparently inadvertently, probably by taking ten times too many of his female companion's super-strength Belgian sleeping pills. Joplin killed herself, likely by accident, with an overdose of high-purity heroin, after learning that her student-drug dealer fiancé from Berkeley was having sex with other women on her West Hollywood pool table. Rumours circulated among hippies that all three were killed by the CIA.

11. This gave rise to a caricature by the satirist-cartoonist Al Capp of a student group called SWINE (Students Wildly Indignant about Nearly Everything). Capp was the creator of the hillbilly Li'l Abner, endlessly bewildered by the seeming insanity of events in the newly emerging sixties world, as were most of Capp's generation.

Abbie Hoffman (above right) visits the University of Oklahoma in 1969 to protest the Vietnam War; and Yippie leader Jerry Rubin (left) speaks at the University of Buffalo in 1970s. Opposition to American military involvement in Southeast Asia had by the late 1960s come to dominate the youth movement. Below, student George Harris sticks carnations into the barrels of National Guardsmen's rifles during the march on the Pentagon in October 1967, giving expression to the pacifist "Flower Power" philosophy that became synonymous with hippie culture. Later the group tried—but failed—to levitate the Pentagon in an "exorgasm" ceremony.

12. New York beatnik poet Allen Ginsberg (1926–1997) wrote the Pentagon invocation, but may have been in Spain on the day it was delivered. Accounts vary. Either way, he was a key personality of the counterculture, from its inception among the beatniks in the early 1950s to its zenith at Woodstock in 1969. He was also a leading figure in the homosexual rights movement triggered by the 1969 Stonewall Riot.

13. The Pentagon protest, involving 150 antiwar groups, from Spanish Civil War veterans to Students for a Democratic Society, was the largest since Vietnam demonstrations had begun in 1965. Attendance estimates ranged from thirty-five to seventy thousand. It turned violent when protestors attacked a side entrance and were driven back with tear gas and rifle butts, while in reply the crowd blocking the main entrance sang "America the Beautiful." Later, military police were ordered to clear the main entrance after the demonstrators' permit expired at 7 p.m., and did so without warning, clubbing protestors with rifle butts. Arrests totaled 681, and about 100 protesters were injured.

Youth International Party (Yippies), launched by archetype hippies Jerry Rubin of Cincinnati and Abbie Hoffman of Worcester, Massachusetts.

By now the movement's most vehement expression was its massive opposition to the Vietnam War. This reached a crescendo on a chilly October afternoon in 1967, when some fifty thousand American Vietnam War protestors went streaming across Washington, D.C.'s Memorial Bridge, from the Lincoln Memorial to the vast, fortress-like Pentagon, global headquarters of the U.S. military establishment. As they thronged before the main entry, they met two hundred U.S. marshals and twenty-five hundred armed military police. The protestors neither attacked nor retreated. Instead, smiling young men and women quietly approached the stone-faced soldiers and inserted flowers into the barrels of their rifles. As they did so a contingent of hippies with wild hair and beards, and even wilder eyes, began an "exorgasm" ceremony intended to levitate the biggest building complex in the world, they said, three hundred feet into the air, turn it

bright orange, make it vibrate, and thus drive out the evil spirits haunting it. A swelling chant arose from ten thousand voices led by the luminaries of the counterculture—Hoffman, Rubin, Allen Ginsberg, and other glassy-eyed radicals.[12] "Demons, Out! Demons, Out! Demons, Out!..." they cried.

It can be stated for the record that the Pentagon did not actually rise; and whether or not any demons evacuated it in 1967, American troops did not evacuate Vietnam for six more years. Though the ceremony was designed as New Left street theater, the band of hippies leading the chant may actually have believed it would work, since people hallucinating on LSD tend to think anything is possible.[13] One thing that was altogether possible and in fact occurring, though rarely comprehended, was the active role of Soviet-sponsored infiltration into the youth movement. It successfully portrayed the Vietnam War as an imperialistic American intervention into the affairs of a small Asiatic nation, rather than a move to contain the advance of international communism further into Southeast Asia (see page 206).

Like King, the movement's organizers were adept at catching media attention.[14] Their pitched battle with police at the 1968 Democratic National Convention in Chicago was broadcast all over the world—and probably elected Republican Richard Nixon that fall, for by now Americans were growing exasperated with youth culture. After six student protesters were shot dead—four by National Guardsmen at Kent State University in Ohio on May 4, 1970, and two more by city and state police at Jackson State University in Mississippi ten days later, the Gallup Poll reported that public opinion sided ten-to-one with the authorities.

The antiwar protest movement produced its first martyrs at Kent State University in May 1970 when Ohio National Guardsmen fired on students, killing four. Here a female student reacts with horror upon seeing the body of one of the slain.

14. The 1968 presidential candidate of the Youth International Party (YIP) was a 150-pound pig named Pigasus. Jerry Rubin delivered the candidate's announcement in Chicago before the big riot. When they were charged with bringing a pig into Chicago, the Yippies' defense counsel William Kunstler retorted that the Democratic Party had just brought thousands of two-legged pigs into Chicago.

Top, a soldier stands guard at a corner in Washington, D.C. in front of the ruins of buildings destroyed during the race riots that followed the assassination of Martin Luther King Jr. in April 1968. Above, the logo of the Black Panthers; right, Huey Newton, founder of the Black Panthers, and cofounder Bobby Seale in a courtroom sketch from 1971. By now the peaceful protests for civil rights had transformed into the violent Black Power movement.

With Nixon's 1972 landslide re-election and the return home of American troops in 1973, the student movement quickly deflated. "When the revolution that the New Left yearned for failed to happen," wrote ex-radical journalists Peter Collier and David Horowitz in their 1989 book *Destructive Generation*, "most of its members disappeared—into health food, jogging, business school, entrepreneurship and yuppiedom" (Yuppies: Young Upwardly Mobiles). A few continued a series of bombings until 1976. The rest gravitated back to the Old Left—the dull, dogmatic Communist Party Marxism run by Moscow that McCarthy had sought to uproot in the fifties and that the New Left of the late sixties had mocked as hopelessly hidebound and unappealing.

But if student power alarmed Americans, they were even more frightened by black power in the slums. African-Americans in 1970 comprised eleven percent of the national population, and about half lived in urban ghettos afflicted with resentment, crime, alcoholism, heroin addiction, underemployment, school truancy, and family breakdown. Ghetto riots and arson broke out in the Watts district of Los Angeles in 1965, in Cleveland and Chicago in 1966, and in Detroit and Newark in 1967. These were not race conflicts, they were eruptions of looting, burning, and mayhem within the black districts, usually in reaction to a police raid or the shooting of a black suspect—and most of their victims were black. After King was murdered in April, 1968, the ghettos erupted in Baltimore, Washington, D.C., and New York City. The total death toll in the sixties' riots numbered well over one hundred, and the destruction gutted whole neighborhoods. Middle-class blacks took advantage of new housing laws to move to white suburbs, leaving the ghettos poorer and more leaderless than ever.

African-Americans in 1970 comprised 11 percent of the national population. Half lived in ghettos afflicted with resentment, crime, heroin addiction, alcoholism, and family breakdown.

In this milieu the Black Panther Party arose, founded in Oakland, California by petty criminal Huey Newton and former Black Muslim Bobby Seale. The Panthers traveled about armed in public and their original goal was to protect blacks from police brutality. However, as events grew more turbulent, the Panthers grew more radical and left wing, issuing a ten-point manifesto of impossible political demands, conducting a running battle with police and the FBI, and raising money through crime. Much admired by white liberals for their "radical chic," they played a romantic role for a few short years and then, like the decade that spawned them, vanished into obscurity, destroyed by police infiltration, arrests, and internal vendettas.

By the end of the decade, there was a universal sense that, for better or worse, America had profoundly changed itself, and the rest of the world along with it. Enthusiasts of the counterculture were confident that the future would be environmentally friendly, socially and racially benign, spiritually broad-minded, and militarily peaceful. Conservatives, on the other hand, saw that in ten short years, the U.S. per-capita rate of violent crime had doubled, the divorce rate had doubled, drug use was rampant, illegitimacy was rising as fast as the birth rate was sinking, and welfare caseload had quadrupled.[15] As Christian psychologist James Dobson wrote of the "permissive absurdities" of the sixties in his landmark book *Dare to Discipline* (1970), "Never has a society abandoned its concept of morality more suddenly."

However, though the world had changed, there was also a gathering realization that the touted Age of Aquarius had come and gone. Its last great moment— the last hippie "happening"—occurred on a remote dairy farm an hour from the little town of Woodstock, New York. In this bucolic setting in August, 1969, four hippies organized an outdoor rock concert that drew half the biggest-name pop

15. Violent crime would not peak until 1992, at 760 incidents per 100,000 people. U.S. divorce peaked in 1982 at 23 cases per 1,000 married women, though this did not reflect the breakup of unmarried couples whose numbers continued to rise into the twenty-first century. As of 2012, none of these indices had returned to anything like the low level of 1960.

2cd set

music from the original soundtrack and more

woodstock

joan baez · butterfield blues band · canned heat · joe cocker · country joe & the fish · crosby, stills, nash & young · arlo guthrie · richie havens · jimi hendrix · jefferson airplane · country joe mcdonald · santana · john b. sebastian · sha-na-na · sly & the family stone · ten years after · the who

Cotillion

A crowd scene at the Woodstock music festival held in upstate New York in August 1969, and, inset, the iconic image from the record album. Half a million fans—ten times the number expected—showed up to watch the concert of big-name American and British rock acts, and to revel in the drugs, the sex and the mud. It became a cherished memory for the counterculture, and would turn into the culture of the American nation.

music acts in America and Britain, and half a million fans from across the country for a three-day "Aquarian Exposition" of "peace and music." It was pure counterculture. The event was ordered by town officials not to proceed, but it did anyway. The massive stage wasn't expected to be ready, but it was. Admission wasn't supposed to be free, but as mile upon mile of youthful pilgrims arrived, the sheer press of numbers forced it to be. And with ten times the anticipated audience, food ran out, the toilets were constantly overflowing, and rain poured down through much of the weekend. Yet for all of that, it was cherished as a blessed memory for most who went: three days of sex, drugs, rock 'n' roll, and mud. The last few thousand to leave what had unavoidably become a stinking mire voluntarily gathered up all the discarded clothing, lost shoes, empty marijuana baggies, sopping sleeping bags, bottles, watermelon rinds, and discarded lawn chairs, and piled it all up in the form of a gigantic peace sign.

The decade of youth had ended. Whether they had grown up remained to be seen, but one conclusion seemed inescapable: the counterculture would now become the culture. ■

The evolution of a revolution

Kinsey's study of American sex was shocking, and the data behind it is still kept secret, but the real cause of the sexual revolution came later, with the development of the Pill

Harvard-trained entomologist Alfred C. Kinsey—with his bow tie and his hair parted in the center of his pate—would seem an unlikely "father of the sexual revolution," but such is the title that history has bestowed on him. Originally a specialist in wasps, to outward appearances he was a dull, decent, respectable, workaholic professor; a happily married husband and father in the uneventful Midwest university town of Bloomington, Indiana. But there was much more to Kinsey than met the eye, and in 1948, aged fifty-four, he and two campus colleagues published a book that shook America, and with it the world.

Sexual Behavior in the Human Male, a turgid, purportedly scientific tome of 675 pages, alleged with clinical sobriety and hundreds of graphs that over one-third of American white men had had a homosexual experience, that ten percent were lifelong homosexuals[1], that half had at some point cheated on their wives, that over two-thirds had had sex with prostitutes, that the average male age of first intercourse was seventeen, that almost all adolescents masturbated at least once a week and a few twice a day, that over half of men think about sex once or several times a day, that half or more of farm boys had sex with farm animals, that

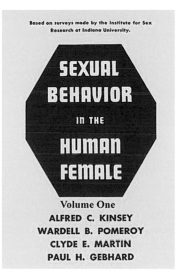

Dr. Kinsey with his wife, Clara, in 1954 arriving at the airport in Lima. "The doctor is conducting a two-week study of Peruvian sex habits," said the Associated Press caption of the day. His bombshell books on male and female sexuality (right), released in 1948 and 1953, excited the American public with statistics purporting to prove, among other revelations, that two-thirds of men had been with prostitutes and ten percent of the population were homosexual. Such statistics were later discredited, and it was also revealed that Kinsey and Clara were personally involved in wife-swapping and same-sex experiments with friends and associates.

1. The ten percent figure is an oft-repeated oversimplification of Kinsey's findings, which were more nuanced. The true number remains a matter of controversy; results vary, depending on the meaning of the question and methodology of the survey. Since the early 1990s, numerous surveys have put the number closer to two percent of adult males. For example, the Guttmacher Institute, an affiliate of Planned Parenthood, published a survey in 1993 reporting that of sexually active men, aged twenty to thirty-nine, 2.3% had engaged in same-sex sexual activity in the last ten years, and 1.1% said that they had engaged only in homosexual acts.

A collector's copy of the first issue of Playboy magazine from December 1953, with sexpot film-star Marilyn Monroe on the cover (and inside as the nude centerfold). Publisher Hugh Hefner said he was "filling a publishing need only slightly less important than one just taken care of by the Kinsey Report."

2. A thorough and relentless scrutiny of the reported Kinsey data was published by Judith Reisman and Edward Eichel in *Kinsey, Sex and Fraud* (1990). In response, the Kinsey Institute issued a formal statement: "Dr. Kinsey was not a pedophile in any shape or form. He did not carry out experiments on children; he did not hire, collaborate, or persuade people to carry out experiments on children. He did not falsify research findings and there is absolutely no evidence that his research 'opened flood gates for the sexual abuse of children.'"

half of married American couples engaged in oral sex, and that thirty percent of men had received homosexual fellatio.

This stunned the country—first that anyone would know and discuss such things, and second, that sexual practices, especially deviant, unnatural ones, were apparently so common. In 1948 some seventy percent of Americans claimed affiliation with a church, and churches took their cue from Saint Paul: "It is shameful even to mention what the disobedient do in secret"(Ephesians 5:12). Normal conjugal sex was not something people talked about in polite company, or took too seriously in coarse company. Deviant sex was not something they were supposed to even think about. As a result, protested Kinsey, much more was known about the sexual behavior of animals than of humans.

Kinsey was the first American of any prominence to pursue the subject, starting quietly in 1938 when students began asking him questions about sex and were willing in turn to answer his questions in return. Since then, with help from Indiana University colleagues Wardell Pomeroy and Clyde Martin, he had interviewed fifty-three hundred white males and more than fifty-nine hundred white women (for a female sequel report that was published in 1953). The interviews were cataloged and tabulated using a secret code to protect confidentiality, and the database has never been publicly released.

Kinsey always defended his work by asserting that as a scientist he was not interested in moral "taboos," just in reporting the reality of human behavior. When some faculty colleagues accused him of weakening the morals of youth, he counteraccused them of succumbing to a stifling, flat-earth obscurantism. He declared in a 1940 address to biology teachers: "Unless one subscribes to an absolutist philosophy, and believes in the intrinsic rightness and wrongness of things, it is very difficult to understand what social interests are concerned in much of the human animal's sexual activity."

Evidence abounds, however, that Kinsey had a personal moral (or immoral) agenda of his own, perhaps in reaction to his severe Methodist upbringing in Hoboken, New Jersey. Doubts have overhung his work from the time it was published to the present. Statisticians immediately rejected his sample of American males—up to one quarter of whom were prisoners, most of them sex offenders, and five percent or more male prostitutes. How, they demanded, could the proclivities of such subjects typify those of ordinary Americans?

This prompted the American Statistical Association to conclude in 1954 that "many of the most...provocative" findings and claims "fall below the level of good scientific writing" (though the report had high praise for the interview methodology). As well, famous psychologist Abraham Maslow offered to help Kinsey correct for "volunteer error" (a tendency he had noticed for sexually active people to talk about their sex lives, while the less active decline), but Kinsey would not cooperate. Subsequent efforts by Kinsey and his institute to correct for the reporting bias, especially in regard to homosexuality, have met with considerable scepticism.

Even more disturbing to many was that Kinsey refused to categorize any sexual practices as "abnormal" or "deviant"—even pedophilia. Indeed, he presented evidence and argument that young children, even infants, could enjoy and benefit from sexual orgasm. Critics like the conservative social commentator Judith Reisman strongly suspect he conducted his own experiments on children.[2] He was secretly a sadomasochistic homosexual, a fact well known to his friends. His associates disclosed long after he died in 1956 that he also routinely directed and filmed wife-swapping and same-sex experiments with themselves, their spouses, his own spouse, Clara, and interested others in his attic. Confirmation of these rumors and reports is said to be locked in the Kinsey Institute's vault.

Despite the scandals and criticisms, Kinsey's amoral approach to human sexuality—his insistence that all sexuality is normal and natural—has served as the basis for sex education and therapy ever since and became a powerful factor boosting the homeschooling movement and the proliferation of Christian schools. Another early enthusiast for his new doctrine was a budding, ambitious entrepreneur named Hugh Hefner, who at the age of twenty-seven in 1953 published the first edition of *Playboy*. Though the pictures of a naked Marilyn Monroe probably accounted for most of the fifty thousand pilot-edition copies sold, he modestly commented within it, "We believe...we are filling a publishing need only slightly less important than one just taken care of by the Kinsey Report."

Neither Kinsey's book nor his philosophy, however, would have changed human sexual behavior very much had it not been for something else. In 1951 a significant meeting took place in New York between birth control advocate Margaret Sanger, her wealthy patroness Katharine McCormick, and Gregory Pincus, a Massachusetts biochemist and expert in the new field of synthetic hormones. Could Dr. Pincus, the women asked, invent a "perfect" orally-consumed contraceptive—soon—and in large volume? With a commitment of $125,000 from McCormick, Pincus said yes.

According to the 1995 book *The Pill* by Bernard Asbell, it took nine years and two million dollars, but Pincus did it. He and others figured out the hormonal formula to fool a woman's body into thinking she was pregnant when she wasn't, thereby suppressing ovulation and preventing impregnation. Next, they figured out how to extract and process the required massive quantity of progesterone from an inedible wild yam they discovered in the jungles of Mexico. By 1957, after extensive testing on women volunteers in the U.S., Puerto Rico, Haiti, and Mexico, the U.S. Food and Drug Administration approved the new Searle drug Enovid for treatment of menstrual disorders, and in 1960 for use as a contraceptive.

The sexual revolution followed. Never before had women been able to reliably disconnect sexual intercourse from procreation. Spermicidal concoctions of all kinds had been used for years, even containing toxic fluids like Lysol, but they didn't work well, if at all. Mr. Goodyear's vulcanized rubber prophylactics, introduced in 1839, weren't much better, and neither was the most common birth control method—premature withdrawal. By 1960 the average American woman had four children, and for many that was enough. Now, unbeknownst to anyone but her doctor, she had unilateral control over her fertility. For women who didn't suffer or didn't mind the side effects, the Pill (as it instantly became known) was a gift from heaven. Before it was legalized for contraception, half a million American women were using it anyway (ostensibly for menstrual

problems). By 1963 users had risen to 2.3 million, and by 1965 to six million.

University of Chicago social scientist Tom W. Smith, citing earlier surveys, has reported that the percentage of women who were virgins at marriage had been dropping through the century, from about ninety percent before the First World War to about fifty percent in the 1950s. After the Pill it sank to twenty percent. This was in part because women in the sixties married later than they did in the family-minded fifties. But that too was Pill related, according to feminist author Nancy Cohen in her 2012 book *Delirium*. Female enrollment in universities spiked upward as soon as the Pill became available. Women began entering professions in large numbers, and the U.S. total fertility rate (average number of children per woman) began to drop. Cohen says this was because women were no longer forced to choose between getting married to have sex, and having a career. Without the Pill there would have been no sexual revolution, she says; and without the sexual revolution, there would have been no feminist revolution, for in her view they were a single event. ∎

> *Even more disturbing, Kinsey refused to categorize any sexual practices as 'abnormal'— even pedophilia.*

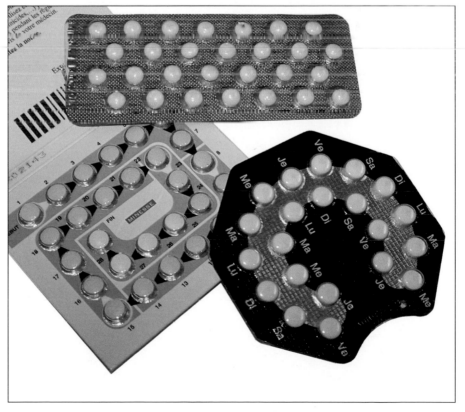

Hefner's magazine and the birth control pill, a selection of which appears below, touched off the sexual revolution that changed much of the world in the 1960s.

FEAR GOD AND KEEP HIS COMMANDMENTS. FOR THIS IS THE WHOLE DUTY OF MAN. ECC 12:13-14

Christians protest the increasingly powerful gay-rights movement, marching along Bourbon Street, New Orleans, in September, 2010. For more than a decade, the push to legitimize and promote homosexuality had made great strides in a culture war that pitted traditional religions of all faiths against the forces of libertinism and its many permutations.

LET THE WICKED FORSAKE HIS WAY

HOMO SEX THE WICKED SHALL BE TURNED INTO

ARE YOU GOD'S BARF?

HOMO SEX IS OF THE DEVIL!

CHAPTER 12

Christianity is rejected as the quest for liberty fuels a war for license

As gay activists smash into Saint Patrick's Cathedral, and nonviolent antiabortionists are beaten, it's plain that a Culture War is on, and the Christians are losing

In the vaulted, neo-Gothic solemnity of Saint Patrick's Cathedral, an echoing cavern of calm in the honking, hectic heart of New York City, Cardinal John O'Connor was at the high altar celebrating a Sunday morning Mass before a large congregation on December 10, 1989. Suddenly the heavy doors swung open and hundreds of yelling young men came streaming into the nave, blocking the aisles, chaining themselves to pews, shoving stunned congregants aside, waving blasphemous signs, and shrieking, "You're killing us!" Before police arrived to haul forty-three of the trespassers away in handcuffs they had brought the service to a stop and had desecrated the consecrated bread.

The so-called "culture wars" of the western world had been going on since the eighteenth-century Enlightenment. But this exhibition signaled that they were entering a new phase. For these were homosexual activists and they were symbolically giving notice that if Christianity did not yield to their demands for a new moral order, then they would work to destroy Christianity.[1]

That same year, on another front, thousands of silent "rescuers"—men and women, young and old, black and white, and almost all churchgoers, Protestant and Catholic—began blocking access to abortion facilities in Pittsburgh, West Hartford, and Los Angeles. It was a form of nonviolent passive resistance. Several hundred protesters would converge on a target clinic before it opened in the morning, crawl up to it on hands and knees, sit on the sidewalk, link arms, sing softly or pray silently, then go absolutely limp when police arrived to clear them away.

1. However much Archbishop O'Connor might have hated the sin, there was little evidence he hated the sinner. In fact, quite the contrary. At Saint Clare's Hospital he opened the first AIDS hospice in the U.S. and personally ministered to dying homosexuals. This did not discourage gay hatred of his Christian "judgmentalism," however. In a federally funded art catalog, gay activist David Wojnarowicz said of him, "This fat cannibal from that house of walking swastikas on Fifth Avenue should lose his church tax-exempt status and pay retroactive taxes from the last couple of centuries." When O'Connor died in 2000, the mainstream arts weekly *Time Out New York* pronounced "good riddance" to the "pious creep."

Former presidential candidate and Catholic Patrick Buchanan. "There is a religious war going on in our country for the soul of America," he declared. "It is a cultural war, as critical to the kind of nation we will one day be as was the Cold War itself."

2. For years the Gallup poll had asked Americans, "Did you, yourself, happen to attend church or synagogue in the last seven days?" and Christians were heartened by a constant 40-plus percent response, decade after decade. Self-reported good behavior (voting, charitable giving) is notoriously exaggerated, however, three separate studies in the 1990s lowered the number to between twenty and thirty percent. Either way, the United States remained the most church-going nation in the developed world.

The police response was not nonviolent, however. Michigan academic William B. Allen, chairman of the U.S. Commission on Civil Rights, gathered numerous documented cases of unprovoked clubbing, broken arms, broken fingers, miscarriages from physical abuse, neglect of serious injuries while arrestees were in custody, and public stripping of women. All this was in striking contrast to the civil rights protests of the 1960s. Unlike then, the Department of Justice refused to investigate, the national media remained aloof, and nothing was done. By 1992 over forty thousand American rescuers had been arrested. "There is a religious war going on in our country for the soul of America," declared presidential candidate Pat Buchanan, a Catholic Christian. "It is a cultural war, as critical to the kind of nation we will one day be as was the Cold War itself."

This conflict over the shape and mores of the future America had been developing since the sexual revolution of the 1960s (see page 209). When sociologist James Davison Hunter produced his book *Culture Wars* in 1991 the name stuck. It examined the widening gulf and deepening contempt between religious moral conservatives on one side and secular liberal-progressives on the other. This war, said Hunter, was an irreconcilable, winner-take-all argument over whether standards of human law and goodness are to be determined by God or by government. As the 1990s unfolded, the issues dividing Americans were no longer geopolitical and economic; they were social and moral, and especially sexual—abortion and gay rights. Connected to these were myriad others—divorce, the diminishing role and rights of men, parental authority over children, freedom of speech and religion, moral limits on new biotechnology, censorship, the purpose of news and entertainment media, standards in art and literature, school curriculum, and academic freedom. Hunter points out that while most Americans found these issues perplexing, and perhaps overly abstract, virtually everyone was being affected by them.

It was primarily an argument over moral authority. Going in one direction were the progressives—the antipoverty, antimilitary, antifamily, and antichurch groups and coalitions that had emerged since the sixties. Progressivism, says Hunter, referring to the late twentieth-century usage of the term, had become a synthesis of three ideas: liberalism (maximum individual freedom), modernism (the past was oppressive, especially to women, gays, and racial minorities), and secular humanism (morality is subjective). It seeks, he said, an ever-expanding social role for the state, the ongoing removal of sexual and other traditional cultural "taboos," and the systematic elimination of Christian authority and influence in public life.

The moral conservatives opposing them consisted of people who in the past would probably have been more against each other than united: many Catholics, some Protestants, plus Mormons, Orthodox Jews, and "natural law" nonbelievers. These groups now banded together to defend traditional values. In fact, it had become clear and commonplace that the great divide of western religion was no longer between denominations but within them. For the same progressive-conservative dichotomy that now divided America was similarly rending faith groups. You believed either in moral progress or in the Bible. In other advanced countries, Christian culture for the most part was quietly dissolving—but not in rights-conscious America, where a large and assertive minority still went to

Above left, an American hydrogen bomb test in 1952. At right, a scene from the 1983 TV movie The Day After, *which depicts a nuclear attack on Kansas City, watched by a hundred million viewers; and a couple of the best-selling books of the era, positing impending doom. A general mood of foreboding gripped the populace, inhibiting social activism. This would soon change.*

church.[2] And the French political theorist Alexis de Tocqueville had said long ago in the 1830s that in America, all ideas are publicly contested, and sooner or later they all end up in court.

The euphoric optimism of the late 1960s—the "Age of Aquarius" to its youthful enthusiasts—was short-lived. In the early 1970s it succumbed to widespread pessimism—notwithstanding America's withdrawal from Vietnam beginning in 1971, suspension of military conscription in 1973, ongoing federal expansion of welfare entitlements, and court-ordered desegregation of schools. The seventies sank ever more deeply into dire fears and forebodings, says British-American historian of religion Philip Jenkins in his book *Decade of Nightmares* (2006). Bookshelves and media were filled with dread prophecies—mass starvation, industrial poisoning, an incipient ice age, a nuclear Armageddon, serial rapists, drug gangs, corporate greed. End-times prophecies surged through the evangelical churches, spurred by Hal Lindsey's *The Late Great Planet Earth*, which that sold more than twenty million copies in fifty-four languages, and was the number one nonfiction best seller of the decade according to the *New York Times*. All of which inhibited social activism. Why save this world if you're about to be raptured out of it?

Early in the 1970s, however, came the development that would gradually reignite cultural conflict. In the U.S. Supreme Court's 1973 *Roe v. Wade* ruling, the justices struck down all state laws against abortion, which had been illegal in virtually all states since the 1820s, save in some cases when pregnancy resulted from rape or incest.[3] Though feminists urged an unrestricted abortion right, the issue was

3. The laws of the colonies and early republic, descending from English Common Law, allowed abortion up to the point of "quickening," when the fetus begins to move inside the mother—usually at or shortly after four months' gestation. More serious criminal prohibitions against both doctors and patients were legislated across the entire Union in the latter nineteenth century.

The New York Times

"All the News That's Fit to Print"

LATE CITY EDITION

NEW YORK, TUESDAY, JANUARY 23, 1973

15 CENTS

VOL. CXXII. No. 42,003

LYNDON JOHNSON, 36TH PRESIDENT, IS DEAD; WAS ARCHITECT OF 'GREAT SOCIETY' PROGRAM

High Court Rules Abortions Legal the First 3 Months

State Bans Ruled Out Until Last 10 Weeks

National Guidelines Set by 7-to-2 Vote

37 MILLION CARS RECALLED BY G.M. TO CORRECT FLAW

Cardinals Shocked —Reaction Mixed

KISSINGER IN PARIS; CEREMONIAL SITE CHOSEN FOR TALKS

NATION IS SHOCKED

Citizens Join Leaders in Voicing Sorrow and Paying Tribute

STRICKEN AT HOME

Apparent Heart Attack Comes as Country Mourns Truman

The front page of the January 23, 1973 edition of the New York Times, *reporting the previous day's* Roe v. Wade *ruling by the Supreme Court striking down all state laws against abortion. The landmark decision, overshadowed by the death of former President Lyndon B. Johnson, was at first dismissed by the Protestant majority as a "Catholic issue." This was to change in a few years when the ramifications began to appear clearly grotesque to traditionalists of all faiths.*

too inflammatory for any politicians to seriously champion it. *Roe v. Wade* saved them the trouble.

Initially, opposition to the decision was largely confined to Catholics. For several years it was dismissed by the Protestant majority as a "Catholic issue" like contraception, which Protestant churches had accepted over the previous three decades. Only later did leading Protestants come to realize that abortion required the tearing apart of a live human individual, formed in the image of God and capable within the first trimester of feeling pain.[4] Because of this initial Protestant-Catholic divide, abortion was not the issue that began the formation of what became the Religious Right.

That arose out of the Equal Rights Amendment, first introduced into Congress in 1923 but never able to command a majority of both houses until 1972. It then became the proposed twenty-fifth amendment to the U.S. Constitution, declaring: "Equality of rights under the law shall not be denied or abridged by the United States or by any State on account of sex. The Congress shall have the power to enforce, by appropriate legislation, the provisions of this article." The first sentence sought to entrench and expand the many concessions made to women since the Kennedy administration, writes Nancy Cohen in her 2012 chronicle of moral conservatism, *Delirium.* The second sentence in the amendment would enable Washington to supersede state legislatures.

To take effect the ERA required ratification from three-quarters—or thirty-eight—of the state legislatures by 1979. Within its first year it gained virtual rubber-stamp approval from thirty. Gallup reported that three-quarters of U.S. voters

Feminists, led by New York congresswoman and gay-rights activist Bella Abzug (wearing a hat), march in New York in 1980 to celebrate the sixtieth anniversary of the Nineteenth Amendment (women's right to vote), and to advocate for the Equal Rights Amendment to the constitution, which would have allowed the U.S. Congress to circumvent state legislatures on matters of sexual equality.

Formidable Republican organizer and conservative activist Phyllis Schlafly at a government hearing in Kansas City, Missouri, in 1976, voicing opposition to the Equal Rights Amendment. Largely because of Schlafly and the network of conservatives she helped marshal, the two-thirds of state support needed to ratify the ERA never materialized.

supported it, and booster organizations such as the National Organization for Women (NOW), sensing little resistance from the rest, assumed they had hit a home run. Such was not the case, however. By 1977 the number of ratifying states had stalled at thirty-five, three states short of success—and then, one by one, some began rescinding their earlier assent, and the ERA unexpectedly died.

The person most blamed (or credited) with stopping it was a woman—Phyllis Schlafly of Illinois, mother of six, lawyer, and formidable Republican organizer. All the reasons feminists advanced in support of the ERA became Schlafly's case for rejecting it. She was a lifelong anti-Communist, one who still shared the hard right convictions of Senator Barry Goldwater, the 1964 Republican presidential candidate slaughtered at the polls by Lyndon Johnson. Schlafly was among a nucleus of determined Christian laity who, starting in the 1950s, spent the next half century pushing the Republicans to the right. (Among others were Paul Weyrich, cofounder of the Heritage Foundation; William F. Buckley, founder of the *National Review*; and author and political thinker Russell Kirk.)

To stop the ERA, however, Schlafly needed a much larger network than her existing mailing list of three thousand names. Author Cohen recounts how her anti-ERA pamphlets soon caught the eye of some women members of the Church of Christ, one of the most conservative evangelical Protestant churches in the South, and the first of many Bible-based denominations to fling themselves into the campaign. Lottie Beth Hobbs of Texas and like-minded supporters joined Schlafly's board. Her mailing list swelled to thirty-five thousand. New to politics, they brought with them a tone and temperament unfamiliar to party veterans like Schlafly—heavily scriptural, cloyingly feminine, sometimes ridiculously overstated, but altogether relentless. By 1975 an army of female

Paul Weyrich

William F. Buckley

Lottie Beth Hobbs

4. The early church inherited from Judaism a proscription on abortion—a prohibition the rest of the Mediterranean world found peculiar. Drug-induced and crude surgical abortions were common throughout the Roman Empire. The earliest explicit condemnation in Christian records appears in the *Didache*, preserved as the Teachings of the Twelve Apostles and reflecting very early post-apostolic Christian belief and practice. Included in a list of sins leading to spiritual death it cited "murder" of "a child by abortion" or by infant exposure after birth. (The Jewish tradition is opposed to abortion, but permits it in cases where the fetus is an "aggressor," meaning that it threatens the life of the mother.)

National Organization for Women (NOW) founder and president Betty Friedan (second from left) is pictured with fellow women's liberationists in a 1968 photograph. The outspoken Friedan was author of The Feminine Mystique (1963), which claimed most American women were unhappy with their lives as housewives and mothers. A zealous proponent of the ERA, Friedan called Phyllis Schlafly a traitor to her sex, and recommended she be burned at the stake.

antifeminists throughout the nonratified states were inviting governors and legislators to polite but meaningful visits over afternoon tea, and sending them home-baked bread accompanied by politically pointed poems.

Amid all the cultural confusion and social eccentricities of the 1970s, the ERA was not a top-of-mind interest for most Americans, and only hard-core feminists had come to see the significance of this improbable, implacable new political force that had blocked them. The new anti-ERA activists prided themselves in being ladylike. Their feminist opponents were not so inhibited. Betty Friedan, cofounder of NOW (the National Organization for Women) and author of The Feminine Mystique, called Schlafly a traitor to her sex and said she should be burned at the stake.

Even so, social conservatism had discovered its strength. Evangelical Christians in 1972 had a twenty-eight percent lower voting turnout than the white American average, even in the South where they were socially predominant. Like other southerners, most Christians who did vote traditionally supported the Democratic Party, of which the South had lost control since the desegregation battles of the sixties. But in 1968 and especially in 1972, southerners opted by a large margin for Republican presidential candidate Richard Nixon.

If they imagined Nixon privately subscribed to either their fundamental Biblical convictions or to their standards of personal decorum, they were soon disabused of the illusion. This became clear from the profane content of Nixon's own audiotapes of himself and his senior staff. They were discovered and published during the Watergate hearings in 1973, which drove him from office in disgrace in 1974. His impressive series of domestic and international achievements were all but forgotten after it was revealed that in private he was a foul-mouthed, vindictive, manipulative, rationalizing paranoid. His White House exit did not particularly discredit American Christianity. Except for a nominal affiliation with Quakerism, Nixon was not seen as religious. But what did affect Christians—or soon would—was the jailing of his staff special counsel, chief hatchet-man and dirty-tricks maestro, Charles Colson. Before and during his seven-month incarceration in an Alabama federal prison this rough, cynical, politically ruthless former Marine captain read C. S. Lewis's Mere Christianity, and gave his life to Christ. Any suspicion it was merely a parole-seeking pretense would be disproven twenty years later when he emerged as one of the most effective Christian leaders of the culture war.

After Nixon's expulsion in 1974, evangelicals were drawn back to the Democratic Party by the 1976 presidential bid of Democratic candidate Jimmy Carter, a quiet, unassuming Georgia peanut farmer whose folksy exterior concealed a profound egocentricity, where Nixon's darker qualities had betrayed a fundamental insecurity. Carter squeaked to victory by two percentage points, thanks in large part to the return of the "Solid South." Unlike the more private Episcopalianism of his Republican opponent, Gerald Ford, Carter was a self-declared Baptist, the first "born-again" president in U.S. history (though the major media had little idea what the term meant), at a time when evangelicals were starting to want some connection between personal faith and political office.

But Carter soon disappointed both them and most other Americans. He seemed overwhelmed by a series of increasingly severe economic and military shocks between 1976 and 1980. The Arab countries forced a second spike in the price of oil, Communist insurgencies were taking over in Central America, inflation was hitting double digits, the federal deficit was reaching alarming proportions, Iran had fallen to radical Islamists and fifty-two American citizens had been taken hostage, the Soviets were deploying new intermediate-range missiles across eastern Europe pointed at the West, and in December, 1979 the Soviets invaded and occupied Afghanistan.

Despite Carter's mass unpopularity, there was among middle-ground Americans widespread fear of his hawkish Republican opponent, Ronald Reagan. Only in the final days of the 1980 campaign did Reagan pull ahead, to win by a comfortable ten-point margin.[5] Carter had assumed he still had the normally quiescent evangelical Protestants firmly in his camp—for why would they want to switch sides and make a former actor from godless Hollywood America's first divorced president? Reagan, who had been raised in his mother's Disciples of Christ Church and called himself a born-again Christian, systematically tapped the rising and expanding but hitherto-ignored political networks of the fundamentalist churches.

By 1980 the new mass-audience television preachers of the evangelical world—Jerry Falwell, Pat Robertson, James Robison, Jim Bakker, and numerous

5. Ronald Reagan began his political career in the 1950s as something of a right-wing scold, but by 1980 he played a genial, relaxed, grandfatherly figure and master of epigram. "Recession is when your neighbor loses his job," he once explained. "Depression is when you lose yours. And recovery is when Jimmy Carter loses his." On abortion he commented, "I've noticed that everyone who is for abortion has already been born." And about being seventy-three years old in the 1984 presidential candidates' debate, he quipped of his fifty-six-year-old opponent, Walter Mondale, "I will not make age an issue in this campaign. I am not going to exploit, for political purposes, my opponent's youth and inexperience."

This 1991 photo of living presidents taken in the Oval Office of the White House shows incumbent George H. W. Bush (center) with (left to right) Gerald Ford, Richard Nixon, Ronald Reagan, and Jimmy Carter. After Nixon's Watergate scandal, evangelical Christians were drawn back to the Democratic Party, helping elect the "born-again" Carter in 1976. But they soon became disillusioned and joined the "New Right" coalition that swept Reagan (and later Bush) to power, starting in 1980.

others—were inveighing regularly against abortion, feminism, and homosexual rights as antifamily, anti-Christian, and un-American. Both Carter and his wife, Rosalynn, had turned out to be unacceptably liberal on the new socio-moral issues, leaving the Democratic evangelical wing feeling betrayed. Reagan had been socially liberal too as governor of California, but he now changed course. "I know you can't endorse me," he told a political throng of fifteen thousand evangelical conservatives. "But I want you to know that I endorse you."

This marked the emergence of Reagan's "New Right"—an unprecedented, broad coalition of pro-Israel Jewish ex-liberals, smaller-government Goldwater libertarians, pro-defense anti-Communists, and populist moral conservatives. The binding thought among these fractious partners was that domestically the federal

Dobson, with his soft, cheerful radio voice and clinical approach, concentrated on speaking to parents, not to politicians, leaving that to the flamboyant preachers.

government should lack both the means (money) and the motivation (progressivism) to pursue anti-Christian policies. Internationally it should invest heavily on defense and anti-Communist alliances.

Within this new coalition, Reagan paid least attention to what was now being dubbed the "Christian Right," whose most active element was the Moral Majority, founded in 1979.[6] But Reagan did give the Christian Right significant concessions: opposition to the ERA, rhetorical rejection of abortion and defunding of groups providing or promoting it outside the U.S., tax breaks to homeschoolers, and a Family Protection Act that gave conservatives control of women's and family issues. More to the point, Reagan gave moral conservatives a level of public respect they got nowhere else.

Inevitably, this New Right coalition evolved over time, especially after the end of the Cold War in 1991 and the rise of Islamic terrorism. Through it all, however,

By the 1980s, mass-audience TV preachers, including the soon-to-be-disgraced Jim Bakker (shown here in 1987 with his then-wife Tammy Faye), were inveighing against abortion, feminism, and homosexuality. Among them were Pat Robertson (top right) and Moral Majority founder Jerry Falwell (bottom right), both of whom helped tighten the Christian Right's hold on the Republican Party.

the Christian Right gradually lost its hold on the Republican Party, while the party's so-called old-guard "blue bloods" quietly resumed control. Even so, it remained loyally Republican if only on the grounds it had nowhere else to go. Author Nancy Cohen, whose contempt for what she calls "sexual fundamentalists" is unconcealed, concludes that moral conservatives provided a consistent forty percent of the Republicans' strength, much too large for the party to ignore or expel, and not nearly enough by itself to win.

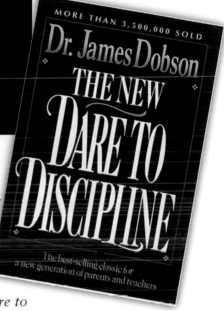

Focus on the Family founder James Dobson and his controversial 1970 parental-help book. By the 1990s his radio ministry was reaching many millions throughout the English-speaking world and Dobson stirred his considerable audience to resist gay rights, abortion, euthanasia, and all aspects of what Christians were now calling the "culture of death," the term used in Pope John Paul II's encyclical Evangelium Vitae *(The Gospel of Life).*

Meanwhile, the original leadership of the Christian Right began to change. The national following of Lynchburg Virginia Baptist pastor Jerry Falwell sagged as the 1990s progressed, due to his continual intemperate statements and unwise endorsements, such as his backing of an unfounded video documentary accusing the Clinton presidency of murder. Much the same fate now began to overtake Pat Robertson, and for much the same reasons. There now emerged an evangelical leader more effective than either of them, however, in James Dobson. A psychologist rather than a clergyman, Dobson became well known to North American evangelicals after he published his controversial 1970 parental-help book *Dare to Discipline*, countering the now ubiquitous permissive child-rearing advice of Benjamin Spock. (*Dare* had sold 3.5 million copies by 2008.) In 1977 he started a radio ministry called Focus on the Family, founded solidly on evangelical, Biblical principles regarding marriage, sexuality, parenting, schooling, family worship, and citizenship. By the 1990s, it was reaching many millions of people throughout the English-speaking world, and the Focus ministry had 1,200 employees.

Dobson, with his soft, cheerful radio voice and clinical approach to problems, concentrated in the 1970s and 1980s on speaking to parents, not politicians, leaving the latter field to the more flamboyant and famous preachers. But by the 1990s, seeing the culture war being lost, Dobson plunged into it directly, bringing his formidable organizational resources with him, and stirring his enormous audience to resist gay rights, abortion, euthanasia, secular intolerance, and all aspects of what Christians were starting to call the "culture of death."

After Pat Buchanan's ringing 1992 declaration of the culture war at the GOP convention, the post-Reagan Republicans under George Bush (Sr.) lost the presidency to Democrat Bill Clinton, the first baby-boomer and the first committed moral progressive to occupy the White House. By now America's cultural conservatives had learned to talk less openly about Christianity. By adopting a more secular rhetoric about families and constitutional freedoms, they inserted themselves all through the Republican Party, in such numbers as to guarantee that it steered consistently to the right on social issues, something it had never done before.

Clinton proved to be a sexual liberal in more than state policy. After it was revealed in his second term that, contrary to his initial denial, he had engaged in

6. One Moral Majority leader, Liberty University founder Jerry Falwell, would later recall, "Early in his first term, I met privately with President Reagan in the Oval Office to communicate to our new leader a list of the major concerns of the so-called 'religious right.' I was so impressed with his crisp and convictioned responses, making it very clear to me that he was as pro-life, pro-family, pro-national defense and pro-Israel as we were. I left that meeting with a fire burning in my heart."

sex with an intern in his office on nine occasions, the Republican-controlled Congress in 1998 sought to impeach him for obstruction of justice (urging witnesses to lie) and perjury (for lying himself under oath). His presidency narrowly survived. Of even greater chagrin to moral conservatives, however, was that through it all he remained almost as popular as before, with an approval rating of about sixty percent until his term ran out in 2000. Had he been allowed to seek a third term he would probably have won.

This was disheartening to a great many conservatives, prominent among them the veteran activist Paul Weyrich. He pronounced the culture war effectively lost for the present,

A 1998 radio station billboard in Cleveland spoofs President Bill Clinton and Monica Lewinsky, the intern who performed oral sex on the president in the White House. The act led to an unsuccessful impeachment case against a president whose public approval ratings remained at around sixty percent throughout his term, despite his various sexual indiscretions. "I no longer believe that there is a moral majority," lamented veteran conservative activist Paul Weyrich. "I do not believe that a majority of Americans actually shares our values."

7. Weyrich's enthusiasm for political activism revived somewhat with the reelection of George W. Bush in 2004. By then he was in a wheelchair, after spinal complications caused by a 1996 fall on ice. The godfather of the New Right died in 2008, at age 66.

8. In their 2011 book *American Grace*, prominent social scientists Robert Putnam and David Campbell conclude that based on the available survey data, Christian Right organizers were as unpopular with Americans as Muslims and atheists. How much of this antipathy resulted from broad media opposition to traditionalist views on almost any issue, the survey did not attempt to ascertain.

and called for a change of strategy. In a famous open letter he wrote, "I no longer believe that there is a moral majority. I do not believe that a majority of Americans actually shares our values.... This is why, even when we win in politics [i.e. get politicians with the right values elected], our victories fail to translate into the kind of policies we believe are important."

Weyrich and many others were concluding by now that it was impossible to reverse moral progressivism by political action.[7] It amounted to attacking the symptoms rather than curing the disease. It was, after all, a *culture* war, and "culture" is far bigger, broader, and deeper than mere government and the democratic process that in theory controls it. Conservatives had always understood this, of course, but they were wrong to think that most Americans were on their side. They might have been in the 1970s, but a generation later evidence was proliferating, even from reputable, Christian-friendly sources (such as Pew Research Center and the Barna Group), that with each passing decade, American values and moral expectations were shifting away from the traditional, if not into a conscious embrace of progressivism, at least away from conservatism.[8] By the opening of the new millennium polls showed that most Americans were now predisposed to equal rights for women and homosexuals, and wanted less religion in politics.

In fact, it was becoming increasingly clear that the institutional fortresses apart from government that change or preserve any culture are the schools and universities, the churches and their secular equivalents, the professions and the media. By the end of the millennium these had all been largely captured, intimidated, or co-opted by radical homosexuals and feminists. In the previous generation all the defaults had changed. Conservatives now had to convince people they were right on each and every issue. The progressive case was now assumed. The culture war might not yet be lost, but so far the Christians had lost all the battles.

One key battle concerned the psychological description of homosexuality. Was it healthy or was it a disorder? In 1970, homosexuals launched a concerted campaign to persuade the psychiatric profession to endorse homosexuality as normal, natural, and healthy. If they could win psychiatry, the disciplines of psychology, social science, education, and theology would follow. In his important book *Homosexuality and the Politics of Truth* (1996) psychiatrist Jeffrey Satinover, a practicing Orthodox Jew, recounts how homosexual activists achieved this goal in three short years.

As recently as 1963 a psychiatric report to the New York Committee on Public Health had confirmed what most psychiatrists had always said—that homosexuality is a serious mental disorder. However, in 1970, a homosexual faction within the American Psychiatric Association ridiculed and shouted down an APA presenter at the annual national convention. Wishing to avoid another such scene, in 1971 the pro-homosexual psychiatrists were given a special panel to lay out their complaints and demands, and at the next convention a nonpsychiatrist broke in, grabbed the microphone, and declared, "Psychiatry is the enemy incarnate." Without any new evidence to support their decision, and allowing for only minimal debate, the APA's Committee on Nomenclature recommended that homosexuality be stricken from the list of mental disorders. When APA dissenters demanded a vote of the whole association in 1973, the National Gay Task Force mailed the APA membership to urge acceptance. Only one-third of the APA membership actually voted. Though most of those who did supported delisting homosexuality as a pathology, a survey of practitioners four years later found that sixty-nine percent disagreed with the decision.

The point of Satinover's book was that homosexual politics had trumped psychiatric medical science ever since. Homosexuality was never considered an illness in the same sense as cancer or measles, but like many compulsions characterized by self-destructive moods and behaviors it was considered a disorder.[9] The author marvels that since 1973 homosexual science has managed to convince the world (falsely in his view) that same-sex inclination is inborn, normal, and irreversible—and that any doubt about this arises from "homophobia."

Having won the battle with the psychiatric profession, nothing now prevented the gay movement from winning the argument everywhere else, with one profession after another. The movement for acceptance and affirmation was not even derailed by the devastation wrought by AIDS (Acquired Immunodeficiency Syndrome) starting in 1981. By 1988 the disease had killed over thirty thousand American homosexuals. Strangely enough, AIDS strengthened the gay movement, by enhancing the status of homosexuals

9. The medical case against homosexual practice rests on a number of surveys of self-reported homosexual activities and outcomes: A "gay lifestyle" involves an average of fifty, often anonymous, sexual partners during one lifetime. It also involves vulnerability to unique diseases such as gay bowel syndrome, lasting damage to the sphincter muscle, and high exposure to often fatal diseases such as AIDS, hepatitis, and rectal cancer. Statistically, there is a much increased risk of suicide. Together, these reportedly produce a twenty-five to thirty-year reduction in average life expectancy.

A gaggle of "gay pride" parade participants pose for a picture in New York City in 2006. Deemed a serious mental disorder by the American psychiatric majority until 1973, homosexuality was delisted from the Diagnostic and Statistical Manual of Mental Disorders (DSM) *that year after a gay faction within the American Psychiatric Association shouted down an APA presenter at the national convention. Only a third of the APA membership bothered voting on delisting, and four years later sixty-nine percent disagreed with the decision.*

Heath Ledger and Jake Gyllenhaal, both heterosexual, portray gay cowboys in the extremely profitable 2004 movie Brokeback Mountain. *Homosexual celebrities (below from left): comedienne Rosie O'Donnell, CNN presenter Anderson Cooper, pop star Elton John, and talk show host Ellen DeGeneres. Following the AIDS epidemic, which successfully transformed the public image of homosexuals into that of noble victim, acceptance of gays grew to the point where they became a staple of network television and pervaded the various spheres of society. By 2012, nine states had legalized same-sex marriage and others appeared likely to follow.*

10. Throughout the HIV/AIDS epidemic in the U.S., roughly half of its victims were homosexuals, ten percent homosexual intravenous drug users, one-quarter other drug injectors, ten percent heterosexuals, and a few percentage points in other categories, such as newborns infected *in utero* by diseased mothers and recipients of infected blood transfusions. In 2012 an estimated 1.2 million Americans were HIV-positive, but the AIDS death toll had been reduced from a high of fifty-four thousand in 1995 to approximately 17,000 in the opening years of the twenty-first century.

as victims. By the 1990s, most active homosexuals could count former friends and lovers who had died a painful and lingering death from Kaposi's Sarcoma, liver disease, or fungal infections.[10]

All through the 1980s and into the 1990s, the AIDS juggernaut advanced, as did the gay-rights movement. "Gay pride" parades across America each June grew larger, more ubiquitous, and more indecent. In major cities they became almost orgiastic displays of public nudity, garish costumes, and lewd gestures, though this did not dissuade prominent political and community figures from leading them. Police departments established gay liaison task forces to combat hate crimes, and high schools, far from educating youth about the hazardous reality of homosexual practice, instead condoned and promoted it by opening "gay-straight" student clubs under the guise of antibullying initiatives.

Soon multinational corporations were adopting such things as gay-friendly policies on health insurance, and by the turn of the century homosexual characters and celebrities pervaded network television talk shows, reality shows, dramas, and comedies—to such an extent that a 2011 Gallup survey found thirty-five percent of Americans estimating that homosexuals comprised over one-quarter of the U.S. population. (The actual homosexual percentage has long been known to be less than three percent among men and less than two percent of women.) By 2012 nine states had legalized same-sex marriage, and others appeared likely to follow. Some Christian cultural warriors pointed to AIDS as God's judgment on the new America, but few people paid much attention, especially after the epidemic crested in 1992, and new drugs improved the odds for many who contracted it. So gayness continued to permeate the culture. Mainline clergy rarely mentioned it until demands for homosexual marriage arose, and the televangelists could not compete with nonstop "normalization" television programs, bolstered by the legal, social, and teaching professions.

Gay activism, of course, was only one blade of the progressive shears. The

First- and second-wave feminism are contrasted in these two photos: to the left, Suffragettes march in Washington, DC, in 1913; below, women's liberationists marching in the same city in 1970. Third-wave feminism erupted through the ensuing decades, emanating from the new women's studies departments in universities, whose practitioners came to dominate the faculties of secular campuses with their antisexist language codes, their female staffing and promotion quotas, and their vague but menacing rules against sexual harassment.

A key battle that the Christians won

The number of American youngsters schooled at home nears two million in 2007 after the courts uphold the primary right of parents to control their children's education

Culture war activists found themselves fighting a retreat on issues of sexual morality, but they made big strides forward in a very different area: education. As judicial and educational officialdom turned against Christianity in the sixties, banning school prayer, Bible study, creation science curriculum, and even Christmas pageants, Protestants came to appreciate English essayist G. K. Chesterton's dictum, "The government did not have such power over us when it could send men to the stake, as it does now when it can send them to the elementary school."

Heeding the biblical injunction to "train up the child in the way he should go" (Proverbs 22:6), fundamental Protestants responded in the sixties and seventies by starting private, church-based Christian schools teaching a Bible-based curriculum. Catholics had long ago established their own schools, usually privately funded and made financially possible by the massive support of religious sisters teaching for very low wages. When the number of these sisters began to drop precipitously in the late twentieth century, many parochial schools had to close. On the Protestant side, the Seventh Day Adventists operate the second largest denominational school system in the world.

As state-directed sex education courses diligently removed the moral element in sex education lessons, the trend toward home education rapidly spread among both Protestant and Catholic families. This whole drift, naturally, aroused resistance from the secular educational establishment, but here the spirit of the age and the thinking of the judiciary actually favored the Christians: they were exercising their constitutionally-enshrined right of religious choice. However, they were also violating the core principle being asserted by the public schools—that state educators should outrank parents in the raising of children, an assertion that actually finds little support in American law.

Compulsory mass education began in North America with the Massachusetts Bay colony's Ye Olde Deluder, Satan Act of 1647, which set fines for any community that failed to provide "common schooling" to all. This impulse to legislate virtue was not unique to Puritans. Pennsylvania constitutional founding father Benjamin Rush, for example, argued in 1786 that only government-mandated schools could elevate the primary loyalty of Americans from the family to the Republic.

Horace Mann, the father of today's government school system in the United States, wrote in 1846 lauding Massachusetts for its "parental" style of government, due to what he perceived as widespread parental neglect and incompetence in raising and

A teacher with her pupils in front of a sod schoolhouse in Oklahoma Territory, circa 1895. Schooling in America had by now become the province of government, formulated fifty years earlier by Horace Mann, who saw the service as "moral philanthropy" designed to compensate for neglect by parents whom he considered "sunken into depravity." However, by the 1960s, a growing number of American parents began to see private and homeschools as an alternative to a public system that was itself veering toward depravity.

A Michigan mother leads her homeschooled children in the Pledge of Allegiance in 1990. Homeschooling in the United States soared in the ensuing decade, and by 2007 close to two million children were being taught at home.

educating the young. "Parents," wrote one of Mann's associates in the *Common School Journal* in 1841, "although the most sunken in depravity themselves, receive with gratitude the services of...moral philanthropy in behalf of their families." Another public school advocate went further: "The child is not in school for knowledge. He is there to live, and to put his life, nurtured in the school, into the community," progressive education pioneer Francis Parker told the National Education Association in 1895. (This organization, dedicated since 1857 to mandatory school attendance and higher teacher pay, was by 2012 the biggest union in the U.S.)

Not until the 1960s, however, did this implicit distrust of families in general and of religious families in particular become obvious and acute. Evangelical Christians then began opting out and setting up church-based day schools. Depending on the size of the church or churches involved, enrollment ranged from a few dozen to hundreds. Running battles ensued in virtually all state and provincial jurisdictions over curriculum, teacher credentials, and testing. But these schools persisted and eventually were accepted. U.S. enrollment in Protestant private religious schools rose from almost nil before 1970, to two million in the opening decade of the twenty-first century—four percent of America's school-age population. Catholic school enrollment was sliding downward to 2.2 million in 2009, while nonreligious private school enrollment was stable at 1.3 million students. However, more than eight out of ten American children still went to government schools.

Most Protestant schools were strikingly different from their public competitors. Private-school teachers, often lacking professional training, were nonunionized, were paid considerably less, and were religiously motivated. Curriculum in all subjects was almost invariably Bible based or biblically referenced, and often designed on an individualized, "mastery learning" model in which each student progresses at his or her own pace from one short unit to the next. There were protracted arguments with the professional teaching establishment on two major points: did this approach teach children to think independently rather than merely memorize, and did it prepare them socially to enter North American society? Both questions resist factual answers, so the debate raged on.

Since North Americans had been imbued for well over a century in the belief that only common schooling integrates society, there was widespread suspicion among both experts and the public that any schooling aimed at preserving religious and social differences would foster ignorance and intolerance. For example, the popular 2004 Lindsay Lohan movie *Mean Girls* opened with a vignette of six little hillbilly kids, one of them gravely intoning, "And on the third day, God created the Remington bolt-action rifle so that man could fight the dinosaurs. And the homosexuals." The other children respond in unison, "Amen."

In fact, the reverse is true, according to a large continental survey of Christian school graduates in 2011 by Cardus, a Hamilton, Ontario social research think tank. It did find that overall Protestant private school students consistently

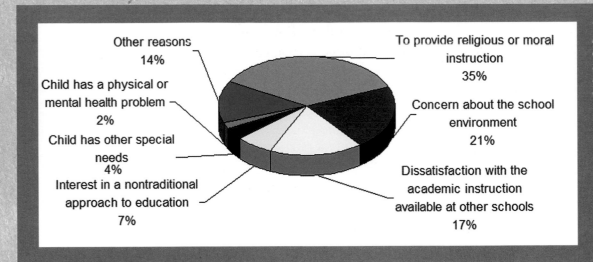

Other reasons
14%

Child has a physical or
mental health problem
2%

Child has other special
needs
4%

Interest in a nontraditional
approach to education
7%

To provide religious or moral
instruction
35%

Concern about the school
environment
21%

Dissatisfaction with the
academic instruction
available at other schools
17%

This chart was produced by the U.S. Department of Education in 2007, to show the reasons for choosing homeschooling over the public system.

score slightly below Catholic and public school averages on standardized tests. However, once they became adults, despite slightly lower average incomes, they ranked significantly higher than any other group in marital stability, number of children, dedication of time and money to civic participation and to local and foreign charities, church attendance, family and private prayer, and respect for authority. Interestingly, Cardus found Protestant graduates the least likely group—by far—to support political parties, join protest demonstrations, or discuss political issues; and it found Bible-based schooling to have reduced political engagement rather than to have encouraged it.[1]

Protestant private school enrollment leveled off in the early twenty-first century, partly because since the 1990s, many Christians had begun opting for homeschooling. By 2007, one and a half million American children were being taught primarily by their parents, and the increase showed no sign of stopping, according to the National Center for Education Statistics (NCES). By some counts, the figure was higher, more like two million. The NCES found that the most common reason for homeschooling (36 percent) was religion; other primary motives cited were family independence, family convenience, or better academics, made possible by the steadily improving curricula available for home-educated children.

If church-based schooling had alarmed the educational establishment in the sixties and seventies, homeschooling in the eighties and nineties horrified it, and for the same reasons: the questionable competence of parents to teach, lack of government oversight, uncontrolled curriculum, and—as ever—the fear that homebound children would enter adulthood "unsocialized." Homeschooling parents had equally sharp criticisms of the state schooling systems: that teachers were careless or too burdened to teach effectively; there was a lack of accountability; the curriculum was often poor, and that the kind of "socialization" often learned in public school was inadequate if not pernicious. In addition, to many parents, the grouping of large numbers of people of the same age in a sealed environment called "school" creates the most unnatural society imaginable.

By 2000, *Time* magazine was reporting that homeschooling scores on Scholastic Aptitude Tests (SATs), American College Tests (ACTs), and other performance tests were averaging five to ten percentage points ahead of national norms, and Ivy League universities were eagerly enrolling homeschooled students because they could think for themselves. Moreover, the constitutional safeguards which protected church schools protected homeschools as well, and by 2005 every state and province allowed the practice, with widely-varying degrees of attempted regulatory oversight and public financial support. Unable to ban the practice, there was a growing movement to accommodate it (and shore up school system revenues) by allowing blended home-and-school academic, sports, and cultural programming.

In his 2009 book *Write These Laws on Your Children*, Robert Kunzman, a former teacher and education professor, detailed the progress of six homeschool families over several years. In every case he found homeschooling had succeeded, although both he and the parents he observed knew personally of other cases where homeschooling amounted to simple neglect. The very nature of homeschooling, he notes, precludes any knowledge of how common this is, because the only parents who allow assessments are the conscientious ones.

To internationally prominent traditional-family advocate Allan Carlson of Rockford, Illinois, homeschooling was a "fundamental revolution, recovering a vital family function lost to the aggressive state a century-and-a-half earlier." In his 2005 book *Fractured Generations*, he observes that homeschool families had more children, fewer mothers working full time (almost none), and spent almost all available hours and resources making homeschooling work. What for many began as a somewhat frightening challenge ended up redefining and reinforcing the whole family enterprise. However modest their numbers, Carlson foresaw homeschoolers having a major impact in rebuilding North American society.

1. It seems impossible to many secularists that anyone holding absolute biblical views of good and evil can be broad-minded and tolerant of contradiction. However, evolutionary psychologist Jonathan Haidt, a self-described liberal atheist, shows in his 2012 book *The Righteous Mind* how conservatives are more broad-minded than liberals (in the literal sense that their moral thinking is broader). He posits that humanity has inherited six preprogrammed areas of moral concern, and that while liberals understand two of them—care and fairness—and ignore the rest, conservatives process all six at once—the other four being loyalty, authority, sanctity, and liberty/oppression. From this Haidt concludes that the liberal Left probably cannot win America's culture war.

other was radical feminism. Its agenda was different but feminists were just as determined as gays to shred America's traditional virtues and values. Feminism already had a long, diverse history in North America and Europe, dating back well into the nineteenth century. The significant difference between the suffragette progressives of the early "first-wave" feminism, and the progressive sexual revolutionaries of the "second wave" in the sixties and seventies, was their attitude towards family. Early feminists wanted the right to vote so that they could close bars and bawdy houses and strengthen and protect home and family. Second-wavers wanted to get out of the home and to radically redefine the family. They found ridiculous the belief of the counterrevolutionaries—Schlafly, Hobbs, and the rest—that the man must be the family breadwinner and decision maker, the woman should be home raising children, and the primary virtue of children should be obedience.

The initial goal of the rebirthed women's movement in the sixties was to gain formal equality with men—equal pay and an equal right to professional careers, an equal right to promiscuous sex made possible by legalized birth control and abortion, shared domestic duties, and so forth. As 1960s optimism gave way to 1970s paranoia and beyond, however, feminism moved into a third wave, one

To third-wave feminism, power is real and objective, truth unreal and subjective; institutions such as the family are exploitative social constructs.

emanating mainly from the new women's studies departments opening in universities across North America, starting with Cornell in 1969. The common philosophy was "postmodern deconstruction"—the idea that power is real and objective, truth is unreal and subjective, and institutions such as the family are arbitrary social constructs through which the powerful (men) exploit the weak (women)—and a vast, complex literature of victimology followed.

More indoctrination than scholarship, and with more emphasis on action than objectivity, academic feminism soon came to dominate many faculties of secular campuses. It intimidated teachers and students alike with vigorously enforced antisexist language codes of pharisaic subtlety, special female staffing and promotion quotas, bewilderingly vague but very menacing rules against sexual harassment, and the replacement of courses on the Judeo-Christian history and intellectual heritage of the western world with courses on Christian persecution of witchcraft, and the concept that all heterosexual sex is rape.

The impact of this third-wave "victimhood" feminism (sometimes called "gender feminism") radiated outward from academia into corporate America, family and criminal law, social professions and medicine, news and entertainment media, and, of course, government. In her landmark book *Who Stole Feminism?* (1995), Christina Hoff Sommers (a self-described equal-rights feminist of the earlier school) provides an example of how easily and effectively such victimhood claims were propagated. In 1991 the American Association of University Women (AAUW), a long-established and credible academic group, started a national campaign to stop schools from "shortchanging girls." Major news media across

U.S. President Barack Obama is shown on the Fox News network's Web site on May 9, 2012, declaring, "At a certain point I've just concluded that for me personally, it is important for me, it is important for me to go ahead and affirm that I think same-sex couples should be able to get married."

North America took up the cause. It was entirely based on an AAUW-commissioned survey of three thousand school children by a Washington consultant, which found that between grades four and ten, the number of girls with high self-esteem (a term the study never defined) drops in half—from sixty percent to twenty-nine.

On the basis of this tiny factoid, and bolstered by the feminist spirit of the age, North American educators launched a frenzied and prolonged drive to create "girl-friendly" classroom innovations—ignoring the fact that more girls than boys already graduated and with higher averages, that more girls than boys were enrolling in university, that classroom teachers favored girls and not boys, and that much of the raw data collected by the pollster contradicted the AAUW's conclusions. Yet not one newspaper or television network challenged any of it.

Had feminism remained in its second stage, conservatives might have fared better in the culture war. But with the turn of the twenty-first century, the third wave remained very much in charge of American cultural institutions, and America's culture war appeared to be moving inexorably against conservatives. However, there were some changes. Until now, initiatives had been led almost entirely by lay people. Among prelates, for every stalwart like New York's Cardinal O'Connor there had been three or four progressives like Archbishop Rembert Weakland of Milwaukee, Cardinal Joseph Bernardin of Chicago, Cardinal Roger Mahony of Los Angeles, and Auxiliary Bishop Thomas Gumbleton of Detroit who either ignored the struggle entirely, or even appeared subtly to support the other side. Since the 1990s, however, the Vatican had been steadily promoting younger conservatives to the episcopate, and these now led a counterattack. In May, 2012, forty-three Catholic employers, including thirteen of America's 195 Catholic dioceses, sued the government for infringing their First Amendment religious freedom. Remarkably, not one U.S. bishop dissented. Even more significantly, the lawsuit was supported by sixty Protestant and Orthodox Jewish social organizations.

The outcome of this mid-election lawsuit was unknowable when this volume was written, but it was the first concrete result of a milestone reached three years earlier. In 2009, a manifesto titled the Manhattan Declaration was published, pronouncing an anathema on the main tenets underlying the new moral order: "We will not comply," it warned, "with any edict that compels us or the institutions we lead to participate in or facilitate abortions, embryo-destructive research, assisted suicide, euthanasia, or any other act that violates the principle of the profound, inherent, and equal dignity of every member of the human family"—even if necessary by acts of civil disobedience.

In content, the statement merely summarized what culture warriors had been saying all along. What set it apart was that it was signed by over one hundred and fifty of the North America's most senior clergy, seminary presidents, and other leaders of the Catholic, evangelical, and Eastern Orthodox churches. Strangely, never had something so simple and effective been accomplished during the four decades of the culture war. Hitherto it had been fought by lay Christians, with minimal participation, and often outright obstruction, by officialdom in most church traditions, cautiously content to stay within their silos of doctrinal difference and tax-exempt ecclesiastical safety. Now they were directly engaged.

At the Stonewall Inn, the New York site of the 1969 riots that ignited the gay-rights movement, a customer emerges on the day of the president's declaration, and reads a sign that says, "Obama supports gay marriage. Let's Drink."

The man who spearheaded this ecumenical *tour de force*, assisted by three prominent Catholic and evangelical theologians, was the aging Nixon Watergate felon Charles Colson. When he got out of jail in 1975 he founded a ministry for prisoners—people who are probably the least publicly appealing clientele there is. He lobbied for more lenient and constructive forms of criminal punishment, and he built his Prison Fellowship into an international evangelical support group for convicts, their families, and their victims. He then added numerous other initiatives, mostly aimed at building conservative interchurch solidarity in an increasingly anti-Christian climate. By the time he died following a brain hemorrhage in 2012, the Manhattan Declaration had drawn the online endorsement of over half a million North Americans.

As an evangelical convert, Colson understood quite well that between the various church traditions lay significant differences on specific points of theology. But like Billy Graham, Pope John Paul II, and many other great twentieth-century Christians, he saw something he believed is more important. As he told *Touchstone* magazine in 1999, "[Christian] disunity works against God's purposes. Until we're really one, the world will not know that Christ was sent by the Father. And so we have to work towards that always—not settling for a lowest common denominator, but always working in the service of Truth. We must try to bring people together in their beliefs, capitalizing on and strengthening the things that we believe in together, and keeping in perspective the things on which we disagree." ∎

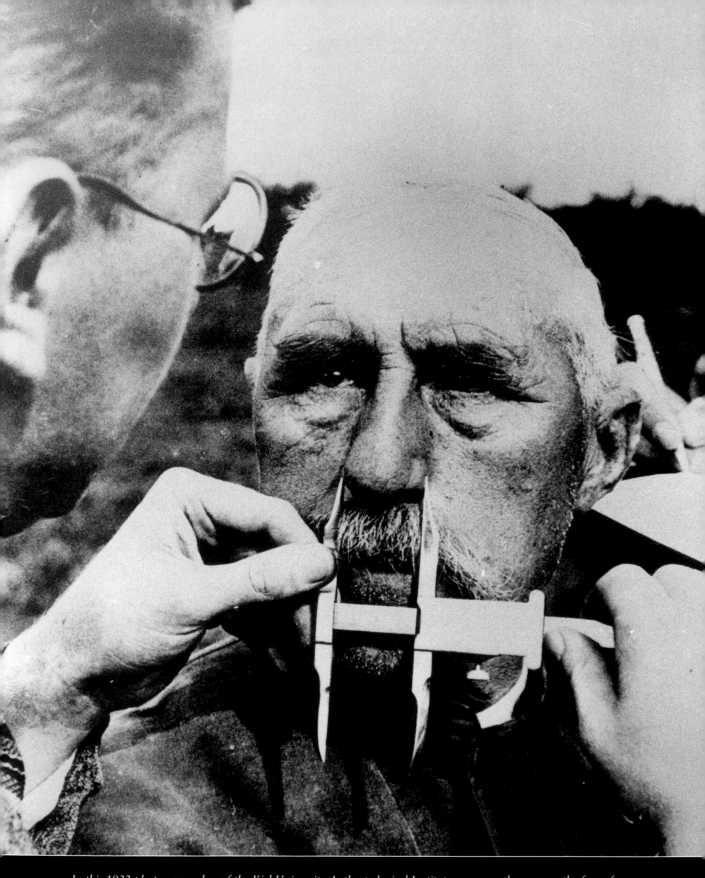

In this 1932 photo, a member of the Kiel University Anthropological Institute measures the nose on the face of an inhabitant of a village in northern Germany to determine racial qualities. Pseudosciences such as phrenology—the measurement and recording of various physical and mental attributes—were practiced widely in Germany and the United States in the 1920s as part of a eugenics campaign to identify the genetically inferior and to stop them from propagating by means of sterilization and later, in Germany, through extermination. Thus, it was widely believed, soci-

CHAPTER 13

If science overrules all, the scientific miracle's dark side will triumph

Study the horror of eugenics, warn the pessimists, and beware the lab-coated zealots of scientism— in which technology dictates right and wrong

Both for those who believe in God and for those who don't—theists and atheists alike—the natural universe consists of a constant procession of events, each caused by a prior event, and itself the cause of a consequent event. The cue hits the billiard ball, transferring energy to it, which carries the ball across the table, where it transfers energy to another billiard ball, which comes to rest after transferring its remaining energy as heat to the billiard table and thence to the atmosphere, and so on. The continuum of cause and effect goes on all over the natural universe all the time, making everything happen, from the flutter of a leaf in the wind to the movement of the red stars.

Though some atheists concede there is evidence of "random conduct" within the natural order whose cause is beyond our capacity to decipher, they nevertheless declare that the natural order is all that exists. In the words of the atheist superstar Carl Sagan, whose thirteen-part series on science was long the most-watched show on American public television, "The Cosmos is all that is or was or ever will be." It was a memorable assertion, but it was not, as philosophers were quick to point out, a scientific one.

To the theist, however, there is something else—something outside this whole process, something above and beyond the natural—namely the *super*natural. This Something Else is what brought the natural universe into being, say the theists. Science cannot prove them right, of course, but neither can it prove them wrong, for science by its own definition confines itself to what happens within nature's

Part of the front cover of the August 1929 edition of Eugenics, *and American eugenics proponents (left to right) Harry Laughlin, Madison Grant, and Charles Davenport. The main hurdle to genetic perfection, said Grant, was that too many people cherished "a mistaken regard for what they believe to be divine laws."*

1. People find things much easier to believe if they happen gradually, observes Christian essayist G. K. Chesterton in *The Everlasting Man* (1925), but this inclination is hardly reasonable. The witch of classical mythology who turns sailors into pigs, for instance, is not readily embraced by the modern mind as something that actually happened. Now suppose that a naval gentleman of your acquaintance begins in his early thirties to show distinctly odd traits. His nose is growing larger and larger. By forty he is discovered to be developing a small tail, and at fifty his voice is changing in the strangest way. Would this be somehow more believable? Chesterton didn't think so.

cause and effect order. Any allusion to the existence or nonexistence of something outside this natural order cannot be a scientific statement. Thus science can prove neither the atheist's case nor the theist's, and Sagan's assertion had wildly exceeded the scientific capability.

Theism in one form or another has existed since history began, whereas atheism is generally viewed as dating back little farther than the Enlightenment, but this is not so. Wherever civilizations have appeared, both views turn up. What has changed, however, is the posture of atheism. After Charles Darwin's nineteenth-century theory of evolution, atheists saw no further need for a Mind behind the natural world. The world's species in effect created themselves through a process of evolution, they reasoned, with strong traits overcoming weak ones as new species "evolved." But the changes were gradual, Darwin concluded, occurring over enormous periods of time.[1] Darwin's famous book was called *On the Origin of Species*, and therein lay an irony. His book describes a system that offers to explain how the species of nature come about. But since it does not attempt to explain how the system itself came about, it does not in fact describe the origin of species.

Armed with this assertion and citing all the astounding recent advances in technology, atheism proclaimed theists to be the enemies of science and themselves its champions. They marched forward into the twentieth century, powerful, aggressive, and condemnatory. Only the "scientific" view of reality must be taught to school children, they declared, and theistic ideas should now be regarded as mere personal opinions, confined to home and church, and denied any significant role in the shaping of law and public policy. Theists objected, asserting that what Darwin propounded was a theory, not a fact, and in any case did not explain how this entire evolutionary complex came to be.

The debate raged throughout the twentieth century. Early on, the atheist position became known as "naturalism," because it asserted that knowledge of nature and its cause and effect system was the only kind of knowledge that could be recognized as valid. Naturalism later came to be called "scientism," because it held that only the scientifically ascertainable could be regarded as known. These conclusions were not scientific but philosophical. Small wonder, therefore, that scientism was soon to emerge as a political philosophy.

This came about through one obvious deficiency in scientism. Science can assert how human beings behave, but not how they *ought to* behave. Words like *should* or *ought to* do not belong in the scientific vocabulary. Morality, to the atheists, being outside the scientific field, must therefore be unknowable. But to the disciples of scientism, this was not a deficiency but an opportunity. If moral rules were not scientifically valid, why need we bother with them?

Furthermore, they said, science had now demonstrated that human conduct, like everything else in nature, ran on strict cause-and-effect rules. Morality implied that

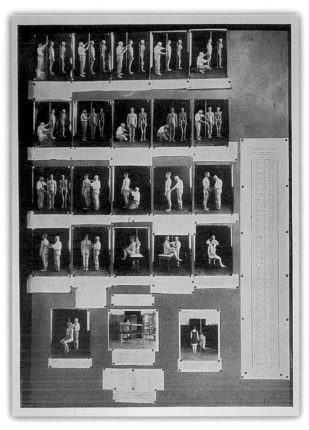

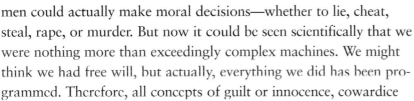

men could actually make moral decisions—whether to lie, cheat, steal, rape, or murder. But now it could be seen scientifically that we were nothing more than exceedingly complex machines. We might think we had free will, but actually, everything we did has been programmed. Therefore, all concepts of guilt or innocence, cowardice or heroism, goodness or evil, cruelty or compassion could now be viewed as delusions. The old moral order, they concluded, was a product of religion, which had now been discredited. All the old rules had been repealed, and we must develop a new morality.

To the naturalists, Charles Darwin and the contemporary scientist Gregor Mendel had shown how this could be done. Just as we selectively breed animals to obtain certain good qualities in their young, surely human beings could be similarly programmed. More importantly, by restricting by law who was permitted to have children, undesirable human qualities could be eradicated. Thus was born at the turn of the twentieth century, what called itself "the science of eugenics." Its birthplace was Britain and its development is described in the previous volume. But the eugenics movement did not thrive in Britain, where its legislative initiatives were thwarted by a combination of Catholic and Laborite members of Parliament. However, in the United States, and to some degree in Canada, it found sweeping success, and there the world would see the first instance of scientism come to power in a democratic country.

One reason for eugenic success in America was the promotional skill of the people behind it—men like Charles Benedict Davenport (1866–1944), the Harvard zoologist, who wrote the "creed" of eugenics whose aims he summarized in 1912: "Prevent the feeble-minded, drunkards, paupers, sex offenders and the criminalistic from having children or marrying their like, or cousins, or any person belonging to a neuropathic strain." In one generation, he predicted, "the crop of defectives will be reduced to practically nothing." Davenport's chief lieutenant was Harry Hamilton Laughlin, a man so wholly dedicated to the cause that he was not afraid to denounce the charitable programs that Americans so admired. By comforting and sustaining the weak and helpless, he observed, they doubtless "relieved much suffering," but they obstructed scientific progress. The central problem, wrote Madison Grant, the program's chief publicist, was that so

Pictured left are the winners of a "Fitter Families" contest in Kansas some time in the 1920s. Families deemed to best fit the ideal genetic profile were rewarded and publicized to promote the cause of eugenics. The series of photos below, displayed at Harry Laughlin's Second International Exhibition of Eugenics held in 1921 in New York, show a doctor measuring up an ideal Nordic specimen.

Alexis Carrel

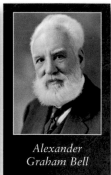

Alexander Graham Bell

John Harvey Kellogg

many people cherished "a mistaken regard for what they believe to be divine laws."

Davenport and Laughlin founded and developed the Eugenics Record Office at their Cold Spring Harbor Laboratory on Long Island, New York, which over the next thirty years would send out hundreds of young women to compile detailed records on 534,625 Americans whom they deemed to be "defective." Sixty thousand of them would face sterilization, many of the males by compulsory castration. But the eugenicists saw this as barely a beginning. Their initial goal was to sterilize fourteen million people in the United States and millions more worldwide, thus replacing the "lower tenth" of the human race with "pure Nordic stock."

Funding such a vast undertaking was not beyond Charles Davenport's capability. He persuaded the Carnegie Foundation to bankroll the Eugenics Record Office. Soon the Rockefeller Foundation began pouring in more thousands. In 1910, further vast sums arrived after Davenport persuaded Mary Harriman, widow of recently deceased Union Pacific Railroad tycoon Ned Harriman, to throw open her vast inheritance to the eugenics cause.[2] In 1914, Dr. John Harvey Kellogg, brother and partner of the Corn Flakes king, founded the Race Betterment Foundation at Battle Creek, Michigan. The funding seemed boundless.

With a program so authoritatively endorsed, it could hardly be otherwise. The renowned inventor of the telephone, Alexander Graham Bell, was a foremost advocate, along with Alexis Carrel, winner of a Nobel prize for medicine; O. P. Austin, chief of the U.S. Bureau of Statistics; senior Harvard professors E. B. Cannon and Robert DeCourcy Ward; Princeton psychiatrist Stewart Paton; Yale public affairs professor Irving Fisher; and University of Chicago economist James Field. Invitations for Americans to attend the First International Congress on Eugenics in 1912 in London went out over the signature of Secretary of State P. C. Knox to the presidents of the National Academy of Sciences, the American Academy of Political and Social Sciences, the American Economic Association, the American Philosophical Association, and to every national medical society in the country. Could such a galaxy of expertise possibly be deceived?

Who would challenge the credibility of a man like ophthalmologist Lucien Howe, for example, credited with saving the sight of thousands of newborns by bathing their eyes with very diluted silver nitrate drops to prevent neonatal infection? Howe was also a zealous eugenicist, and historian Edwin Black in his *War Against the Weak* (2003) describes in detail Howe's zealous campaign to forcibly sterilize blind people and forbid them to marry. This led to marital prohibitions in some states on purely racist grounds. Not only black/white marriages were forbidden, but white/Asian marriages in Montana, and white/Native American marriages in other states. Delaware criminalized marriages between people on welfare.

Next Howe wanted eugenic sterilization and marital prohibition for all people of "weak eyesight," plus their siblings and children, but here he encountered stubborn resistance. Three times the New York State Assembly voted down his ideas, and he died before he could launch a fourth campaign.[3] But Howe had produced one proposal that was adopted in other states: that anyone even suspected of a physical, psychological, or economic deficiency must post a $14,000

2. Edward Henry "Ned" Harriman and his wife Mary were parents of W. Averell Harriman (1891–1986), former U.S. ambassador to Britain and to the Soviet Union, secretary of commerce in the Truman government, forty-eighth governor of New York State, and twice defeated as a candidate for the Democratic presidential nomination.

3. Historian Edwin Black cites a draft law that the ophthalmology wing of the American Medical Association placed before the New York Assembly. It reads: "When a man and woman contemplate marriage, if a visual defect exists in one or both of the contracting parties, or in the family of either, so apparent that any taxpayer fears that the children of such a union are liable to become public charges, for which that taxpayer would probably be assessed, then such taxpayer…may apply to the county judge for an injunction against such a marriage." The judge would then "appoint at least two experts to advise him concerning the probabilities of the further transmission of the eye defect." The experts were specified as a qualified ophthalmologist and "a person especially well versed in distinguishing family traits which are apt to reappear."

bond ($140,000 in 2010) for a marriage certificate, redeemable by the state if their progeny became a public burden.

Clergy of liberal theology leapt on the genetic bandwagon. The American historian Christine Rosen cites in her book *Preaching Eugenics* (2004), for example: Harry Emerson Fosdick of New York, who extolled "the humanitarian desire to take advantage of this scientific control of life"; celebrated Episcopalian rector Phillips Endicott Osgood of Minneapolis, who won the sermon contest sponsored by the American Eugenics Society by exhorting Christians to "keep their bloodlines pure"; and Henry Strong Huntington, editor of *Christian Week* magazine, who somehow discovered through eugenics an interest in nudity. Frolicking through the woods naked with like-minded friends, he rhapsodized, was "poetry incarnate." There were also discordant voices, of course, like the Indiana pastor who insisted that "all human beings are God's children." The secretary of the state board of health, however, dismissed this as "bosh and nonsense," declaring

Holmes, though one of the most respected U.S. jurists, was a religious skeptic, an ardent Darwinian, wholly persuaded that the authority for law must be human, not religious.

that people are what they are "through the stock from which they sprang."

A much more discordant note came in December 1930, when Pope Pius XI condemned eugenics, not for its aims, but for its methods (sterilization and refusal of marriage) and for its presumptions. "Where no crime has taken place, and there is no cause present for grave punishment," his encyclical declared, "public magistrates can never directly harm or tamper with the integrity of the body, either for reasons of eugenics or for any other reason."

Those few Catholic clergy who had in part endorsed the program backed off, but the United States Supreme Court did not. It decided eight to one to uphold state-legislated sterilization. The majority decision was written by Justice Oliver Wendell Holmes, publicly one of the most respected jurists in U.S. history, though privately a religious skeptic, an ardent Darwinian, a despiser of what he called the "do-gooder" inclination of Americans, and a man wholly persuaded that the ultimate authority for law must be of human origin, not religious. Moses, that is, had been repudiated. But there was no immediately obvious successor.

"Eugenical sterilization was now the law of the land," writes historian Black. "The floodgates opened wide." One state after another hastened to enact sterilization legislation. Where there were only 1,422 sterilized persons in public institutions in 1917, the number reached 38,087 by 1941. More than fourteen thousand were in California.

But what legislatures enact and judges rule does not necessarily resolve an issue in a working democracy. Public support for eugenics had never been strong, particularly after the Hearst newspapers launched a campaign against it 1915 with one horror story after another.[4] Some of these came from far-off Britain where an eight-year-old boy reportedly was castrated when found masturbating, and a fifteen-year-old because he allegedly "rubbed himself" against a woman. After thirty-eight children in one Kansas institution had been surgically sterilized,

4. At its peak, the newspaper empire headed by William Randolph Hearst was by far the biggest in America, consisting of thirty major dailies plus a stable of magazines. Hearst was notable for his "yellow" (i.e. sensationalist) journalism, and his focus on eugenics was likely grounded in the emotions it aroused rather than his personal moral outrage. Eventually his papers were running opinion pieces both favoring and opposing the movement.

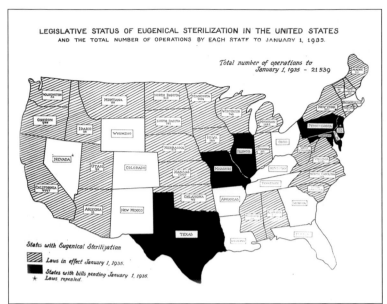

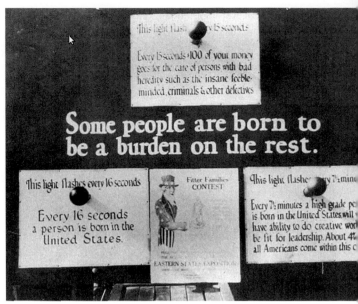

Some people are born to be a burden on the rest.

A 1935 map of the United States showing where eugenics legislation had been enacted and sterilization operations performed; a eugenics advocacy poster at the 1926 Philadelphia Sesqui-Centennial International Exposition; and eminent American jurist Oliver Wendell Holmes at his desk. Despite opposition from the Catholic Church and the Hearst newspapers, the U.S. Supreme Court upheld state-legislated sterilization programs eight to one, with Holmes, an ardent Darwinist, writing the majority decision.

an inquiry found that the superintendent had violated the law by ordering it, although he was neither charged nor fired. There were heartrending stories from poor farm families of the South who cooperated hospitably with the "nice lady" who came to ask them about their family and then found themselves ordered sterilized by the local board of health. But their son and daughter-in-law had only just been married, they pleaded. Naturally they wanted to have children. That was too bad. Progress was progress. All this despite increasing evidence that many of these human "defects" are not in fact genetically transmitted.

But the worst effects of the eugenics revolution were developing overseas. In Germany the Nazis, deeply committed to their "master race" concept, took power in 1933. They launched a ruthless eugenic persecution of Jews, Gypsies, and other "defectives," patterned on American legislation and receiving the active assistance of the American movement. Laughlin threw his monthly *Eugenics News* into such strident support of the Nazi endeavors that an alarmed Carnegie Foundation asked Davenport to muzzle him. Davenport retired in 1934, and Laughlin assumed the leadership. Carnegie had long been unhappy with him, but did not force his retirement until the Second World War broke out in 1939, when it also closed the records office, whose vast files on "defective" Americans were finally seen as useless. After Laughlin died in 1943, it was disclosed that for years he had suffered from epilepsy, a disease he was particularly determined to wipe out through eugenics. He and his wife had no children. Charles Davenport died a bitter and defeated man in February 1944, fifteen months before the Nazi surrender.

Eugenics was seemingly also dead, and its disciples and financial backers quietly but rapidly distanced themselves from it. But the thinking that created it—scientism and the yearning to use science to produce a new type of human being and a new human society—remained fully alive. Moreover, in the opening decades of the twentieth century, it had acquired a propagandist of extraordinary imagination and literary talent. Herbert Gordon "H. G." Wells was converted from evangelical Christianity to the religion of scientism by Oxford biology professor Thomas Huxley, the man known as "Darwin's bulldog" (as described in the previous volume). In the service of scientism, Wells would write nearly one hundred books, many of them classics of science fiction.

As a zealous eugenicist, Wells left Davenport and Laughlin far behind. The goal for humanity, he wrote in *Anticipations* (1903), his first big seller, must be a scientifically planned future, directed by men and women with "beautiful and strong bodies, clear and powerful minds." To produce these there must be "no pity and less benevolence" towards the "unfit"—specifically any individuals with "transmittable diseases, mental disorders, bodily deformations, criminal insanity, or incurable alcoholism." All such must be "put to death humanely."

Not only did he write with confidence on humanity's future, Wells also assumed the ability to reconstruct its past. The first chapters of his *Outline of History* (1919) portray in exhaustive detail exactly how man the beast evolved from his beastly ancestors, largely deduced from the cave drawings of animals found in France and Spain. Wells's *Outline* inspired the Catholic essayist Hilaire Belloc to write a *Companion to the Outline of History*, which chapter by chapter exposed the Wells book as manifest nonsense. Enraged, Wells wrote *Mr. Belloc Objects* (1926), much of it a personal attack on Belloc (including unflattering references to his weight), to which Belloc replied with yet another book, *Mr. Belloc Still Objects* (also 1926).

All this had brought into the fray the redoubtable G. K. Chesterton with his own "outline of history" entitled *The Everlasting Man* (1925). Those cave drawings, Chesterton noted, assuredly did disclose one certain fact about our early

Author H. G. Wells (top) is seen in a turn-of-the-century photograph. Below left is a poster advertising the 1935 film version of one of his many futuristic novels, Things to Come. *An atheist, Darwinist, and keen eugenics supporter, Wells promoted a future with "no pity and less benevolence" toward the "unfit." Wells's positions ignited a verbal war between him and the Anglo-French Catholic writer Hilaire Belloc (below right).*

Joseph Mengele

I admit we have had to infringe on your rights. My own defense is that small claims must give way to great. As far as we know, we are doing what has never been done in the history of man, perhaps never in the history of the universe. We have learned how to jump off this speck of matter on which our species began. Infinity and therefore perhaps eternity is being put into the hands of the human race. You cannot be so small-minded as to think that the right or the life of an individual or of a million individuals are of the slightest importance in comparison with this.

The mindset behind the eugenics phenomenon is here recognizable, but elsewhere Lewis outlined the warning much more specifically. The coming great peril, he declared, would be a sanitized technological despotism which already was becoming apparent. "It is not now done in those sordid 'dens of crime' that Dickens loved to paint. It is not done even in concentration camps and labour camps. But it is conceived and ordered in clean, carpeted, warmed and well-lighted offices, by quiet men with white collars and cut fingernails, and smooth-shaven cheeks, who do not need to raise their voice." They are not "bad men" in the old sense of the word. "They are not men in the old sense at all. They are, if you like, men who have sacrificed their own share of traditional morality in order to devote themselves to the task of deciding what 'Humanity' will henceforth mean" (from the introduction to a 1961 edition of *The Screwtape Letters*).

The coming peril, declared Lewis, would be a sanitized technological despotism, not done in concentration camps, but in clean, carpeted, well-lighted offices.

Lewis's message was clear: any society that replaces the old morality with a new man-made code of its own will become an intolerable tyranny. Man's so-called "dominion over nature" would come to mean the dominion of some few men over most other men. Lewis was particularly conscious of the dangers and delusions inherent in all forms of utopianism, observes British columnist Philip Vander Elst, "whether social, scientific or religious," and scientism through its various manifestations represented all three. "In a word," Lewis wrote, "it is the belief that the supreme moral end is the perpetuation of our own species, and this is to be pursued even if, in the process of being fitted for survival, our species has to be stripped of all those things for which we value it—of pity, of happiness, and of freedom."

Meanwhile, the attack upon religion gathered momentum, notwithstanding setbacks on the eugenics front. It was assumed, writes historian Alister McGrath in *The Twilight of Atheism: the Rise and Fall of Disbelief in the Modern World* (2006), that sooner or later this war between science and religion "could only lead to the elimination of religious belief as a relic of a superstitious age that was now long behind us." Three views held sway in academe, writes McGrath: that science represented liberation from superstition; that science provided proof where religion rested on myth and legend; that evolution had made belief in God impossible.

An increasing emphasis was laid on the erosion of intellectual progress by religion. Because of religion's degenerative effect, wrote Julian Huxley in 1936, "humanity will gradually destroy itself within; it will decay in its very core and

6. For clarity, brevity, sanity, and comedy, David Berlinski is arguably the most effective champion of religion against the assault of scientism since G. K. Chesterton and C. S. Lewis. But Berlinski describes himself as "a secular Jew whose religious education did not take." He speaks, therefore, as a nonbeliever. He regards the current defense of religion as wholly inadequate, and dedicated his book, *The Devil's Delusion: Atheism and Its Scientific Pretensions* (2008), to his maternal grandfather, who perished at Auschwitz. He is writing, that is, in defense of the faith of his grandfather.

essence, if this slow but relentless process is not checked." Science, on the other hand, promised "a sublime society." Scientists, declaimed Oxford chemistry professor Peter Atkins, "are the summit of knowledge, beacons of rationality, and intellectually honest," and "there is no reason to suppose that science cannot deal with every aspect of existence, since science is the apotheosis of the intellect and the consummation of the Renaissance."

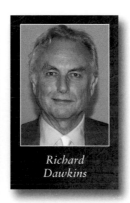

C. S. Lewis's space trilogy, shown above, attacked the eugenicist utopianism of H. G. Wells. The third book in the series, That Hideous Strength, *portrays a society where man-made "scientific" codes of conduct have replaced the old morality and created an intolerable cruelty. "In a word," Lewis wrote, "it is the belief that the supreme moral end is the perpetuation of our own species, and this is to be pursued even if, in the process of being fitted for survival, our species has to be stripped of all those things for which we value it—of pity, of happiness, and of freedom."*

As the century unfolded, observes philosopher and mathematician David Berlinski, the continuing attacks on religious belief had the effect of consolidating religious skepticism around science.[6] "From cosmology to biology, its narratives became *the* narratives... Like any militant church, this one [science] places a familiar demand before all others: 'Thou shalt have no other gods before me.'" It also acquired the equivalent to a bench of bishops: Nobel physics laureate Steven Weinberg ("I think one of the great historical contributions of science is to weaken the hold of religion"); particle physicist Victor J. Stenger ("The belief in supernatural forces remains to this day a yoke on the neck of humanity"); evolutionary biologist Richard Dawkins ("The Universe we observe has precisely the properties we should expect if there is, at bottom, no design, no purpose, no evil, no good, nothing but blind pitiless existence"); Nobel molecular biologist laureate James Watson ("The biggest advantage to believing in God is you don't have to understand anything, no physics, no biology").[7]

Darwin's theory was advanced as fact in the media and accepted as such by the intelligentsia. High school textbooks offered detailed illustrations showing how man emerged through *piscaform* and *simian* stages to his present state. Black moths survive in sooty industrial districts where white moths do not (thus demonstrating evolution at work today), and how the fossil record traces the gradual progress of species from lower to higher—all indisputable evidence of evolutionary development. There could be no further argument.

But argument there was, and from an unexpected source—the law faculty of the University of California, Berkeley. Professor Phillip E. Johnson, who was raised a nominal Congregationalist, turned nominal skeptic in university, and then, after a failed marriage, became a born-again Presbyterian Christian, and

7. One notable dissenter from this "bishops' bench" of atheist scientists was French geneticist and pediatrician Jérôme Lejeune (1926–1994), who identified the chromosomal abnormality that causes Down syndrome, or Trisomy 21. His research revolutionized the field of genetics, but Lejeune was horrified to see his findings lead to a steep increase in eugenic abortions, a development he described as "beyond heartbreaking." (A 2009 study in the *British Medical Journal* reported that ninety percent of babies diagnosed *in utero* with Trisomy 21 are aborted.) Lejeune's later years were dedicated to pro-life advocacy at the urging of Pope John Paul II; in 1997 the Catholic Church opened his cause for canonization.

Julian Huxley

Steven Weinberg

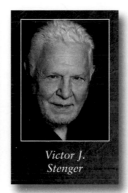

Victor J. Stenger

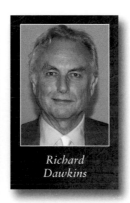

Richard Dawkins

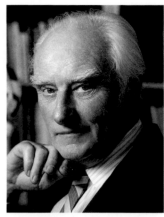

The DNA model built in 1953 by the English molecular biologist Francis Crick (top right) and the American James Watson (bottom). Both men were vigorous opponents of Intelligent Design. "The biggest advantage to believing in God," said Watson, "is you don't have to understand anything: no physics, no biology." Crick proposed that "Darwin Day" be created as a national holiday in Britain.

decided to examine as a lawyer the credibility of the evidence for the evolutionary thesis. Why, for instance, after one hundred forty years of intensive searching, was the "missing link" still missing? Johnson called his book *Darwin on Trial*, and it took him ten years to find a publisher. The big publishing houses make big money publishing expensive textbooks written by the big names in the sciences, and they proved reluctant to see Johnson's skeptical opus reach print.

They had good reason. For Johnson did not challenge evolution on the basis of the Bible, but on what he saw as the inadequacy of supporting scientific evidence, indeed often of its total absence. Where, he asked, were the transitional species—half fish-half lizard, or half lizard-half bird, and the tens of thousands of other transitionals that must have occurred in a gradual evolution such as Darwin described. Where were the fossil or skeletal remains to authenticate those detailed textbook illustrations of evolving man? It turned out that there weren't any. And as for the celebrated black moths, when the sooty districts were cleaned up, the white moths returned. So much for evolution.

When Johnson finally got his book published in 1993, it became an overnight best seller. Devout evolutionists turned on its author with something approaching hysteria, which proved unwise on their part. The fury of their attack focused so much attention on *Darwin on Trial* that over the next ten years Johnson wrote seven more books, and gave rise to a philosophical movement called Intelligent Design (ID). Meanwhile, in *The Design Inference* (1998) and *Intelligent Design* (1999), mathematician and philosopher William Dembski of Southwestern Baptist Theological Seminary provided the philosophical explanation of ID, which was of course, like Carl Sagan's declamation, not a scientific assertion but a philosophical position. It was, however, enough to set Christian parents demanding that schools teach Darwin theory as theory, not fact, and that its deficiencies be taught as well.

One deficiency in particular had been raised in 1972, by preeminent evolutionary biologist Stephen Jay Gould and paleontologist Niles Eldridge. They held that evolutionary change more often occurs in short bursts after long periods with no change at all, and the reason transitional species remained undiscovered was that there weren't very many—maybe none at all. That is, while Gould remained an evolutionist, he dismissed the assumption that the changes must occur gradually. Noted paleontologist Robert Carroll also affirmed this, beginning one paper with the statement: "Most of the fossil record does not support a strictly gradualistic account of evolution." Eugene Koonin of the National Center of Biotechnical Information also agreed. "Major transitions in biological evolution show the same pattern of sudden emergence at a new level of complexity," he wrote. The new types "appear rapidly and fully equipped," and "no intermediate forms between the different types are detectable." Berlinski, however, saw this as more than an incidental amendment to Darwin's original theory. It eliminated the core idea of natural selection. "A gradualistic account of evolution is precisely what Darwin's theory demands. It is the heart and soul of the theory."

There was a further upsetting development for atheists. When the twentieth century began, many scientists assumed the universe had no beginning and would never end, but in 1929 Edwin Hubble discovered that its galaxies are moving outward and away from one another at an increasing speed. This, and the discovery in 1964 of microwave background by American radio astronomers Arno Penzias and Robert Wilson, led to the theory that the universe had begun with an immense explosion—the big bang. Then by a billions-to-one chance, its founding elements coalesced in just the right proportions to permit it to do what it now does. By the end of the twentieth century, most scientists had subscribed to the "big bang" theory. That is, they had concluded the universe did have a starting point, while leaving unanswered the same old conundrum: Who or what provided it?

The American astronomer Edwin Hubble and the hundred inch Hooker Telescope, at the time the world's largest, with which he measured the shifts in the galaxies that led him in the 1930s to determine that the universe was expanding. This revelation led to the confirmation of the big bang theory, which gave the universe a starting point, something hitherto denied by many scientists who held that the universe had always existed. It reopened the old question: Who or what created the Big Bang?

Francis Collins, head of the Human Genome Project, is shown here being sworn in as the director of the U.S. National Institutes of Health in 2009. Seen by some as America's greatest living scientist, Collins alarmed many of his peers when, after reading C.S. Lewis's Mere Christianity, *he became a convert to the Christian faith.*

Finally, in 2003, there came out of Washington the announcement that after thirteen years of research, the Human Genome Project—a team effort of American, British, Japanese, Chinese, French, and German scientists—had identified the twenty to twenty-five thousand genes in human DNA. This opened vast new avenues of research for medicine, many of them undeniably beneficial, but it also opened vast new possible manipulations of human genetics, many of them undeniably dangerous. The announcement was made by the project's leader, Francis Collins. What the announcement did not disclose was that Collins, whom some were calling the greatest American scientist, was in fact a convert to the Christian faith—drawn to it, he later revealed, through the writings of C. S. Lewis (see chapter 19). Collins's book, *The Language of God*, is must reading for every literate Christian at the dawn of the third Christian millennium.

Nor was Collins the only scientist turning toward God. Others also were moving in that direction. Collins quotes cosmologist Robert Jastrow, leading American scientist in the Apollo space program, who remained agnostic but acknowledged one reality: "For the scientist, who has lived by his faith in the power of reason, the story ends like a bad dream. He has scaled the mountains of ignorance; he is about to conquer the highest peak; as he pulls himself over the final rock, he is greeted by a band of theologians who have been sitting there for centuries." ■

Armageddon: a scientific scenario

The atomic age furnished humans with the ability to destroy themselves, and the horrors portrayed by the scientists by far outdo the biblical ones

"It is almost certain that the end of the world will come within the next hundred years, and humanity should begin setting up colonies on Mars to escape this disaster."

This prophecy, made in January 2012, was neither a product of end-times theology nor a new forecast for the Rapture by the Pentecostals. It was, in fact, an observation made by Stephen Hawking, arguably the world's preeminent theoretical physicist, in response to a caller on a BBC open line science show, and it exemplifies a remarkable change that was becoming evident in the last half of the twentieth century. No longer were visions of Doomsday restricted to biblical circles. Scientists had become active in the field, and many of their forecasts were fully as fearsome as anything inspired by the Book of Revelation.

These prophecies of possible disaster began after the Americans dropped the first atomic bombs on Hiroshima and Nagasaki on August 6 and 9, 1945, bringing about the surrender of Japan six days later. As the destructive capability of nuclear weapons soared in the ensuing decades, a chilling truth became clear: for the first time in history, man had the capability to destroy himself. As more and more nations acquired nuclear arms, the likelihood of such an end rose accordingly. Science, in short, while conferring unfathomable powers on humanity, had also made possible humanity's self-annihilation.

The response of governments to this new reality was one of ill-concealed bafflement. During the 1950s and '60s, civil defense systems were instituted in major cities throughout the developed world, although scientific assessments of the magnitude of potential damage soon made defense measures appear close to futile. In England, for example, an organization called Scientists Against

The atom bomb explodes over Nagasaki in 1945, and (inset) an array of the various intercontinental missiles from the Cold War era. For the first time in history, man had acquired the capability to destroy himself.

Stephen Hawking

1. As Wells was rising in his science-fiction career, the greatest collection of physicists ever to assemble convened at Brussels in 1927, twenty-nine in all, to discuss quantum physics. Commenting on their group photograph, science writer Sheila Jones notes in *The Quantum Ten: A Story of Passion, Tragedy, Ambition and Science* (2007) that at that time the renowned physicist Niels Bohr was no longer on speaking terms with the renowned physicist Werner Heisenberg because they had fought over wave-particle duality. Neither was Heisenberg speaking to the renowned physicist Wolfgang Pauli because he was helping Bohr with the duality problem. Pauli meanwhile was despairing because he had been turned down for a professorship, while the renowned physicist Max Born had just suffered another nervous breakdown over his philandering wife. Here, then, was a contemporary sample of Wells's serenely rational human elite.

Nuclear Arms produced a careful study of what would happen if the most probable foe, the Soviet Union, loosed an attack. What they predicted was nothing less than a clinically calibrated horror story.

In approximately one-millionth of a second, the nuclear explosion would release heat tens of million of times more intense than any high explosive used in the Second World War. Deaths would depend on the scale of the attack, set out in the report as levels "A" through "K" ("A" represented forty megatons of bombs, and "K" four hundred megatons—the latter well within the Soviet capability.) An A-level attack would result in five million deaths and ten million total casualties. A K-level attack would produce forty-two million deaths and forty-seven million casualties; only seven million people of a total population of fifty-four million would survive uninjured. Forty-two million would be dead. This assumed a night attack when people would be at home. In a day attack with much of the population packed in crowded downtown offices and factories the toll would be significantly greater.

In a K-level attack more than half of the United Kingdom's land area would be contaminated by nuclear fallout, and more than half its housing facilities destroyed. Since gas and oil pipelines, electric power, and all forms of transportation would be incapacitated, starvation, infectious disease, and radiation sickness would make any human survival problematic. Whether human life survived anywhere else would depend, of course, on the dimensions of the original attack. In the case of a world war, human survival of any kind would become questionable.

American scientists, equally alarmed, established in 1945 the *Bulletin of the Atomic Scientists*, with seventeen Nobel laureates on its board of directors. The *Bulletin* was aimed at the nontechnical reader, detailing nuclear developments as they occurred, and provided public speakers, op-ed pieces, and magazine articles to carry its dire messages. In 1947, it set up what it called "the Doomsday Clock." When events moved the world closer to the "Nuclear Armageddon," the clock was moved closer to midnight. When developments made an open clash less likely, it was moved the other way.

When established, for example, the clock was set at seven minutes to midnight. When the Soviet Union acquired and exploded its first atomic bomb in 1949, it was moved up to three minutes to midnight. In 1953, when the U.S. and Soviet Russia tested thermonuclear devices within nine months of one another, it was moved up to two minutes. It was not changed during the Cuban missile crisis of 1962 because the crisis was over before the clock could be changed. The U.S.-Soviet Partial Test Ban Treaty in 1963 saw it moved back to twelve minutes. The proliferation of nuclear capability to include China, India, and Pakistan, then perhaps to "rogue states" like Iran and North Korea put it ahead to five minutes. The clock is still managed by the *Bulletin of Atomic Scientists*, but has been modified to include "climate change."

In the late 1990s, a new threat to planetary security was added into the calculations with the discovery of "global warming," later known as "climate change," a rise in global temperatures since the late nineteenth century, believed to be caused by increasing concentrations of greenhouse gases produced by fossil fuels and deforestation. The executive editor of the magazine *Scientific American*, Fred Guterl, in his book, *The Fate of the Species: Why the Human Race May Cause Its Own Extinction and How We can Stop It* (2012), sees climate change as the chief threat and envisions within even a few short years the world turned into an uninhabitable desert.

He explores other possible environmental calamities—superbugs, microbes immune to antibiotics, terrorists who might specialize in biological attack, but he leaves a major gap by not fulfilling the implicit promise of his title. He never explains just how we can stop extinction. As critic Gaylord Dold commented at the time in the McClatchy Newspapers, "There is hardly a word about politics, not a mention of religion, ethnicity or migration." Science got

> *The doomsayer Stephen Hawking's observations are instructive, not for what they assert, but for what they ignore.*

us into this, Guterl seems to assume, and science presumably will have to get us out. Just how this would work he does not specify.

But it certainly raises the question of whether dire restrictions and arbitrary action necessary to meet these threats could be accomplished by democratic governments. If not, then presumably by some kind of autocracy. But run by whom? Are we moving toward government by a scientific elite, the benevolent despotism envisioned in the novels of science-fiction writer H. G. Wells, who assumed that scientists would not be prone to the pride and arrogance of lesser men, and would therefore preserve peace, justice, and prosperity?[1]

Even the doomsayer Stephen Hawking becomes uncharacteristically reticent on this point. He sees nuclear war, climate change, or disease all capable of wiping out humanity, and he is absolutely certain of one thing. Religion must play no significant role in the future. Following publication of his book *A Brief History of Time* (1988), he took to making pronouncements on various subjects ever more distantly removed from theoretical physics. On heaven: "There is no heaven or afterlife for broken-down computers; that is a fairy story for people afraid of the dark." On women: "They are a complete mystery, though I spend most of the day thinking about them." On God: "God is not necessary; the universe was made by the big bang."

Perhaps most revealing, however, is Hawking's observation: "Almost all of us must sometimes wonder: Why are we here? Where do we come from? Traditionally, these are questions for philosophy, but philosophy is dead. Philosophers have not kept up with modern developments in science. Particularly physics." He continues: "Scientists have become the bearers of the torch of discovery in our quest for knowledge." New theories "lead us to a new and very different picture of the universe and our place in it." His observations are instructive, not for what they assert, but for what they ignore, notably the fact that science can offer no information as to how humans *should* behave. It can tell us what humans *do*, but not what they *should do* or *ought to do*.

Of one thing Hawking seems assured: religion is passé. As another notable physicist, Nobel laureate Steven Weinberg, at a 2007 conference entitled "Beyond Belief: Science, Religion, Reason and Survival":

The environmental group Greenpeace flies a helium-filled snowman at the 2007 G8 Summit in Germany, publicizing the phenomenon of climate change as man-made. Science has produced most of the modern world's potential catastrophes, but has trouble telling us what can be done about them, and especially what ought to be done.

"Religion is an insult to human dignity. With or without it, you would have good people doing good things and evil people doing evil things. But for good people to do evil things, that takes religion."

Weinberg was warmly applauded, notes mathematician and essayist David Berlinski in *The Devil's Delusion: Atheism and Its Scientific Pretensions* (2008), "but not one member of his audience asked the question one might have thought pertinent: Just *who* has imposed on the suffering human race poison gas, barbed wire, high explosives, experiments in eugenics, the formula for Zyklon B, heavy artillery, pseudo-scientific justifications for mass murder, cluster bombs, attack submarines, napalm, intercontinental ballistic missiles, military space platforms, and nuclear weapons? If memory serves, it was not the Vatican." ∎

Evangelical pastor Joel Osteen delivers a sermon to more than sixteen thousand spectators at his Lakewood megachurch in Houston, Texas, in October 2008. Though it sprang from the fundamentalist tent revivals of the early twentieth century, by the 1970s evangelicalism was building—and filling—church auditoriums the size of sports arenas.

How a lanky farm kid made the 20th century an evangelical victory

With massive rallies for Christ across the world Billy Graham turned a shaky Protestant tradition into a virile gospel vehicle in a very secular age

North American Protestantism entered the second half of the twentieth century strong in numbers but weakened in spirit, bedeviled by doubts, division, and strife. To illustrate just how far it had fallen, historian George Marsden cites the confident assertion of the president of Boston University, William Warren, (in 1873) that American Christians had publicly won every argument worth winning (*The Evangelicals*, 1975). Marsden contrasts that with the cutting comment by atheist H. L. Mencken a half century later that anyone still publicly professing Christianity in educated company could expect to meet open derision. Protestantism had fared ill in the new century, its previous hegemony challenged by massive Catholic immigration, its culture mocked by intellectuals, and its theology rendered seemingly obsolete by science.

By 1950 there were three major strands within Protestantism. They are better described as divergent tendencies rather than as distinct denominations, for the denominational alignment amongst them was—and remains—complex. The first and predominant division comprised the Modernists who, to remain "relevant," had largely renounced scriptural literalism and supernatural beliefs (see chapter 3). Such thinking was to be found in varying degrees at the top of most pre-Civil War mainline denominations—the Episcopalians, American Baptists (but notably not the Southern Baptists), most Presbyterians, United Methodists, Evangelical Lutherans (but not the Missouri Synod Lutherans), and the United Church of Christ, to name only the largest.[1] In 1950 they could still claim the at

1. The American term "mainline Protestant" does not mean "mainstream Christianity." It came into use during the theological controversies over Modernism of the early twentieth century, according to church historian D. Michael Lindsay's *Faith in the Halls of Power: How Evangelicals Joined the American Elite* (2007). The Modernist churches were the large, long-established, modernizing suburban churches along the old main line of the Pennsylvania Railroad west of Philadelphia, in contrast to the more independent and biblically literalist congregations throughout rural America, especially in the South. The term "main line" came to be applied to that whole region of the metropolitan area, embracing several municipalities.

least nominal adherence of most American Protestants, and Protestants collectively still outnumbered Roman Catholics, though the latter formed by far the largest single denomination in the U.S. and Canada.

The second significant but much smaller Protestant stream were the fundamentalists—those who held fast to the "five fundamental" supernatural beliefs of historic Protestant Christianity: the inerrant authority of the Bible; that Jesus, being God, performed physical miracles; that he was born of a virgin; that his physical death on a Roman cross atoned for human sin; and that he rose physically from death and will physically return to earth. Fundamentalism had as yet relatively few churches and seminaries of its own, though these were being established. In addition, an unknowable but large number of "Bible-believing" fundamentalists remained in Modernist mainstream church pews, though not in their leadership.

By the century's end, evangelicalism would become by far the dominant form of American Protestantism, leaving the fundamentalists behind in numbers, dollars, and influence.

At the dawn of the twentieth century, the third Protestant tendency was emerging from among the fundamentalists: people designating themselves as "new evangelicals." By the century's end, evangelicalism would become by far the dominant form of North American Protestantism, leaving both fundamentalist and mainline adherence far behind in numbers, dollars, and influence. However, this distinction between evangelicals and fundamentalists at the mid-century was more cultural than doctrinal; the doctrinal differences did not emerge until the century's closing decades.

The first and many would say the greatest of the evangelical leaders came from a family of modestly prosperous, Bible-believing dairy farmers outside Charlotte, North Carolina. He was born in 1918, and grew into an engaging, mischievous, unscholarly string bean of a youth of the sort everyone likes, especially girls. As a teen in the early thirties, his dreams centered not on God but on baseball. He aspired to be a professional player and the greatest moment of his life up until then came when he shook hands with baseball's greatest star of the early twentieth century, Babe Ruth. The youth's name was Billy Graham.

His life changed in 1934 when, by chance, he delivered a truckload of young people one fall evening to a month-long local tent revival led by an old-style, hellfire Southern evangelist named Mordecai Ham. Seeing the throng of four thousand, Graham stayed to watch. In one evening, Ham convinced Graham that though he was scripturally grounded, well behaved, and active in the church, his faith was superficial. "This man," Graham would later recount with awe, "would stand up there and point his finger at you, and name all the sins you had committed. It made you think your mother had been talking to him." Billy kept coming back as the revival progressed. To avoid Ham's accusing finger and sweeping, searching stare, Billy joined the choir to sit behind him, though he couldn't sing. But at the revival's end, when the rest of the choir sang the evangelical hymn "Almost persuaded now to believe," Billy went forward, as he said, "almost persuaded but lost!" He thus committed his whole life to Christ.

2. Catholics could be racist too, as seen in the 1930s Detroit radio ministry of Father Charles Coughlin. Though initially enthusiastic about the New Deal, by 1934 Coughlin was calling Roosevelt a pawn of Jewish bankers, and by 1938 greeting public rallies with the Nazi salute. Neither the American Catholic hierarchy nor the Vatican could persuade Detroit Bishop Michael Gallagher to silence his priest, though Gallagher's successor, Archbishop Edward F. Mooney, did so. Eventually the federal government revoked Coughlin's broadcast rights and denied him access to the mails. He died in 1979 at age eighty-eight, still writing pamphlets against communism.

Ham was a well-known fundamentalist of precisely the sort Graham would politely distance himself from over the next twenty years—sincere, blunt, and uncompromising on scriptural doctrine—but also judgmental, racist, authoritarian, and unconvincing to most Americans. Many fundamentalists of the twenties and thirties were openly racist and xenophobic, active in the resurgent Ku Klux Klan of the 1920s, and preaching an anti-Catholic, anti-Jewish, antiblack gospel of white Protestant supremacy in the Depression.[2] Even after anxieties over such things eased following the Second World War, fundamentalist Christians retained a reputation for being "militant, schismatic, antischolarly," and generally belligerent, in the description of historian John Gerstner (*The Evangelicals*, 1975).

Graham's call to preach came while he was attending the Florida Bible Institute (nicknamed "the FBI") in the mid-thirties, a new school which attracted visits from the era's best-known radio evangelists. Graham found meeting them thrilling—partly to hear what they said, partly because he was always fascinated by fame, and partly to study their style. Like most good preachers, he was more interested in opening hearts than in filling minds—more in preaching salvation than in debating theology. He led his first tent revival at age twenty. It went so well he was sure that God was showing him his true calling. He switched that summer from Presbyterian to Baptist and was ordained a minister.

Graham pretty much ignored the Second World War

In a 1910 photograph (below left), a solemn rural crowd attends one of the tent revivals popular during the first decades of the century; Billy Sunday (below right), the professional baseball player turned evangelist, strikes one of his "turning out Satan" poses for the camera in 1908; and hellfire southern evangelist Mordecai Ham (top) promotes one of his tent revival meetings from a van in the early 1930s. "This man," said Billy Graham of Ham, "would stand up there and point his finger at you, and name all the sins you had committed. It made you think your mother had been talking to him."

3. After three very productive years at the unaccredited FBI, Graham earned a degree in sociology at Wheaton College near Chicago, then the fundamentalist equivalent of Harvard. It was there he met and married a student named Ruth Bell, a missionary's daaughter who had grown up in the squalid poverty and cultural hostility of China. Until she married Graham, her ambition had been to conduct her own evangelistic mission to Tibet where, she prayed, she would be martyred. Their marriage was a happy one, producing five children. Graham relied heavily on her counsel and encouragement until she died in 2007.

4. Many of Graham's youth ministry associates remained with him lifelong. Not so Charles Templeton of Toronto. Troubled by what he saw as the superficiality of the conversions they were effecting, Templeton quit the YFC team and enrolled in Princeton Theological Seminary, which in the 1950s could still be described as neo-orthodox and broadly Reformed, and inclusive of all the trends in the Presbyterian Church. He encouraged Graham to do likewise. Graham did agree to read some new higher criticism and subjectivist theology, but found it so weakened his faith he soon stopped. The two remained friends after Templeton in 1957 declared himself agnostic.

Norman Vincent Peale, photographed in 1964, and inset, his famous 1952 self-help book, The Power of Positive Thinking, *which stayed on the* New York Times *best-seller list for 186 weeks, and which had, by the end of the century, sold more than five million copies. Peale was a mainline Reformed Church pastor in New York who became extraordinarily wealthy and famous by combining Christianity and psychology.*

after the army rejected him as a battlefront chaplain due to pastoral inexperience. He enrolled in Wheaton College and married.[3] His first salaried ministry was as field representative for a new postwar, Chicago-based evangelistic team called Youth for Christ. (By 2012 it carried a payroll of twenty-two thousand people working in one hundred seventeen countries.) There he joined a core of young evangelists like himself who were quite uninterested in the sectarian rivalries and scriptural battlegrounds that so preoccupied their elders. They came from all branches of Protestantism, including the theologically drifting mainline churches. Their only task, as they saw it, was "loving Jesus supremely," by winning souls who would otherwise burn in hell.[4]

A more auspicious time to evangelize could hardly be conceived. Postwar American society craved two things—prosperity and religion. From this arose Graham's recurrent prediction that a major revival was about to sweep across America. It soon became apparent that he envisioned something far more substantial than the kind of fashionable positive thinking then being preached by the much acclaimed Norman Vincent Peale.[5] People were starting large families and returning to churches in huge numbers. Prewar confidence in the moral promise of science and socialism had been thoroughly shaken by Nazi gas chambers and Soviet gulags, both the work of atheist regimes. A pervasive awareness of the reality of sin and the need for forgiveness had taken hold—everywhere, that is, except in the leadership of the mainline denominations, which continued tracking leftward toward secular utopianism while the rest of society swung back to the right. Any remaining popular faith in one-world utopianism ended when the Soviets, aided by widespread Communist subversion in the West, exploded their first test atomic bomb on the Kazakhstan steppe in 1949.

The young Billy Graham as a student at Wheaton College in the early 1940s, and, left, being greeted dockside by a group of fans on his return from his 1954 Crusade for Christ, during which he preached to more than two and half million in Britain, Sweden, Finland, Holland, Germany, and France.

Graham soon progressed from youth missions in high schools to full-blown citywide evangelistic crusades in the late forties. Highly organized and heavily promoted as interdenominational events, they were immensely popular. Many Americans had concluded that since slave states like Russia were officially atheist, a patriotic American should be Christian. And since mainline churches were soon growing pacifist and ever more left wing, people began gravitating in ever-growing numbers to evangelical "born-again" churches and preachers, especially Graham.

He had a knack of gaining affection and respect from hostile individuals and difficult audiences. William Martin's excellent Graham biography (*A Prophet With Honor*, 1991) recounts Graham's 1954 address to students at the ultra-left-wing London School of Economics. He had just stepped nervously to the podium when one student suddenly leaped in front of it and began cavorting like an ape—in plain mockery of Graham's creationist rejection of evolution. The students all laughed. Graham laughed too, and then said, "He reminds me of my ancestors." The students laughed even louder, this time in appreciation rather than derision. Then Graham added, "Of course, all my ancestors came from Britain." That brought the house down, writes Martin, and, whether or not any students got saved, they listened with open ears to everything he said.

Humor was not much a part of Graham's preaching, however, and he learned to avoid relying on the kind of sentimental anecdotes so popular with many preachers. His dress went from attention getting and bizarre as a youth preacher, to conservative as an adult. He went to great lengths to avoid the odor of sexual and financial scandal that had clung to so many itinerant, nondenominational ministries. Early on, he established the "Billy Graham Rule" that forbade him or any other leader of his ministry from being alone in any room with a woman not his wife. He also put himself on a published salary, adequate but not lavish. He moderated the Carolina twang in his speech. He used guest celebrities to

5. Author of *The Power of Positive Thinking* (1952), best-selling manual of the burgeoning self-help industry, Peale (1898–1993) was a mainline Reformed Church pastor in New York. Like Graham, Peale's energetic output of inspirational speeches, sermons, books, and broadcasts made him one of the most recognized and admired men in America. Graham thought highly of him. Other evangelicals, however, have categorized Peale as an unregenerate materialist whose main message was for people to lay up treasures on earth rather than in heaven.

Denigration of evangelists by the "enlightened" intelligentsia was nothing new. This 1812 painting by the English caricaturist William Hogarth, entitled Credulity, Superstition and Fanaticism, *is believed to depict the preacher George Whitefield, mentor to John Wesley, dangling puppets of a witch and a devil before a congregation in various states of ecstasy, grief, and horror. To the right of the preacher a "scale of vociferation" measures his oratory, rising from "natural tone" to "bull roar."*

encourage the public to fill his rented stadiums and auditoriums.

There he would pace the stage, scanning his audience with mesmerizing intensity, watching for the subtle cues to change his subject or cadence. He cared not at all that he often sounded unsophisticated to educated people—as, for instance, in describing the end-times, when scripture says the dead will arise from their graves to be judged by Christ. "Wait till those gravestones start popping open like popcorn in a popper! Oh boy! Won't it be wonderful when those gravestones start popping!" Even worse, he would act out Bible stories in modern slang, leaping around the stage to portray different characters, and hamming it up so much that his wife Ruth would cringe, and eventually got him to stop. All the same, people loved it.

Graham is not usually ranked above history's greatest revivalists—Billy Sunday, Dwight Moody, Charles Finney, George Whitefield, and John Wesley—but he's in the same league. Attendance at his crusades was remarkable, sometimes astonishing: three hundred fifty thousand in over eight weeks in Los Angeles in 1949;[6] one-half million each in Portland and Atlanta in 1950; three hundred thousand in Washington DC, and another half million in Dallas in 1952; two million in Britain over twelve weeks in 1954 (including "relay" crowds hearing him live via telephone line over loudspeakers in local churches); nearly two and a half million in New York in 1957 over three months; four million in New Zealand and Australia in 1959; three million in Seoul, Korea in 1973. These were just a few of the big ones; there were hundreds of smaller ones.

Graham was the first major televangelist, and the best known worldwide. As his ministry grew, he was backed eventually by a staff of hundreds, and bolstered by tens of thousands of volunteers. Before he was forced into retirement by Parkinson's disease in 2005, Graham had preached in person to eighty million people and to countless more via radio and television. He was the first truly global evangelical preacher, and for five decades ranked as one of the ten most admired men in America.

Throughout his career Graham never really changed his basic sermon. He usually began with a scattering of current news stories (often badly mangled) to show that the world was going to hell—because of communism, youth rebellion, materialism, moral relativism, etc.—and then moved to the straight gospel message that only by repenting and surrendering one's whole life to Jesus could anyone hope to live forever in heaven. There was nothing complicated about it, nothing gimmicky, and Graham never shrank from instilling fear of eternal damnation in his audience, though with age he came to place greater emphasis on grace and mercy.

His new evangelical preaching aligned with all five points of the fundamentalists. The rift that opened between them was over practice, not doctrine. As Graham began attracting vast audiences to his crusades, he encouraged—and then insisted—that mainline Protestant churches help fill them. Few were eager to do so, fearing that many of their members might never come back. They could be lured instead to evangelical/fundamentalist churches. Better, however, to be seen as part of the same crusade than opposed to it, so most pitched in. Graham made a point of never criticizing any denomination, not even Catholic—for as he put it in 1957, "God has people in all churches."[7] This comment—and the broad ecumenism of his new magazine *Christianity Today*—caused a furor among fundamentalists. The few of their leading lights who had not already done so, such as Bob Jones, founder of Bob Jones University in South Carolina, and evangelist and fundamentalist newspaper publisher John Rice, severed their ties.

Thus a rupture that began in the early 1940s was complete in 1957. Graham stood widely accused by leading fundamentalists of fellowship with false Christians—"those who preach apostasy" and a "non-redemptive gospel." *Christianity Today*'s founding editor, Carl Henry, a firm born-again Christian himself, countercharged that fundamentalism evinced "a harsh temperament, a spirit of lovelessness and strife, contributed by much of its leadership." In the end

The public mood was moving away from salvation to personal freedom. No longer would any one form of Christianity be regarded as the 'American way.'

it came down to this: fundamentalists emphasized above all purity of biblical belief, and refused fellowship with any who did not vigorously espouse their core tenets to the exclusion of all others; for as Saint Paul had said (2 Corinthians 6:14) "Come out from among them [the nonbelievers] and be ye separate." Evangelicals, in contrast, emphasized the preeminence of Christ's "great commission," (Matthew 28:19): "Go ye therefore, and teach all nations, baptizing them in the name of the Father, and of the Son, and of the Holy Spirit, teaching them to observe all things whatsoever I have commanded you."

By now the postwar religious boom had run its course. Gone were the days when Congress would pass a special exemption for Billy Graham to preach from the steps of the Capitol, as it did in 1952, or add such words as "[one nation] under God" to the Pledge of Allegiance, as it did in 1954. By 1958 American courts were banning the Lord's Prayer in public schools, and the public mood in the free world was moving away from national salvation toward personal freedom. No longer would evangelical Christianity—or any other form of Christianity—be automatically equated with the "American way."

Graham was just as aware as the fundamentalists that the Bible, though morally demanding of individuals, does not preach any specific political, social, or economic philosophy. Never did Christ or the apostles preach explicitly for or against imperialism, democracy, communism, war, slavery, the sale of alcohol, social equality, or progressive taxation. According to the Bible, the sole explicit mandate of Christianity is to preach the way of personal salvation by total faith

6. The Los Angeles crusade was struggling until one evening a small crowd of local newsmen showed sudden interest, encouraged by a two-word telegram from the famous and enigmatic newspaper tycoon William Randolph Hearst: "Puff Graham." Hearst and Graham never met or corresponded, but Hearst—though something of a California hedonist—approved of religion in general (his newspapers had bolstered Billy Sunday in the twenties), and of Graham's strong anti-Communist message. Hearst died two years later.

7. Leading up to Graham's 1964 crusade in Boston, the city's Catholic archbishop, Cardinal Richard Cushing, declared enthusiastically that Graham preached Christ crucified, and that any Catholic would be stronger for hearing his message. He urged young Catholics to attend the event, and older ones to pray for its success. In a forty-five minute televised conversation with Graham, Cushing said that if the Catholic Church in America had a few more men like Graham its future would be secure, and Graham replied that he found himself "much closer to Roman Catholic traditions than to some of the more liberal Protestants."

The 1963 Billy Graham Crusade at the Los Angeles Coliseum set an all-time attendance record for the facility of 134,254. By now Graham was augmenting his crowds with members of mainline Protestant churches, institutions which he made a point of never criticizing. "God has people in all churches," Graham was fond of saying, causing a furor among fundamentalists.

in Christ through the church. As journalist Richard Wheeler forcefully points out in his 1974 book *Pagans in the Pulpit,* all Christian social or political lessons must be inferred; as for what the Bible actually says, it gives as much comfort—and discomfort—to the political right as to the left.

Yet from the earliest days of the Church, the spiritual conversion of humanity seems naturally to bring with it a strong desire to reform humanity socially and politically. The evangelical tradition going back to Charles Finney in the northeastern states was to add momentum to revivals by attaching social and political causes to the gospel—antislavery, teetotalism, alleviation of poverty, and female suffrage, among others. Southerners like Graham had beheld with rising dismay progressivism and Modernism in the mainline churches elevate these ancillary interests to the primary mission of the faith while the Bible was virtually abandoned.

In reaction, the fundamentalist/evangelical movements had largely renounced any kind of social and political activism, thereby lapsing into indifference. In their view, discipleship (i.e., discipline) demanded a godly personal life; the outward signs of which were an ordered family and church life, one proof of which was complete abstinence from cursing, drinking, and smoking. Their disinterest in secular social reform was compounded by a growing conviction among many, after the state of Israel was established in 1948, that the end-times were about to happen. The Lord Jesus would now return to rule the earth "with a rod of iron" and would look after all such matters.

As political issues go, Graham's anticommunism had been safe enough—it had been a fundamentalist article of faith since the twenties—but by the late 1950s important new causes were arising. The most dangerous to evangelical unity was the rising clamor for racial desegregation of the South. Hailing as he did from the old Confederacy, Graham knew the racial issue to be volatile, but early on positioned himself against segregation. He considered it unchristian. The apostle Paul said that the church does not distinguish between races; free association between Jews and gentile nations was the practice of the early church (with great scandal to Jews at the time). In 1952, six years before the Montgomery bus boycott (see chapter 11), Graham began insisting (with a couple of lapses) that there be no racial seating divisions at his revivals—even in Southern states where mixed seating was against both law and custom. For preaching that God judges the heart, not the skin, Graham turned many white Southerners against him. Racists preferred the fundamentalists, many of whom remained staunchly pro-segregation.[8]

Graham said he could see no justification for legal color bars at all; but like most Southern liberals he would have preferred to allow progress to be made over time, not forced by judges and politicians in Washington. His "gradualism" provoked scorn from more radical mainline clergy and Southern blacks. Among them was Martin Luther King Jr., who preached at Graham's New York crusade in 1957. Though King disagreed with Graham's gradualism and Graham disagreed with King's radical agenda and civil disobedience, they remained amicable, and both sought an end to segregation.

Another sign of changed times for Graham was the razor-thin presidential victory of John F. Kennedy over Richard Nixon in 1960. For eight years Graham had enjoyed personal access to and friendship with Republican President Dwight Eisenhower, probably America's most openly religious president. Graham was

8. President Bill Clinton recounted to evangelist Pat Robertson in 2008, "Neighborhood after neighborhood after neighborhood in my state [Arkansas] was on the verge of violence, yet tens of thousands of black and white Christians were there together in a football stadium. And when [Graham] issued the call at the end of this message, thousands came down holding hands, arm in arm, crying. It was the beginning of the end of the old South in my home state. I will never forget it."

Billy Graham allied himself with virtually every U.S. president through his sixty-year preaching career, the exception being Harry S. Truman (who considered Graham a self-aggrandizing "counterfeit"). Here Graham can be seen with Richard Nixon (left) at a crusade in 1970, with John F. Kennedy at a dinner in 1962, and with former presidents (left to right) Jimmy Carter, George H.W. Bush, and Bill Clinton at the dedication of the Billy Graham Library in 2007.

Conservatively inclined evangelicals, while deeply admiring of Graham's undoubted evangelical accomplishments, are far less positive about his politics. In his autobiography, *Just As I Am*, they note, Graham proves himself a thoroughgoing liberal. All his political causes were liberal causes. He is delighted to report that President Johnson described him as a great liberal, and he said little on the abortion question. However, the politician Graham supported most unreservedly and ultimately to his own dismay was the Republican Richard Nixon. Thereafter, he vowed no further political alliances. Yet he was warmly devoted to Bill Clinton and promoted Clinton's wife, Hillary, as a presidential candidate in his last crusade.

even closer to Ike's vice president, Nixon, a man of his own generation. The evangelist refrained (as ever) from criticizing Kennedy's Catholicism during the 1960 campaign, but had actively supported Nixon. Nevertheless, Graham established friendly although not close relations with the Kennedy White House. After Kennedy's 1963 assassination, Graham, much to his surprise, was warmly received by President Lyndon Johnson. They became good friends—partly because the association served their mutual interest, partly because of Graham's continued anticommunism and support for the war in Vietnam and Great Society welfare programs, and partly because of Johnson's personal fundamentalist background in Texas. He was the first serving president to attend a Graham crusade.[9]

In religion, as in everything else, the sixties were a watershed. Ancient prejudices, principles, and national virtues—about race, sex, parental authority, manliness, manners, patriotism, public prayer and religious belief—appeared to be collapsing on all sides. In 1966 *Time* magazine asked on its cover "Is God Dead?" What it meant, of course, was "Is Christianity finished?"

Mainline Protestant denominations apparently thought it was. Seeing society moving once again in a left-liberal direction, they spoke with growing confidence and stridency against the Vietnam War, the arms race, racism, capitalism, and traditional belief (see subchapter, page 289). Theologically they joined a strong secular transition from Modernism (adapting God to science) to post-Modernism (God is whatever you conceive him to be). Based on this new subjectivism, and despite the absence of new scholarly support of any significance, they asserted their biblical skepticism more strongly than ever.

Yet an odd thing happened on the way to God's funeral. Through all the tumult of that turbulent decade, Graham's massive ministry changed

A 2008 Christmas spectacular at the Thomas Road Baptist Church in Lynchburg, Virginia (right), founded by Jerry Falwell (above) in the late sixties, along with the Christian liberal arts campus Liberty University. By the second decade of the twenty-first century, Thomas Road had a membership of twenty-four thousand.

neither its message nor its course, and just got bigger and bigger. While membership in mainline Modernist churches began to sag and then plummet, evangelical and fundamentalist churches continued to grow, and new ones to appear. New Protestant televangelists—some later to become disreputable, others not—were building mass audiences. The sixties saw the rise of the first megachurches, with memberships far above previous norms, some exceeding ten thousand. The era also produced the spectacular if short-lived Jesus Movement.[10]

In 1966, a dynamic young pastor named Jerry Falwell established Thomas Road Baptist Church in Lynchburg, Virginia. By the end of the decade it would seat three thousand people at once, and by the end of the century reported average weekly attendance of more than thirteen thousand. It launched a radio broadcast, then a television program, and opened a large mission hospice for alcoholics. In 1971, Falwell founded the Christian liberal arts campus Liberty University, which by 2012 had grown to a residential enrollment of over twelve thousand and online course enrollment of eighty thousand more.

Another pastor who rose to prominence in the sixties was Pat Robertson. The son of a Virginia federal senator, he served as a Marine in Korea, and afterward trained in law.[11] Then he underwent a serious conversion to evangelical

10. The Jesus Movement emerged within the hippie counterculture during the sixties and early seventies, spreading from the West Coast across North America and over to Europe, and fostering in America the development of both the Christian Right and the Christian Left. It persuaded tens of thousands of young people to live in communes, bearing names like the Shiloh Communities and the Children of God. The movement reached its zenith in 1972 when it attracted eighty thousand to what it called Explo '72 in Dallas. Its most lasting impact upon the churches came with its adaptation of the music of then hippies to the message of the gospel.

When the tapes revealed Nixon to be a foul-mouthed, manipulative cynic, Graham reacted with tears and vomiting after forcing himself to read the transcript.

Christianity. Ordained a Southern Baptist minister in 1961, like Graham, he found his vocation in religious broadcasting, and more than Graham in politics.

All three men—Falwell, Robertson, and Graham—plainly saw political involvement as necessary to their evangelism in various ways. Graham, after his good friend Richard Nixon won the presidency for the Republicans in 1968, found himself back in constant contact with world decision makers in the White House. His own role soon went far beyond spiritual counsel to partisan advice and cooperation. Even more than with Lyndon Johnson, Graham was aware that at a purely political level he was using and being used by Nixon; after all, that is how politics works. At a deeper spiritual level, however, he remained convinced that he was doing God's work, not just the Republican Party's, and after Nixon, his ongoing political alliances favored the Democrats.

As the sixties reached their chaotic finale with ghetto riots, slain students, drug addiction, and a pervasive sense of social disorder, Graham publicly lauded and promoted Nixon as a great Christian leader. And when in 1973 it began to look likely that Nixon had sanctioned criminal behavior by his own staff during his 1972 reelection campaign and then helped try to cover it up (see chapter 12), Graham remained loyal almost to the end. At first he belittled the Watergate "escapade," and as incriminating evidence mounted, he saw Nixon as King David, a holy hero beset by small-minded critics. When the Watergate tapes revealed Nixon to be a foul-mouthed and manipulative cynic, Graham, after forcing himself to read the transcript, reacted with weeping and vomiting. Strangely,

11. Pat Robertson served in the Korean War, but managed, likely through help from his senator father, to stay safely in the rear— apparently stocking liquor in officers' clubs. When he ran for the Republican presidential nomination in 1986, his claim that he was a decorated "combat veteran" proved highly embarrassing when soldiers who remembered him said it was untrue. Worse, he sued one of them for defamation for thirty-five million dollars, but backed down before trial and paid the man's court costs.

The endless quest for the end-times

Crowds jeered the Millerites when the earth failed to vanish, but the day would come when their descendants ran the second biggest Christian school system in the world

On October 22 of the year 1844, thousands of men, women, and children from the northern United States—up to half a million by some estimates—left their houses, trudged to the hilltops, even climbed into apple trees, to await the Second Coming of Jesus. Some had made white "ascension robes" and many had quit their jobs and sold their homes and goods because, they were convinced, at midnight a great trumpet would sound, the heavens would break open, and Jesus Christ would come in power and glory to draw all true believers up into paradise. And all their scornful former friends and neighbors ("Babylonians") would be consigned to eternal perdition.

Midnight passed, Jesus did not appear, and there came the Great Disappointment. The faithful wept and lamented until dawn. The ridicule they had suffered on their way up was as nothing to what greeted them going back down. Many were so embarrassed they left town; some left Christianity entirely. Few would ever again heed the likes of William Miller, the self-

taught Baptist whose complex scriptural analysis over twenty years had persuaded him and so many others that the world would end in 1844. A tiny remnant of Miller's original following held on and formed the Seventh Day Adventist Church, which would one day operate the second largest denominational school system in the world, after the Roman Catholics.[1]

Early nineteenth-century New England, however, was alive with theological innovation, as was Britain, and many people were delving into "eschatology," the study of what will come at the end of life and at the end of the world. This involved elaborately interpreting numerous Bible prophecies by Daniel, Ezekiel, Isaiah, Jesus, Paul, Peter, and the writer of the Book of Revelation.

In the 1830s, even before the Great Disappointment, an Anglican priest named John Darby was working out a new interpretation called "premillennial dispensationalism," which was then spread from Britain to Protestant Europe by a new sect called the Plymouth Brethren.[2] Revivalist Dwight Moody

Fifteenth-century German painter Stefan Lochner's The Last Judgment. *Medieval and Renaissance millennialism enjoyed a rebirth in nineteenth-century America as various branches of evangelical Christianity attempted to put a date on Armageddon—an enthusiasm that continued into the next century and became known as end-times eschatology.*

In 2011 the eighty-nine-year-old American Christian radio broadcaster Harold Camping (left) became the latest in a long line of prognosticators to set a date for the end of the world and the Second Coming, as displayed on his Judgment Bus, shown here parked outside Camping's California radio station. According to one source, 254 such dates have been predicted through the centuries, beginning with that of the Jew Thaddeus in 44 AD.

brought it to America in the 1870s, and over the next century it became the official or quasi-official belief of most evangelical and fundamentalist churches—though it has developed numerous variations. Because it rejects the general Christian understanding of the previous centuries, both Catholic and Protestant, it met resistance, and even some evangelicals still reject it entirely.

By interpreting and counting forward from a lengthy and difficult prophecy of Daniel in the sixth century BC, and considering what Jesus said later and what the apostle Paul wrote in his first letter to Christians in Thessalonica, Darby concluded that the world is nearing an end. Before it does, Jesus will revisit the earth secretly and remove into heaven all true believers, living and deceased. The living left behind will suffer for seven years the worst calamities ever to befall humanity, and then Jesus will appear in force at Armageddon with all his angels and saints. God will vanquish and imprison Satan and destroy his chieftains. This will usher in a thousand-year reign of peace on earth.

Then, said Darby, Satan will be released from prison, rally his still potent forces which have been biding their time, and they will meet a final and eternal defeat. Satan will be cast into hell forever, with all his friends and allies. There will come a Second Judgment, the dead will rise from their graves, and those living and those now raised will be sent to heaven or to hell. The earth as we have known it will be dissolved in fire, and God will create a new eternal earth and a new heaven.

Traditional Christian eschatology, following the teaching of Saint Augustine, is less complex. It was held that Daniel prophesied that four great earthly kingdoms would precede the coming of God's kingdom on earth: the Babylonian empire, the Persian, the Hellenic, and the Roman, at which point Jesus appeared and founded his kingdom in the form of the Christian Church. The millennium spoken of in Revelation is an era not to be reckoned neatly as one thousand years but simply as a long time, and a time, less of peace than of faith, when the demons of paganism are driven back by the church.

According to the traditional view, most of the dire future events Jesus prophesied to his disciples concerned the horrifying siege of Jerusalem and the destruction of the Jewish Temple unleashed by the Romans forty years later (see volume 1, chapter 9). However, he also made clear that at the end of the age there will be widespread apostasy, terrible tribulation, and a resurgence of Satan's power over the earth. Then out of mercy Christ will return with his angels and saints, defeat Satan and his legions, judge the living and the dead, and create a new earth and a new heaven.

Perhaps the greatest difference between the two major eschatologies is over what Jesus meant when he proclaimed (repeatedly) that "the kingdom of God is at hand." Until 1830, even most Protestants believed, as did the Fathers of early Christianity, that the kingdom and the Church were the same thing, though by the Church they did not include the visible church on earth, but only the Church in heaven. Dispensationalists, in contrast, believe Jesus meant reestablishment of the ancient Hebrew kingdom of David, and that when the Jews rejected Jesus, God chose to hold back the millennium until they are convinced. That is why there has been such interest among dispensationalists since 1948 in the creation and defense of the State of Israel. Dispensationalists commonly believe that the end-times will begin when the Jews rebuild the Temple and resume animal sacrifices, and that Jesus will reign over the earth from Jerusalem.

All Christians do still agree on one thing: the Day of the Lord could come soon, with dispensationalists insisting that it *will* come soon. With a few unfortunate exceptions, they have refrained from precise date setting, partly because Jesus warned us not to do it and partly because it makes Christians look like fools when they're wrong. ∎

1. Miller's ideas were dismissed in the white South as just another ridiculous Yankee notion, along with banking and the abolition of slavery. However, black slaves sweating in the cotton fields were heard to sing about Jesus coming soon to deliver them.

2. In addition to numerous evangelical church denominations, the nineteenth century incubated the Mormons, Christian Science, and the Jehovah's Witnesses. The Witnesses have predicted the Second Coming on seven different dates between 1914 and 1994 (see volume 11, page 157).

he afterward expressed strong disapproval of Nixon's foul language, not that he had probably lied to Congress and obstructed justice.[12]

Graham said afterward he had learned a sharp lesson from the Watergate affair, writes biographer Martin, namely that he must never again "get that close to someone in office." In later years he retained his quasi-official status as Protestant chaplain to most presidents, but avoided politics until Bill and Hillary Clinton came on the scene. Besides, Graham's main focus in 1974 was on something very different—the first genuine worldwide congress of evangelical leaders. That summer it brought two thousand four hundred clergy and lay activists of all races and colors, both sexes, and from all inhabited continents to Lausanne, Switzerland. The International Congress on World Evangelization in ten days was to lay the groundwork for the completion of Christ's great commission. Much advance effort was made to reduce the risk that the congress would hang up on two vital issues: how much latitude to allow cultural and national differences within the faith, and how best to balance Christian evangelism with social, moral, and political activism.

For example, should converts from Islam be allowed to continue their lifelong discipline of prayer five times daily, simply switching their prayer from Allah to God the Father, Son, and Holy Spirit? Earlier western missionaries had often been far from flexible on such points. How much tolerance should be afforded to antibiblical native social customs—such as polygamy or adultery? Should evangelicals support justifiable rebellions? Is evangelical Christianity inherently capitalist, or can it also be socialist? Should western values as regards the role and rights of women be expected of converts in more puritanical and patriarchal cultures? If no native evangelist is available for a mission, is a western substitute better than

A modern view of Lausanne, Switzerland, site of the 1974 International Congress on World Evangelization, which Graham helped organize alongside World Vision. The congress brought together twenty-four hundred Bible-believing clergy and lay activists of all races and colors to reach a consensus on how much latitude to give cultural and national differences within the faith, and how best to balance Christian evangelism with social, moral, and political activism. Among the sensitive questions considered: How much tolerance should be accorded witch doctors and polygamists?

none? Should evangelical churches cooperate with each other and with nonevangelical Christians? What about with Buddhists or animist witch doctors? Hundreds of such questions were urgently in need of clear answers.

What was not open to debate was whether Christians should stop preaching the gospel in deference to an opposing majority or official faith in any country, be it Hindu, Muslim, tribal animism, or Communist atheism. Though the mainline churches' decision in the 1930s to ally with other religions and shift their missionary purpose from preaching the gospel to social work had ruptured Protestantism, this was not a point evangelicals were willing to concede.

Believers from hundreds of isolated and beleaguered missions around the globe realized, many for the first time, that they were a crucial part of a worldwide army.

Nor did they. The overarching answer to all questions, summarized in the Lausanne Covenant and developed in considerable practical detail, was that the church is neither right wing nor left wing, has no superior national language, and no national culture has any inherently superior position within it. It has only one constant task—to preach salvation in Christ through the gospel. Social action of all sorts—political, economic, and cultural—derives from that prime imperative, and is to be encouraged where necessary, but must never supersede it.

Lausanne—which many third-world evangelicals consider Billy Graham's greatest achievement—came to a powerful consensus on even the stickiest differences. Exhilarated believers from hundreds of isolated and beleaguered mission outposts around the globe realized, many for the first time, that they were a crucial part of a worldwide army of preachers offering salvation in Christ to everyone on the planet. Lausanne bolstered initiatives like World Vision, founded in 1950 to support evangelical foreign missions, which had played a major part in organizing the congress. (World Vision in 2008 had a budget of $2.6 billion and 44,500 employees, ninety percent of them working in their own countries scattered all across the earth.)

Meanwhile, in the United States evangelical Christians were being recruited by 1980 into the new Religious Right, or Moral Majority, to elect Ronald Reagan and take over the Republican Party. They had reason to do this; in fact some saw themselves as being driven into it. The Supreme Court's *Roe v. Wade* decision in 1973, which had made abortion the pivotal issue in what was shaping up as a cultural war, had changed the political landscape. Evangelicals now saw issues of faith lying beneath the political issues. They also saw that the Democrats were making it clear they had no place for anyone who was going to oppose the new social order. So, despised as they were by the so-called "blue bloods" of the Republican Party, it offered the only place evangelicals could fight in the cultural war.

The Moral Majority's highest-profile promoters were the above-mentioned televangelists, Jerry Falwell and Pat Robertson. Graham, better known than either of them, politely wished them well. In *Christianity Today* he cautioned them not to let politics blur their spiritual focus. "In my earlier days," he explained to a 1980 media conference, "I tended to identify the Kingdom of God with the American way of life. I don't think like that now." He was beginning by now to

12. Graham kept in touch with Nixon until the latter died in 1994, and said that Nixon became increasingly spiritual after leaving office. Graham urged people not to judge the man, because after all "there's a little bit of Watergate in all of us." He blamed much of Nixon's misfortunes on sleeping pills, for "all through history drugs and demons have gone together." And after John F. Kennedy's presidential sexual escapades were exposed in 1975, Graham said in favor of Nixon, "At least he didn't have nude women running around the private quarters of the White House."

An eighty-six-year-old Graham is assisted to the podium by his son Franklin for the last night of his final crusade in 2005 before an adoring throng of sixty thousand in a New York City park. By now evangelicalism was well ensconced in the new political right, an affiliation that Graham had tried to avoid.

wind down and hand things over to the eldest of his five children, Franklin. In 2005, shortly before his wife died, "America's pastor" struggled to the microphone leaning on a walker and preached his last crusade to an adoring throng of sixty thousand in a New York City park. He was eighty-six.

But while it's easy to say "evangelism first, activism second," politics has a way of sidelining everything else—something it soon began doing in the United States. Whether its political venture had strengthened or compromised American evangelicalism it was too early to say. However, in the opening years of the twenty-first century, evangelical churches certainly appeared to remain generally robust, though their overall membership had crested.[13]

Moreover, a serious problem appeared to have developed. Churches cannot seal themselves off from the culture in which their members live, along with the unsaved people they are trying to convert. The anti-authoritarianism which sank such lasting social roots in the sixties, and the pervasive ethos of relativism that came with it, inevitably affected the churches. It became customary for people—including many Christians—to say and think: "After all, we cannot really and truly *know* anything." Or, "That's your truth, but not mine." Or, "Jesus is about love and wouldn't send anyone to hell." Or, "All religions are really saying the same thing." Or, "I'm into spirituality, not religion." Or, "People are basically good." All these statements are counterbiblical, and yet the thoughts they express have become so culturally ingrained that few pastors dare challenge them.

Since its origins, Protestantism has talked about being "washed in the blood of Christ." Above or near most Catholic altars is the likeness of a tortured man spiked to a cross. The central message of all biblical and creedal Christianity has been that God so hates sin, and so loves humanity, that he entered his own creation and died on a cross to atone for sin's hellish consequences, and to save for all eternity those who truly believe in him. But how can churches convince people this is true if people have come to believe that truth and God, sin, and hell—if they exist at all—are whatever you conceive them to be? This condition is called religious post-Modernism.

A Protestant strength, especially in America, has always been innovation—though it brings with it a tendency toward faddishness. In the early seventies, Trinity College, Illinois, student and youth pastor Bill Hybels reasoned that the way to get post-Modernists into church, is to apply consumer marketing techniques to evangelism, starting with a customer survey: "What would you want from a church?" From the survey's answers he built Willow Creek Community Church in the Chicago suburb of South Barrington, with average weekly attendance by 2011

13. The evangelical denomination with by far the most members, the Southern Baptists, saw their membership peak in 2006 at 16.3 million and then begin a slow but steady decline.

The megachurch phenomenon blossomed in the late sixties and seventies, and remained robust into the new millennium. Clockwise from top left: a scene from a nativity play in front of the Crystal Cathedral in Garden Grove, California; President Bill Clinton answers questions on his spiritual well-being posed by Willow Creek Community Church founder Bill Hybels; a crowd at Houston's Lakewood Church on opening day, July 16, 2005; and churchgoers at Willow Creek watch video monitors as pastor Bo Boshers preaches during a Sunday service in April 1995.

of twenty-four thousand (including five electronically tied-in outlying congregations in the Chicago area), making it the third-largest church in the U.S.[14]

What the market wanted, he found, was a friendly, busy community with plenty of social support and outreach. What it did *not* want was "churchiness"—crosses, pews, stained-glass windows, moralistic preachiness, and money collections. In stages, Hybels built a nondenominational campus—a massive steel and glass, seven thousand-seat auditorium and office complex, with a lake and fountain on one side, and on the other a stadium-sized, color-coded parking lot with Sunday morning traffic directors and a shuttle service. There's not a cross in sight; from outside, the place could pass for a modern college or corporate office complex, and inside it feels like (and is) a vast, very up-to-date concert hall. Sunday worship services (or "gatherings"—two in English, one in Spanish) start with loud electric music and usually include a lot of professional musical and dramatic presentations on a twenty-eight foot, high-definition LED video screen.

Most of Keller's parishioners are young professionals: brokers and lawyers. They don't want loud sound, but to find why they are alive and what to do.

There is some audience singing, some scripture and a lively sermon. About the only day of the year there isn't nonstop activity is Christmas, when everyone stays home to be with family.

Yet despite all its departures from past practice, Willow Creek's theology is generally acknowledged to be straight five-point fundamentalism—though much of the emphasis in the auditorium is on good feelings and community, not on the Bible. The more serious Christianity takes place in smaller groupings and gatherings; this on the premise that once people are in the seats, some will immerse themselves fully in the faith, but not if they never start. This became known as the "seeker-friendly" church model, and spread rapidly across evangelical North America.

A different American seeker-friendly approach is demonstrated by Redeemer Presbyterian in Manhattan. Pastored by Tim Keller, aided by his wife Kathy, evangelical Presbyterians who arrived from Pennsylvania in 1989, it grew from zero to five thousand in three locations over the next twenty years. Keller, formerly a professor from Virginia, delivers the sermon from all three pulpits each Sunday, in a calm, quiet voice, and sticks to a straight Calvinist gospel message. There are no fancy electronics, congregants worship from simple printed service sheets with mostly traditional hymns accompanied by an organ and a brass quartet (there's a jazz service in the evening).

Keller's parishioners are mostly twenty- and thirty-something professionals: accountants, brokers, lawyers. They don't want excitement—loud sound and bright lights. Working as so many do in the most stressful jobs in the world, they get excitement enough during the week. They want to know why they are alive, and what beyond making money they should be doing. Keller, author of the best seller *The Reason for God* (2009), has insisted that it was not actually hard to find and bring them together. If approached intelligently and sympathetically—whether

14. The Hartford Institute for Religion Research defines a megachurch as Protestant, led by a strong pastor (almost invariably a man), having congregational and community activities almost daily, and self-reported average weekly attendance of two thousand or more. In its report for 2008 Hartford listed twelve hundred such churches in the U.S., most often evangelical, very often independent (nondenominational), and more often than not in the suburbs of large cities in the South. Hartford estimated that if U.S. Catholic parishes of similar size were included, it would add about three thousand churches to the list. The phenomenon crested in the early eighties.

they have heard the gospel before or not—people will often respond positively. By 2012 Keller had helped plant sixty-five new Bible-based churches in New York area, only ten of which were of his own denomination.

However, it is one thing to change the way the message is delivered, and quite another to change the message itself. The latter appears to be the goal—or at least the effect—of the "emergent church," the latest phenomenon to hit the English-speaking evangelical world. Like the seeker-friendly churches of the seventies and eighties, the "emergents" trace their origins to the sixties, but only came to wide notice in the nineties. To reach young post-Modernists, an association of U.S. church innovators started up as the Leadership Network. One of its early participants was the highly effective Mark Driscoll, sometimes styled the "cussin' pastor" because he is in many ways unconventional. In 1996 at the age of twenty-five he founded the amazingly prolific Mars Hill Church in Seattle (which by 2012 had opened fourteen of its own associate churches and helped plant over four hundred others). Driscoll soon realized that some of his Network colleagues were more than innovative—they had renounced Christianity altogether. He ascribed to the extreme emergents eight heretical speculations (or conversations, as the emergents prefer) which cast in doubt all five evangelical fundamentals.

Mark Driscoll, the so-called "cussin' pastor," delivers one of his entertaining sermons—part fire-and-brimstone, part stand-up routine—at the Mars Hill Church in Seattle in 2009. Starting at age twenty-five in 1996, Driscoll has opened fourteen associate churches and helped "plant" four hundred others.

The "emerging church" movement—like the mainline Modernist shift one century earlier—was diverse enough to resist easy categorization. Just as mainstream evangelicalism tilts noticeably to the political right and to biblical literalism, the opposite was true of emergents: they tilted to the left and toward heterodoxy (mixing of various Christian traditions). Regardless of degree and direction, however, emergents insisted that they be accepted as evangelicals, just as a century ago Modernists insisted on being seen as Christians.

Maryland musician, author, and lecturer Brian McLaren (age forty-four in 2000) was seen as the most prominent emergent apologist in the early twenty-first century, and among the most extreme. Like all emergents, he rejected the belief that humans can know any truth absolutely, and that the evangelical insistence on the absolute, exclusive truth of scripture, and on salvation being in Christ alone, is impossibly misguided. He held that the real message of Jesus was misconstrued from the beginning by the early church—it was about the kingdom of God on earth, not in heaven. Evangelicals, he argued, would be fulfilling the great commission better if they helped inner city drug addicts, prostitutes, and poor people rather than rich Republicans, and if they sought common ground with other religions rather than consigning them to hell as disbelievers. McLaren argues that evangelicals should listen to everyone's personal story, and help that individual relate his own life to scripture. Rather than guessing endlessly and wrongly about when this world will end, they should focus on building the kingdom of God on earth. Rather than dismissing out of hand the rituals, mysteries, traditions, and stories of other, older forms of Christianity, experience and adapt them.

The titles of McLaren's books indicate his beliefs: *A New Kind of Christian* (2001), *The Story We Find Ourselves In* (2003), *The Secret Message of Jesus* (2006), *Everything Must Change* (2007), and *Finding Our Way Again* (2008)—to

Brian McClaren   Tim Keller   Don Carson

name only a few. Don Carson, an internationally recognized theologian from Trinity Evangelical Divinity School in Illinois, was among several traditionalists to critique emergents' voluminous writings in the 2000s. In *Becoming Conversant with the Emerging Church* (2005) he found in them a mix of good and bad—but mostly bad. On the most controversial points, perhaps to deflect accusations of heresy or to avoid inconsistency, emergents tend to ask leading questions rather than make definitive statements. After all, anyone who states absolutely that all absolutes are false soon suffers Mark Twain's amusing retort that "All generalizations are false, including this one." It is much more effective to ask, "Are absolutes even possible?" and then quietly to proceed on the assumption that they are not.

Carson notes that at the core of their position, McLaren and other emergent post-Modernists rely on a false antithesis between knowing something is true, and knowing something absolutely in every detail. Only God can have complete knowledge of anything. But that does not mean humans cannot know anything at all; we can know something to be true without knowing every last detail about it. And the whole record of the New Testament, says Carson, is that Jesus did know absolutely what was true and necessary for salvation because he is God, and that any contrary teaching, to the extent of its inconsistency, is false.

It was impossible to assess in 2012 how far emergent thinking had infiltrated evangelicalism. Its champions had been published by the world's premier religious houses, and translated and distributed to Christians worldwide. Emergent conferences were drawing large and growing participation. If it was just another Protestant fad, it was certainly one of the bigger ones.

One thing at least was clear. As Carson and other traditionalists maintained, emergence in its extreme forms had emptied Christianity of meaning, no less than Modernism had done a century earlier when in order to remain "relevant" it shattered Protestant Christianity, and became ever less relevant in the process. The emergents could assuredly contend that they were "up-to-date," but it seemed the lesson of twenty centuries of Christian experience that the more a thing is up-to-date, the sooner it will go out of date. Permanence, in other words, is not the product of relevance. Or as journalist G. K. Chesterton once put it: "Whenever I'm told that the gaslight is here to stay, I know that it's about to go." ∎

The sad saga of the 'Seven Sisters'

The postwar era began well for the seven mainline churches, but when they quit God to preach left-wing causes, their numbers fell from 50% of the population to 8%

The unexpected resurgence of North American Christianity after the Second World War benefited all major faith traditions, but not equally. Roman Catholicism and evangelical/Pentecostal fundamentalism both grew sturdily in numbers and influence in the second half of the century, to the point where Catholicism became the largest single denomination on the continent, and the churches of the evangelical Southern Baptist Convention would surpass Methodism as the largest Protestant denomination in the United States. The Methodists were one of America's mainline Protestant churches—sometimes called Protestantism's "seven sisters."[1] Up into the middle years of the cen-

tury, their views, goals, and theology could be taken generally as the American Christian consensus. During the century's closing decades, however, this changed signally, as their doctrinal positions slid into ambivalence, their membership plunged and they became culturally and politically irrelevant.

Their looming implosion was not evident, however, when the boys came home from the Second World War in 1945 to get married and raise families in new, boxy little bungalows in the treeless suburbs rolling out like synthetic carpet around North American cities. New churches were appearing all through these new neighborhoods and most were still mainline Protestant, because that was America's old-time religion, and the traditional was

1. America's seven significant mainline denominations in the twentieth century were, from largest to smallest, the United Methodist, the Evangelical Lutherans in America, the Presbyterian Church (U.S.), the Episcopal Church (the American Anglicans), American Baptist (separate from the Southern Baptists), the United Church of Christ, and the Disciples of Christ. There were in addition many smaller ones of similar theology and tradition. The largest equivalents in Canada are the United Church, the Anglican Church, the Lutheran Church, and the Reformed Church in America.

An archetypal American family emerges from their Episcopal church in this early 1950s photo taken in New York. In the postwar boom, churches were proliferating in the new suburbs and most were of the mainline Protestant denominations. In the ensuing decades, however, these churches would fall empty as the flocks lost interest in Christianity, or switched to the burgeoning evangelical denominations.

Thomas Oden: a supporter of all left-wing causes in the 1950s and 1960s, he was later to revert.

what most young American families seemed to want. All too often, however, it wasn't what they got from mainline churches.

The mainline leadership faced two postwar challenges: to regain its earlier moral and cultural authority in an increasingly secular age, and to continue on its prewar progressive, socialist track. However, America had changed. The moral authority previously exercised by mainline churches was shifting—indeed, had already shifted—to the rising secular "social sciences," burgeoning in the universities and adopted as well by seminaries across the spectrum. These new disciplines had always been encouraged by the mainliners because they had in the past at least acknowledged the social utility of traditional Christian morals. But now the social scientists had discovered they could ignore Christianity entirely, even attack or undermine it. So the Jesus-as-sociologist formula was quietly discarded.

Moreover, though the horrors of totalitarian atheism were well known and much deplored in the postwar western world, and though religion, especially Christianity, was enjoying a popular resurgence, North Americans favored the evangelical Christianity of Billy Graham or the resolute doctrinal stability of Roman Catholicism. In 1949, a good citizen believed in God, went to church, and opposed godless communism. But most influential mainline Protestant leaders still leaned, if not to Marxism, at least to democratic socialism as a necessary antidote to what they saw as capitalist exploitation. In this they also found greater acceptance, if not among their congregations, at least among the secularist academics whose interest lay in the study of Man, not of God, a concept they were rapidly relegating to church-run seminaries.

Typical of this reorientation was the Methodist postwar theology student Thomas Oden, destined to venture deeply into the schools of new theology and emerge from them as the champion of what he would call paleo-orthodoxy. But as a Depression kid from Oklahoma and a self-described "movement person" at the progressive Methodist Asbury seminary in Kentucky, he supported any and all left-wing causes whether Christian or not: pacifism, socialism, abortion rights, and civil rights. His doctoral thesis in the late 1950s was on "demythologization," a term invented by the German theologian Rudolf Bultmann for interpreting scripture divorced from what was considered mythological forms of belief. Though more radical than his establishment elders, Oden's differences with them were merely a matter of degree. Mainline magazines like *Christian Century* continued to pronounce with left-liberal moral certitude on every conceivable socio-political issue, from atomic war to trade unionism. And as essayist Laurence Moore writes in *Between the Times* (1989), mainline Protestant views soon became indistinguishable from center-left secular opinion throughout North America.

It was notable that most of this leftist, secularist penchant was centered in the upper echelons of each mainline church—in its seminaries, in its publications, and in the mainline National Council of Churches, established in 1950. The average churchgoer remained comfortably oblivious to most of it, however, and postwar mainline church membership continued to grow. Meanwhile, the leadership patiently waited, serenely confident, or so it appeared, that the political wind would soon shift and youth in particular would see the light and wisdom of their thinking. And indeed, youth did. When the black civil rights movement exploded in the segregated southern U.S. in the late 1950s, the mainline churches—far more than others—leaped into the fray in defense of the oppressed. After desegregation came the baby-boom social revolution of the 1960s, which the mainliners embraced with enthusiasm, even excitement. Theologically speaking, they marched around their own ecclesiastical Jericho and cheered when the walls came tumbling down.

All mainline churches tolerated or encouraged scriptural revisionism and moral and doctrinal relativism in the sixties, but the Episcopalians (Anglicans) did it with the most panache. They produced, for example, James Pike, bishop of San Francisco. A maestro of media-savvy shock value, Pike could catch and ride every new wave. Pike's face, according to Joseph Bottum in the journal *First Things* (August/September 2008) was "in every photograph, his signature on every petition, and his blessing on every cause."

> In 1949, a good citizen believed in God, went to church, and opposed communism.

In the early 1950s, he had been boldly anti-Communist, and by 1962, when he made the cover of *Time* magazine, he was boldly pacifist, feminist, and anti-Christian. By the latter 1960s, he had denied the Virgin Birth, the Resurrection, the existence of hell, the divinity of Jesus, the Holy Spirit, and the necessity of God's grace to be saved. Though such views had actually become quietly commonplace among mainline clergy, Pike was so flagrant about it he was put on trial for heresy by his brother bishops, quit the church over it, and announced himself to be a gnostic.[2]

Pike was famous but not otherwise unusual; the aforementioned Thomas Oden, by now a theology professor at Drew University in New Jersey, was into everything from the "deep-seeking" nondogmatic spiritualism of Esalen in Big Sur, California, to tarot cards, astrology, and the occult. He was at one, that is, with the mainline churches in the 1960s. He shared the passionate, self-righteous conviction among many, especially the young, that America had nothing to teach the world and much for which to apologize: nuclear weapons, industrial pollution, military and religious imperialism, capitalism, consumerism, vicious racial prejudice, and puritanical sexual stupidity—and all these on a scale that made it at least as bad as communism, if not worse. From the desegregation march on Birmingham in 1963 to the march on the Pentagon in 1967, mainline Protestants were in the front lines. Along with angry Marxists, drugged hippies, and urban terrorists, they advocated loudly for draft dodgers, Black Panthers, abortion, Communist insurgency movements worldwide, unilateral disarmament, legalized pot, gay rights, and an immediate exit from Vietnam.

Meanwhile, as the causes espoused by the mainline churches in Britain strayed like those in America ever more wildly from the lofty into the loony, and as their congregations likewise dwindled, it fell to the Christian convert and journalist Malcolm Muggeridge to describe the lamentable spectacle of the once-august bench of bishops of the Church of England. "If there is one thing more unedifying than a ruling class in a position of dominance," he writes in *Jesus Rediscovered* (1977), "it is a ruling class like ours on the run. They are capable of every folly and misjudgment, mistake their enemies for friends, and feel bound to go out of their way to encourage whatever and whoever seeks their destruction. In their fore-

San Francisco Bishop James A. Pike, fingers his peace symbol during a speech given to members of the Baha'i faith in 1967, calling for a renewal in modern churches that will "enable more and more people to turn on without drugs." A maestro of media-savvy shock value, Pike could catch and ride every new wave, and by the late 1960s was denying the Virgin Birth, the Resurrection, the existence of hell, the divinity of Jesus, the Holy Spirit, and the necessity of God's grace to be saved.

front today one notes a bizarre contingent of crazed figures in purple and black cassocks."

Hitching a current social, moral, or political cause to Christian evangelism had been a constant feature of American evangelicalism since the Second Great Awakening in the early nineteenth century: Sunday-rest laws, antislavery, antidrinking, women's suffrage, child welfare, and public health. C. S. Lewis (in *The Screwtape Letters*, 1942) depicted the mentality of such movements within the faith which he summed up as "Christianity and Water." Some of his examples: "Christianity and *the Crisis*, Christianity and *Vegetarianism*, Christianity and *Spelling Reform*." Any of these may be worthy, he wrote, but they are secondary. "Mere Christianity" dies if something else becomes the main point. In mainline Protestant upper echelons, that had happened; and as the gulf between the pulpit and the pews widened, the hitherto unthinkable occurred. While Catholic and evangelical/Pentecostal churches kept growing, mainline Protestant membership after 1967 leveled off and then began to slide steadily downward—taking with it, of course, attendant personal disciplines such as daily prayer and Bible reading, the exercise

2. James Pike (1913–1969), Episcopalian bishop of San Francisco, led in many ways a sad life: alcoholic, promiscuous, twice divorced, and thrice married. His son committed suicide in 1966, prompting the grieving father to delve into occult practices. The ex-bishop died at age fifty-six by falling sixty feet from a cliff while trying to hike out of the Judean desert. He and his third wife, Diane, searching for data on the "historical Jesus," had driven ill prepared into the desert. The car broke down. While Diane went for help, Pike was to stay with the vehicle. When she returned with several rescuers, Pike had wandered off. His body was found later.

of personal virtue, and lay witness and outreach in the community.

Any serious mainline expectation that church attendance would swell by preaching a secular gospel to an increasingly secular public vanished with the 1972 book *Why Conservative Churches Are Growing* by Dean Kelley. He was a former mainline Methodist minister who had joined the executive board of the National Council of Churches and later served on the board of the American Civil Liberties Union. Kelley flagged what was clearly a long-term trend working against any churches that stressed politics above personal salvation. Anyone who endorsed the secular gospel did not need a church; there were citizen action groups and political parties for things like disarmament and abortion. And those who wanted God in their lives weren't going to get it in a church focused on ending sexism and healing the environment. It hardly mattered whether the departed faithful were opting for conservative evangelical churches or for none at all; either way, they were leaving mainline Protestantism. Between the 1960s and the new millennium, total mainline adherence fell steadily from over fifty percent of Americans in the 1960s to eight percent.

"Weigh the benefits," argues Thomas Reeves scathingly in *The Empty Church* (1998). "Sunday with the family at the beach, or in church listening to a sermon about

> Anyone who agreed with the 'secular gospel' had no need of a church

AIDS? Studying for an exam, or hearing that the consolations and promises of the Bible are not 'really' or 'literally' true?" After Kelley's prominent book, however, mainline leaders did not rethink their direction. As North Americans polarized with the culture war, mainline Protestants continued to sound too religious for the secular left, and too secular left for the religious right. Yet they persisted, and as each new decade brought new cultural enthusiasms, causes, and slogans, some mainline leaders would predict a resurgence of interest among the young, and others would say that even if more members left, God had called the churches to preach a secular gospel to a secular world. The optimists would forever echo leftist Episcopal priest Malcolm Boyd, who said in the 1960s, "There is a new Christian movement springing up in this country when many are saying that the church is dying." And the fatalists would repeat the other perennial sixties article of faith, by "boasting," says Reeves, "of what they saw as their exceptional enlightenment and decrying the inability and unwillingness of Christians in general to share in their commitment to 'higher' causes."

In fact, the mainline churches were often accused through the ensuing decades of being "stuck in the sixties" in much the same way as the whole secular left. In 2004, the Institute on Religion & Democracy (IRD) reviewed the annual resolutions between 2000 and 2003 adopted by four of the largest mainline U.S. churches, as well as those of the National Council of Churches (NCC) and the World Council of Churches (WCC). In those four years, on average seven out of ten criticisms regarding human rights were directed against either Israel (thirty-seven percent) or the U.S. (thirty-two). By contrast, only five of the fifteen worst human rights violators in the world were mentioned, sparingly—but not China, the largest of the world's worst offenders, and few criticisms were made of Muslim atrocities against Christians through much of the Middle East. Nor did the IRD note any admission by the mainline groups that they were holding Israel and the U.S. to a higher standard than anyone else. After communism fell in the early 1990s, two separate mainline apologies were made (one from the NCC, another from the WCC) for never having understood or addressed Communist persecution of Christians—though the problem was well known to any who paid attention. Nevertheless the mainline denominations continued as lopsided as before.

According to critic Reeves in *The Empty Church*, the secular gospel is built into the leadership system of all mainline churches, because for decades the Left has controlled their national budgets and offices. When, for example, the influential leftist professor Thomas Oden experienced a radical conversion to mere Christianity in the 1970s (he was appalled and shaken by the absolute feminist insistence upon abortion), he was immediately sidelined and shunned. In Reeves's assessment, the mainline church laity continues to be more moderate or conservative on average than the leadership, but "are no match for zealous, ideological interest groups" who continue to "support, appoint, and elect each other" to decision-making positions. Unable to do much about it, conservative laymen "tend to stay out of

the political side of church life." Various lay attempts in the 1970s and 1980s to restore traditional Protestant Christianity to the mainline soon sputtered out, and liberal dominance seemed permanent.

It was unknowable in 2012 whether or when any of the imploding mainline establishments might fold. With membership declining from attrition, desertion, a low birthrate, and no discernible new interest among unchurched youth, their future certainly appeared bleak. However, even skeptics like Reeves refused in 1998 to rule out a resurrection for all or some, however improbable.

With the new millennium came a new development: the confessing movement. Unlike the earlier reform efforts, which garnered roughly one percent of mainline membership, the confessing movement claims the support of about ten percent in the Presbyterian Church, and has gained significant influence in several United Methodist regional conferences. Methodist professor Oden is in a confessing church congregation. Confessing leaders, though unable to wrest overall control from the current left-liberal elite, work within existing churches to evangelize, build local church attendance, restore belief in the divinity of Christ and in the need of all people for repentance and forgiveness, defend biblical teachings, and preach the Christian gospel rather than the secular one. Many recovering mainline congregations rely for evangelization on the Alpha program (see sidebar, page 412).

John Wesley, Methodism's eighteenth-century English founder, once said, "I am not afraid that the people called Methodists should ever cease to exist, either in Europe or America. But I am afraid lest they should exist only as a dead sect, having the form of religion without the power. And this will undoubtedly be the case unless they hold fast the doctrine, spirit and discipline with which they first set out." ■

A young member of the Great I Am Church of God in Claremont, California, reacts tearfully during prayers at a Pentecostal service in 2006. In the course of a century, Pentecostalism, with its direct appeal to the spirit, has burgeoned into a "third force" among churches—after Catholicism and Orthodoxy (viewed as one) and historical Protestantism—with more than two hundred million adherents worldwide.

CHAPTER 15

In less than a century, more than 200 million accept Pentecostalism

Born out of the post-Civil War 'holiness movement,' it emerges from the Los Angeles warehouse district to make 'speaking in tongues' a world phenomenon

The outburst of North American revivalism that produced twentieth-century Protestant fundamentalism also gave rise to something in many ways quite different. "Pentecostalism" appeared in Los Angeles in 1906, with press reports of worshippers uttering incomprehensible sounds they called "speaking in tongues." Most people dismissed this as the kind of faddish silliness for which the West Coast was already becoming notorious, and many fundamentalists disowned it as unchristian, even diabolical. Nobody—except Pentecostals—foresaw it exploding within a few decades into the world's most vigorously expansive form of Christianity. It is now often called—and not just by Pentecostals—Christianity's "third force" (after Catholicism/Orthodoxy and historical Protestantism).

Pentecostals say they take the meaning of the Bible even more literally than the most fundamental of fundamentalists. Beyond asserting the reality of miracles in general, and of Christ's physical Resurrection, they further claim to have revived a form of worship that disappeared shortly after the age of the apostles: the practice of talking in unknown languages. Although not all Pentecostals possess this gift, they believe it is the sure sign of someone having been saved or, as they put it, "baptized by the Holy Spirit."

The 1906 Azusa Street Revival, recognized as the birth of U.S. Pentecostalism, took place over three years in a derelict two-story church building in a Los Angeles warehouse district. It drew in local black Angelinos and smaller numbers of Latinos, Asians, and whites, and attracted a swelling contingent of curious visitors

Pentecostalism grew out of the belief by those in the late nineteenth-century holiness movement, notably Kansan faith-healer Charles Parham (top center), that the movement was losing its vigor, becoming too intellectual, and no longer possessed its original miraculous powers. Accordingly Parham established a Bible school for young missionaries in an empty Topeka mansion called Stone's Folly (right). His students included William Seymour (top left), who launched the Azusa Street Revival in Los Angeles, the first Pentecostal church at which parishioners fainted and spoke in tongues during services, drawing ridicule from such quarters as the Los Angeles Daily Times (top right).

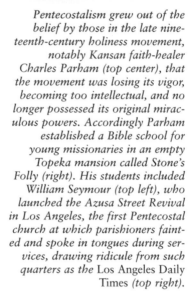

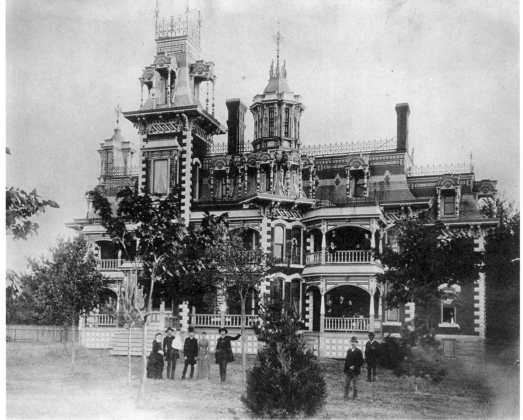

from far and wide. Its leader and founder, William Seymour, was a short, stocky black man with one eye blinded by smallpox, whose mother had been a slave in Louisiana and whose father was a black Union Army soldier in the Civil War.

Like many late nineteenth-century Protestants, black and white alike, Seymour had grown up in the interdenominational "holiness movement" that spread through North American Christianity after the Civil War. By the 1880s, there were holiness adherents in all the mainline churches, especially among the then-dominant Methodists. Holiness focused on reaching a heroic level of personal purity, piety, and virtue, the attainment of which depended upon a one-time adult experience of being "born again"—something Jesus had said was essential for salvation (John 3:3).

There was nothing prissy, fussy or feminine about holiness Christianity, even though many of its most effective leaders and apologists were women (in which regard it was progressively ahead of its time). It was tough-minded, assertive, evangelistic, moralistic and uncompromising.[1] Furthermore, it was as acceptable in the rural areas and western frontiers as in the tumultuously industrializing cities of the Northeast.[1]

By 1900, "holiness" was losing its vigor among the more educated and prosperous classes, who were now intellectualizing and theologizing it into tame respectability. Such at least was the feeling among younger, poorer, and more rural and Southern enthusiasts. One of these, Charles Parham, an obscure itinerant faith healer in Topeka, Kansas, became seized by the idea that the church lacked more than its original holiness. Also absent, he declared, was the power of the Holy Spirit that had enabled believers to perform the amazing acts of healing, exorcism, courage, and prophecy through which God converted the Roman Empire. Like many other zealous Protestants, Parham was also a convinced dispensationalist (see sidebar, page 280) and believed the world would soon end with Christ's return. It made sense to him that at this time God would restore to his church these original miraculous powers in order to save as many as possible in the last days.

In 1900 Parham began a Bible school for young missionaries. Having no money, he located it in an empty house called Stone's Folly, an unfinished Topeka mansion so named for the over-ambitious entrepreneur who had built and lost it. The only text book at Bethel Bible School was the Bible itself, and to occupy his several dozen students while he was away for a speaking engagement, Parham once asked them to see if it offered any unmistakable outward proof that an individual has received the Holy Spirit.

When he returned several days later, the students were ready. According to the Book of Acts, they told him, the descent of the Holy Spirit upon the first Christians had consistently been accompanied by speaking in tongues. Parham was impressed and on New Year's Eve, 1900, teacher and students prayed together long into the night. Precisely following Acts, student Agnes Ozman requested that Parham lay his hands on her head and ask God to give her the Holy Spirit.

To their astonishment and delight, Ozman's companions all heard her suddenly talking in what sounded to them like Chinese, while a halo of light appeared around her head. They all testified that for three days this thirty-year-old unilingual farm woman could no longer write in English, only in Chinese characters.[2] "I talked several languages, and it was clearly manifest when a new dialect was spoken," Ozman herself later related. "I had the added joy and glory my heart longed for, and a depth of the presence of the Lord within that I had never known before. It was as if rivers of living water were proceeding from my innermost being."

Soon most of the Bethel Christians, including Parham, could speak in tongues. They were convinced that these were real languages, but this was not easy to prove in Topeka, Kansas, in that era. In any case, the phenomenon of "glossolalia" (Greek *glossa*, "language," and *laleo*, "speak") is as puzzling today as it was for first-century Christians The Acts of the Apostles (2:5–13) recounts that on Pentecost individual apostles suddenly began speaking in human languages

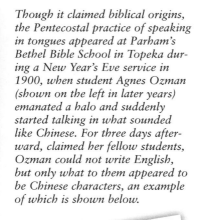

Though it claimed biblical origins, the Pentecostal practice of speaking in tongues appeared at Parham's Bethel Bible School in Topeka during a New Year's Eve service in 1900, when student Agnes Ozman (shown on the left in later years) emanated a halo and suddenly started talking in what sounded like Chinese. For three days afterward, claimed her fellow students, Ozman could not write English, but only what to them appeared to be Chinese characters, an example of which is shown below.

1. Some few "holiness" believers proclaimed themselves "sinless." In 1891, for instance, a holiness Quaker named Amos Kenworthy, a burly and uncouth broom maker from Indiana, claimed that he had not sinned for twenty-one years. Similarly, Abner Crumpler, founder of the Holiness Church of North Carolina, remarked in 1896 that he had been free of any sin for nine years.

2. This is the account of the first experience of glossolalia as recorded by founder Charles Parham and generally accepted among Pentecostals. Agnes Ozman's version of events differs on some points, but not substantially. Two students who quit Bethel Bible School complained that the others were fanatical, but did not criticize Parham.

This image by the thirteenth-century English illuminator William de Brailes depicts the apostles during Pentecost, when, according to Acts 2:4, the Holy Spirit descended upon them, and they "began to speak with other languages, as the Spirit gave them utterance." This speaking in actual foreign languages—or xenoglossia—is a foundational tenet of Pentecostalism, although usually church members practice glossolalia, whereby the "language" they speak is of no known provenance, and requires church-appointed interpreters to decode.

3. The *Topeka Daily Capital* also reported that when Bethel students took Agnes Ozman's spirit-directed writing to a local Chinese man for translation, he "threw up his hands in bewilderment. 'Me no understand,' he protested. 'Takee to Jap'," meaning to someone who could read Japanese.

they had never learned, but which throngs of foreigners visiting Jerusalem knew and recognized—languages from Mesopotamia, Asia Minor, Arabia, North Africa, and Rome.

The technical term for this—someone speaking a human language he has never learned—is "xenoglossia." However, the apostle Paul in his first letter to the church at Corinth appears to refer at length (in chapters 12 through 14) to some Christians also speaking true glossolalia, which can sound like a human language yet is usually taken to be gibberish. Whichever it was, all such practices seemingly had vanished from the church by the early fourth century.

It is noteworthy that Parham saw no use in glossolalia as such, and remained certain that twenty-one actual xenoglossic languages had been uttered at Stone's Folly. Fixed in his mind was the idea that God was preparing him and his disciples to convert foreign nations prior to the Second Coming, and he told the *Topeka Daily Capital* that the gift of xenoglossia was of practical assistance to that end. He went to some lengths to prove the languages were real, though contemporary news reporters considered the evidence dubious.[3]

Parham's Topeka venture ended later that year when the American Bible Society, owner of Stone's Folly, sold it to a local bootlegger. (Perhaps fittingly, it burned to the ground five months later, but in another century there would be a Catholic parish church on the site, whose charismatic members sometimes spoke in tongues.) Parham next opened a Bible school in Houston, where his students included William Seymour, thirty-five, who would shortly launch the Azusa Street Revival in Los Angeles. Meanwhile, Texas segregation laws required that he sit outside the classroom, listening to the lessons through a half-open door.

In early 1906, Seymour was invited by a holiness congregation in Los Angeles to become its assistant pastor. In his first sermon to this small black church, he commended tongue speech as the only sure evidence that a believer has been saved. A notably humble man, he acknowledged that he himself had not yet received the much-prized gift, but this novel salvation thesis was rejected immediately by the local holiness leadership as inconsistent with the denomination's beliefs, leaving him unemployed.

The penniless minister found shelter with a kindly church member, and some of the congregation, eager to explore glossolalia, conducted several days of intense worship in this man's home. On April 9, Seymour and seven others fell to the floor, consumed with ecstasy and testifying in tongues, which caused his host's young daughter to flee from the house, terrified by this "holy rolling." Shortly thereafter, the crowd expanded to the point that Seymour had to preach on the front porch, which soon collapsed (without injury to anyone), prompting the move to sturdier quarters on Azusa Street.

American church services at the time, even among nonliturgical Protestants, were typically restrained, decorous affairs, with ordered routines, pews in neat rows, printed hymnals, robed choirs, stained glass, and steeples. Not at Azusa, which had no formal program at all. Its earliest pulpit consisted of two packing crates; elder Seymour would sit praying for hours behind this makeshift structure, his head buried inside the upper box. Then he would emerge to preach with the soul-searing passion of the South, challenging his hearers: "Be emphatic! Ask for salvation, sanctification, the baptism with the Holy Ghost, or divine healing."

Thousands responded by speaking in tongues on the spot, or spontaneously and freely reacting in other ways to what they deemed to be the prompting of the Holy Spirit. White and black, Latino and Asian, they shouted out, sang individually, sat murmuring in trances, danced, hugged (interracially at times), jerked, fainted, performed spontaneous exorcisms, and wept with each other. Descriptions of this borderline pandemonium, published in religious newspapers, alerted the country and then the world.[4]

The charismatic revival continued daily from ten in the morning until midnight or later, for more than three years—one thousand days in the Pentecostal narrative—though some sources consider it to have lasted several years longer. In many ways it was reminiscent of the bedlam that sometimes erupted at the mass camp meetings of the Second Great Awakening a hundred years earlier with people shrieking and groaning, falling into trances, testifying with sudden eloquence

White and black, Latino and Asian, they shouted out, sang, murmured in trances, danced, hugged, jerked, fainted, and wept in borderline pandemonium.

at great length, jerking spasmodically, laughing uncontrollably, and lying for hours as though dead (see volume 11, chapter 5).

The Azusa pioneers pried open a "charism" (Greek for divine power) or, some would say, a chasm, that has in varying degrees divided North American Christendom ever since.[5] Critics saw in it chaos, vulgarity, and occasionally something close to insanity, convincing many that its source was diabolical. But the worshippers themselves claimed that a sense of irresistible harmony swept through their ranks, unpredictable as a tornado yet as precise, bringing to oppressed souls a profound sense of peace.

Participants claimed a precedent in King David's dancing with joyous abandon before the Ark of the Covenant, shocking the more staid members of his court, and not least his princess wife Michal. David was a lowborn shepherd, and Pentecostals have always felt a strong affinity for and with the poor, and an urge to ignore or flout conventions. Above all, the Azusans cited the apostles and the early church. On the day of Pentecost, when Jesus' one hundred and twenty newly inspired disciples issued from their hideout and astonished the citizens and pilgrims of Jerusalem, they were so strangely merry and boisterous that their leader, Simon Peter, had to insist they were not drunk. Some onlookers were unconvinced, but the Bible says the number of Christians swelled that day to three thousand.

Pentecostals, as they soon were commonly known, shortly reached a consensus, contrary to Charles Parham, that language-specific xenoglossia was not the only legitimate form of tongue speaking. Though meaningless to human ears, glossolalia came to be accepted as a "spirit language" by which God speaks through the believer, back to God himself. Those who do it—and they are now

4. Charles Parham, although notably broad-minded on race and gender issues for his time and place, was nevertheless horrified by the abandoned physical contact occurring among races and sexes at the exuberant Azusa services. He consequently made comments so crude that they have stained his memory ever since.

5. Though Pentecostals unquestionably popularized "tongue speech," there were some precedents. Scottish adherents of the Presbyterian schismatic Edward Irving reportedly practiced it in the 1830s, as did American disciples of the Australian prophet Alexander Dowie in the later 1800s. Glossolalia was also known among Christian Union holiness believers in North Carolina and Tennessee in the late 1800s, and occurred as well during a massive spiritual revival in Wales in 1904–1905. Also, some Azusa worshippers were "Jumpers," a tongue-speaking Russian sect that had fled Armenia to avoid annihilation by the Turks, as predicted by their prophets.

The queen and king of faith healing

Sister Aimee and Oral Roberts left an indelible print on 20th-century Christianity, though her sad demise and his fiscally disastrous hospital cloud both their stories

One thing that put Pentecostalism on the world map of Christianity was its belief in faith healing—meaning that without any medicine God will cure goiters, pain, cancer, and even raise the dead—which built the careers of two of its most famous early preachers, Aimee Semple McPherson and Oral Roberts.

Sister Aimee, as she was to become known, was more famous after the First World War than the redoubtable evangelist baseballer Billy Sunday had been before it. Born Aimee Elizabeth Kennedy, she was raised poor on a farm near Ingersoll, Ontario, and had both the stylish beauty of movie actress Mary Pickford and the fiery resolve of Joan of Arc. She became convinced in her early teens that God wanted her to preach, but since women preachers were as yet unheard-of, she could only puzzle about it at first. In 1907 she attended a Pentecostal mission in Toronto, where she first spoke in tongues and fell in love with the Irish preacher, Robert Semple. Six months later, just before her eighteenth birthday, they married, and two years later were on a ship, bound to preach in Hong Kong. There, surrounded by poor Chinese living mainly on rats and insects, they both immediately caught malaria, and two months later Robert was dead. Aimee, before heading back to San Francisco two months later, gave birth to their daughter.

She went to New York, destitute and more uncertain than ever what God expected of her. There she joined her mother, Minnie, serving in a Salvation Army soup kitchen in the teeming immigrant slums. She met and soon married a decent young salesman, Harold McPherson, and bore him a son a year later, in March 1913. Harold struggled to content her with housewifery, but soon after giving birth she almost died of appendicitis. During this crisis she said she heard God again calling her to preach. Before he divorced her in 1921, Harold tried, off and on, to accept and assist her vocation as she organized tent revivals in Ontario, up and down the seaboard states, and then westward to the Pentecostal mecca of Los Angeles. Aimee may well have been the first woman to drive across America. Meanwhile, Minnie permanently left her own aging husband, James, on the farm in Ontario to stay in Los Angeles to help her daughter.

Aimee's bewildering combination of biblical zeal, headstrong resourcefulness, and showbiz panache rapidly made her the most famous woman in America. In 1922 she toured Australia, in 1923 she founded the 5,300-seat Angelus Temple in Los Angeles, in 1924 she became America's first female national radio broadcaster, and in 1926 she vanished mysteriously while swimming in the Pacific, and was assumed drowned. A month later she wandered out of the Mexican desert, still looking like Greta Garbo despite (she said) having been held by kidnappers in a remote adobe shack and having trekked twenty miles to escape. No evidence could be found to support this tale, and much was found to discredit it, but no charge was pursued. From her Temple stronghold in 1927 she founded the Pentecostal Foursquare Gospel Church (eight million members in one hundred and forty-four countries in 2006). Though she became more reclusive in the

Above, celebrity evangelist Aimee Semple McPherson is greeted by a throng of her followers at the Los Angeles station after her tour of Europe and the Holy Land in 1931. Below, her Angelus Temple, still used for worship services in 2005. Inset, "Sister Aimee" in the mid-1920s. Her bewildering combination of biblical zeal, headstrong resourcefulness, and showbiz panache rapidly made her the most famous woman in America.

Oral Roberts at a crusade meeting in 1962. By now Roberts, with the aid of television, had increased his reach to the point where he was rivaling Billy Graham. Roberts, more than anyone, changed Pentecostalism from its original emphasis on holiness to a desire for physical well-being and material prosperity.

1930s, she continued to preach, help the poor, and provoke scandalous gossip until she died of a sleeping pill overdose (accidental or deliberate) in 1944, aged fifty-three.

Through all of this, Semple McPherson was careful to keep Pentecostal tongue speaking in the background because it drove away people from other churches, but she could not do the same with faith healing. Her services were besieged by unfortunates with every disease imaginable, who were impossible to ignore and so numerous as to make preaching—her preeminent calling—all but impossible. She tried delegating the healing ministry to subordinates, but it remained for many people their main expectation of her. So Sister Aimee cured them in the hundreds and thousands, or so they said. Those who couldn't come in person would put their hands on the radio as she preached, hoping and praying for relief.

Soon after her sun had set, there came Oral Roberts—a very different, less complicated personality. He grew up in the same rural poverty she had, son of a Pentecostal pastor in Oklahoma. After a brief round of dissipated teen rebellion, Roberts almost died of tuberculosis at age seventeen in 1935. He felt that God had spared him so he could preach, and he spent the Second World War pastoring little churches and raising a family with a wife to whom he remained faithful until she died in 2005. In 1947, Roberts quit his hand-to-mouth ministry. He was convinced that God did not want him to remain poor. God told him to go out and buy a Buick and heal the sick. He never looked back.

Over the next five years his ministry outgrew his first two-thousand-seat tent, and then a seven-thousand seater, and then a twelve thousand. In 1954, he increased his reach exponentially by starting a weekly television program, and he was soon rivalling—and sometimes passing—the audience and recognition level of Billy Graham. Unlike Graham, however, and unlike Aimee Semple McPherson, Roberts was not ecumenical. He kept a tight tie to the Pentecostal churches.

In fact, Roberts more than anyone changed Pentecostalism from its original emphasis on "holiness" (heroic moral sacrifice) to a desire for physical well-being and prosperity. He called it "seed faith": for any person with absolute, genuine faith in God, God will give whatever he asks. Though Roberts himself lived very comfortably, he was never seriously accused of the undue profiteering so characteristic of his televangelist successors. What he *was* often accused of was faith-healing humbug. This, however, comes with the territory. People either believe in it or they don't; proof or disproof is in the heart of the beholder.

He was also guilty of serious mismanagement as his empire expanded. In 1963 he founded Oral Roberts University in Tulsa, Oklahoma, accredited in 1971, which became the preeminent campus of the Pentecostal faith. It was Roberts' response, he said, to a direct command from God to "build Me a university." Though it flourished, it almost sank after Roberts added a City of Faith Medical and Research Center in 1981. With three towers, the tallest sixty stories, it was a colossal financial failure, and Roberts humiliated himself by pleading in 1987 that if donors did not send him eight million dollars right away, God would "call him home." Donors in fact sent him nine million, but in 1989 he had to sell the property anyway, and a large portion of it was still empty in 2012.

It was his last hurrah. A major donor pushed Roberts into a figurehead role to rescue his university, and his family suffered the same vicissitudes—divorce, homosexuality, estrangement—as other prominent televangelist dynasties.

God called Oral Roberts home in 2009 at age ninety-one. For all the mockery and disappointments he suffered later in life, he was unquestionably one of twentieth-century Christianity's greatest leaders. ∎

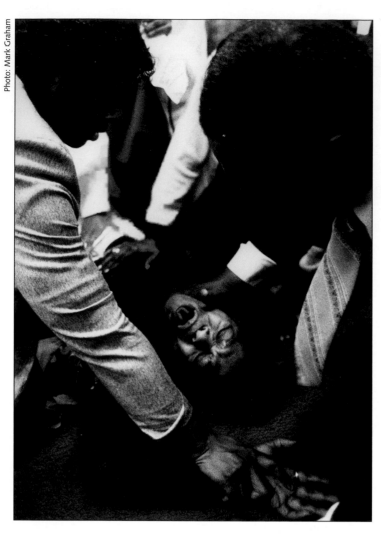

A woman writhes and speaks in tongues during a present-day service at a Southern American Pentecostal church. Such displays, a hallmark of Pentecostalism, have been denounced by those from other evangelical churches as unholy if not ridiculous. Early twentieth-century Baptist writer and theologian Clarence Larkin described such scenes as "more characteristic of demon possession than a work of the Holy Spirit."

many, from across the Christian spectrum—say that in private prayer they remain in charge of their faculties, and that it helps them discover how to handle any difficult or perplexing situation, giving them peace and a sense of spiritual direction.

In public worship it is typically confined to Pentecostal-type churches, and the tongue speaker is supposed to remain silent unless there is a recognized interpreter present who can translate. Paul declared that it was good to pray in tongues privately, though not in church if the congregation could not know what was being said. He also noted that the Holy Spirit gave specific abilities to some but not to everyone, listing the powers of prophecy, healing, other miracles, exorcism, tongues, and the interpretation of tongues (1 Corinthians 12:8–28). Tongue speaking united Pentecostals, but set other Christian churches against them. Evangelical churches, in particular, insisted that the early Christians, including Paul, practiced only xenoglossia, not glossolalia, and that the gift ceased once the faith had spread so far that it was no longer needed.

Pentecostalism was denounced broadly and bitterly as unholy, and not solely because of tongues. Michael L. Brown, professor of Jewish Messianic Studies and founder of the charismatic evangelical FIRE School of Ministry in North Carolina, records in his 1996 book *From Holy Laughter to Holy Fire* that Pentecostalism was categorically condemned by many of the most respected evangelical preachers and scholars of the era. G. Campbell Morgan called it "the last vomit of Satan." To evangelical Congregationalist scholar Reuben Torrey, it was "emphatically not of God, and had been founded by a sodomite" (a reference to a Texas criminal charge leveled against Parham in 1907 but never tried, for lack of proof). Harry Allen Ironside, a renowned Moody Bible teacher, called the goings-on at Azusa "exhibitions worthy of a madhouse." William Baxter Godbey, a Wesleyan evangelist who brought thousands to Christ, dismissed Pentecostal leaders as "Satan's preachers, jugglers, necromancers, enchanters, magicians, and all sorts or mendicants." Clarence Larkin, a Baptist pastor whose sermons on dispensationalism shaped conservative Protestant theology in the early twentieth century, stood aghast at worshippers "writhing in contortions" and creating scenes "more characteristic of demon possession than a work of the Holy Spirit."

Yet Pentecostalism quickly spread, and not just across North America. It began to travel the world. Parham's role soon ceased to be central, and William Seymour followed him into obscurity as the faithful fanned out far and wide.[6] One particularly striking aspect was that, unlike most other evangelical ministries, no single strong leader played a central role, yet as early as 1907, missionaries simply issued from Azusa Street like shock troops, reaching more than twenty-five nations in two years.

By century's end, Vinson Synan of Regent University, Virginia, counted twenty-six denominations, mostly North American, claiming descent from Azusa participants. In *The Holiness-Pentecostal Tradition* (1997), Synan calculated that Pentecostal denominations had 217 million members worldwide as of 1997. If charismatics and "third wavers" in other denominations were included, this type of Christian totaled 463 million. The Pew Forum published similar but higher figures in 2011. It concluded that of the world's estimated 2.2 billion Christians, 1.1 billion were Catholic and 800 million Protestant—and of the latter, the largest denomination was Pentecostal, at 279 million. In addition, Pew estimated that there were 305 million charismatic believers in other denominations.

Charles Peter Wagner, former missionary and a noted professor at Fuller Theological Seminary, has held that the Pentecostal/charismatic flood represents the fastest growing voluntary, nonpolitical movement in humanity's history. It rapidly fostered independent churches in Asia, Africa, and Latin America, on a scale unprecedented in many regions. Synan concurs: "As the second-largest family of Christians after the Roman Catholic Church, the Pentecostal churches can now justifiably be called a major Christian 'tradition'." The Azusa missionaries lacked training and money, but not confidence. The first issue of their first publication, *The Apostolic Faith*, proclaimed, "Many are speaking in new tongues and some are on their way to the foreign fields, with the [God-supplied] gift of the language." Congregants earnestly tried to discover what languages they were speaking, so as to know where God wanted them to go. This confidence invariably proved ill founded.

Most American Pentecostal missionaries knew virtually nothing about foreign cultures and religions, quite typically dismissing the lot, from the Buddhist focus on divine compassion to Confucian veneration of ancestors, as demon inspired. Further, women constituted perhaps two-thirds of the first missionary wave at a time when even western women were only beginning to be taken seriously for work outside the home. Rail and steamship now made it easy to reach foreign cities, but survival was not guaranteed after that. Many missionaries would lose children and spouses to tropical illnesses.

Despite daunting hurdles, most of these missions succeeded. *The Bridegroom's Messenger* claimed in December 1908, for example, that sixty missionaries had received Spirit baptism in India, while fifteen missionary societies had "witnesses to Pentecost" in twenty-eight stations throughout Hinduism's ancestral homeland. The entire

6. Charles Parham remained the acknowledged originator of Pentecostal Christianity, but was soon eclipsed by its rapid expansion. William Seymour, who was honored as a bishop by his congregants, died in 1922 and is buried with his wife, Jennie, in Evergreen Memorial Park (Los Angeles), under the simple inscription, "Our Pastor." Seymour was largely forgotten until 1972, when Yale historian Sidney Ahlstrom proclaimed him "the most influential black leader in American religious history." In 2012, the site of his Azusa Street Church was occupied by Little Tokyo's Japanese American Cultural and Community Center Plaza.

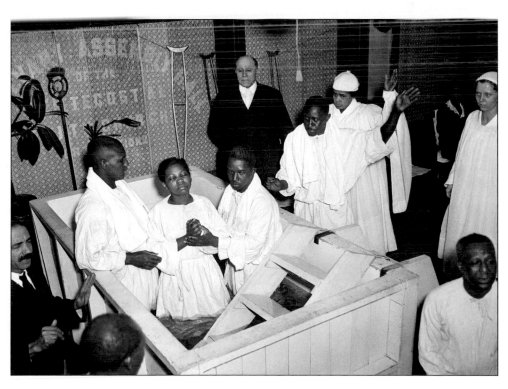

An April 1934 baptism ceremony at the Pentecostal Faith Church of All Nations in Harlem, New York. Crutches, discarded by the beneficiaries of faith healing, can be seen in the background. By now the Pentecostal movement had spread like a fire, not only throughout North America, but to the third-world countries of Africa, Asia and South America. Charles Peter Wagner, a professor at California's evangelical Fuller Theological Seminary, holds that Pentecostalism is the fastest-growing voluntary movement in the history of humanity.

Pentecostal development in the sub-continent had occurred within one year, and its acceptance there was far from unique.

Pentecostals have their own explanation for this rapid success. They claim that the Azusa missionaries were not launching an international movement so much as linking one up that already existed. Major studies of early Pentecostalism in Argentina, Chile, Ghana, Korea, the Philippines, South Africa, and South India have concluded that largely autonomous outpourings "with essentially shared beliefs and expectations" apparently occurred around the globe during the first decade of the twentieth century.

Young and old members of the Hallelujah Village Church in Vellore, India, sing songs of praise at a modern-day Pentecostal service. India was the first of the third-world countries in which Pentecostalism took root, thanks in large part to Pandita Ramabai (inset), a Hindu woman who converted to Christianity in the late nineteenth century and initiated revival-style meetings at her mission between Bombay (now Mumbai) and Pune.

So writes the Irish theologian-historian Alister McGrath in *Christianity's Dangerous Idea* (2007). In India, for example, charismatic worship was reported in 1905 in the northeast Khassia Hills, and in 1901 in central India near Mumbai (Bombay) and Pune. In the latter community, Pandita Ramabai had established the Mukti Mission in 1889, helping poverty-stricken widows and other outcast women. In 1901, Ramabai, a high-caste Hindu before her conversion, initiated revival-style meetings, blazing a trail that would soon be followed by American Pentecostals.

Chronicler Helen S. Dyer described in her 1905 report *Pandita Ramabai: The Great Revival*, "The next evening, while Ramabai was expounding John 8 in her usual quiet way, the Holy Spirit descended with power, and all the girls began to pray aloud so that she had to cease talking. Little children, middle-sized girls, and young women wept bitterly and confessed their sins. Some few saw visions and experienced the power of God and things too deep to be described. Two little girls had the spirit of prayer poured on them in such torrents that they continued to pray for hours. They were transformed with heavenly light shining on their faces."

A contemporary but entirely independent surge was the Welsh Revival during 1904–1905. Its meetings, described as continuing far into the night and notable for high emotion, healings, and speaking in tongues, are said to have generated as many as one hundred thousand conversions.

Aside from divine inspiration, several explanations have been proposed for the speed of Pentecostalism's success. Being less hierarchical, it attached relatively small importance to education and clerical rank, and more readily transferred authority to indigenous converts. New charismatic churches quickly became self-propagating and even self-supporting offshoots, outside the control of Euro-Americans. Moreover, Pentecostal theology takes seriously all forms of spiritual power, especially angels, demons, and miraculous occurrences. While western culture now tends to dismiss such manifestations as psychologically induced superstitions, most people in Asia, Africa, and Latin America still very much believe in them.

Then too, American Pentecostals were generally poor, and understood the poverty of those to whom they preached. Although other missionary enterprises could probably say the same, Pentecostals were especially concerned about physical needs as well as spiritual salvation. Not all Azusa's spirit-baptized adherents went abroad, however. The well-known holiness pastor William Durham, for example, returned to his North Avenue Mission in Chicago in 1907, where he electrified thousands with Pentecostal-style meetings that sometimes ran all night. This nurtured many more proselytizers.

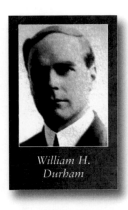

William H. Durham

Schisms appeared almost as fast as new congregations. In 1911, Durham and Seymour had a falling out over some of the fine points of sanctification, with Durham preaching a doctrine of the "finished work" of Christ on the cross. Most Pentecostals agreed with Durham, and the Azusa church came to an end. An even more serious schism occurred in 1916 with the emergence of "oneness" Pentecostalism. These believers maintain that God is a single spirit who expresses himself as Father, Son, and earthly spiritual presence. Baptism should therefore be in the name of Jesus alone, not the biblical formula "in the name of the Father, Son, and Holy Spirit" (Matthew 28:19).

Adding to such divisions as these was America's endemic racism, most acute in the South but prevalent everywhere. For instance, lynching of blacks (along with Mexicans and occasionally immigrants) was a popular theme for postcards until such gruesome souvenirs were banned from the mail in 1908. Given this kind of social pressure, Azusa Street's interracial amity proved more truce than triumph. Elsewhere, denominational segregation became typical across the movement, although there were exceptions at the congregational level among oneness brethren.[7]

Since then, North American Pentecostal Christianity has gone through two distinct phases. Prior to its broader acceptance by other churches in the 1960s, it was derided and shunned, and in response became notoriously belligerent and insular. Far from weakening Pentecostalism, however, isolation seemed to strengthen it. Pentecostal evangelists recruited newcomers more aggressively and successfully than did those of other churches, even faster than the Southern Baptists. Millions of North Americans discovered satisfaction and sanctification in the lively exercise of Holy Spirit power—immediate, exuberant, spontaneous, scriptural, and intensely personal. As mainstream denominations declined from sedate to sedentary, and fundamentalists thundered against mysticism in the church, Pentecostals went rollicking ahead on their own.

Paul Alexander, a theology professor at Azusa Pacific University, explored the attraction of Pentecostalism in his 2009 book *Signs and Wonders*. Although he grew up a fourth-generation Pentecostal in Kansas, Alexander later switched to a Lutheran confession, while continuing to hold his earlier denomination in high regard. He describes how Pentecostals are encouraged to think positively always, and to rely on God to guide them in everything. They pray for miracles, great and small, and often believe they get them. They prefer the Spirit to spirits. They were the first denomination to switch from traditional church hymns to loud contemporary praise music. Their worship style is two-way—preachers get constant feedback and encouragement with the congregation shouting "Amen!", "Hallelujah!"

7. By the 1920s, the major denominations within classical Pentecostalism had been formed: Assemblies of God, founded in 1914; International Church of the Foursquare Gospel, 1927; Church of God in Christ, an African-American denomination that adopted Pentecostalism in 1907; Church of God, a Tennessee denomination that became Pentecostal in 1907; International Pentecostal Holiness Church, formed in 1911; United Pentecostal Church International, a merger of oneness Pentecostal churches, in 1945; and Pentecostal Assemblies of the World, a oneness merger that began in 1914. In 2012 the *New International Dictionary of Pentecostal and Charismatic Movements* listed more than seven hundred Pentecostal denominations globally.

Among the more outlandish iterations of early Pentecostalism was snake handling, denominations of which were begun in 1910 by George Went Hensley, who was inspired by the invocation in Mark 16: 17–18: "And these signs shall follow them that believe: In my name shall they cast out devils; they shall speak with new tongues. They shall take up serpents; and if they drink any deadly thing, it shall not hurt them; they shall lay hands on the sick, and they shall recover." Hensley died from snakebites in 1955. Though forbidden by Pentecostalism generally, instances of the slithery practice are reported to this day in rural areas of the southern U.S. and western Canada. Here coalminers handle snakes at a Pentecostal service in Harlan County, Kentucky, in 1946.

"Praise the Lord!" and "Preach it!" Their faith culture is one of storytelling, starting with the Bible, rather than of theological abstraction, and they are very good at helping and trusting each other. They believe firmly in the daily reality and relevance of dreams, prophecies, tongues, healings, and angelic and demonic powers.

Things changed for Pentecostalism quite suddenly in the 1960s when other churches recognized that the third force was here to stay and began trying to understand its strange success, which enabled Pentecostals to become more ecumenical and less defensive. In 1960, tongue speaking and Holy Spirit baptism broke out in an Episcopal (Anglican) church in the Los Angeles suburb of Van Nuys, beginning with its well-educated head pastor, Reverend Dennis Bennett. After that hit the press, the same thing began to happen elsewhere: at a Presbyterian church in New Jersey; then a Baptist church in the same state; then an Episcopal parish in Wheaton, Illinois. Christian students in significant numbers at Yale, Princeton, UCLA, Harvard, Stanford, and Wheaton were spirit baptized. In his 1964 book *They Speak with Other Tongues*, journalist John Sherrill relates how within three years the awareness and exercise of charismatic gifts swept through mainstream American Christianity, even Roman Catholicism. "Charism" became a key word of the Second Vatican Council, to which Pope John XXIII frequently referred as a "new Pentecost" (see chapter 10).

As charismatic Christianity spread into other denominations both Catholic and Protestant in the 1960s, it did not usually lead to internal doctrinal strife, as many had feared. Catholic charismatics on the whole remained good Catholics, and Protestants remained good Protestants within their various denominational boundaries. The main difference between them and the Pentecostals, says Roger G. Robins in his 2010 book *Pentecostalism in America*, is that Pentecostals deem tongue speaking the definitive sign of spirit baptism, while charismatics rank it equally with other spiritual gifts, such as healing, discernment of spirits, and prophecy. Spirit baptism (or in the Catholic faith, charismatic renewal) operates within the existing doctrinal understanding of the believer, acting not upon the mind but upon the heart.

The Catholic charismatic renewal—which is practical Pentecostalism expressed in Catholic language, theology, and imagery—began in 1967 on four Midwestern American college campuses and quietly exploded. Greeted with cautious approval by most bishops, by the turn of the century it was active in two hundred and thirty countries among more than one hundred million adherents.

Introduction of the charismatic gifts moved with similar ease through the older mainline Protestant denominations, but encountered barriers among evan-

The Catholic charismatic renewal was greeted with cautious approval by most bishops. It became active in 230 countries with one hundred million adherents.

gelicals and such fundamentalists as the powerful Southern Baptists and Missouri Synod Lutherans. Within these diverse Bible-based churches, some are nondispensationalist, and see Pentecostalism as a return of the third-century Montanist heresy, condemned at the time for its apocalyptic end-times certainty, harsh morality, and ecstatic worship. Others are dispensationalist, holding apocalyptic beliefs of their own, but reject Pentecostalism's ecstatic, mystical, experiential approach. They all reject its anti-trinitarian "oneness" sects, as being equivalent to Mormonism and the Jehovah's Witnesses.

But despite such resistance, by the closing decades of the twentieth century, evangelicalism was becoming increasingly charismatic in feeling, language, and worship style. Gordon T. Smith, a prolific evangelical scholar at Regent College, Vancouver, notes in his essay "Conversion and Redemption" in the authoritative 2011 *Oxford Handbook of Evangelical Theology*, that the pattern of revivalism which sustained evangelicalism for two centuries had lost its appeal. Based on the convert intellectually accepting certain defined biblical propositions about personal salvation, evangelicalism put little emphasis on personal spiritual experiences, continuing discipleship after the conversion feeling wears off, or the sacramental role of the church. These, as it happens, are all strengths within Pentecostalism and charismatic Christianity. As a result, many of the largest new churches and ministries in the new century, although not explicitly Pentecostal, were noticeably charismatic.

Indeed, the only possible vulnerability of the Pentecostal/evangelical churches in the twenty-first century appeared to lie in their success, and more specifically the

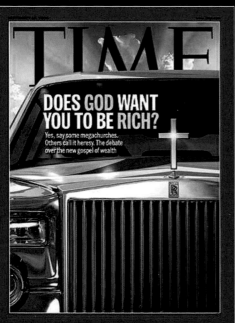

The success of the Pentecostal movement has materially enriched some of its influential pastors—a situation that resulted in a Senate investigation which, if nothing else, shed light on their lavish lifestyles and inspired a Time magazine cover story. Among the richest were (counterclockwise from bottom right) Kenneth Copeland, Creflo A. Dollar, and Joyce Meyer, whose Canadair Challenger jet is pictured above her. These preachers attribute their wealth to what they call "prosperity theology." They contend that certain biblical passages—including the parable the talents (Matthew 25:14–30)— promise that faith and good works will result in personal prosperity.

financial wealth of their most prominent and influential pastors, especially those with national and international television followings in North and South America and Korea. A four-year U.S. Senate investigation (which chose for legal reasons not to compel evidence) was unable to assess precisely how much went to the featured televangelists. But it briefly described the lavish lifestyles of half a dozen of them: Kenneth and Gloria Copeland of Texas (Pentecostal), Creflo and Taffi Dollar of Georgia (charismatic independent), Benny Hinn of Texas (charismatic independent), Eddie Long of Georgia (charismatic Baptist), Joyce and David Meyer of Missouri (charismatic independent), and Paula and Randy White of Florida (charismatic independent)—all of them obviously spending millions of dollars a year on salaries, expenses, personal mansions, fancy cars, and private jets.

Television ministries are legally tax-exempt religious organizations like churches, and operate as unaccountably as private companies governed by close friends or family members. Similar criticisms are often directed at megachurches, but their incomes cannot match that of the media ministries. The six listed above amounted to billion-dollar conglomerates of church and charitable enterprises, linked to for-profit investments that were shielded from effective IRS examination by the religious exemption of the parent church. And these were just the largest at the time. They had been preceded by a long and sordid succession of sex and money scandals going back to the bankruptcy of Jim Bakker (Pentecostal), his Praise The Lord empire, and his five-year imprisonment in 1989 on twenty-eight counts of fraud and conspiracy.[8] Yet despite the scandals, believers remained willing to support ever more television ministries.

Paul Alexander devotes a chapter of *Signs and Wonders* to an increasing belief in prosperity theology among Pentecostal/charismatics in America, and he cites even worse examples in Korea and Brazil. Prosperity theology is based on the notion that God does not want people to be poor, and therefore pours out his blessings on the virtuous. Author Alexander agrees with the first point, crediting it as key to Pentecostal success in the third world. If "prosperity" is taken simply to mean sufficiency, lifting people out of urban slums and destitute rural villages all over the world, who could be against it? But the super ministries have turned it into plain greed by encouraging reciprocal greed in their audiences: "If you give this ministry one hundred dollars, you will receive one-hundredfold in return."

Televangelizing prosperity preachers are the face of Pentecostalism most visible to the outside world, one that many noncharismatic Christians and non-Christians alike find quite repellent. But the strength of the third force of Christianity lies elsewhere, in the army of ordinary believers and speakers in tongues who for a hundred years have exceeded everyone's expectations—except, that is, their own. ■

8. Jim Bakker was not the only televangelist to make undesirable news in the 1980s. Jimmy Swaggart (Pentecostal), was defrocked in 1988 as an Assemblies of God minister for involvement with prostitutes, and continued his broadcast ministry as an independent Pentecostal. Faith healer Peter Popoff (independent charismatic) almost lost his multi-million-dollar ministry in 1987, when it was revealed that his amazing knowledge of people in his audiences arrived by an in-ear receiver rather than from the Holy Spirit. But by 1998 he was back in business, and in 2005 he and his wife drew a combined salary of nearly one million dollars.

Pope John Paul II occupies the archbishop's chair at Wawel Cathedral in Krakow in 1979 during the first of his many visits to his homeland as pope. The surprise death of predecessor John Paul I after thirty-three days, paved the way for this fifty-eight-year-old junior cardinal, Poland's Karol Wojtyla, to become the first Slavic pope in history.

CHAPTER 16

How the genius of JPII transformed the papacy and foiled its traducers

Facing dissent in Europe, Marxism in Latin America, clerical pedophilia, and four would-be assassins, he found one loyal ally: it was called the laity

I talian churchmen have a word for what they want in a new pontiff: he must be *papabile* (literally "pope-able"). Does he have the wit, character, and spiritual strength to be a bridge (Latin *pons*, whence "pontiff") between God and man, and to keep peace between the Vatican and the national and political factions, cultures, and traditions within the billion-member Roman Catholic Church? When Pope Paul VI died in 1978 (see chapter 10, page 190), Catholicism was in trouble. According to Catholic historian George Weigel in *Witness to Hope* (2001), the church was so thoroughly divided between modernizers and traditionalists by 1978 that the men who flew into Rome to choose a successor were prepared for a long stay. On August 25, 111 red-robed cardinals sang the medieval hymn "*Veni Creator Spiritus*" (Come, Holy Ghost) as they processed in sweltering heat from Mass in Saint Peter's Basilica into the ornate Sistine Chapel—there to be locked inside for however long it would take.[1]

Conclave deliberations are secret under pain of excommunication, but it is widely believed that the initial votes favored the staunchly traditionalist Italian Giuseppe Siri, bishop of Genoa. The progressive vote for modernization, initially favorable to Vatican official Sergio Pignedoli, by the end of day two had swung decisively to a third Italian, Venice Archbishop Albino Luciani. That happened, reportedly, because a fourth Italian, Cardinal Archbishop of Florence Giovanni Benelli, though *papabile* himself, had pressed the case for the quiet, unassuming Venetian. Before uttering the crucial "*accepto*" (I accept), Luciani

1. A modern conclave contains up to 120 cardinals of voting age (under 80), almost half from Europe, and almost half of those from Italy. Each vote, called a "scrutiny," proceeds mostly in silence. Between scrutinies, cardinals informally discuss the evolving options. There are no formal nomination meetings, parties, or candidate speeches. A cardinal writes the name of his designate on a numbered ballot. Canon law requires only that his choice be a baptized male Catholic (even himself), though candidates are invariably cardinals. The moment an elected candidate says the word "*accepto*," he is the pope.

2. It seems to have become the assumption of papal conclaves that he who wants the job shouldn't get it. It wasn't always so. Gregory VI is known to have bought the office from the corrupt Benedict IX in the eleventh century just to get him to leave. The famously hedonist and fun-loving Medici pope Leo X, upon his election in 1513, was said (by an enemy) to have exulted, "God has given us the papacy; let us enjoy it."

is said to have buried his head in his hands and said, "May God forgive you for what you have done."[2]

Luciani's appearance on the basilica balcony as Pope John Paul I came as a surprise to media and onlookers, since he wasn't thought to be in consideration. Yet the short, smiling pontiff with working-class sympathies was so friendly and funny, and so unlike his austere and erudite predecessor, the press loved him and people warmed to him instantly. They liked that he was the first pope in many centuries to refuse a coronation with the triple tiara, the first to refer to himself as "I" and not "we", and that he spoke well in simple language.

The cardinals who had elected John Paul I were, says Weigel, unaware that their new man had been suffering serious heart problems, because he did not tell them. He simply bowed his head and accepted their decision as the will of God. They discovered his condition only thirty-three days after his installment, when a household nun found him sitting dead in bed on the morning of September 29, apparently killed by a heart attack.[3]

This escalated the perception of problems in the church to outright crisis. What now? Historians agree that the cardinals who converged once again on Rome were convinced that with Luciani's untimely death, God was telling them something—but what? Both traditionalists and progressives remained firm in their opposing positions, and Luciani had seemed the best compromise.

This mood of somber preoccupation was evidenced by Karol Wojtyla, the junior of Poland's two cardinals. Born in 1920, Wojtyla had lived

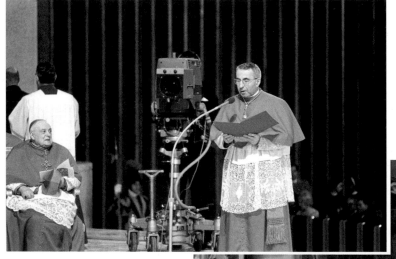

On the right, the conclave of cardinals gathers at Saint Peter's Basilica before entering the Sistine Chapel, where they will elect a successor to the recently deceased John Paul I (shown standing in inset above, five years earlier, as Cardinal Albino Luciani).

Karol Wojtyla during his First Communion in Poland around 1931; and as a young priest in the 1950s enjoying one of his athletic pursuits, kayaking. At his ordination in 1946, Poland's Communist government recognized him as an ally, a mistake that would eventually lead to their overthrow. His opposition to the regime imposed upon Poland by the Soviet Union would later define his reign as pope.

most of his life under totalitarian regimes—first Nazism and then communism. He had from his youth a passion for culture, especially drama, as well as sports, hiking, and kayaking. However, he had spent much of his adolescent years resisting the Nazis by working in a Catholic cultural underground, and was accepted as a clandestine seminarian in Krakow. By war's end (for Poland) in 1944, Wojtyla's small family had all died of natural causes, and he went into the Catholic priesthood. His ordination in 1946 set him in opposition to the new Communist regime imposed on Poland by the Soviet Union. Wojtyla considered Catholic Christianity, not communism, to be the true essence and foundation of Polish culture, and though the Vatican after Yalta pursued a policy of reluctant acceptance of Soviet hegemony in Eastern Europe, Wojtyla never did agree with leaving half the continent in slavery.

He was philosophically trained, reform minded, and likable. By 1978, he had risen to archbishop of Krakow and cardinal, had traveled in international church circles, and had voted in the August conclave. He had barely returned to Poland when the news arrived that John Paul I was dead. He immediately went to his chapel to pray. His friends in Krakow noticed that he was strangely quiet as he prepared to return to Rome. There had long been a premonition among some of them that he would one day become pope—though as everyone knew, no Slav had ever been pope and Italians had held the post since 1523, so what were the odds? But then there was a story that as a young priest Wojtyla had visited the famous miracle-working friar Padre Pio in Italy in 1947, who had prophesied (so went the legend) that one day Wojtyla would be pope. Indeed, a small number of first-round ballots were said to have named him in the August conclave. While Catholics in Italy were praying fervently that their own local favorite would now be chosen, the Poles closest to Wojtyla, unwilling to lose

3. The pope's sudden death generated abundant conspiracy theories, the most common that he was one of a half-dozen people murdered by officials in or close to the allegedly corrupt Vatican Bank. However, though bank-related murders did occur, it has been convincingly disproved that John Paul I was one of them. Even so, anyone who finds such theories impossibly far-fetched might well heed the comment of nineteenth-century cardinal John Henry Newman: "The Rock of Saint Peter on its summit enjoys a pure and serene atmosphere, but there is a great deal of Roman malaria at the foot of it." Moreover, by 2011, mainstream secular media—*Forbes, der Spiegel*, and many others—were reporting regularly on the Vatican Bank's failure to satisfy Europe's increasingly stiff banking disclosure standards.

him, were praying fervently that he would be passed over and come home.

Voting in this second 1978 conclave went into a third day. The accepted story has it that once again Siri of Genoa garnered the traditionalists' support and that this time Benelli of Florence outpaced him with progressive votes. Neither cardinal, however, gathered the necessary two-thirds plus one vote. That distinction fell in the eighth round to Karol Wojtyla, aged fifty-eight, because, according to author Weigel, he was seen as (a) a strong doctrinal conservative, (b) a modernizer though not a Modernist, (c) a bishop of exceptional experience, intelligence, character, and personality, (d) fluent in the ten most common languages of the Catholic world, and (e) not from Italy. Many cardinals were convinced that Luciani's death was a signal from God to search farther afield.

If the throng in Saint Peter's Square had been surprised in August, they were totally baffled by the complete stranger who stepped to the loggia balustrade on October 16—and (being mostly Romans) they were suspicious. "*Chi è?*" they asked each other dubiously. "Who's he?" "Is he an Asian...a Negro?" In booming, fluent Italian, John Paul II answered: "Praised be Jesus Christ!... We are still

French journalist André Frossard sensed something strangely magnificent. 'This is not a pope from Poland,' he wrote, 'but a pope from Galilee.'

grieved after the death of our beloved John Paul I. And now the eminent cardinals have called a new bishop of Rome. They have called him from a far country—far, but always near through the communion of faith and the Christian tradition." Because he spoke their national language so well—and even better their religious one—the crowd soon began cheering, louder and louder. A Polish pope! There was something inspiring about this new man. They felt it instantly, as would millions of others in years to come. French journalist André Frossard, a convert from atheism, sensed in John Paul II something strangely magnificent. He said, "This is not a pope from Poland; this is a pope from Galilee."

By choosing the papal name of his predecessor, John Paul signaled his commitment to completing the changes called for by Vatican II thirteen years earlier—which he soon told the Roman curia must be their highest priority. Like the first John Paul he eschewed a coronation, and broke precedent by receiving the homage of his brother cardinals standing rather than enthroned. He preferred people not to kiss his ring, though he never made an issue of it. He said Catholics should understand that the "Constantinian era" of the church was over—by which he meant the politically powerful medieval and early-modern papacy. The only power of the church, declared John Paul, lies in the mystery of the cross and Resurrection; and the church must not speak in the language of force, but of love and charity.

He was soon recognized as tireless. He rose at 5:30, prayed, read the news, said Mass at 7:30, spent most mornings from 9:30 to 11:00 writing or editing sermons, speeches, and encyclicals in his spacious, modestly furnished Vatican apartment. He started his official business at 11:00. Unlike other popes, he took charge of his own chapel, his own private lunch and supper company, and his own summer residence. Whenever he wasn't working, eating, or sleeping, he was praying. He watched few movies, and relaxed by walking and reading philosophy.

John Paul II had a gift for media messaging. Upon his election, for example, he found out that Poland's Communist television monopoly had scheduled three hours for his two-hour inaugural Mass; so he stretched the event to three to deprive them of the concluding hour he knew they would otherwise devote to hostile commentary. His famous sermon that morning—"Be not afraid—open wide the doors for Christ!"—was unabashed,

John Paul II rides through the streets of Mexico City in January 1979 during his first foreign trip as pope. Preaching in fluent Spanish to a crowd so dense he had to be brought to the outdoor altar by helicopter, the pope called for "urgent reforms" in government to help the poor. By this, he would later clarify, he did not mean Marxism.

powerful evangelism. After the Mass he left the basilica and went alone to the crowd outside, blessed a group of handicapped people, hugged a small boy who broke past security to give him flowers, and waved aloft his big crozier like a flag. They cheered and cheered, and went on cheering after he had returned to his apartment, where he waved some more from the window. Finally he told them, laughing, that it was time for everyone to eat lunch, "even the pope."

For the Roman curia and their three thousand staff, the Vatican's quiet, predictable routines were suddenly a thing of the past. This pope often welcomed unscheduled outsiders, especially Poles, into his home, he set his own agenda, and he moved with exhausting speed. Three months after his installation, in January 1979, upon invitation by Latin American bishops, John Paul conducted a major tour of Mexico—a country run by a revolutionary government intolerant of the church and constitutionally anticlerical. But it was like the bursting of a dam. He was welcomed at the airport by the Mexican president, priests and nuns broke the law by appearing in religious dress in public, and one million Mexicans showered him with flowers along his five-mile route into Mexico City.

The Mexican visit was a preview of John Paul's long reign. Preaching in fluent, self-taught Spanish to a crowd of Indians in southern Mexico so dense he had to be brought to the outdoor altar by helicopter, he promised to bring "real help" in pressing for economic and political justice for the poor. This, he said, required "bold changes" and "urgent reforms" in Latin America.[4] Yet the very next day he warned the third decennial assembly of Latin American bishops that the extreme, Marxist forms of "liberation theology" which pervaded so many of their countries, and were being preached by so many of their radicalized priests, were contrary to Catholic beliefs and must be stopped.

Secular media and the radical Catholic left immediately accused the pope of hypocrisy. How could he demand liberation in Poland while seeking to suppress it in Latin America? How could he demand freedom and equality for Eastern Bloc Christians while resisting the same thing for women within his own church? Answering such questions would occupy the first half of his twenty-seven-year papacy—for in the pope's view, they arose from a fatally flawed twentieth-century

4. Talk of Latin American political reform was more than mere platitude. One year later, Salvadoran archbishop Oscar Romero was shot to death while lifting the chalice above the altar during Mass in a hospital chapel. Though opposed to Marxist liberation theology, Romero fearlessly advocated for political and economic reforms, and for a peaceful, negotiated end to the brutal civil war between right and left. For this he was martyred, probably by a right-wing death squad. To the chagrin of the right-wing Salvadoran government, Pope John Paul prayed at his tomb during his visit to that country in 1983.

conception of freedom. Marxism is Marxism, whether in the incubation stage contained in the more extreme forms of Latin American liberation theology, or in the tottering and fossilized regimes of the Soviet empire. Communism is not, for example, like Aristotelian or Platonic philosophy, which can be adapted to and completed by Christianity. Marxism—like radical feminism—fundamentally misapprehends the nature of man, and its absolute demands must therefore produce not freedom but oppression.

John Paul's Mexican trip ended with the sight of a million small handheld mirrors flashing and twinkling in the sun toward his departing plane to bid him farewell. He flew home to Rome, to keep an important appointment of a kind rare among popes. To remind everyone that he was actually bishop of Rome, and not only "vicar of Christ on earth," he officiated at the marriage of a young woman of no great social consequence named Vittoria Janni whom he had met in church at Christmas. The daughter of a Roman street cleaner, she was engaged to a young man named Mario Maltese, and she asked John Paul if he would perform the ceremony. He smiled and agreed. Also, by popular demand, he started leading each month's first Saturday recitation of the rosary across the whole world on Vatican radio. He preached to thirteen thousand Italian soldiers, and was photographed grinning in a plumed helmet. News media had never seen a

At bottom, Karol Wojtyla returns to Krakow as Pope John Paul II in June 1979, arriving by helicopter, and met by his cousins (the two little girls being led by a priest). Inset above, during the pope's fourth pilgrimage to Poland in post-Communist 1991, Solidarity leader Lech Walesa greets him with a kiss to the papal ring, a practice John Paul tolerated but wished would end.

pope like this, nor had the world. By spring time Rome's tourist council estimated that John Paul had drawn a record five million visitors to the Eternal City.

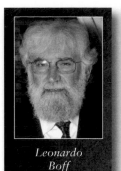
Leonardo Boff

Charles Curran

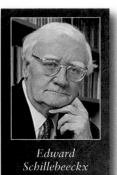
Edward Schillebeeckx

Paul Collins

Indeed, John Paul was such a natural star it would be possible to see his papacy as a kind of continual evangelistic rock tour. Weigel recounts in *Witness to Hope* how in June, 1979, John Paul made a triumphal visit to Poland (see chapter 17), and in October the first papal visit in history to both Ireland and the United States. In New York, Mayor Edward Koch introduced himself by saying, "Your Holiness, I am the mayor," to which the pope replied, "I shall try to be a good citizen." Greeting tens of thousands of exuberant youth in Madison Square Garden arena, he stood waving up to them from his Ford Bronco "popemobile" as it slowly circled the rink. A high school band blared out the triumphant theme from the boxing movie *Rocky* and the kids chanted "John Paul Two—We love you!" and the pope chanted back through the sound system, "Woo hoo woo—John Paul Two—He loves you!" At one point the pope actually imitated a rock drummer and then thrust both thumbs in the air while the crowd erupted in a happy bedlam wilder than the Garden ever gave the New York Rangers.

In the Midwest, after hearing John Paul preach under a hot sun to the largest crowd in the history of Iowa, an admiring Protestant pastor said to his Catholic neighbor, "You got a pope who knows how to pope!" In Chicago the Poles in the crowd sang their traditional well-wishing song *Sto lat!* so long, loudly, and often that the pope joked, "If they keep this up Americans will think it's the Polish national anthem." Recessing from Mass in the Cathedral of the Holy Cross in Boston he veered aside into the congregation to greet a young woman named Jane De Martino in a wheelchair, paralyzed by a traffic accident. He took her hand, kissed her, whispered something to her, and gave her a little white and gold rosary. A nearby policeman burst into tears.

Such behavior by a pontiff was as novel to Catholics as it was to everyone else, and it is safe to assert that most loved it. Not so Catholic progressives, however—those who wanted more local and national autonomy from Rome, a married priesthood, women priests, homosexual priests, a permissive policy on divorce, contraception and abortion, a liturgy less about God and more about people, more emphasis on government programs and less on salvation through the sacraments. People of this view had come to dominate many—perhaps most—dioceses of the western world after Vatican II, and John Paul's nonstop evangelistic road show kept hammering home the message that these changes would not happen.

Like most popes, John Paul moved as quickly as possible to appoint a supportive curia. Key to this was his 1981 recruitment of Bavarian priest and theologian Joseph Ratzinger, installed by Paul VI only four years earlier as archbishop of Munich. Ratzinger and Wojtyla had first connected at the August 1978 conclave. Now John Paul persuaded Ratzinger to head the Vatican's Congregation for the Doctrine of the Faith (CDF), the Catholic Church's highest doctrinal

The nun who won over the world

They were Calcutta's human trash who didn't matter, but to Mother Teresa they did,
and by becoming their servant she drew 4,000 helpers to give hope to India's hopeless

The slums of Calcutta (now Kolkata) in the 1940s were a miasma of almost inconceivable misery, where tens of thousands of people per square mile lived in squalor and disease. Acquisition of clean food and water was a daily struggle on streets flowing with garbage and raw sewage. The tropical climate ensured stifling heat punctuated by seasonal monsoons, while Bengal's recurring famines brought streams of refugees from the countryside, most of whom would join the existing hordes of homeless beggars. For the poorest of the poor—the abandoned children, the lepers, the dying— death was generally imminent. But it was precisely to these unfortunate souls that in 1946 a diminutive nun named Agnes Gonxha Bojaxhiu chose, entirely single-handed, to dedicate her life.

Single-handed, that is, except for God. The woman who would be known to history as Mother Teresa reached her remarkable decision while traveling through Calcutta's wretched slums to the annual retreat of her order. A Sister of Loreto, then thirty-six, she reflected upon the desperation she observed from her train window, and her life purpose suddenly came into focus. Author Joan Graff, in *Mother Teresa* (1988), quotes her later recollection of that crucial decision: "I was to leave the convent and help the poor, while living among them. It was an order. To fail would have been to break the faith."

Her faith would be severely tested. Conditions worsened with the outbreak of hostilities between Bengali Muslims and Hindus in August 1946, and orderly British rule crumbled during the preparations for India's partition. By 1948, when she received permission to leave her order, Calcutta was seething with ethnic hatred and its slums were more horrifying than ever. But into them she went, alone, and began to experience all the consequences of her resolve. "The poverty of the poor must be so hard for them," she wrote in her diary. "While looking for a home I walked and walked till my arms and legs ached... Then the comfort of Loreto (her former order) came to tempt me. 'You have only to say the word and all that will be yours again,' the Tempter kept on saying." (Quoted in *Mother Teresa: A Complete Authorized Biography,* by Kathryn Spink, 1997.)

Instead, being nearly as poor as the beggars surrounding her, she simply joined them and set to work. But before long the novelty of her lone and humble enterprise led to a certain reputation; young women arrived, eager to help her, supplies began to be donated, and government officials publicly applauded this unique undertaking. From the beginning, however, Mother Teresa refused state administrative intervention; her work must remain apolitical.

Her own early life was the source of this principle. She was born August 1910 into an Albanian family at Skopje, the capital of Macedonia, then an Ottoman province. Nationalist feeling ran high in the Turkish-controlled Balkan territories, and her father was involved in politics. His suspicious death in 1918 deeply affected the eight-year-old girl. Her Roman Catholic faith, while a source of consolation, also underlined her family's minority status in a country dominated by Islam and by Orthodox Christianity. At age eighteen, Agnes left the tensions of her homeland for a life of service to the Catholic Church.

Joining the Sisters of Loreto, she spent the first year of her novitiate at Loreto Abbey in Rathfarnham, Ireland. Her studies continued after traveling to Darjeeling, India. She chose the name Teresa upon taking religious vows at twenty-one, and for the next fifteen years taught in convent schools, learning three languages along the way. Many of her students would later follow her to Calcutta's unforgiving streets.

With Vatican permission these women formed the nucleus of the Missionaries of Charity, founded as a diocesan congregation in 1950. By 1955, they had established the City of Peace (a leprosy hospice), the Children's Home of the Immaculate Heart (an orphanage), and the first Home for the Dying. Momentum continued as donations increased and new volunteers arrived. In response to persistent demand, the Missionaries of Charity Brothers was established in 1963. Mother Teresa meanwhile nurtured a growing desire to expand the work outside the city.

Although canon law forbade such action until the Missionaries of Charity had achieved ten years of service, by 1959 the archbishop of Calcutta allowed the opening of other Indian foundations. Prime Minister Jawaharlal Nehru attended the inauguration of the Delhi children's home, thus guaranteeing a national profile. Soon the first overseas operation opened in

The Albanian nun Agnes Gonxha Bojaxhiu, known to the world as Mother Teresa, was called at age thirty-six to live with and assist the poor on the streets of Calcutta, as she is shown doing here in a 1976 photo. In 1979 she was awarded the Nobel Peace Prize, and donated the proceeds to the poor of India.

Venezuela, a modest affair with five Sisters providing care to impoverished peasants. A papal audience in 1965 led to the founding of a house for refugees in Rome, a children's home in Tanzania, and an Australian rehabilitation clinic for juvenile addicts.

This global outreach drew the attention of Malcolm Muggeridge, a British media personality whose 1969 BBC documentary, *Something Beautiful for God*, brought international fame to Mother Teresa's work. Best known for world-weary cynicism, Muggeridge surprised viewers with a reverential portrayal of the Missionaries of Charity. Public reaction was immediate and donations soared. Among numerous awards bestowed upon the Missionaries' founder was the Nobel Peace Prize; she requested that the accompanying $192,000 be donated to India's poor. Her Nobel Lecture in December 1979 was notable for its condemnation of contemporary morality: "I feel the greatest destroyer of peace today is abortion," she declared, "because it is a direct war, a direct killing—direct murder by the mother herself."

Commentators cited such remarks as proof of a political agenda, and the politicized nature of the abortion issue ensured that her vehemently pro-life position would generate criticism. In the 1980s, it was her association with people of dubious credibility that provided her opponents with ammunition. In 1981, she accepted the *Legion d'Honneur* from Haitian dictator Jean-Claude Duvalier. In 1987, her trip to Albania included a visit to the grave of former Communist leader Enver Hoxha. The acceptance of a $1.25 million donation from Charles Keating, convicted in the 1980s U.S. savings-and-loan scam, and her subsequent refusal to acknowledge calls to return the money, elicited guilt-by-association charges. Some Bengalis objected to the portrayal of Calcutta as a hopeless environment.

Meanwhile, disturbing allegations emerged of negligent medical care provided by the Missionaries of Charity. In 1994, Dr. Robin Fox, editor of the respected British medical journal *The Lancet*, visited a Missionaries hospice in Calcutta. His accusations of caregiver incompetence were later corroborated by former volunteers. More serious was Dr. Fox's assertion that the withholding of pain medication for patients was unethical and deliberate. And while the Missionaries of Charity weathered this storm of controversy, Mother Teresa silently struggled through a profound crisis of her own.

Always careful to present a public image of gentle strength, in private life she questioned her faith, her work, herself. Her correspondence, released posthumously as *Come Be My Light: The Private Writings of the 'Saint of Calcutta'* (editor Brian Kolodiejchuk, 2007), reveals what is recognizably the state described as the "dark night of the soul," experienced by her namesake Thérèse of Lisieux, Saint Anthony, Saint John of the Cross, and numerous others, typically those far advanced in the spiritual life. They must rely on pure, naked faith, not the affirmed and assisted faith of the "normal" Christian. Thus she feels abandoned by God, lacking palpable, normal affirmations from him.

"I have no faith—I dare not utter the words and thoughts that crowd in my heart and make me suffer untold agony," she wrote. Her ubiquitous smile? "A mask." Her doubts were starkly expressed: "What do I labor for? If there be no God—there can be no soul—if there is no soul then Jesus you are

Mother Teresa leaves the Missionaries of Charity residence in the Bronx holding the hand of Diana, Princess of Wales, in June 1997. In this, the year of her death, Mother Teresa had become as big an international celebrity as Diana, who had espoused selected charities, and died in an automobile crash that same year. Unlike the jet-setting princess, however, Teresa lived with those she helped, and, six years later, was beatified by Pope John Paul II for her selfless service to the poor.

also not true." In her final years, however, she expressed a sense of peaceful resolution: "God is in love with us and keeps giving Himself to the world—through you—through me." Eventually she recognized her mysterious suffering as an imprint of Christ's Passion on her soul.

This very human woman achieved tremendously in the name of the faith. When she died in 1997, some four thousand Missionaries of Charity sisters and brothers were caring for countless disadvantaged persons worldwide. In 1999, the Gallup Poll reported that Americans considered her "Most admired person of the twentieth century." The government of India gave her a state funeral, which spoke volumes since India is a predominantly Hindu country. Pope John Paul II beatified her in 2003, remarkably soon after her death, and her example serves as an ideal for millions. But Mother Teresa herself put most succinctly the essence of the choice she made in 1946: "Only in Heaven will we see how much we owe to the poor for helping us to love God better because of them." ■

Australia's controversial Cardinal George Pell, shown here preaching in Sydney, was the focus of liberal criticism in the late John Paul/early Benedict period. The liberals charged that Pell's "overemphasis" on obedience to papal diktat, and his disregard for individual conscience, was contrary to Catholic tradition. Laughing, Pell retorted, "If every individual's personal conscience is supreme, my conscientious viewpoint is as good as the view of this crew, and there is no way of resolving the dispute between us."

5. Among the several key doctrinal conclusions of Vatican I, Collins cites as the most significant that of "papal primacy," which decreed that the bishop of Rome holds authority over the "clergy and faithful, of whatever rite and dignity, both singly and collectively...not only in matters concerning faith and morals, but also in those which regard the discipline and government of the church throughout the world." Collins argues that Vatican I overextended the traditional understanding. The primacy doctrine is distinct from the same council's "papal infallibility" pronouncement, which describes a seldom-invoked and heavily circumscribed papal power to further define existing doctrines.

authority under the pope. By the 1980s it had serious work to do, and it wasted no time in doing it. The most striking thing about it, however, was how gently it proceeded—on the logic that bishops, rather than Rome, should be the first line of defense against error.

In 1984, the CDF formally condemned Marxism-based forms of liberation theology. In 1985, it politely but firmly rapped the literary knuckles of Brazilian priest, liberation theologian, and author Leonardo Boff, leading him to quit the priesthood eight years later. In 1986, it canceled the Catholic teaching certificate of American priest and ethics professor Charles Curran; he remained Catholic and switched to a Methodist university. Also in 1986, it corrected Dutch Dominican Modernist Edward Schillebeeckx but did not condemn his books or excommunicate him. That same year it rectified permissive interpretations of earlier Vatican statements about homosexuality, reiterating that same-sex practices are intrinsically disordered and always immoral. In 1987, it warned bishops of the moral repugnancy of most new forms of human reproductive technology, and of scientific experiments with human embryos.

Any hope the Vatican II progressives harbored when the reformer Karol Wojtyla became John Paul II had vanished by the 1990s. He may have been in some ways a modernizer, but not in the areas they most wanted. One such disappointee was Australian priest Paul Collins, a prolific and skillful polemicist. He ran afoul of the CDF over his 1997 book *Papal Power*.

The Collins thesis, repeated in later books such as *God's New Man* (2006), holds that the Catholic Church changed fundamentally—much for the worse—when it formally adopted a policy in the First Vatican Council (1869–1870) that the pope is all-powerful over the church.[5] After a disagreeable exchange with Prefect Ratzinger's CDF, Collins left the priesthood in 2001. He nevertheless added his name to a formal 2006 doctrinal complaint to the CDF by twenty-four noted Catholic liberals against controversial conservative Australian cardinal George Pell. His "overemphasis" on obedience to papal teaching, and his disregard for individual conscience, they charged, were contrary to Catholic tradition. Asked about it by news media, Pell actually laughed, and suggested his critics were being logically inconsistent: "If every individual's personal conscience is supreme, my conscientious viewpoint is as good as the view of this crew, and there is no way of resolving the dispute between us." (The CDF did not respond to the complaint.)

If there was ever a death knell for Vatican II progressivism it tolled in October, 1992 with the release of the new *Catechism of the Catholic Church*, a six-year project overseen by Ratzinger and eleven other cardinals and bishops. Written by dozens of contributing scholars, it had gone through nine drafts. In eight hundred pages, item by item, it laid out all facets of basic Catholic faith.

In the process it answered authoritatively all the questions about faith and morals that had been troubling the church for thirty years. It did not satisfy Catholic dissenters, who remained numerous in the first world, especially Europe; but it left no more room for doubt among the laity—whether or not they agreed—as to where their church stands on every contended point.

As John Paul II steadily pursued his course, visiting one hundred thirty nations, inaugurating a biennial papal World Youth Day around the globe, preaching about social justice, religious liberty, human dignity, and salvation through faith in Christ, his critics were reduced to grinding their teeth. Collins, for example, complained that the world no longer associated "Roman Catholicism" with the local bishop and the neighborhood church. It was now wholly personified by this traveling, telegenic pope, who monopolized the media limelight and appointed into the hierarchy, in the description of prominent progressive Catholic priest and novelist Andrew Greeley, "mean-spirited careerists—inept, incompetent, insensitive bureaucrats."

Critics of John Paul's departure from progressivism were confounded by the unprecedented popularity of this travelling pontiff who became a virtual rock star in the course of his visits to 130 nations, drawing immense crowds wherever he went, and charming politicians and religious leaders of all stripes. At bottom, the multitudes gather in the Polish shrine city of Czestochowa for John Paul's sixth visit there in 1991. Below right, he greets the Dalai Lama during one of the Buddhist leader's eight visits to the Vatican. Below left, John Paul waves to a Paris crowd from the bulletproof "popemobile" (a precaution instituted after the 1981 assassination attempt) during the 1997 World Youth Day.

His many critics knew that John Paul had forged an unbreakable bond of affection with the laity. The biggest problems he saw in the church were centered in the hierarchy. John Paul was determined, clearly, to find and promote traditionalist clergy as quickly as possible, to the highest possible level—even if it meant, as it often did, bypassing progressives who were already in line for advancement. Most Catholic priests are ordained and promoted by bishops, but all bishops and cardinals are chosen only with papal approval; and it was here that struggles were most intense.

In the early church, when congregations were small and the earthly reward for a bishop's mitre was very often martyrdom, bishops were chosen by their priests, often with the participation of the educated laity, subject to neighboring bishops being willing to consecrate them. When the church became larger, wealthier, and more influential, the secular influence was assumed by kings and emperors, an inevitability that worked well when the monarchs were themselves pious Christians. When the kingdoms of northwestern Europe and Britain turned Protestant, their views were no longer relevant. Since the Reformation, and since Vatican I, secular government involvement has given way to papal authority,

Nowhere did episcopal oversight cause John Paul worse headaches than in Europe, where a culture of moral relativism had infected most dioceses.

mainly through the "nuncios" (Vatican diplomats) assigned to each country. Local bishops and national bishops' councils, though they still initiate the selection process, leave the final scrutiny and choice of short-listed candidates to the nuncios, the Vatican Congregation for Bishops, and the pope.

Nowhere did episcopal oversight cause John Paul worse headaches than in Europe, where a culture of moral relativism and sacramental lassitude had infected most dioceses as local bishops tried to remain relevant to Europe's emerging post-Christian culture. In 1986, against local wishes and advice, the pope imposed an obscure but orthodox Benedictine priest named Hans Groer as archbishop of Vienna, a key see that had long been leading in a progressive direction. In 1995, Groer was credibly accused of homosexual abuse over twenty years, some involving adolescent minors, and he retired in disgrace. Groer categorically denied all charges. Ratzinger wanted an investigation; John Paul did not.

Three other Austrian conservatives were appointed as bishops against local preferences in the 1980s. In the Swiss diocese of Chur a storm broke in 1988 when the Vatican preemptively installed a young priest named Wolfgang Haas, first as coadjutor bishop, and then as archbishop two years later. This led to demonstrations outside the cathedral, and added momentum to the new "We Are Church" (WAC) lay movement spreading across Europe from Austria.

In 1997, WAC presented a petition to Vatican officials containing, it said, two and a half million signatures supporting the now-standard list of progressive demands. Almost all of the signatures—about ninety percent—came from the Germanic countries. Elsewhere, including North America, the petition effort fell flat: in the U.S., for example, despite media fanfare and a goal of one million signatures, organizers were chagrined to gather only thirty-seven thousand in a nation of sixty-one million Roman Catholics. Maureen Fiedler, the dynamic dissident nun who spearheaded it, later conceded: "We overestimated the theological maturity and underestimated the pietism of the Catholic laity."

Progressives became increasingly perplexed by the laity, especially the young. Even churchgoing Catholics were known to overwhelmingly disobey Catholic doctrinal demands, and to openly disagree with disciplines such as an exclusively male, celibate clergy; yet they continued to cherish John Paul. But this was explained by sociologist Franco Ferrarotti of the University of Rome. Modern people, especially the young, he said, know they can do what they want, but they like to be told authoritatively what is right, even if they choose to ignore it. Not only was John Paul telling them, he did it with obviously deep conviction and compassion.

This portrait of the aging pontiff was produced by the English painter James Gillick during the final year of John Paul's life, after he began to experience severe suffering from Parkinson's disease. But he eschewed seclusion, slowly dying in public as he had lived.

His papacy reached its zenith with the millennial celebrations marking the two-thousandth year since the birth of Christ. By then he was already visibly ill with Parkinson's disease, which became steadily more debilitating and obvious. Some said he was also suffering lingering effects from a near-fatal gunshot wound from a Turkish professional assassin in 1981 (see sidebar, page 32 and chapter 17, page 341). Fewer people were granted an audience. He grew weak and would fall asleep in meetings, his hands began to shake, he walked hunched over, and was often visibly in pain. Rather than seclude himself, however, he still spent as much time as he could in the public eye—slowly dying in public as he had lived. In 2003 Ratzinger acknowledged that the pope was very ill and urged the faithful to pray for him. That October the pope appointed 26 new cardinals of voting age (under 80) to bring the college up to strength.

He sat silently through the Easter celebrations of 2005, due to a recent tracheotomy to keep him breathing, and he died peacefully in his bed two weeks later. He was eighty-four and had been pope for over twenty-six years—second

only to the thirty-one-year record of Pius IX in the latter nineteenth century. There followed the biggest, most witnessed funeral in the history of mankind, televised live around the globe with leaders in attendance from almost every nation on earth—including the U.S. president and two former presidents, the prime minister of the Russian Republic, and the Prince of Wales and the parliamentary leaders of the United Kingdom. Among thousands of clergy present were leaders of Protestant, Eastern Orthodox, and Jewish faiths. But most who came

Above, in Krakow, a crowd mourns the death of their beloved son in April 2005. Below, the then dean of the College of Cardinals, Joseph Ratzinger (later Pope Benedict XVI), conducts the Requiem Mass at Saint Peter's, a record-breaking event attended by about ninety heads of state. Close to four million flocked to Rome for the funeral.

were lay people, numbering some two million, including perhaps one-half million Poles. The influx doubled Rome's population, producing logistical and security problems on an unprecedented scale. They came to honor the life of a man who had represented something important and good across the world. Many Catholics, even some cardinals, were already appending the unofficial tag "the great" to his name, which—if it sticks—would make him the fourth "great" pope after the apostle Peter. (The others were Saint Leo I, Saint Gregory I, and Saint Nicholas I—fifth, sixth and ninth centuries respectively).[6]

After the prescribed nine days of mourning for John Paul, the cardinals—almost none of whom had voted in conclave before—were locked into the Sistine chapel to choose a successor. One of the few who had been present in 1978 was Joseph Ratzinger, longtime doctrinal enforcer and now also dean of the College of Cardinals, and as such the president of the conclave. Neither Catholic liberals nor London bookies were listing him among the *papabili*, because he was too old (almost seventy-eight and anxious to retire), too authoritarian (nicknamed "God's Rottweiler"), and too much a Nazi-era German (as a teen he had been drafted into the Hitler Youth to support a Bavarian anti-aircraft crew).

Yet despite all this, the choice fell on him with the fourth scrutiny. In his 2005 book *Pope Benedict XVI*, Ratzinger's countryman and longtime friend Heinz-Joachim Fischer says the conclave had good reasons. Ratzinger was calm, careful, and competent—a necessary relief after the "tempestuous style" of John Paul. He knew the Vatican inside out, and having been in Rome since 1981, could serve as Roman bishop and Italian primate—an important consideration which usually favored Italians. Given his age, he would not likely reign for a quarter-century as John Paul had—another plus. But most important, for all his "bad cop" reputation, the cardinals found him gracious, gentle, orthodox, articulate in six Catholic

Neither Catholic liberals nor London bookies were favoring Ratzinger because he was too old and too authoritarian (nickname: 'God's Rottweiler').

vernacular languages plus Latin, Hebrew, and Greek, and personally warm. When voting began, while the Italians divided four ways, Ratzinger was named by sixty cardinals, according to Fischer's inside information, and on the fourth count passed the required seventy-seven.

As usual, the result was a surprise, and the early predictions for his papacy proved wrong. He continued, with reduced frequency, his predecessor's papal pilgrimages, especially World Youth Day, and in September 2012 made a controversial—and highly successful—visit to Lebanon, at a time when just over the border Syrians were in a state of civil war. But by 2012 he was eighty-five, and as his health grew more uncertain, he faced two major problems from the past which he could neither shelve nor solve.

One was the long-festering aforementioned Vatican Bank scandal, involving possible money laundering and murder (see footnote, page 313). It climaxed in May 2012 with the publication of the book *His Holiness* by Gianluigi Nuzzi, a noted Italian journalist bringing charges of secrecy, cronyism, and corruption against the Vatican—and specifically against Benedict's secretary of state (effectively the pope's prime minister) Cardinal Tarcisio Bertone. There was scant chance of the Vatican Bank scandal going away any time soon.

Far worse, at least from a public relations perspective, was a clerical sexual abuse scandal that had rocked the church with growing force since the 1980s. It involved priests, bishops, and religious who had seduced minors from across the Catholic world, especially in Europe, North America, and Australia from the 1960s to the 1980s. Worse still, there was consistent evidence of Catholic prelates concealing these crimes, a pattern which some victims claimed extended

6. Acceding to popular demand, Benedict XVI suspended the rule that the "cause" of any prospective saint must wait at least five years after death. In 2009 it was declared that John Paul II was "venerable," in having lived a life of heroic virtue. In 2011, with Vatican confirmation of one posthumous miraculous cure credited to him, he was proclaimed as "blessed." As of 2012 he was expected to be named a saint within a few more years.

Blows that shattered the priestly image

Grievous tales, billions in damages, children's lives ruined, recurrent cover-ups—
the Catholic Church reels after judgment falls on the sexual sin of 4 percent of the clergy

In a courtroom in Abbeville, Louisiana, eleven-year-old witness Scott Gastal testified to a judge that when he was seven, just after his first day as a Catholic altar boy, he had been sodomized so forcefully he had to be hospitalized. The perpetrator, a man who kept a loaded gun beside his bed, had warned him not to talk about this to anyone. But even if little Scott had been able to rise above his fear, guilt, shame, and confusion, who would have believed him? The rapist was his parish priest, Father Gilbert Gauthe.

The nationwide media exposé of child abuse by Catholic priests that followed Gauthe's 1985 criminal conviction left the impression that he must have been be a vicious ogre. Perhaps he was, but he had been immensely popular in his parishes—especially with his victims, of whom there were officially thirty-seven, but more likely seventy, and possibly a hundred.

Until the mid-1980s, priestly celibacy was admired in American popular culture as proof of selflessness. Henceforth priests would often be portrayed as sociopathic sexual predators. In one diocese after another, horrific, heartbreaking tales hit the media, attended by million-dollar lawsuits.

Pedophilia aside, young Father Gauthe was in several ways typical of many North American Catholic seminarians of the 1960s: theologically shallow, morally ambivalent, uncertain of his vocation, but in high demand as the ranks of the Catholic clergy aged and thinned. He first served as an assistant priest, starting in 1972, at Broussard, nearby the small oil patch city of Lafayette in his home state of Louisiana.

Gauthe's slightly effeminate manner didn't bother the local Cajun farmers and oil riggers because he was a robust outdoorsman, loved guns, and would shoot low-flying geese from his parish belfry. Women liked him because he was young and handsome, a lively socializer and a bit of a rebel. He gave soaring funeral orations, and used his CB radio scanner to rush to the scene of traffic accidents and help police. Best of all, he loved children and they loved him. He took them camping in the bayou, he was chaplain to the Boy Scouts and the school basketball team. They were forever popping over to the rectory to play his video games, and because of him they stayed in church.

As New Orleans author Jason Berry recounts in his 1992 book *Lead Us Not Into Temptation*, Gauthe went after boys aged seven to nine—altar boys and their friends—and lost interest in them after puberty. The children kept the secret: this was the man from whom their own mothers received Christ in Communion, while they themselves held the communion paten, the man who knew and forgave the secret sins of their own fathers. Parents, by ones and twos, became aware of his foul activities, but not the extent of them. And what could one family do? Police wouldn't believe it and it would rupture the community. Nuns suspected it, but felt they could only try, in vain, to keep little boys away from him.

Before long Gauthe's priestly superiors knew that he was up to something, but they had no wish to know more, nor any apparent conception how driven pedophiles are, or how dishonest and manipulative they are with everyone, including themselves; nor did they appreciate how destructive to children and families his behavior really was. Hearing Gauthe's vague admission that he had lightly fondled one or two boys, they sent him off for treatment, and forgot about it when he returned. He served in four rural parishes, molesting as he went.

The diocese discovered the gravity and extent of his crimes in 1983, when a swampland alligator farmer learned that Gauthe had seduced three of his four boys. When the diocesan vicar general told this man that Gauthe could not be removed because there was no one to replace him, he replied, "You either get him out of here or someone's gonna kill the son of a bitch and it might be me." That got Gauthe packed off permanently for out-of-state treatment. Three years of tangled criminal and civil trial proceedings followed, during which church lawyers, insurance companies, and clergy tried to limit the damage by hiding what Gauthe had done. Gauthe was sentenced in 1985 to twenty years in prison without parole. Upon his release eleven years later, he immediately fondled a three-year-old boy in Texas. He spent the next decade in and out of jail.

But the horrific tales and horrendous insurance settlements ($20 million in Lafayette alone, $3 billion nationwide) were just beginning. To what extent the problem was, clinically speaking, pedophilia (compulsive sex with prepubescents), and to what extent a common form of homosexuality (sex with postpubescent male minors) was much debated by academics. Regardless, every case brought heartbreak.

For example, after her first Communion at age eight, Stacie White of Cleveland, Ohio was first molested and then repeatedly penetrated in her own bed by Father Martin Louis. Her devout parents thought he was praying with her before bedtime. In fact he was lying in her bed with his hand over her mouth, telling her as he raped her that "God knows about this; it's okay. You know, I'm part of God." (White later forgave him, remained Catholic, and went to visit him in prison.)

By the 1990s, as the exposé spread from North America to Europe, a definite pattern had emerged—one that persisted into the twenty-first century, as many thousands of claims went to court. The same pattern seen in Lafayette—official indifference, then reticence, and then deliberate obfuscation—was repeated in dozens of other dioceses across North America. Many victims and their parents left the church. "I'd look at the priests on the altar," one victimized Louisiana father told Jason Berry, "and I'd wonder if this one does women, or that one is gay, or if this other one is a pedophile. I can't help it. Every time I see a priest I wonder what kind of sicko this one is."

The problem, inevitably, landed on national bishops' conferences to solve—a job for which they were juridically and financially ill equipped. Not until 2002 did the American

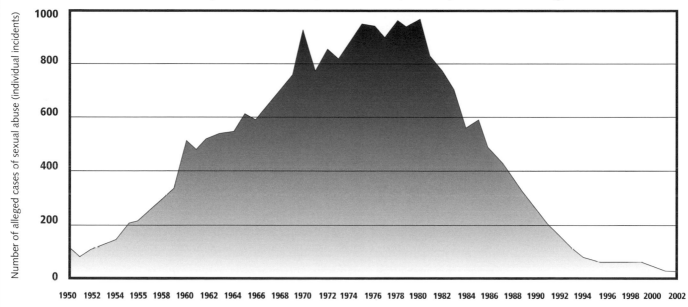

Sexual Abuse by U.S. Priests

Total number of reported incidents, 1950–2002, in the year of their alleged occurrence

Number of alleged cases of sexual abuse (individual incidents)

1000
800
600
400
200
0

1950 1952 1954 1955 1958 1960 1962 1964 1966 1968 1970 1972 1974 1976 1978 1980 1982 1984 1986 1988 1990 1992 1994 1996 1998 2000 2002

Source: John Jay College Report, "Causes and Context of Sexual Abuse of Minors by Catholic Priests in the United States, 1950–2010"

conference undertake to discover how many victims and victimizers it might have, and to decide from that how to handle it. Their massive study, "Causes and Context of Sexual Abuse of Minors by Catholic Priests in the United States, 1950–2010," was cofunded by the U.S. Justice Department and conducted by the secular John Jay College of Criminal Justice in Manhattan. It cataloged and analyzed every plausible complaint to every U.S. Catholic diocese since 1950, and released its final report in 2011.

Over the fifty-two years, U.S. bishops had received ten thousand allegations of sexual abuse of minors against forty-four hundred priests—four percent of the priests in service in those years. Eighteen percent of the victims were up to ten years old at the time of the offense, forty-six percent eleven to fourteen, and thirty-one percent fifteen to seventeen. Though most of the allegations came in after 1991, most of the alleged acts—over eighty percent—had taken place by 1981. This suggested to the researchers that the problem emerged from the "anything goes" ethos of America's sexual revolution. Priests trained under the sterner seminary regime of the 1940s and '50s proved no more immune than the more permissively trained priests of the 1960s and '70s. However, the authors gave several reasons for supposing that because far fewer crimes had been alleged as having occurred since the early 1980s, far fewer crimes had in fact been perpetrated.

From the very imperfect data available from other, non-Catholic sources, the John Jay report also suggested that:

• A similar percentage of Protestant ministers (two to three percent) sexually molested minors in the 1980s.

• Eighty-one percent of victims were male.

• The risk of a minor being sexually abused in the early 1990s (by which time public reporting had improved) was twenty-two times higher with a school teacher than with a Catholic priest, fifty times higher from a day care attendant, and seventeen times higher with a parent.

• The suspected influx of homosexual priests in the 1980s did not stop the rate of sexual abuse from dramatically declining.

Events, however, gave one pause. One day after the 2011 report was released with much fanfare, Kansas City police charged local Catholic priest Shawn Ratigan, 45, with possessing hundreds of mildly pornographic pictures (clothed but suggestive) of little girls, five in particular, which he had somehow furtively taken in local schools and churches. Police found out only because the local vicar general (reportedly) ignored his bishop, Robert Finn, and told them. Just as Father Gauthe was the first U.S. priest jailed for pedophilia, Bishop Finn in 2012 became the first prelate criminally sentenced (to probation, not jail) for failing to protect children. At long last U.S. judges were making it clear that bishops will be punished for turning a blind or indulgent eye to pedophilia.

The American Catholic laity, meanwhile, appeared to have taken the controversy in stride. According to Gallup's annual church-attendance survey, weekly Catholic attendance dipped briefly only after the worst year of the media crisis, 2002, and otherwise held fairly steady from 1985 to 2009. ■

7. American news stories about the issue mushroomed from some forty each year in the late 1980s to two hundred and forty in 1992 and more than four hundred in 1993, involving all major U.S. news outlets, and with some reports running in installments to book length.

Pope Benedict XVI celebrates an evening vigil service in Saint Peter's Square to mark the end of the Church's Year of the Priest in 2010. The year had proved a formidable one, as two scandals—one concerning clerical child abuse, the other the Vatican Bank—continued to plague the Vatican. Seated in front of Benedict (to his right) is papal butler Paolo Gabriele, later arrested by Vatican police for stealing private correspondence, purportedly to reveal new malfeasance to the pope.

all the way to Rome. By 2011, the cost of compensating victims had reached $3 billion in the U.S. alone, and had bankrupted eight U.S. dioceses. Ireland was similarly enmeshed. As wave after wave of lawsuits and headlines hit the church after the mid-1980s, the crisis just got worse. Before the story broke, bishops in the worst-affected dioceses (especially Boston and Los Angeles) tried to preserve the trustworthy reputation of the priesthood by buying silence from victims, shuffling offending priests to new dioceses, browbeating victims and parents, and stonewalling police investigations—thereby marking the whole church as untrustworthy.[7]

Benedict XVI, though more responsive to the abuse charges than John Paul II had been, appeared unruffled by these storms—knowing that the abuse epidemic actually ended in the 1990s. Besides, any church with a celibate male clergy tends to be suspect, even when it isn't guilty. He was a child in Bavaria when the Nazis used a sexual incident to enflame the always-latent paranoid suspicion of ordinary people about bestial practices among a celibate clergy—fantasies of secret sexual orgies, satanic rituals, and the murder of illegitimate infants by harems of nuns. Such lascivious speculations are as old as Christianity. In his 1996 book *Pedophiles and Priests*, Catholic-turned-Episcopalian author Philip Jenkins traces them back through the political pornography of the secular revolutions, to some of the more lurid and ludicrous accusations of Protestant Reformers, to the medieval ribaldry of Chaucer, to pagan defamations of the

nascent church. Even if there were never particular misdeeds by particular clergy (as indeed there always are, sometimes more, sometimes less), the imagination of fallen humanity will assume that the church is forever sunk in them.

Catholicism entered its third millennium buffeted by many crosscurrents but still, apparently, quite seaworthy. The banking and sexual scandals, the dearth of priests, the huge unhappiness of its aging radicals, and the moral disobedience of its laity—all these were problems, to be sure, but not of a magnitude it had never faced before. At a deeper and more lasting level it had, thanks to John Paul and Benedict, some powerful forces working in its favor.

Most obvious of these was the fact that Catholicism had lost its fortress mentality, an arrogant "we're-right-and-you're-wrong" holdover from its long struggles against the Reformation, the Enlightenment, and the post-Enlightenment. These struggles left a legacy of defensive ecclesiastical paralysis. The new theology of Christian humanism that guided the two post-Vatican II teaching and preaching popes was quite unlike the arid, rigid intellectual Thomism previously prevalent; and it enabled the church to open many new channels of communication with Protestant and Orthodox Christians, with Muslims and Jews, with women, with people of no religion, with those left wondering why their materialist revolutionary philosophies had so signally backfired. To all of these, the church could now explain John Paul's great insight that human nature is rooted in acts of self-giving, not self-assertion. Historian George Weigel says John Paul and Benedict both saw this as the mainspring of Vatican II, and it informed everything they did to bring the council to full fruition.

There was thus within the church, at least outside of radical-progressive circles, a growing sense of spiritual recovery. This did not amount to a confident expectation of clear sailing in fair weather; far from it. Such has never been the lot of Christ's church for very long. But it did mean that however stormy the seas of the third millennium may get, and however large or small the crew, the authority of the captain was clear and the course of the ship was known to everyone on board. ■

A West German man pounds on the Berlin Wall at the Brandenburg Gate on November 11, 1989, while East German guards watch with an air of bemusement from atop the notorious rampart. Built twenty-eight years earlier to keep the citizens of East Germany from escaping to the West, the wall had become a symbol of the seventy-eight-year-old Soviet system which, with the help of Christians inside and outside the Iron Curtain, was about to be relegated to the dustbin of history.

CHAPTER 17

How defiant Christians triggered the collapse of the Soviet colossus

Led by a pope the Red government once thought safe, the people of Poland beard their Communist masters, and Marxism's European bastion fast crashes down

In the final stage of the Second World War, during a discussion of the future of Eastern Europe, British Prime Minister Winston Churchill advised Joseph Stalin to have regard for the views of the Vatican. "How many divisions does the pope have?" Stalin scoffed. "You can tell my son Joseph," the reigning Pope Pius XII was said to have remarked, "that he will meet my divisions in heaven." For Stalin's successor nearly half a century later, however, the answer was to come rather sooner than heaven. In fact, the whole Soviet colossus was by then crashing down, and a successor of Pius XII was in no small measure helping to bring this about. He had, that is, divisions enough.

Certainly at the close of the Second World War, a Soviet collapse seemed, and was, far from imminent. Soviet troops pushing back Hitler's armies were initially welcomed as liberators in Eastern Europe. But soon they revealed themselves as conquerors, installing everywhere local Communist governments, with their own armies, gulags, and secret police. These satellite regimes, though Marxist, became far from enamoured of Soviet Russia, and some were less draconian than the Soviets toward religion.

In Czechoslovakia, for example, the Communist government supported the Protestants while oppressing the Catholic Church. The policy backfired. The Catholic churches, though ascendant, had never enjoyed vast popular support before. Now they began to fill up with dissatisfied Protestants who hated communism. So the underlying Marxist contempt for all religions gradually began drawing Protestants and Catholics together, despite more than five centuries of bitter rivalry.

Rioters surround a captured Russian tank during the Polish October workers' uprising of 1956. The protest had strong religious overtones and resulted in an easing of Soviet control, which allowed for the limited continuance of Catholic practice. One Catholic leader who emerged in the 1960s as especially adept at resisting the state was Bishop Karol Wojtyla, the future Pope John Paul II, shown below during a pastoral visitation to Krakow in 1967.

In Hungary, Communist rule gravitated toward the Stalinist model, imposing a ruinous five-year economic plan, seizing all church-run schools, and imprisoning religious leaders such as Cardinal Joseph Mindszenty. Historians have cited the strong religious faith of Hungarians, some two-thirds of whom were Catholic, as a major element in the nation's 1956 revolution. Initially a protest by intellectuals, it quickly led to a general uprising, the brief overthrow of the regime, the liberation of political prisoners (including Mindszenty, who would live for the next fifteen years in the U.S. embassy), and the flight of hundreds of thousands of people to the West. But when the new government declared it wanted no part of the Soviet Union's military alliance—the Warsaw Pact—Soviet tanks and troops rolled in, brutally suppressed the revolt, and reimposed a puppet regime. This caused serious splits in Communist parties in western Europe and many defections. The blinders about the Soviet "workers' paradise" were coming off.

Of all the countries in the Soviet Union's new empire, Poland was both the most populous and the most problematic. It was also the most strategically placed, lying between East Germany and the Soviet Union. The politburo in Moscow was concerned enough about its stability to assign a Soviet marshal as its defense minister. The most troublesome piece of the Polish puzzle was the Catholic Church, which had a far stronger claim on the Poles' hearts than the Communists, having kept the national hope burning during the nineteenth century when Poland had been parceled out amongst its neighbors. Because the new Communist regime was unwilling to try destroying the church for fear of turning the population entirely against it, the church became the unofficial opposition.

So while one side had the guns, the other had the hearts of the people. The Polish Communists tried many of the antireligion propaganda strategies developed by the Soviets but these proved even less effective in Poland than they had in Russia. In the "Polish October" of 1956, a workers' uprising for more pay became a popular protest with strong nationalist and religious overtones, one that saw the Soviet-appointed defense minister sent home to Moscow, while hundreds of symbols of Soviet supremacy were destroyed. In an astonishing show of solidarity, fully ninety-five percent of all parents petitioned the government for the teaching of Catholic catechism in the state schools. Anxious not to trigger an uprising followed by a Soviet invasion, the government complied. When it reneged three years later, the church instituted its own twice-weekly religious classes with nearly one hundred percent attendance.

Wojtyla was not considered radical. The Communists thought him manageable and malleable and, to their later regret, pushed the church to promote him.

Poland was, in fact, so Catholic a country that before the century's end it would be exporting surplus priests to North America. However, in the 1950s the Communists saw hope in the next generation because it was being taught socialist values in state schools. This too failed because most teachers were practicing Catholics. For the government, therefore, the problem seemed unsolvable. The longer Poland remained Communist, the more Catholic it got. As in Czechoslovakia, and in defiance of Marxist theory, communism, so long as it was in power, was making people more Christian, not less. Though the government occasionally murdered especially influential priests, it generally preferred to fight the church indirectly, by refusing jobs or university entrance to known believers, or by keeping churches out of its new satellite towns. One Catholic leader who emerged in the 1960s as especially adept at resisting the state with equally indirect tactics was Karol Wojtyla, consecrated as archbishop in 1958 at the age of thirty-eight.[1]

Had it been left to Poland's bishops alone, it is unlikely that Wojtyla would have been installed in the historic Krakow archdiocese, because while he was well liked, he was seen by many as soft on communism. In fact, according to Helen Whitney and Jane Barnes, who made *John Paul II: The Millennial Pope* for the Public Broadcasting Service, he was initially ranked seventh on Cardinal Stefan Wyszynski's list. "He was known for his intelligence, for being personable and open-minded, a priest who would compromise in the interest of building churches

1. As a priest and auxiliary bishop of Krakow, Karol Wojtyla drew the attention of the regime when the local authorities expropriated the diocesan seminary. Wojtyla came to see Lucjan Motyka, the Communist leader in Krakow, and negotiated a deal: one floor for the regime, the rest for the church. Motyka was reportedly so astonished to meet a bishop who could compromise that he reported the encounter in detail to Warsaw: here was a man they could work with. Other secret reports on Wojtyla described him as an intellectual, poorly organized, and apolitical—a decisive underestimation.

and seminaries," they wrote. "He was not considered radical. The Communists thought he would be manageable, malleable, even a poet," and (much to their later regret) leaned successfully on the church to promote him. The filmmakers recount how General Wojciech Jaruzelski, the last Communist leader of Poland, later "admitted that one of the great ironies of the regime he served was how much they had underestimated Wojtyla. 'My Communist colleagues decided that the bishops ahead of Karol Wojtyla on the list of candidates were not good for the state, so they pushed Karol Wojtyla. The Holy Spirit works in mysterious ways.'"

When the regime jailed a priest for failing to pay his taxes (a favorite tactic), Bishop Wojtyla announced that he personally would celebrate the prisoner's masses. The priest was released. To counter the regime's stolid refusal to allow new churches to be built in its model workers' towns, claiming there was no demand for them, Wojtyla sent his priests door-to-door recruiting parishioners, and presented officialdom with the resulting hefty membership lists. In such a

The workers' town of Nowa Huta, shown at the bottom under a bleak midwinter sun, was one of the Soviet regime's satellite towns, which the Polish government of General Wojciech Jaruzelski, above right, had tried to keep church-free. But membership drives organized by Bishop Wojtyla persuaded the authorities to allow the construction of the Ark Church, below, just outside of the town's borders.

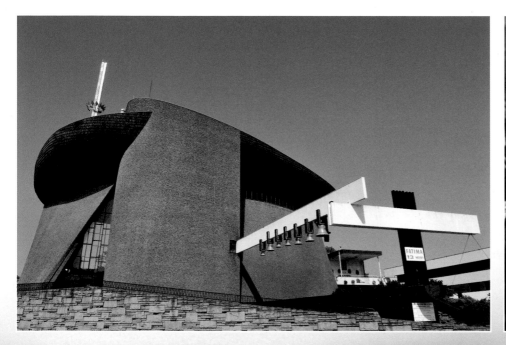

way, writes John O'Sullivan in *The President, The Pope and the Prime Minister*
(2006), he enabled the construction of the renowned Ark Church outside the
workers' town of Nowa Huta, dominated by a huge steel crucified Christ forged
in the Lenin Steelworks. Wojtyla had celebrated masses on major feast days on
the proposed site for half a decade to expose the government's refusal to grant
building permits. Crosses were repeatedly erected and repeatedly pushed down by
government bulldozers. Eventually, Wojtyla and the state agreed to compromise.
The Ark Church would go up, but just outside the town border.

While the young bishop was developing his indirect resistance to totalitarianism, the Vatican was reaching an uneasy accord with the Soviet Union called
Ostpolitik.[2] Forged in the era of Pope John XXIII and furthered by Paul VI and
Cardinal Agostino Casaroli, a longtime Vatican diplomat, this rapprochement
was mostly pragmatic. communism, clearly, would rule in Eastern Europe for the
long term. There was also in *Ostpolitik*, however, a strong whiff of an enduring
western intellectual infatuation with socialism, even among Catholic clergy, and
especially in Latin America, where by the 1960s younger clergy were using a new
liberation theology to put Christ on the side of the poor by aligning him with
Marxist rebels. In sum then, the Soviets made minor allowances for a titular
Catholic presence in Eastern Europe, while the Vatican promised to discourage
Catholic underground operations there. This all had understandably little appeal
for any Catholic actually living behind the Iron Curtain who wasn't on the secret
police payroll.

Nonetheless, *Ostpolitik* contributed indirectly to the erosion of Soviet power
by promoting the 1975 Helsinki Accords, which the Vatican signed along with
thirty-four other states. By these accords, the national borders of Eastern Europe
at the end of Second World War were permanently ratified, and all signatories
vowed to keep a human rights watch on each other. The Soviets believed they had
achieved something (their wartime acquisitions guaranteed) for nothing. But the

2. *Ostpolitik* began as the term
for West German efforts to cooperate with East Germany and other
Soviet Bloc countries but was reap-
plied to the Vatican's policy of rapprochement with the Soviet Union.
Both were premised on the latter's
apparent permanence and power.
Under it, the Vatican let
Communist governments help vet
the selection of prelates, and throttled back on underground church
activities in countries with strong
Catholic presences such as
Lithuania, Byelorussia, and
Ukraine. In return it won tolera-
tion for surviving church institutions. However, it left many
Catholics behind the Iron Curtain
feeling betrayed. How the Soviets
viewed *Ostpolitik* was indicated by
the reaction of Aristov, the Soviet
Ambassador to Poland, upon the
election of Karol Wojtyla as pope,
who noted, "It will clearly be more
difficult to use the Vatican as a
moderating influence on the Polish
episcopate."

Police use tear gas to break up a Solidarity demonstration in the port town of Gdansk, Poland, in May of 1982. Fighting occurred in several Polish cities, resulting in curfews and thousands of arrests, following imposition of martial law and a ban on labor unions by the Polish leadership. With the implicit support of Pope John Paul II several waves of illegal strikes swept the country and by the end of the decade the regime gave up, negotiating a new deal with Solidarity and legalizing free unions and free elections.

human rights component—pushed by the Vatican—turned out to be far from nothing. Throughout the Soviet Bloc both secular and religious rights advocates coalesced, and, calling themselves Helsinki Monitoring Groups, compiled rights violations and reported them to international bodies as prescribed by the Accords. The Soviet Union, of course, suppressed them internally, but this only emphasized to the outside world its hypocrisy and cynicism.

In Poland there evolved a variation of the good-cop, bad-cop routine. Cardinal Stefan Wyszynski fought a very public battle in defense of church institutions and rights while Bishop Wojtyla encouraged a low-key but widespread discussion involving secular and Catholic intellectuals about the direction Polish culture should go. According to author O'Sullivan, this strategy baffled the Communists because the discussion did not so much attack the government as ignore it.

This approach widened when Wojtyla violated the spirit of *Ostpolitik* by clandestinely ordaining priests for Czechoslovakia. (The Vatican had agreed to restrict Czech bishops from ordaining priests for Czech churches. Wojtyla was ordaining Polish priests for Czech churches.) The Polish government deemed at least three of Wojtyla's sermons during the 1970s to be seditious, but by now the church had gained such popular support that the regime dared not jail Wojtyla as it had Wyszynski, for three years in the 1950s.

In 1976, Wojtyla acted even more provocatively, organizing a fund to support the families of protesters jailed or injured and hospitalized by the police. When Wojtyla's election as pope surprised the world in 1978 (see chapter 16) Vadim Pavlov, chief KGB agent in Warsaw, immediately dispatched a very accurate reassessment to the Soviet politburo. "Wojtyla holds extreme anti-Communist views, openly opposing the socialist system." When Moscow remonstrated against the Polish government for allowing a Polish cardinal to be elected pope, the Poles responded that their country would be easier to govern with him in Rome. The Polish government was therefore prepared to join the Polish people, however insincerely, in congratulating the new pope. "What particularly perturbed the KGB," according to Vasili Mitrokhin, the KGB archivist who defected to Britain in 1992 with thirty years of secret files, "was the evidence that among many [Communist party] members, even some senior officials, the joy was genuine."

As Pope John Paul II, Wojtyla soon confirmed the Soviets' worst fears. Off to Vilnius, the capital of the oppressed Baltic country of Lithuania, he sent his cardinal's cap to lie on the altar at the Marian shrine at Ostra Brama. He also appointed a Lithuanian as his adviser on Eastern Europe. While visiting Assisi, when a voice from the crowd shouted, "Don't forget the 'church of silence'," a reference to the Catholic Church behind the Iron Curtain, the pope responded, "It's not a 'church of silence' anymore. Because it speaks with my voice."

The original *Ostpolitik* had been aimed at preserving Catholic institutions. But John Paul, according to his preeminent biographer George Weigel, saw the institutional church as servant and protector of the Christian faith, which needed cultural and individual freedom to thrive. He sent a Christmas sermon to his old diocese which called on Poland to emulate her patron saint, Saint Stanislaw, who had been martyred in 1079 for criticizing the Polish king. The government censored the printed version but pastors read it in full from their pulpits. In 1979, he put fire in the belly of Czechoslovakia's Cardinal Tomasek, turning a timid octogenarian into, as Weigel put it, "one of Czechoslovak communism's fiercest and most feared critics," and he similarly emboldened Ukrainian Cardinal Joseph Slipyi.

The microfilm that changed history

The secret police found the manuscript, and its safekeeper ended up dead, but Solzhenitsyn's monumental testimony escaped Russia and hastened the Soviet downfall

After five days of brutal KGB interrogation in August 1973, Elizaveta Voronyanskaya, aged sixty seven, long the confidante and typist of the dissident writer Alexander Solzhenitsyn, broke down and revealed the whereabouts of his most vital manuscript. She was found days later in her Leningrad apartment, an apparent suicide by hanging, due to trauma and guilt. Some suspected the KGB had simply finished their job, but they had failed in one essential respect. A microfilm copy of the manuscript they sought to suppress had already been smuggled out of the Soviet Union, and *The Gulag Archipelago* was published in France that December.

This book, a detailed account of life and death in Russia's vast political prison system, was described by American diplomat George Kennan as "the most powerful single indictment of a political regime ever to be levied in modern times" and has been credited with dealing a death blow to the Soviet system. Its author unquestionably knew his subject, having spent eight years as a Gulag prisoner and nine more writing his searing exposé. For publishing it, he would spend another twenty-one in exile from Russia.

Solzhenitsyn, coincidentally, was born in Kilovodsk, northern Caucasus, on December 11, 1918, just when the Bolshevik state and the Gulag were being created. His widowed mother, Taissia, twenty-three, was the well-educated daughter of a formerly wealthy Ukrainian. She never remarried, but moved with her lively young son to Rostov-on-Don, northeast of Moscow, where they lived in tenements without plumbing on her meager wages as a typist. "I spent my childhood in queues for bread, for milk, for meal," he would write. But during vacations with a wealthy aunt, he spent hours in her library, reading by age ten such volumes as Tolstoy's *War and Peace*.

Alexander Solzhenitsyn in 1953 upon his release from the Gulag camp at Ekibastuz, which inspired The Gulag Archipelago. *The book has been described as "the most powerful single indictment of a political regime ever to be levied in modern times."*

The pope's first major move proved a decisive one: his nine-day, six-city, thirty-nine-sermon visit to Poland in June, 1979. It was a triumph that drew one third of the population into massive displays of spiritual unity and political defiance, and managed to leave many with the sense they had experienced a personal encounter with the pope. The Polish leadership had resisted pressure from their own lower echelons, and from other Warsaw Pact governments, to forbid John Paul entry. In the end, they believed that refusing the pope would stir up more popular unrest than admitting him and, in the short term, they were right. Despite the huge crowds and occasional government harassment, all events were peaceful and positive. John Paul told his vast audiences that only when individuals and governments submit to a higher moral law, "the dignity of the human person [can] be respected and universally recognized."

Everywhere he went he preached that the way for Poles to transform the nation was to transform themselves. Near Nowa Huta, where he had helped secure the

Alexander Solzhenitsyn (center, seated) in 1975 during his appearance on the French television program Apostrophes.

Poland, East Prussia, and Berlin.

His careworn mother Taissia died of tuberculosis in 1944, at age forty-nine, and the following year, Alexander was arrested for mocking Stalin in a letter to a friend. Detained for six months at Moscow's dreaded Lubyanka Prison, he was interrogated twice and sentenced to eight years' hard labor, followed by internal exile for life. He spent almost a year in slave camps where "you worked until the skin came off your hands and your fingers froze," and the beds were planks, garments often threadbare, and rations meager. But he claimed to know atomic physics (having read an American book on the subject) and was transferred to the Mavrino research center in Moscow. Here conditions were markedly better and he met one Dmitri Panin, whose arguments furthered his gradual disillusionment with Marxism.

Biographer Joseph Pearce, in *Solzhenitsyn: A Soul in Exile* (1999), calls his subject a Soviet propaganda success story. Abandoning Orthodox Christianity for Marxist-Leninism, he was disinclined to question the state. He studied literature by correspondence, then took a degree in mathematics and physics at Rostov University, where he met Natalya Reshetovskaya, a chemistry student and accomplished pianist. They married in April 1940, both aged twenty-one. A fledgling physics teacher when Hitler invaded Russia in 1941, Solzhenitsyn joined the army, where he became captain in an artillery brigade. He also found time to write poems, short stories, and letters, observing that "one cannot become a great Russian writer without being a soldier at the front." And he witnessed the horrific revenge of Red Army soldiers—urged by Stalin to show no mercy—as they advanced into

Then Natalya asked for a divorce, fearing that as the wife of a political prisoner she would lose her job, and moved in with another man. Prisoner Solzhenitsyn, transferred to a labor camp in Ekibastuz, Kazakhstan, simultaneously began the most dispiriting and physically grueling years of his sentence. In 1951 he was found to have cancer, and while recovering from the consequent operation, rediscovered his Christian faith, a conversion he summarized: "First comes the fight for survival, then the discovery of life, then God."[1] The fight for survival continued when he was released from prison at age thirty-five and permanently exiled to Kok-Terek in southern Kazakhstan. He was treated again for aggressive abdominal cancer in an Uzbekistan

building of the famous Ark Church, he declared: "You have built the church. Now build your lives with the Gospel." The visit was transformative at a personal level for many, Weigel recounts in *Witness to Hope* (2001). "The pope had delivered what the comrades had promised"—that being a wave of communal feeling and fellowship for which the best word was *solidarnosc*—solidarity. This was the name ultimately selected by Polish workers who struck illegally to protest an increase in prices of consumer goods imposed by Communist leader Edward Gierek. Though Gierek had stayed in power for more than a decade by keeping prices down with foreign loans, now, in 1980, he had to placate Polish farmers with realistic food pricing.

This in turn set off a wildcat strike, one that was too big and, this time, too peaceful, for the government to respond with tanks and guns. The papal visit, Weigel believes, had imbued in the strikers a new dignity, patience, and willingness to form coalitions, a sense of identity that extended well beyond their narrow self-interest as individual unions. The strike grew to include the Gdansk shipyard, and

hospital, an experience he fictionalized in *Cancer Ward*.

Just as he arrived at Kok-Terek, however, came the news of Stalin's death. Successor Nikita Khrushchev favored liberalization, and in 1956 Solzhenitsyn was released from exile. He moved to Ryazan, south of Moscow, and Natalya left her common-law husband to remarry him. Khrushchev, intent upon exposing Stalin's viciousness, approved publication in 1962 of Solzhenitsyn's novel, *One Day in the Life of Ivan Denisovich*, a candid, caustic, and critical description of the Gulag. Published in Russia and the U.S., it made Solzhenitsyn an acclaimed author at age forty-four.

But under Khrushchev's successor, hardliner Leonid Brezhnev, his work was again considered subversive. Although he was somewhat protected by his international reputation and such influential friends as cellist Mstislav Rostropovich, in 1965 the KGB seized most of his texts. He had always taken extreme precautions with *The Gulag Archipelago* manuscript, however. Begun in 1958, it also included a history of the Gulag and testimonies received by letter from other prisoners. Solzhenitsyn began to write in secluded locations, including a cabin in Estonia, and never kept a complete copy in any one place. For research, typing, and concealment he had many courageous, code-named collaborators.

These included the unfortunate Voronyanskaya, and he would write about them in *The Invisible Allies*. But they did not include his wife Natalya, a successful chemist and a religious skeptic who resented his prolonged absences and austere life. She later denounced his novels as exaggerations and married a KGB agent. However in 1968, Solzhenitsyn met Natalya "Alya" Svetlova, aged twenty-eight, a mathematician who admired his writing. Alya had a six-year-old son; by the time they married in 1972 she had borne Solzhenitsyn two sons as well, and would soon produce a third. She would also provide steady support in the years ahead.

In 1969, Solzhenitsyn had been expelled from the Soviet Writers Union, and was later denied permission to publish in the USSR. His work circulated through the *samizdat* or underground press, however, and in the West he became a rising star with the publication of *Cancer Ward* and of *The First*

Circle, a fictionalized account of Mavrino. But he dared not travel to Sweden in 1970 to receive his Nobel Prize in Literature, for fear he would be barred from returning to Russia.

With publication of *The Gulag Archipelago*, Soviet authorities lost all patience. Its author was arrested on February 12, 1974, and deported to Germany the next day. Six weeks later he was reunited with Alya and his sons in Switzerland and the family moved to Vermont two years later. But the West's initial enthusiasm for this gaunt, bearded dissident gradually cooled. In a biting Harvard commencement address in 1978, for example, he excoriated the West (in Russian) for its stultifying consumerism, political impotence, and sensationalistic media. Said media took to portraying him as a brave but preachy reactionary.

Never fluent in English, he toiled on his epic historical novel, *The Red Wheel*, while donating all royalties from the best-selling *Gulag Archipelago* to political prisoners and their families. But then came another reversal of fortune, this time of global proportions: the fall in 1991 of the Soviet Union. Solzhenitsyn returned to his beloved Russia in 1995. Courted by some as a potent visionary and dismissed by others as a spent force, he continued writing and speaking until in 2003 he died of heart failure at eighty-nine.

While opinions on his literary gifts vary, few deny his moral courage or the influence of his work. "The simple step of a simple courageous man is not to participate in lies," he declared in his 1970 Nobel lecture—then added, "But writers and artists can do much more: defeat the lie!" That Alexander Solzhenitsyn fully met this challenge, few would dispute. ∎

1. In his book *Loving God*, Charles Colson provides detail on Solzhenitsyn's conversion. While Solzhenitsyn was recovering from his operation in the cancer ward, a doctor, Boris Kornfeld, told him of his own conversion from that of a persecuted Jew to a confessing Christian. He said it had given him a sense of freedom, even there in the Gulag, to do what was right, not what he was ordered to do. That night Boris Kornfeld was murdered. His confession did not die, however, but lived on in the life of Alexander Solzhenitsyn.

3. Solidarity grew to ten million members from all walks of life through the transformation of a rail workers' strike with narrow objectives into a national movement for human rights, thanks in large part to Pope John Paul II's 1979 visit to Poland. This reversed the course of history as prescribed by communism's founding visionary Karl Marx. As he predicted in *The Communist Manifesto*, true socialism would be achieved only after the proletariat became aware of itself as an oppressed class and threw off its chains (wage slavery, government, and religion). Now in Poland, inspired by Christian faith, the workers realized their essential solidarity with Poles of all classes and began the process of throwing off the chains which divided them (socialism, the Polish United Workers' Party, and the Soviet Union).

Top, Lech Walesa, the charismatic thirty-seven-year-old leader of Solidarity, speaks to a crowd in the Polish city of Bydgoszcz, where Polish farmers had threatened to turn what was a peaceful protest into a violent revolution in March 1981. By now what had begun as a 1970 workers' strike to protest an increase in the prices of consumer goods, had become a mass movement for religious freedom, human rights, and the release of political prisoners. Below, Walesa is shown playing with his daughter before a portrait of Pope John Paul II, whose support of the strikers had convinced the initially reluctant Polish bishops to unanimously support the Solidarity movement.

then blossomed into a national movement that would include ten million members—one-quarter of the nation, all under the name Solidarity.[3] Its charismatic young leader, Lech Walesa, successfully expanded its goals to include not only the right to strike, but religious freedom, human rights, and the release of political prisoners. It stopped just short of calling for the end of communism.

Despite the early adoption of Christian symbolism by the strikers, the Catholic Church in Poland at first kept its distance, even criticising the workers. But after a timely intervention by John Paul, who maintained his own links to the strikers, the nation's bishops unanimously endorsed the movement. The regime capitulated, providing the Soviet Bloc's first recognition of self-governing trade unions, as well as of free speech. Instantly more than thirty independent unions sprang into being. When he signed the Gdansk Accord with the government, Walesa used a gaudy souvenir pen from the pope's visit. Later he said, "The Holy Father, through his meetings, demonstrated how numerous we were. He told us not to be afraid."

Moscow remained irate and the settlement was short-lived. The Soviet leadership had failed to persuade the Polish government to deny the pope entry, and then, with the shipyard strike, to impose martial law. They now installed a Polish general, Wojciech Jaruzelski, as prime minister, and in 1981, after Solidarity staged a four-hour general "warning strike" involving virtually every working

Pole, Jaruzelski declared martial law and outlawed Solidarity.

That same year Pope John Paul II was very nearly permanently removed as a threat to Soviet hegemony. On May 13, as he was circling Saint Peter's Square in a white jeep, a Turkish professional killer named Mehmet Ali Agca shot him twice with a nine-millimeter semi-automatic pistol, only narrowly missing vital organs. The pope survived to forgive his would-be assassin, his body weakened but his belief in being chosen by God for great purpose only strengthened.

The question whether the Soviets had ordered the shooting remains open. They would have been the chief beneficiaries. The Italians also arrested and tried a suspected accomplice from Bulgaria, a Soviet satellite, who was acquitted, partly because he had a convincing alibi. But a decade later his alibi was blown when he was identified in photographs of the assassination attempt standing near Agca in Saint Peter's Square. The Bulgarian secret service, says O'Sullivan in *The President, the Pope and the Prime Minister*, "would never have dared to embark on such an enormity without explicit Soviet instruction." Agca later made remarks suggesting Soviet involvement and in 2002, an investigation by the Italian Parliament concluded "beyond all reasonable doubt" that the Soviets had ordered the pope's assassination.[4]

The Polish leadership maintained martial law until 1983, and even afterwards kept the ban on Solidarity and other independent unions. The Polish secret police continued to murder dissidents, most notably the priest Jerzy Popieluszko in 1984 (beatified by the Catholic Church in 2010). Jaruzelski would later maintain that he had imposed martial law to keep the Soviets, supported by other Warsaw Pact countries, from squashing Poland the way they had rebellions in Hungary and Czechoslovakia. (Though historians doubt the Soviets would have resorted to invasion, an opinion survey in Poland twenty years later indicated most Poles thought Jaruzelski made the right move.)

4. Four known attempts were made on John Paul's life. A year after this incident he was stabbed with a bayonet while on a pilgrimage to Fatima, Portugal, by a deranged fascist priest named Fernández y Krohn; the injury was superficial and little was disclosed at the time. In 1995, an astute policewoman in Manila discovered and aborted an attempted bombing during the pope's appearance at World Youth Day in the Philippines, where John Paul had drawn a crowd of over five million; the crime was later ascribed to agents of the Muslim terrorist group al-Qaeda. On a 1997 trip to Sarajevo, Bosnian security officials found a bomb planted under a bridge he would be crossing.

Father Jerzy Popieluszko is pictured here on a mural in the south-central Polish town of Ostrowiec, commemorating the thirty-year anniversary of the Solidarity movement. Popieluszko, later beatified by the Vatican, was murdered by the Polish secret police in 1984, as part of a crackdown on dissidents.

The newly erected Berlin Wall is shown here in 1961, the iconic Brandenburg Gate captured within the Soviet sector of the city. On the facing page, a German map of the day shows the division of the city. East Germany had always been the most successful emulator of the Soviet model, surpassing it in the quality of its industrial output and even rivaling it in the medal count of its Olympic sports teams. Unlike other Soviet states, however, the German Democratic Republic adopted a different policy toward religion, allowing its mostly Protestant churches to retain their property and encouraging them to provide social services.

5. The Orange Alternative fought the Polish Communist regime through mockery, using as its trademark cartoon dwarves. When other groups painted antiregime slogans on walls, and the police painted over these with white spots, the Orange Alternative would superimpose dwarf images. Mocking the Hegelian-Marxist formulation that each economic stage was a "thesis" that created its own "antithesis," which would overthrow it to form a "synthesis," the Orange Alternative declared, "The thesis is the antiregime slogan. The antithesis is the spot and the synthesis is the dwarf." The Alternative staged huge demonstrations without apparent purpose (identified by people in dwarf caps), confounding police by providing no grounds for charges. They counted it a success when they provoked the police to arrest, in one case, sixty-four Poles dressed as Santa Claus. "Help the Militia," proclaimed one typical slogan. "Beat yourself up." People in other Warsaw Pact countries would later adopt orange as a sign of dissent.

However, repression of Solidarity simply begat more radical and underground organizations such as Fighting Solidarity, which specialized in graffiti and pamphleteering, the Federation of Fighting Youth, and the absurdist Orange Alternative.[5]

As Poland's managed economy collapsed in the mid-1980s, a million Poles fled the country (hijacking eleven airliners along the way), and when, in 1988, the military government responded with a referendum promising economic and political reforms, most voters refused to participate. Several waves of illegal strikes swept the country and eventually the regime gave up, negotiating a new deal with Solidarity (though it was still illegal), and legalizing free unions and free elections. When the first such election finally occurred in 1989, the Communists suffered a stunning defeat. Solidarity won every seat available to it but one (which was won by an independent) and its candidate became prime minister. Jaruzelski was elected president (he was the only candidate) but as soon as free presidential elections followed, Walesa won that position.

Of all Eastern Bloc countries, East Germany had always been the most successful emulator of the Soviet model, managing to surpass it with the quality of its industrial output and even to rival its Olympic teams. It adopted a different policy toward religion, letting churches retain their property, and encouraging them to provide social services for the old, the handicapped, and the mentally ill. On the dark side, the German Democratic Republic employed an army of one hundred thousand paid informants who infiltrated every facet of the culture including the churches. This had the same effect as in other totalitarian countries, of creating what American political analyst David Steele called "a culture of silence" and of mistrust that the Christian churches ultimately would bring down.

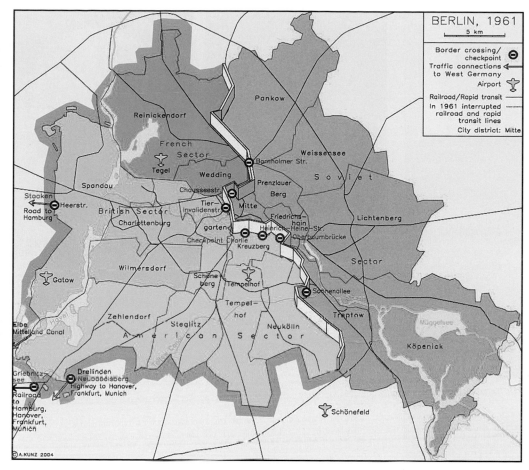

Inspired by the writings of Dietrich Bonhoeffer, the pastor and theologian who died resisting Hitler, some East German Protestant churches stood up to the regime, at first in small ways (for example, defending conscientious objectors who had been drafted into the armed forces). Other churches openly supported the regime in the manner of Russian Orthodoxy, while yet others played a dual role, endorsing the regime publicly while encouraging and protecting dissenters within their ranks. The smaller Catholic Church managed to open a seminary at Erfurt in 1952 to provide training for priests in most of East Germany. The college produced 417 priests before it was dissolved on February 15, 1978.

Things began to change in the 1970s when some Protestant churches started holding youth services that included folk music, poetry, and, most dangerous of all in the regime's view, free and open discussion. The discussions came to focus on "peace" in a way critical of East Germany's warlike stance against the West, and these soon grew into an annual "Ten Days for Peace" multimedia event drawing tens of thousands from across the country. The Communist regime attempted petty acts of harassment such as staging air-raid drills during performances, but otherwise took a hands-off approach, perhaps because of the generally religious atmosphere and the orderly conduct of the participants.

Youth pastors like Friedrich Schorlemmer and Rainer Eppelmann were early leaders, and suffered imprisonment for it. Schorlemmer cunningly chose as his symbol the Soviet sculpture of a sword being hammered into a plowshare.[6] There were so many imitators, the regime banned it.

As David Steele wrote in his contribution to the 1994 book *Religion, The Missing Dimension of Statecraft*, the Protestant churches by the mid-1980s were

6. From the book of the prophet Micah 4:3, "And he shall judge among many people, and rebuke strong nations afar off; and they shall beat their swords into plowshares, and their spears into pruning hooks: nation shall not lift up a sword against nation, neither shall they learn war any more." The Soviets gave the United Nations a sculpture titled "Let Us Beat Our Swords into Plowshares" in 1959. It did not credit the Bible.

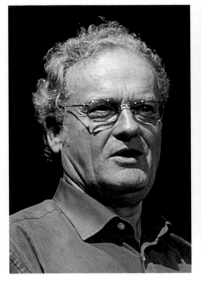

Youth pastors Friedrich Schorlemmer (top left) and Rainer Eppelmann were early leaders of the anti-Communist movement which used a message of peace to attack the warlike East German regime and cannily chose as their symbol the Soviet sculpture depicting—though without attribution— the pacifist biblical injunction to beat one's swords into ploughshares (Micah 4:3; Isaiah 2:3–4). The sculpture is shown here outside the United Nations headquarters in New York, to which it was given by the USSR in 1959.

providing havens of "reconciliation, dialogue, participation and community" in contrast to the sense of alienation and paranoia that had so long prevailed everywhere else. The discussions had widened to women's rights, the environment, and, most provocatively of all, emigration to West Germany. When government pressure caused the church leadership to cancel the Ten Days event in Berlin in 1987, a spontaneous grassroots "Church from Below" group staged its own events in Berlin churches, with the tacit approval of the leadership. Historian Arvan Gordon called this impromptu defiance "the opening of the last act in the collapse" of the German Democratic Republic.

When the government itself staged a rally in East Berlin of two hundred thousand supporters in January, 1988, dissidents disrupted the march. The regime cracked down with selective raids on churches and many arrests. Caught in these was Vera Wollenberger, a founder of the Church from Below and a self-proclaimed Christian socialist with no desire to leave East Germany. The regime deported her anyway. But this fueled more calls for an open emigration policy.

Some Communist leaders called for a harsher response to dissent, while others considered the situation already hopeless: the generation born and indoctrinated under socialism was thoroughly disaffected and, thanks to the churches, openly rebellious. Push finally came to shove in Leipzig, at the Lutheran Saint Nikolai Church, a massive and beautiful medieval edifice in the city core. Weekly prayers and discussions begun by Pastor Christian Führer in 1980 had grown by 1989 into marches by tens of thousands. "In church," Führer later told journalists, "people had learned to turn fear into courage...to have hope and to have strength."

On October 9, 1989, even though an intensive government response by soldiers and paramilitary police with orders to shoot to kill was widely rumored, seventy thousand met at Saint Nikolai and marched peacefully through the city. Government forces refused to shoot civilians armed only with candles. The next week, two hundred thousand marched. They were doubtless emboldened by Soviet leader Mikhail Gorbachev's public liberalization policy, while the regime was equally demoralized by Gorbachev's unpublished declaration that the one million Soviet troops in East Germany would not support the regime.

In another month the pivotal blow fell. The citizenry demolished the notorious Berlin Wall built to bar East Germans from flight to West Germany. Early in 1990, the country's first free elections since 1933 brought the Christian Democrats to power with a mandate to seek reunification with West Germany. One by one the other Communist regimes negotiated democratic reforms that removed the Communists from office peacefully; Romania alone resorted to violence. Hungary, while still Communist itself, had opened its border to East Germans seeking entry to West Germany, even before the destruction of the Berlin Wall. Soon Hungary itself was free.

All this was made possible by the collapse of the Soviet Union's will and power. Though most western observers believed throughout the 1980s that the USSR was the same superpower it had been in previous decades, in fact its command economy was failing under the pressure to supply consumer goods to a growing population and enough weaponry to the armed forces to match that of the United States and its allies. Moreover, the Soviet Union's nine-year attempt to take Afghanistan, launched in 1979, had finally forced an economic collapse.

During the crucial decade leading to the Soviet demise, the U.S. commander in chief was President Ronald Reagan. Reagan had also survived an assassination attempt shortly before the attempt made on the pope. Like John Paul, he came away believing God had altered the bullet's trajectory and saved his life. In his journal he wrote, "Whatever happens now I owe my life to God and will try serve Him in whatever way I can." According to biographer O'Sullivan, Reagan "thought he knew the great purpose for which God had spared him. It was to hasten the collapse of communism."

These two postage stamps reflect converging points of view on the changes occurring in the Eastern Bloc. A 1990 West German stamp (top) celebrates the huge candle-lit marches outside Leipzig's Saint Nikolai Church of the previous year, with the caption "We are the people." The 1988 Soviet Russian stamp celebrating perestroika (restructuring), declares "Restructuring is the reliance on the living creativity of the masses." perestroika and its companion, Glasnost (openness), would pave the way for the momentous changes about to come.

President Ronald Reagan walks with John Paul II through an ornamental garden in Miami during the pope's 1987 visit. Following the assassination attempt upon him, the president pledged to serve God in whatever way he could. He came to believe that God's great purpose for him was to hasten the collapse of communism.

An artist's conception of the Space Laser Defense System, part of the Strategic Defense Initiative (known as Star Wars), launched by Reagan in 1984. Designed to destroy nuclear ballistic missiles in space, it carried such a potentially high cost that countering it helped bring about the fall of the Soviet Union. Below, far right, Reagan takes a chip out of the remains of the Berlin Wall during a postpresidential visit in 1990. Three years earlier, speaking in front of the Brandenburg Gate on the West German side, Reagan had famously importuned Soviet Leader Mikhail Gorbachev (near right): "Mr. Gorbachev, tear down this wall!"

Reagan, a Democrat turned Republican, was a former Hollywood actor and two-term governor of California who had groomed himself for the presidency by closely studying national and international affairs. He had never agreed with *Ostpolitik* or the concept of "peaceful coexistence," and once summarized his goal in the Cold War as, "We win and they lose." As he recovered from his wound, which had politically strengthened his hand in Congress, he developed the strategy that would bring the USSR down, first with economic sanctions over the imposition of martial law in Poland, and then, with the promotion of the Strategic Defense Initiative (SDI). Universally dubbed "star wars" after the popular movie, SDI would have created an antiballistic missile system which, he insisted, would make all nuclear weapons obsolete. Whether it was technically feasible may well have been beside the point in Reagan's grand vision. The logic of the Cold War required the Soviet Union to spend trillions of rubles it did not have to try to match SDI; and this proved its undoing.

That, anyway, is a Republican explanation for the Soviet collapse. Democrats have another one. Overall, they say, the collapse was the combination of many things—the inefficiency of Communist economics, the Afghanistan war, the arms race with the U.S., the hollowness of atheistic materialism, and envy of the western standard of living. One thing is agreed upon. The suddenness of the collapse surprised everyone.

The man presiding over the downfall was Mikhail Gorbachev, who as Communist party general secretary took over Soviet leadership in 1985. A reformer fully a generation younger than his predecessors, Gorbachev attempted Soviet renovation through the policies of *perestroika* (economic restructuring) and *glasnost* (recognition of human rights). Under the former, he sought to make the Soviet Union economically competitive, and to reduce the size and cost of the military. He had no interest in sustaining the Cold War or suppressing religion. Though not a Christian, when he met with the pope he introduced John Paul to his wife with the words, "I have the honor to introduce the highest moral authority on earth."

Citizens carrying a huge Russian flag in the new red, blue, and white colors celebrate in Red Square on August 22, 1991, the day following the attempted coup by Soviet hardliners to take back control of government. That year saw the dissolution of the Soviet Union as one republic after another declared independence. In three years the alliance of militantly atheist regimes had fallen apart.

But Gorbachev tried to use the meeting to enlist the pope in backing a new European alliance led by a reformed Soviet Union against America. Countering this, John Paul pressed for full religious freedom. In the end only the pope got his way.

While Reagan pressured the Soviet Union from outside its borders, dissenters worked from within. Michael Bourdeaux, the Anglican priest whose Keston College in England had provided the West its most reliable window on Soviet oppression of religion, wrote in 1977: "A democratic (usually called 'dissident') movement has emerged, disunited, but openly calling for the most far reaching changes in Soviet society. It has profoundly affected the psychology of the intelligentsia. The church has been active in this from the beginning. Individuals and sometimes large groups from among Russian and Georgian Orthodox, Baptists, Pentecostals, Adventists, Catholics of both Eastern and Latin Rite have come very close to the point of formulating a common cause."

As Gorbachev loosened restrictions and released prisoners, their protests and calls for change only increased. His efforts to salvage the Soviet Union failed as his country disintegrated into competing factions and nations, and his partly liberated economy failed. As one by one the constituent Soviet national republics voted for secession, the western ones sought the blessing of their instantly-revived Christian churches, especially in Lithuania, Ukraine, and Byelorussia.

Gorbachev's liberalization revealed the enduring Christian faith of ordinary people, as well as the hollowness of communism's atheist materialism.

In Lithuania, the demise of communism began fifteen years before the Berlin Wall fell, when five young Catholics illegally used their trial for high treason to expose Soviet oppression of religion and stir the courage and conscience of the people. In 1988, Lithuanians welcomed home their exiled archbishop Julijonas Steponavicius. In Ukraine, the Eastern Catholic Church had been officially merged into Russian Orthodoxy by Stalin, but it now emerged, four million strong.

In Russia itself, when old-guard Communists sought to reverse the tide and staged a *coup d'état* to unseat Gorbachev, the Russian Orthodox Church itself was suffering from internal dissent. But in the end, Patriarch Alexii II stood by the reforms of the new regime, while many Orthodox clergy among the newly elected congress appeared prominently among the crowds that rushed to the Russian parliament to resist the tanks and troops sent by the Marxist adherents.

Gorbachev's liberalization, in the end, revealed both the enduring Christian faith of many ordinary people, and the emptiness of communism's atheist materialism. The number of active Orthodox parishes grew from seven thousand in 1985 to twenty-seven thousand in 2006, while the number of clergy more than quadrupled to twenty-nine thousand. And as the Russian Orthodox leadership enjoyed new influence and prestige, those who had suffered in prison for their faith called for the leaders to repent of their many compromises with the Communist regime.

Over three short years the alliance of atheist regimes led by the Soviet Union had fallen apart. The new, democratic governments of central Europe that replaced them willingly restored much of the property that had been taken from churches and removed the invisible restrictions on Christianity.

Even so, after four generations of communism, the system's collapse left Eastern Europe in a state of economic and social ruin. The churches which had struggled only to survive and minister to their people in the minimal ways their political overlords had allowed now found themselves with new problems. No longer the heroes of resistance, they lost popularity by opposing popular trends and practices such as abortion, or by forming political alliances with conservative political movements. In Poland, the Catholic Church heavily involved itself in an open war against materialist consumerism which, the Poles were warned, would prove an even more dangerous foe than communism. The man who issued that warning was Pope John Paul II. The church secured its longtime goal of religious instruction in the state schools without public discussion. Among its successes, as the old Communist system collapsed, was creation of a network of dozens of charities and its own informal network of social assistance at the parish level.

In Russia, Orthodoxy built churches and claimed three-quarters of the population as members but counted on only four percent to attend weekly, while seeking state restrictions on Catholic and evangelical Protestant missions. The country meanwhile endured a decline in health standards unprecedented in the industrial world: life expectancy dropped by five years due to mounting malnutrition, alcoholism, homicide, suicide, and smoking. Its abortion rate—seventy-three terminations for every hundred live births—was the world's highest in 2011. The Orthodox Church, backed by public policy makers and worried about Russia's population decline, led a campaign to restrict abortion. Gone was state oppression but social stability was also gone. Instead, there was turmoil from licentiousness, political corruption, criminal opportunism, and gangsterism.

Christians in the formerly Communist countries could nonetheless take heart from the unnamed millions who had died for their faith. Resistance seemed hopeless against the all-powerful Communist regime, but they fought and died anyway. Some have been acknowledged publicly as martyrs. Their successors were left with the huge task of reviving the heart and soul of Eastern Europe. ■

Patriarch Alexii II of Moscow releases a dove at Christ the Savior Cathedral to mark Annunciation Day 2011. Alexii was among the Orthodox clergy in Russia who stood by the reforms of the post-Communist regime. In the two decades after the fall of communism, Orthodoxy built churches and claimed three-quarters of the population as members. Unfortunately only four percent of the population actually attended church, and licentiousness and gangsterism continued to plague the country.

One of the lucky ones who survived the Nazis' Auschwitz extermination camp, Aaron Stern, his camp tattoo still visible, is seen here in the uniform of the Haganah, the paramilitary force that would become the national army after the creation of the State of Israel on May 15, 1948. The Jewish homeland would, through the rest of the century and into the next, become the catalyst for Islamic rage.

CHAPTER 18

How the Jewish quest for a homeland turned into a cauldron of war

Russian pogroms and the Nazi Holocaust spur calls for a State of Israel, but to the Arabs it's perceived as an island of infidels fouling a vast Muslim sea

The rugged mountains, rocky plains, and green valleys of the Holy Land contain few valuable natural resources. Potable water is scarce and most of the land is too rough and too dry to farm. Though it was for millennia a military buffer zone between East and West, it no longer offers much strategic geographic advantage to anyone. Yet despite this, it remains one of the world's most contested pieces of real estate, because of its importance to the world's three great monotheistic religions. Jews see it as the land God gave specially to them; to Christians it is the place of Christ's birth, ministry, Crucifixion, and Resurrection; and to Muslims it is their most sacred site outside Arabia, and a problematic island of infidels in the great Islamic sea.

In the twentieth century, more than in most others, this epicenter of conflict would once again send shock waves around the world. The fall of the Muslim Ottoman Empire after the First World War would combine with the horror of the Holocaust in Europe in the Second to create an opportunity for the rebirth of the Jewish homeland. This in turn would be the catalyst for a global explosion of Islamic rage against Jews and against a western world which had served as the clumsy midwife to the birth of the new State of Israel. For modern secularists, it would represent a "clash of civilizations," but many Christians would see it simply as historic Islam back on the warpath.

The Jews were driven from their biblical land after they rebelled against the Roman Empire. In 70 AD three legions descended upon them, demolished their great Temple in Jerusalem, and thereby ended the ancient ritual sacrifice of animals

1. While the Koran urges relative tolerance of conquered Jews and Christians, who are termed *dhimmis*, what this means in practice is determined by Muslim jurists. One code adopted widely throughout the Ottoman Empire and still enforced in parts of the Muslim world decrees that the dhimmis be perpetually "humiliated." They must not ride horses, camels, or donkeys. They must live in smaller houses than Muslims. They must not hold public office. They must not display crosses or ring church bells. They must not recite the Bible aloud. They must not openly display wine or pork. They must never address a Muslim, unless first spoken to. Their clothing must be subject to Muslim regulation. They must be permanently subject to a special tax; if they default in payment, they instantly lose dhimmi status and may be slain or taken with their wives and children into slavery.

to atone for the sins of the people. As Christ had forewarned forty years earlier, the legions left "not one stone upon another" (Mark 13:2). The end of the Temple also marked the end of the Jewish prophets, the holy men who for nearly ten centuries had declared to Israel and the world the power and goodness of God. Even the Jewish name for the country, Judea, disappeared; the Romans thereafter officially named the area Palestine. The banished Jewish survivors fled east and west through the Roman and Persian empires. Their religion, centered for centuries on animal sacrifice in the Jerusalem Temple, they changed to one without blood sacrifice and based in the local Jewish synagogue; it became known as Judaism. Yet for two millennia they longed to return. Their prayer at each Yom Kippur (Day of Atonement) has been "Next year in Jerusalem."

However, most Jews did not seek converts. The only ones who did were the ostracized Jewish sect known as the Christians, who in the great dispersion proclaimed Jesus as the Jewish Messiah foreseen by the prophets and in whose bloody death by crucifixion they discerned the reality which the sacrifices of the Temple had prefigured. They began captivating the imagination and adherence of people all over the Roman and Persian empires. By the third century AD the Christians were so numerous that the Roman authorities, doubting their loyalty to the empire, loosed upon these followers of Christ a series of persecutions. But the courage of Christian martyrs so moved people that by the fourth century the empire itself became Christian and the paganism of the ancient world disappeared, never to return. Even the city of Jerusalem, whence Jews had mostly been

The destruction of the Temple in Jerusalem by the Romans in 70 AD as depicted by the mid-nineteenth-century romanticist Italian painter Francesco Hayez. The banished survivors fled east and west, refashioning the religion of the Temple into the religion of the synagogue, and for two millennia they longed to return.

The Wailing Wall in Jerusalem, photographed in the early 1900s, where pilgrims lament the long-ago destruction of the Temple. At the time, Jerusalem was still part of the declining Ottoman Empire, and home to a small cohort of tolerated Jews. But in the late nineteenth century the Viennese journalist Theodore Herzl, shown below en route to Palestine in 1898, founded the World Zionist Congress to advocate for a new Jewish home-land in the Holy Land. The increasing number of Jews fleeing the various persecutions of the twentieth century would create a rapidly growing population at odds with the Arabs living in the region.

banished, became a predominantly Christian city. Another three hundred years later came a further convulsion. The armies of Mohammed conquered Arabia, then burst forth, conquering the Persian Empire and much of the Roman one and imposing Islamic religious government and law as they swept with fire and sword through the Middle East and North Africa. As kindred "peoples of the Book" Christians and Jews were tolerated, but distinctly and definably as second class subjects.[1] Even so the Jews prospered. They became bankers to both Christian and Islamic rulers, gaining ever higher status in government, the professions, the arts, and sciences, until periodic persecutions (Christian and Islamic) would descend upon them and kill them or banish them and reduce them to penury and misery. Then, always irrepressible, they would rise again.

Through it all, a large-scale return to the Holy Land remained an undying hope. Except for the partial recapture of the region by Christian Crusaders in the eleventh and twelfth centuries, control of Palestine lay in Muslim hands for the better part of thirteen hundred years. Though they cherished the Dome of the Rock in Jerusalem, where they believe Mohammed rose briefly to heaven, the Holy Land never held quite as much religious significance for Muslims as it did for Jews and Christians; Islam's holiest place is Mecca in Arabia. Palestine came under the Muslim rule of the Turkish Ottomans in 1517 when Süleyman the Magnificent seized it from the Muslim Mamluks. To prevent sectarian strife, Süleyman recognized three communities within it—Muslim, Christian, and Jewish. He rebuilt its crumbled walls and public facilities and launched it on a prolonged and unusual period of peace. In 1700 the small Jewish minority in the city numbered about twelve hundred.[2] However, the decline of the Ottoman Empire saw a decline in Jerusalem, whose total population was down to eight thousand by the mid-nineteenth century.

The humanist ideals of Europe's eighteenth-century Enlightenment renewed Jewish hope of acceptance in Christian lands, but their optimism was short-lived. With the new ideas came ultranationalism and anti-Semitic racism, so that a yearning for their own land was kindled anew. Theodor Herzl, a Viennese journalist, gave voice to it: the only way to achieve safety and security for his people

2. Jerusalem's Jewish population was doubled later that year to about twenty-four hundred when a contingent of immigrants led by the preacher Judah HeHasid arrived from Europe, a forerunner of Zionism. About half their number had perished during the journey. His colonists built the Hurva Synagogue, the main Jewish place of worship until 1948 when it was destroyed by the Arabs. It was rebuilt in 2010.

The looming revival of conflict over the Holy Land was made manifest in the prescient writing of a Lebanese Christian scholar named Najib Azuri, who foresaw in 1905 the awakening of the Arab nation and the quiet effort of the Jews to reconstitute the ancient kingdom of Israel: "These two movements are destined to fight each other endlessly until one overcomes the other. The fate of the entire world hinges on the final result of this struggle."

was through the establishment of a Jewish state, he argued. He founded the World Zionist Congress in 1897 to advocate for a new nation, which he envisioned as secular, pluralistic, and socialist. Argentina and East Africa were among the locations considered, but Jewish scripture mentioned only *Eretz Yisrael*, the ancient Holy Land, and settling there soon became the movement's sole objective.

Many Jews were already on the move. Violent pogroms in late nineteenth-century Tsarist Russia and elsewhere in eastern Europe drove out four million, more than half to the United States, and some few to Palestine in accord with the emerging Zionist impulse. The latter formed a vanguard for two waves that followed them, pushing the Jewish population there to fifty thousand by the dawn of the twentieth century. The indigenous Palestinian Jews, who had been living relatively peaceably with their Arab neighbors for generations, did not welcome them, but like the Arabs they were rapidly overwhelmed by the European culture of the newcomers.

The waning Ottoman Empire clung to life through the nineteenth century by entering into a series of strategic alliances with various European nations that were competing for commercial control of the Ottoman lands. Fatally, the Ottomans allied with Germany in the First World War. Seeing a chance to at last

The 1916 Sykes-Picot agreement divided the Middle East between Britain and France, with Britain taking control of the Holy Land (shown on map, right). Two years later British foreign secretary Lord Arthur Balfour (below left) signed the famous declaration (shown to the right of Balfour) that endorsed "the establishment in Palestine of a national home for the Jewish people." After the Great War ended, the Balfour Declaration was adopted by the League of Nations as part of the British mandate for Palestine. Bottom, members of two Zionist settlement societies gather in the desert near Jaffa in 1909 to cast lots for building sites in what will become the city of Tel Aviv.

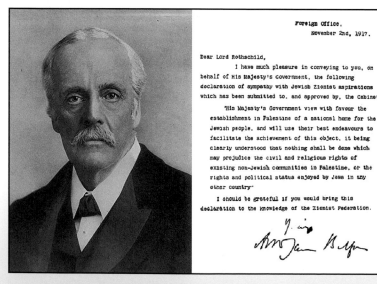

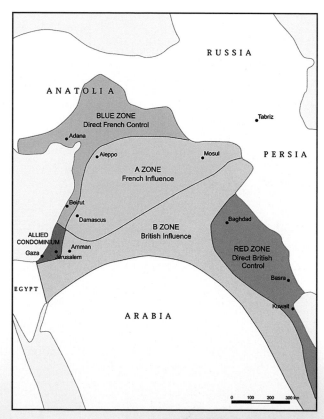

British police forces in Jerusalem (below) attempt to contain an Arab mob protesting measures protecting immigrant Jews in 1933; (at left) in 1936, Jews carry the bodies of seventeen victims of Arab race riots. Incoming western Jews had naively believed the Arabs would welcome them with tolerance and gratitude for lifting them out of economic and technological stagnation. Instead, the indigenous Palestinian population saw the newcomers as a new kind of colonizer. British efforts to reconcile the conflicts proved ineffectual.

throw off the Ottoman yoke, and with British support, the Arabs launched a full-scale revolt. The Ottoman sultan, who styled himself leader of all Sunni Muslims, appealed for pan-Islamic unity by proclaiming *jihad* (holy war) against Britain and its allies, France in Lebanon and Syria, and Italy in Libya. It fell on deaf ears throughout most of the Muslim world, and the Ottoman collapse was assured. But it was a dark moment for Islam. The Turks thereafter looked to the secularized West for economic and technological salvation. The Arabs, riven by tribal and sectarian divisions, appeared powerless. For the Zionists of Europe, the hour of their great return seemed at hand. No one in the Arab world perceived this with a greater sense of foreboding than the Muslim inhabitants of Palestine.[3]

Even before the First World War ended, the Allied powers had started planning the partition of the Middle East. The 1916 Sykes-Picot agreement divided the region between Britain and France, with Britain taking control of the Holy Land. Among British policy makers, including Prime Minister David Lloyd George, there were numerous "Gentile Zionists" who supported restoration of the Jewish homeland. They had strategic objectives too, not least currying favor among American Jews and rising Protestant churches who saw the rebirth of Israel as precursor to fulfillment of the biblical prophecy of the Second Coming. A year later came the famous Balfour Declaration, issued by British Foreign Secretary Arthur Balfour, which endorsed "the establishment in Palestine of a national home for the

Imam Hassan al-Banna founded the Islamist Society of Muslim Brothers (the Muslim Brotherhood) in Egypt in 1928 in reaction to the secularism creeping into the post-Ottoman Arab world. Modernist leaders tried to suppress the movement, but its brand of violent Muslim extremism would persist into the next century. Beneath his portrait, members of the Muslim Brotherhood are shown in 2006 (above) celebrating al-Banna's centenary; (inset right) the organization's emblem, and (top right) a group of Brotherhood fighters during the 1948 Arab-Israeli war.

Jewish people." Though carefully worded to uphold "the civil and religious rights of the non-Jewish communities in Palestine," the statement lent enormous legitimacy to the Zionist project, especially after it was adopted by the League of Nations as part of the British mandate for Palestine.

The Jewish population grew rapidly in the 1920s through immigration by Zionists and refugees from continuing persecution in Europe. They tended to be wealthier than the impoverished Palestinian Arabs, and with the support of international Zionism they purchased large amounts of land for new Jewish settlements. Many hoped the indigenous Arab population would demonstrate the same tolerance toward Jews observed since the days of Süleyman. Then too, perhaps the skills they were introducing might lift the Arabs from what the newcomers saw as economic and technological stagnation. The Palestinians—both the Islamic majority and the Christian minority—were beginning to perceive things differently. To them, the Christian West was colonizing their land with Jews it didn't want. On the other hand, with Turkey now gone, the Palestinians (who traditionally considered themselves part of Syria) now wanted to have their own state, something the planners of postwar Europe endorsed.

British efforts to reconcile these conflicting aspirations proved ineffectual, and violent confrontations between Jews and Arabs began. Arab nationalist movements proliferated, targeting both Britons and Jews. In Egypt, Syria, and elsewhere, the British and French slowly ceded control to self-governing Arab authorities. But in strife-torn Palestine, there was no such option.

As the Great Depression took hold, western nations began closing their doors to Jews fleeing increased anti-Semitism in Europe, especially Germany, which left many Jews with no place to go but Palestine. Between 1930 and 1935, the Jewish population there doubled to nearly four hundred thousand, almost a third of the total population. As they acquired land from Arab landowners, the previous Arab tenants became a dispossessed peasantry. Terrorist groups such as the Black Hand emerged and attacked both Jewish settlers and the British. The Jews responded in kind. Tit-for-tat terrorism became and would remain the modus operandi of the conflict.

In 1936, Arab nationalists, supported by volunteers from neighboring countries, conducted a general strike and a nationwide tax revolt, accompanied by armed attacks on Jewish settlements and British installations. British authorities and Jewish militias struck back. Palestinian leaders were arrested, sometimes tortured, and sent to a detention camp. The uprising, called the "Great Revolt" by Palestinians, continued for the better part of three years. Meanwhile a British government inquiry, recognizing an "irrepressible conflict...between two national communities within the narrow bounds of one small country," proposed a "two-state solution" granting eighty percent of the land to the Palestinians, twenty to the Jews. The Jews agreed; the Palestinians emphatically did not.

Meanwhile, former Ottoman provinces were made independent countries, their borders drawn by the Great War victors, some becoming client states of western powers, some tribal despotisms, and some autocracies ruled by brute force. But many of these were quietly abandoning Islamic law, dismaying the pious and thereby giving rise in Egypt in 1928 to the Society of Muslim Brothers,

Saudi Arabia would become the richest of the Arab nations and the primary financier of the spread of Islamic fundamentalism across the Muslim world.

or Muslim Brotherhood, whose credo was (and remained as of 2012): "Allah is our objective; the Koran is our law, the Prophet is our leader; Jihad is our way; and death for the sake of Allah is the highest of our aspirations." Convinced that such Muslim medievalism was not the way of the future, the more secular Arab leaders tried to thwart it, but it grew steadily.

The outbreak of the Second World War in 1939 changed things in the Middle East. Needing Arab allies against Germany, the British abandoned their commitment to a Jewish state, promised to halt Jewish expansion, and to create a Palestinian state within a decade. When the war ended in 1945, however, and it became known that two-thirds of the Jewish population of Europe had been exterminated in the Nazi Holocaust, the need for a Zionist state returned to the British—and the world's—political agenda.

By then a new Middle Eastern factor had acquired major international significance. Western governments and companies had gained control of the oceans of oil beneath Arab lands, most importantly in what would soon become Saudi Arabia, spiritual homeland of Islam, whose oil reserves seemed unlimited. Extremely poor, consisting almost entirely of inhospitable desert, the country had been dominated by two tribal leaders: Hussein bin Ali and Abdul-Aziz bin Saud. The latter was a descendant of the ancient House of Saud, which three centuries earlier had allied through marriage with Muhammad ibn Abdul Wahhab, founder of a fanatically ultra-orthodox Sunni Muslim sect called the Wahhabi. Both men were British proxies during the war, and Hussein, whose territory included the holy cities of Mecca and Medina, had led the Arab revolt against the Ottomans.[4]

Wahhabism was strong among the fierce Bedouin tribesmen of the desert interior, and bin Saud harnessed their religious and martial fervor in a movement called the Brethren. In one battle with Hussein loyalists over an oasis town,

4. Hussein's son Faisal was a key military leader in the Arab Revolt against the Ottomans. He developed a close relationship with British Middle East archaeologist turned intelligence officer T.E. Lawrence, hero in the 1962 movie epic *Lawrence of Arabia*. They shared a vision of a pan-Arab state that would unite the Sunni and Shi'a under a modern, moderate form of Islamic government. The victory of the Wahhabist Saud clan over the Husseins on the Arabian Peninsula ensured that this did not happen.

eleven hundred camel-mounted and primitively armed Brethren warriors overwhelmed a much better equipped rival force that outnumbered them five to one. Through such triumphs, the House of Saud gained full control of the most of the peninsula by 1932, and the Kingdom of Saudi Arabia was born. It would become the richest of the Arab nations and primary financier of the spread of Islamic fundamentalism across the Muslim world in the twentieth century.

The British worked hard to keep their Arab puppet governments quiescent during the Second World War, banning Jewish immigration to Palestine. When the Shah of Iran favored Germany, the British put his son on the throne. They also deposed a pro-Axis regime in Iraq. Tens of thousands of Palestinian Jews fought for the Allies as did some Palestinian Arabs. But other Arabs saw a German victory as their best hope to regain their country. One was the Grand Mufti of Jerusalem, Haj Amin al-Husseini, a leader in the 1936 uprising exiled to Germany, who viewed Hitler's Final Solution to the Jewish problem as a final solution to the Palestine problem as well.

But the German Holocaust so powerfully strengthened the Zionist cause that international support for it became almost universal, including from the United States and (initially) the Soviet Union, the new global superpowers. However, there was one

The long agony of Christian Egypt

After a short lull in Muslim discrimination, militant Islam returns, violence erupts anew, and thousands flee—but hope revives with the 'Arab Spring'

The bomb that exploded shortly after midnight on New Year's Day in 2011 outside the Saints Coptic Church in Alexandria, killing twenty-one Christian worshippers and wounding nearly eighty, signaled the beginning of religious and civil violence and revolutionary political upheaval that would rock Egypt. Hours later, as angry Coptic Christians clashed with police in the streets, torching cars and throwing rocks, President Hosni Mubarak, eighty-two, appeared on television. "This sinful act is part of a series of efforts to drive a wedge between Copts and Muslims," he declared, "but Allah has aborted the plotters' plan and turned it against them. We are all in this together and will face up to terrorism and defeat it."

Within seven weeks, however, Mubarak's thirty years in power was ended by the so-called "Arab Spring"—a wave of public protest and revolt that swept much of the Middle East. But the optimism implicit in the term "Arab Spring," invented by the western media, begged an obvious question: was this widespread unrest and rebellion evidence of a new popular desire for freedom and democracy, or a new opportunity for Islamist hard-liners to impose Muslim oppression on Christians and other minorities where previous secular regimes (however corrupt and/or authoritarian) had enforced greater tolerance?

After eighteen days of massive street demonstrations against his repressive and corrupt regime, during which 846 people were killed, an exultant crowd of thousands in Cairo's Tahrir Square cheered the news that Mubarak had resigned. His replacement, Egypt's Supreme Council of Armed Forces (SCAF), promised to amend the constitution and hold free elections. However, Egypt's Christians, an estimated minority of ten percent of the country's eighty-three million inhabitants, had more reason to fear than to celebrate.

Ethnically and religiously, the Copts trace their ancestry

Top, Egyptian protesters set fires and form barricades during the lead-up to the so-called Arab Spring in Cairo's Tahrir Square in 2011. Above right, Coptic Christians hold a blood-spattered poster of Christ aloft as they chant, "With our blood and soul we redeem the cross," after a morning Mass inside Alexandria's Saints Church on January 2, 2011. The previous day a Muslim bomb had exploded outside the church, killing twenty-one worshippers. The resignation of President Hosni Mubarak, above left, in February 2011, brought the promise of free elections, but subsequent events gave Coptic Christians more reason to fear than to celebrate.

back to pre-Arab and even pre-Christian times. According to tradition, they began to embrace Christianity in 55 AD, when the evangelist Mark preached the gospel in Alexandria, and Saint Mark is considered the first Coptic pope. Anti-Christian persecutions by Rome's pagan emperors ended in 306 AD, but for Egyptian Christians their tribulations had scarcely begun. In 451 the Coptic Church rejected a doctrine about Christ worked out at the Council of Chalcedon, which the Roman emperor (now ruling from Constantinople) had assembled to combat the Nestorian heresy.[1] For this rejection the Copts suffered more torture, death, and forfeiture of land.

Thus when Muslim Arab armies invaded Egypt in 641, the Christian population welcomed them, hoping that Islam's new yoke would be lighter than Constantinople's—or Persia's, whose most recent occupation had ended only thirteen years earlier. They hoped in vain. To Muslims they were *dhimmis*, the historic Muslim term denoting the second-class status of Christians and Jews, and extended in more recent times to Hindus, Buddhists, and others. As such they were subjected over the centuries to outright persecution at worst, and at best systemic exploitation through the *jizya* tax levied specially on dhimmis.[2]

By the tenth century, Arabic had become Egypt's vernacular language, and Coptic was relegated to church use only. Although the Copts maintained the distinctive blue cross tattoo on the right wrist, their stringent regime of 251 fast days, their monastic tradition, veneration of their martyrs and of the Virgin Mary, Coptic Christianity had experienced slow, steady decline.

Hosni Mubarak took power in October 1981, after his peace-seeking predecessor, Anwar Sadat, was assassinated by Muslim extremists. Mubarak imposed permanent martial law, and never lifted it. He was resolutely secularist and to a degree tolerant of Christianity. However, Muslim-Christian intermarriage was still not recognized, and Christians were barred from high government office. But they were otherwise legally protected, and Mubarak was endorsed by Pope Shenouda III, the Orthodox patriarch of Alexandria, representing ninety-five percent of Egypt's Christian minority.

Yet despite martial law, Islamism grew in strength and hostility. In the last years of Mubarak's regime, according to a November 2011 report by the Washington-based organization Freedom House, violence against Christians "increased dramatically." It documented fifty-three incidents of "communal conflict" between January 2008 and January 2010, thought to be caused largely by Salafist extremists, a fundamentalist strand of Egypt's Sunni Islamic majority.

After Mubarak fell, violence increased. Typically, some rumoured religious insult or indignity would trigger a Muslim attack, setting off a Christian protest, followed by deadly street fighting. According to an October 2011 report by Human Rights Watch, six months earlier a Muslim mob had burned Two Martyrs Church in Atif, fifteen miles south of Cairo, over an alleged affair involving a Muslim woman and a Coptic man. Two thousand Copts, mostly poor people such as garbage collectors, blocked Cairo streets in protest, leading to thirteen people being killed and some 140 injured. Two months later, twenty-three were killed and 232 injured after Salafists torched the churches of Saint Mena and Saint Mary, burning the latter to the ground, with ensuing street battles. The apparent cause was a rumor that Christians had forcibly confined a woman who wanted to convert to Islam.

The deadliest single episode to follow Mubarak's ouster, however, was not the work of Salifist fundamentalists. It occurred in October 2011, when Egyptian soldiers opened fire on demonstrators outside a Cairo television station, and drove armored vehicles into ten thousand reportedly peaceful protestors, mostly Christians, angered by the failure of the SCAF to act on yet another church burning. Reported casualties were twenty-eight killed (including one Muslim and one policeman) and over three hundred wounded.

When Egyptians went to the polls in June 2012, forty percent of the seats went to the ostensibly moderate Freedom and Justice Party of the Muslim Brotherhood, and twenty-five percent to the Salafist Al-Nour party. President Mohammed Morsi, sixty, an engineer who had taught briefly at California State University, moved swiftly to secure control of the SCAF. In late November he granted himself sweeping powers, resulting in more rioting, and accusations that he was betraying the Arab Spring.

By 2012 a major Christian exodus was under way. The Cairo-based Egyptian Union of Human Rights Organizations claimed that nearly one hundred thousand Copts had emigrated in 2011 alone, swelling an outflow that had been going on for years. Many went south, crossing Sudan to Ethiopia, the only Christian-majority country left in northern Africa, where most Christians belong to the kindred Ethiopian Orthodox Church. However, in the previous forty years the number of Egyptian Coptic churches in Ethiopia had grown from seven to one hundred fifty, and the Coptic population to four million; in short, there were now half as many Egyptian Christians in Ethiopia as there were in Egypt.

This phenomenon was not confined to Egypt. As radical Islamism grew throughout the Muslim world, from Algeria to Indonesia, Christians were leaving in record numbers from Syria, Iraq, Palestinian Israel, and Pakistan, among others. In the West Bank and Gaza, lands held by the Muslim Palestinian authority, the Christian share of the population had dropped from about twenty percent after the Second World War to under two percent. After the U.S. invaded Iraq in 2003 and ousted Saddam Hussein, rising Islamism caused almost two-thirds of Iraq's 1.3 million Christians to leave their country. A very similar Christian exodus was expected to follow the 2011 Arab Spring outbreak of civil war against much-hated Syrian dictator Hafez al-Assad. Both Assad and Hussein were of the secularist Ba'ath party, and both leaders—whatever their other deficiencies—provided a reasonable level of security to Christians.

Though the situation east of the Mediterranean looked increasingly bleak, encouraging signs began to appear in Egypt. To avoid a repetition of murderous events during Christian holy days in 2010 and 2011, Muslim Egyptians in 2012 turned out in hundreds and thousands to physically surround and shield Christmas celebrations in Christian churches against possible attack by extremists—and were encouraged to do so by the Muslim Brotherhood. On another occasion, when security forces began attacking Muslims praying in a Cairo square during a demonstration, Christian Egyptians rushed in to surround and protect them. Thousands of Egyptian youth were now putting a cross and crescent together on their own Facebook photos, and when Muslim extremists in demonstrations raised their ancient cry of "Allahu Akbar" (God is Great) against Christians, they were drowned out by the answer, "Muslim, Christian, we're all Egyptians."

This augured well for a new Alexandrian patriarch—whom Copts call pope. In November 2012, the Copts elected their 118th spiritual head, Tawadros (Theodore) II. In a traditional ritual during a Liturgy at Cairo's cathedral, a blindfolded choir-

Muslims alike, including President Nasser, and was photographed by news media. The luminous figure of a woman in silent prayer appeared numerous times, sometimes several times a week. The apparition was pronounced genuine by both the Coptic and Catholic churches. Even the Egyptian police could find no evidence of a hoax, though American sociologists determined from a distance that it was an obvious example of mass delusion.

Similar appearances above Coptic churches were also reported in 2009 and 2010, which devotees found entirely unsurprising. After all, they said, it was in Egypt that the Holy Family found refuge for four years from Herod's wrath. Now, Egypt itself needed help. ▪

boy plucked his name from a glass bowl, one of three possible candidates previously selected by two thousand four hundred clerics and prominent laymen. A former pharmacist and long-time priest, Pope Tawadros (whose christened name was Waih Sahby Baqi Soleiman) has since emphasized that the church's role is not political, but spiritual. He particularly noted the need for young people, so heavily influenced by TV, internet, and cell phones, "to be spiritually filled and to engage in a spiritual relationship with God."

Pope Tawadros may have divine assistance. In 1968 and 1971 the Virgin Mary appeared above a Coptic church in Cairo's Zeitoun district, was seen by millions, Christians and

1. Nestorians claimed that Christ had two distinct natures, while Copts were accused of being Monophysites—the opposite error, which holds that Christ's human nature is absorbed into his divine nature. But Copts in fact claim adherence to Miaphysitism, the belief that Christ's humanity and divinity are distinct but united in one nature. (For more on the Copts, see volume 5, pages 144, 171–174).

2. Many Muslims and their sympathizers insist that jizya was simply the dhimmi equivalent of the Muslim zakaat, or alms tax for the poor. Critics, however, contend that typically the jizya was punitively higher than the zakaat (a) to ensure that non-Muslims paid disproportionately for Muslim government, and (b) to encourage the conversion of dhimmi populations to Islam. According to Al-Muwatta, an early Islamic jurist, the jizya—unlike the Muslim zakaat—was to "humble" the dhimmis. Secular Muslim regimes generally abandoned religiously based taxation, but the restoration of jizya was high on the hard-line Islamist priority list in the late twentieth century.

Above, Jewish refugees crowd the deck of the Theodore Herzl *as it arrives in the port of Haifa in April 1947, the banner reading "The Germans destroyed our families and homes—Don't you destroy our hopes." Top right, just over a year later, on May 15, 1948, Prime Minister Ben Gurion reads the proclamation declaring the new Jewish State. Despite the determination of the combined Arab armies to drive the Jews into the sea, the better-equipped and better-led Israelis repelled the Arab attackers. By the time of the UN-imposed truce in 1949, Israel controlled eighty percent of Palestine. In the bottom photo, soldiers from the Israeli Haganah force stand on an Egyptian Air Force Spitfire shot down in the surf during a raid on Tel Aviv airfield. Below left, Israel's new flag, featuring the Magen David (shield of David) between two stripes symbolizing a prayer shawl.*

significant exception. Britain's new Labour government, which supplanted Winston Churchill's at the Second War's end, proved unsympathetic to the plight of the Jews and blocked the emigration of Holocaust survivors to Palestine. The Zionists, already outraged at Britain's 1939 reversal of support for a homeland, turned on their erstwhile protectors with a vengeance.

From 1945 to 1947 underground Zionist militias carried out numerous attacks against British authorities. Bombing British colonial offices in Jerusalem's King David Hotel, they killed ninety-one people. The British had one response: they wanted out of Palestine.[5] They brought their case to the United Nations which in 1947 produced a partition plan splitting Palestine roughly evenly between Arabs and Jews, giving the Jews, based on existing settlements, the productive northern coastal plain, Galilee, and the empty southern Negev Desert, and Palestine the area around Jerusalem, the southern coast around Gaza, and the west bank of the Jordan River. The portion assigned to the Jews contained a large Arab minority. Jerusalem was to be jointly held and internationally administered. Palestinian Arabs saw the plan as a gross injustice. They had pointedly ignored the visiting UN commission which recommended it (unlike the Jews, who had courted the commission), setting a pattern later summarized by Jewish diplomat Abba Eban as, "[Palestinians] never miss an opportunity to miss an opportunity." On May 14, 1948, a provisional Jewish government proclaimed the birth of the State of Israel. Supported by neighboring independent Arab states, the Palestinians resolved to fight.

The new state was born as a battleground. As British troops withdrew, fighting broke out between Palestinian militias and Israeli security forces. On May 15, Egypt, Syria, Jordan, Lebanon, and Iraq sent troops into the newly divided country with one declared objective: the Jews must be "swept into the sea." The Israelis, though outnumbered fifty-to-one, were better equipped, better led, and fighting for their lives. They penetrated deep into Arab Palestinian territory and Syria's Golan Heights until a UN truce was imposed that left Israel in control of nearly eighty percent of Palestine's territory.

The Palestinians were now more thoroughly dispossessed than ever. Hundreds of thousands became refugees on the scraps of land still nominally Palestinian. The inhabitants were almost completely bereft of economic opportunity and political leadership. Even their Arab "allies" preyed on their weakness: Jordan took control of the West Bank and East Jerusalem while Egypt effectively ran the Gaza Strip. Though it was the Palestinians who had started shooting, they could

Hundreds of thousands of refugees dwelt on the scraps of land still Palestinian. They were bereft of opportunities. Their Arab 'allies' preyed upon them.

now convincingly present themselves to the world as betrayed and victimized. In 1972, Palestinian writer Fawaz Turki would portray their destitution: "The nation of Palestine ceased to be. Beneath the glamour [of Israel] lies the tragedy of another people who suffered for no reason, who were uprooted from their homeland, and who had never in their history practiced persecution in their *rencontre* with the Jews, but who were made to pay the price of a crime [the Holocaust] committed by others."

As sad and powerful as the plight of the Palestinians was in the western world, it was no match for the heroic narrative of the Jews of Israel. It was celebrated in literature and films, especially the 1956 Leon Uris novel *Exodus*, a runaway international best seller that was made into a Hollywood blockbuster. The western world's postwar baby boom generation was in the main enthralled by the birth of Israel. Its early secular, socialist orientation resonated with their own youthful liberal philosophical views, and its story of a people's liberation from the Holocaust, from British colonialism, and from implacable Arab enemies echoed their devout belief in the universal right to self-determination—a right, however, that they did not extend to the Palestinians.

The birth of the State of Israel fueled Arab nationalism as never before. Beyond Palestine, in the 1960s it was personified in one Arab leader, Egyptian president Gamal Abdul Nasser. Widely traveled, well read, and movie-star handsome, Nasser fought the Israelis in Palestine as a young officer during the 1948–49 war and witnessed the humiliation of the Arab armies. He gained power in a 1952 military coup. A modernist with little time for Islamic fundamentalism,

5. Gravely weakened by the Second World War, Britain's once mighty empire was unraveling in South Asia as well as the Middle East. Independence and partition arrived simultaneously for Hindu India and Muslim Pakistan in 1947. Within a decade, the latter would become one of the world's first and larger Islamic republics. Pakistan was not as theologically strict as some of the Islamic republics that followed, but radical Islamism would flourish there and foment jihad throughout the region.

he became the foremost champion of pan-Arab nationalism in the Middle East. During his nearly twenty-year rule the Arab-Israeli conflict would become a defining characteristic of pan-Arabism.

Nasser's first confrontation with Israel came in 1956, when he announced the nationalization of the Suez Canal, a passage vital not only to the western powers but also to the Soviet Union, which was gaining influence in Egypt and supplying weapons to the Nasser regime. While the U.S., fearful of driving Arab nations into the Soviet orbit, sought diplomatic solutions, Britain and France secretly conspired with Israel to invade Egypt and seize the canal. After fierce fighting on the Sinai Peninsula, where the Israelis again whipped their Arab opponents, the conflict was eventually ended through diplomatic efforts led by Canadian external affairs minister (and future prime minister) Lester Pearson, and the deployment of the first-ever UN peacekeeping force.

Smoke rises from oil tanks beside the Suez Canal following the initial Anglo-French assault of Port Said, Egypt, on November 5, 1956. Egypt's President Gamal Abdul Nasser (top left), a champion of an-Arab nationalism, an enemy of Israel, and, increasingly, a friend of the Soviet Union, had nationalized the canal, thus threatening this vital French and English link to their Middle Eastern oil. After fierce fighting in the Sinai Peninsula, where the Israelis once again beat their Arab opponents, the conflict was eventually ended by the diplomatic efforts of Canadian foreign minister (and future prime minister) Lester Pearson, top right.

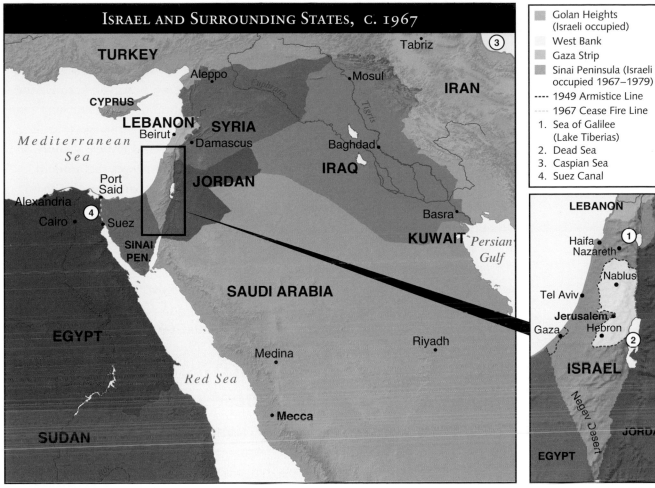

ISRAEL AND SURROUNDING STATES, C. 1967

Golan Heights (Israeli occupied)
West Bank
Gaza Strip
Sinai Peninsula (Israeli occupied 1967–1979)
---- 1949 Armistice Line
····· 1967 Cease Fire Line
1. Sea of Galilee (Lake Tiberias)
2. Dead Sea
3. Caspian Sea
4. Suez Canal

The stalemate ended what became known as the second Arab-Israeli war. Attempts to build pan-Arab nationalism continued, hampered by political disunity but bolstered by ever-rising oil wealth. "There will be no peace on Israel's border because we demand vengeance," declared Nasser, "and vengeance is Israel's death." Faced with annihilation, the Israelis opted to develop the ultimate deterrent, nuclear weapons. France provided the technology to build a reactor capable of producing the material needed for atomic bombs, and while Israel has never admitted to possessing them, it is well understood that the country was nuclear capable as early as 1960. The threat of nuclear retaliation provided Israel with some protection from all-out invasion by Arab armies, but could not prevent the ever-increasing guerrilla violence inside the country and along its borders.

Moreover, the Palestinians now acquired leadership. In 1959, a young Cairo-raised Palestinian named Yasser Arafat founded a militant group called Fatah. From other Arab countries he gathered financing, and fighters from among their Palestinian refugees. By the mid-1960s Fatah was launching regular attacks against the Israelis. Soon his name became synonymous with Palestinian nationalism, and the Palestine Liberation Organization (PLO) came into being. Attacks by Fatah and others, brutal Israeli reprisals, coupled with escalating border skirmishes between Syrian and Israeli forces, were a primary catalyst for a third Arab-Israeli conflict. Hostilities began when Israel attacked Egypt, ending an uneasy decade-long truce. Supported by the Soviets, Egypt joined a concerted Arab attack on Israel in 1967. In the ensuing Six-Day War, Israel routed the Egyptians from Gaza and the Sinai, the Jordanians from the West Bank, and the Syrians from the Golan Heights.[6]

6. After the Six-Day War, Israel's military superiority over its Arab enemies became the stuff of legend—and humor. One joke described a large Arab army column moving through the desert and spotting an Israeli soldier atop a sand dune. The commander first dispatched a patrol to deal with him and it didn't come back, then a platoon which likewise failed to return, and finally an entire company. Finally, one wounded soldier returned and said, "It's a trap. There are two of them." The joke exemplified western admiration for the Israelis and contempt for the Arabs.

Sayyid Qutb

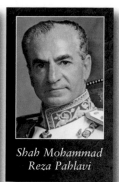

*Shah Mohammad
Reza Pahlavi*

Six years later Egypt and Syria tried to recoup their losses with surprise attacks across the Sinai and the Golan Heights. Like its predecessors, the fourth Arab-Israeli war (also known as the Yom Kippur War) ended victoriously for Israel, still in control of most of the land it conquered in 1967. It was not an unequivocal victory, however, because the war united the Arab members of the Organization of Petroleum Exporting Countries (OPEC) behind a five-month oil embargo that quadrupled prices and left much of the western world critically short. It was the most effective demonstration of pan-Arab power the modern world had ever seen, and put enormous pressure on Israel and its main ally, the U.S., to negotiate a return of the occupied Palestinian territories.

Still, Israel's battlefield triumphs had firmly established its status as the regional military superpower. Fear of an Arab invasion receded. The original terms of partition, dividing Palestine roughly equally between Jews and Arabs, no longer described the reality, and Israeli settlements steadily proliferated in the occupied territories. Some were approved by the government, others were not. All were justified on the grounds that they were indispensable to Israel's long-term security.

But the fanaticism of the Munich assassins evidenced a much wider movement whose basis was religious. A threat to traditional Islam was increasingly seen.

The communal kibbutz settlements flourished like never before—or since—in the 1960s and 1970s. They dated back to the first *aliyah* (going up, or ascent) when Europeans Jews with little or no agricultural experience formed collectives to build economically sustainable farms and later manufacturing operations and protect themselves from often hostile Arab neighbors. These were the romantic pioneers of Israeli lore, the workers of the "Miracle in the Desert" who used drip irrigation to coax crops and prosperity from barren ground, and who doubled as volunteer citizen-soldiers. Predominantly socialist and secular, they attracted tens of thousands of like-minded young foreigners from numerous western countries. Their experiences helped shape the West's view of Israel as a plucky underdog bringing civilization, democracy, and freedom to a primitive Arab backwater.

But one million Palestinians now lived under Israeli military occupation. The neighboring Arab states, Jordan and Egypt in particular, loath to tangle with a nuclear-armed Israel that had repeatedly bested them in battle, turned to diplomacy to regain occupied lands in exchange for durable peace agreements. Under Nasser's successor, President Anwar Sadat, Egypt detached itself from the Soviet Union and became a client of U.S. development aid and military support. King Hussein of Jordan, meanwhile, took military action to drive Palestinian militants out of his country. The sole tool left to the Palestinians now was terrorism. Already much in vogue among Irish republicans, Basque separatists, and ultraleft groups like the Red Brigades in Italy, the Red Army Faction in Germany, the Weather Underground in the U.S., and the *Front de Libération du Québec* in Canada, bombings, airplane hijackings, and political assassinations were everywhere making headlines.

The worst terrorist action of the period was orchestrated by the Palestinian group Black September when it kidnapped and killed eleven Israeli athletes at the 1972

Munich Olympics. Broadcast live around the world, their brazen invasion of the athletes' village and subsequent slaughter of their hostages announced the arrival of Islamic terrorism as a global phenomenon. Western media and governments scrambled to develop counterterrorism strategies, and the Israeli secret service launched a decades-long covert effort which successfully hunted down and assassinated Black September and PLO members believed involved in the "Munich Massacre."

But the fanaticism of the Munich assassins evidenced a much wider movement whose basis was no longer national but religious. The rise of Israel, the fate of the Palestinians, the recurrent Arab defeat in war, the triumph of western technology, and the influence of the secular West's moral decadence in Middle Eastern life and culture were increasingly seen as a threat to traditional Islam and to the Koran. One of the first to pronounce this view had been Sayyid Qutb, an Egyptian writer and scholar. Though a secularist in his youth, Qutb became a zealous convert to Islam and a key figure in the rise of the Muslim Brotherhood, the revivalist group born in Egypt in 1928 that in mere decades would grow to millions of members worldwide.

Qutb spent two years in the U.S. in the late 1940s, and wrote influential books describing American degeneracy in minute and sometimes titillating detail. His works also excoriated modern Arab society and government as suffering from a "new age of ignorance," which he likened to the pagan Arab world before Mohammed. Qutb was executed in Egypt in 1966 for allegedly plotting President Nasser's assassination. Princeton historian Bernard Lewis, in his book *The Crisis of Islam; Holy War and Unholy Terror* (2003), says that Qutb's ideas "became a regular part of the vocabulary and ideology of Islamic fundamentalists," especially among those mullahs who toppled the government of Iran in 1979 and replaced it with an ultra-orthodox Muslim theocracy.

Columns of smoke pour from the wreckage of three airliners hijacked by the Palestine Liberation Organization (PLO) and incinerated in the Jordan desert in 1970. Below left, PLO leader Yasser Arafat meets supporters in Tehran, Iran, in the early 1980s, following the revolution and the installation of the Ayatollah Khomeini (right).

Two U.S. Marine Corps tanks patrol the streets of Baghdad in April 2003 during the Second Gulf War against Iraq. Below, bronze sculptures of Iraqi despot Saddam Hussein, which once sat atop towers in Saddam's Republican Palace, sit in a yard of the palace grounds in 2005 following the American-led defeat of Iraq. Osama bin Laden (bottom right) had initially offered to assist the Saudis, whose oilfields were threatened by Iraq's invasion of Kuwait during the First Gulf War, but was rejected and forced to move his jihadist training operations to Afghanistan.

7. The Iranian revolution unfolded quickly, catching many in the West by surprise. Its radical Islamic character was soon revealed, however, when an organized brigade of students invaded and occupied the U.S. Embassy in Tehran and took fifty-two of its staff hostage for 444 days. The pretext was that the U.S. was a threat to the revolution, and to back the new regime's demand for the return for execution of the exiled Shah, who was undergoing medical treatment in the U.S., a nation Ayatollah Khomeini labeled "the Great Satan."

Under Mohammad Reza Pahlavi, the Shah installed by the British during the Second World War, Iran had become one of the richest and most secularized states in the Muslim world. But Iranian leftists and liberals resented the ostentatious wealth and undemocratic structure of the Pahlavi monarchy, while traditionalist Muslims despised its modernist reforms in areas such as equal rights for women. Both groups were viciously persecuted under Pahlavi's increasingly authoritarian rule, and both played key roles in the 1979 revolution that ended it. The aftermath brought the return of exiled Shia cleric Ayatollah Ruhollah Khomeini and the creation of an Islamic republic, which moved quickly to marginalize its erstwhile allies in the liberal intelligentsia by closing their newspapers, banning their political parties, and violently suppressing their protests.[7]

Radical Islam was on the rise throughout the Middle East. Also in 1979, the Soviet Union responded to the ever-growing threat of uprisings within its Muslim-dominated republics by invading Afghanistan, a country then governed by a Moscow-backed Communist proxy. Mujahideen guerrillas, with heavy American support, tormented the mighty Soviet military machine for a decade, bleeding it steadily of money, morale, and men, until the Russians finally gave up and went home. For radicalized Islam, however, the war served another, much larger purpose. With active American assistance starting in 1982, Afghanistan became an American-funded incubator and training ground for "freedom fighters" from all over the Muslim world; and when the Soviets left Afghanistan in 1989, so did the Islamist fighters, going home to spread jihad terror from Algeria to Indonesia. What America had helped unleash on the Soviet Union prior to its collapse in 1991 would now rebound on itself and the rest of the free world.

Foremost among their Islamist antagonists was Osama bin Laden, scion of a wealthy Saudi family with close ties to the House of Saud. Born in Riyadh in the late 1950s, the son of a billionaire construction magnate and his tenth wife, bin Laden was raised in the puritanical Wahhabi Muslim tradition and became an active jihadist at the outset of the Soviet-Afghan war, when he was in his early thirties. He used his considerable personal wealth to recruit and train fighters in

When the Soviets left, Afghanistan became a training ground for 'freedom fighters' who then went home to spread jihad terror all over the Muslim world.

Pakistani camps for the war in Afghanistan, which earned him a devoted following among his coreligionists. Late in the war, the tall, bearded ascetic founded al-Qaeda, literally "the Base," with the objective of conducting jihad against the enemies of Sunni Islam through a global network of militants. As early as 1990, evidence was emerging of al-Qaeda-linked terrorist plots against the west, including plans and one attempt to blow up skyscrapers in New York.

The artificial Arab world constructed by the western powers at the dawn of the twentieth century continued to unravel during its last decade. The brutal, despotic Sunni regime of Saddam Hussein in Iraq, after nearly bankrupting itself in an eight-year, U.S.-supported war against the new Shiite Islamic republic of Iran, tried to expand its oil holdings by invading Kuwait in 1990. Bin Laden offered his Islamist fighters to the Saudis, whose own oilfields were threatened by the invasion, but the Saudis instead joined an American-led coalition of more than forty countries that quickly repulsed the Iraqis.[8]

Bin Laden, now completely estranged and soon to be exiled from his Arabian homeland, moved his jihadist training operations first to the Muslim-controlled Republic of Sudan, and then back to Afghanistan, where the mujahideen victors over the Soviets had established the world's purest and nastiest religious government. The Taliban regime forbade education for girls, forced women to wear full face coverings, banned most kinds of public entertainment, and enforced the Sharia law that included public stoning of women for adultery. It was one of the few places on earth that would accept bin Laden, whom western intelligence agencies had conclusively linked to several terrorist actions. Shortly after his arrival in Afghanistan in 1996, he declared war on the United States and later issued a *fatwa*

8. Saddam Hussein's Iraq was Baathist, a secular Arab nationalist movement. As long as he was in power, traditionalist Islam was a marginal political force in Iraq. However, an international coalition led by the U.S. and Britain invaded the country in 2003 and toppled the regime, ostensibly to rid the region of Hussein's "weapons of mass destruction." During the nine-year occupation by western forces that followed, the country was wracked by sectarian violence between Sunni, Shi'a, and Kurdish Muslims. After ten years of chaos and the execution of Hussein, Islamists had gained far more influence than they ever had under Hussein.

explicitly calling for Muslims to kill Jews, Americans, and their allies.

Bin Laden's al-Qaeda was far from the only Islamist terrorist group spreading murder and mayhem in the last decades of the twentieth century. Others appeared in many Muslim countries, but Lebanon was a particularly rich spawning ground. This former French mandate was mired in civil war from the mid-1970s to the early 1990s. The departed French had left the pro-West Maronite Christian minority in a dominant position, but it was slowly overwhelmed by the rising Muslim population, greatly expanded by the arrival of several hundred thousand Palestinian refugees after 1948. Yasser Arafat's PLO conducted terrorist operations within the country, and used it as a base to export terror into Israel. Islamic Jihad and Hezbollah, two Iranian-backed Lebanese terrorist groups, were founded during the civil war. The former was credited with a 1983 suicide bomb attack on U.S. and French peacekeeping troops in Beirut that killed nearly three hundred people including 241 American soldiers, the largest single-day U.S. military loss of life since the Second World War.

The Lebanese civil war was also the scene of a massacre of civilians in Palestinian refugee camps that possibly did more to undermine western goodwill toward Israel than any other single incident. In response to cross-border attacks from the PLO and others, Israel invaded and occupied Lebanon in 1982. In September of that year, a Christian militia group called the Phalangists, aided by Israel security forces, entered the Sabra and Shatila Palestinian refugee slums of Beirut and went on a forty-eight-hour rampage that left somewhere between eight hundred and four thousand people dead, including many women and children. Later investigation by the Israeli government and others revealed that the Israeli army, under the leadership of future prime minister Ariel Sharon, did little or nothing to stop the slaughter.

In the end, Israel paid dearly for turning a blind eye. The favorable opinion of westerners had been shifting, as awareness of the protracted Palestinian refugee problem grew, and with the Israeli election of a right-wing Likud government in 1977. More hawkish than Labor, and with strong political ties to Israel's rising population of hard-line Orthodox Jews, Likud would hold power for most of the rest of the century and beyond. It alienated left-wingers and liberals in the West who had identified with the more secular and socialist Labor governments that founded and built modern Israel. Over time, the western intelligentsia first came to see moral equivalence between Palestinian terrorist attacks and Israeli reprisals, and then began to view Israel as the villain. Other factors hastened this process—

A Maronite priest lends his support to South Lebanese army fighters in 1985 in Beirut during the Lebanese civil war. The former French mandate was mired in strife from the mid-1970s to the early 1990s as the pro-West Maronite Christian government was slowly overwhelmed by the rising Muslim population, swollen by the arrival of tens of thousands of Palestinian refugees, and became the spawning ground for the Islamic Jihad and Hezbollah.

Israel's nuclear arsenal, the continued expansion of Israeli settlements within occupied territories, and the construction of an 850-mile wall around the West Bank to help thwart suicide bombers.

Meanwhile, in western Europe there developed another cause of religious conflict. Muslim immigrant populations grew rapidly, while the birth rate of non-Muslims fell to alarmingly low levels. Mosques and Islamic religious schools proliferated, often funded by Saudi Wahabbis, and were sometimes discovered to be teaching jihadism and producing native-born terrorists. In short, the process of assimilation that had worked with earlier immigrant generations did not work with Muslims. They were not coming as settlers, but as colonists who brought their own society with them. Leftists in the West blamed this "radicalization of Islam" on Israel. Western Christians, knowledgeable of history, had another theory. The man who "radicalized" Islam, they said, was Mohammed. (See volume 5.)

The defining moment in this new western polarization over Israel and Islam occurred on September 11, 2001, when nineteen terrorists, sponsored and trained by bin Laden's al-Qaeda, hijacked four commercial aircraft filled with passengers and turned them into suicide bombs aimed at symbols of American global hegemony in New York and Washington DC. Nearly three thousand civilians were killed, and out of the rubble of the twin towers of the World Trade Center and the smoldering hole in the Pentagon and a scorched field in Pennsylvania where the last plane crashed there emerged an entirely new geopolitical dynamic.

The incumbent U.S. president, Texas Republican George W. Bush, proclaimed a "war on terrorism" and within weeks launched a UN-sanctioned multinational invasion of Afghanistan to depose the Taliban and destroy al-Qaeda. He succeeded in the former but not the latter, and bin Laden's organization went on to score murderous blows against other western civilian targets in London and Bali, plus dozens of bombings aimed at westerners or non-Sunni Muslims, particularly Iraq and Pakistan. Al-Qaeda-linked or inspired terrorists also struck in the capitals of Russia, India, and Spain, while dozens more plots around the world were uncovered before they could be executed.

The U.S. and its allies, shakily supported by a United Nations that was increasingly split between western developed nations and a growing bloc of largely Muslim third world governments, spent most of the first decade of the twenty-first century trying to stabilize the governments they established in Iraq and Afghanistan, with inconclusive results. Billions of dollars and thousands of lives were spent on the effort. The "peace process" in the Middle East had made some progress in the 1990s when a more moderate PLO under an aging and increasingly corrupt Arafat had finally begun to accept the principle of a "two-state solution" for Israel and the Palestinians. This, however, fell apart with Arafat's death in 2004. The terrorist group Hamas filled the Palestinian power vacuum in Gaza, precipitating a renewed wave of suicide bombings and rocket attacks against Israel. Israeli public opinion hardened against any form of compromise. Seemingly gone forever was the original Zionist vision of Jews living in harmony with their Arab neighbors. Parliament gave the government carte blanche to use troops and targeted assassinations to protect the nation's security.

The Middle East heartland of Islam ended the first decade of the new century on what was to many a more hopeful note: the "Arab Spring." It began on a small-city street in quiet Tunisia, when local police confiscated the wheelbarrow of fruit a young vendor named Mohamed Bouazizi was hoping to sell that day to support his otherwise destitute family. Unable to pay the required bribe, on January 4, 2011, the exasperated man stood outside the town hall, shouted "How do you expect me to make a living?", thoroughly doused himself with gasoline, lit a match, and died in the flames. The tragedy triggered outrage against the coercive corruption endemic to the Muslim Middle East, and spread in strong waves from Tunisia across much of the region. By the end of 2012, massive, spontaneous, often bloody popular uprisings had driven governments from office in Tunisia, Libya, Egypt, and Yemen, wrested reforms from many others, and had ignited an ongoing civil war in Syria.

It remained quite unclear whether the Arab Spring would beget greater government respect for civil rights—especially of religion—in these notoriously repressive countries, or would bring worse repression under newly legitimized Islamist political parties backed by terrorist militias. As this volume was published in 2013, it could go either way. Each country's history and political circum-

stances were quite different. For example, Islamist political parties were generally doing well in elections after the unpopular governments were pushed out, but that did not necessarily put them in charge of either the government or the army.

The answer will be knowable in due course by whether the number of Christians slain each year for their beliefs rises or falls. The Center for the Study of Global Christianity, based in South Hamilton, Massachusetts, estimated in 2011 that every year approximately one hundred thousand Christians have been targeted and killed because of their faith, most often in Muslim countries like Egypt. After the Arab Spring arrived, PBS reported that an estimated ninety-three thousand Coptic Christians left that country, presumably fearing worse to come—just as after the fall of Saddam Hussein's secularist government, two thirds of the country's 1.5 million Christians left Iraq, either as émigrés or refugees. According to PBS, some experts were predicting that the total Christian population of the Middle East, some twelve million in 2012, would be halved that within a decade.

Pessimists looked back nine hundred years to the launching of the Crusades, one century after the end of the first Christian millennium, which was an attempt to restore Christian lands conquered by Islam. After nearly three hundred years, the attempt failed. The state of Israel, they would say, is a similar attempt by Jews to regain their lost land at the end of the second millennium. Need we be surprised if it should fail? Optimists see in a phenomenon like the Arab Spring a sure sign that the old ways are changing and a new era of democracy and civil rights is coming to the Middle East. Only one thing seemed certain. Either the pessimists or the optimists will prove right, but this time it won't take three hundred years to find out. ■

WOMEN, MEN, KINGS, EMPERORS, CITIES AND REALMS

When Jill stopped crying she found she was dreadfully thirsty. The birds had ceased singing and there was perfect silence in the forest, except for one small persistent sound, the sound of running water.

She went cautiously from tree to tree. It grew clearer every moment and, sooner than she expected, she came to an open glade and saw the stream, bright as glass, running across the turf a stone's throw away. But although the sight of the water made her feel ten times thirstier than before, she stood as still as if she had been turned into stone.

And she had a very good reason; just on this side of the stream lay the Lion. She knew at once it had seen her, for its eyes looked straight into hers and then turned away—as if it knew her quite well and didn't think much of her.

"If you're thirsty, you may drink." It was the voice of the Lion, not like a man's, deeper, wilder and stronger.

"May I—could I—would you mind going away while I do?" said Jill.

The Lion answered this only by a look and a very low growl. As Jill gazed at its motionless bulk, she realized she might as well have asked the whole mountain to move.

The delicious rippling noise of the stream was driving her nearly frantic. "Will you promise not to—do anything to me?" said Jill.

"I make no promise," said the Lion.

"Do you eat little girls?" she said.

"I have swallowed up girls and boys, women and men, kings and emperors, cities and realms," said the Lion. It didn't say this as if it were boasting, nor as if it were sorry, nor as if it were angry. It just said it.

"Oh dear!" said Jill. "I suppose I must go and look for another stream then."

"There is no other stream," said the Lion.

From: *The Silver Chair*
in C. S. Lewis's The Chronicles of Narnia
where the great Lion Aslan represents Jesus Christ

CHAPTER 19

Myth to masterpiece: the irresistible advance of 'Mere Christianity'

As the West's intelligentsia abandon the gospel, a novelist, a journalist, and an Oxford don produce a new vision of the old faith its foes cannot rebut

With Karl Marx assailing Christianity through the medium of economics, Thomas Huxley ("Darwin's Bulldog") through the medium of science, and Sigmund Freud through the medium of sexuality, early twentieth-century Christians might be forgiven for wondering: Just how will God respond? Surely we will not be left without some means of rebuttal. How are we to fight back? God's answer—as would later become apparent, at least to many Christians—was already in preparation. Yet it first came, not from a towering figure of wide academic acclaim or scientific renown, but from an unpretentious Scottish country pastor, whose dearest desire was to become a preacher, and who had been dismissed by his first, and only, congregation. Further, it took the form, not of some momentous Marxist, Darwinian, or Freudian manifesto, but of a fairy tale. The name of that failed preacher was George MacDonald, and the name of his fairy tale was *Phantastes*. It went to the printer some six months before Charles Darwin published *On the Origin of Species*.

Darwin's book set fire to the intellectual world and much else. MacDonald's fairy tales, *Phantastes* and others, thrilled many adults who had a taste for such things. In particular, they fired the imaginations of two men who had never met each other, and had never met MacDonald. Both averred that his fairy tales changed the direction of their thinking and of their lives, and they in turn would change the thinking and the lives of multitudes of others. One of these men was G. K. Chesterton; the other was C. S. Lewis. In the twentieth century, their writings

1. Many assume that Lewis used the title "Mere Christianity" ironically, indicating that its readers would rapidly discover there is nothing "mere" about it. But John G. West, program director of the Discovery Institute, writes on a C. S. Lewis website that he adopted the term from a book entitled *Reasons for the Christian Religion*, by Richard Baxter, a much-read seventeenth-century popular theologian. "I am a CHRISTIAN, a MEER CHRISTIAN," wrote Baxter, "of no other Religion; and the Church that I am of is the Christian Church, and hath been visible wherever the Christian Religion and Church hath been visible: But must you know what Sect or Party I am of? I am against all Sects and dividing Parties."

would bring throngs of converts into the Christian faith in both its Catholic and Protestant manifestations, including some of the literary giants of the era. The sales of their books would run into the hundreds of millions, and their influence would extend into the twenty-first century.

From their work and that of a dozen academics or writers allied with them, all either English or living in England, there emerged a portrayal of what Lewis succinctly described as "the belief that has been common to nearly all Christians at all times"—the belief, that is, shared by all the major Christian denominations. Over a fifty-year period, roughly the first half of the twentieth century, this portrayal would come forth in an avalanche of epic poems, novels, radio and stage plays, essays, short stories, broadcast talks, fairy tales, and polemical argument. In its entirety it could be described by the title which Lewis originally applied to a radio series he made for the BBC: "Mere Christianity."[1]

By the end of the twentieth century, it was becoming clear that "Mere Christianity" could stand its ground intellectually against all the furies hurled against the traditional faith by atheists, agnostics, secularists, and professional media skeptics alike. To ordinary thoughtful people as well it proved far more compelling than any of the dreary alternatives the world could contrive against it or offer in its stead.

But the seed had apparently been sown by George MacDonald, the unsuccessful preacher, born in 1824 to a Scottish farm family in Aberdeenshire. MacDonald's boyhood, writes Richard H. Reis in his 1989 biography, "was set in a traditional rural atmosphere compounded of Calvinist hellfire, oatcakes, horsemanship, agricultural virtues and exploration of neighborhood ruins and wilderness." Contrary to Freudian theory, he revered his father who, although a Congregationalist, was prone to value his own biblically drawn conclusions over

A portrait of the writer and cleric George MacDonald painted by Sir George Reid in 1868, and some illustrations from his popular late nineteenth-century fantasy books The Princess and the Goblin *and* Phantastes. *For G. K. Chesterton the former was "a book that has made a difference to my whole existence." For C. S. Lewis, after reading the latter discovered, "I knew I had crossed a great frontier."*

PHANTASTES
A Færy Romance

GEORGE MACDONALD

THE PRINCESS AND THE GOBLIN

those of his church. Young George clearly shared this independence of view. He graduated from the University of Aberdeen with a master's degree in chemistry, and then studied instead for the Congregationalist ministry.

When he assumed his first pastorate, however, things soon went wrong. MacDonald was something of a universalist, believing that salvation was conferred by Christ on all people, not just upon an elect few, so in 1853, his church elders fired him as a heretic. He decided that he must earn his living with his pen, difficult as this might be. By then he had married Louisa Powell, the slender daughter of a London leather merchant, and she had already borne the first of their eleven children. For several years they lived close to dire poverty, while George turned out essays that were rarely read, sermons that were never preached, and beautifully rhymed poetry that the critics faulted as lacking depth. Even worse, he suffered chronic lung problems, a lifelong affliction, which had carried away his mother, father, and two brothers and would claim four of his own young children.

The family was financially rescued by Lady Byron, the widow of the great poet; she became MacDonald's patron. In 1858, he published *Phantastes*, the first of his fairy tales, which received little immediate attention although it exhibited his extraordinary aptitude for storytelling—in fact, for mythmaking. Five years later came his first realistic novel, *David Elginbrod*, which demonstrated that he also possessed after all an aptitude for making money with his pen.[2] A profusion of such novels followed, all best sellers, and by 1877, nearly thirty years before his death in 1905, MacDonald found himself wealthy and celebrated. Queen Victoria awarded him a civil list pension, and he toured America as a literary luminary, but the novels that made his fortune were not destined for posterity. What did last were the fairy tales, for adults and children, as well as his three books of "unspoken" (meaning unpreached) sermons.

In the 1873 cartoon (left), the hirsute MacDonald is already recognized as a celebrity novelist. Something of a universalist, he had alienated himself from his Congregationalist church twenty years earlier, and was forced to seek a living with his pen for himself, his wife, and their eleven children. The family was financially rescued by the patronage of Lady Byron (right), who kept the MacDonalds afloat until his books began selling in the 1860s.

2. Better remembered than George MacDonald's first novel is the four-line epitaph he included for one of its characters:

Here lies Martin Elginbrod,
Hae mercy on my soul Lord God,
as I would do were I Lord God,
and ye were Martin Elginbrod!

The appeal of fairy tales for adults is one of those phenomena that seems self-evident to many—perhaps most—adults and totally baffling to others. This is also true of certain jokes, which meet with gales of laughter from some, and cold incomprehension from others. To explain why a fairy tale is interesting is about as hopeless as explaining why a joke is funny. Either you appreciate it or you don't. However, if there be any doubt as to the magnitude of the audience for adult fairy tales, one need only cite the sales data on J. R. R. Tolkien's magnificent opus, *Lord of the Rings,* termed by its author a fairy tale. By 2012 it was to sell more than 150 million copies.

Similarly, Chesterton's infatuation with MacDonald seems almost boundless. He wrote that *The Princess and the Goblin,* which MacDonald published in 1872, "helped me see in a special way from the start," and that it was "a book that has made a difference to my whole existence. Of all the stories I have read, it remains the most real, the most realistic, in the exact sense of the phrase the most life-like." He derived from MacDonald, he said, "a child-like joy as a uniquely human reaction, and as proof of the existence of God."

MacDonald saw that to redeem his creatures God must descend into the temporal world since all creatures, unlike God, exist in time.

His appreciation went well beyond the fairy tales, to include MacDonald's concepts of God and Christ as elucidated in his *Unspoken Sermons.* MacDonald, he wrote, "escaped the theological environment of his upbringing and developed a complete alternative theology." In it, Chesterton discerned the first faint signs of a reunited Christendom:

> When he comes to be more carefully studied as a mystic, as I think he will be when people discover the possibility of collecting jewels scattered in a rather irregular setting, it will be found, I fancy, that he stands for a rather important turning point in the history of Christendom, as representing the particular Christian nation of the Scots. As Protestants speak of the morning stars of the Reformation, we may be allowed to note such names here and there as the morning stars of the Reunion. *(From Chesterton's introduction to the biography of George and Louisa MacDonald, written by their son, Dr. Greville MacDonald.)*

MacDonald's "alternative theology" lay not in compromising the miraculous but in magnifying it. That is, writes biographer Richard Reis, he saw that "in dealing with his creatures, God must descend from his timelessness into the temporal world, since all creatures, unlike their creator, exist in time." In short, if God was to rescue a fallen humanity, he must enter the realm of time to achieve it. The Christian concept of God being incarnated as a human being was therefore inescapable, for only thus could the deliverance of man be accomplished.

Lewis, destined to become one of the century's most powerful advocates of Christianity, both intellectually and imaginatively, would unequivocally ascribe his conversion to MacDonald's initial influence. The quality that enchanted him in the fairy tales, he said, "turned out to be the quality of the real universe, the divine, magical, terrifying and ecstatic reality in which we all live." When he first picked up *Phantastes*, "nothing was further from my thoughts than Christianity." Yet after he read it, "I knew I had crossed a great frontier... I have never concealed the fact that I regard him as my master. Indeed I fancy that I have never written a book in which I did not quote him."

MacDonald's work appeared during the late Victorian era, which historian Christopher Dawson, a Chesterton convert, describes as "the low water mark in the Christian world"—a period, that is, when many if not most leading thinkers in both the sciences and the humanities, in Europe and America, firmly rejected the doctrines of the Christian faith. Nevertheless, in the brief Edwardian period that followed (named for King

Edward VII takes an oath on the Bible during his coronation at Westminster Abbey in 1902. In the brief Edwardian period that followed, most people clung at least nominally to Christian morality, though they knew almost nothing about it. After the disillusionment of the First World War, however, such traditionalism would be under steady attack.

Edward VII, 1901–1910), most people still clung at least nominally to Christian morality. "The Edwardians," observes Professor John Coates in *Chesterton and the Edwardian Cultural Crisis* (1984), "though no longer guided by the sources of Christian wisdom, had not yet abandoned the Christian moral tradition which they had inherited but which they scarcely understood." By the 1920s, however, even Christian morals would be under attack. Novelist Evelyn Waugh, in his masterpiece *Brideshead Revisited*, has the character Charles Ryder casually summarize the interwar attitude:

> The view implicit in my education was that the basic narrative of Christianity had long been exposed as a myth, and that opinion was now divided as to whether its ethical teaching was of present value, a division in which the main weight went against it; religion was a hobby which some people professed and others did not; at the best it was slightly ornamental, at the worst it was the province of "complexes" and "inhibitions"—catchwords of the decade— and of the intolerance, hypocrisy, and sheer stupidity attributed to it for centuries. No one had ever suggested to me that these quaint observances expressed a coherent philosophical system and intransigent historical claims; nor, had they done so, would I have been much interested.

In much the same vein, Robert Blatchford, editor of the widely respected socialist newspaper *The Clarion*, formally pronounced the death of the Christian faith in a series of columns published between 1903 and 1905: "There is no escape from that conclusion," he wrote. "The case for science is complete." Against the resulting fusillade of objections from Christian readers, he stood his ground: "My object is not so much to help to destroy an obsolete religion, as to help build up a better religion in its place. It will be a big job, and I shall be tired before it is through. But I shall do it." In succeeding columns he went farther. "To build a cathedral, and to spend our tears and pity on a Saviour who was crucified nearly two thousand years ago, while women and little children are being crucified in our midst, without pity and without help, is cant, and sentimentality, and a mockery of God."

In a column in July 1904, he went even farther: "Before we can propagate our religion of Determinism and Humanism, we must first clear the ground of Free Will, of Sin against God, and the belief in the divine inspiration of the Bible." His ideas gained vast popularity. His pamphlet "Merrie England" sold over a million copies, and in January 1905, he was able to declare: "A religion which will not bear the truth will have to go, no matter how dear to some of us it may be." Besides, in his new religion, man need no longer bear the burden of sin. He writes:

> Now, then, did God make Adam? He did. Did God make the faculties of his brain? He did. Did God make his curiosity strong and his obedience weak? He did. Then, if this man Adam was so made that his desire would overcome his obedience, was it not a foregone conclusion that he would eat the apple? It was. In that case, what becomes of the freedom of the will?

His triumphant conclusion followed: Since God is responsible for human existence, God is responsible for all human acts. "If any reader can show me any escape from that conclusion, I shall be glad to hear from him."

Blatchford could issue his challenges in confident anticipation of the same hapless responses that Christians had been making since this sort of attack began, late in the previous century. Protestants would cite the authority of the Bible against him; Catholics could cite the authority of the church. Since he despised and rejected both, these were not compelling arguments. Or they might say he was bound for hell, but he didn't believe in that either. His opponents perforce had to endure in silence or in rage, the latter often furnishing Blatchford with new grounds to attack them as latent inquisitors.

But then, out of London's Kensington district, there appeared the Fat Man: a journalist, a wit, a poet, an essayist, and an exuberant consumer of food and alcohol though he had never once been seen drunk. Behind his ebullient exterior there lay what would eventually come to be widely recognized as one of the most intelligent minds of the twentieth century. But the immediate impression chiefly inspired by Gilbert Keith Chesterton ("GKC" to many) was what some would call joviality and others would more accurately discern as joy. Chesterton nominated himself to respond to columnist Blatchford, a man whose person and sincerity he profoundly respected, but whose theology he regarded as patent nonsense. In a succession of columns in the *London Daily News* he began to show why it was nonsense, citing neither the Bible nor the church but only what he called Common

Robert Peel Glanville Blatchford photographed in 1900, and, above, the May Day 1895 number of his socialist newspaper The Clarion. *His championing of determinism and humanism met with limp resistance from the ill-instructed Christians of the day until a journalist named Chesterton arrived on the scene.*

Sense. For one thing, he noted that this Christian habit of blaming man, not God, for human sin kept cropping up…

> …in the most unlikely places. Even in *The Clarion*, for instance, I have seen writers impose grave blame on their political opponents and to those who adulterate milk and butter and rack-rent slums. But you, on your principle, hold these men guiltless. Why do you not come to their rescue? Why this exaggerated tenderness for the reputation of Adam, a gentleman who has been dead for some time? Shake off this exaggerated respect for the Old Testament. Clear yourself, Mr. Blatchford, from these Hebraic mists.

Something else, Chesterton continued, greatly puzzled him. How could Blatchford so much as scold, say, some clerk—call him Ruggles—for making a mistake, if it wasn't Ruggles's fault at all but God's, for making Ruggles prone to error? On the basis of his principles, all Blatchford could reasonably say would be: "My dear blameless Ruggles, the anger of God against you has once more driven you, a helpless victim, to put your boots on my desk and upset the ink on the ledger. Let us weep together." If that was the way errant employees were treated at *The Clarion*, Chesterton added, he would apply immediately to work there.

Blatchford did not respond well to this line of attack. It might be "witty and brilliant," he conceded, yet it "cannot be seriously regarded as a contribution to a theological debate." When he began to realize that far from stirring outrage, he was now being laughed at, it was he who became outraged. "If Mr. Chesterton does not regard the universe of science as grander and nobler, as well as a larger scheme than that of Genesis, I can only say that I cannot agree with him." He deplored Chesterton's undue flippancy. "Mr. Chesterton can think clearly enough, and write clearly enough. It is only because he finds it cheaper and easier to show off than to reason that he descends to the levity of which he is too often guilty." Blatchford then reasserted his first and foundational premise—that Christianity simply "is not true."

But behind Chesterton's frivolity lay a highly relevant observation. By exonerating the human race of all personal responsibility, Blatchford was attacking not just Christianity but the basis of the justice system of the western world, which rests on the assumption that man must take responsibility for what he does because he is actually capable of doing otherwise. And on what basis was Blatchford so emphatically advancing this theory? On the flat assertion that "Christianity is not true"— which he was offering as an unproven certitude, in fact a dogma. "So I now find," wrote Chesterton, "that you have got into communication with that absolute truth which agnostics have hitherto failed to reach. You have a supernatural assurance, an assurance beyond argument."

The Blatchford-Chesterton clash raged on for months, Chesterton obviously enjoying it immensely.[3] Blatchford, who did not enjoy it at all, would remain persuaded until his death in 1943, at age ninety-two, that Chesterton must have been play-acting. He found it incomprehensible that a man of such obvious intelligence and erudition could sincerely accept as true the creedal assertions of the Christian faith.

3. GKC was famous, among other things, for his delight in argument. Not untypically, a Chinese waiter in a Fleet Street restaurant, where he would sometimes work on his combative columns, told a Chesterton acquaintance: "Your friend, that big man, he very intelligent. He eat and he laugh. Then he take up a pencil and he write. Then he laugh at what he write."

G. K. Chesterton, in a sketch by Alfred Priest done in the first decade of the twentieth century. This young man nominated himself to respond to editor Blatchford, whose person and sincerity he profoundly respected, but whose theology he regarded as patent nonsense. Chesterton's joyful jousting with the agnostic had a notable wakening effect on Britain's Christian community. Defending the faith, they found, could be fun.

Chesterton as a slender young man. His performance at school and college were unimpressive. And although he manifested great talent, he was almost totally disorganized and would remain so for the rest of his life.

4. Anglicanism throughout much of the twentieth century was roughly divided into three parties. The Anglo-Catholic "high church" preserved many of the Catholic traditions inherited from the Middle Ages and earlier. The "low church" hewed more closely to the eighteenth-century practices of John Wesley and discouraged ritual. Each of these was a relatively small minority; most Anglicans belonged to neither. In the nineteenth century a third party came into being, the "broad church," which by the twentieth had turned into the Modernist movement.

Others found it not incomprehensible but exhilarating. Chesterton's confrontation with the agnostic editor had a notable wakening effect on the much-beleaguered Christian community in Britain. Suddenly, Christians who read newspapers, particularly young people, became aware of several realities: For one, they discovered they could fight back, that they were indeed *supposed* to fight back. For another, they could win arguments. Their elders, the intelligentsia like Blatchford, were often quite unconsciously spouting errant absurdity. Young Christians realized that not only could they rationally defend their faith, they could hold up to ridicule the manifold deficiencies of the substitute concoctions being advanced against it. Best of all, they could revel in all this, just as Chesterton did. Defending the faith could be *fun*. Who would have believed it?

Life for Chesterton was not always fun, however. Born into the family of a London estate agent in 1874, his performance at Saint Paul's School and the Slade School of Art was unimpressive. Though he manifested great talent, he was almost totally disorganized and would remain so for the rest of his life. "Am in Market Harborough," he one day telegraphed to his wife. "Where should I be?" He could quote poetry from memory in quantities as vast as they were inaccurate, though the inaccuracies not infrequently were an improvement on the original. Introducing a selection of Chesterton essays entitled *Prophet of Orthodoxy* (1997), its editor, Russell Sparkes, recalls the exasperation of a London publisher who found thirteen errors on one page of a Chesterton manuscript, plus four misquotations in four lines of poetry. Such inaccuracy, he fumed, would ruin the reputation of his publishing house. But the book was Chesterton's biography of the poet-playwright Robert Browning (1903), and became a best seller.

Yet when Chesterton graduated from art school, the zest for life which he would later reflect was largely absent. His art skills were undeveloped, and he had trouble finding challenging work. Two factors changed him. One was a young woman named Frances Blogg, five years his senior, who saw great potential in this tall man in his rumpled hat and cape, carrying a sword stick, a cigar usually drooping from his lips. Frances's mother seriously disagreed, labeling him "an opinionated scarecrow." When he proposed marriage in the summer of 1898, he was a minor editor in a publishing house, earning £60 a year. He would have to make at least £300 for them to survive, said Frances, £500 for them to live comfortably. So challenged, Chesterton wangled a columnist job on the *Daily Mail* which with freelance income raised him to sufficiency by January 1901. They were married on June 28. It was the beginning, writes Sparkes, of a lifetime love affair.

The other factor was George MacDonald's *Phantastes*, which opened his hitherto agnostic mind to the possibility of a world or worlds beyond this one. Together with Frances, a devout Anglican, he began to piece together what he thought was his own religion. By 1904, he discovered to his surprise that it had already been pieced together for him in what was called the Apostles' Creed. That year Chesterton joined the Anglo-Catholic tradition in the Anglican Church, Frances staunchly by his side.[4] But in the course of raising his income, he had become involved in another love affair, notably with Fleet Street. He became infatuated with journalism. Though Wikipedia in 2012 was citing his work in philosophy, ontology, poetry, plays, journalism, public lectures and debates, literary and art criticism, biography, Christian apologetics, and fiction—including fantasy and detective fiction—Chesterton himself had rejected such a description. He considered himself a journalist, he said—nothing more.

Another idiosyncrasy was that he was not ashamed of being old-fashioned, rather cherishing obsolescence. Thus he was not overawed, for instance, at the newly appreciated magnitude of the universe. Philosopher Herbert Spencer had lately "popularized the contemptible notion the size of the solar system ought to overawe the spiritual dogma of man," Chesterton observed. "But why should man surrender his dignity to the solar system any more than to a whale? It is quite futile to argue that man is small compared to the cosmos; for man was always small compared to the nearest tree."

Since he found himself at odds with most current thinking, Chesterton decided to collect his adversaries into a single package and attack them all at once, publishing *Heretics* in 1905. A "heretic," notes the bemused historian Jay P. Corrin in *G. K. Chesterton & Hilaire Belloc: The Battle Against Modernity* (1981) was almost anybody Chesterton disagreed with, not excluding most of the leading publicists of the day, whom he "unmercifully rebuked." Its central argument, however, was crystal clear: that in the name of progress and "efficiency" fundamental institutions of society—family, church, Christmas, pubs—were being dangerously undermined, all in the supposed service of science. Men's minds were being left "derelict in a sea of uncertainty." The targets of this assault not unnaturally demanded to know where Chesterton himself stood, so in 1908 he produced *Orthodoxy*, an assertion of traditionalist Christianity, presented with all his boundless insight and imagination.

By now, he had found two allies, whose thinking was much in accord with his own on the paramount issues of the time. One was Hilaire Belloc, a French-born historian and ardent Catholic, who like Chesterton rejected both capitalism and socialism in favor of what came to be called "distributism."[5] Like many other Edwardians, one of them Chesterton, Belloc acquired a reputation for anti-Semitism,

5. Distributism, an economic philosophy developed in the early twentieth century, seeks to fulfill the teachings of Pope Leo XIII. It advocated a society in which property ownership was widely distributed rather than centralized under the control of the state or concentrated in the hands of a few individuals. It regarded both socialism and unbridled capitalism as equally flawed and exploitative. Chesterton was its most powerful advocate in Britain, and a Catholic community was developed at Ditchling in Sussex as a pilot project. Although the community did not survive, it significantly influenced the thinking of the notable economist E. F. Schumacher, whose collected essays, *Small Is Beautiful: Economics as Though People Matter* (1973), was named by the *Times Literary Supplement* in 1995 as one of the hundred most influential books published after the Second World War. Schumacher became a convert to Catholicism.

Left, GKC with wife, Frances, at their Beaconsfield, Buckinghamshire, home in 1926. She had seen great potential in the shambling man with the sword cane and rumpled cape. Their marriage in 1901 was the beginning of a lifetime love affair. In the 1932 oil painting on the right, Sir James Gunn nicely captures the self-described "Three Musketeers" who together took on the fashionable skeptics of the interwar period. From left, Chesterton, Maurice Baring, and Hilaire Belloc.

George Bernard Shaw is shown to the right in a Soviet painting from 1937 during an admiring visit to a Moscow factory as part of the socialist playwright's 1937 world tour. Above, Shaw and his fellow socialist H. G. Wells are caricatured by the Polish-born Mark Wayner around the same time. The debates between the Chesterton-Belloc-Baring trio and the Shaw-Wells duo evolved into single combat between GBS and GKC, two affectionate rivals whose dramatically staged debates would entertain the paying public for three decades.

largely founded on the claim that no devout Jew could become a patriot, because his ultimate loyalty lay elsewhere. (The fact that the same charge could be laid against Catholics, whose religious loyalty must lie to Rome, was not addressed by Belloc, though it was by others.) In that case, the Jews contended, where could they live? Immediately appreciating this point, Chesterton became an ardent Zionist, powerfully urging the creation of a state of Israel, and when the Hitler holocaust began in Germany, no denunciations were louder than his.

The third of the "Three Musketeers," as they called themselves, was Maurice Baring, poet, novelist, essayist, and playwright. Chesterton labeled the three: "Baring" (i.e., Maurice), "Over Baring" (Belloc), and "Past Baring" (himself). By the last years of the Edwardian decade (Blatchford having faded into background), the Musketeers had taken on two of the major heavyweights on the agnostic side, George Bernard Shaw and H. G. Wells. Baring was the least confrontational of the three, but his work could be powerfully influential. In *Open Letter on the Decay of Faith* (1906), for example, he wrote:

> I desire you to remember that we are Europe; we are a great people. The faith is not an accident among us, nor an imposition, nor a garment; it is bone of our bone and flesh of our flesh; it is a philosophy made by and making ourselves. We have adorned, explained, enlarged it; we have given it visible form. This is the service we Europeans have done to God. In return, he has made us Christians.

The contest between the Chesterton-Belloc-Baring trio and the Shaw-Wells duo soon came down to a one-on-one contest between Chesterton and Shaw which in various forms went on for the next thirty years. Their debates became well-attended, dramatically staged events, very unlike the Blatchford affair, because the opponents were much more evenly matched. There were other distinctions as well. They soon came to like and deeply admire one another, with Shaw, who was fourteen years older, assuming the role of an elder brother. He justly chided Chesterton for financial carelessness, and unjustly for sheer laziness in not writing plays. But Shaw actually knew that, whatever else Chesterton's shortcomings might be, he was certainly not lazy. Between his newspaper columns, his freelance essays, his novels, the few plays that Shaw finally forced him to write (all tremendously successful), and the long series of crime stories centered on his fictional priest-detective Father Brown, Chesterton was arguably doing the work of three men. He was, Shaw acknowledged, "a man of colossal genius."

But it was neither genius nor overwork that caused a dark shadow to fall over his life during the First World War. This shadow centered on his younger brother Cecil, an outspoken anti-Semite, who had taken over a weekly paper started by Belloc, renaming it the *New Witness*. Britain's Liberal government in 1912 was rocked by scandal. Godfrey Isaacs, managing director of the American Marconi Company was discovered to have sold Marconi shares to Lloyd George, Britain's Chancellor of the Exchequer, to Isaacs's brother Sir Rufus Isaacs, and to the chief whip of the Liberal Party, for £1.06 a share.

The government, in secret, subsequently awarded a huge contract to the Marconi Company, nearly quadrupling the value of its stock, whereupon the recipients sold. In the uproar that followed, Cecil's paper accused Godfrey Isaacs of illegal share promotion and pronounced the whole scandal a typical Jewish affair. Isaacs laid charges of criminal libel against Cecil, and proved them. The penalty was light, a £100 fine, but the humiliated Cecil resigned from the *New Witness*. He joined the army, survived three wounds, and died in a French military hospital of a kidney ailment twenty-five days after the war ended. His trial and death so devastated his elder brother that GKC fell into a deep depression.

Not until 1922 did he emerge from his despair, when he decided after long hesitation to join the Catholic Church. The reason he delayed so long, writes historian Joseph Pearce in *Literary Converts: Spiritual Inspiration in an Age of Unbelief* (1999) was that Frances steadfastly refused to become Catholic. Finally Gilbert acted alone, and for four years they lived in spiritual isolation. It was a serious dilemma for Frances, Pearce writes, who knew she must not forsake her faith solely for her husband's sake. Jesus had specifically warned

Alec Guinness plays a game of chess as Chesterton's detective in the 1954 film Father Brown. *Guinness was one of a growing circle of high-profile Catholic converts in mid-century. His own path to the faith began during filming of Father Brown,* when he was mistaken for a real priest by a small boy.

Chesterton's works had shaken England's cultural establishment and a surprising number of improbables dropped out and became part of the Catholic Revival. Included in the distinguished group were the poetess Edith Sitwell (left), as painted by Roger Fry; and (clockwise from top left) Sir John Randolph ("Shane") Leslie, Christopher Dawson, Ronald Knox, Theodore Maynard, Compton Mackenzie, Alfred Noyes, Robert Speaight, and E. T. Whittaker.

against that (Luke 14:26). At length, she quietly consulted the local Catholic priest, was received into the church without fanfare, and soon the accustomed domestic order reasserted itself. Instead of helping her husband find his place in the Book of Common Prayer and nudging when to stand, sit, or kneel, she was doing the same thing in the Catholic Mass. It was noted, moreover, that she was a far more outwardly devout Catholic than he.

Chesterton lived for another fourteen years, and died of congenital heart failure in his home at Beaconsfield, Buckinghamshire, at age sixty-two. His last words were a greeting to his wife. After a Requiem Mass in London at Westminster Cathedral, he was buried in the Beaconsfield Catholic Cemetery. Frances died two years later from a type of cancer, according to Sparkes, known to follow depression caused by bereavement. In Victorian terms, she died of a broken heart. Had Chesterton lived fourteen years longer, he would have learned that his old adversary Shaw, in the months before his death in 1950, was discovered to have been exchanging letters with an elderly and very holy Catholic nun for some years. Their subject was prayer, something with which Shaw had become much taken up. Chesterton would have been greatly gratified. Perhaps he had won the final debate.

Chesterton's last years had been far from idle. Out of loyalty to his brother, he took over the *New Witness*, changing its name to *GK's Weekly* at the suggestion of Shaw, who held that otherwise the publication had no chance of survival. Chesterton kept it going, meeting the rigors of editorial deadlines almost to the day of his death, tirelessly promoting the flagging cause of distributism and inveighing against the evils of Nazism.

His legend continued to flourish. In fact, writes Reverend Ian Boyd, president of the Chesterton Institute and editor of the *Chesterton Review* (which he founded in 1974), there are two legendary and seemingly incompatible Chestertons. The first is the rollicking comrade of the early years, the bard of the beer drinker, verbally brawling with all comers, jeering the abstemious, and rejoicing in the zest of being alive. The other is the piously Catholic later Chesterton, photographed visiting with the aged and with children, consort of nuns and priests, and arguably the premier Catholic apologist in Britain, Europe, and the United States. As his celebrity among Catholics soared, however, it diminished among Protestants and secularists.

Which of these legends—the early Edwardian or the later Catholic—is the "real" Chesterton," or did one simply turn into the other? Father Boyd, having posed the question, offers an answer. The commonality between the two, he writes, can be described as sacramentalism. "Convinced that God can be found in material realities, Chesterton developed a religious critique of life which he presents in all his writings, ultimately based on a belief that God is present in creation through sign and symbol... He seldom wrote about directly religious subjects, but in the events of everyday, or in a piece of chalk, or in a city street, he found the central religious mystery." In both Chestertons, says Boyd, the same assumption underlies what he says, does, and writes, for the two are in fact one.

Chesterton was shaking up England's cultural establishment. The most improbable people—novelists, poets, dramatists, biographers—had begun to take Christianity seriously.

Following his conversion, Chesterton had three monumental books left to write: biographies of Saint Thomas Aquinas and Saint Francis, and a history of Christianity which he entitled *The Everlasting Man*. Among its early readers was an Oxford don, an atheist who was vigilantly resisting an increasingly persuasive suspicion that, no matter how distressing the possibility, Christianity might actually be true. *The Everlasting Man*, as C. S. Lewis would later acknowledge, pushed him significantly closer to this unwelcome possibility. But the notion that he himself would one day be recognized worldwide as Chesterton's effectual successor would have shocked him at the time.

That day was still far down the road, however, and Chesterton's works and persona were meanwhile shaking England's cultural establishment to its core. The most improbable people—accomplished and recognized novelists, poets, essayists, dramatists, biographers—began to take Christianity seriously, a score or more of them becoming Catholic (and two becoming Anglican). The story of this Catholic Revival, as it came to be called, is recounted in entertaining but convincing detail in Pearce's *Literary Converts*.

This irruption—for so it was regarded by conventional people—began with an announcement widely considered scandalous. When Edward White Benson, the archbishop of Canterbury, died of a heart attack in 1896, he left three sons who all were destined to become distinguished British writers. Eight years later, it was disclosed that the youngest, Robert Hugh Benson, who had dutifully followed his father into the Anglican clergy, had decided to become a Catholic, which in high social circles was regarded as nothing less than appalling.[6] Such conversions admittedly had been common enough a half century earlier in the Oxford Movement. Still, a son of the archbishop of Canterbury! It seemed excessive. Worse yet, Robert Benson began training for the Catholic priesthood the following year.

6. Robert Hugh Benson's eldest brother, A. C. Benson (Arthur Christopher), was a widely published poet and essayist who wrote the words to the patriotic song, "Land of Hope and Glory" to the tune of Edward Elgar's "Pomp and Circumstance March No. 1." The middle brother, E. F. Benson (Edward Frederick), wrote a number of highly popular novels between the two world wars, some of which were made into a television series during the 1980s under the title *Mapp and Lucia*. All three brothers specialized in horror or ghost stories. None had children, or indeed ever married. A sister, Margaret, also childless, became a noted Egyptologist. Two other children of Archbishop Edward White Benson died young.

That the journalist Chesterton was behind this, none doubted, not least on account of his book, *Orthodoxy*. While he had himself remained an Anglican for fourteen years after its publication, *Orthodoxy* was being extensively read by young people, who found it more compatible with Catholicism than with Anglicanism as practiced in most English churches. In 1906, there came another conversion incident, when a promising Anglican priest named Lewis Watt became a Jesuit. In 1908, the Irish peer Sir John Randolph Leslie, first cousin of Winston Churchill, took the name Shane Leslie while at Cambridge and declared himself Catholic. At Oxford that year, another future writer of note, Edward Ingram Watkin, also announced his conversion.

Moreover, while at university, Watkin had met a truly obnoxious agnostic—quick, clever, and of devastating wit, whose sarcasms against Christianity so enraged him that he once picked up a lawn chair and crashed it down on

Knox realized that the new generation of theologians were drifting in a fog of skepticism, and that the main danger to the Church of England arose from Modernism.

the fellow's head. When the ensuing brawl had been broken up, their "discussions" continued for another three years, after which the determined agnostic also became a Catholic Christian. This young man, Christopher Dawson, would be one of Christianity's greatest historians, and his friendship with Watkin lifelong.

Even more specifically a Chestertonian convert was Ronald Knox, son of another Anglican bishop. When Knox left Eton for Oxford, he later reminisced, "my views were orthodox above the average. My oracle was G. K. Chesterton—he is still." After an outstanding career at both Eton and Oxford, he was ordained an Anglican priest in 1912. But he gradually realized, he wrote, that "the new generation of Anglican theologians were drifting into a fog of skepticism," and he "became convinced that the main danger to the Church of England arose not from Protestantism but from Modernism." Even so, Knox was reluctant to abandon his church. Then four of his friends, all future writers, converted within four years: Theodore Maynard in 1913, Compton Mackenzie in 1914, Francis Dudley in 1915, and Julien Green in 1916. Knox himself followed them in 1917 and was made a Catholic priest a year later. During a spectacular career, he would turn out theological treatises, radio plays, detective stories, biographies, and an English translation of the Bible.[7]

Not everyone was enthralled by this surge into dogmatic religion—Sir Arnold Lunn, for example. Son of a Methodist minister, Lunn was a champion skier who invented slalom racing in 1922, organized the first world championship in slalom and downhill racing in 1931, and was knighted for these and other such accomplishments. He early rejected his family's Christian heritage, and as a resolute agnostic launched an intensive campaign against Christianity in general and Catholicism in particular. In 1924, he published *Roman Converts*—in bitter criticism of such turncoats as Cardinals Newman and Manning, scientist Joseph Tyrell, Chesterton, and Knox.

7. In January 1926 the newly formed BBC broadcast a drama in which rowdy strikers went wild in downtown London, vandalizing art galleries and public buildings, and threatening revolution. A snowstorm simultaneously tied up other communication and transportation facilities, so that thousands panicked, assuming that the story was true. The producer was the Catholic academic Ronald Knox, but the show, intended as a hoax, was in no way related to his religion. Twelve years would elapse before a similar scare would panic Americans, that one the work of Orson Welles.

It unnerved him somewhat that the latter two, the only ones left alive, took it sportingly and even applauded his forthright language. However, religion was not Lunn's only issue. He lamented as well the increasing self-preoccupation of the age, the rejection of reason in every area but science, and the general disposition that only material things can have any reality. These concerns he published in 1930 under the title *Flight from Reason*. As it became evident that he was in fact far closer to the Christians than he was to the materialists, he began an exchange of letters with Knox (later published under the title *Difficulties*). The outcome was Lunn's conversion to Catholicism, for which he became an irrepressible champion until his death in 1974.

In the decade of the 1920s and early 1930s, conversions to "the Roman faith" continued unabated: Christopher Hollis, biographer, historian, and politician in 1924; poet and literary critic Alfred Noyes (noted among much else for the hoofbeat rhythm in "The Highwayman") in 1927; actor-biographer Robert Speaight in 1929; editor-publisher Brocard Sewell (who later became a Carmelite friar) in 1931; math-physicist E. T. Whittaker in 1930. Also in 1930 came the conversion of a writer considered by some to be the century's best English language novelist, Evelyn Waugh. The years after the Second World War would see a number of others, among them poet Edith Sitwell in 1955, and actor Alec Guinness in 1956.

The memorial in Mürren, Switzerland to Sir Arnold Henry Moore Lunn, downhill skiing pioneer and reluctant, but eventually avid, convert to Catholicism. For the last forty years of his life, Lunn was the faith's irrepressible champion.

One figure often included in this Chesterton-driven English Catholic Revival, incidentally, was not born English, detested Chesterton, and became Anglican, not Roman Catholic. This was Thomas Stearns Eliot, who hailed from St. Louis, Missouri, and after taking his Harvard degree moved to Oxford on a scholarship. Perceived throughout the English-speaking world to be the poet laureate of the dominant Modernist philosophical and theological movements of the twentieth century, Eliot is often cited as its most influential poet. Works like *The Love Song of J. Alfred Prufrock* (1915), *Gerontion* (1920), *The Waste Land* (1922), and *The Hollow Men* (1925) were cherished by the oncoming generation as embodying the core cynicism born of the First World War. They emphatically did not endear Eliot to Chesterton, who pilloried his works both by rational argument and ridicule. How wistfully young people would recite the closing verse of *The Hollow Men*:

> This is the way the world ends,
> This is the way the world ends,
> This is the way the world ends,
> Not with a bang but a whimper.

To which Chesterton replied with a verse of his own, written on behalf of those who did not share Eliot's doleful Modernistic temperament:

> Some sneer, some snigger, some simper;
> In the youth where *we* laughed and sang,
> And *they* may end with a whimper
> But *we* will end with a bang.

The question ultimately arose, however: did Eliot himself really share that sentiment? Historian Pearce makes the case that Eliot never was a Modernist, that his early poems had been misinterpreted, and that he arguably was not recommending morbidity but depicting Modernism's futility. In 1927, he declared himself a classicist, a royalist, and an Anglo-Catholic—none of them faintly compatible with Modernism. He also became a naturalized British subject. "It is hard to imagine," writes Pearce, "the impact that Eliot's conversion to Anglo-Catholicism had on the army of moderns who idolized his poetry for its pessimism and its undertones of despair." One such was Virginia Woolf, reigning queen of Bloomsbury, who alerted the group to the Eliot tragedy:

> I have had a shameful and most distressing interview with dear Tom Eliot who may be called dead to us all from this day forward. He has become an Anglo-Catholic believer in God and immortality, and goes to church. I was shocked. A corpse would seem to me more credible than he is. I mean there's something obscene in a living person sitting by the fire and believing in God.

"But it's better," Chesterton retorted, "than sitting *in* the fire and *not* believing in God."

After his conversion, both Eliot's work and its message notably changed. Now came his plays: *The Rock* (1934), *Murder in the Cathedral* (1935) on the assassination of Archbishop Thomas Becket, *The Family Reunion* (1939), *The Cocktail Party* (1943), *The Confidential Clerk* (1953), and *The Elder Statesman* (1958), all with Christian implications or assertions. Meanwhile, he directly approached Chesterton. Perhaps they should talk, he said. They did, and Chesterton began contributing to a magazine which Eliot edited.

Chesterton's life was now drawing to a close, and in 1931 his successor, C. S. Lewis, had been as he himself described it "dragged kicking and screaming" into the Christian religion. Dragged, that is, by the sheer rationality of the Christian case as he discovered it. (Lewis's story runs as a subchapter beginning on page 397.) Yet Lewis knew better than most that reason alone rarely brings a person to commitment in Christ, though it serves indispensably to remove obstacles to such a commitment. More potent than reason is what some call the "moral imagination." A compelling story, a perceptive poem, a movie, a painting, a song, a symphony or oratorio, a spring morning, can cause an individual to *want* to believe,

The poet and playwright T. S. Eliot photographed in the late 1940s diagramming a play in his office at the Institute of Advanced Study at Princeton University; below right, a 1970 production of his Murder in the Cathedral, *actually staged in Canterbury Cathedral. Eliot, one-time darling of the post-First World war Bloomsbury Group, alarmed old friends with his conversion to Anglo-Catholicism in 1927. "I was shocked," reported Virginia Woolf, after a visit with Eliot. "I mean there's something obscene in a living person sitting by the fire and believing in God." Chesterton rejoined: "But it's better than sitting in the fire and not believing in God."*

C. S. Lewis puffs on a cigarette during a 1946 interview in his office at Oxford University's Magdalen College, whose "dreaming spires" can be seen in the exterior photograph on the left. Having been brought to the faith in part by Chesterton, Lewis's career at Oxford would be thwarted by his faith, although his book sales and the popularity of his lectures would place him among the most influential dons of the day.

and such a desire is invariably fulfilled. "To him who knocks," said Jesus Christ, "it will be opened." Thus Lewis's conversion did not begin in 1931, but years before when he first read MacDonald. He had not been dragged kicking and screaming into *Phantastes*, and that's when the die was cast.

He was doubtless aware of other realities. The Oxford of the twentieth century—although it had been founded as a Christian endeavor, abounded in Christian symbols, and nearly all its colleges bore Christian names—could not be accurately described as supportive of its ancestral faith. Christianity naturally was permitted, within well established bounds—in the chapels, of course, and the theological faculties, but always with adequate concession to Britain's increasingly "pluralistic" recognitions, and as fit material for historical inquiry, with certain well recognized provisos. There must be no aspersions of fear or favor or certitude favoring Christianity, and its many discerned sins must be adequately recognized and exposed. As for the other faculties—the physical sciences, social sciences, and medical sciences, and the literary, legal, and philosophical disciplines—well, surely these were no fit theater for the creedal, the doctrinal, or the biblical.

If Lewis was to serve the cause of Christ at all, it was precisely here that a man with his background and aptitudes was most urgently needed. Some would be offended, he knew, and would deplore, scoff, and possibly protest, yet wasn't this the sort of thing that "carrying the cross" was all about? As the record shows, his answer was "yes," he acted accordingly, and his acceptability at Oxford slowly diminished from then on. Though the numerical dimensions of his book sales alone would make him probably the most influential Oxford teacher of his time, and his lectures were some of the best attended, Lewis would never be given a full professorship there.

He had friends there, however, particularly one John Ronald Reuel Tolkien, who like Lewis himself had been a junior line officer on the western front in the

First World War. But they had not met in the trenches. As Tolkien wrote, "By 1918, all but one of my close friends were dead." He and Lewis met later at Oxford. "I have always been told," Lewis noted, "never to trust a Romanist and never to trust a philologist, and Tolkien was both." Yet the devoutly Catholic Tolkien would play the central human role in bringing Lewis into the Christian faith, although like Eliot he became an Anglican. Also, late in the 1930s, Tolkien, Lewis, and several others formed the Inklings, which met weekly at Oxford's Eagle and Child pub to read aloud their current manuscripts.[8] Thus two of the best-selling literary works of the twentieth century—Tolkien's *Lord of the Rings* and Lewis's *Chronicles of Narnia* (120 million copies sold against Tolkien's 150 million)—got their introduction being read aloud in a little English pub.

Lewis's initial entry into the field of Christian literature came in 1933, two years after his conversion. *The Pilgrim's Regress,* modeled on John Bunyan's classic, depicted the experience of his own generation in the intellectual world. Aimed squarely at Modernism, it included some classic skewering—like the Clevers, who live in a large, dark cave, write incomprehensible poetry, and learn by rote a whole vocabulary of cynicism. Although the Clevers endlessly proclaim their fearless independence of all authority, the hero discovers they are actually in the

Insidiously disturbing, the Screwtape Letters *leave the reader wondering whether the thoughts in his mind are his own, or put there by somebody else.*

employ of a little man, named Mr. Mammon, who lives outside the cave. Especially notable as well is Death, who pursues the terrified hero as he flees, mile after mile, through the hill country. "Run as hard and fast and as far as you like," cries Death, "but you cannot escape me." At length, the hero stops and turns, to face death squarely. "In that case," he says, "I will surrender to you now." Abruptly, Death pulls back, saying, "Ah, but you have just escaped me."

Out of the Silent Planet, first of a science fiction trilogy on the rising tide of "scientism," which Lewis saw as a particular peril of the oncoming age, appeared in 1938. *The Problem of Pain,* his first purely apologetic book, was published in 1940, with the Second War under way. It deals directly with what Lewis saw as the most lethal argument facing religion: How could a good God make a world in which such evil things happen?

Six months later the amusing yet somewhat disquieting *Screwtape Letters* began appearing in the *Guardian.* Epistles from the undersecretary of a department in hell to his nephew, a junior tempter on earth, supply suggestions as to what thoughts the younger devil ought to plant in the mind of "the Patient" (representing you or me) to assure his safe delivery to "Our Father Below." Insidiously disturbing, it leaves the reader wondering whether the thoughts running through his mind are his own, or whether they are being put there by something or somebody else.

Later came *The Great Divorce,* its title referring to the divorce between good and evil, heaven and hell, which portrays in convincing allegory how our hour-by-hour, day-by-day moral decisions ultimately turn us into a heavenly or a hellish

8. The Inklings was neither a society nor even a club, since it had no charter, no bylaws, no rules, and no minutes. It was simply a group of men who took to meeting regularly. Besides Lewis and Tolkien, it included at one time or another: Owen Barfield, a lawyer; essayist and editor Charles Williams; Lewis's older brother Warren; Tolkien's son Christopher; children's writer and biographer Roger Lancelyn Green; Adam Fox, a poet and the dean of divinity of Magdalen College; English professor Hugo Dyson; Lewis's physician, R. E. "Humphrey" Havard; New Zealand literary academic J. A. W. Bennett; biographer and historian Lord David Cecil; and Nevill Coghill, literary academic and dramatist.

The Eagle and Child public house in Oxford. The corner table where Lewis, J. R. R. Tolkien, and the other "Inklings" would gather, is commemorated, bottom, with photos and a plaque. Below, a bust of Tolkien at Exeter College, Oxford. The Anglican Lewis and the Catholic Tolkien would read aloud their manuscripts of the Chronicles of Narnia and the Lord of the Rings at the little pub in the late 1930s. The Narnia series would go on to sell more than 120 million copies by century's end, while Tolkien's Lord of the Rings would top 150 million.

creature. "Judgment Day," in other words, is every day. These and some two dozen more works, many of them academic, led to Lewis's first major publishing breakthrough, the strongly Christian Chronicles of Narnia series, destined to become the century's best-selling children's series.

Meanwhile, what has arguably provided his most lasting impact had been initiated by the BBC. During the Battle of Britain, the air force asked Lewis to give talks on Christianity to the personnel at air stations. He agreed, and these led to four BBC radio series on the Christian religion, twenty-eight fifteen-minute programs in all, covering belief in God, belief in Christ, Christian morality, and the doctrine of the Trinity as it applies to the soul of each individual. These talks made Lewis's voice the most familiar on British radio next to Winston Churchill's. Published in book form as *Mere Christianity*, sales in the second decade of the twenty-first century were by one estimate still exceeding seven hundred thousand a year in the U.S. alone. That would be seventy years after the initial BBC broadcasts.

These broadcasts raised an intriguing question. Much of their content seemed to come as a shock to ninety-nine out of one hundred church-attending adult Christians, who seemingly had never before heard that Christianity could be such a fascinating, challenging, life-changing experience. The explanation, of

Dorothy L. Sayers, photographed in the mid-1930s. With acid-tipped pen, she blamed the public's profound ignorance of Christianity on the reluctance of the clergy to teach dogma. Although a trenchant Christian apologist, Sayers is perhaps best known for her contribution to that peculiarly English fiction genre, the murder mystery. She wrote over a dozen novels on the adventures of amateur detective Lord Peter Wimsey, which entertain while gently ridiculing contemporary British society.

course, was the lamentable state of the churches, whose teaching function for most people had ceased with their childhood. But Lewis was sparing of criticism, principally because he wanted to avoid conflict within the Christian family.

Mere Christianity, as he repeatedly pointed out, was not being offered as another version of the Christian faith. He himself had invented no part of it, and he acknowledged a heavy debt to the learning and insight of men like Dawson, Knox, and, of course, Chesterton. Lewis sought to express only what all Christian denominations held in common, he said. His central purpose was to lead people into the existing churches, not to start a new one, and he regarded interdenominational conflict among Christians as one of the most serious obstacles to an outsider considering conversion. Certain issues were admittedly real, but as with disputations between pure mathematicians or between genetic biologists, a layman must be prepared to delve deeply into the issues before he can voice a valid opinion.

One contemporary of Lewis's was not so inhibited in criticizing the clergy, however, namely the detective story writer Dorothy L. Sayers, whose books on popular theology were the equal of his own, although her sales and fame would never match his. Many people consider Sayers' twelve BBC radio plays on the life of Christ, *The Man Born to Be King*, to be the best dramatic representation ever created of the Gospel accounts, and Lewis described as "indispensable" her portrayal of the Trinity in *The Mind of the Maker*.

Sayers was also unlike Lewis in that she was not a convert; the daughter of an Anglican clergyman, she was raised in the bosom of the church. She blamed the widespread public ignorance of Christianity (see facing page) on the reluctance of the clergy to teach dogma, and she made the case with mordant insight and lethal tongue:

> Christ, in his Divine innocence, said to the woman of Samaria, "Ye worship ye know not what" (John 4:2), being apparently under the impression that it might be desirable, on the whole, to know what one was worshipping. He thus showed himself sadly out of touch with the twentieth century mind, for the cry today is: "Away with the tedious complexities of dogma—let us have the simple spirit of worship; just worship, no matter of what!" The only drawback to this demand for a generalized and undirected worship is the practical difficulty of arousing any sort of enthusiasm for the worship of nothing in particular.

Wilt thou be baptized? Nope!

Dorothy L. Sayers presents the catastrophic catechism of the modernistic man; it's all very funny, but it discloses the church's abysmal failure to teach the faith

Where G. K. Chesterton and C. S. Lewis, both converts to Christianity, were generally sparing in their comments on the clergy, their fellow Christian apologist, Dorothy L. Sayers, the daughter of an Anglican clergyman and raised in the church, was much less so. She bitterly deplored the failure of the church to teach Christianity—"dogma," as she unapologetically described it—and in this "catechism" she depicted the way most people in the mid-twentieth century had come to regard the teachings of the church. Over the course of the ensuing fifty years little would change.

Judging by what my young friends tell me, and also by what is said on the subject in anti-Christian literature written by people who ought to have taken a little trouble to find out what they are attacking before attacking it, I have come to the conclusion that a short examination paper on the Christian religion might be very generally answered as follows:

Q: What does the Church think of God the Father?

A: He is omnipotent and holy. He created the world and imposed on man conditions impossible of fulfillment; He is very angry if these are not carried out. He sometimes interferes by means of arbitrary judgements and miracles, distributed with a good deal of favouritism. He likes to be truckled to, and is always ready to pounce on anybody who trips up over a difficulty in the Law, or is having a bit of fun. He is rather like a dictator, only larger and more arbitrary.

Q: What does the Church think of God the Son?

A: He is in some way to be identified with Jesus of Nazareth. It was not His fault that the world was made like this, and, unlike God the Father, He is friendly to man and did his best to reconcile man to God (see *Atonement*). He has a good deal of influence with God, and if you want anything done, it is best to apply to Him.

Q: What does the Church think about God the Holy Ghost?

A: I don't know exactly. He was never seen or heard of till Pentecost. There is a sin against Him which damns you forever, but nobody knows what it is.

Q: What is the doctrine of the Trinity?

A: "The Father incomprehensible, the Son incomprehensible, and the whole thing incomprehensible." It's something put in by theologians to make it more difficult—it's got nothing to do with daily life or ethics.

Q: What was Jesus Christ like in real life?

A: He was a good man—so good as to be called the Son of God. He is to be identified in some way with God the Son (see above). He was meek and mild and preached a simple religion of love and pacifism. He had no sense of humor. Anything in the Bible that suggests another side to His character must be an interpolation, or a paradox invented by G. K. Chesterton. If we try to live like Him, God the Father will let us off being damned hereafter and only have us tortured in this life instead.

Q: What is meant by the Atonement?

A: God wanted to damn everybody, but his vindictive sadism was sated by the crucifixion of His own Son, who was quite innocent, and, therefore, a particularly attractive victim. He now only damns people who don't follow Christ or who never heard of Him.

Q: What does the Church think of sex?

A: God made it necessary to the machinery of the world, and tolerates it, provided the parties (a) are married, and (b) get no pleasure out of it.

Q: What does the Church call Sin?

A: Sex (otherwise than as excepted above); getting drunk; saying "damn", murder, and cruelty to dumb animals; not going to church; most kinds of amusement. "Original sin" means that anything we enjoy doing is wrong.

Q: What is faith?

A: Resolutely shutting your eyes to scientific fact.

Q: What is the human intellect?

A: A barrier to faith.

Q: What are the seven Christian virtues?

A: Respectability; childishness; mental timidity; dull-ness; sentimentality; censoriousness; and depression of the spirits.

Q: Wilt thou be baptized in this Faith?

A: No fear!

I cannot help feeling that as a statement of Christian orthodoxy, these replies are inadequate, if not misleading. But I also cannot help feeling that they do fairly accurately represent what many people take Christian orthodoxy to be, and for this state of affairs I am inclined to blame the orthodox. ∎

From "The Dogma Is the Drama"
An essay in *Creed or Chaos* (1939)
by Dorothy L. Sayers

One result of this shrinking from doctrinal specifics, Sayers contends in the introduction to her radio plays on Jesus Christ, is to strip the Gospel of its staggering implications:

> Of all examples of the classical tragic irony in fact or fiction, this is the greatest—the classic of classics. Beside it, the doom of Oedipus is trifling, and the nemesis of the Oresteian blood-bath a mere domestic incident. For the Christian affirmation is this: that a number of quite commonplace human beings, in an obscure province of the Roman Empire, killed and murdered God Almighty—quite casually, almost as a matter of religious and political routine, and certainly with no notion that they were doing anything out of the way. Their motives, on the whole, were defensible, and in some respects praiseworthy. There was some malice, some weakness, and no doubt some wresting of the law—but no more than we are accustomed to find in the conduct of human affairs. By no jugglings of fate, by no unforeseeable coincidence, by no supernatural machinations, but by that destiny which is character, and by their unimaginative following of their ordinary standards of behavior, they were led, with a ghastly inevitability, to the commission of the crime of crimes. We, the audience, know what they were doing; the whole point and poignancy of the tragedy is lost unless we realize that they did not know. The appalling truth is hidden from all the agonists in the drama.

Dorothy L. Sayers died in 1957, C. S. Lewis in 1963, J. R. R. Tolkien in 1973. Mere Christianity did not die, however, either in book form or as a force for Christian conversion. Year by year, individuals would discover it, including such well known public personalities as C. E. M. Joad, long the "show atheist" of British broadcasting, who converted to Christianity in 1952; Charles Colson, sentenced to prison as the hatchet man of the Nixon administration in the Watergate scandal, who converted in 1973 and spent the rest of his life serving Christian causes, among them the rehabilitation through faith of imprisoned criminals; Tom Monaghan, who sold his Domino's Pizza chain in 1998 and gave a billion dollars to Christian education, the pro-life movement, and various Catholic media agencies; and Francis Collins, former head of the Human Genome Project, who converted to evangelical Christianity in 1977, and in 2006 published a book on the compatibility of Christianity and science.

A poster advertises the 2010 release of the The Voyage of the Dawn Treader, *the third of the seven Narnia books to reach the big screen. The three films cost $560 million to make, and by late 2012 had brought in $1.5 billion at the box office. The movies sparked new interest in C. S. Lewis, and book sales rose accordingly.*

These men all specifically attributed their conversion to "Mere Christianity," and they were just four among many tens of thousands. With the twenty-first century, the movie version of the Narnia series sparked new interest in Lewis, and his book sales rose again. Strengthened by these intellectual champions, among many others, Christians entered their third millennium equipped with a convincing presentation of their faith which for sixty years had stood up solidly against all assaults hurled against it. But with very few exceptions, Mere Christianity was never seriously adopted by leading theological seminaries. Its development was largely the work of laymen—Lewis the professor of English, Sayers the novelist and playwright, Chesterton the journalist, and MacDonald the failed clergyman and writer of fairy tales. It was essentially a layman's religion, and a missionary one.

As such, it may well accord with the great changes afoot in the Christian world, described in the chapter that follows on the Christian charismatic movement in the southern hemisphere and in Asia—the mind and imagination, as it were, reinforcing the spirit. But that lies beyond the time frame of this series, which is confined to history. Prophecy is another line of work. ■

The 'dejected and reluctant convert'

'That which I greatly feared had at last come upon me,' said C. S. Lewis. 'God was God.' And so he began composing 'the Case for Christianity,' which would entice the world

In May 1941, Britain stood alone and vulnerable against a Germany that ruled most of western Europe and was still allied to Soviet Russia in the East. For six months of the previous year, Britain's industries and darkened cities had been blasted by Luftwaffe bombers, and with the spring of 1941 a German invasion was considered imminent. At some point in that perilous spring, the religious department of the British Broadcasting Corporation (BBC) made a decision that was to bring a new and authoritative voice to British radio, second only to that of Prime Minister Winston Churchill himself. That voice was to talk about God, a subject in which Britons had developed a sudden and compelling interest, forty thousand of them having met a violent and premature death in the previous year, with far more maimed and/or left homeless.

That new voice belonged to an Oxford professor of Medieval and Renaissance English literature named Clive Staples Lewis, who in good-humored simple language made what he called the "Case for Christianity"—why Christian belief is reasonable, and why he believed Christ's claims

to be God were (and are) true. He did not quote scripture, and he did not appeal to emotion. He reasoned. This subject and this approach might have drawn a meager audience in peacetime, but in the desperation of war the interest level was high.

Indeed, had Britain not been fighting for her life, it was doubtful that C. S. Lewis, who was neither a clergyman nor a credentialed theologian, would be hosting a national program on Christian theology. The BBC's head of religious programming, James Welch, had read Lewis's first apologetic work published the year before, *The Problem of Pain*. So impressed was he by Lewis's thinking that he decided Lewis should be addressing the nation. Though the professor had never broadcast before, his series of fifteen-minute Sunday evening talks, made from a London broadcast booth over the next three years, were not only immensely popular in themselves, but formed the basis of his best-read Christian book, *Mere Christianity*, published in 1952, and by 1977, twenty-five years after it was published, still selling over two million copies a year.

Lewis was forty-three when he began broadcasting, but was not a lifelong Christian. Born in Belfast in Northern Ireland in 1898, he grew up in a large, rambling suburban house, which he fondly remembered afterward for its "long corridors, empty sunlit rooms, upstairs indoor silences, attics explored in solitude, distant noises of gurgling pipes, and the noise of wind under the tiles." There were memories also, of endless books. Since neither Clive nor Staples appealed to him, he took for himself the name "Jack" at age four, and remained for his life close to his only sibling, a brother named Warren. Together they invented an imaginary world of talking animals they named Boxen. However, this idyllic world ended with their mother's death from cancer when Lewis was ten, and his bereaved solicitor father sent them to boarding school in England. He hated both the school and England, but eventually got over

the second aversion.[1] He also lost his childhood belief in God and became a professing atheist. In 1914 his father sent him to study privately with William T. Kirkpatrick, who taught Lewis to be a rigorous thinker and confirmed him in his religious skepticism. In 1916, Lewis earned a scholarship to University College, Oxford.

He loved and excelled at the academic life, but his sojourn at Oxford was soon interrupted by the First World War. In 1917 he volunteered in the British army, and as a commissioned second lieutenant on the front line experienced the horrors of trench warfare. He was seriously wounded in the arm, leg, and chest by shrapnel from a short-falling British shell at the Battle of Arras in April 1917. After his convalescence in England, the war was over and he was discharged. He went on to a stellar ascent at Oxford, was made a don, and settled in a house just outside the city. In 1919 he published the first of two volumes of poetry, little noted, reflecting both his love for classical literature and his thoroughgoing skepticism of religion.

This rational skepticism coexisted with a

> *Lewis had a potent love for 'northernness,' the harsh, pristine world of Odin, Thor, and Viking longships.*

C. S. Lewis photographed in a field near Magdalen College, Oxford, in 1946. During the preceding war years, this professor of Medieval and Renaissance English had helped bring the British people through the perils of war with his fifteen-minute talks about God that would later bring many to the faith in their published form, Mere Christianity. *Twenty years after its first publication, the book was still selling over two million copies a year.*

lively poetic imagination, however, fed in his childhood and youth by a potent love of mythology, especially Norse—what he called "northernness" in his autobiography *Surprised by Joy*: a sense of "being uplifted into huge regions of northern sky," into the harsh, pristine world of Odin and Thor and the Viking longships. "I desired with an almost sickening intensity something never to be described…and then found myself at the very same moment already falling out of that desire, and wishing I were back in it."

Two writers from a generation earlier initiated his slow return to Christ. At age seventeen, while waiting for a train on a fateful frosty afternoon in Surrey and bound for Oxford to write his entrance exams, he purchased the Everyman edition of George MacDonald's *Phantastes*, and was enthralled by it. In MacDonald he found some of the mythic qualities he so cherished, but here they were presented in a fantastical story invisibly rooted in MacDonald's Christian faith. Lewis wrote, "I did not know (and I was long in learning) the name of the new quality, the bright shadow… I do now. It was holiness."

Also making a significant impact was the work of journalist G. K. Chesterton, especially his robust summary of humanity *The Everlasting Man*, which Lewis read in an infirmary bed in France. He disagreed with Chesterton's arguments, of course, but loved and admired his mind and spirit—and, simply, his manifest goodness. A nonbeliever must be careful what he reads, Lewis later observed; for just as MacDonald had subtly baptized his imagination, Chesterton baptized his intellect.

As a rising Oxford professor in the 1920s, Lewis found himself moving toward theism. It made much more sense out of reality as he experienced it, and drew together the poles of reason and imagination. If existence is merely material and mechanistic, it is meaningless, and so are myth and poetry. But he did not want to mindlessly assent to some sort of wish-fulfillment consolation. He wanted the truth, and that necessitated a drawn-out inner struggle. He later said that he was brought to Christianity like a prodigal, "kicking, struggling, resentful." But he could not escape the conclusion to which he was com-ing—that there was a God. "You must picture me alone in that room in Magdalen, night after night, feeling, whenever my mind lifted even for a second from my work, the steady, unrelenting approach of Him whom I so earnestly desired not to meet," he recounted in *Surprised by Joy*. "That which I greatly feared had at last come upon me. In the Trinity Term of 1929 I gave in, and admitted that God was God, and knelt and prayed: perhaps, that night, the most dejected and reluctant convert in all England."

Two years, and many conversations later, Lewis converted from theism to Christianity, largely due to a dawning understanding of how the Incarnation, execution, and Resurrection of Jesus Christ had fulfilled the yearnings awakened in the great myths. He became convinced that myth had become fact in the central drama of redemption.

His approach was always charitable and calm, never heated or judgmental. In debate he invariably treated opponents with respect, dignity, and good humor. He was instrumental in forming the Socratic Club at Oxford, which pitted Christians against atheists and agnostics in public debate. These bouts featured such champions as Dorothy L. Sayers, J. S. Haldane, J. Bronowski, Konrad Lorenz, and Iris Murdoch.

By the outbreak of the Second World War, Lewis's forthright writing and debating had made him known, certainly within Oxford and in some circles beyond it, as an unusually able Christian apologist. The radio broadcasts made him known across the country. The year following his first radio broadcasts, Lewis wrote a series of imaginary letters, published one at a time in the left-wing newspaper *The Guardian*, consisting of the advice of a senior devil in hell, Screwtape, to a junior tempter on earth. Skewering the ideas of both nonbelievers and Modernist Christians, the installments were hugely popular and were published together as *The Screwtape Letters* in 1942. Lewis said that trying to think like a devil was one of the most depressing exercises of his life, but *Screwtape* remained one of his most popular books. However, not everyone quite got the joke. One country parson cancelled his *Guardian* subscription because much of the advice seemed "positively diabolical."

> Lewis understood how Jesus Christ fulfilled the longings awakened in the great myths. Myth was fact in redemption.

1. In his autobiography *Surprised by Joy*, Lewis recounts among his boarding-school experiences two horrible years at Wynyard School in Watford, Hartfordshire, which he nicknamed "Belsen," after the notorious Nazi concentration camp and where headmaster Robert "Oldie" Capron would beat the pupils capriciously and viciously. In his 2013 biography *C. S. Lewis – A Life: Eccentric Genius, Reluctant Prophet,* historian and theologian Alister McGrath writes that Wynyard was closed in 1910 when Capron was certified insane, and that Lewis confided later in a letter to a young American fan, who asked about his school days, that he "never hated anything as much, not even the front line trenches in World War I."

In the hundreds of letters, essays, articles, and books that flowed from his pen (he detested typewriters) between 1933 and his death in 1963, certain thoughts predominate. At the root of all his apologetics is the conviction that Christianity should be believed because it is true. Moderns all too often reduce it to mere subjective sentiment, but real faith must also convince the intellect. As he wrote in *Mere Christianity*, "I am not asking anyone to accept Christianity if his best reasoning is against it." Whether Christianity is humane, comforting, inspiring, or good for society were to him irrelevant.

Lewis saw modernity confounded by two great philosophical errors: relativism and materialism. Relativism insists that objective moral truth either does not exist or cannot be found. Ultimately, for the rela-

The ten-year-old "Jack" Lewis (standing, right), is shown here in a 1908 photograph with his father, Albert, and elder brother Warren ("Warnie"), in their Irish home. After the First World War, Lewis began a stellar ascent at Oxford, but before the 1920s were over he would come to the painful conclusion that there was indeed a God, describing himself as "the most dejected and reluctant convert in all England." His conversion to Christianity and textual ventures into Christian evangelism, while leading to public success, would deny him a full professorship at Oxford, forcing him to move to Cambridge's Magdalene College (below) in the 1950s.

tivist, everything is subjective—based on one's own feelings. Therefore, says Lewis, modern men and women have ceased to think morally in terms of reason, but rather in feelings and sentiments. We can only talk about preferences, not eternal truths that are there whether we feel them or not. As he put it in *Christian Reflections*, "Unless there is some objective standard of good, over-arching Germans, Japanese, and ourselves alike, whether any of us obey it or not, then of course the Germans are as competent to create their ideology as we are to create ours." Modern thinkers, Lewis points out, are always trying to find new standards on which to build a new morality, but "the human mind has no more power of inventing a new value system than of planting a new sun in the sky or a new primary color in the spectrum."

The other great philosophical opponent to the Christian worldview that Lewis battled was materialism, also known as naturalism, the belief that the physical world of our senses is the only reality. The denial of supernatural reality leaves us with a religion that is only psychology, justice that is only self-protection, politics that are only economics, and love that is really only lust, he countered. "The strength of such a materialist critic," writes Lewis in *The Weight of Glory* (1941), "lies in the words 'merely' or 'nothing but.' He sees all the facts but not the meaning... He is therefore, as regards the matter in hand, in the position of an animal. You have noticed that most dogs cannot understand pointing. You point to a bit of food on the floor; the dog, instead of looking at the floor, sniffs at your finger. A finger is a finger to him, and that is all. His world is all facts and no meaning." The end of such reductionism is this, he writes in *The Abolition of Man* (1943): "You cannot go on 'explaining away' forever: you will find that you have explained explanation itself away." What we need, says Lewis in his book *Miracles* (1947), is a bigger perspective of reality than materialism can offer us. "In science," he writes, "we are only reading the notes to a poem; in Christianity we find the poem itself."

One of Lewis's most powerful reasons for belief in God was his "argument from desire." He notes that it is a common human experience to sense that this world is somehow haunted by realities that are beyond it, as though there was "something more." We often find ourselves longing for something

that transcends this life, for something which is just beyond our grasp. Such an experience may be awakened in us by a sublime sight, hearing beautiful music, or by experiencing romantic love, inspiring a feeling of ecstatic wonder, of something akin to nostalgia, or an unexplainable melancholy. In all of these, it is the feeling of being in the presence of mystery. It was such experiences that brought Lewis to the threshold of faith, and understanding them more deeply that helped him to embrace the God toward whom they pointed.

Lewis had such experiences from the time he was a child, staring out his nursery window toward the distant Castlereagh Hills. He felt the same kind of longing in response to literature, and even in a little toy garden his brother once made of earth and flowers nestled in a little tin container.

This statue of the young Lewis looking into a wardrobe, entitled "The Searcher," was sculpted by Ross Wilson for the city of Belfast in 2008 to honor the native son whose Narnia Chronicles were enjoying such success in written and movie form. As well as evoking the first book of the series, The Lion, the Witch, and the Wardrobe, *the statue also conjures up the longing experienced by Lewis and everybody else, a longing that Lewis saw as evidence of the supernatural.*

All such things awakened a beautiful aching in his heart, "an unsatisfied desire." For nothing on earth could quench the desire these experiences awakened.

The existence of such longings is evidence that there is more to life than we can touch, taste, smell, or feel. All our earthly experiences fall short of fulfilling these longings. So why do we have them? What natural purpose do they serve? "Do fish complain of the sea for being wet?" Lewis once asked. "Or if they did, would that fact itself not strongly suggest that they had not always been, or would not always be, purely aquatic creatures? If you are really a product of a materialistic universe, how is it that you don't feel at home there?" (*A Mind Awake*, 1968). Or, as he proposed in *Mere Christianity*, "If I find in myself a desire which no experience in this world can satisfy, the most probable explanation is that I was made for another world." Lewis believed that this God, the answer to our longings, was not simply the "life force" of the Deists, or the mere metaphor of the Modernists, but a personal God who demands a response from his creation.

Reason, Lewis reminded us, is the organ of truth—the way we come to knowledge. But imagination is the organ of meaning. It helps us make sense of reality and fully experience what truth can only point toward. He understood that our hearts need to be moved, as well as our brains.

In Lewis's works of imagination the gospel is embodied in story, myths, analogies, and allegories in order that we may see it afresh. That was his motivation for writing the seven children's Narnia stories, between 1949 and 1954, creating an imaginary medieval/classical world of talking beasts, pagan demigods, dragons, and giants which adventurous modern English children find their way into and out of. Though adult readers understood them as allegorical Christianity (for which his friend J. R. R. Tolkien heartily disliked them, and said so), Lewis hoped to impart the meaning of the gospel without the burdensome paraphernalia children had in those days of Sunday schools, stained glass, ponderous sermons, and fussy adult churchliness. Narnia was to prepare his readers for the gospel, just as the ancient myths of dying gods prepared

humanity for the time when myth became fact in the person of Jesus Christ.

None of these Christian assertions and endeavors won Lewis many friends at Magdalen College in Oxford. Indeed it was very much the opposite. "There is nothing like worldly success on the part of one academic to make all the others hate him or her," writes A. N. Wilson in *C. S. Lewis: A Biography* (1990). Lewis's undisguised contempt for the blurred thinking behind Oxford's plunge into Modernist subjectivism made him even more foes. (Example: in his novel, *That Hideous Strength*, one trendy professor is described as "a man of straw, a glib examinee in subjects that require no exact knowledge.") Thus in 1954, when Cambridge University offered him the newly established chair of Medieval and Renaissance English Literature, a high distinction, he accepted it, but he continued to live at Oxford, coming home on weekends.

This appointment represented a major change in his life and there had already been another. Up until August of 1952, Lewis's personal and professional life had been virtually one and the same. Then he had an unusual visit from an American woman. Joy Davidman was Jewish, much accomplished as a young poet and promising novelist, an ex-Communist, mother of two in a failing marriage, and a convert to Christianity under the strong influence of Lewis's writings. She had been corresponding with him for three years, and now came to see him. Lewis was much taken with her intellectually, as was his brother, though not his friends. Her acrid New York accent and uninhibited manner, which Lewis found delightful, they found otherwise.

Though he reportedly did not respond romantically to her, she challenged him intellectually and increasingly helped him with his work. When her visa expired and she was ordered home to America, she asked him bluntly if he would marry her to change her immigrant status. He agreed and they were legally wed. Only then did Lewis discover himself hopelessly in love with her, and the following year they were married by an Anglican priest.[2] Their bliss, however, soon fell under a shadow. Joy was discovered to have bone cancer and died three

> *Such longings evidence that there is more to life than what we can touch, taste, smell, or feel. So why do we have them?*

2. Since Joy Davidman had divorced her first husband (William Lindsay Gresham), the Anglican bishop of Oxford refused to allow the marriage. A local priest performed it anyway, clearly violating church discipline. But since Joy's husband had himself been divorced before marrying her, Lewis reasoned that this, by the same church rule, would have nullified her first marriage. So she must have entered the second as a single woman. Such sophistry, however, did not satisfy Tolkien, who severely objected to Lewis's marrying a divorced woman. After Joy's death, Lewis developed a close friendship with Gresham, an alcoholic who had become Christian (and later recanted). Whether Lewis won him back to the faith is not known.

3. "All those hairy old toughs of centurions in Tacitus," writes Lewis in the *Four Loves*. "All pansies? If you can believe that, you can believe anything." In his biography, Wilson ascribes this to Lewis's "simple-mindedness." Whenever Lewis adheres to the current intellectually acceptable view, Wilson finds him brilliant, insightful, rational, progressive. Whenever he departs from it, he is being simple-minded. And since all Lewis's most controversial positions—his Christology, his traditionalist morality, his insistence of an underlying natural law common to all human cultures—are departures from the modernist convention and therefore "simple-minded," Wilson's biography, whatever its pretensions, amounts to an attempt to undermine the credibility of its subject.

Above, Lewis and Joy Davidman (also right), share a quiet moment in 1957. Lewis wrote of her death and his mourning in the book A Grief Observed, *later the basis of a play and the film* Shadowlands *(inset below) starring Anthony Hopkins and Debra Winger. Lewis was deeply taken with the brash New York Jewess with whom he had corresponded for three years before meeting; his friends weren't so keen.*

years later. The loss shook Lewis as nothing had since the death of his mother, and his book, *A Grief Observed*, initially published under a pseudonym, describes as little else ever has the agony of bereavement. He placed beside Joy's grave the memorial lines he had originally written on the death of his close friend Charles Williams:

> *Here the whole world (stars, water, air,*
> *And field, and forest, as they were*
> *Reflected in a single mind)*
> *Like cast off clothes was left behind*
> *In ashes, yet with hopes that she,*
> *Re-born from holy poverty,*
> *In lenten lands, hereafter may*
> *Resume them on her Easter Day*

Lewis died on November 22, 1963, the day President John F. Kennedy was assassinated and Aldous Huxley died. He lived only up to the brink of the grand departures his beloved Church of England was to make from the Christian tradition.

However, he left little doubt where he would have stood on the issues when they arose. In his book, *The Four Loves* (1943), he scorned the notion that all strong male friendships must be implicitly homosexual.[?] The concept of female priests he saw as an invitation to disaster, because it would dig a permanent gulf between Anglicanism on the one hand and the Roman Catholic and Orthodox churches on the other. His fellow apologist, Dorothy L. Sayers, agreed with him.

The epitaph on Lewis's tombstone was, like certain things he himself had written, almost callous. It was taken from Shakespeare's *King Lear*: "All men must endure their going hence," it read. Period. No consolation. Death is real. Get used to the idea. That was the message. Harsh, surely, but also true, commemorating a man who had seen many go hence, some much beloved. It was fitting. ■

Chinese Catholics kneel and worship in front of a church on a hillside in Baoji, in northwest China's Shaanxi province in May 2005. China, along with sub-Saharan Africa and Latin America, had been among the leaders in Christian growth in recent decades, with its numbers rising from four million to fifty million since 1949. The boom has been largely ignored by a western media unwilling to acknowledge Christianity's resurrection outside of the developed world.

CHAPTER 20

The faith rises again as millions join Christ across the third world

The face of Christianity has changed its color as Asia and Africa in teeming numbers embrace the cross, and the high tide of secularism turns

In *The Everlasting Man*, his intriguing history of the Christian faith, G. K. Chesterton conceded that in 1925 the Christian religion might reasonably be considered dead. It had died around the beginning of the twentieth century, he observed, and when he himself died eleven years later he would have found little convincing reason to change his mind. "There are some people who say they wish Christianity to remain as a spirit," he noted in *The Everlasting Man*. "They mean very literally they wish it to remain as a ghost. But it is not going to remain as a ghost. What follows this process of apparent death is not the lingerings of a shade; it is the resurrection of the body." However, he added, the death of Christianity is not a new occurrence. It had died so many times before.

Five times in all, by GKC's count, and he called the closing chapter of his history *The Five Deaths of the Faith*. But only the first death—which came on the first Good Friday—had provided grounds for real despair. The responsible opinion and respected authority of the time was wholly in agreement that this trouble-making Jesus was dead and that his movement, which gave every evidence of being a one-man affair, was sure to die with him. Responsible opinion was mistaken, of course. The first death was followed by the first Resurrection, and in

The cover of a recent edition of his classic 1925 history of Christianity, The Everlasting Man. At the time of the book's publication, the faith was undergoing what GKC termed its "fifth death." As ever, however, he predicted a resurrection that would in fact begin in the final half of the century. The caricature of GKC is by John Herreid from 2006.

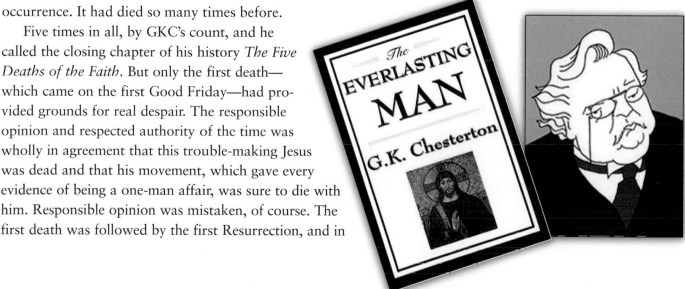

1. Jesus' refusal to take up arms or to convert his following into a military uprising puts him in sharp contrast with Mohammed. The early histories of the two religions, Christianity and Islam, offer a striking contrast. Over its first three hundred years, Christianity won the Roman Empire, largely through the witness of its countless martyrs, slaying no one. When Mohammed realized that to remain in Mecca would probably cost him his life, he left for Medina, formed an army, and began the conquest of Arabia. Islam in its first three hundred years conquered the Mediterranean world and much of Asia by the sword, slaying tens of thousands.

The risen Christ (inset) with Saint Peter (left) and Saint Paul and a pair of angels is depicted here by the Dutch painter Anthonis Mor in 1564. The depiction is of the first Resurrection; Mor and his fellow Renaissance artists were part of what might be termed the third resurrection of the faith—a rebirthing that also included the building of the Gothic cathedrals like the magnificent example in Chartres, France, below.

little more than three hundred years this supposedly dead faith had become the central philosophical and moral rationale of the entire Roman Empire.

After another hundred or so years, the empire itself died (the western half of it anyway), and informed opinion again pronounced the demise of its religion. If the empire perished, men reasoned, how could Christianity survive? Yet even as Rome's western empire was gradually smashed to pieces, a most dumbfounding thing occurred. The same peoples who were doing the smashing began to adopt as their own the religion of their defeated foe, practicing it not only in the Roman lands they had overrun but in many instances transmitting it back to the regions they came from. And that was the second resurrection.

The third death came with fire and fury from the desert. The religion of "the Prophet," according to his sword-wielding followers, was destined to conquer the world, and for a time this seemed quite likely. Mighty Persia fell before them, followed by the ancient Christian lands of Palestine, Syria, Lebanon, and Egypt. Christian North Africa went down, and finally Christian Spain and much of Christian France. The Christendom that once encircled the Mediterranean was now all but destroyed. Rome would be next, vowed the Prophet's swordsmen, and "backward Europe" lay virtually prostrate at their feet. This was the third death. Almost all the Christian lands were gone.

But not quite all. In those that survived, a Christian people only recently

emerged from barbarism mounted a counterattack known to history as the Crusades (from Latin *crux*, cross). That is, they sought to regain by the sword what had been lost to the sword—but the Crusades failed. Such was not the way of Christ. "Could I not have had twelve legions of angels?" he demanded (Matthew 26:53), but he chose instead to suffer.[1] So Christians after that largely took up tools instead of swords; the men of the monasteries rebuilt the infrastructure of the empire, the great Gothic cathedrals appeared, followed by the artistry of the Renaissance, and the Christian universities from which philosophy and the sciences emerged. Civilization was reborn, rooted in a Christianity more powerful than ever. And that was the third resurrection.

A battle had been won but not the war; events now took another turn. Christianity acquired wider acceptance, bringing with it wealth and power and so corrupting its leadership that direction of the faith fell ever more decisively into the hands of kings and princes. Their wars became so-called Christian wars, but the unity of the faithful, for which Jesus had so fervently prayed on the night before his death (John 17:21), was woefully lost. Thus for three of the darkest decades of the Christian era, Protestants and Catholics slew each other by the tens of thousands in a war that turned into a power struggle between Bourbon and Habsburg, and in the end had almost nothing to do with God, Christ, or religion.

Judgment falls upon such error. There is always a price, and the price of the Thirty Years War is known as the Enlightenment. Repelled to the point of nausea by the sordid carnage of these supposed wars of religion, men began to rail and legislate against God. The eighteenth century and early nineteenth were to see a sweeping rebellion against the traditional. In France, the church schools and the churches themselves were defunded. In Italy, the Papal States, the papacy's chief source of revenue, were seized by revolutionaries. Prussia, the ascendant power in Germany, declared war on the Catholic Church and sought to close its schools, while transforming the supine Protestant churches into government departments, a process that went back to the Protestant Reformation. Meanwhile in America, Deism became the non-Christian religion of the elite, and church attendance dropped to six percent of the population. The undeniably brilliant Thomas Jefferson, chief architect of the newly established republic, published a revised version of the Gospels, with all miracles expunged, as well as Jesus' theological teachings. Deism, soon to be known as Unitarianism, would become the religion of most Americans, Jefferson prophesied. The fourth death of the faith was pronounced.

But the fourth resurrection came hard upon the fourth death. When the Catholic Church in France sought funding through public subscription, it was overwhelmed by the huge sums contributed by the faithful, including by many children—far more, in fact, than the French government had ever provided. The church, no longer viewed as a governmental bureaucracy, saw its credibility surge; its moral and spiritual authority grew stronger than they had been since medieval times; and new religious orders were established. In America, spurred by the Second Great Awakening, church membership rose from six to forty-three percent of a population which by the end of the nineteenth century was seventeen times that of Jefferson's day. Deist Unitarianism, far from sweeping the country, was on the wane and by the end of the twentieth century, would account for just one-fifth of one percent of the American population. Most astonishing of all, missions sent out from Europe and America produced by far the greatest growth Christianity had ever experienced, even during those years when it had converted the Roman Empire. And that was the fourth resurrection.

Like an idol to the secularist age over which he reigned, a statue of Charles Darwin sits at London's Natural History Museum. His two books, On the Origin of the Species *and* The Descent of Man, *heralded the fifth of the five deaths of the faith, or so many people, especially in Europe, would assume.*

But by Chesterton's count there were five deaths, and the fifth attack would appear to be the most lethal. It began with Darwin's momentous two books, *On the Origin of Species* (1859) and *The Descent of Man* (1871), which challenged the old "Argument from Design" and took deep root, not only in the scientific community, but among the intelligentsia of both Europe and America. By the time Chesterton published *The Everlasting Man*, serious belief in the existence of God, or even belief in a Mind behind the physical universe, had all but vanished in academic circles. Religious skepticism reigned in the news media and among public school curriculum planners. Small wonder that later in the century, during America's culture war, the Christian Moral Majority was chagrined to discover that it was by no means a majority. Even in America, that is, the faith was dying its fifth death.

The Welsh-born, Cambridge-educated professor Philip Jenkins and one of the thirty-two editions of the book that revealed the tremendous gains being made by Christianity in the third world. "If we want to envision a 'typical' contemporary Christian," he writes, "we should think of a woman living in a village in Nigeria or in a Brazilian favela."

Unobserved by the European and American media, however, or even by much of the Christian press, a curious thing was quietly happening. In October 2002, an article in the *Atlantic Monthly* disclosed that Christianity had for some time been recording astounding growth in Africa and Latin America and also in Asia. Even in Red China it had grown from four million to fifty million since the Communist triumph despite severe government persecution. In India, official figures put the Christian population at twenty-five million, about 2.5 percent of the population. The *World Christian Encyclopedia* put it at 6 percent including what it called *crypto*-Christians (those who believe and worship in secret while publicly professing Hinduism to avoid persecution). This would mean that there were more Christians in India than in Europe. In South Korea, Christianity had become the leading religion, as it had been for some time in the Philippines. There had been phenomenal growth of Pentecostal Christianity throughout Latin America, and all the churches, particularly the Catholic, were growing so astonishingly in Africa that the "Dark Continent" had effectually become the numerical center of the Christian religion. Islam was growing there too, but not nearly as rapidly as Christianity.

The author of the *Atlantic Monthly* piece was Philip Jenkins, Welsh-born, Cambridge-educated, and a professor of history at Pennsylvania State University. His article summarized his new book: *The Next Christendom: The Coming of Global Christianity*, which would go through thirty-two editions in its first ten years. It was not widely reviewed in the general media, however, either because Christianity had ceased to command serious secular interest, or because what Jenkins documented was so much at odds with currently popular perceptions that they didn't know quite how to contend with it.

Moreover, to some the book was plainly offensive. Put bluntly, Jenkins was asserting that the rest of the world did not share the lofty religious skepticism of Europe's literati and America's intellectual elite. Far from leading the modern age, the opinion leaders of the West were now living in a cultural backwater, unaware of what was going on everywhere else. The faith they had assumed to be dead had, unbeknownst to them, become more alive than ever. They stood implicitly accused, that is, of crass ignorance grounded in bigotry. Yet Jenkins' facts were nowhere seriously challenged, and his reasoning nowhere seriously disputed.

Not that many white Christians might be all that receptive to his message in any event. "If we want to envision a 'typical' contemporary Christian," Jenkins writes, "we should think of a woman living in a village in Nigeria or in a Brazilian *favela* [slum]." This, incidentally, is a noteworthy quality he discovers in the new Christendom. The faithful are as a rule very poor. Often they live in hovels in the midst of huge cities, for they have made Christianity a highly urban religion. But the success of Christianity, particularly of Pentecostalism, in vast urban slums is no mystery, declares retired Harvard theologian Harvey Cox. "Sometimes, the only thriving human communities in these vast areas of tar paper shacks and cardboard huts are Pentecostal congregations," he writes. "The fellowship of believers is comparable to a large family gathering." In the Christian communities that grew up in these shantytowns, most of them Pentecostal, writes historian Peter Brown (*The World of Late Antiquity*, 1971), the individual found a home and shelter from the cold impersonal world, much as did the members of the early Christian church within the teeming cities of the late Roman Empire.

But another factor has also been highly significant. Most Pentecostal converts are women, seemingly drawn to the faith by the notable changes that were observed in the earliest men to embrace this faith. No longer would a male, once converted, squander family resources on drinking, gambling, and prostitutes; he would work hard instead to lavish loving care on his wife and children. Historian Elizabeth E. Brusco calls this *The Reformation of Machismo*, the title she gave a 1995 book on Pentecostalism.

Hundreds of thousands of people attend an all-night Pentecostal service held by the Redeemed Church of Christ on a highway in Lagos, Nigeria, in October, 2003. Because congregations are so large, the service is often held outdoors or in airplane hangars, although more recently megachurches, such as the fifty-thousand-seat Faith Tabernacle built by Bishop David Oyedepo (inset) have been built to accommodate the throngs.

Some images from the new Christian pastures in the southern hemisphere. Clockwise from top left: Brazilian evangelicals, part of a membership of two million, pray inside the main Renascer em Cristo temple in Sao Paulo in May 2007. A stained-glass window in the Presbyterian Church of the Torch, Kikuyu, Kenya, depicts Jesus and his flock of Kikuyu women and children in traditional attire. South Koreans bow before the immense Yoido Full Gospel Pentecostal Church in Seoul (capacity: twenty-eight thousand). A bridegroom in the Indian province of Mangalore is anointed with coconut milk in a traditional ceremony incorporated into the Catholic ceremonial.

This annual "March for Jesus" in Sao Paulo, Brazil, in June 2011, attracted about two million people, largely from Brazil's hundreds of Protestant churches, which have made great gains in South America in recent decades. Roman Catholicism, however, continues to hold its own. For although by 2010 there were sixty million Latino Protestants, there were four hundred and twenty million Latinos who were not, most of them still loyal Catholics.

A *Washington Post* account describes as quite typical the experience of Agua Branca Baptist Church, located in one of Sao Paulo's huge slums, which outgrew its rented brick facility and had to buy an enormous tent to accommodate its 1,500-member congregation. But such a number is arguably picayune in the demographics of the new southern Christendom. The Jotabeche Methodist Church in Chile claims eighty thousand members; its cathedral in Santiago seats eighteen thousand. Bishop David Oyedepo's Faith Tabernacle in Nigeria seats a reported fifty thousand in its main auditorium, while one of its many open air evangelical campgrounds covers some twelve thousand acres.[2]

All of them pale, however, beside the Yoido Full Gospel Pentecostal Church in Seoul. Seating at least twenty-eight thousand, Yoido is among the world's biggest churches, and according to the *Guinness Book of World Records* its total membership numbers five hundred thousand, the world's largest independent congregation. The number of Christians in Korea was about three hundred thousand in 1920. By 2010 they numbered about twelve million—three quarters Protestant, mostly Pentecostal, and most of the rest Catholic. But mainline Protestant congregations have also held their own in Korea. The Kwanglim Methodist Church, which had one hundred and fifty members in 1971, forty years later had eighty-five thousand, and there were almost twice as many Presbyterians in Korea as in the United States.

Sometimes the numerical strength of the "southern" Christians becomes publicly noticeable. Several million believers, for example, turn out for the annual March for Jesus in Sao Paulo, which draws faithful from Brazil's hundreds of Protestant churches. Another notable instance is the annual Easter pilgrimage of the million-member Zion Christian Church in South Africa.

But the principal factor behind most of this third world growth is Pentecostalism, whose greatest surge has been in Latin America. In 1940 there were barely a million Latin American Protestants; there are now sixty to seventy million. Their numbers were growing at the rate of about nineteen million a year, wrote Harvey Cox in *Fire from Heaven* in 1969. In Brazil in the 1990s they were

2. David Oyedepo, a Nigerian Christian author who claims a net worth of $150 million, is presiding bishop of the Living Faith Church World Wide, which operates in sixty-three cities in thirty-two African nations. Bishop Oyedepo's church owns four private jets and real estate in Britain and America. He has established two universities, a system of "heritage schools," and a publishing arm that has sold some four million books. Oyedepo himself has written seventy of them. He is widely regarded as the founder of the charismatic movement in Africa. His father was Muslim, but he was raised by his devout Christian grandmother.

opening one new church a week in Rio de Janeiro, and their numbers increased from nine to fifteen percent of the population. This was mostly at the expense of the Catholic Church, whose proportion of the population fell from eighty-four to seventy-four percent. By the twenty-first century, the Pentecostals owned one of the largest TV stations in the country, and had their own political party and their own football team.

The Catholic response to all this has been far more effective than the numbers may indicate, if only because the Pentecostal numbers are frequently found to be exaggerated. At first the reaction chiefly consisted of papal denunciations. Even the generally tolerant Pope John Paul II likened the "sects," as he called them, to

The study group that exploded

How a vigorous Anglican priest in a dying London parish set off a lay movement in which millions discover Christianity, a faith they knew almost nothing about

Christians are instructed to evangelize—to spread the faith to others. That command gained urgency in the late twentieth century, as church attendance steadily sagged and people in the developed world lapsed into unbelief. After Vatican II, Catholic laity were told to evangelize, something they had long been doing through such groups as Catholic Action and the Catholic Truth Society, though the responsibility had hitherto been exercised mainly by the clergy. But how, exactly, did one go about it? Preach on a street corner? Testify in the office lunchroom? Go door-to-door handing out tracts? What do you say? And once you have alarmed and offended all your friends, how do you get them back?

An answer to this universal conundrum did in fact emerge, and spread with exponential speed through all church traditions across the globe in the 1990s. By 2009 it reported having reached fifteen million people in one hundred languages and one hundred and sixty-nine nations. It was called the Alpha program.

Alpha was hatched in—of all places—the chic, cosmopolitan area of central West London, in the spacious, ornate Anglican parish church of Holy Trinity, Brompton. Relatively new by British standards, Holy Trinity was built in the 1820s to serve the elite families of the British Empire. Alpha began there as an unremarkable adult Christian study course in the listless seventies, when public interest in Christianity seemed to have vanished and pews were mostly empty. To meet changing demand in the 1980s the course evolved into an introduction to basic Christianity for those—especially young adults—who knew nothing about the faith but felt an interest. By 2012 the Alpha program, now worldwide, was still run from Holy Trinity by the parish vicar, Reverend Nicky Gumbel.

The standard Alpha course for adults took one evening a week for ten weeks, each lesson beginning with a light meal, followed by a video address from Gumbel in person or from a trained leader, and then small-group discussion. (There were also special Alpha courses for students, youth, prisoners,

seniors, and military personnel.) Each week dealt with one or two themes addressed to participants, beginning with "Is there more to life than this?" and then moving on through Christ, the Crucifixion, prayer, the Bible, the Holy Spirit, the church, resisting temptation, talking to others about God, etc. Each course would usually climax with an entire day or "weekend away." Registrants in any one course typically ranged in number from a dozen to a score, and included a mixture of Christians, lapsed Christians, and never Christian.

Instead of proselytizing strangers, lay Christians now needed only to ask friends and neighbors if they ever considered life's larger questions—and if so, to try out this free course where people from all faith backgrounds got to explore them in a friendly, nonjudgmental way. Yes it was Christian, but nobody expected them to keep coming if it didn't interest them. Just give it a try.

In a 2009 interview with *Guardian* journalist Adam Rutherford, Gumbel explained that Alpha's content evolved somewhat haphazardly, and it certainly is not how most experts would introduce the faith. However, it was found to work well in all circumstances—rich nations and poor; urban, suburban, or rural communities; small-group settings or large. Part of the reason for its success, he said, was its accepting, welcoming spirit. Objections to Christianity were encouraged and answered, and though not all participants were persuaded, many did in fact convert, including many who did not expect to. He found that the most open-minded age group by far were young adults who had no personal knowledge or impression of Christianity at all.

Though Alpha described itself as a bare introduction to agreed-upon Christian essentials, and not a denominational catechism, some Catholics and evangelicals dismissed the training as seriously deficient. The former said it misrepresented and underplayed the nature and meaning of sacraments, and the latter found there was too little about God's holiness and human sinfulness. Regardless, many Catholic bishops approved "Alpha for Catholics"—the same course with a "ravening wolves." But the Latin American church through much of the 1960s and 1970s had been targeted by the Catholic liberation theology movement, whose Marxist inclinations brought John Paul sharply down upon it as well, soon after he became pope. The Latin American move into Pentecostalism paralleled the suppression of liberation theology, but no Marxism is evident in Pentecostalism. Its political affiliations, Jenkins says, range widely.

Meanwhile, a Catholic charismatic movement proved immensely popular, inspiring much greater participation by the laity in the work of the church. This may have slowed the Pentecostal advance, but did not check it. Besides, Jenkins writes, such trends disturb conservative Catholics, because charismatic Catholic services

Alpha movement founder Nicky Gumbel (above left) and an Alpha-organized leadership conference in London in May 2012, which featured, among other things, an interview with former Prime Minister and Catholic convert Tony Blair (right). Born in the Holy Trinity Anglican church in middle-class London in the 1970s, this modern evangelistic program has grown to embrace mainline Protestants, Pentecostals, evangelicals, Orthodox, and Catholics.

warning at the outset that Catholicism has more to add about Communion, baptism, confession, and marriage. Likewise, many fundamental Protestants accepted that Alpha could only get newcomers through the door, where after it fell to pastors and congregations to hold them.

A second criticism, especially from evangelical Protestants, was that Alpha became openly Pentecostal and charismatic, talking in its "weekend away" segment about being filled with the Holy Spirit. This was assumed to mean speaking in tongues, prophecy, and healing. Gumbel acknowledged that this happened when the participants wanted it to, but that Alpha's more conventional participants simply dealt with the subject in whatever manner their church approved of.

Among other things, Alpha demonstrated how far practical ecumenism had traveled in half a century. Designed and initiated by mainline Protestants, it was accepted intact and used by Pentecostals, evangelicals, Orthodox, and Catholics. The reality of the third millennium is that Christians increasingly focus more on where they agree than on where they differ. This affects everything, even how they speak.

An Alpha pamphlet quotes one church leader as follows: "It is necessary to awaken in believers a full relationship with Christ, mankind's only savior. Only from a personal relationship with Jesus can effective evangelization develop." The writer was not Billy Graham or Oral Roberts. It was Pope John Paul II. ∎

Telesphore Mpundu, Catholic archbishop of Lusaka, blesses the palm leaves held by Christians outside Zambia's Supreme Court on Palm Sunday, 2012. Zambia was declared a Christian country in 1991, part of a growing trend in sub-Saharan Africa. Where, in 1900 there had been just ten million Christians, there were almost four hundred million by 2012, roughly half the population.

tend to look so Protestant. Jenkins also reminds readers that even after decades of Protestant growth, Catholicism is still overwhelmingly the largest religious presence in Latin America. Against the sixty million Latinos who are Protestants, some four hundred and twenty million others remain in the Catholic Church.

The seeds the missionaries had sown sprang vigorously to life, generating the astonishing rise of homegrown Christianity. This represents a remarkable victory.

A very different picture emerges in Africa, where Catholic growth played a central role in the twentieth-century Christian advance. Where there were sixteen million African Catholics in 1955, there were fifty-five million in 1978, and one hundred and forty million in 2006. At that time one-eighth of the world's Catholics were Africans, and one-sixth predictably will be Africans by 2025. As of 2006 there were 426 African bishops and 27,000 priests. In Nigeria alone, which counted around eighteen million Catholics, parishes offered five to six masses on a Sunday and still many people had to listen outside. One Nigerian seminary at last count had a thousand students; the biggest American seminary enrolled about two hundred.

Jenkins describes overall Christian growth in Africa as "staggering." In 1900, there were ten million Christians there. By 2000, there were three hundred and sixty million. If the growth rate of 2.3 percent per year holds—by no means a certainty, of course—the Christian population of the continent predictably will double in thirty years. Zambia declared itself a Christian nation in 1991. The Cathedral of Our Lady of Peace, built with Zambian government aid starting in 1991, claims to be the largest Catholic Church in the world, bigger even than Saint Peter's in Rome.

Whatever else these various developments might imply, they resoundingly evidence the singular success achieved by European and American missions to the

3. The turn to Christianity was significantly aided by the failure of the nationalist movements which followed the European exodus. In many countries, independence produced a new political elite who took over for itself the economic position of the former colonialists. The vast majority of the people became disillusioned with nationalism and therefore turned to something else.

third world in the nineteenth century. Up to the 1950s, the brave and selfless missionary was something of a hero to congregations at home, but after 1950 his image suffered a grievous and growing denigration as secularism gained ground in the latter years of the twentieth century. "At their worst," Jenkins notes, "missions were presented as a cynical arm of ruthless, racist, colonial exploitation."

The very word "missionary" conjured up visions of "redneck zealots forcing starving children to be baptized before they get a few crusts of bread," observed journalist Nicholas Kristof in the *New York Times*, before rebutting such a picture as false. The best evidence against such negativity comes from people whom the missionaries won as converts. When the colonial powers withdrew and independence movements swept the third world, the seeds they had sown sprang vigorously to life, generating the astonishing rise of homegrown Christianity now observable. This represents a remarkable victory.[3]

It has not been without cost, however. Particularly in Africa, political turmoil often followed the withdrawal of the European powers. In Uganda, for instance, Anglican Archbishop Janani Luwum was murdered either by or on the orders of psychopathic autocrat Idi Amin, for opposing the government. In the Congo, Cardinal Emile Biayenda was assassinated in 1977, for resisting the government's crackdown on the church. Numerous political murders of Christians occurred in Kenya and Zimbabwe. And in Latin America, Bishop Oscar Romero of El Salvador was shot while saying Mass. He had publicly rebuked soldiers who were Christians for following government orders and shooting Christian citizens.

Violence notwithstanding, Jenkins is confident that Christian growth will continue all over the third world throughout the twenty-first century, but it will not be a peaceful process. Christianity's ancient enemy, Islam, will oppose it in every possible way, including terrorism and vigorous persecution, as already demonstrated in Nigeria, Indonesia, Sudan, the Philippines, and more lately in the Middle East and Egypt. Nor will all the violence be occasioned by Islam; already there have been some jarring incidents.

Below left, the bodies of children killed in sectarian violence in the village of Dogo-Nahawa, central Nigeria, in March 2010, when fighting between Christian and Muslim youths claimed more than two hundred lives. Top right, a grainy photo from 1980 shows nuns and others grieving over the body of Archbishop Oscar Romero of San Salvador, shortly after he was shot by government forces while he raised the chalice during Mass. Bottom left, Archbishop Janani Luwum of Uganda who was killed by dictator Idi Amin's forces in 1977; and, right, Cardinal Emile Biayenda, who was assassinated the same year during political unrest in the Congo. Although the rise of homegrown Christianity in the post-colonial regions has been remarkable, it has not been without cost.

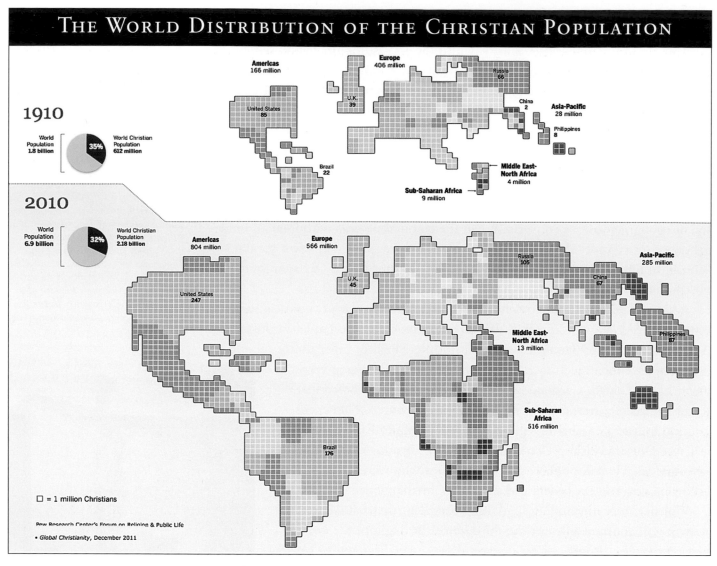

1910

World Population 1.8 billion — 35% — World Christian Population 612 million

Americas 166 million · Europe 406 million · Russia 66 · United States 85 · U.K. 39 · China 2 · Asia-Pacific 28 million · Philippines 8 · Brazil 22 · Middle East-North Africa 4 million · Sub-Saharan Africa 9 million

2010

World Population 6.9 billion — 32% — World Christian Population 2.18 billion

Americas 804 million · Europe 566 million · Russia 105 · United States 247 · U.K. 45 · China 67 · Asia-Pacific 285 million · Philippines 87 · Brazil 176 · Middle East-North Africa 13 million · Sub-Saharan Africa 516 million

☐ = 1 million Christians

Pew Research Center's Forum on Religion & Public Life
• *Global Christianity*, December 2011

This "weighted" map of the world, produced by the Pew Forum on Religion and Public Life, shows each country's relative size based on its Christian population.

4. The decline of Europe is notable, writes historian Jenkins, even in terms of current population trends. A table of the world's twelve biggest cities, based on population estimates for 2015, shows Tokyo at 26.4 million; Mumbai 26.1, Lagos 23.2, Dhaka 21.1, Sao Paulo 20.4, Karachi 19.2, Mexico City 19.2, Shanghai 19.1, Jakarta 17.3, Kolkata (Calcutta) 17.3, Delhi 16.8, and Metro Manila, 16.8. (The 2010 census shows "metropolitan New York" at 18.9, so it could be listed as ninth. It is notable that all European metro areas were under 11 million in 2011.

Such was the intertribal mass murder in Rwanda in 1994, for example, where Anglican and Catholic bishops, priests, and even nuns took part in the slaughter. One Ugandan church organized a general suicide which claimed a thousand lives. There was also the expulsion of tens of thousands of Pentecostals and evangelicals by their Catholic neighbors in Mexico's Chiapas province, in the opening years of the twenty-first century. But such tragedies are characteristic in periods of sweeping religious change, as witness the horrors of the Frankish court when Christianity was being reestablished after the fall of the Roman Empire, or the Anabaptist fanaticism at Münster during the Protestant Reformation.

In sum, as the twentieth century ended, a notable religious transformation had radically moved the population center of the Christian faith. Where in 1800 only one percent of Protestant Christians lived outside Europe and North America, by 1900 this had risen to ten percent. Taking Christianity as a whole by the year 2000, sixty-six percent of all Catholics and Protestants lived outside Christianity's old Euro-American heartland. Already, Jenkins notes, Christianity's demographic centers of gravity were no longer Geneva, Rome, Athens, Paris, London, New York; they were Kinshasa, Buenos Aires, Addis Ababa, and Manila.

Such a shift of geographic center is certainly no new phenomenon for Christianity, which began in the lands bordering the eastern Mediterranean, and then moved to southern Europe, then to northern and eastern Europe, then across the Atlantic to America. Now it is moving again, into the southern hemisphere and Asia. "God goes," observes the American columnist Philip Yancey, "where he is wanted."

This change is in line with a general shift in population. In 1900, thirty-two percent of the world's peoples lived in Europe, North America, or the lands of the former Soviet Union. By 1970, this had shrunk to twenty-three percent, and if present trends continue it will be down to ten or twelve percent by 2050.[4]

The chief factor in this spectacle of a diminishing Europe is the fall in the European fertility rate, caused chiefly by the reluctance of twentieth-century parents to have children. To maintain a stable population, a rate of 2.1 children per woman of childbearing age is required. Germany's rate by 2012 stood at 1.3, Italy's at 1.2, Spain's at 1.1. All former Soviet states are now in the range of 1.2. If Germany were to cut off immigration to protect its culture, as some in that country have demanded, its population by 2050 would have shrunk by one quarter—unless German women should somehow recover an interest in motherhood. By that time, however, the absence of young people would have created a sociological crisis.

Besides shunning motherhood, Europe during the twentieth century had also all but abandoned the Christian faith (which may to some degree explain the rejection of the parental role).[5] Published figures on religious affiliation from some countries do not appear to sustain this claim, but neither do they even remotely reflect the reality. Although the vast majority of Britain's sixty million people are still held to be Anglican, for instance, at Easter less than one million show up at church. One survey in 2000 found that forty-four percent of Britons claimed no religious affiliation whatever, a rise from thirty-one percent in 1931. Another found that more than half of young adults do not believe Jesus existed as a person. If present trends hold, Jenkins concludes, England's churches will be abandoned in a generation or two.

The situation in Germany is much the same. Twenty-seven million are listed as members of the German Evangelical Church, but less than a million attend its services. In France, almost the whole population is listed as Catholic, but less than eight percent attend Mass. The attendance figures from Scandinavian countries are even more dismal: Sweden five percent, Norway and Denmark three percent. Canada claims twenty percent, yet two of its major non-Catholic churches have suffered calamitous losses. Between 1961 and 2000, the United Church (a union

5. In one of his most effectively polemic poems, the English novelist, storyteller, and poet Rudyard Kipling (1865–1936) foretold how the modern world's new "isms" would destroy or cripple any society that seriously adopted them. Referring to three in particular— pacifism, communism, and libertinism—he called them "the gods of the market place" and showed how each would inevitably be overthrown by the "gods of the copybook headings," the old moral adages appearing at the head of each page in the "copybooks" by which children used to be taught handwriting. The verse on libertinism reads:

On the first Feminian Sandstones we were promised the Fuller Life

(Which started by loving our neighbour and ended by loving his wife)

Till our women had no more children and the men lost reason and faith,

And the Gods of the Copybook Headings said: "The Wages of Sin is Death."

Congregants at the Richmond Chinese Alliance Church, near Vancouver, British Columbia, sing hymns to music provided by the Sinfonia Mosaic orchestra. As immigration becomes increasingly necessary to fill the void left by the West's disenchantment with parenthood, the prevailing skin color of North American congregations has noticeably changed. In Vancouver, for example, fifty Christian congregations have Chinese, Korean, Vietnamese, or Filipino names.

The priceless gift of notoriety

How Dan Brown's purported exposé focused attention on the Opus Dei phenomenon, a 90,000-member new Catholic order, not sinister but doubtless very appreciative

From the blood and smoke of the Spanish Civil War emerged, perhaps fittingly, one of modern Catholicism's most intriguing movements. Opus Dei is a twentieth-century order, mainly of laymen and women, from scientists and corporate executives to cleaning ladies, but also including priests. In 2012, it claimed over ninety thousand members spread across the globe.

What showered public attention on Opus Dei, however, was novelist Dan Brown's 2002 best-seller *The Da Vinci Code*, which is largely an anti-Vatican, gnostic conspiracy fantasy. The effect of Brown's tale is to undermine orthodoxy and conventional history. For dramatic effect, his villain is a murderous albino giant serving loyally as an Opus Dei monk (though Opus Dei does not include monks). Brown found special fascination in the Opus Dei practice of self-mortification, the deliberate self-infliction of mild pain. In addition to serious fasting, it can include use of the "cilice" (a small barbed chain worn around an arm or thigh for part of the day, tightly enough to hurt but not enough to draw blood). "The Discipline" may also include mild self-flagellation over the bare shoulders with a light corded whip or leather belt (such as John Paul II used regularly). The devout regard it as the spiritual equivalent of physical fitness exercises.

These traditional Catholic self-disciplines, however, are neither required nor the purpose of Opus Dei. The vision for the order came to Josemaria Escriva de Belaguer from God, he said, in his native Spain in 1928. It came "whole and entire."[1] Unique in church history, Opus Dei (Latin for "the Work of God," or simply "the Work") would be a secular order composed of, quite revolutionarily for its time, clergy and lay members, men and eventually women, on a mission of sanctification through their secular careers and jobs. Even the most mundane tasks, if carried out wholeheartedly and offered up to God, can be holy in themselves, Escriva believed, and he admonished his flock to "sanctify work, sanctify oneself in work, and sanctify others through work."

In an article in *First Things*, historian Alister McGrath perceives similar thinking in, incidentally, the theology of the Protestant John Calvin and Martin Luther:

> Whereas monastic spirituality regarded vocation as a calling *out* of the world into the desert or the monastery, Luther and Calvin regarded vocation as a calling *into* the everyday world...Work was thus seen as an activity by which Christians could deepen their faith, leading it on to new qualities of commitment to God. Activity within the world, motivated, informed, and sanctioned by Christian faith, was the supreme means by which the believer could demonstrate his or her commitment and thankfulness to God. To do anything for God, and to do it well, was the fundamental hallmark of authentic Christian faith. Diligence and dedication in one's everyday life are, Calvin thought, a proper response to God.

Paul Bethany playing the Opus Dei "monk" best known to the world, through the success of the anti-Catholic blockbuster movie The Da Vinci Code *(2003). Bottom left, some considerably less menacing seminarians attend lessons at the Opus Dei University of the Holy Cross in Rome in 2008. Devised by Josemaria Escriva de Belaguer (right), after experiencing a vision in 1928, Opus Dei ("Work of God") would become an international secular order composed of clergy and lay members on a mission of sanctification through their own secular work.*

Escriva's early apostolate was obstructed by the outbreak of the Spanish Civil War, which forced him to spend months feigning insanity in a Madrid asylum before fleeing to the northern town of Burgos in friendly Nationalist territory. After Franco's victory Escriva found many recruits for his new venture among the optimistic, idealistic youth of battered Madrid. He focused, if not quite officially, on the social and intellectual elite, envisioning a Catholic intelligentsia to answer Europe's new secularist left. For instance, the order soon had members in Franco's cabinet, who established nominal Opus Dei control of the Spanish Council of Scientific Research.

Having solidly grounded itself in Spain, by 1950 Opus Dei was spreading through Europe and was designated by Pope Pius XII as an institution of "pontifical right." This meant its

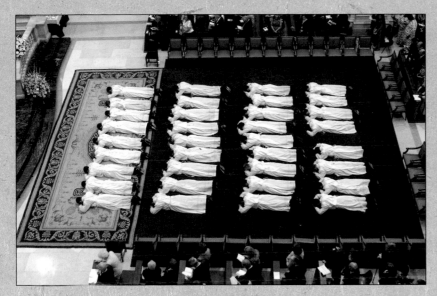

Left, newly ordained deacons prostrate themselves before the altar during an ordination Mass at the Basilica of Saint Eugene in Rome, celebrated by Bishop Javier Echevarria, head of Opus Dei. Right, a "cilice," the spiked chain that Opus Dei members may wear for part of the day around the arm or thigh as a means of self-mortification.

priests were not under regional diocesan jurisdiction, and answered only to the pope. Its independence was confirmed and strengthened by John Paul II in 1982.

Opus Dei continued to expand. Escriva would dispatch several priests and lay "numeraries" to a nation he considered ripe for the Work. They would begin to cultivate upper- and middle-class Catholics and open a residence. If this attracted members, they would undertake what they called "corporate works" or charitable activities. This usually meant founding schools. Many of the teachers would be Opus Dei members, though many were not. Opus Dei served only for spiritual direction, leaving the actual educating to secular professionals. In Spain, one of Opus Dei's business schools is ranked as among the world's best by the secular British newsmagazine *The Economist.*

The organization's inner structure remained little changed since the 1940s. Ordained Opus Dei priests serve beneath the prelate, originally Monsignor Escriva, and minister to a lay branch consisting of men and women called numeraries, celibates who vow themselves to poverty, obedience, and chastity and live in Opus Dei residences. There are also supernumeraries, typically married members who live with their families; numerary assistants, who serve as housekeepers in Work residences and are exclusively female; associates, who are celibate members who live at home; and co-operators, nonmembers who provide assistance, prayers, and often money to the Work.

Support for the order within the church has never been unanimous. Initially, conservative Catholics sensed a strong whiff of anticlericalism in the secular mission of the work. It has often been falsely portrayed as a secret society, and assumed to be the special agent of a sinister Vatican. More recently, its recruiting methods have drawn fire, with former members claiming Opus Dei's techniques amount to brainwashing. Opus Dei admits that in the past it encouraged some underage prospects to hide their association from their fami-

lies, but now encourages the full knowledge and involvement of a potential recruit's family. They further point out that everyone has freely joined and may freely leave. However, some who have left dispute this, most famously Maria del Carmen Tapia in her book *Inside Opus Dei.* She among others has claimed to have suffered what amounted to psychological torture, and then blackmail and intimidation after leaving the order. Opus Dei's responses to such claims have ranged from outright denial to ambiguity.

But perhaps their most serious accusation is that Opus Dei is equivalent to a cult of personality surrounding "The Founder," Escriva. Former members, some personally close to him, have described him as a petty tyrant, alternately charming useful outsiders and berating terrified subordinates with crude obscenities, and constantly promoting his future sainthood. His defenders reply that no saint was ever without sin, and point out Escriva's innumerable good works and dedication to the church.

For non-Catholics at the turn of the twenty-first century, Opus Dei's image was undoubtedly informed mainly by *The Da Vinci Code.* Tom Hanks, the star of the Hollywood film version, perhaps produced the most apt disclaimer for Brown's story, which he stressed was only that—fiction. Brown himself, keen to keep interest in the book alive, at one point claimed it was historical. To this, Hanks scoffed: "My heritage, and that of my wife, suggests that our sins have been taken away, not our brains."

In fact, by their commitment to sanctifying ordinary life and work, Opus Dei anticipated the Second Vatican Council by three decades. The task, handed down from "the saint of everyday life," is to find God in all things, in all places, at all times.

1. Escriva died in 1975 at age seventy-three, and was recognized as a saint by Pope John Paul II in 2002.

The impact of the new Christians on old churches was startlingly exemplified at the 1998 Lambeth Conference of Bishops of the worldwide Anglican Church, where western bishops proposed the ordination of homosexual priests. The proposal was shelved, due to the numerical weight of the African and Asian bishops, but not before Nigerian bishop Emmanuel Chukwuma (left) attempted to exorcise the "homosexual demons" from the Reverend Richard Kirker (right), leader of the Lesbian and Gay Christian Movement, whom Chukwuma accused of "killing the church."

6. The U.S. Constitution itself makes no mention of a separation of church and state. The First Amendment states simply: "Congress shall make no law respecting an establishment of religion, or prohibiting the free exercise thereof." The concept of a "wall" separating religion from political activity appears only in a letter of Thomas Jefferson. But that letter was cited by the U.S. Supreme Court in 1947 as evidence that such a wall was what the framers of the Constitution intended. With the "wall" thereby recognized, some contend that religion should not be allowed any voice whatever in the shaping of public policy. Since most, if not all, laws reflect a moral principle at some level, and since the morality of religious people is based on religious authority, the result of such a contention must be the effectual disenfranchisement of all religious people. American Christians, however, have shown no inclination to withdraw from public debate. Their religion continues to be very active in it.

of Methodists, Congregationalists, and some Presbyterians) lost forty percent of its members, the Anglican fifty-three percent. American attendance overall held up well at forty-three percent, but arguably was chiefly sustained by immigration from Latin America.

However sweeping the new Christian presence in the third world, Jenkins predicts that its impact will be just as startling in first world churches. In many American and European congregations, prevailing skin color noticeably changed over the last two decades of the twentieth century. Once almost wholly white, it was becoming a melange of yellow, black, white, and many shades of brown.

This reflects the movement of southern peoples into the northern hemisphere, as immigration becomes increasingly necessary to fill the void left by the West's disenchantment with parenthood. Some of the changes are already evident in Euro-American church life. Of two thousand Pentecostal churches in the New York City area, most are predominantly Latino. In Vancouver, Canada, some fifty Christian congregations have Chinese, Korean, Vietnamese, or Filipino names. Two-thirds of Chinese-Americans attend Christian churches. About half the active congregations in the Boston-Cambridge area, according to Jenkins, worship in a language other than English. After the passage of the 1965 Immigration Act, at least sixty-six percent of newcomers were Christian, and just eight percent Muslim. About three quarters of Arab-Americans are Christian, chiefly from Palestine, Lebanon, and Egypt.

Facts such as these disclose something largely unknown to Americans, Jenkins concludes: that the United States is not, in terms of religious affiliation anyway, a multicultural nation. It is a now distinctly Christian one and immigration is making it moreso. About ninety-five percent of Americans with a declared religious affiliation are Christian, and the remaining four to five percent are Jews, Muslims, Buddhists, and Hindus.

The impact of these new Christians on the old churches was startlingly exemplified at the 1998 Lambeth Conference of bishops of the worldwide Anglican Church. American and Canadian bishops advanced a motion to permit the ordination of homosexuals to the ministry, expecting it to pass easily. But it did not pass at all. The issue was shelved, largely due to the numerical weight of the African and Asian bishops. When American and Canadian bishops began ordaining gays anyway, four Anglican archbishops from Africa, one from Australia, and one from England boycotted the next Lambeth conference in 2008, threatening the church with the loss of its strongest constituency of support.

Christians of the third world, Jenkins emphasizes, are far more conservative and traditionalist than those of Europe and America. Much like those of the early church, they believe strongly that God performs miracles in daily life, and that the "freedoms" advanced by many of the old churches are in fact radical departures from biblical and Christian teaching. As their influence becomes stronger, sharp conflict can be expected.

In the Zambian town of Chirundu, near the Zimbabwean border, a barber shaves a customer in a shop decorated with football posters and a large poster of Jesus. Christians of the third world are like those of the primitive church in that they believe strongly that God performs miracles in daily life.

Jenkins also discerns a source of even sharper strife. The separation of church and state, a principle enshrined in the U.S. Constitution, is almost unknown in the third world.[6] Church leaders there are expected to be moral leaders in the shaping of the law, a function they have fulfilled since colonial days. Anglican clergy championed the campaign against South African apartheid. Zambia's first president, Kenneth Kaunda, was the son of a Presbyterian minister. Tanzania's first president, Julius Nyerere, taught in the Catholic mission schools. Churches in Brazil form their own political parties. People reared in such an environment will not easily separate church from state, and as they form an ever greater presence in America and Europe they can be expected to assert their religious convictions politically. Who will be there to oppose them? The children of the present Euro-American generation will be too few for their opinions to carry much weight.

So this, whatever it may portend, appears to be the fifth resurrection of the Christian faith that Chesterton predicted. He did not live to see it, but he knew it would come to pass—because it always had. *Heaven and earth shall pass away, but my words shall not pass away.* That was the prophecy of Jesus Christ (Matthew 24:35), Chesterton noted, and over the succeeding twenty centuries it clearly was being fulfilled: "If men really learn to apply reason to the accumulating facts of so crushing a story, it would seem that sooner or later even its enemies will learn from their incessant and interminable disappointments not to look for anything so simple as its death.

"They will watch for it to stumble; they will watch for it to err; they will no longer watch for it to end. Insensibly, even unconsciously, they will in their own silent anticipations fulfill the relative terms of that astounding prophecy; they will forget to watch for the mere extinction of what has so often been vainly extinguished; and will learn instinctively to look first for the coming of the comet or the freezing of the star." ■

BIBLIOGRAPHY

Alberti, Luciano. *Music of the Western World*. Trans. Richard Pierce. New York: Crown Publishers, 1974.

Alexander, Paul. *Signs & Wonders: Why Pentecostalism Is the World's Fastest Growing Faith*. San Francisco, CA: Jossey-Bass, 2009.

Alfeyev, Hilarion. *Orthodox Christianity: The History and Canonical Structure of the Orthodox Church*. Yonkers, New York: St. Vladimir's Seminary Press, 2011.

Allen, John L. Jr. *Opus Dei: An Objective Look Behind the Myths and Reality of the Most Controversial Force in the Catholic Church*. London: Image, 2007.

Andrews, James F, ed. *Paul VI: Critical Appraisals*. New York: Bruce Publishing Company, 1970.

Annussek, Greg. *Hitler's Raid to Save Mussolini: The Most Infamous Commando Operation of World War II*. Cambridge, MA: De Capo Press, 2005.

Arvidson, Stefan. *Aryan Idols: Indo-European Mythology as Ideology and Science*. Trans. Sonia Wichmann. Chicago: The University of Chicago Press, 2006.

Asbell, Bernard *The Pill: A Biography of the Drug That Changed the World*. New York: Random House, 1995.

Augstein, Rudolf. *Konrad Adenauer*. London: Secker & Warburg, 1964.

Bailey, Betty Jane and Bailey, J. Martin. *Who Are the Christians in the Middle East?* Second Edition, Grand Rapids, MI: William B. Eerdmans, 2010.

Bajema, Carl Jay, ed. *Eugenics Then and Now*. New York: Dowden, Hutchinson & Ross, 1976.

Baker, Nicholson. *Human Smoke: The Beginnings of World War II, the End of Civilization*, New York, Simon & Schuster, 2008.

Barraclough, Geoffrey, ed. *The Times Atlas of World History, Revised Edition*. London: Times Books Limited, 1984.

Beevor, Antony. *The Second World War*. New York, Little, Brown and Company, 2012.

Berkouwer, G. C. *The Second Vatican Council and the New Catholicism*. Grand Rapids, MI: William B. Eerdmans, 1965.

Berlinski, David. *The Devil's Delusion: Atheism and Its Scientific Pretensions*. New York: Crown Forum, 2008.

Berry, Jason. *Lead Us Not into Temptation: Catholic Priests and the Sexual Abuse of Children*. Champaign, IL: University of Illinois Press, 1992.

Berryman, Phillip. *Liberation Theology: Essential Facts about the Revolutionary Movement in Latin America—and Beyond*. Oak Park, IL: Meyer Stone Books, 1987.

Bertone, Tarcisio. *The Last Secret of Fatima*. With Guiseppe de Carli. New York: Doubleday, 2008.

Bertrand, Michael. *Race, Rock, and Elvis*. Champaign, IL: University of Illinois Press, 2000.

Black, Edwin. *War Against the Weak: Eugenics and America's Campaign to Create a Master Race*. New York: Four Walls Eight Windows, 2003.

Bloom, Harold, ed. *Bloom's Modern Critical Views: Henrik Ibsen*. New York: InfoBase Learning, 2011.

Bostdorff, Denise M. *Proclaiming the Truman Doctrine: The Cold War Call to Arms*. College Station, TX: Texas A&M UP, 2008.

Bryant, Mark. *World War I in Cartoons*. London, Grub Street Publishing, 2006.

Brook-Shepherd, Gordon. *The Last Habsburg*. New York: Weybright and Talley, 1968.

Carrillo, Elisa A. *Alcide De Gasperi: The Long Apprenticeship*. Notre Dame, IN: University of Notre Dame Press, 1965.

Carson, D. A. *Becoming Conversant with the Emerging Church: Understanding a Movement and Its Implications*. Grand Rapids, MI: Zondervan, 2005.

Chesterton, G. K. *Orthodoxy*. New York: Doubleday, 2001.

——. *The Everlasting Man*. New York: Doubleday, 1955.

——. *Heretics*. London: John Lane, 1928.

Christenson, Cornelia V. *Kinsey: A Biography*. Bloomington IN: Indiana UP, 1971.

Christopher, Andrew and Vasili Mitrokhin. *The Mitrokhin Archive: The KGB in Europe and the West*. London: Allen Lane, 1999.

Christopher, Joe R. *C. S. Lewis*. Boston: Twayne Publishers, 1987.

Churchill, Winston S. *The Second World War: The Gathering Storm*, Boston, Houghton Mifflin, 1948.

——. *The Second World War: Their Finest Hour*, Boston, Houghton Mifflin, 1949

Cohen, Nancy L. *Delirium: How the Sexual Counterrevolution Is Polarizing America*. Berkeley, CA: Counterpoint, 2012.

Collier, Peter and David Horowitz. *Destructive Generation: Second Thoughts About the Sixties*. New York: Summit Books, 1989.

Collins, Francis S. *The Language of God: A Scientist Presents Evidence for Belief*. New York: Free Press, 2007.

Collins, Paul. *God's New Man: The Election of Benedict XVI and the Legacy of John Paul II*. London, UK: Continuum, 2005.

Confino, Alon. *Foundational Pasts: The Holocaust as Historical Understanding*. London: Cambridge UP, 2012.

Conquest, Robert. *V.I. Lenin*. New York: Viking Press, 1972.

Cooper, Stephen. *The Politics of Ernest Hemingway*. Ann Arbor, MI: UMI Research Press, 1985.

Corrin, J .P. *G. K. Chesterton and Hilaire Belloc: The Battle Against Modernity*. Athens, OH: Ohio UP, 1981.

Courtois, Stephane, et al. *The Black Book of Communism*. Cambridge, MA: Harvard UP, 1999.

Dale, Alzina Stone. *Maker and Craftsman: The Story of Dorothy L. Sayers*. Grand Rapids, MI: William B. Eerdmans, 1978.

Douglas, Emily Taft. *Margaret Sanger: Pioneer of the Future*. New York: Holt, Reinhart and Winston, 1970.

Dowty, Alan. *Israel/Palestine*. Cambridge, UK: Polity, 2012.

Dwork, Deborah and Robert Jan van Pelt. *Holocaust: A History*. New York: W. W. Norton, 2002.

Eden, Guy. *Portrait of Churchill*. New York: Hutchingson & Co, 1945.

Ellwood, Sheelagh. *Franco*. New York: Longman, 1994.

Emmons, Caroline S. ed. *Cold War and McCarthy Era: People and Perspectives*. Santa Barbara, CA: ABC-CLIO, 2010.

Farmer, Brian. *Radical Islam in the West: Ideology and Challenge*. Jefferson, NC: McFarland and Company, 2011.

Fattorini, Emma. *Hitler, Mussolini and the Vatican: Pope Pius XI and the Speech That Was Never Made*. Trans. Carl Ipsen. Cambridge, UK, Polity Press, 2011.

Fischer, Fritz. *Germany's Aims in the First World War*, Düsseldorf, Droste Verlag und Druckerei GmbH, 1961.

Fischer, Heinz-Joachim. *Pope Benedict XVI: A Personal Portrait*. New York: Crossroad Publishing Company, 2005.

Fleming, Brian. *The Vatican Pimpernel: The Wartime Exploits of Monsignor Hugh O'Flaherty*. Wilton, Cork, Ireland: Collins Publishing, 2008.

Fletcher, William C. *A Study in Survival: The Church in Russia*. New York: Macmillan, 1965.

——. *The Russian Orthodox Church Underground, 1917-1970*. London: Oxford UP, 1971.

Furlong, William B. *GBS/GKC: Shaw and Chesterton, the Metaphysical Jesters*. State College, PA: Pennsylvania State UP, 1970.

Fussell, Paul. *Doing Battle: The Making of a Skeptic*, New York, Little, Brown and Company, 1996.

Geelan, P. J.M. and D. C. Twichett, eds. *The Times Atlas of China*. London: Times Books Limited, 1974.

Giangreco, D. M. *Hell to Pay: Operation Downfall and the Invasion of Japan*. Annapolis, MD: Naval Institute Press, 2009.

Gildea, Robert. *France Since 1945*. Oxford: Oxford UP, 2002.

Glenny, Misha. *The Fall of Yugoslavia: The Third Balkan War*. Toronto: Penguin Books Canada, 1993.

Gordon, Arvan. "The Church and Change in the GDR" *Religion in Communist Lands*. 18 (1990), 138-154.

Graham, Helen. *The Spanish Civil War: A Very Short Introduction*. Oxford: Oxford UP, 2005.

Graziosi, Andrea. *Stalinism, Collectivization and the Great Famine*. Cambridge, MA: Ukrainian Studies Fund, 2009.

Greeley, Andrew M. *The New Agenda*. Colorado Springs, CO: Image Books, 1975.

Gregory, Paul R. *Lenin's Brain and Other Tales from the Secret Soviet Archives*. Stanford, CA: Hoover Institution Press, 2008.

Haidt, Jonathan. *The Righteous Mind: Why Good People Are Divided by Politics and Religion*. New York: Parthenon Books, 2012.

Hall, Richard C. *The Modern Balkans: A History*, London, Reaktion Books Ltd., 2011.

Hanley, Boniface, OFM. *No Strangers to Violence, No Strangers to Love*. Notre Dame, IN: Ave Maria Press, 1983.

Himmelfarb, Gertrude. "From Clapham to Bloomsbury." *Commentary Magazine*, February 1985.

Hitchcock, James. *The Decline and Fall of Radical Catholicism*. New York: Herder and Herder, 1971.

Hitchcock, William I. *France Restored: Cold War Diplomacy and the Quest for Leadership in Europe*. Chapel Hill, NC: University of North Carolina Press, 1998.

Hitchens, Christopher. *The Missionary Position: Mother Teresa in Theory and Practice*. New York: Verso, 1995.

Ho, Louis K. *The Dragon and the Cross: Why European Christianity Failed to Take Root in China*. Edmonton, AB: Xulon Press, 2009.

Hovhannisyan, Nikolay. *The Armenian Genocide. Armenocide. Causes, Commission, Consequences*. Yerevan: National Academy of Sciences Institute of Oriental Studies, 2002.

Hunter, James Davidson. *Culture Wars*. New York: Basic Books, 1991.

Irving, David. *Hitler's War*. New York: Avon Books, 1990.

Jägerstätter, Franz. *Letters and Writings from Prison*. Trans. Robert Krieg. Maryknoll, NY: Orbis, 2009.

Jenkins, Philip. *Decade of Nightmares: The End of the Sixties and the Making of Eighties America*. Oxford, UK: Oxford UP, 2006.

——. *The Next Christendom*. Oxford, UK: Oxford UP, 2011.

——. *Pedophiles and Priests: Anatomy of a Contemporary Crisis*. Oxford, UK: Oxford UP, 1996.

John Paul II, Pope. *Memory and Identity: Conversations at the Dawn of a Millennium*. New York: Rizzoli, 2005.

Johnson, Paul. *Intellectuals*. London: Weidenfeld and Nicolson, 1988.

Johnson, Phillip. *Darwin on Trial*. Downers Grove, IL: InterVarsity Press, 1993.

——. *Defeating Darwinism by Opening Minds*. Downers Grove, IL: InterVarsity Press, 1997.

Keegan, John. *The Second World War*. New York: Viking Penguin, 1989.

Kelley, Dean M. *Why Conservative Churches are Growing*. Atlanta, GA: Mercer UP, 1996.

Kepel, Gilles. *Jihad: The Trail of Political Islam*. Cambridge, MA: Belknap Press, 2002.

Kevles, Daniel J. *In the Name of Eugenics: Genetics and the Uses of Human Heredity*. New York: Harvard UP, 1985.

Keyserlingk, Robert Wendelin. *Fathers of Europe: Patriots of Peace*. Montreal: Palm Publishers, 1972.

Khosrokhavar, Farhad. *Suicide Bombers: Allah's New Martyrs*. London: Pluto Press, 2005.

Kidder, Annemarie S. *Ultimate Price: Testimonies of Christians Who Resisted the Third Reich*. Maryknoll, NY: Orbis Books, 2012.

Kunzman, Robert. *Write These Laws on Your Children: Inside the World of Conservative Christian Homeschooling*. Boston, MA: Beacon Press, 2009.

Lafayette, Bernard. *The Role of Religion in the Civil Rights Movement*. Self-published paper, 2004.

Lang, Michael. *The Road to Woodstock*. New York: Ecco/HarperCollins, 2009.

Lapide, Pinchas. *The Last Three Popes and the Jews*. Bristol, UK: Hawthorn Books, 1967.

Larson, Edward J. *Summer for the Gods: The Scopes*

Trial and America's Continuing Debate Over Science and Religion. New York: Basic Books, 1997.

Lewis, Bernard. *The End of Modern History in the Middle East.* Standford, CA: Hoover Institution Press, 2011.

Lewis, C.S. *On Stories: And Other Essays on Literature.* London: Harcourt Brace Jovanovich, 1982.

———. *The Great Divorce.* New York: HarperOne, 2009.

———. *Mere Christianity.* San Fransisco: Harper, 2001.

———. *Pilgrim's Regress.* Melbourne, AUS: Collins, 1977.

———. *The Screwtape Letters.* San Francisco: Harper, 2001.

Lewy, Guenter. *The Catholic Church and Nazi Germany.* New York: Da Capo Press, 1964.

Li, Zhensheng. *Red-color News Soldier: A Chinese Photographer's Odyssey Through the Cultural Revolution.* London: Phaidon Press, 2003.

Lochery, Neill. *The View From the Fence: The Arab-Israeli Conflict from the Present to Its Roots.* New York: Continuum, 2005.

Lowe, Peter. *The Origins of the Korean War.* New York: Addison Wesley Longman, 1997.

Lukacs, John. *A History of the Cold War.* Garden City, NY: Doubleday, 1961.

MacDonald, George. *Phantastes.* London: J.M. Dent, 1915.

———. *The Princess and the Goblin.* New York: Books of Wonder, 1986.

MacDonald, Michael H. *The Riddle of Joy: G. K. Chesterton and C. S. Lewis.* Grand Rapids, MI: William B. Eerdmans, 1989.

Machan, Tibor R. *Ayn Rand.* New York. Peter Lang, 1999.

MacMillian, Margaret. *Paris 1919: Six Months That Changed the World.* New York: Random House, 2003.

Malinski, Mieczyslaw. *Pope John Paul II: The Life of Karol Wojtyla.* Washington DC: Seabury Press, 1979.

Mark, Chi-Kwan *China and the World since 1945: An International History.* New York: Routledge, 2011.

Marsh, Christopher. *Religion and the State in Russia and China.* London: Continuum International, 2011.

Martin, William. *A Prophet with Honor: The Billy Graham Story.* New York: Harper Perennial, 1992.

McGrath, Alister. *The Twilight of Atheism: The Rise and Fall of Disbelief in the Modern World.* New York: Doubleday, 2006.

———. *Christianity's Dangerous Idea: The Protestant Revolution—A History from the Sixteenth Century to the Twenty-First.* New York: HarperCollins, 2008.

———. *C. S. Lewis—A Life: Eccentric Genius, Reluctant Prophet.* Carol Stream, IL: Tyndale House Publishers, 2013.

Mencken, H. L. *A Religious Orgy in Tennessee: A Reporter's Account of the Scopes Monkey Trial.* Brooklyn, NY: Melville House Publishing, 2006.

Metaxas, Eric. *Bonhoeffer: Pastor, Martyr, Prophet, Spy.* Nashville, TN: Thomas Nelson, 2010.

Miller, Robert Moats. *Harry Emerson Fosdick: Preacher, Pastor, Prophet.* New York: Oxford UP, 1985.

Mills, Nicolaus. *Winning the Peace: The Marshall Plan and America's Coming of Age as a Superpower.* Hoboken, NJ: John Wiley and Sons, 2008.

Mojzes, Paul. *Balkan Genocides: Holocaust and Ethnic Cleansing in the Twentieth Century.* Lanham, MD: Rowman and Littlefield Publishers, 2011.

Molony, John N. *The Emergence of Political Catholicism in Italy.* London, UK: Croom Helm, 1977.

Mueller, Michael. *Canaris: The Life and Death of Hitler's Spymaster.* Trans. Geoffrey Brooks. Annapolis, MD: Naval Institute Press, 2007.

Muggeridge, Anne Roche. *The Desolate City: Revolution in the Catholic Church.* Toronto: McClelland and Stewart, 1986.

———. *The Gates of Hell.* Toronto: McClelland and Stewart, 1975.

Muggeridge, Malcolm. *Something Beautiful for God.* New York: Harper & Row Publishers, 1971.

Murphy, Paul I. and R. Rene Arlington. *La Popessa.* New York: Warner Books, 1983.

Nichols, Aidan. *G. K. Chesterton, Theologian.* Manchester, NH: Sophia Institute Press, 2009.

Niemoeller, Sibylle Sarah. *Crowns, Crosses, and Stars: My Youth in Prussia, Surviving Hitler, and a Life Beyond.* West Lafayette, IN: Purdue UP, 2012.

Noel, Gerard. *Pius XII: The Hound of Hitler.* London: Continuum, 2008.

Noll, Mark, David William Bebbington, and George A. Rawlyk, *Evangelicalism: Comparative Studies of Popular Protestantism in North America, the British Isles, and Beyond 1700-1900.* Oxford, UK: Oxford UP, 1994.

O'Connell, Marvin R. *Critics on Trial: An Introduction to the Catholic Modernist Crisis.* Washington DC: The Catholic UP, 1994.

O'Sullivan, John. *The President, the Pope, and the Prime Minister: Three Who Changed the World.* Washington DC: Regnery Publishing, 2006.

Papini, Roberto. *The Christian Democrat International.* New York: Rowman & Littlefield, 1997.

Patterson, George N. *Christianity in Communist China.* Waco, TX: Word Books, 1970.

Pearce, Joseph. *Solzhenitsyn: A Soul in Exile.* San Francisco: Ignatius Press, 2011.

Peris, Daniel. "Commissars in Red Cassocks: Former Priests in the League of the Militant Godless." *Slavic Review* 54 (1995): 340–384.

Poewe, Karla. *New Religions and the Nazis.* New York: Routledge, 2006.

Ponchaud, François. *Cambodia: Year Zero.* New York: Holt, Rinehart, and Winston, 1978.

Pospielovsky, Dimitry. *The Russian Church Under the Soviet Regime 1917–1982.* Yonkers, NY: St. Vladimir's Seminary Press, 1984.

Powell, David E. *Antireligious Propaganda in Soviet Union: A Study of Mass Persuasion.* Cambridge, MA: MIT Press, 1975.

Prager, Dennis and Joseph Telushkin. *Why the Jews? The Reason for Antisemitism.* New York: Simon and Schuster, 1983.

Prittie, Terence. *Konrad Adenauer, 1876–1967.* London: Tom Stacey Ltd, 1972.

Ready, William. *The Tolkien Relation.* Chicago: Henry Regnery, 1968.

Reeves, Thomas C. *The Empty Church: Does Organized Religion Matter Anymore?* New York: Simon and Schuster, 1996.

Reisman, Judith A. and Edward W. Eichel. *Kinsey, Sex and Fraud: The Indoctrination of a People: An Investigation Into the Human Sexuality Research of Alfred C. Kinsey, Wardell B. Pomeroy, Clyde F. Martin and Paul H. Gebhard.* Lafayette, LA: Lochinvar, 1990.

Ridley, Jasper. *Mussolini.* London: Constable and Company, 1997.

Roberts, Andrew. *The Storm of War: A New History of the Second World War,* New York, HarperCollins Publishers, 2011.

Roberts, Elizabeth Mauchline. *Stalin: Man of Steel.* London: Methuen Educational, 1968.

Rychlak, Ronald. *Hitler, the War, and the Pope.* Huntington, IL: Our Sunday Visitor, 2000.

Sanchez, Antonio Cazorla. *Fear and Progress: Ordinary Lives in Franco's Spain, 1939–1975.* West Sussex, UK: Wiley-Blackwell, 2010.

Satinover, Jeffrey. *Homosexuality and the Politics of Truth.* Grand Rapids, MI: Baker Books, 1996.

Scholl, Inge. *The White Rose: Munich 1942–1943.* Middletown, CT: Wesleyan UP, 1983.

Schrader, Helena P. *The Blockade Breakers: The Berlin Airlift.* London: History Press UK, 2008.

Sherrill, John. *They Speak with Other Tongues.* Grand Rapids, MI: Chosen Books, 1964.

Shirer, William. *The Rise and Fall of the Third Reich: A History of Nazi Germany.* New York: Simon & Schuster, 1960.

Shlaes, Amity. *The Forgotten Man: A New History of the Great Depression.* New York: HarperCollins, 2007.

Sivan, Emmanuel. *Radical Islam: Medieval Theology and Modern Politics.* New Haven, CT: Yale UP, 1985.

Smith, Bradley F. *Adolf Hitler: His Family, Childhood, and Youth.* Stanford, CA: The Hoover Institute on War, Revolution, and Peace, 1967.

Snape, Michael. *God and the British Soldier: Religion and the British Soldier in the First and Second World Wars.* New York: Routledge, 2005.

Solzhenitsyn, Alexander I. *The Gulag Archipelago: An Experiment in Literary Investigation.* Trans.Thomas P. Whitney and Harry Willets. Abridged Edward E. Ericson. Toronto: Harper Perennial Modern Classics, 2007.

Sommers, Christina Hoff. *Who Stole Feminism? How Women Have Betrayed Women.* New York: Simon and Schuster, 1995.

Sparkes, Russell, ed. *Prophet of Orthodoxy: the Wisdom of G.K. Chesterton.* London: Fount, 1997.

Steele, David. *At the Front Lines of the Revolution: East Germany's Churches Give Succor to the Purveyors of Change, in Religion, the Missing Dimension of Statecraft.* New York: Oxford UP, 1994.

Strachan, Hew. *The First World War,* London, Penguin Books Ltd., 2003.

Srinivasa Iyengar, K. R. *Lytton Strachey: A Critical Study.* Port Washington, NY: Kennikat Press, 1967.

Synan, Vinson. *The Holiness-Pentecostal Tradition: Charismatic Movements in the Twentieth Century.* Grand Rapids, MI: William B. Eerdmans (1997).

Tapia, María del Carmen. *Inside Opus Dei: The True, Unfinished Story.* New York: Continuum, 2006.

Taylor, A.J.P. *The Origins of the Second World War,* New York, Simon & Schuster Inc., 1961.

Taylor, S.J. *Stalin's Apologist: Walter Duranty, The New York Times's Man in Moscow.* New York: Oxford UP, 1990.

Toynbee, Arnold. *A Study of History.* Oxford, UK: Oxford UP, 1972.

———. *Armenia Atrocities: The Murder of a Nation,* London, Hodder & Stoughton, 1915.

Tracy, Kathleen. *Elvis Presley: a Biography.* Westport, CT: Greenwood Press, 2007.

Tucker, Spencer C. *The Great War 1914–1918.* Bloomington IN: Indiana UP, 1998.

Wakin, Edward. *A Lonely Minority: The Modern Story of Egypt's Copts.* New York: William Morrow and Company, 1963.

Waugh, Evelyn. *Brideshead Revisited.* New York: Penguin Classics, 2000.

Weigel, George. *Witness to Hope: The Biography of Pope John Paul II.* New York: HarperCollins, 1999.

———. *Against the Grain: Christianity and Democracy, War and Peace.* New York: Crossroad Publishing Company, 2008.

Weikart, Richard. *From Darwin to Hitler: Eugenics and Racism in Germany.* New York: Palgrave Macmillan, 2004

Weitz, Eric D. *Weimar Germany: Promise and Tragedy.* Princeton, NJ: Princeton UP, 2007.

Wells, David F. and John D. Woodbridge, eds. *The Evangelicals: What They Believe, Who They Are, What They Are Changing.* Nashville, TN: Abingdon Press, 1975.

Wilkinson, Alan. *The Church of England and the First World War.* London: SPCK, 1978.

Williams, Beryl. *The Russian Revolution 1917–21.* Oxford UK: Basil Blackwell, 1987.

Williams, Donald T.Y. *Mere Humanity: G. K. Chesterton, C. S. Lewis, and J. R. R. Tolkien on the Human Condition.* Nashville, TN: Broadman & Holman, 2006.

Wills, Garry. *Bare Ruined Choirs: Doubt, Prophecy, and Radical Religion.* Garden City, New York: Doubleday, 1972.

Wilson, A.N. *C. S. Lewis: A Biography.* New York: Ballantine Books, 1990.

Wiltgen, Ralph M. *The Rhine Flows into the Tiber.* New York: Hawthorn Books, 1967.

Wolfe, Gregory. *Malcolm Muggeridge: A Biography.* Grand Rapids, MI: William B. Eerdmans, 1997.

Wolfe, Jesse. *Bloomsbury, Modernism, and the Reinvention of Intimacy.* Cambridge, UK: Cambridge UP, 2011.

Woolf, S.J. ed. *The Rebirth of Italy 1943–50.* London: Longman Group, 1972.

Zahn, Gordon. *In Solitary Witness: The Life and Death of Franz Jägerstätter.* Collegeville, MN: Liturgical Press, 1964.

Zernov, Nicolas. *The Russian Religious Renaissance of the Twentieth Century.* New York: Harper & Row, 1963.

PHOTOGRAPHIC CREDITS

113 top courtesy Chris John Beckett; 128 photo by Yousuf Karsh; 386 bottom row, third from left courtesy St Joseph's College (Brooklyn, NY); 400 top photo courtesy Marion E. Wade Center

Akg Images
5 bottom © IAM; 62 lower © akg-images; 82 © akg-images; 86 © akg-images; 87 top inset © akg-images/ RIA Nowosti; 89 © akg-images/ullstein bild; 91 bottom © akg-images/ullstein bild; 106 © akg-images; 177 © akg-images; 183 inset below © Yvan Travert/akg-images; 250 © akg-images; 258 bottom right © Bildarchiv Pisarek/akg-images; 259 top right © akg-images; 384 top right © akg-images; 394 © akg-images

Art Resource
100 right © bpk Berlin/ Art Resource, NY; 145 bottom © National Army Museum/The Art Archive at Art Resource, NY

Associated Press
122 © Associated Press; 127 centre left © Associated Press; 180 top © Associated Press; 180 inset Associated Press; 181 Associated Press; 218 top © Associated Press, inset © Associated Press; 227 left © Associated Press; 268 © Associated Press; 285 right lower © Associated Press, bottom © Associated Press; 303 © Associated Press; 336 © Bettmann/Corbis/ AP Images; 372 inset © Associated Press; 390 © Associated Press; 411 © Associated Press

Bridgeman
0 © Staatliche Kunstsammlungen Dresden/ Bridgeman Art Library / © Estate of Otto Dix / SODRAC (2012); 4 bottom © SZ Photo/scherl/The Bridgeman Art Library, inset: © Bridgeman Art Library; 7 bottom © Bridgeman Art Library; 10 bottom left © Bridgeman Art Library; 12 © Bridgeman Art Library; 14 left © Bridgeman Art Library, right © Bridgeman Art Library; 15 bottom © Bridgeman Art Library; inset © Bridgeman Art Library; 17 © Bridgeman Art Library; 20 © Bridgeman Art Library; 22 bottom inset © Look and Learn/Bridgeman Art Library, top © Bridgeman Art Library; 28 right © Bridgeman Art Library; 29 © Bridgeman Art Library; 30 © Bridgeman Art Library; 35 © Bridgeman Art Library; 37 © Bridgeman Art Library; 40 © Bridgeman Art Library; 54 © Bridgeman Art Library; 58 top right © Christie's Images/Bridgeman Art Library, top center © The Bloomsbury Workshop/Bridgeman Art Library; 59 © Bridgeman Art Library; 98 top right © Bridgeman Art Library, bottom right © Bridgeman Art Library; 102 © Bridgeman Art Library; 108 © Bridgeman Art Library; 112 top © Bridgeman Art Library; 116 top right © Bridgeman Art Library, bottom © Galerie Bilderwelt/Bridgeman Art Library; 117 top inset © Bridgeman Art Library, bottom © Bridgeman Art Library; 134 left © Galerie Bilderwelt/Bridgeman Art Library, right Bridge Art Library; 149 top © Herbert Art Gallery & Museum, Bridgeman Art Library; 149 lower left © Bridgeman Art Library; 153 © Bridgeman Art Library; 160 inset © Bridgeman Art Library; 167 © Bridgeman Art Library; 170 bottom © Peter Newark/Bridgeman Art Library; 171 bottom © AA World Travel Library/Bridgeman Art Library, top left © Bridgeman Art Library, 174 © Bridgeman Art Library; 192 top Bridgeman Art Library; 206 top left © Bridgeman Art Library, top right © Bridgeman Art Library; 207 top left © Peter Newark Military Pictures/ Bridgeman Art Library, bottom left © Peter Newark Military Pictures/ Bridgeman Art Library; 274 © Stapleton Collection/Bridgeman Art Library; 310 © Forum/UIG/Bridgeman Art Library; 316 inset © Forum/UIG/Bridgeman Art Library, bottom © Forum/UIG/Bridgeman Art Library; 321 bottom © Forum/UIG/Bridgeman Art Library, inset right © Private Collection/Bridgeman Art Library; 323 © Study for a portrait of Pope John Paul II, Gillick, James/Private Collection/Bridgeman Art Library; 324 top © Forum/UIG/Bridgeman Art Library; 340 top © Forum/UIG/ Bridgeman Art Library; 391 top © Look and Learn/ Bridgeman Art Library

Contact Press Images
172 © Contact Press Images

Corbis
31 © Junius B. Wood/National Geographic Society/Corbis; 32 © VATICAN/Reuters/Corbis; 70 © Bettman/CORBIS; 34 © Bettmann/CORBIS; 78 © Daisy Gilardini/Science Faction/Corbis; 83 top © Bettmann/CORBIS; 85 bottom © Hulton-Deutsch Collection/CORBIS; 90 right © Ira Wyman/Sygma/Corbis; 113 bottom right © Bettmann/CORBIS; 114 left © BettmanN/CORBIS; 120 © CORBIS; 135 top © Berliner Vertag/Archiv/dpa/CORBIS; 139 top © CORBIS, inset left © Bettmann/CORBIS; 143 left © Bettmann/CORBIS; 144 top © Ansa/CORBIS; 164 bottom © Bettmann/CORBIS; 168 bottom © NICKY LOH/Reuters/Corbis; 169 top © Bettmann/CORBIS, bottom © Baldwin H. Ward & Kathryn C. Ward/CORBIS;

170 top © CORBIS; 183 top © Bettmann/CORBIS; 186 top © Imaginechina/COR-BIS, bottom right © Michael Reynolds/epa/CORBIS; 198 © Dpa/dpa/CORBIS; 200 © Manfred Rehm/dpa/CORBIS; 202 bottom © Bettmann/CORBIS, inset © Bettmann/CORBIS; 203 © Bettmann/CORBIS; 205 © Inediz Reports/Demotix/COR-BIS; 206 bottom © Bettmann/CORBIS; 207 top right © Bettmann/CORBIS, bottom right © Jacques Pavlovsky/Sygman/CORBIS; 208 © Henry Diltz/CORBIS; 210 © CORBIS; 211 © Bettmann/CORBIS; 213 inset © Bettmann/CORBIS; 215 top © Bettmann/CORBIS, bottom © Bettmann/CORBIS; 220 top left © Ted Streshinsky/CORBIS; 221 top left © Henry Diltz/CORBIS; 223 © Bettmann/CORBIS; 226 top © Elliott Landy/CORBIS; 234 bottom © Bettmann/CORBIS; 238 bottom left © Douglas Kirkland/CORBIS; 240 Wally McNamee/CORBIS; 242 top © Kimberly French/Focus Features/Bureau L.A. Collection/CORBIS; 248 © Mark Avery/ZUMA Press/CORBIS; 249 © ANDREW GOMBERT/epa/CORBIS; 271 bottom left © Kirn Vintage Stock/CORBIS; 273 top left © Bettmann/CORBIS; 277 lower right © Robert Padget/Reuters/CORBIS, upper right © CORBIS; 284 © Aristide Economopoulos/Star Ledger/CORBIS; 284 top left © Bill Nation/Sygma/CORBIS; 291 © Bettmann/CORBIS; 300 top © Bettmann/CORBIS; 312 bottom © Bettmann/CORBIS; 315 © Bettmann/CORBIS; 318 © JP Laffont/Sygma/CORBIS; 319 © Mike Segar/Reuters/CORBIS; 321 © Gianni Giansanti/Sygma/CORBIS; 328 © Alessandra Benedetti/CORBIS; 330 © Reuters/CORBIS; 332 top © Bettmann/COR-BIS; 334 inset left © Jean-Baptiste Rabouan/Hemis/CORBIS, inset right © Bettmann/CORBIS; 338 © Richard Melloul/Sygma/CORBIS; 340 inset © Alain Nogues/Sygma/CORBIS; 342 © CORBIS; 346 bottom right © Michael Probst/Reuters/CORBIS; 347 © Peter Turnley/CORBIS; 350 Bettmann/CORBIS; 354 bottom © Bettmann/CORBIS; 355 top © Austrian Archives/CORBIS, bottom © CORBIS; 356 top left © Jamal Nasrallah/epa/CORBIS; 358 inset © Bettmann/COR-BIS, bottom © Bettmann/CORBIS; 359 top © Carlos Cazalis/CORBIS, bottom right © Shawn Baldwin/CORBIS; 361 top left © Khaled Elfiqi/epa/CORBIS; 362 top left © Hulton-Deutsch Collection/CORBIS, top right © Bettmann/CORBIS, lower right © CORBIS; 364 inset right © Bettmann/CORBIS; 367 top © Bettmann/CORBIS, inset left © Michel Setboun/CORBIS; 370 © Patrick Chauvel/Sygma/CORBIS; 373 top right © Christopher Morris/VII/CORBIS; 379 © Bettmann/CORBIS; 381 © Historical Picture Archive/CORBIS; 390 bottom © Hulton-Deutsch Collection/CORBIS; 403 © ImagineChina/CORBIS; 410 top right © Nigel; 419 top left © Eidon Frustaci/Demotix/CORBIS, top right © Orjan F. Ellingvag/CORBIS; Pavitt/JAI/COR-BIS, top left © Caetano Barreira/X01990/Reuters/CORBIS; 415 bottom left © STR/epa/CORBIS; 421 © Gideon Mendel/CORBIS

Getty Images
Title page © Time & Life Pictures/Getty Images; 52 © Time & Life Pictures/Getty Images; 60 © Time & Life Picture/Getty Images; 66 © Getty Images; 124 © Time & Life Pictures/Getty Images; 125 top © Time & Life Pictures/Getty Images; 126 © Popperfoto/Getty Images; 130 © Getty Images; 131 inset © Time & Life Pictures/Getty Images; 132 inset © Getty Images; 132 bottom © Getty Images; 136 © Getty Images; 137 inset lower right © Getty Images, upper right © Getty Images; 140 top © 2004 Getty Images; 146 below © Getty Images, inset top © Getty Images; 147 inset © Getty Images; 154 © Time & Life Pictures/Getty Images; 158 © Time & Life Pictures/Getty Images; 160 top © 2008 Getty Images; 161 left © Time & Life Pictures/Getty Images; 163 left © Time & Life Pictures/Getty Images; 197 top left © Mondadori via Getty Images; 221 right © Time & Life Pictures/Getty Images; 222 bottom © Washington Post/Getty Images; 235 top © Time & Life Pictures/Getty Images; 284 top right © AFP/Getty Images; 289 © SuperStock/Getty Images; 294 © Getty Images; 301 Time & Life Pictures/Getty Images; © 308 bottom © Time & Life Pictures/Getty Images; 345 bottom © Time & Life Pictures/Getty Images; 385 © Getty Images; 391 bottom © Time & Life Pictures/Getty Images; 409 bottom © Getty Images; 410 centre © Godong/Getty Images; 418 bottom left © Getty Images

National Portrait Gallery
376 bottom left © National Portrait Gallery, London; 380 bottom © National Portrait Gallery, London; 383 bottom right © National Portrait Gallery, London; 384 top left © reserved; collection National Portrait Gallery, London

The Pew Forum on Religion & Public Life
416 © 2010 The Pew Forum on Religion & Public Life

Reuters
420 left © Reuters/Kieran Doherty

INDEX

El Salvador 315, 415
Eldridge, Niles 263
Eliot, T.S. 59, 389-390
Ellis, Havelock 71, 72
embryo research 248
emergent church 287-288
Empty Church, The (Reeves) 292, 293
Enabling Act (1933) 105, 109-110, 143
end-times 174, 233, 265, 276, 280-281, 298, 355
England
    bombing of, in WW II 126, 132, 133
    Christian population 417
English Common Law 233
Enigma code 132
Enlightenment 407
Enver, Ismail 19
Episcopal Church. *See* Anglicans, Church of England
Epistles, Pauline 228, 275, 298, 302
Eppelmann, Rainer 343, 344
equal rights activism 247
Equal Rights Amendment 234-236, 238
Esalen 291
eschatology. *See* end-times
espionage 57
Estonia 129, 130
Ethiopia 107, 360
Ethiopian (languages) 118
Ethiopian Orthodox Church 360
eugenics 1, 66, 68, 253-254
    Christian support 255
    in Germany 256, 258-259
    Supreme Court decision 255-256
Eugenics Record Office 254, 256
Europe
    alliances in WW I 2-3
    birth rate and population 416-417
    educational reforms 75
    map, after WW I 15, 331, 335
    map, after WW II 157
    post-war reconstruction 158-167
euthanasia 111, 152, 248
evangelical churches 270, 273, 275-276, 279, 284
    congress, international 282-283
    and other faiths 283, 287
    Pentecostals, disagreement with 302, 307
    in the U.S. 236-237, 238
Evangelical Lutherans in America. *See* Lutherans, Lutheranism
evangelism 293
    China 173-176, 185-186
    Russia 88-89
    United States 291
Everlasting Man, The (Chesterton) 387, 399, 405
evolution, theory of 40, 47, 52, 66-67, 252, 260-262
    scientific evidence 262-263
Exodus (movie) 363
Explo '72 (Dallas) 279
exposure of infants 235
Eysenck, Hans 62

F

FBI 217
Faisal bin Hussein 357
faith healing 300, 301
Faith Tabernacle (Lagos, Nigeria) 411
Falange Party (Spain) 113
Falkenhayn, Erich von 6-7
Falwell, Jerry 237, 238, 239, 278, 279, 283
Family Protection Act 238
famine
    China 179
    USSR 81, 91. *See also* Holodomor
Fangcheng Fellowship 185
Farmer, James 215
farms, farming. *See* USSR—agricultural reform
Fascism 106-107, 112
Fatah (political movement) 365
Fatima (Portugal) 32
Faubus, Orval 216
Faulhaber, Michael von 152
Federal Republic of Germany. *See* Germany
Federation of Fighting Youth (Poland) 342
Fedotov, Ivan 90
feminism 58, 72, 221, 232, 234-235, 240, 248
    attitude towards family 229, 247
Feng Jianguo 185
Ferrarotti, Franco 323
Fiedler, Maureen 323
Field, James 254
Fighting Solidarity (Poland) 342
Final Solution. *See* Holocaust
Finland 9, 129
    Russia, conflict with 130
Finn, Robert 327
First Jesus Church (Fujian, China) 186
Fischer, Heinz-Joachim 325
Fisher, Irving 254
Five Fundamentals 46, 47, 48, 51
Five Year Plans (USSR) 80-81, 93
Fletcher, William 25, 82-83, 84
Foch, Ferdinand 11, 12, 15
Focus on the Family 239
folk tales 175
Ford, Gerald 237
Formosa. *See* Taiwan
Forster, E.M. 57, 59
Fortune, Reo 69
Fosdick, Harry 46-47, 49, 53, 255
Foursquare Gospel Church 300-301, 305
Fourteen Points (Wilson) 14
Fox, Adam 392
Fox, Robin 319
France
    casualties in WW II 148
    Cold War 156
    colonies 135, 206
    Germany, relations with 124, 128, 162, 166-167
    government, post-WW II 158-160
    invasion under Hitler 130-131

    navy 132
    Republic, third 5
    and Soviet Union 124, 158
    WW I 4-5
France, Anatole 13
Franco, Francisco 107, 150
    Hitler, relationship with 113, 126
    Soviet Union, relations with 114
Franco-Prussian War 1
Franz Ferdinand, Archduke of Austria 2-3
Franz Joseph I, Emperor of Austria 2
Frederick II (the Great), King of Prussia 123
Free Democratic Party (Germany) 166
Free Speech movement 221
free will, doctrine of 253
Freedom and Justice Party (Egypt) 360
freedom of speech 340
Freedom Rides 215, 216
Freeman, Derek 64, 65, 69
Freikorps 100, 101
Freud, Sigmund 59-61, 63
    detractors 62
Friedan, Betty 236
Frings, Joseph 195, 196
Frossard, Andre 314
Fry, Roger 58
Fuchida, Mitsuo 137
Führer, Christian 344
fundamentalists, Christian 48, 50, 239, 270-271, 276, 283, 286, 408
    growth of, in the sixties 279
    origin 46, 51, 234
    political clout 235-238
    rift with Billy Graham 275, 277
fundamentalists, Islamic 358, 367, 368-371. *See also* Salafist sect (Islam); Wahhabi sect (Islam)

G

Gajowniczek, Franciszek 153
Galen, Clemens von, Bp. of Münster 111, 152
Gallagher, Michael, Bp. of Detroit 270
Gallipoli campaign (1915-1916) 8
Gandhi, Mohandas 215
Gao Yongjiu 184
Garnett, David 58
Gasperi, Alcide De 156, 161, 162
Gastal, Scott 326
Gauthe, Gilbert 326
gay pride parades 241, 242
gay rights. *See* homosexuality
Gaza Strip 362, 363
Gdansk Accord 340
Gdansk shipyard 339
Geheime Staatspolizei. *See* Gestapo
Gehre, Ludwig 151
Genesis, Book of (OT) 52, 68
genetics, human. *See* Human Genome Project
genocide 8, 16-19, 144. *See also* Armenia, Armenians—genocide; Holocaust; Holodomor
George V, King of Great Britain 13

George VI, King of Great Britain 128
Gerlich, Fritz 108, 115
German Christian Church 108-109
German Democratic Republic. *See* Germany
German Evangelical Church 109, 151, 152, 417
Germany
    armaments 116, 129, 141
    armed forces, in WW II 123. *See also* Luftwaffe; SA (Sturmabteilung); SS (Protection Squad)
    birth rate 417
    bombing of 126, 139, 140
    casualties in WW II 98, 145, 148
    Christian church under Hitler 108-109
    and churches, post-WW II 342-343
    Cold War 156, 162-166
    colonies 15, 100
    communism, threat of 100
    conditions of peace after WW I 12-15, 100
    counterintelligence agency. *See* Abwehr
    demilitarized zone, occupation of 124
    division, post WW II 162
    economic reconstruction 166
    economy after WW I 101
    France, conflict with 1, 126, 128
    government under Hitler 110-112
    Italy, alliance with 107
    in the Mediterranean 133
    and Poland 117
    postwar government 162, 166, 335, 342-344
    1st Reich 1
    2nd Reich 1, 98
    3rd Reich 110, 111, 115-141
    reunification 345
    Russia, conflicts with 6, 85, 133-135
    U.S. loans, dependence on 103
    Weimar Republic 12, 100-101, 103
    World War I 1-4, 6-13, 98. *See also individual battles*
Germogen, Bp. of Tobolsk 24
Gerstner, John 271
Gestapo 104
Gibraltar 113, 150
Gierek, Edward 339
Gillick, James 323
Gilson, Etienne 49
Ginsberg, Allen 220, 222
glasnost 347
Gleichschaltung 110-111
global warming. *See* climate change
glossolalia. *See* tongues, speaking in
Gobineau, Arthur de 98
"God is Dead" movement 278
Godbey, William 302
Goebbels, Joseph 103, 105, 111, 115, 126, 148

casualties in WW II 148
Cold War 156
Communism, threat of 144
post WW II 156, 160-162
in WW I 3, 8, 14
in WW II 107, 126, 140-141, 144
Iwo Jima, battle of (1945) 138

J

Jackson State University 223
Jagger, Mick 219
Japan 15, 126, 135
bombing of 138, 148
casualties in WW II 148
invasion of U.S. 135-137
Jaruzelski, Wojciech 334, 340-342
Jastrow, Robert 264
Jefferson, Thomas 407, 420
Jefferson Airplane 219, 220
Jehovah's Witnesses 307
in Russia 30-31
Jenkins. Philip 189, 233, 328, 408,
413-416, 420, 421
Jerusalem 352-353, 362
population 353
Wailing Wall 353
in WW I 11
Jerusalem, siege of (70) 281
Jesuits 5, 43, 53, 204
Jesus Christ 352, 399, 406
divinity 44, 45, 203
in Modernist theology 41, 42, 44,
48, 49
Resurrection 40, 47, 48
Jesus Family (China) 175, 178, 184
Jesus Movement 279
jihad. See terrorism
Jim Crow laws 212-214, 216
Jin Luxian 179, 187-189
Jing Dianyang 175, 178, 184
Joad, C.E.M. 396
Jodl, Alfred 125, 126
Joffre, Joseph-Jacques-Césaire 4, 7
John XXIII, Pope 33, 191-196, 200,
306, 335
John, Elton 242
John, Gospel of (NT) 296, 407
John Jay College of Criminal Justice
(Manhattan) 327
John Paul I, Pope 311-312, 313
John Paul II, Pope 32-33, 203, 205,
310, 328, 412-413, 418, 419
assassination attempts 322, 341
as bishop in Poland 332, 333-336
death and funeral 323-324
early years 312-313
election as pope 314-315, 336
legacy 329
Mexico, initial visit to 315-316
opposition to Communism 313,
335-337, 347-348
Poland, visits to 337-340
and reformists 317, 320, 322-323
travels 317, 321
Johnson, Lyndon 206-207, 211,

217, 278
Johnson, Phillip 68, 261-262
Jones, Bob 275
Jones, Sheila 266
Joplin, Janis 220, 221
Jordan 363, 366
Jotabeche Methodist Church
(Santiago, Chile) 411
Juan Carlos, king of Spain 114
Judaism, Jews. See also anti-
Semitism; Holocaust; Israel (modern state); Zionism
and abortion 235
in the ancient world 120, 277,
351-352
and the Catholic Church 144, 199
as a chosen people 120-121
in Croatia 144
and end-times 281
in Germany 118-119, 121, 356
in Greece 191
in Italy 144
under Muslim conquerors 352, 353
refugees in WW II 113, 114
in Russia 30
in the United States 238
Jude, Apostle 16
Jumpers 299
Jutland, battle of (1916) 9

K

KGB 86-87
Kaas, Ludwig 108, 109
Kappler, Herbert 153
Karl I, Emperor of Austria 12-13
Katzen-Ellenbogen, Edwin 258-259
Kaunda, Kenneth 421
Kazakhstan 338
Keating, Charles 319
Keitel, Wilhelm 125, 126
Keller, Timothy 218, 286-287, 288
Kelley, Dean 292
Kellogg, John 254
Kennan, George 337
Kennedy, Jackie 202
Kennedy, John F. 197, 202, 206, 211,
217, 277-278
Kennedy, Robert 202, 203, 217
Kent, Peter 144
Kent State University 223
Kenya 415
Kerensky, Alexander 22, 23
Kesey, Ken 219
Kesselring, Albert 140-141
Keston College (England) 88
Keynes, John Maynard 56-57, 58
Khomeini, Ruhollah, Ayatollah
367, 368
Khrushchev, Nikita 88, 89, 339
kibbutz settlements 366
Kilpatrick, W. H. 74
Kim Il-sung 170
King, Martin Luther 202, 214-218,
225, 277
Kinsey, Alfred 210, 227-228

Kinsey Institute 228, 229
Kipling, Rudyard 417
Kirk, Russell 235
Kirker, Richard 420
Kirkpatrick, William 398
Kitchener, Horatio 5
Kleist, Ewald von 131
Knox, P.C. 254
Knox, Ronald 388-389, 394
Kochurov, John 23
Kolbe, Maximilian 152
Kolkata (India) 318
Kolodiejchuk, Brian 319
Koonin, Eugene 263
Koran 352
Korea 81, 135, 161, 167, 266, 408
Christian population 411
Korean War 170-171
Korin, Pavel 30
Kornfeld, Boris 339
Kristallnacht 126, 128
Kristof, Nicholas 415
Krogman, W. 140
Krohn, Fernández y 322
Krutch, Joseph 68
Kryuchkov, Gennady 89
Ku Klux Klan 214, 271
Kucharski, Heinz 151
Kung, H.H. 177
Küng, Hans 52, 195, 196, 200
Kung Pinmei 178, 179, 188
Kunstler, William 223
Kunzman, Robert 246
Kursk, battle of (1943) 145, 148
Kustodiev, Boris 31
Kuwait 369
Kwanglim Methodist Church (Seoul)
411

L

LSD. See drug culture
labor unions 160, 202
Lady Chatterley's Lover (Lawrence) 59
Lafayette, Bernard 215
LaGuardia, Fiorello 161
Lakewood Church (Houston) 285
Lambeth Conference (1998) 420
Lang, Cosmo, Abp. of Canterbury
125, 128
Lange, Hermann 152
Laos 206
Lapide, Pinchas 144
Larkin, Clarence 302
Larson, Edward 66, 68
Lateran Seminary 156, 157
Lateran Treaty (1929) 107, 143
Latin (language) 195, 203, 204
Latin America 199. See also under
individual countries
Christianity, growth of 408, 411-
412, 414
political reform 315
Latvia 129, 130
Laughlin, Harry 252, 253-254, 256

Lausanne Covenant (1974) 283
Lawrence, D.H. 58, 59
Lawrence, Jerome 68
Lawrence, T.E. 11, 357
Lawson, James 215
League of Nations 14, 15, 107,
116, 124
League of the Militant Godless 29-
30, 83
Leary, Timothy 220, 221
Lebanon 325, 370
Ledger, Heath 242
Ledien, Curt 151
Lee, Ivy 47
Lee, Robert 68
Lefebvre, Marcel 203
Legion of Mary 178
Lehnert, Josefine. See Pascalina, Sister
Lejeune, Jérôme 261
LeMay, Curtis 139, 164, 165, 206
Lemkin, Raphael 17
Lend-Lease program 137
Lenin, Vladimir 22, 26, 30, 37, 80
Leningrad. See St. Petersburg
(Russia)
Lennon, John 218, 219
Leo I, Pope 324
Leo X, Pope 312
Leo XIII, Pope 41, 43-44, 48, 53, 383
Leslie, John (Shane) 388
Levittown (N.Y.) 210
Lewis, Bernard 367
Lewis, C.S. 6, 10, 396
as apologist 399, 400-402
conversion 378, 390-392, 399
death 403
early life 398
influence of Chesterton 387, 399
influence of MacDonald 375, 376,
391, 399
legacy 375-376
marriage 402
on pacifism 15-16
writings 259-260, 392-393, 399,
401-403
Lewis, John 215
Lewis, Warren 392, 398
Lewy, Guenter 153
Li Tianen 184-185
Li Zhisui 169
Lian Xi 173-174
liberation theology. See theology, lib-
eration
Liberty University (Lynchburg, Va.) 279
Libya 372
Lichtenberg, Bernard 152-153
Liebknecht, Karl 100
Liepert, Hans 151
Lifton, Robert 178
L'il Abner (comic strip) 221
Lindsay, D. Michael 269
Lindsey, Hal 233
Lippman. Walter 68
literacy (U.S.) 77
Lithuania 129, 130, 335, 336, 348
Little Flock (China) 174-175, 184

communism, legacy of 349
destruction of armaments 133
and Fatima 33
France, relations with 158
in Germany, postwar 162
Jews, persecution of 354
Korea, involvement in 170
monarchy, fall of 9
post WW II 156, 158, 163-165
in WW I 2, 8, 9
in WW II 85, 129, 130, 133-135
Russian Orthodox Church 21-24,
348-349
in North America 25
reform, under Soviets 27, 36
seminaries 84. 85
under Stalin 82-85
suppression under Bolsheviks 23-26
Russian Orthodox Church Outside
Russia (ROCOR) 85
Rutherford, Adam 412
Rwanda 119, 416
Rychlak, Ronald 144, 152

S

SA (Sturmabteilung) 102, 105, 108,
111, 115
SCAF. See Supreme Council of
Armed Forces (Egypt)
SDI. See Strategic Defense Initiative
SDS. See Students for a Democratic
Society
SS (Protection Squad) 105, 115
SSPX. See Society of Saint Pius X
Sack, Karl 151
Sackville-West, Vita 58
Sacred Heart Cathedral (Guangzhou,
China) 186
sacred union (France) 5
Sadat, Anwar 360, 366
Sagan, Carl 251-252
St. Ignatius Catholic Cathedral
(Shanghai) 188
St. Nicholas Orthodox Church
(Harbin, China) 172
St. Nikolai Church (Leipzig) 344
St. Paul's Cathedral (London) 131, 133
St. Petersburg (Russia) 27
siege (1941-1944) 134
sainthood, process of declaring 325
Salafist sect (Islam) 360
Salkahazi, Sara 153
salvation (Christian doctrine) 53
samizdat (definition) 339
Samoa 64-65, 69
San Francisco 219, 220
Sanger, Margaret 69, 229
personality 70-72
Sanger, William 70-71, 72
Sanjurjo, Jose 113
Santos, Lucia dos 32-33
Sarikamsh, battle of (1914-1915) 17
Satan 281
Satinover, Jeffrey 241
Saud, Abdul-Aziz bin 357, 358

Saudi Arabia 357-358
Sawatsky, Gerhard 36
Sayers, Dorothy 55, 399, 403
writings 394-396
Scarlet and the Black (movie) 153
Schacht, Hjalmar 116
Schaeffer, Francis 48, 49
Schellenberg, David 36
Schillebeeckx, Edward 52, 320
Schlafly, Phyllis 235, 247
Schleicher, Kurt von 104
Schlieffen, Alfred von 2
Schlieffen Plan 2-3
Schliemann, Heinrich 101
Schmorell, Alexander 151
Scholl, Hans 151, 152
Scholl, Sophie 151
schools. See also homeschooling
in Russia 30
in the United States 47, 66, 233
Schorlemmer, Friedrich 343, 344
Schrader, Helena 164, 165
Schumaker, E.F. 383
Schuman, Robert 156-158, 160, 165,
166-167
Schuman Plan 166-167
Schuschnigg, Kurt von 125, 126
Schutzstaffel. See SS (Protection
Squad)
science 35, 251-252
science and religion 40-41, 43, 51, 52,
66-68, 193, 260-261, 267, 396
scientism (philosophy) 252, 256-
257, 260
opposition from Christians 259
Scientists Against Nuclear Arms
265-266
Scopes, John 66-68
Scopes trial 50, 66-68
Screwtape Letters (Lewis) 291,
392, 399
Seale, Bobby 224, 225
Second Coming. See end-times
Second Great Awakening 291, 407
Second Vatican Council. See councils
of the church—Vatican Council,
2nd
secrets of Fatima. See Mary, mother
of Jesus
secular humanism. See progressivism
secularism 290-292. See also cultural
revolution
segregation. See civil rights movement; racism (U.S.)
Selasssie, Haile 107
Selincourt, Hugh de 71
seminaries 21, 25, 37, 45, 46, 177,
204-205, 249, 290, 343, 414
Semitic languages 118
Semple, Robert 300
Seoul (Korea) 170
Serbia 2, 3, 144
Sergius, Metropolitan of Moscow 29,
30, 36-37, 84-86
Sergius of Radonezh 25
"seven sisters" 289
Seventh Day Adventists 244, 280

Sewell, Brocard 389
sex education 244
sexual morality 56, 58, 63-64, 210-211
sexuality, study of 227-229
Seymour, William 296, 298-299,
302, 303, 305
Shangri-la, origin of 175
Shankman, Paul 65
Sharon, Ariel 370
Shaw, George Bernard 384-385, 386
Shenouda III, patriarch of the Coptic
Church 360
Sherrill, John 306
shipping, during WW I 10
Shirer, William 103, 105, 116,
124, 153
Shoah. See Holocaust
Shuttlesworth, Fred 215
Siberian Seven 90
Sicily, battle for (1943) 140
Silesia 117
Simonds, Herbert 71
Sinatra, Frank 161, 162
Singapore 135, 138
sins, seven deadly 55
Siri, Giuseppe, Bp. of Genoa 311, 314
Sisters of Loreto 318
Sitwell, Edith 389
Six-Day War (Arab-Israel) 365
Sixties Revolution. See cultural revo-
lution (U.S.)
Sixtus affair 13
skepticism 42
Skorzeny, Otto 106
slavery 179, 213
Slee, J. Noah 71
Slick, Grace 219
Slipyi, Joseph, Metropolitan of
Ukrainian Uniates 86, 337
Slovakia. See Czechoslovakia
Smith, Gordon 307
Smith, Tom 229
Snape, Michael 5
social gospel movement 51
social ministry 283
socialism, democratic 290
Society of Jesus. See Jesuits
Society of Muslim Brothers. See
Muslim Brotherhood
Society of Saint Pius X 203
Socratic Club (Oxford) 399
sola scriptura (doctrine) 198
Solidarity movement 339-342
Solzhenitsyn, Alexander 81-82,
337-339
Somme, battle of (1916) 7-8
Somme, 2nd battle of (1918) 9
Sommers, Christina 247
Soong family 177
Sophie, Duchess of Hohenberg 2-3
South Africa 421
Southern Baptist Convention 51,
269, 284, 289
Soviet Union. See USSR

Spain 112-114
political chaos in 1930s 112
U.S., alliance with 114
WW II, role in 113
Spanish Civil War 107, 112-113
outcomes 114
Spanish Council of Scientific
Research 418
Sparkes, Russell 382, 386
Speaight, Robert 389
Speer, Albert 122
Spellman, Francis 204
Spencer, Herbert 383
Spink, Kathryn 318
Spock, Benjamin 69, 210, 239
Stalin, Joseph 30, 37, 80, 83, 88, 93,
95, 149, 331
allied with Britain and U.S. 139
China, relations with 168
and Germany, postwar 163, 165
Great Terror 84-85
Russia, invasion of 133
Stalingrad 135, 141, 145
Stanislaw, Bp. of Krakow 337
Star Wars (defense system). See
Strategic Defense Initiative
Stauffenberg, Claus von 153
steel, manufacture of, post-war 167
Steele, David 342, 343
Stein, Edith 152
Stein, Rosa 152
Stelbrink, Karl 152
Stenger, Victor 261
Stephen, James 58
Steponavicius, Julijonas, Abp. of
Vilnius 348
sterilization. See eugenics
sterilization laws 111
Stern, Aaron 350
Stewart, Lyman 46
stock market crash (U.S., 1929) 103
Stone's Folly (Topeka, Kn) 296, 297,
298
Stonewall Riot (1969) 221, 222
Stormtroopers. See SA
(Sturmabteilung)
Strachey, James 59
Strachey, Lytton 56
Straight, Michael 57
Strasser, Gregor 103
Strategic Defense Initiative 346-347
Streseman, Gustav 103
Strutt, Edward 13
Studdert Kennedy, G.A. 5
Students for a Democratic Society
221, 222
Sturzo, Luigi 106, 107
Stuttgart Declaration of Guilt 152
submarines. See U-boats
Sudan 369, 415
Sudetenland. See Czechoslovakia
Suez Canal 133, 139, 364
suffragettes 243
suicide, assisted 248
Süleyman (the Magnificent), caliph 353
Sun Yat-sen 168, 177

Do you have Volumes One through Eleven?

The amazing history of the world-wide Christian faith, from the founding of the Church at Pentecost until today.

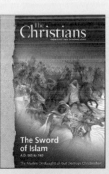

Volume 1
A.D. 30 to A.D. 70

Volume 2
A.D. 70 to A.D. 250

Volume 3
A.D. 250 to A.D. 350

Volume 4
A.D. 350 to A.D. 565

Volume 5
A.D. 565 to A.D. 740

Volume 6
A.D. 740 to A.D. 1100

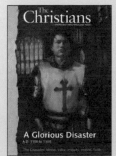

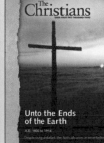

Volume 7
A.D. 1100 to A.D. 1300

Volume 8
A.D. 1300 to A.D. 1500

Volume 9
A.D. 1500 to A.D. 1600

Volume 10
A.D. 1600 to A.D. 1800

Volume 11
A.D. 1800 to A.D. 1914

Volume 12
A.D. 1914 to A.D. 2001